# PETRETTI'S

# COLLECTIBLES
# PRICE GUIDE
# 10TH EDITION

## Allan Petretti

Dubuque, Iowa

Inquiries may be directed to:
Allan Petretti
21 South Lake Dr., Hackensack, NJ 07601

"Coca-Cola" and "Coke"
are registered trade marks which identify the same product of The Coca-Cola Company


Printed in the United States of America
All Rights Reserved

Library of Congress Catalog Card Number: 97-72679
ISBN 0-930625-76-5

Other books by Allan Petretti:
*Petretti's Soda-Pop Collectibles Price Guide*

Editor: Allan W. Miller
Art Director: Jaro Šebek
Assistant Editor: Elizabeth Stephan
Assistant Designers: Lynn Bradshaw, Carla Goldhammer
Production Assistants: Chris Gross, Aaron Wilbers,
    Dan Bockenstedt, Barb Brown-Loney, Robert Buss,
    Joyce Powers, Jim Maddox, Paula Hopkins,
    Miriam Hoffman, Judy Ludowitz, Cindy Berns

To order additional copies of this book
or a catalog please contact:

Antique Trader Books
P.O. Box 1050
Dubuque, Iowa 52004-1050
1-800-334-7165

 ANTIQUE TRADER BOOKS
Division of Landmark Specialty Publications

# ACKNOWLEDGMENTS

*Producing a book such as this is just not possible without a little help from your friends. Listed below are some of the people who have contributed to this book over the years. I consider all of them my friends. I would also like to thank all of you who have called or written to say how much you've enjoyed the book. Those kind comments have made all the long hours and hard work worth while.*

Sharon & Joe Happle
Bert Hansen
Margaret Almond
Gordon Breslow
Thaddeous Krom
Freddy Brewer
Ron Paradoski
John Morgerson
Jeff Brady
Bob Nance
Jay & Joan Millman

Bill & Jan Schmidt
Don & Donna Arnold
Bill & Kay Hendricks
Dr. & Mrs. Eugene
Brinker
Jeff Wright
Irv & Dot Shirley
Larry Schulz
James McDonald
Robert Rentzer
Neal Selznick

Larry & Nancy Werner
Jack Kelly
Phil Perdue
Richard Bostwick
Ted Oswalt
Dave Goddard
Susan Anievas
Dave Baker
Gary Metz
Billy Osborne
Harper Lieper

Robert & Audrey Flinn
Jerry Jacobs
Bill Whitaker
Robert Nelson
Vincent Jacono
Rudy LeCoadic
Chuck Hardy
Fred Maney
Scott Rosenman
Chuck Campbell
Joe Davis

Blaine Martin
Robert Morawic
Don Brunjes
Greg Barney, Sr.
John Wise
James D. Julia, Inc.
Darryl Kirbo
Larry Dikeman
Randy Inman

*With Special Thanks To . . .*

Thom & Frances Thompson

*Thom has always been my number 1 supporter, ever since the first edition he has unselfishly offered his knowledge and collection, to help make this book better. Thom & Frances are among the countries top collectors. This book wouldn't be what it is today without their help.*

Rodger Robinson

*For supplying photographs of some of his great cardboard cutouts and signs.*

Don & Marty Weinberger

*Who allowed me to photograph some beautiful pieces from their extensive collection.*

Dann & Jinx Perszyk

*For supplying great black and white and color photos from their collection.*

John Barbier

*His time and energy on the "magazine ad" section of this book is much appreciated.*

Jim Meehan

*His expertise and help with the bottle section of this book was very helpful, as well as his research on Kay Displays*

Randy Schaeffer & Bill Bateman

*The C.C. Tray-ders (Randy & Bill) through their research and writings especially during their years producing "The Coca-Cola Collectors News" have brought forth more information about the history of Coca-Cola than all other sources put together.*

Leonard J. and Joseph L. Schiff

*Authors of "Edward Payson Baird; Inventor, Industrialist, Enterpreneur" for their help with the "Baird Clock" section of this book.*

Gael & Rosalie deCourtivron

*Their collection of toys is one of the best in the country and have always made it available to me. Their help in expanding this section of the book is much appreciated.*

The Coca-Cola Company/Phillip F. Mooney, Archives Manager

*For supplying me with photos for this book, and always extending an invitation from The Archives for any help I might need.*

Pop Poppenheimer (1922–1988)

*One of the best known collectors of Coca-Cola memorabilia passed away in 1988. Pop was so well liked among the collecting community that anyone who knew him will never forget him. . . . He will be missed. Pop and his wife Belle were among the first to make their collection available to me for this book.*

Danny Ragsdale

*For his hours of bottle photography, that helped expand that section of the book is most appreciated.*

Alan Wright

*For allowing photography of his extensive bottle collection*

Bob Newman

*For allowing photography of some rare pieces from his extensive collection.*

Marc Cardelli

*For supplying some photo's of pieces in his collection*

John Yarbrough

*For supplying some photos of pieces in his collection*

*To my wonderful wife Rannie and my three great children, Dante, Deana & Vito
who have shared their husband and father with Coca-Cola for all these years . . . I Love You All.*

# CONTENTS

# CONTENTS

# INTRODUCTION

Only in America could a product that was created with such humble beginnings, and which sold for pennies and has been around for over 110 years, become the most well-known trademarked product in history. That trademark is so well known, in fact, that it is not only part of our history, but has truly become part of what we call "Americana".

The fascination with the product Coca-Cola, the company, and its advertising has become the focal point for a legion of fans from all over the world who collect memorabilia associated with this company.

While some wonder in amazement how a five-cent soda fountain drink has evolved into a timeless "Mega Giant" of American business, others who collect and study this great company's history find it to be no mystery. It started with a great product, with a unique taste, and a total mystique surrounding its ingredients. That was combined with the most dynamic, progressive and complete advertising campaign in history. It is this advertising, its look, uniqueness, and rarity, that is the core of what we now know as Coca-Cola collectibles.

The quality and quantity of the advertising produced by The Coca-Cola Company over the years has created an appreciation and desire for it as well as a wealth of material for today's collectors to accumulate, search for and lust after. Even though The Coca-Cola Company produced this advertising in mass quantities, finding quality examples from any era is becoming more and more difficult, especially considering the number of new collectors entering the market in recent years.

Quality, quantity and rarity. If I had to pick the three words that best describe the reasons why people collect this memorabilia, these would be the perfect three. For those of you who have not experienced or seen first hand the quality and beauty of this wonderful advertising, you are in for a treat. As you go through this book you will view some of the most creative and beautiful artwork produced by America's best artists and advertising companies. The consistent quality of the advertising produced by these people was no accident. That smile that you get when you look at this artwork and remember a simpler time is no coincidence. The pretty girls, couples at the beach, leisure time and sports—the things that are supposed to make you smile. This theme is evident throughout Coca-Cola advertising and was created to make you feel good. It's the memories of the past—the good times, and even the bad—that people are eager to recapture, and even though it's impossible to relive an event from the past, owning something that reminds us of another time, makes us feel better. But quality alone surely cannot account for the high numbers of individuals who are fascinated by the advertising used by this company. The quantity of material used to sell this five cent soft drink is absolutely incredible, and by quantity I do not necessarily mean shear numbers of one particular item. But rather the vast numbers of objects used to carry the message that, "When thirsty, you should drink a Coke." One of the things that amazes many when they first start to collect Coca-Cola memorabilia is the wide variety of items to be collected. Because of this variety, it is not uncommon for many to specialize in only one area within Coca-Cola collectibles—bottles, serving trays, calendars and periodical advertising are just a few examples. Because the company did so much advertising in specific areas, it is quite possible to build a formidable and yet never complete collection in only one

specialty area. Many collectors soon realize that with the limitless number of items to collect, specializing allows you to assemble an impressive collection in the area that best suits your interests. The thing that I like best about this extremely wide variety of Coca-Cola collectibles is the fact that there is an area, a particular object or a price range, that seems to fit every type of collector: from young children to teens, and from newly married couples to big time investors and collectors. There just seems to be a perfect level for everyone.

One would certainly think that with all the advertising produced by The Coca-Cola Company, and with all the collectors seeking this memorabilia, that we have seen everything. Not so! The one thing that continually creates the challenge for Coca-Cola collectors is how rare some of these objects are. It is a fact that we continue to uncover items that were previously unheard of. These discoveries, especially when they are early or highly desirable pieces, are what keep collectors' interest peaked. The chance of uncovering one piece that is so rare that it could possibly be unique, is one of the key elements that make collecting this memorabilia so exciting. Remember, if this memorabilia was easy to find, the challenge would be gone, as well as the value.

Because the popularity of this memorabilia grows each year, it becomes necessary to have a book that is updated periodically, and which tracks the value of this much sought after memorabilia. This helps collectors keep aware of what is happening in a very fast-moving market. For those of you who have followed this book over the years, you will find this edition much different and quite unique.

While the words "Price Guide" are in the title, and everything in the book is assigned a value, this is much more than a price guide. Even though you will find over six thousand photos here, this is also much more than a picture (wish) book. Even with all the quality color plates of some of the rarest Coca-Cola memorabilia ever seen, this is much more than a coffee table book. And, with all the current fantasy and reproduction information compiled here, this still is much more than a book on reproductions. With this latest edition, the amount of information that has been added has truly made this a "total" book on the subject. Yet it is much more than an information or history book of The Coca-Cola Company. This total book is what I call the "text book" of Coca-Cola collectibles.

The fact that this book is designed by a collector, for collectors, makes it the most important tool you will need to make important decisions to improve your collection and increase your investment. One of the most significant changes you will find here is the introduction of an Image Identification System. With the extensive and ever growing number of images found in this book, it becomes necessary to be able to identify and access these images easily. The identification system and how it is used will be explained in detail on a proceeding page. With the consistently growing number of collectors and the demand for updated information at an all time high, additions to this book such as history, slogans, logos, competitors, manufacturers, and artists, as well as back-up support information that can be found no where else, will assist you in becoming a more informed and knowledgeable collector.

No matter how many photos or pages of information are added to this book, and no matter how much I try to downplay the importance of pricing, it is a fact that prices are considered the most important part of this book by a majority of today's collectors. It is most important that you understand that the values shown are just one small element of the entire book. These values are not placed arbitrarily—a great amount of research and tracking goes into the evaluation of this memorabilia. These values and what they represent are one person's opinion and are only given so you, the collector or dealer, can have an approximation as to the value of a particular collectible that you are about to purchase or sell. In fact, the real value is set by people other than myself. What the value actually comes down to is the piece itself: its condition, its rarity, the asking price and, most importantly, how badly you as the buyer want that particular piece. After that, this book or anything else means nothing.

All I can do is offer you this information as a "guide" for you to use or not, to assist you in making those difficult decisions on whether to buy or not to buy, or determining what to sell an item for. So please consider this while reviewing this book, and try not to take the values shown too seriously; they are actually set to be flexible.

As I state throughout the book, the values shown are based on what I call "average price for average condition." Using a standard of "Mint" condition on which to base values does a disservice to collectors because most pieces found today are not in mint or even near mint condition. In fact, most pieces found today are in excellent "8" condition, or what I call "average." So, the prices shown are based on this standard of "8" condition. If a piece is found in better condition the value will be higher, and in lesser condition the price will be lower. This flexibility allows both buyer and seller the ability to point out condition in a positive or negative view, in order to be in a better bargaining position to either buy or sell the piece. There is just too much of a disparity in value between pieces in different condition to be setting values with total disregard to condition. So, to use this book effectively, it is important not to rely on the values shown as absolute or "set in stone," and when all is said and done it is you who determines the value, not others. I feel it is very important that price guide authors explain to readers how prices shown in their books are determined, and on what condition these values are based.

I am personally very frustrated when attempting to use a price guide that makes no mention of condition. I have noticed some important changes in the market concerning condition and how it effects values. This trend has been growing over the past few years; collectors are becoming more interested in condition. They seem to be more conscious and demanding with their condition requirements when adding a piece to their collection. The reasons are obvious. With the ever-growing prices on quality pieces, the concern with investment potential becomes an important factor when paying these current prices. Many would rather wait until they find a piece in the condition they feel comfortable with, rather than settle for less. The assumption being that the better the quality the better the appreciation over the years. This change, and the continual movement in that direction, is very important to understand when using this book, because the gap between the value of a piece in near mint to mint condition and the same piece in good or very good condition seems to get larger each year. This simply means that a piece in near mint condition selling for $500 may only sell for $100 in good or very good condition,

and a lot less than that in poor condition. Try to keep this "value to condition" ratio in mind when buying or selling.

One of the biggest problems facing today's collectors is the continual onslaught of unauthorized reproduction and phony Coca-Cola collectibles. Note the use of the word "unauthorized." It is important that you understand that when an item is produced which incorporates the name or trademark of The Coca-Cola Company without authorization to do so, is counterfeiting. These counterfeit items have no part in the history of The Coca-Cola Company. I personally find these counterfeit items insulting to collectors and without value, in the same way that a counterfeit twenty dollar bill has no value. Many people over the years have totally misunderstood my point concerning these unauthorized, counterfeit pieces, and they object to my use of the word "worthless." The individuals who produce this phony material are attempting to capitalize on the good name, hard work and reputation of The Coca-Cola Company by selling illegal, unauthorized collectibles. If anyone truly feels these items have any value, all they need to do is ask The Coca-Cola Company. Hopefully, the additions made to the fantasy and reproduction section of this book (which, by the way, you will find in no other Coca-Cola Price Guide) will help you make those important decisions regarding counterfeits. Keep in mind, however, that as the popularity and value of Coca-Cola collectibles continue to rise, these counterfeit pieces become more and more prevalent. And, it is virtually impossible to show everything being produced.

I have always made an effort in this book to supply readers with backup and support information regarding individual pieces or particular groups of items in the form of "lead in" pages or boxed-in notes. In that tradition I have expanded support information with this edition. My hope is that this information will help you better understand how or why some of this material was used, if it is common or rare, and what to look for when faced with the decision to buy or not to buy. In addition, an expanded "Collector Assistance" section should prove to be helpful to today's collectors who can use as much help as they can get to protect their collection and investment.

As anyone who has been involved in Coca-Cola collectibles for any length of time knows, it is virtually impossible for any book, even one as extensive as this one, to cover the subject completely. There are some areas of collecting that have obviously been left out of this edition. For the most part, this book covers Coca-Cola collectibles produced from 1886 to the early 1970s. Many long time collectors consider the early 1970s—when the wave logo started—as a cut off point for traditional collecting. I am not sure that I follow that belief anymore. However, I cut off coverage at this time mainly because this is where my main interest ends, and tracing values of pre-1970s pieces is a big enough job. I will not add items to this book that I cannot cover properly or with accurate and pertinent information. However, some exceptional or unusual pieces have been included from the 1970s to 1980s time period. One area of collecting that has been excluded here, to the surprise of some, is vending machines. Lack of extensive information, and personal interest over the years has kept me from including them. There are a number of excellent books on vending machines and more information on those publications can be found in the back of this book. Other areas of collecting that you will not find in this book include "Made

# INTRODUCTION

for Collectors Market" items such as music boxes, polar bears and catalog items. Also, 75th and 100th Anniversary pieces, commemorative bottles, pin sets (such as Disney, Olympics, state flags, sports) and others are just too recent to be included here. If a piece you have is not shown in the book, do not assume the piece is rare. Both rare and common pieces have sometimes been left out of this book simply because it is just impossible to show everything that is available.

Hopefully, this introduction has helped you understand what you can expect to get from this book, and also helped you

to understand what has been included and what has been excluded, and why. I hope I have given you a better understanding of how the book has been developed and how it should be used to be most effective. Also, as you review the book, I hope you find it as interesting and helpful as I intended it to be. Please take the time to read my explanation concerning how I developed the values shown. Before passing judgement regarding values that you may feel are too high or too low, consider all the factors that go into pricing this material and the responsibility involved.

## ABOUT THE AUTHOR

Being in the printing and advertising business with an interest in history provided a natural opportunity for Allan Petretti to become interested in collecting the advertising of The Coca-Cola Company. By the early 1970s he was a devoted collector and was among the early group of organized collectors. A member of The Coca-Cola Collectors' Club, he created, organized and conducted the first club auction at the San Diego convention in 1978. Beginning in 1976, he published his first mail-bid auction. Twenty-one years and forty-two auctions later, these semi-annual auctions have become one of the main sources of quality Coca-Cola and other soda-pop memorabilia, selling over 52,000 pieces.

This continuous buying, selling, evaluating and staying on top of current market values, combined with a vast library of photographs, created the perfect opportunity to produce a book which showed and evaluated Coca-Cola memorabilia. Since 1977, when the first edition of this book was produced, it has become the main source of information and current pricing for thousands and thousands of today's collectors. *Petretti's Coca-Cola Collectible Price Guide*, now in its 10th edition, is not only considered the "bible" to most collectors, but has also become the standard by which many other price guides follow. With his strong distaste for illegal, unauthorized Coca-Cola collectibles, Mr. Petretti has become a leading opponent of counterfeit material and insists on uncovering and showing as much of it as possible in his books. Most recently he has

produced *Petretti's Soda-Pop Collectible Price Guide*. In its first edition, this in the only book which deals with the entire soda-pop collectibles' field.

Allan Petretti's many appearances on nationally syndicated television and radio shows include "Personal FX," "Smart Money with the Dolans," "Whatchagot" with Harry Rinker, and "Rinker on Collectibles." In addition, he is a regular talk show guest on radio stations nationwide. Mr. Petretti also writes a regular column for the *Antique Trader Weekly*, *Gameroom Magazine*, as well as writing feature articles for a number of antique publications. He also does seminars around the country to Coca-Cola Collectors' groups. Mr. Petretti also has been interviewed by *The Wall Street Journal, USA Today, The Robb Report* (Investibles), and collectible columnists from all over the country. He is also called upon to conduct appraisals for insurance companies and private collections.

Writing on Coca-Cola collectibles, as well as buying and selling on a full time basis, Mr. Petretti has become one of the foremost authorities on values and market trends of Coca-Cola memorabilia in the country.

Correspondence from fellow collectors and any information on rare and unusual items is always welcome. Write to:

Allan Petretti
21 South Lake Drive
Hackensack, NJ 07601

# VALUE-CONDITION-INVESTMENT POTENTIAL

The following chart shows in detail the condition on which my book prices are based. Values shown are based on excellent or "8" condition, which I call average. As the condition rises so does value, as well as dropping in lesser condition. The chart also indicates how the value and condition relates to investment potential.

| 1934 TRAY | | CONDITION | VALUE | NOTE |
|---|---|---|---|---|
| | 10 | MINT | $1,800.00*<br><br><br><br>$1,700.00 | *The price difference in the Mint category can be justified by brighter colors and higher shine.*<br><br>*Remember—Mint means Mint, Flawless, Perfect, no visible marks. There is no "Mint, Except . . ."*<br><br>*Investment Potential $$$$$$* |
| | 9.8 | NEAR MINT ++ | $1,400.00 | *The Near Mint category has a wider range, and abused more than any other category.* |
| | 9.5 | NEAR MINT + | $1,300.00 | *Every chip or scratch could lower the value.*<br><br>*Remember—Near Mint means just about perfect, with only minor problems.* |
| | 9 | NEAR MINT | $1,200.00 | *Investment Potential $$$$$* |
| | 8.9 | EXCELLENT ++ | AVERAGE CONDITION | *This is the category that most pieces fall into. It is in this range of condition that book prices are based. Most pieces are not found in Mint condition, this is the average or middle ground.* |
| | 8.5 | EXCELLENT + | $1,000.00 | |
| | 8 | EXCELLENT | AVERAGE PRICE | *Investment Potential $$$$* |
| | 7 | VERY GOOD | $700.00 | *Desirability, Displayability, Re-sale potential, and Collectibility, begin to drop at this point. Also notice how prices drop faster than they rise.* |
| | 6 | GOOD + | $500.00 | |
| | 5 | GOOD | $375.00 | *Investment Potential $$* |
| | 4 | FAIR | $200.00 | *Collectibility is gone at this point, even as a filler piece. It's very questionable if the piece is even worth having.* |
| | 3 | | | *Remember—Rare pieces are certainly as exception.* |
| | 1–2 | POOR | $1.00–$50.00 | *Investment Potential $* |

(In the EXCELLENT section, vertically: BOOK PRICES FALL IN THIS RANGE)

Investment Potential—$$$$$$ = The Best     $$$$$ = Super     $$$$ = Excellent     $$ = Not very good     $ = Bad

*This chart does not mean that pieces in Mint condition will be worth double book price. The 1934 tray is above average in desirability, and because of this, top dollar, Mint condition price, is higher than other trays, or pieces of less desirability. Each piece has to be evaluated on its merits, desirability, condition, etc. In some cases, top dollar, Mint condition price may only be 10% over book price.

With all the thousands of images in this book, it becomes necessary to be able to access these images easily. This Identification System not only allows us to identify and access an individual image quickly, but also enables collectors and dealers to find a particular item in the book without going through complete sections. By knowing the number of the piece, it can be found by looking it up in the numerical index in the back of the book. Listed next to the image identification number will be the page or pages that image appears on. Once familiar with this "Image Identification System" number, pointing out pieces to potential buyers, or quickly accessing a photo, will be very easy.

Because of the extensive number of images, as well as the thousands and thousands yet to be identified by this system, it becomes necessary to use a three-letter category code followed by a six-digit number. Keep in mind that this code number does not necessarily follow the chronological order of the piece. The last three digits allows us to give additional information to the reader about this particular piece—if it is a variation, part of a set, a piece of a larger display, if its boxed, and other pertinent information.

Below, you will find information on how this "Image Identification System" works as well as an alphabetical listing of identification codes. This system consists of three parts. First is a set of code letters. The first letter in the code is always the same "P" which identifies the book in which the system is used *Petretti's Coca Cola Collectibles Price Guide* (P). The next two letters are the actual item's identification code, for example, "CA"—calendar. (A complete listing of the codes follows.) The next three digits is the actual image number (remember these numbers are not necessarily in order of the piece's chronological order). The three-digit code number is followed by a decimal point (.) and then three additional letters or digits. This series of letters and numbers allows additional information to be known about that particular piece, for example:

| | |
|---|---|
| .000 | - no additional information needed |
| .001 | - variation no. 1 |
| .S00 | - complete set |
| .S01 | - no. 1 of set |
| .B00 | - in original box or package |
| .BS0 | - complete set in box or package |
| .P01 | - part no. 1 of a multi-piece sign or object |
| .F00 | - foreign |

| **Example 1** | 1915 calendar w/bottle .......PCA036.002 | 1943 airplane hanger ..........PCS355.S18 |
|---|---|---|
| 1921 calendar ...............PCA045.000 | 1915 calendar w/color variation .PCA036.003 | no. 18 of set |
| **Example 2** | **Example 4** | **Example 5** |
| 1921 calendar (top only) .......PCA045.P01 | 1943 airplane hangers .........PCS355.S00 | 1933 Metalcraft toy truck .......PTC005.000 |
| **Example 3** | (cardboard signs) set of 20 | 1933 Metalcraft toy truck .......PTC005.B00 |
| 1915 calendar w/glass ........PCA036.001 | 1943 airplane hanger ..........PCS355.S01 | in original box |
| | no. 1 of set | |

PAN - Anniversary items

PBL - Blotters
PBM - Bookmarks
PBN - Books, notebooks, tablets
PBA - Bottles (amber straight side type)
PBC - Bottle Carriers
PBG - Bottles (clear, green, etc. - straight side)
PBD - Bottle Displays
PBY - Bottles (display type)
PBF - Bottles (flavor type)
PBT - Bottles (Hobbleskirt or commemorative type)
PBH - Bottles (Hutchinson type)
PBQ - Bottles (24 oz., 28 oz., quart size)
PBS - Bottles (seltzer type)

PCA - Calendars
PCN - Cans
PCC - Canvas or Cloth Signs
PCS - Cardboard or Celluloid Signs
PCD - Cardboard Diecuts
PCB - Change Receivers, Plates Bowls
PCG - Chewing Gum
PCL - Clocks
PCH - Clothing, Patches
PCO - Commemorative Items
PCE - Coolers (electric & vending machines)
PCI - Coolers (ice chests)
PCP - Coolers (picnic)
PCT - Coupons, Tradecards, Postcards

PDE - Decals and Stickers

PDS - Dispensers
PDF - Display Frames
PDP - Display Pieces
PDR - Display Racks

PES - Educational Material (school stuff, etc.)

PFS - Flange Signs
PFN - Fans, Napkins, Coasters
PFA - Fantasy and Recent Items
PFE - Festoons

PGA - Games
PGC - Glasses, Cups, Mugs
PGS - Glass Signs

PKP - Knives, Ice Picks, Silverware, Etc.

PLE - Letterhead, Letters, Envelopes, Invoices
PLS - Light-up Signs and Lamps

PMB - Menu Boards
PMI - Miniatures
PMC - Mirrors (pocket), celluloid items
PMD - Miscellaneous 3-D items
PMS - Miscellaneous Signs
PMU - Music

POP - Openers
POA - Original Art

PPM - Paper Material

PPS - Paper Signs
PPA - Periodical Advertising
PPH - Photos
PPJ - Pins, Buttons, Jewelry, Fobs
PPL - Playing Cards
PPC - Porcelain Signs

PRA - Radios, Music Boxes
PRC - Relative Collectibles
PRE - Reproductions
PRB - Rip-off Brands

PSS - Salesman Samples
PSP - Small Collectibles
PSM - Smoking Material (matches, lighters, etc.)
PSR - Sports Related
PST - Straws
PSC - Syrup Containers

PTM - Serving Trays (misc. or foreign)
PTO - Serving Trays (oval or round)
PTR - Serving Trays (rectangle)

PTH - Thermometers
PTN - Tin Signs
PTT - Tip Trays/Change Trays
PTY - Toys
PTC - Toy Trucks and Cars
PTS - Trolley Signs

PVA - Vienna Art Plates

PWC - Wallets, Change Purses, etc.

# HISTORY OF THE COCA-COLA COMPANY AND ORGANIZED COCA-COLA COLLECTING

The History of The Coca-Cola Company is an incredible story that has been written about many times. While some of the books written about this company have created controversy, it is not the intent of this brief outlined sketch to either confirm or deny any of these stories. Rather, the intent is to give the collector an overview of how this company has evolved over the years, in order to better understand the history of the objects that are collected. A somewhat different approach has been taken with the following historic account. By breaking it down into eras, it not only recounts the history, but also explains to collectors some of the advertising used during those eras. Hopefully, this outlined history, along with the information on how this history relates to the objects we collect, will be helpful to many of you. Keep in mind that this is not intended to be a detailed in-depth account, but rather a sketch for you to better understand the origin and growth of The Coca-Cola Company.

The history of this soft drink sold by it's trademarked name "Coca-Cola" is certainly one of the most interesting stories of an American business. Originated from an idea conceived over one hundred and ten years ago, Coca-Cola has become the most popular and largest selling soft drink of all time.

The creator of Coca-Cola, Dr. John Stith Pemberton, was born in 1831 in Knoxville, Georgia. Attending schools in both Columbus and Rome, Georgia, he later went on to study at Southern Botanico Medical College of Georgia. After obtaining a degree in pharmacy, he began his career as a druggist in Oglethorp, Georgia. In 1853, Pemberton married Anna Lewis, and the following year she gave birth to their only child, Charles Ney Pemberton. In 1855, the Pemberton family moved to Columbus, Georgia where he became a popular and successful druggist. While Pemberton's business was pharmacy, he also practiced medicine and did perform some minor surgery. However, a great deal of his success and income was derived from the sales of proprietary medicines. With the outbreak of war, Pemberton, now in his thirties, enlisted as a First Lieutenant in 1862. During 1862 and 1863, he served as Captain and eventually as Colonel of Company K, Robinson's Georgia Cavalry. In 1865, with the war actually over, Pemberton was seriously injured in one of the last engagements with Union soldiers. Recuperated but badly scarred, Pemberton attempted to rebuild his business. Towards that end he formed a partnership with well-to-do physician, Dr. Austin Walker. The relationship between Pemberton and Walker flourished, and in the late 1860s Pemberton began producing his own line of proprietary medicines, including a product which claimed to purify the blood—Extract of Stillingia—as well as Globe Flower Cough Syrup, and others. With a fine laboratory and profitable business in Columbus, Pemberton felt only true success would only come by moving to Atlanta, which he did in 1869. Continuing his experimenting with proprietary medicines, he developed an impressive list of products including Gingerine, Indian Queen Hair Dye, Triplex Pills, and a number of other cures, elixirs, perfumes and drinks. Pemberton's desire to create the perfect medicine and drink led him to experimenting with a remarkable substance,

JOHN STITH PEMBERTON

derived from coca leaves, which was supposed to aid digestion and extend life. Burdened with financial problems complicated by a fire which destroyed much of his business, Pemberton began to rebuild his business and he continued to experiment to develop his line of medicines. His combination of wine and coca became known as "Pemberton's French Wine Coca." Although it imitated other products on the market at the time, including Vin Mariani, Pemberton felt his product was much better and the answer to his desire for a perfect product. But the temperance movement which began in the 1870s was now gaining strength, and by 1886 the use of wine in medicine was about to come to an end.

Another product being developed by Pemberton was Coca-Cola, which, by the way, was listed along with French Wine Coca and other products like Gingerine on his letterhead at the time. With constant experimenting with this Coca-and-Cola drink, he finally felt it was right, and as the legend goes, it went to the Venable soda fountain at Jacob's Pharmacy to be tried out. It is important to point out at this time that any product developed by, or represented by, Dr. J.S. Pemberton is part of the history of Coca-Cola and very collectible. Although overlooked for the most part, these pre-Coca-Cola collectibles are now gaining in popularity and value, and I might add that products and advertising associated with either Venable's soda fountain or Jacobs' Pharmacy are also very collectible. The popularity of this new so-called "temperance drink" grew with the addition of carbonated water. Pemberton was finally pleased with his product and began devoting much of his time to it. While Pemberton was still creating and perfecting his then-unnamed product, two business men attempting to sell a printing machine came to Atlanta. Frank Robinson and his partner David Doe, from Maine, approached Pemberton with a deal and, along with Pemberton's partner at the time, Ed Holland, the four men started the "Pemberton Chemical Company." Robinson soon forgot his printing equipment and began devoting his entire attention to producing and promoting Coca-Cola (by the way, he created the name Coca-Cola). Robinson was very excited with the new product, and with very little available money promoted Coca-Cola well through the use of oilcloth banners, newspaper ads, and free sample tickets. In addition, there is evidence that paper posters and streetcar signs were also used. These very early advertising pieces are almost unheard of in the Coca-Cola collecting community, and anything from this era is considered extremely rare.

By the Spring of 1887, one partner of the Pemberton Chemical Company, David Doe, decided to call it quits. M.P. Alexander, a pharmacist from Memphis, took his place and the company pushed forward with much needed cash and additional help—including the addition of one Woolfolk Walker and Pemberton's son Charles, as the company's salesmen. In 1887, Dr. Pemberton applied for a patent for the Coca-Cola trademark, which was granted in June of 1887. In July of 1887, for some unknown reason, Pemberton sold the majority of his interest in Coca-Cola to Willis Venable and George Lowndes. Pemberton retained the remaining interest for his son, Charles. From July of 1887, when Pemberton sold his majority interest, until December of that year, much confusion and many transactions took place, including many new names and claims being introduced. Some of these names like A.O. Murphy, J.C. Mayfield, Mrs. Dozier, and others would play an important part in the future of The Coca-Cola Company some years later.

In early 1888, with the enticing of Frank Robinson, an

**ASA CANDLER**

Atlanta druggist named Asa Candler, who was interested in obtaining new products, became interested in Coca-Cola and soon he began taking control. With part of the interest owned by Joseph Jacobs of Jacobs' Pharmacy, Candler was able to acquire his share, and in March of 1888 Candler, Charles Pemberton, Woolfolk Walker, and his sister Mrs. M.C. Dozier, filed to incorporate The Coca-Cola Company. Within weeks of the incorporation on April 14, 1888, Charles Pemberton was bought out for $550, and on April 17, Candler bought half of the interest owned jointly by Walker and Dozier. During the summer of 1888, Dr. Pemberton died of cancer. The death of this well known and popular gentleman ended the first era in history of The Coca-Cola Company.

Asa Candler continued to acquire control of Coca-Cola, and in August of 1888 bought out Walker and Dozier for a grand total of $1,000. So, after a great deal of change, transfers and buy-outs, Asa Candler, for the most part, took complete control as the sole proprietor of Coca-Cola.

Asa Candler's life began on December 30, 1851, one of eleven children of Sam and Martha Candler of Villa Rica, Georgia. As a youth during the Civil War, Candler received little education but did complete some high school education after the war. In 1870, Candler quit school and became an apprentice in a drugstore in Cartersville, Georgia. While working and living at the drugstore, Candler kept his dream of becoming a doctor alive by studying chemistry and medicine in his spare time. Over the next couple of years, Candler felt his main interest was in becoming a druggist and he gave up hope of being a physician. But he felt this could best be done in the big city of Atlanta. Candler arrived in Atlanta in January of 1873 with hopes of landing a position with a local druggist. Disappointed that the job was not available, he canvassed all of Atlanta until he got lucky at a drug store owned by George Howard. Candler worked hard for his boss, and in 1877, Howard offered Candler and another employee, Marcellus Hallman, an opportunity to buy one of his stores. The

partnership was good, and with hard work, smart business deals and luck they had built in a couple of years a very good business. In 1878, Asa Candler married Lucy Howard, his former boss' daughter, even though Dr. Howard felt his daughter was much too young. In December of 1878, Lucy gave birth to a son, Charles Howard Candler, who was the first of five children—four boys and a girl. In 1881, after ending his partnership with Marcellus Hallman, Asa Candler entered into a partnership with his father-in-law, Dr. George Howard, and in 1886 bought out his interest and the company became Asa G. Candler and Company.

Atlanta was a boom town in 1886 and Candler, at thirty-five years old, was on his way to building his fortune. Before taking total control of Coca-Cola, Candler bought the rights to an impressive list of proprietary medicines and other products including Electric Bitters, De-Lec-Ta-Lave, King's New Discover, Everlasting Cologne, Bucklen's Arnica Salve, and others. Any advertising relating to these products that were owned and distributed by Asa Candler, including the very popular Botanic Blood Balm (B.B.B.) which came later in 1889, is very collectible. Trade cards, calendars, ads (especially when mentioning Asa Candler, Wholesale Druggist) are an important part of the history of Coca-Cola and are becoming more popular and valuable as collectors better understand their history. From 1888 to 1890, Candler conducted his wholesale and retail drug business on Peachtree Street in Atlanta, with Frank Robinson handling the manufacturing of Coca-Cola and one man handling sales of not only his patent medicines but Coca-Cola as well. With business doing well another salesman, Sam Dobbs, Candler's nephew, was added to the payroll. With the sales of Coca-Cola consistently growing during this time, Candler realized the potential of his soda fountain drink and began divesting himself of all of his patent medicines with the exception of De-Lec-Ta-Lave and B.B.B., which were still selling very well.

By 1891, Candler sold his drug business and moved his Coca-Cola manufacturing business to 42 1/2 Decatur Street, after selling off De-Lec-Ta-Lave and B.B.B. He filed to incorporate The Coca-Cola Company on December 29, 1891. With the sales of Coca-Cola continuing to soar, Candler sought to spread out his sales and shares in his new company and he found an investor in Boston. Seth Fowle & Sons, Proprietary Druggists, bought fifty shares of stock along with all rights to the New England area for the next twenty years. It proved to be a great move. The New England area was flooded with advertising, and sales skyrocketed. Because of this early relationship between Fowle and Coca-Cola, some rare and unusual pieces have come out of the New England area over the years. Seth Fowle also published *The Coca-Cola News* in the 1890s and early 1900s. These small fold-over papers were directed to drug stores and soda fountains in the New England area, and they are considered rare today.

During the early 1890s, with sales continually on the increase, a considerable amount of advertising was produced incorporating the distinctive Coca-Cola script logo on signs, calendars, newspaper ads, and any place else where the public could notice that now-recognizable trademark. While this early advertising was for the most part medicinal, the product was called "Delicious and Refreshing" right from the start. These advertising pieces proclaiming that Coca-Cola was the "Ideal Brain Tonic," "Cures Headache," and "Relieves

Exhaustion" among others, are the most valuable, rare and interesting of all Coca-Cola memorabilia, and highly in demand by collectors. By 1894, free drink "tickets" were being used, as they were earlier, to get people to try the product. These tickets were mailed out and handed out by the thousands. The system of giving away free drink tickets worked well, and began a practice that was continued by Coca-Cola for many years. These free drink tickets are always collectible, especially the early versions.

By 1895, the product Coca-Cola was being sold in every state and territory in the United states. As the 1890s were coming to an end, The Coca-Cola Company slowly continued to lessen its medicinal claims, many ads and advertising pieces simply claimed that Coca-Cola was "Delicious and Refreshing." This practice continued as Congress passed a tax on proprietary medicines, and not beverages. With the Internal Revenue ruling that Coca-Cola was a drug, it was ordered to pay the tax. A long battle with the government continued until it was finally decided, in 1902, that Coca-Cola was indeed a soft drink. However, as the turn of the century came to an end, occasional mention of "Relief for Headache" and other benefits remained.

During the last half of the 1890s, syrup plants and branch offices were opened in Dallas, Chicago, Los Angeles, Philadelphia and, in 1899, an office in New York City was added, continuing the company's growth and acceptance of the product by the American people. Just before the turn of the century, in July of 1899, something happened that was so important that it would change the history of Coca-Cola from that point on. Two lawyers from Tennessee, Benjamin Franklin Thomas and Joseph Brown Whitehead, finally, after repeated attempts, entered into an agreement with Asa Candler to sell the product Coca-Cola in bottles. Candler, not thinking very highly of the idea, signed the contact believing that with this franchise he had very little to lose. The fact is that this contract had huge implications for the Coca-Cola business and started a franchising system that turned out to be enormous and way beyond all expectations. With this, company approved franchised bottling, the practice of putting the product in a bottle, began. Five years earlier, Joseph Biedenharn of Vicksburg, Mississippi, who sold Coca-Cola at his soda fountain, felt it could be sold in bottles to people who lived in areas that had no soda fountain. At the time Asa Candler was not impressed. So, technically, the Thomas and Whitehead contract was the beginning of company-authorized bottling and their timing was just perfect.

By 1900, the cumbersome, difficult-to-use Hutchinson stoppered bottles were being replaced with a new bottle designed with a top that allowed a metal crown to be crimped and sealed over it. This crown would change the course of the bottling industry from that point on, and the impact on collectors of these early bottling attempts is tremendous. Hutchinson bottles are becoming more and more valuable as collectors insist on having examples of them in their collections. Values of these bottles have increased steadily over the years.

Brown and Whitehead flourished, both hard-working businessmen that became the forerunners—the "Parent Bottlers"—who were now experiencing phenomenal sales and reaching rural areas that fountain sales could not normally reach. But because of differences that they just could not agree

on, they decided to split their territory and by the following decade three hundred and seventy-nine bottling plants were in operation. With the task still much larger than the two men could handle, they decided to further divide their large domain. This resulted in the formation of four parent bottling companies.

Even though Joseph Biedenharn had been bottling Coca-Cola without a contract since 1894, he finally agreed to a formal contract for The Coca-Cola Bottling Company. Many bottlers followed as The Coca-Cola Bottling business flourished. Although the product was the same, the package varied from bottler to bottler. The large variety of bottles used has created a wealth of resources for today's collectors to search for a wide range of variations. This lack of uniformity would soon end.

Along with the bottling sales successes went continued success with syrup sales through soda fountains. The sale of syrup in 1900 for 370,877 gallons was exceeded by one million gallons annually by 1904. The combination of popular soda fountains and a progressive bottling industry marked a time of exceptional growth. By 1917, gallonage sales skyrocketed to over twelve million annually. With consistent growth and great leadership, and while serving as mayor of Atlanta, Asa G. Candler decided to give his business to his wife and five children, while keeping only seven shares in his name. In less than two years the most important business transaction the South had ever seen took place. The Coca-Cola Company was sold for $25,000,000. The majority ownership at the time of the sale was held by Asa Candler's five children, Judge J.S. Candler, Sam Dobbs, Frank Robinson and Samuel L. Willard. The sale of the company was consummated on September 12, 1919.

On the purchasing side was Ernest Woodruff, backed by The Trust Company of Georgia, of which Woodruff was President. Along with the Chase National Bank and the Guaranty Trust Company of New York City, the new company was incorporated in the state of Delaware. Ernest Woodruff expanded the facilities of The Coca-Cola Company and added a syrup plant in New Orleans in 1919. The continual growth under Ernest Woodruff leadership brought an end to the Candler era.

The Coca-Cola Company was poising itself for a period of growth that was unprecedented, but first it had to correct some problems. From the beginning, as Coca-Cola gained popularity, the company battled off hoards of imitators who attempted to capitalize on this product's success. (This subject is covered in more detail in another section of this book, "Coca-Cola and the Competition.") While Harold Hirsh was in full charge of The Coca-Cola Company's legal affairs and continually fought and won these battles with the imitators in the courts, he became increasingly frustrated with non-uniformity of the Coca-Cola bottle.

The bottles used by the hundreds of bottlers around the country varied too much from clear to several shades of green, and from light amber to dark amber. The sizes varied, as did the shapes; some used labels and some did not. The result was a hodgepodge of bottles that looked just like all other pop bottles of the time. Coca-Cola needed a new package, a bottle that would stand out far and above any other. Convincing bottlers of the need for an expensive new bottle would not be easy, but Harold Hirsch, at the 1914 Bottlers Convention, stressed the importance of spending the money now for the protection it would bring in the future. In June of 1915, a number of glass manufacturers were asked to create a distinctive package for Coca-Cola. It was an employee of The Root Glass Company, while experimenting, who came up with an unusual sample that would later become known as the "Hobbleskirt" design. At The Coca-Cola Bottlers Convention in 1916, the design of the bottle was accepted. However, getting all the bottlers to switch over to the more expensive bottle would take a number of years.

By the summer of 1917 new problems arose. With the United States entering World War I, it became necessary to ration sugar. The Company recommended that bottlers make no attempt to expand their market because of the effect this lack of sugar would have on syrup production. The Coca-Cola Company used the problem to its benefit, asking the public for its patience and producing patriotic ads to show that the company was behind the war effort. In 1919, with the war over, the recovery from rationing of sugar was quick for The Coca-Cola Company and sales made a dramatic upward swing: from 10,314,727 gallons in 1918 to 18,730,167 in 1919.

The advertising created by The Coca-Cola Company during the teens was fabulous. The company had a vision of what the "All American Girl" looked like, and demanded it on its advertising. "The Coca-Cola Girls" of the teens are among the most beautiful of all their advertising. Starting in 1914 the calendars produced by the company became larger and featured full-body images, dressed in the latest fashions of the day. These girls, even though different models, had the same look—the eyes, parted mouth, and the hair, it was all part of that look—the "Girl Next Door" look. These calendars are the highlight of collectible Coca-Cola advertising during the teens.

**ROBERT W. WOODRUFF**

By 1923, Robert Winship Woodruff, the thirty-three-year-old son of Ernest and Emily Winship Woodruff, took over as President of The Coca-Cola Company. Robert was born in 1889 in Columbus, Georgia, and was brought to Atlanta in 1893. He attended school near his home in Inman Park, and then Georgia Military Academy. His early employment included The General Pipe and Foundry Company in Atlanta, The General Fire Extinguisher Company, and The Atlantic Ice & Coal Company as purchasing agent. On October 17, 1912 he married Miss Nell Hodgson of Athens, Georgia. After his marriage he took a job with the White Motor Company and within a year was a branch manager in Atlanta. By 1916 he was elected to the Board of Directors of The Trust Company of Georgia. He was only twenty-seven years old. After a stint in the war with the motor corps, Woodruff became Vice President of the White Company in 1922, but resigned in 1923 to become President of The Coca-Cola Company.

The Woodruff era was to mark a dramatic change in the advertising of Coca-Cola. The D'arcy Advertising Company took on the Coca-Cola account at the same time Robert Woodruff took over presidency of The Coca-Cola Company, mainly because D'arcy employee Archie Laney Lee, a former reporter for the *Atlanta Georgian*, was a personal friend of Woodruff. The business relationship strengthened their personal relationship, and the results had an incredible positive effect on the company's advertising that would last for the next quarter of a century.

With standardization of the bottle back in 1916, Robert Woodruff felt it necessary to continue the process. The next big move to standardize the bottlers came in 1924, with the formation of a Standardization Committee. Woodruff felt that Coca-Cola in bottles was the future of the Coca-Cola business. The committee, headed by Charles V. Rainwater, held its first meeting and recommended a standard design for trucks, cases, stationery, checks and many other things including uniforms for drivers. Subsequent meetings resulted in the development of standardized plans for bottling plants. In 1929, the committee published a booklet titled *Coca-Cola Bottler's Standards*. The booklet presented the rules of standardization along with specifications and actual samples. These books are prized collector items. Since the standardization committee started in the 1920s, The Coca-Cola Company has continued standardization to this day. With standardization in place and in light of Woodruff's favorable feelings toward bottle sales, he called for increased advertising that emphasized Coca-Cola in bottles. The policy showed big results from 1923 to 1928. While fountain sales grew twenty percent, bottle sales increased by sixty-five percent.

The "Bottle vs. Fountain" advertising creates some interesting variations for today's collectors. The same artwork modified with a glass for fountain sales or a bottle for bottle sales provide perfect additions to collections. The advertising that Woodruff and Lee developed presented Coca-Cola as much more than a soft drink. It was actually part of your life, distinctive and enjoyed by every segment of society, and meant to symbolize the pleasant things that life had to offer. By 1925 the planned nationwide use of billboards to advertise Coca-Cola was shared by The Coca-Cola Company and local bottlers. In 1927, The Coca-Cola Company used commercial radio to advertise and continued the practice for the next twenty-five years until the advent television.

Many other ground-breaking advertising campaigns went into effect in the 1920s. Archie Lee's use of the word "Pause" in Coca-Cola advertising led to one of the greatest expressions of American advertising: "The Pause That Refreshes." The late 1920s also saw the first "Big City" electric sign, spectacular in New York's Times Square. During the Depression of the early and mid-1930s, Lee continued creating advertising landmarks by hiring artist Haddon Sundblum, who produced the Santa Claus image that we are now so familiar with as a yearly tradition. During the early 1930s, The Coca-Cola Company began associating Coca-Cola with food. The slogan "Natural Partner of Good Things to Eat" continued the process of showing that Coca-Cola is more than just a drink for when you were thirsty. Good at home, at work, with food and everywhere!

The advertising of the late 1920s changed dramatically as the 1930s unfolded. The flappers and pretty girls that were earlier displayed on calendars were now replaced by the

"Down Home" images of young boys fishing, with great artwork by Norman Rockwell, N.C. Wyeth and others. Since calendars were mainly brought into the home, these images were important to The Coca-Cola Company, which wished to portray Coca-Cola as a family drink that was as popular with the children as the grown ups. The connection of Coca-Cola at home carried through the late 1930s with the introduction of the open top six-bottle carton, letting consumers know that it was "So easy to take home."

In 1940, one of the most successful advertising and public relations campaigns in the company's history was launched with publication of the first of a series of three booklets titled *Flower Arranging in the Home*. Over five million of these booklets were given away over the next three years, continuing the growing sales of Coca-Cola by the six-pack for home use. As sales continually skyrocketed, Archie Lee continued to come up with ground-breaking advertising including the use of the trademark "Coke" making its first appearance in national advertising in 1941. In 1942 "Coke" was highlighted by the image of "The Little Sprite," or what collectors now call "The Sprite Boy." This little pixie, created by Archie Lee and delineated by Haddon Sunblom, helped emphasize the connection between "Coke" and "Coca-Cola."

As America entered World War II, Robert Woodruff set the direction of The Coca-Cola Company's business efforts by stating "We will see that every man in uniform gets a bottle of Coca-Cola for five cents wherever he is and whatever it costs." During the war sixty-four bottling operations were set up as close to battle areas as possible. During the war over 5,000,000,000 bottles of Coke were consumed by the men and women of the armed forces. By 1946, over one hundred and fifty Coca-Cola Bottling Plants were in operation around the world in the former areas of military operations. World War II affected the entire world, with very few exceptions. With so many countries in economic ruin it would be quite a while before many could enjoy a normal economy, and not until the 1950s did Coca-Cola reopen many of those markets. In 1949, the first plant to produce Coca-Cola syrup outside the United States was in Brussels, Belgium.

War-time advertising produced by The Coca-Cola Company is always of special interest to collectors. Because of the war effort, metal was not used in advertising, which meant no serving trays, tin signs, etc. But advertising must go on and go on it did. With wood and masonite replacing the tin signs, companies that produced specialty advertising like Kay Displays, Inc., flourished. Magazine advertising was increased with beautiful, colorful patriotic ads showing our service people in uniform. These gave the country a sense of pride. The war effort showed up in much of the company's advertising with sets of signs called "Airplane Hangers" which depicted our aircraft winning the air battles of the war. This wartime advertising is always very popular among collectors, with the cream of the crop being a set of cardboard cutouts showing service women from the five branches of the services, enjoying a glass or bottle of Coke. Produced in a small set as well as a full-size set, these are certainly among the best advertising done during this period.

With the war over and our servicemen coming home, the United States was preparing for a period of prosperity and relaxation. The 1950s saw the servicemen home with their families, picnics, ballgames and leisure time—meaning Coke

time—and Americans drank it like never before. It took The Coca-Cola Company until 1944 to sell its first billion gallons of syrup, with the second billion gallons being sold by 1953. Collectors should note that with the leisure and fun times of the early '50s came an influx of picnic coolers by The Coca-Cola Company. Between ballgames, picnics and the beach, the need to keep those Cokes cold was very important and the use of picnic coolers became very popular. Because of this, most of the picnic coolers from the '50s and '60s are fairly common today. With the world starting to get back to some type of normalcy in the 1950s, Coca-Cola was quickly becoming a worldwide drink with no other soft drink ever enjoying such world wide popularity.

The 1950s added a whole new dimension to Coca-Cola advertising—television. The Coca-Cola Company was well aware that television was not only revolutionizing entertainment in the home, but everywhere, and they took advantage of it. The Coca-Cola Company sponsored a Thanksgiving special in 1950 which featured Edgar Bergen and Charlie McCarthy, marking their first TV appearance. This show was followed by a Christmas special "One Hour in Wonderland" which starred Edgar Bergen and Walt Disney's animated characters. In the later '50s, Coca-Cola and Disney — would team up again, sponsoring "The Mickey Mouse Club." Because of the baby boom of post World War II, The Coca-Cola Company felt it important to reach children, and what better way than via television. In 1951 they sponsored "The Adventures of Kit Carson," which starred Bill Williams. The popular cowboy was a big hit with the kids. In 1953, seeking to appeal to all age groups, they sponsored Eddie Fisher in "Coke Time," another popular show that resulted in exactly what Coca-Cola was looking for: A family show with appeal beyond just the kids. These early television shows resulted in a tremendous amount of related material to collect, from records, toys, premiums, posters and magazine ads to a cardboard cutout of Eddie Fisher. These TV-related collectibles are very popular with a generation that remembers these shows so vividly.

In 1955, Coca-Cola introduced a number of new packages. A twenty-six ounce family size and two king size bottles: a ten ounce and a twelve ounce with a modified hobbleskirt design. The mid-1950s saw big changes in American life, new entertainment resources like TV, and a resurgence of traditional recreation activities such as bowling, roller skating and movies were putting a big dent in the popularity of the drug store soda fountain. Big time supermarkets were putting the corner grocery stores out of business. Rock and roll was taking over the teens, and the automobile had become much more important than just a means of taking you to work. In 1954 a chain of hamburger stands owned by two brothers named McDonald were bought out by Ray Kroc. With his hamburgers and fries he offered customers Coca-Cola, starting a relationship which proved to be fantastic for both McDonald's and Coca-Cola.

With music becoming more popular in American life than ever before, Coca-Cola and its advertising company, McCann-Erickson attempted to keep up with the popular music of the day. New advertising initiatives included The McGuire Sisters, Ricky Nelson, Anita Bryant and a very popular program, the "Hi-Fi" club. The "Hi-Fi" club was a series of dance parties sponsored by the local radio stations and Coca-Cola bottlers.

(More detailed information on the "Hi-Fi" club can be found later in this book).

By 1962, J. Paul Austin became the President of The Coca-Cola Company. Austin, a graduate of Harvard Law School who commanded a PT Boat in World War II, would lead The Coca-Cola Company into a whole new decade with the addition of newly created diet drink, Tab. In 1963, Mc Cann-Erickison and Coca-Cola needed a song—a theme that would sum up everything that was needed to be said about Coca-Cola in one short verse—and they found it. Written by Bill Backer, the song and campaign "Things Go Better With Coke" became so popular that it was heard and seen everywhere. The 1963 "Things Go Better" campaign created a whole new area of collectibles, including music boxes, musical lighters, novelties, signs and a whole new "fresh" look to Coca-Cola advertising.

These 1960s collectibles are becoming more and more popular. By 1965 the soft drink industry was doing very well, with an annual two hundred and sixty drink per capita, and Coca-Cola held forty-one percent of the market. The mid-1960s also saw the addition of Duncan Foods products such as Minute Maid Orange Juice and Hi-C to The Coca-Cola family. These new additions were advertised as refreshing drinks that could be enjoyed any time of the day, and they were sold in vending machines.

By the late 1960s a new Coke theme song was heard everywhere. The song and the campaign "It's the real thing" flooded the airwaves. At the same time, The Coca-Cola Company felt it needed a new look and hired the New York firm of Lippincott and Margulies to create that new look. The result was the "Dynamic Ribbon" or as collectors call it, the "Wave Logo." Although advertising produced after this point is very collectible, that is basically where this book ends. While the 1970s saw many changes in Coca-Cola, it was on March 7, 1985 that Robert Woodruff died at the age of ninety five. That ended the Woodruff era.

## THE HISTORY OF ORGANIZED COCA-COLA COLLECTING

While we have quite a bit of information showing that people saved or collected advertising and production material produced by The Coca-Cola Company as far back as the 1930s and 1940s, organized collecting did not start until the very early 1970s. At first I was amazed to find small classified ads in company publications from the 1940s from people seeking ceramic syrup dispensers from the 1890s, old advertising, and early bottling equipment. But then I said "Why would that be so strange?" That is exactly what we look for today. While I guess this great advertising has always been admired and saved by collectors, it was not until fairly recent times that these collectors started to interact and become aware of others with the same interest. In the early 1970s The Coca-Cola Company went through a nostalgia craze with a campaign that offered to "Bring Back the Good Ole Trays." Showing and offering these reproduction trays sparked a lot of interest in history and nostalgia fans alike. In 1972, *The Illustrated Guide to the Collectibles of Coca-Cola*, by Cecil Munsey, continued to draw attention to this beautiful artwork as collector interest grew.

While early efforts to organize collectors tried and failed, one collector from Memphis, Tennessee, Bob Buffaloe, succeeded. On no budget at all he published a newsletter that drew all these strangers into a group. Most were amazed that others shared their interest. Bob organized the first convention in Atlanta in 1975, and The Coca-Cola Collectors Club (then known as The Cola Clan) was on its way. With a newsletter that became more informative and inclusive and with more enthusiasts joining the ranks, the conventions became an annual event. The second convention in Elizabethtown, Kentucky, featured the opening of Bill and Jan Schmidt's museum at their bottling plant. Many long timers like myself look back at this event as possibly the very best convention. These conventions became the focal point of the collecting community, something that we anxiously waited for to meet new friends with the same interest, to buy and sell to and stay up to all hours of the night talking Coca-Cola. As the years went on, the ranks grew and the early conventions at Huntsville, San Diego, and Nashville became bigger and better, with the first convention auction being conducted in San Diego. As popularity and values grew, Coca-Cola memorabilia became more and more accepted among advertising collectors and main stream collectors in general. Today it has evolved as one of the top collectibles for long term steady growth.

Much of the information during these early years came from Wilbur Kurtz, Jr., The Coca-Cola Company's archivist. He was a great story teller, with many anecdotes. His love of history and Coca-Cola made him the perfect spokesman for the growing group of Coca-Cola collectors. While some of the information supplied was not totally accurate, it made for great stories. Unfortunately, some of this misinformation stayed with collectors and has become part of history. Compounding the problem was a set of price guides produced in the 1970s that were very helpful on one hand, but contributed to this misinformation on the other hand. It is this unfactual information that is most difficult to eliminate from collectors' minds. For example, the story that Lillian Russell appeared on Coca-Cola advertising, when in fact it was actually a misidentified Lillian Nordica. This, along with other incorrect facts, die hard in the minds of collectors.

As the 1970s went in the 1980s The Coca-Cola Collectors Club grew in numbers and went through a very educational time period with the help of Randy Schaeffer and Bill Bateman—two historians who corrected much misinformation while at the helm of the club newsletter. Big changes have taken place since then, with a club that quite possibly has lost sight of its intended purpose: the organization of a group of people with a common interest, studying, collecting and dealing in the history of The Coca-Cola Company and it's memorabilia. It is mis-direction that I personally hope does not continue.

# CALENDARS

It is not a coincidence that calendars appear first in this book. They have been, since my first day as a collector of Coca-Cola memorabilia, my main interest. I would consider trading any tray or sign I owned for that one particular calendar that I needed. Everyone who collects and enjoys the advertising and production material of The Coca-Cola Company, even those who collect anything with that famous trademark, will admit that there is that one area of collecting that is most fascinating to them. Because of the beautiful artwork and colors, along with the fact that they are rare, calendars have become the most important pieces in my collection.

Many people do not realize the importance of the calendar as a marketing tool in the days before radio or television. Of course there were newspaper and magazine ads and signs which brought the product before the public eye, but the calendar was much more than that. This was a useful product that was given away to consumers with the hope that they would hang them in their homes, both to remind them of the date and that Coca-Cola was "delicious and refreshing." It obviously worked, and worked well. The Coca-Cola Company realized this, producing at least one type of calendar every year beginning in 1891. In some cases a few different calendars were produced in one year.

During my early years of collecting, there was only one group of price guides available on Coca-Cola collectibles, and the discrepancies between the calendars shown in these books and the calendars that I was purchasing were very obvious. It soon became clear that many of the calendar pads shown were switched or altered in some way. Those price guides, unfortunately, are still available, showing the misdated and altered calendars. With this book, I hope to clear up those discrepancies.

Prior to 1914, the sizes of calendars were not very consistent. I have made every attempt to give correct sizes whenever possible. The size of the complete calendar (including pad), made between 1914 and 1919, is approximately 13" x 32". From 1920 to 1922, they measured 12" x 32". All of these calendars were equipped with a metal strip and hanger at the top. From 1923 to 1940, the size was approximately 12" x 24", again with metal strip and hanger. In 1926, however, the calendar changed drastically, measuring 10 1/2" x 18 5/8" and printed on a medium-weight card stock. It also had a hole drilled at the top for hanging (replacing the standard metal strip). 1926 was also the first year that the calendar had a cover sheet over the pad which simply said "1926 Compliments of The Coca-Cola Co., Atlanta, GA." The standard use of cover sheets over the pad didn't start until after 1930.

Another interesting aspect of Coca-Cola calendars is the glass and bottle variations. Because of the obvious difference between fountain and bottle sales, two calendars were issued in certain years, one showing the model holding a glass and one holding a bottle. In some of these cases, one type of calendar may be rarer than the other, depending on how many have turned up over the years. The following is a list of calendars that have been printed in two separate versions of glass and bottle: 1904, 1914, 1915, 1916, 1917, 1919 (knitting girl), 1920, 1923, and 1927. The bottle version of the 1923 calendar is very unusual in that the bottle is embossed "8 oz." rather than the standard "6 1/2 oz." which is the size of the bottle used at that time. The 1927 calendar also has a slightly different variation. On one calendar there is a large bottle inset with a border around it on the lower left hand side, and another has no bottle at all. There is also a glass variation on the 1928 distributor calendar. In 1918, and from 1921 to 1930 (with the exception of 1923 and 1927), calendars show both glass and bottle, and from 1931 on they show bottles only.

As any collector who actively seeks Coca-Cola calendars knows, they are not easy to find. Anything prior to 1914 is considered rare, and anything prior to 1910 is very rare. Despite the rarity of these early calendars, the value drops drastically if they are found without a pad or a sheet attached, or trimmed from their original size.

After 1940, there was a major change in Coca-Cola calendars. From 1941 through the 1960s, they were made as multiple-page-type calendars, usually consisting of six pages plus a cover sheet, with two months on each page.

The condition of the calendar, as with any Coca-Cola collectible, is most important in determining value. The prices you see on calendars in this book reflect examples in nice clean, presentable condition. Examples in poor condition or without a pad will certainly be worth less, and mint untouched examples could certainly be worth more.

There are a few things to keep in mind when purchasing a calendar. First, be sure that it has not been trimmed from its original size. (The measurement information provided earlier should be helpful.) The pad or sheet attached is also very important. Make sure it is the correct year for the calendar. If it is not a full pad, take note as to how many sheets are attached. One sheet attached (other than the last sheet) is acceptable as long as you realize that you are buying an altered calendar. If a calendar is trimmed or has a partial or no pad at all, or had been mounted to poster board, it can not be called mint.

In this section of the book, you will find the most complete collection of Coca-Cola calendars ever assembled, including stock calendars, foreign, and small size "home" or "reference" calendars, all of which are very interesting. Very few calendars known to exist are absent from this publication. Whether you are a die-hard calendar collector like myself, or if you just happen to have a few in your collection, I hope you will agree with me that calendars are certainly the most beautiful of all Coca-Cola collectibles.

PCA005.001
1891   6 $^1/_2$" x 9" . . . . . . $15,000

Note: Pre-1900 calendars are
considered very rare.

PCA010.000
1896   6 $^1/_2$" x 10 $^1/_2$" . . . . . . . $20,000
Photo Courtesy: Gordon Breslow

PCA009.000
1895   7" x 14"
Cut down as shown . . . . . . . . . . $2,000
Complete calendar with pad . . . $20,000
Photo Courtesy: Richard Bostwick

PCA011.000
1897 Cut down as shown . . . . . . . $4,500
Complete calendar with pad . . . $15,000

Note: Additional calendars can be
found on color pages 49-54.

PCA006.000
1892 . . . . . . . . . . . . . . . . . . . . $25,000
Photo Courtesy: The Coca-Cola Co., Atlanta GA

PCA012.001
1898   7 $^3/_8$" x 13" . . . . . . . . . . . $12,000
Photo Courtesy: Gordon Breslow

PCA005.000
1891   6 $^1/_2$" x 9" . . . . . . . . . . . $15,000
Photo Courtesy: Gordon Breslow

PCA013.000
1899   7 ³/₈" x 13" . . . . . . . . . . $12,000
Photo Courtesy: Gordon Breslow

PCA013.001
1899   7 ¹/₄" x 12 ³/₄" . . . . . . . $12,000
Photo Courtesy: Joe Happle

PCA013.002
1899   7 ³/₈" x 13" . . . . . . . . . . $10,000
Photo Courtesy: Author's Collection

*Note: All of these early calendars are considered very rare.*

PCA014.000
1900   7 ¹/₄" x 12 ³/₄" . . . . . . $15,000
Photo Courtesy: Bob Nance

PCA014.001
1900   7 ¹/₄" x 12 ³/₄" . . . . . . $15,000

PCA015.000
1901   7 ³/₈" x 13" . . . . . . . . . . $7,500

Photos Courtesy: The Coca-Cola Co., Atlanta, GA

# CALENDARS
## GLASS AND BOTTLE VARIATIONS

PCA035.001

1914 . . . . . . . . . . . . . . $6,000

With bottle, Rare

PCA035.000

1914 . . . . . . . . . . . . . . $2,000

Photos Courtesy: Gordon Breslow

PCA036.002

1915 . . . . . . . . . . . . . . . . $8,500

With bottle, Rare

*Note: The bottle version of both the 1914 and 1915 calendars are considered rare. Both required extensive "artwork alterations" to accommodate the bottle. Notice the complete re-positioning of arm and hand on the 1914 and lowering of the arm on the 1915. In contrast, the 1916, 1917, 1919, and 1920 required simply adding the bottle.*

*Note: Additional calendars can be found on color pages 49-54.*

PCA037.001

1916 . . . . . . . . . . . . . . $2,500

With bottle

PCA037.000

1916 . . . . . . . . . . . . . . $2,500

With glass

PCA036.001

1915 . . . . . . . . . . . . . . $4,800

With glass. There are two different color variations of the 1915 calendar. One logo is gray and red and another is all red.

*Note: It's interesting that while some variation calendars are rare, others like the 1916 and 1919 have turned up pretty much the same over the years.*

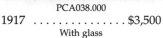

PCA038.000
1917 . . . . . . . . . . . . . . $3,500
With glass

PCA038.001
1917 . . . . . . . . . . . . . . $3,000
With bottle

PCA040.000
1919 . . . . . . . . . . . . $4,000
With glass

PCA040.001
1919 . . . . . . . . . . . . $4,000
With bottle

*Note: The artwork on the 1919 calendar is very interesting and colorful. It has always been very popular with collectors. This has made it somewhat difficult to find. The glass and bottle variations seem to have turned up evenly over the years.*

*Note: The bottle version of the 1927 calendar is completely different from all other variations. The bottle version has also turned up more often over the years. Values shown are based on examples in complete condition of 8.5 or better. Examples in lesser condition will have much less value.*

*Note: Additional calendars can be found on color pages 49-54.*

PCA051.001
1927 . . . . . . . . . . . . $1,500
With glass

PCA051.000
1927 . . . . . . . . . . . . $1,200
With glass and bottle

PCA041.000
1918  5" x 9" ...... $450
June Caprice

PCA042.000
1919  6 ¼" x 10 ½" ........ $4,000
Marion Davies

PCA043.000
1916  8" x 15" ......... $3,200
Miss Pearl White, Rare (This calendar
was a magazine insert piece)

*Note: The June Caprice Distributor
Calendar has always been considered
a common piece. Condition must
be nice to warrant this price.*

PCA051.002
1927  7" x 13" .............. $1,600

PCA052.001
1928  8" x 14" ............. $850
Regulation glass

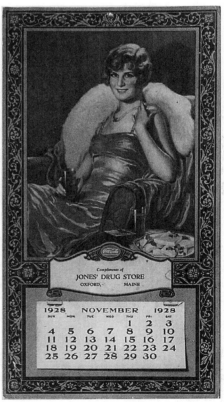

PCA052.002
1928  8" x 14" ............... $900
Unmarked straight side glass

# CALENDARS
★★★ Indicates that the calendar has been reproduced (See the repro section of this book)

PCA035.000
1914 . . . . . . $2,000
★★★

PCA036.001
1915 . . . . . . . $4,800

PCA037.001
1916 . . . . . . . . $2,500

PCA038.001
1917 . . . . . . . $3,000

PCA039.000
1918 . . . . . . . $5,000

*Note: Prices shown on these calendars are based on examples in Excellent condition with partial or full pads. Examples in Mint condition with full pads will be worth more. Items in less than Excellent condition, or without pad, will be worth much less.*

PCA040.001
1919 . . . . . . . $4,000

PCA044.001
1920 . . . . . . $2,800
With bottle

PCA044.000
1920 . . . . . . $2,800
With glass

PCA045.000
1921 . . . . . . . $1,800

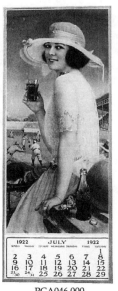

PCA046.000
1922 . . . . . . . $2,400

# CALENDARS

★★★ Indicates that the calendar has been reproduced (See the repro section of this book)

PCA047.001

1923 . . . . . . . . . . . $1,000

With glass

PCA047.000

1923 . . . . . . . . . . . $1,000

With bottle

PCA048.000

1924 . . . . . . . . . . . $1,500

★★★

PCA049.000

1925 . . . . . . . . . . . $1,200

★★★

Note: Prices shown on these calendars are based on examples in Excellent condition with partial or full pads. Examples in Mint condition with full pads will be worth more. Items in less than Excellent condition, or without a pad, will be worth much less.

PCA050.000

1926 . . . . . . . . . $1,800

PCA051.000

1927 . . . . . . . . . . . $1,200

PCA052.000

1928 . . . . . . . . . . . $1,200

★★★

PCA053.000

1929 . . . . . . . . . . . $1,500

PCA054.000

1930 . . . . . . . . . . . $1,200

# CALENDARS
★★★ Indicates that the calendar has been reproduced (See the repro section of this book)

PCA055.000

1931 . . . . . . . . . $1,000

PCA056.000

1932 . . . . . . . . . $800

PCA057.000

1933 . . . . . . . . . $800

PCA058.000

1934 . . . . . . . . . $800

PCA059.000

1935 . . . . . . . . . $750

★★★

PCA060.000

1936 . . . . . . . . . $900

PCA061.000

1937 . . . . . . . . . $750

PCA062.000

1938 . . . . . . . . . $750

PCA063.000

1939 . . . . . . . . . $600

PCA064.000

1940 . . . . . . . . . $600

# CALENDARS

PCA066.000

1942 . . . . . . . . . . . . $385

PCA067.000

1943 . . . . . . . . . . $550

PCA068.000

1944 . . . . . . . . . . $375

PCA065.000

1941 . . . . . . . . . . . . . . . . . . . . . . $450

PCA069.000

1945 . . . . . . . . . . $385

PCA070.000

1946 . . . . . . . . . . $700

PCA071.000

1947 . . . . . . . . $350

PCA072.000

1948 . . . . . . . . . . $350

PCA073.000

1949 . . . . . . . . . . $250

PCA074.000

1950 . . . . . . . . . . $250

PCA075.000

1951 . . . . . . . . . . . . . . . . . $175

PCA076.000

1952 . . . . . . . . . . . . . . $185

PCA077.000

1953 . . . . . . . . . $185

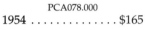

PCA078.000

1954 . . . . . . . . . . . . . $165

PCA079.000

1955 . . . . . . . . . . . . . . . . . . . . . $100

PCA080.000

1956 . . . . . . . . $85

USA

PCA081.000

1957 . . . . . . . . . $100

PCA080.001

1957 . . . . . . . . . . . . . . . . . . . . $60

Canada

PCA082.000

1958 . . . . . . . . $65

PCA083.000

1959 . . . . . . . . . $85

PCA084.000

1960 . . . . . . . . . . $60

PCA088.000

1964 . . . . . . . $60

PCA089.000

1965 . . . . . . . $60

PCA090.000

1966 . . . . . $60

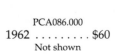

PCA085.000

1961 . . . . . . . $60

PCA086.000

1962 . . . . . . . . $60

Not shown

PCA087.000

1963 . . . . . . . . . . . . . $60

PCA091.000

1967 . . . . . . . $60

PCA092.000

1968 . . . . . . . . . $60

PCA093.000

1969 . . . . . . . $60

# CALENDARS

PCA094.000
1970 . . . . . . . $6

PCA095.000
1971 . . . . . . . . . $20

PCA101.000
1972 . . . . . . .$6

PCA096.000
1972 . . . . . . . . . . . . . $20

PRE049.000
1973 . . . . . . . . . . . . . . . . . $35

PCA097.000
1973 . . . . . . . . . $15

PCA098.000
1973 . . . . . . . . . . . . $25
Cloth

PCA099.000
1974 . . . . . . . . . . . $25
Cloth

PCA100.000
1974 . . . . . . . $25

PCA103.000
1975 . . . . . . . . . . . . . . . $10

PCA102.000
1975 . . . . . . . . $15

PCA105.000
1977 . . . . . . . . . . . . $10

PCA109.000
1978 . . . . . . . . $6

PCA106.000
1979 . . . . . . . . . $6

PCA108.000
1980 . . . . . . . . . $10

PCA107.000
1980 . . . . . . . $6

PCA110.000
1982 . . . . . . . . $6

PCA111.000
1983 . . . . . . . $6

PCA112.000
1984 . . . . . . . . $6

PCA113.000
1986 . . . . . . . . $5

# CALENDARS
## HOME OR REFERENCE CALENDARS

PCA130.000

1954 . . . . . . . . . . . . . . . . . $35

PCA131.000

1955 . . . . . . . . . . . . . . . $35

PCA132.000

1956 . . . . . . . . . . . . . . $25

PCA133.000

1957 . . . . . . . . . . . $25

PCA134.000

1958 . . . . . . . . . . . $15

PCA135.000

1959 . . . . . . . . . . . $15

PCA136.000

1960 . . . . . . . . . $15

PCA137.000

1961 . . . . . . . . . . $15

PCA138.000

1962 . . . . . . . . . $15

PCA139.00

1963 . . . . . . . . . . . . . $15

PCA140.000

1964 . . . . . . . . . . . $15

PCA141.000

1965 . . . . . . . . . . . . . $15

PCA142.000

1966 . . . . . . . . . . . $15

PCA143.000

1967 . . . . . . . . . . . . . $10

PCA144.000

1968 . . . . . . . . . . . . . $10

PCA145.000

1969 . . . . . . . . . . . . . $5

PCA146.000

1970 . . . . . . . . . . . . . $5

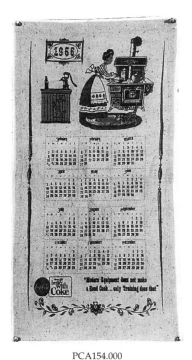

PCA154.000

1966 . . . . . . . . . . . . . . . . . . . $50

Cloth "Kitchen" calendar

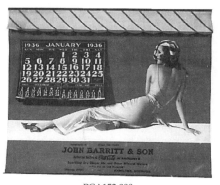

PCA152.000

1936 . . . . . . . . . . . . . . . . . . . . . . . $375

Distributor calendar, Hamilton, Bermuda

PCA149.000

1953  16" x 33"  . . . . . . . . . . $400

PCA153.000

1949 . . . . . . . . . . . . . . . . . . . $375

Local bottler

Note: The Boy Scout Calendars shown are all
"Stock" calendars with art  by Norman Rockwell.

PCA148.000

1946  . . . . . . . . . . . . . . . . . . . $550

PCA150.000

1973 . . . . . . . . . . . . . . . . $45

Houston Bottling Co.

PCA151.000

1949  6 1/2" x 11 1/2"  . .$350

PCA147.000

1945 . . . . . . . . . . . . . . . . . $550

# CALENDARS
## (FOREIGN)

PCA158.000

1948 . . . . . . . . . . $175

Canada

PCA160.000

1951 . . . . . . . . . . . . . $85

Italian

PCA159.000

1950 . . . . . . . . . . . . . . $100

South America

PCA164.000

1958 . . . . . . . $50

Canada

PCA163.000

1956 . . . . . . . $50

Canada

PCA080.002

1957 . . . . . . . . . . . . . . . $60

Canada

PCA165.000

1954 . . . . . . . . . . . . . . . . . . . $500

Hong Kong

PCA157.000

1947 . . . . . . . . . . $175

Canada

PCA161.000

1952 . . . . . . . $65

Canada

PCA166.000

1944 . . . . . . . . . . . . . . . . . . . $750

Mexico

PCA156.000

1943 Top only . . . . . . $100
Complete . . . . . . . . . $350

Canada

PCA162.000

1955 . . . . . . . $60

Canada

PCA155.000

1941 . . . . . . . . . . . $450

Canada

— 32 —

# COCA-COLA CHEWING GUM

The "Coca-Cola Gum Company" was chartered in Atlanta, Georgia, on March 17, 1903 by Atlanta businessmen David B. Carson, William L. Clark and George C. Rogers with an initial investment of $15,000. A contract was signed by Asa G. Candler, president of The Coca-Cola Company, on March 23, 1903, allowing the gum company the sole right to use the said copyrighted words (Coca-Cola) in connection with the manufacturing, advertising, labeling, packing and selling of chewing gum."

The company was very innovative, ordering vending machines as early as April of 1903. During the next couple of years some super Coca-Cola Gum-related advertising was produced, including the bookmarks and a Hilda Clark cardboard poster.

It is assumed that Coca-Cola syrup was one of the ingredients of the chewing gum, as a 1904 ad states "contains the delightful tonic properties of Coca-Cola."

A group of Richmond, Virginia, investors chartered a company named "Franklin Manufacturing Company" and bought all the machinery and assets of the "Coca-Cola Gum Company" of Atlanta by deed dated April 1, 1905. This new company relocated the business to 2405 E. Franklin Street in Richmond, Virginia. (A three story warehouse that had been a tobacco warehouse, and even served as a Confederate hospital during the Civil War. This building block today houses a paper and box manufacturing company.) The name of the company probably originated from the street name.

In 1911, the name of the company was changed to "Franklin Caro Company, Inc." (although the Inc. was omitted on most of the advertising). Most of the investors in the company were engaged in other businesses, and stock ownership and officers changed many times through the years. The company made a strong effort over the years to persuade Coca-Cola bottlers to sell the gum through their route men. Some ads appeared in *The Coca-Cola Bottler* magazine promoting this. The gum was also carried by wholesale mail order grocers, and ads for the gum appeared in their catalogs. A few salesmen did call on retail accounts in the Richmond, Virginia, Washington D.C., eastern Virginia and North Carolina areas, but the most extensive marketing was done by mail to the Coca-Cola bottlers.

In 1913, the business moved to 200 South Sixth Street in Richmond, Virginia, a four story brick warehouse building (it is no longer standing). From 1914 through 1916, the business prospered and the company added additional brands of gum to its inventory. Until 1911 the only brand was the "Coca-Cola Pepsin Gum." "Caro Gum" was added in 1914, "Honeyfruit"

in 1915, and "Richmint" in 1916. By 1912, they were also marketing different flavors of the "Coca-Cola Gum": "Peppermint Pepsin," "Spearmint Pepsin" and "Wintergreen Pepsin" (wrappers indicate the latter two were later labeled "Spearmint Flavor" and "Wintergreen Flavor.")

In December of 1912, the Franklin Caro Company applied to the U.S. Patent Office to register the trademark "Coca-Cola" as it applied to the chewing gum. After approximately two years of questioning by, and explanation to, the Examiner of Trademarks, the Patent Office agreed to pass the application. When the application was published on November 3, 1914 in the *Official Gazette*, The Coca-Cola Company immediately filed an opposition with the Patent Office. On November 23, 1914, The Franklin Caro Company withdrew their application under threat of Coca-Cola not ratifying the original 1903 contract, which was still valid.

Franklin Caro Company applied again to the Patent Office for trademark registration on June 8, 1915, but this time for registration of the name "Coca-Cola Gum." Again, this was approved by the Patent Office and published in the *Official Gazette* on September 7, 1915. Again The Coca-Cola Company filed a very lengthy opposition with the Patent Office, which in turn asked for a response from Franklin Caro. Several extensions were tendered to Franklin Caro for their response, but when they failed to formally respond, the opposition was sustained and judgment rendered by the Patent Office in favor of The Coca-Cola Company on September 29, 1916.

However, Franklin Caro Company was successful in registering the trademark "Coca-Cola" in Canada (Jan. 31, 1916) and in Newfoundland (Feb. 14, 1916). In August of 1915 (even as the above patent attempts were being made), the principal stockholders wishing to sell the business advised The Coca-Cola Company of their intentions. Under a clause in the 1903 agreement, The Coca-Cola Company retained the right of the first refusal should a sale be contemplated. Negotiations with Harold Hirsch, council for Coca-Cola, and Sam Dobbs, a direct contact to Franklin Caro Company, carried on for nearly nine months before The Coca-Cola Company finally tendered an offer of $7,000 on June 30, 1916 to buy the existing contract between the two companies. This offer was for the "Coca-Cola Gum" name only, not the physical assets. This offer was not accepted, and the gum company changed ownership again, this time through the influx of new investors into the business. Officers also changed at this time.

The company was never on a sound financial basis after 1916. War rationing hurt the business, as did the inflated price

of sugar immediately after the war, coupled with mismanagement, and with gum companies such as Wrigley's and Beechnut producing a better quality gum and using a more aggressive marketing and advertising campaign. The business continued to lose money. Heavily in debt, the "Franklin Caro Company" filed bankruptcy on February 28, 1921.

A bankruptcy sale was held May 25, 1921 and the company was bought by a group of investors headed by Richmond businessman A. Stanley Kratz for $40,000. The company was reorganized under the name "Franklin Caro Gum Company, Inc.," and a former officer of the company was installed as president. Another flavor of gum, "Velvet," was added in 1923, and the company added a line of roasted peanuts—called "Ole Virginia Smithfield"—in late 1923. The company had made an attempt in these last years to improve the quality of its gum by increasing the chicle content, but this was too little, too late. Sales decreased yearly, and records of sales showed practically no repeat orders of Coca-Cola Gum. The use of three flavors under the Coca-Cola brand name did little to help the market for the gum.

The Coca-Cola Company, after a couple of months of negotiations (and surreptitiously through a third party, a Julius H. Wyman of Baltimore, MD), bought all the assets, stock, machinery, registrations, and contract for $20,000 in November of 1924 to prevent other firms from buying the company and actively using the "Coca-Cola" brand. In a memo to Robert Woodruff it was stated that "no firm could use it more atrociously as to quality" than Franklin Caro had. The gum company was then liquidated. The "Franklin Caro Gum Co."

was succeeded by the "Smithfield Products Company, Inc.," which was owned by the Coca-Cola Company and was chartered on January 20, 1925. There is some evidence they did continue to produce the roasted peanuts and honeyfruit gum under the "Smithfield" name for a short time. All of the chewing gum brand registrations were transferred to this company in the fall of 1925, but I have found no physical proof that Coca-Cola Gum was manufactured or marketed by them.

There is evidence that The Coca-Cola Co. considered marketing candy, cigars, and chewing gum with the Coca-Cola trademark on them in the early 1940s. A May, 1940 pamphlet, although questionable, depicts these products. A memo of September, 1941 outlines a trial marketing study. Labels and wrappers were printed, of which a quantity of gum wrappers are available. This venture died either because of World War II or, more probably, due to a decision to not allow the Coca-Cola logo on products other than the drink.

Rumor has it—and I have found some evidence of the fact—that The Coca-Cola Company did sell "Coca-Cola Gum" periodically in small quantities after 1925. I am told this was done to protect the registration of the Coca-Cola Gum brand. But, for all practical purposes, the gum was produced only from 1903 through 1924.

I want to offer a special thanks to Phil Mooney of The Coca-Cola Company and Bill Ricketts, both of whom provided me with much of the information pertinent to this chronology. Without their help this could not have been written. (Submitted by Thom Thompson, Versailles, Kentucky.)

PCG022.000
1914-1916  5 $\frac{1}{4}$" x 7 $\frac{3}{4}$"  . . . . $14,000
"Dutch Girl", chewing gum cardboard cutout,
counter display piece, Very Rare. Photo
Courtesy: Thom Thompson, Versailles, KY

PCG021.000
c.1914-1916  14" x 20 $\frac{1}{2}$"  . . . $15,000
"Dutch Boy", chewing gum cardboard cutout,
window display piece, Photo Courtesy:
Thaddeus Krom, Maywood, NJ

PCG020.000
1903-1905  4 $\frac{1}{2}$" x 11 $\frac{1}{2}$"  . . . . $10,000
"Baby", Coca-Cola chewing gum hanger, card-
board cutout, Very Rare. Photo Courtesy: John
Yarbrough, Shaw, MS

PCG023.000
c.1914  6 $\frac{1}{2}$" x 14"  . . . . . . . . . . . . . $8,000
Sign, tin, embossed, Very Rare, Southern Can Co.,
Balto. MD. (three colors, red, green, white)
Photo Courtesy: Joe Happle

PCG024.000
c.1908  11"  . . . . . . . . . . . . . . . . . . . $8,000
Sign, cardboard, embossed gold corners and wood
grain border, Photo Courtesy: Jan Perry, Chicago, IL

PCG025.000
c.1916  . . . . . . . . . . . . . . . . . . . . $10,000
Coca-Cola chewing gum free offer, two-part window
display piece, Rare. Photo Courtesy: Joe Happle

PCG026.000
c.1905-1911 . . . . . . . . . . . . $2,200
With embossed lid add . . . $200
Pepsin Gum jar with paper label

PCG027.000
c.1912 . . . . . . . . . . . . . . . $2,000
Franklin Caro jar and lid, (square corner jar) with Coca-Cola paper label

PCG028.000
c.1912-1914 . . . . . . . . . . . $2,000
Franklin Caro jar and lid, (bevel corner jar) with Coca-Cola paper label

PCG029.000
c.1903-1905 . . . . . . . $2,200
Coca-Cola Chewing Gum jar, with Coca-Cola paper label

PCG030.000
c.1905-1911 . . . . . . . . . . . . $750
With embossed lid add . . . $200
Coca-Cola Pepsin Gum jar, (bevel corners—square corner Pepsin Jar is earlier)

PCG031.000
c.1903-1905 . . . . . . . . . . . . . . . $750
With embossed lid add . . . . . . . $200
Coca-Cola Chewing Gum jar

# COCA-COLA CHEWING GUM

Dates indicated are probable dates these particular wrapper designs were in use, based on information on letterhead and advertising. Few wrappers survive, being the disposable item they were. Beware, I have seen some wrappers reproduced by color xerographic means. Wrappers with original gum are worth more. (Photos Courtesy: Thom Thompson)

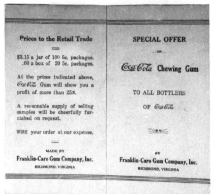

PCG044.000
c.1940 . . . . . . . . . . . . . . $150
Spearmint flavor gum, five-piece package wrapper. Questionable that this was ever actually marketed, see preface.

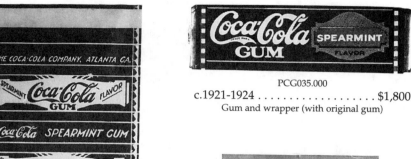

PCG035.000
c.1921-1924 . . . . . . . . . . . . . . . . . $1,800
Gum and wrapper (with original gum)

PCG037.000
c.1913-1916 . . . . . . . . $1,000
Spearmint flavor wrapper

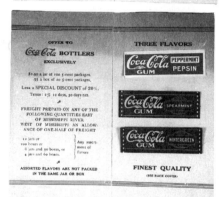

PCG043.000
c.1921-1923  6 1/4" x 6 1/2" . . . . $3,000
Price card (folder), showing front and back (prices and three sample pieces of gum)

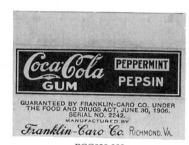

PCG039.000
c.1913-1916 . . . . . . . . . . $1,000
Peppermint pepsin wrapper

PCG040.000
c.1911-1913 . . . . . . . . . $1,000
Spearmint pepsin wrapper

PCG041.000
c.1921-1924 . . . . . . . . . $1,800
Wintergreen flavor gum and wrapper (with original gum)

PCG042.000
c.1916-1920 . . . . . . . . $1,000
Peppermint pepsin wrapper

PCG038.000
c.1916-1920 . . . . . . . $1,000
Spearmint flavor wrapper

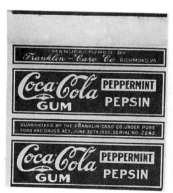

PCG046.000
c.1916-1920 . . . . . . $1,000
Peppermint pepsin, five-piece package wrapper

PCG045.000
c.1915-1924 . . . . . $100
Honey-Fruit brand, five-piece package wrapper

PCG036.000
c.1903-1905  4 1/2" . . . . . . . . . . . . . . . . . . . . . . $3,000
Rolled piece of gum for automatic gum dispenser, gum and wrapper

PCG051.000

c. 1925 . . . . . . . . . . . . $300

Honey-Fruit Gum counter card. This card shows the manufacturer to be Smithfield Products Co., Richmond, VA.

PCG033.P01

c.1903-1905 7" x 8 1/2" . . $2,000

Sign, porcelain, Rare. This sign would have been attached above and at the back of the Doremus Automatic Vending Machine that dispensed the rolled gum.

PCG050.000

c.1916 . . . . . . . . . . . . . . . . . . . . . $1,500

Shipping box, cardboard, held 20 packages of gum (box only)

Note: Some of the Doremus machines came on the market in the mid-1970s with advertising etched on the glass. The machines and gum were (and are) authentic, but the advertising was added by a dealer of the period attempting to enhance the value of machines he had for sale. This machine has been shown in a price guide with the spurious glass. These same machines were also used by cigar manufacturers in the early 1900s.

PCG049.000

c.1920s . . . . . . . . . . . . . . . . . . . . . $300

Honey Fruit Chewing Gum counterdisplay box, product of Franklin Caro Co. (box only)

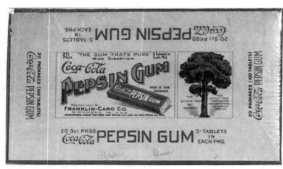

PCG047.000

c.1912 . . . . . . . . . . . . . . . . . . . . . $2,500

Shipping box cover wrap for box to hold 20 packages of gum

PCG048.000

c.1920s . . . . . . . . . . . . . . . . . . . . . $2,500

Coca-Cola Chewing Gum counter display box (box only)

PCG052.000

c.1913 12 1/2" x 6 1/4" . . . . . . . . . . . . $400

Coca-Cola Chewing Gum shipping box, wood. These boxes were used to ship the glass counter display jars filled with 100 packages of gum.

PCG063.000

c.1912-1916 . . . . . . . . . . . . . . . . . . . . . . . . . . . . . $2,000

Chewing gum fan, Rare. Photo Courtesy: Thaddeus Krom

PCG054.000

PCG055.000

PCG053.000

Photo Courtesy:
Thaddeus Krom

Photo Courtesy: Thom
Thompson

Photo Courtesy: John
Barbier

1903-1904 2" x 6" . . . . . . . . . . . . . . . . . . . . $2,000 Each

Coca-Cola Chewing Gum bookmarks, Rare

PCG068.000

1914 . . . . . . . . . . $175

Letterhead

PCG065.000

1916 . . . . . . . . . . . . . $350

Letterhead (probable 1914 to
1920 usage)

PCG060.000

1904 . . . . . . . . . . . $1,500

Coca-Cola Chewing Gum trade
card, Louisiana Purchase
Exposition, St. Louis, MO
(Electricity Building), Rare. Photo
Courtesy: Thom Thompson

PCG061.000

c.1912-1914 . . . . . . . . . . . . . . . . . . . . . . . . . . . . . $2,600

Chewing gum fan, Rare. This fan pictures all children. A fan also exists
picturing young women. Photo Courtesy: Phil Perdue Louisville, KY

PCG067.000

1908 . . . . . . . . . . . . . . . . . $350

Letterhead (probable 1905 to 1911 usage)

PCG069.000

1914 . . . . . . . . . . . . . . . . . . . $200

Letterhead showing "Caro" Pepsin gum

PCG066.000

1914 . . . . . . . . . . . . . . . . . . . $500

Letterhead (probable 1912 to 1914 usage)

PCG064.000

1921 . . . . . . . . . . . . . . . . . . . $350

Letterhead (probable 1921 to 1924 usage)

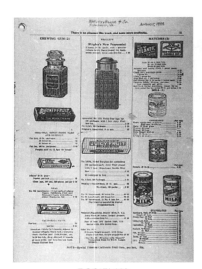

PCG071.000

August 1922 . . . . . . . . . . . . . $200

"Harvey, Blair & Co." Catalog

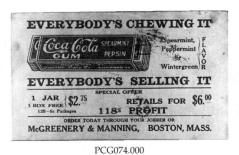

PCG074.000

1912 . . . . . . . . . . . . . . . . . . . . . . $1,200

"Special Offer" postcard. Photo Courtesy:
Thom Thompson

PCG073.000

c.1908 . . . . . . . . . . . . . . . . . . . . . $500

Coca-Cola Pepsin Gum postcard, Washington
Monument, Richmond, VA

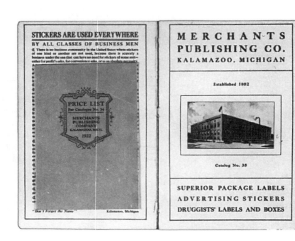

PCG075.000

PCG070.000

June 1918 . . . . . . . . . . . . . . . . . . . $200

"Harvey, Blair & Co." wholesale grocery catalog
with page showing andpricing Coca-Cola gum

1923 . . . . . . . . . . . . . . . . . . . . . . . $300

"Merchants Publishing Co." catalog showing printed
labels, including a "Coca-Cola Pepsin Chewing
Gum" Jar Label (this example would date from
c.1912), hardbound book and price list

PCG072.000

Spring 1919 . . . . . . . . . . . . . . . . . $225

"Southern Bargain House" wholesale department
store and grocery catalog,with page showing prices
of Coca-Cola Gum

# COCA-COLA CHEWING GUM

Very few ads for the Coca-Cola Chewing Gum exist. The only national distribution was that in *Everybody's Magazine*. Each of those ads ran in several issues and are the most common of all gum collectibles. The other ads are for local distribution. All ads shown on this page appeared in the black and white. (Most photos courtesy: Thom Thompson)

PCG077.000
1904  1" x 2 ³/₄" . . . . . . . . . . . . . . . . $50
*Ad, Everybody's Magazine*

PCG082.000
1914  approx. 1 ¹/₂" x 6" . . . . . . . . . $100
Ad appearing on 1914 "Washington Nationals" baseball score card,

PCG080.000
October 1912  3 ¹/₂" x 4 ¹/₂" . . . . . . $125
Ad appearing in *The Coca-Cola Bottler*

PCG078.000
1906 and 1907  1" x 2 ³/₄" . . . . . . . . . $45
*Ad, Everybody's Magazine*

### COCA-COLA PEPSIN GUM

suits the boy. It will suit you and your boy. No adulteration in Coca-Cola Gum. It is all gum and stays big. Don't melt. Made of the best grade of Mexican chicle gum and finest flavorings and Pepsin used in its preparation. It aids digestion and gives comfort after a hearty meal.

**COCA-COLA PEPSIN GUM HAS A LASTING FLAVOR**

20 5-cent packages, box . . . . . 60c

PCG085.000
1908 . . . . . . . . . . . . . . . . . . . . . . . $100
Ad from Peter Van Schaak & Sons, Chicago wholesale drug catalog

PCG083.000
1916  5 ¹/₂" x 8" . . . . . . . . . . . $225
Ad from Richmond, VA City Directory

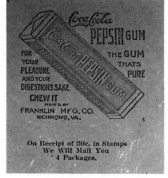

PCG084.000
3 ¹/₂" x 5 ¹/₂" . . . . . . . $150
Ad from 1907 "Guide to Richmond and Vicinity"

PCG081.000
1905  1" x 2 ³/₄" . . . . . . . . . . . . . $45
*Ad, Everybody's Magazine*

PCG079.000
1914-15  1 ¹/₂" x 5 ¹/₄" . . . . . . . . . . . $100
Ad from winter "Bijou Theater Programme" Richmond, VA

PCG086.000
February 1913  1 ¹/₂" x 6" . . . . . . . . . . . . . . . . . . . . . . . . . . . . . . . . . . . . $125
Ad appearing in "Poli's Popular Players" program, Washington D.C.

— 41 —

PPS024.000
1910  20" x 30"  . . . . . . . . . . . . . . . $5,000
"Gibson Girl", metal strip at top and bottom

PPS087.000
1899  Trimmed as shown  . . . . . . $3,500
Complete in Excellent condition  . $15,000
"Hilda Clark", Very Rare

> Note: Preserving and framing these early paper signs is very important. Mounting and cleaning should only be done by someone knowledgeable in paper preservation.

PPS025.000
1927  20" x 32"  . . . . . . . . . . . . . . . $1,800
"Bathing Beauty"

PPS026.000
1921  20" x 32"  . . . . . . . . . . . . . . . $2,000

# PAPER SIGNS

PPS029.000
1932  11" x 21 $^1/_2$" . . $2,400
"Lupe Velez"

PPS030.000
1936  14 $^1/_2$" x 22" . . . . . . . . . . . $1,000
"Chinatown"

PPS027.000          PPS028.000
1929  10" x 30" . . . . . . . . . . . $2,000 Each
Metal strip top and bottom

*Note: Advertising with movie stars, celebrities, or sports personalities as the subject matter is more valuable than advertising with an unidentified model.*

PPS031.000          PPS032.000          PPS033.000          PPS034.000
1920s  12" x 20" . . . . . . . . . . . . . . . . . . . . . . . . . . . . . . . . . . . . . $1,000 Each
Paper hangers, metal strip at top and bottom

— 43 —

PPS035.000
1939  19" x 57" . . . . . . . . . . . . . . . . . $600

PPS036.000
1950s 13" x 41" . . . . . . . . . . . . . . . . . $75

PPS038.000
1950s 18" x 60" . . . . . . . . . . . . . . . . . $400

PPS037.000
Late 1950s 14" x 36" . . . . . . . . . . . . . . $65

PPS039.000
1937 19" x 58" . . . . . . . . . . . . . . . . . $750

PPS040.000
c.1920s 11 3/4" x 33 1/2" . . . . . . . . . $1,000

PPS041.000

PPS042.000
1940s . . . . . . . . . . . . . . . . . . . . . . $50 Each

PPS043.000
1950s . . . . . . . . . . . . . . . . . . . . . . . . . $30

PPS044.000
1940s . . . . . . . . . . . . . . . . . . . . . . . . . $30

PPS045.000
1960s 19" x 57" . . . . . . . . . . . . . . . . . $85

DOES ENTERTAINING FRIGHTEN YOU? SEND 10¢ FOR THIS BOOK ON HOME ENTERTAINING

The Coca-Cola Company
Atlanta, Ga.

PPS046.000
1930s 11" x 21" . . . . . . . . . . . . . . . . . $425

Taste Treat

For Outdoor Living at its Brightest

Brighten Your Meals With
Coke

PPS050.000
1955 16" x 27" . . . . . . . . . $100

PPS049.000
1930  10" x 30" . . . . $1,600

"LET'S LISTEN IN"
Coca-Cola on the Air
EVERY WEDNESDAY EVENING
N.B.C. Coast-to-coast Network

PPS048.000
1930 8" x 26" . . . . . . . . . . . . . . . . . . . $425

Come in...we have
Coca-Cola
5¢

PPS051.000
1951 10" x 25" . . . . . . . . . . . . . . . . . . $225

Drink Coca-Cola
Delicious and Refreshing

Tune In
31-piece Orchestra
Graham McNamee
Grantland Rice

EVERY WEDNESDAY EVENING · N.B.C. NETWORK

PPS047.000
1920s 8" x 26" . . . . . . . . . . . . . . . . . . $375

Take some home today!
Coca-Cola
Delicious and Refreshing
6 BOTTLES 25¢
PLUS DEPOSIT

PPS052.000
1951 10" x 25" . . . . . . . . . . . . . . . . . . $125

THE BEST STOP SIGN

in these United States is used by Toonerville's One-Man Police Force

...But he has no patent on it

· · · · ·

Every Coca-Cola Dealer can Stop More Nickels

by using this same stop sign

DO YOUR PART—

1. Put Up More Advertising
2. Increase Your Dealer's Sales
3. Win a Toonerville Cash Prize

PPS054.000
1930  12" x 18" . . . . . . . . . . . . . $200
Toonerville

Good with food

Coke
Coca-Cola
Delicious and Refreshing

PPS053.000
1950s 11" x 24" . . . . . . . . . . . . . . . . . $65

PPS080.S00
1950s .....$30 each
Channel cards

PPS055.000
c.1927 10" x 16" piece . . $100

PPS056.000
1920s 10" x 16" piece . . $65

Crepe paper window decoration (used from rolls)

PCS375.001
1950s . . . . . . . . . . . . . . . . . . . . . . . . . . . $30
Channel card

Note: A Channel Card is a cardboard sign that slides into a metal channel around the top of the soda fountain.

PCS376.001
1960s . . . . . . . . . . . . . . . . . . . $15
Channel card

PCS377.001          PCS377.002
1950s . . . . . . . . . . . . . . . . . . . . . . $50 Each
Channel cards

PPS079.S00
1930s . . . . . . . . $35 Each
Window banners, paper

PCS375.002
1950s . . . . . . . . . . . . . . . $75
Channel card in wire hanger

PCS374.001

PCS376.002
1960s . . . . . . . . . . . . . . . $15
Channel card

PCS427.000
1950s 12" x 15" . . . . . . . . . . . . . . . . $40
Cardboard

PCS374.002
1950s . . . . . . . . . . . . . . $18 Each
Channel cards

PCS373.S01          PCS373.S02          PCS373.S03          PCS373.S04          PCS373.S05

1950s 12" x 15" . . . . . . . . . . . . . . . . . . . . . . . . . . . . . . . . . . . . . . . . . . . . . . . . . . . . . . . . . . $40 Each

Hanging signs, cardboard

PPS057.000
1935  10 3/4" x 23"  . . . . . . . . . . . . . . $450
Ray Noble, window banner

PPS058.S00
c.1937  . . . . . . . . . . . . . . . . . . . . . . . $375
"Home Refreshment" store display (complete)

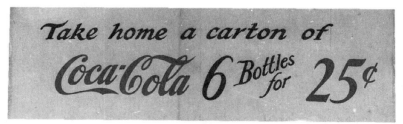

PPS059.000
1930s  8" x 22"  . . . . . . . . . . . . . . . . . $100

PPS060.000
1930s  4 1/2" x 25"  . . . . . . . . . . . . . . . $65

PPS061.000
1950s  11" x 32"  . . . . . . . . . . . . . . . . . $25

PPS062.000
1955  14" x 20"  . . . . . . . . . . . . . $85

PPS063.000
1950s  14 1/2" x 20 1/2"  . . . . . . . . $25

PPS064.000
1955  20" x 36"  . . . . . . . . . . . . . . . . . $125

PPS065.000
1958  20" x 36"  . . . . . . . . . . . . . . . . . $100

# PAPER SIGNS

PPS066.000
1950s  11" x 22"  . . . . . . . . . . . . . . . . . $75

PPS067.000
1949  11" x 22"  . . . . . . . . . . . . . $150

PPS068.000
1952  11" x 22"  . . . . . . . . . . . . .$75

PPS069.000
1950s  11" x 24 $\frac{1}{2}$"  . . . . . . . . . . . . . . $60

PPS052.000
1951  11" x 22"  . . . . . . . . . . . . . $100

PPS072.000
1960s  13" x 22"  . . . $50
Paper cutout

PPS071.000
Late 1940s  36" x 52"  . . . . .$250
Amsterdam

PPS073.000
1970s . . . . . . . . . . . . . $15

PPS074.000
1980  22" x 28"  . . . . . . . . . . . . . $15 Each
Marvel Comics/Coca-Cola

PPS075.000

PPS076.000
1953  . . . . . . . . . . . . . . . . . . . . . . . . $40
Canadian (French) paper cutout

— 48 —

# CALENDARS

PCA005.000

1891  6 $^1/_2$" x 9"  . . . . . . . . .$15,000

Thought to be the first calendar used by Coca-Cola, Rare.

Photo Courtesy: Gordon Breslow

PCA010.000

1896  6 $^1/_2$" x 10 $^1/_2$"  . . . . . . .$20,000

Rare.

Photo Courtesy: Gordon Breslow

PCA012.002

1898  7 $^1/_4$" x 12 $^3/_4$"  . . . . .$18,000

Rare.

Photo Courtesy: Author's Collection

PCA013.002

1899  7 $^3/_8$" x 13"  . . . . . . . . . .$10,000

Rare.

Photo Courtesy: Author's Collection

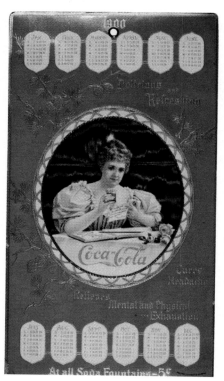

PCA014.001

1900  7 $^1/_4$" x 12 $^3/_4$"  . . . . . .$15,000

Rare.

Photo Courtesy: Gordon Breslow

PCA015.000

1901  7 $^3/_8$" x 13"  . . . . . . . . . . .$7,500

Photo Courtesy: Gordon Breslow

PCA016.000

1901  7 5/8" x 11"  . . . . . . . . . . . .$10,000

PCA018.001

1903  7 3/4" x 15"  . . . . . . .$6,000

PCA018.000

1903  7 3/4" x 15"  . . . . . . .$6,000

*NOTE: Shown above are two different versions of the 1903 calendar. On the right is copyright 1902. On the left is copyright 1901, with a logo variation.*

PCA017.000

1902  7 1/2" x 14 1/2"  . . . . . .$8,500

PCA019.000

1904  7 3/4" x 15 1/4"  . . . . . . .$4,500

PCA020.000

1905  7 3/4" x 15 1/4"  . . . . . . .$6,000

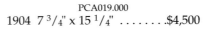

PCA021.000
1906  7 ³/₄" x 14 ¹/₄"  . . . . . .$6,500

PCA022.000
1907  7" x 14"  . . . . . . . . . . .$7,500

PCA023.000
1908  7" x 14"  . . . . . . . . . . .$5,500

PCA024.000
1909  11" x 20 ¹/₂"  . . . . . . . .$8,500
Rare.
Photo Courtesty: Gordon Breslow

PCA025.000
1910  15" x 26"  . . . . . . . . . . .$10,000
"Happy Days", Rare.
Photo Courtesy: Author's Collection,

PCA030.000
1913  16" x 28"  . . . . . . . . . . . . .$8,500
Bottlers' Calendar
Photo Courtesy: Author's Collection

# CALENDARS
## (Hamilton King Art)

> *Note: Artist "Hamilton King" painted the very beautiful "Coca-Cola Girls" for the calendars from 1910 to 1913. All of this art work was used on trolley car signs for the same years.*

PCA026.000
1910  8 3/4" x 17 1/2" . . . . . . $6,500

PCA027.000
1911  10 1/2" x 17 3/4" . . . . . . . . . . $6,000

PCA028.001
1912  12 1/4" x 30 3/4"  . . $6,500
Large version, Rare

PCA028.000
1912  9 3/4" x 19 3/4"  . . . . . $5,000
Small version

PCA029.000
1913  13 1/2" x 22 1/2"  . . . . . . . . . $4,000

# CALENDARS

PCA035.000

1914 . . . . . . . . . . . $2,000

PCA036.000

1915 . . . . . . . . . . . . . $4,800

PCA039.000

1918 . . . . . . . . . . . . $5,000

*Note: Calendars shown must have partial or full pad, and be in Excellent or Better condition to warrant these prices.*

PCA040.000

1919 . . . . . . . . . . . . . . .$4,000

PCA046.000

1922 . . . . . . . . . . . . . .$2,400

*Note: All of these calendars are also shown in the black and white section.*

PCA055.000

1931 . . . . . . . . . . . . . . . . . $1,000

Norman Rockwell art

— 53 —

PCA043.000

1916  8" x 15"  . . . . . . .$3,200

Miss Pearl White (This calendar
was actually a magazine insert
piece.)

PCA149.001

1958  11" x 23"  . . .$400

(Rockwell Art) Boy Scouts

PCA170.000

1964  7 1/4" x 10 1/4"  . . . . .$200

Cub Scouts

PCA169.000

1953  16" x 33 1/2"  . . . . . . . . . . . . .$1,500

"Kentucky Derby" showing all the Derby winners
over the years, Rare

Photo Courtesy: Gordon Breslow

PCA172.000

1950s  3 3/4" x 5"  . . . . . . . . .$125

"Pause for Living" Perpetual Calendar
with original box

PCA168.000

1943  14" x 29"  . . . . .$500

South America

PCA151.000

1949  8" x 14 1/2"  . . .$350

(Rockwell Art) Boy Scouts

PCA171.000

1946  6 1/2" x 11 1/2"  . .$375

(Rockwell Art) Boy Scouts

PCG076.000
1903  14 $^1/_2$" x 19 $^1/_2$"  . . . . . . . . . $18,000
Hilda Clark Coca-Cola Chewing Gum sign, cardboard, easel back, die-cut, embossed, Very Rare.
Photo Courtesy: Thaddeus Krom, Maywood, NJ

# COCA-COLA CHEWING GUM

PCG035.000
c.1921-1924 . . . . . . . . . . . . . . . . . .$1800
Gum and Wrapper.
Photo courtesy: Nostalgia Publications

PCG087.000
c.1903  4 $^1/_2$" x 10 $^1/_2$" . . . . . . . . .$15,000
Cardboard sign easel back, embossed, die cut, Rare.
(Kaufmann and Strauss Co., NY).
Photo Courtesy: Chuck Campbell

PCG024.000
c.1908  11" . . . . . . . . . . . . . . . . . . . . .$8,000
Cardboard sign  (Embossed gold corners and wood
grain border).
Photo courtesy: Scott Rosenman

PCG023.000
c.1914  6 $^1/_2$" x 14" . . . . . . . . . . . . . .$8,000
Sign, tin,  emobssed, Very Rare.
("Southern Can Co., Balto.MD.")
Photo Courtesy: Joe Happle

PCG021.000
c.1914-1916  14" x 20 $^1/_2$"  . . . . . . $15,000
"Dutch Boy" Chewing Gum cutout, cardboard, Very
Rare. Photo Courtesy: Thaddeus Krom, Maywood, NJ

*Note: Prices are based on items in Excellent condition. Items in
Near Mint to Mint condition could be worth more, and in Poor condition that
same item would be worth far less.*

# COCA-COLA CHEWING GUM

1903-1904   Aprox 2" x 6" . . . . . . . . . . . . . . . . . . . . . . . . . . . . . . . . . . . . . . . . . . . . . . . . . . . . . . . . . . . . . . . . . . . . . . . . . .$2,000 each

Coca-Cola Chewing Gum Bookmarks, Rare.
Photos courtesy: (First 5) Thaddeus Krom

PCG053.000

PCG054.000

PCG056.000

PCG057.000

PCG058.000

PCG059.000
Photo Courtesy: Jim Alexander

PCG034.000
c.1912 . . . . . . . . . . . . . . . . . . . . . . . $4,500
Coca-Cola Pepsin Gum tin (held five sticks of gum), Rare

PCG020.000
1903-1905  4 1/2" x 11 1/2"  . .$10,000
"Baby" Chewing Gum hanger cutout,
cardboard, Very Rare

PCG032.000
c.1903-1905 . . . . . . . . . . . $12,000
Doremus Vending Machine with cylindrical
gum and tin top sign, Very Rare

PCG033.000
c.1903 . . . . . . . . . . . . . . . . . . . . . . $12,000
Doremus Vending Machine with cylindrical gum
and porcelain top sign, Very Rare

*Note: The two Doremus Automatic Vending Machines shown are 21" high with top sign and 6" wide. The top signs are 7" x 8 1/2". One version is lithographed tin and the other is porcelain. Keep in mind, these machines were mainly used as cigar vendors. Some had a cigar cutter attached to side.*

*Note: Special thanks to Bill Enes and Thom Thompson for making these photos possible.*

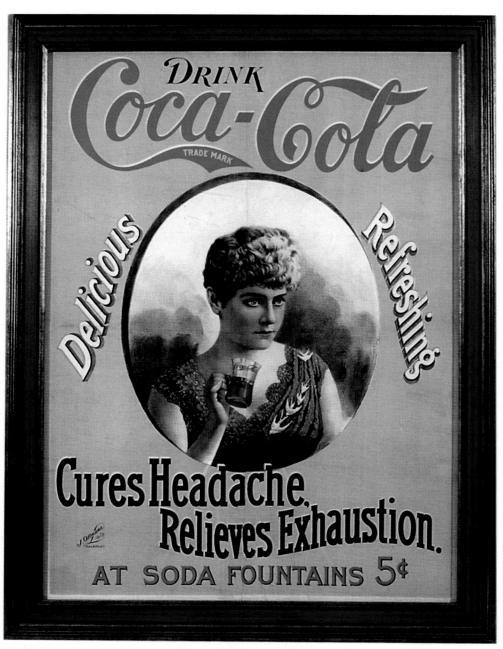

PPS010.000
c.1896   30" x 40"  . . . . . . . . . . . . .$20,000
Cameo paper sign, printed by J. Ottman Litho,
Co., N.Y. , Pre-1900 paper signs are Very Rare

PPS015.000
1901  14 $\frac{1}{2}$" x 19 $\frac{1}{4}$" . . . . . . . . . $15,000
"Girl With Yellow Roses", Photo courtesy: Author's
Collection. Note: Beware of repros of this piece.
Original has "copyrighted 1898 Wolf & Co., Phila."
lower right corner. One repro has a signature
on left corner of table and cross (+) mark or
marks on chest or table.

PPS016.001
1902  14 $\frac{3}{4}$" x 19 $\frac{1}{2}$" . . . . . . . . . $15,000
"Bottle Sales". Photo Courtesy: Chris Daniel

PPS016.000
1902  14 $\frac{3}{4}$" x 19 $\frac{1}{2}$" . . . . . . . . . $15,000
"Fountain Sales". Photo Courtesy: Author's Collection

PPS017.000
1903  14 $\frac{3}{4}$" x 19 $\frac{1}{2}$" . . . . . . . . . $15,000
"Hilda Clark". Photo Courtesy: Author's Collection

PPS018.000
1904  14 $^1/_2$" x 19 $^1/_2$" . . . . . . . . . $12,000
Lillian Nordica, metal strip top and bottom, Rare.
Photo Courtesy: Author's Collection

PPS019.000
1908  14" x 22"  . . . . . . . . . . . . . . $15,000
"Good to the Last Drop", metal strip top and bottom, Very Rare. Photo Courtesy: Author's Collection

PPS020.000
1913  18" x 24"  . . . . . . . . . . . . . $10,000
"Which" Coca-Cola or Goldelle Ginger Ale, Rare.
Photo Courtesy: Dave Baker

PPS021.000
c.1908  18" x 24"  . . . . . . . . . . . . $10,000
Gold Seal Ginger Ale and Coca-Cola, Rare.
Photo Courtesy: Joe Happle

# PAPER SIGNS

PPS014.000
1901  15" x 20"  . . . . . . . . . . . . . . . . $8,000
"Hilda Clark"

PPS022.000
1912  16" x 24"  . . . . . . . . . . . . . . . .$5,000
Printed by Ketterlinus Co., Philadelphia, PA

PPS023.000
c. 1912 16" x 22"  . . . . . . . . . . . . . . . $5,000
Printed by Ketterlinus Co., Philadelphia, PA

PPS080.000
c.1908  16 $\frac{1}{2}$" x 46" . . . . . . . . . . . .$3,500
Unusual paper sign with Bottler's name, Rare

PPS081.000
1920s  13" x 22"  . . . . . . . . . . . . . . .$1,600
Heavy Paper

PPS082.000
1920s  29 $\frac{1}{2}$" x 43" . . . . . . . . . . . . . . . . . . . . . . .$8,000
Very Rare. Printed by "The Forbes Lithograph Mfg. Co. Boston, MA."
Photo Courtesy: Author's Collection

Note: The sign on the right was
offered to bottlers and shown in
advertising price lists from 1928
through 1933. Called a "Fibre
sign" the size was listed (incor-
rectly) as 30" x 60". Suggested
use was indoors as well as outside
at fairs, circuses, and carnivals.
The price actually dropped from
$120 per 1,000 in 1928 to $100
per 1,000 in 1933.

PPS083.000
1928-1933  28" x 57" . . . . . . . . . . . .$2.800
Heavy Paper, printed by "The M C A Sign Co.
Massillon, OH", Rare.
Photo Courtesy: Author's Collection

Trolley cars, also called street cars, were first introduced in New York City in 1831. Originally, the trolleys were horse drawn carriages which operated on tracks in the street. As the end of the nineteenth century approached, most major American cities built street railways, but it was not until the electric street cars were introduced that the street railways really came into widespread use. The first electric trolley was installed in Richmond, Virginia, in 1887.

The electric street car, which was powered by electric wires above or below the street, revolutionized American cities by providing the public with low cost, convenient transportation.

Similarly, cable cars, intro-duced in San Francisco in 1873, were used in hilly cities because they were thought to be safer in that type of situation. These cable cars were pulled along the tracks by an endless, engine-driven cable onto which the cars were attached.

By the turn of the century, the East and Midwest regions, with their expanded interurban service, had a street railway system larger than that of their railroad system. Unfortunately, mostly because of the ever-growing popularity of the automobile, the street railway system began to decline and eventually die. Now, cable cars can only be found in San Francisco and electric trolleys in only a handful of cities. But, in their time and because of their low cost and convenience, the trolleys were a popular form of public transportation and, therefore, an excellent place for companies such as Lucky Strike, Nabisco, and of course, The Coca-Cola Company, to target their advertising. This advertising came in the form of cardboard signs which collectors have dubbed "street car signs" or "trolley car signs." They are unmistakable because all are a standard size of 11" x 20 1/2", printed on a lightweight, flexible cardboard. The size of these signs was very important, because they were inserted into metal brackets which became stock items when the cars were made, and the selling and

changing of the signs was done by advertising agencies, many of which specialized in trolley advertising.

Young boys, hired by the ad agencies, usually handled the actual changing of old signs and replacing them with new ones. One boy would stab the sign with a sharp, pointed stick, and lift it out with one swift motion. Another boy would follow and pick up the old signs. And, yet another boy would insert new signs into the brackets. With the demise of the trolley as a major form of transportation, signs similar to trolley car signs came into use on buses and subways.

For collectors, trolley car signs have always been one of the most desirable and sought after of all the signs used by The Coca-Cola Company to advertise their product. Unfortunately, early ones are very rare. Because of the type of material they were made of and their exposure to the heat and the cold, many of the trolley car signs, rare and otherwise, are found in rough condition. Many of the signs are found discolored due to smoke from smoking passengers.

On the following pages you will find the largest number of trolley car signs ever shown in one book, many of which are quite rare, as my estimated values will show. Keep in mind, however, that even though a large number of signs are shown in this book, this is just a sampling of the many used by The Coca-Cola Company over the years.

My personal favorites are signs which are representative of other advertising used for that particular year. In the years 1910, 1911, 1912, and 1913, for example, the artist Hamilton King's artwork was used on trays, calendars, magazine ads, and trolley car signs. Those are rare and very desirable. Finding signs which go along with the theme of other advertising of a particular year is always exciting and many such examples do exist. Other signs have been found with artwork that was not used on any other advertising. In any case, all are interesting and are very sought after by collectors.

PCS014.000

c.1907 . . . . . . . . . . . . . . . . . . . . . . . $2,800

"Relieves Fatigue"

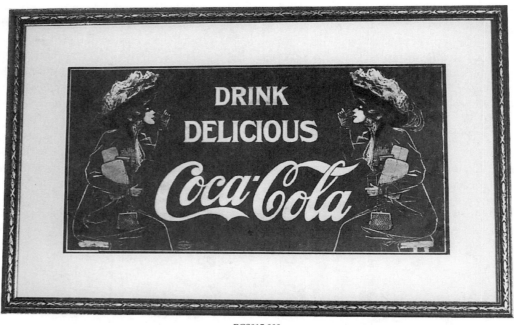

PCS015.000

1912 . . . . . . . . . . . . . . . . . . . . . . . $3,800

"Hamilton King Art", Rare

# TROLLEY SIGNS
*11" x 20 1/2" Cardboard*

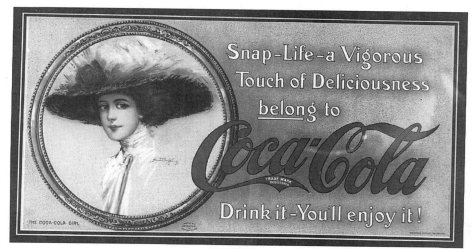

Note:
Additional
Trolley Signs
can
be found on
color pages
178-180.

PCS016.000
1910 . . . . . . . . . . . . . . . . . . . . . . . . . $5,500
Featuring "The Coca-Cola Girl" by Hamilton King
and printed by Wolf & Co., Philadelphia, PA

PCS017.000
1914 . . . . . . . . . . . . . . . . . . . . . . . . $4,500
"Two Girls"

PCS018.000
1918 . . . . . . . . . . . . . . . . . . . . . . $1,500
World War I sugar rationing facts

— 67 —

*Note:
Additional
Trolley Signs
can be found
on color pages
178-180.*

PCS019.000

c.1907 . . . . . . . . . . . . . . . . . . . . . . . . $2,000

PCS021.000

1927 . . . . . . . . . . . . . . . . . . . . . . . . $1,800

Art by Fred Mizen

PCS020.000

c.1909 . . . . . . . . . . . . . . . . . . . . . . . . $2,600

PCS022.000

c.1905 . . . . . . . . . . . . . . . . . . . . . . . . $2,000

PCS023.000

c.1918 . . . . . . . . . . . . . . . . . . . . . . . . $4,000

PCS024.000

c.1913 . . . . . . . . . . . . . . . . . . . . . . . . $2,200

PCS025.000

c.1918 . . . . . . . . . . . . . . . . . . . . . . . . $950

PCS026.000

c.1914 . . . . . . . . . . . . . . . . . . . . . . . . $800

PCS027.000

c.1913 . . . . . . . . . . . . . . . . . . . . . . . . $3,500

PCS028.000

c.1918 . . . . . . . . . . . . . . . . . . . . . . . . $500

# CARDBOARD DISPLAY PIECES

PCD030.000
1931  19" x 27" . . . . . . . . . . . . . . . $2,500
Rockwell Art cardboard cutout
(must be complete)

PCD029.000
1930  18" x 42" . . . . . . . . . . . . . . . $1,800

PCS031.000
1906  19" x 26" . . . . . . . . . . . . . . . $10,000
"Juanita" cardboard, easel back, embossed center,
with gold trim

PCD031.000
1935  18" x 36" . . . . . . . . . . . . . . . $2,800
Rockwell Art, Printed by Snyder & Black
(must be complete)

— 70 —

PCD027.000

1922 . . . . . . . . . . . . . . . . . . . . . . . . . . . . . . . . . . . . . . $8,500

Summer

PCD028.S01

PCD028.S02

Complete Display PCD028.S00

PCD028.S03

1927 . . . . . . . . . . . . . . . . . . . . . . . . . . . . . . . . . . . . . . $5,500

Fall three-piece "Leaf"

PCD032.000

c.1922 . . . . . . . . . . . . . . . . . . . . . $15,000

"Four Seasons" window display. Note: The "Four
Seasons" window display has been mistakenly called
"One of a Kind" by some dealers. While this is a
beautiful and rare piece, it is far from "One of a
Kind." The price shown is for items in Average
condition, examples in less than desirable condition
will be worth much less.

PCD033.000

1922  32" x 42" . . . . . . . . . . . . . . . . $3,500

PCD035.000

1921  32" x 42" . . . . . . . . . . . . . . . $4,000

PCD034.000

c.1913 . . . . . . . . . . . . . . . . . . . . . $7,000

"Cameo" foldout window display

# CARDBOARD CUTOUTS

Prices are based on examples in Excellent or Better condition. Pieces that have been trimmed or in less than Excellent condition, will be worth less. Sizes are all approximate.

PCD038.000
1926  28" x 42"  . . . . . . . . . . . . . . . . . $4,000

PCD037.000
c.1912  28" x 38"  . . . . . . . . . . . . . . . $7,500

PCD036.000
c.1916  36" x 40"  . . . . . . . . . . . . . . $6,500

PCD039.000
c.1922  23" x 40"  . . . . . . . . . . . . $4,500

— 73 —

PCD040.S02

PCD040.S01

PCD040.S03

PCD040.S00 c.1926  Complete 3-piece display . . . . . . . . . . . . . . . . . . . . . . . . . . . . . . . . . . . . . . . . . . . . . . . $6,000
Center piece only, 3-D, 24" x 36" . . . . . . . . . . . . . . . . . . . . . . . . . . . . . . . . . . . . . . . . . . . . . . . . . . . . $4,000
End pieces only 14" x 18" . . . . . . . . . . . . . . . . . . . . . . . . . . . . . . . . . . . . . . . . . . . . . . . . . . . . $750 Each
Window display. Printed by Niagara Litho, Buffalo, NY. Note: This display also had a cardboard balloon with ribbon attached to her wrist.

PCD041.000

c. 1948  14" x 20" . . . . . . . . . . . . . . . . . $285

PCD042.000

1949  14" x 18" . . . . . . . . . . . . . . . . . $750

3-D

# CARDBOARD CUTOUTS

PCD043.000
1940  12" x 17" . . . . . . . . . . . . . $600
Canada

PCD044.000
1937  32" x 40" . . . . . . . . . . . . . . . $1,800

PCD045.P01
1940s  19" x 22" . . . . . . . . . . . . . . . . $800
3-D

PCD046.000
1958  29" x 34 $\frac{1}{2}$" . . . . . . . . . . . . . $385
3-D

PCD047.000
1933  7 $\frac{1}{2}$" x 11" . . . . . . . . . . . $475

PCD049.P01
1944  19" x 15 ¹/₂" . . . . . . . . . . . . . . $450

PCD048.000
1926  18" x 32" . . . . . . . . . . . . . . . . . $2,500
"Umbrella Girl" with glass.
Note: There is also a bottle version of this
cutout shown on a color plate in this book.

PCD052.000
1948  . . . . . . . . . . . . $1,200

PCD051.000
1932  23" x 30" . . . . . . . . . . . . . . $2,000

PCD050.000
1949  27" x 31" . . . . . . . $700

PCD053.000
Early 1900s  . . . . . . . . . . . . . . . . . $6,500
"Girl in Horseless Carriage", Very Rare.
Photo Courtesy: Don & Donna Arnold

# CARDBOARD CUTOUTS

PCD054.000
1956 18" x 19" . . . . . . . . . . . . . $375

PCD057.S01
1951 14$^{1}/_{2}$" x 17" . . . . . . . . . . $375
Snyder & Black

PCD056.000
1944 15" x 19" . . . . . . . . . . . . . . . . . . . . . $2,500
Niagara Litho, Rare. This piece could either be used as a hanging sign or a stand-up. There is also a "Sprite Boy" version.
Photo Courtesy: Authors Collection

PCD055.000
1950 14" x 20" . . . . . $385
Niagara Litho

PCD059.000
1948 17" x 18" . . . . . . . . . . . . . . . . . . $650
3-D

PCD058.000
1954 13" x 20" . . . . . . . . . . . . . $600
Niagara Litho, 3-D

# CARDBOARD CUTOUTS

PCD060.000
1937  19" x 25 $^1/_2$"  . . . . . . . $500

PFE039.P01
1942  17" x 26"  . . . . . . . . . . . . . . . . . . . . . . . . . . . . . $475
3-D, (Part of a Festoon)

PCD062.000
1950s  13" x 18"  . . . . . $200
3-D, 2-sided

PCD061.000
1960s  12" x 18"  . . . . . $175
3-D

PFE040.P01
1945  20"  . . . . . . . . . . . . . . . . . . . . . . . $385
3-D, (Part of a Festoon)

PCD063.000
1956  16" x 19"  . . . . . . . . . . . $285
3-D

> *Note: Pieces from Festoons (Backbar Displays) are very interesting and collectible. Prices will vary on these, but keep in mind they are only part of a much larger display and worth only a percentage of what the complete display would be worth.*

> *Note: Remember condition is the most important factor when determining value.*

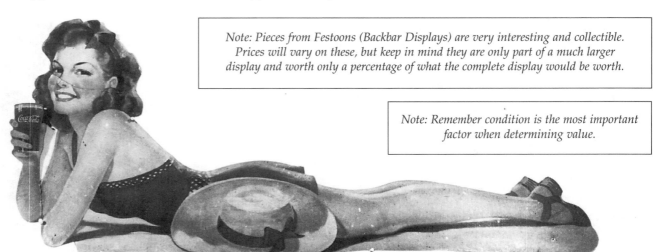

PFE041.P02
1940s  45"  . . . . . . . . . . . . . . . . . . . . . .$425
3-D, (Part of a Festoon)

PCD064.P02
1953  12" x 20"  . . . . . . . . . . $200
Niagara Litho

PCD065.P02
1950s  21 $^1/_2$" x 20"  . . . . $185

PCD066.000
1948  26" x 42"  . . . . . . . . . . . . . . . . $2,000

PCD069.000
1964  24" x 58"  . . . $350

PCD067.000
1924  24" x 40" (as shown)  . . . . . . . $2,700

PCD068.000
1952  18" x 36"  . . . . . . . . . . . . . . . . . $550

# CARDBOARD CUTOUTS

PCD070.000
1938  41" x 43" . . . . . . . . . . . . . . . . $2,200
3-D window display, Printed by Niagara Litho Co., NY

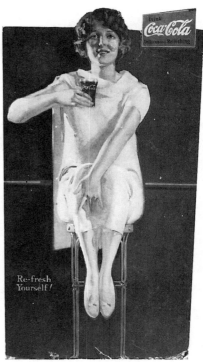

PCD071.000
c.1926  16" x 19 $^1/_2$" . . . . . . $3,000

PCD072.000
1952  21" x 30" . . . . . . $250

PCD073.000
1956  24" x 35" . . . . . . . . . . . . $325

PCD074.000
1952  20" x 28" . . . $385

PCD075.000
1960s  28" x 36" . . . . . . . . $185

PCD076.000
1956  15" x 18" . . . . . . . . . . . $385
3-D, easel back

PCD077.000
1953  24" x 35" . . . . . . $300

# CARDBOARD CUTOUTS (MOVIE STARS)

PCD078.S02

PCD078.S01
1933

PCD078.S03

PCD078.S00 Complete 3-piece display . . . . . . . . . . . . . . . . . . . . . . . . . . . . . . . $6,500
Center piece only, 20" x 26" . . . . . . . . . . . . . . . . . . . . . . . . . . . . . . . . . . . 4,600
End piece, 13" x 20 $^1/_2$" . . . . . . . . . . . . . . . . . . . . . . . . . . . . . . . . . . . . $900 Each
"Movie Window Display"

PCD079.000
1933  10" x 20" . . $1,800
Claudette Colbert

PCD081.000
1932  13" x 16" . . . . . . . . . . . . . . . $1,300
June Collyer

PCD080.000
1933  10" x 20" . . . $1,800
Claudette Colbert

# MOVIE STARS AND CELEBRITIES

Right from the beginning, The Coca-Cola Company realized the importance of celebrity endorsements. Performers and singers like Hilda Clark and Lillian Nordica shown with a glass or bottle of Coca-Cola lent an air of sophistication. Celebrities dressed in the latest styles of the day had a big impact on the buying public. These early celebrity endorsements obviously worked; both Hilda Clark and Lillian Nordica were used for consecutive years in different and colorful images. As the years went on the company occasionally used movie stars and celebrities, but it was not until the 1930s, which was a boom decade for Hollywood and the motion picture industry, that they used them extensively. Books, radio and movie magazines glamorized the bigger than life stars who were idolized by millions of movie goers. The Coca-Cola Company capitalized on these stars' popularity by featuring them on periodical advertising, serving trays, cardboard signs, and cutout window displays. Movie star and celebrity advertising pieces are among the most desirable of all Coca-Cola memorabilia.

Usually the actors and celebrities seen enjoying an ice cold Coke were the big stars of the day: Jean Harlow, Clark Gable, Claudette Colbert, Joan Crawford and many other stars of the 1930s silver screen.

Without exception, movie stars who appear are identified on the finished piece of advertising. Frankly I doubt if any of these stars would lend their image without proper acknowledgement. Nevertheless, I still hear from collectors who insist that the piece they have, showing an unidentified model, is Rock Hudson, Marilyn Monroe, Ted Williams or others. We have no information that any of these stars ever did any advertising for Coca-Cola, so remember: Do not assume that an image on a piece of advertising, especially a product like Coca-Cola, is that of a movie star, a sports star or a celebrity unless it is identified as that star. Also keep in mind that most of this movie star and celebrity advertising is very desirable and sought after, making it rare. In above average or near mint condition it can be considered very rare.

---

The following is a list of movie stars and celebrities pre-1960 (excluding sports). This list is by no means complete, but it is a good representation of the celebrities who have lent their name and image to advertise Coca-Cola.

| KEY: | Authors(A) | Movies (MS) |
|---|---|---|
| | Ziegfield Follies (Z) | Radio (R) |
| | Television(TV) | |
| | Music (singer, opera, composer, or conductor) (M) | |

---

Ida Bailey Allen (A)
Diana Allen (MS)
Adrienne Ames (MS)
Richard Arlen (MS)
Lionel Barrymore (MS)
Wallace Beery (MS)
Tony Bennett (M)
Edgar Bergen (R)
Joan Blondell (MS)
Billie Burke (MS)
Sue Carol (MS)
Hilda Clark (M)
Louise Closser Hale (MS)
Claudette Colbert (MS)
June Collyer (MS)
Velma Connor (Z)
Jackie Cooper (MS)
Joan Crawford (MS)
George Cukor (MS)
Marion Davies (MS)
Frances Dee (MS)
Morton Downey (M)
Marie Dressler (MS)
Madge Evans (MS)
Percy Faith (M)
Eddie Fisher (M)
Clark Gable (MS)
Wynne Gibson (MS)
Cary Grant (MS)
Louise Clo Hale (MS)
Lionel Hampton (M)
Jean Harlow (MS)
Phillips Holmes (MS)

Benita Hume (MS)
Spike Jones (M)
Leonard W. Joy (M)
Kay Kayser (M)
Andre Kostelanetz (M)
Lola Lane (MS)
Mario Lanza (M)
Laura LaPlante (MS)
Evelyn Law (Z)
Carole Lombard (MS)
Edmund Lowe (MS)
Dorothy Mackaill (MS)
Frederic March (MS)
Sari Maritza (MS)
Florine McKinney (MS)
The McGuire Sisters (M)
Graham McNamee (R)
Grant Mitches (MS)
Karen Morley (MS)
Ricky Nelson (TV, M)
Ray Noble (M)
Lillian Nordica (M)
Maureen O'Sullivan (MS)
Gene Raymond (MS)
Grantland Rice (R)
Singin Sam (M)
Larry Steele (M)
Genevieve Tobin (MS)
Lupe Velez (MS)
Johnny Weismuller (MS)
Pearl White (MS)
Bill Williams (Kit Carson) (TV)
Loretta Young (MS)

# CARDBOARD CUTOUTS (MOVIE STARS)

PCD082.000

1932 . . . . . . . . . . . . . . . . . . . . . . . . $4,000

Joan Blondell

PCD083.000

1932 . . . . . . . . . . . . . . . . . . . . . . . . $4,000

Sue Carol

Note: Coca-Cola advertising featuring movie stars are always desirable and sought after by collectors. Cutouts in Poor condition will be worth much less than values shown.

PCD084.000

1933 . . . . . . . . . . . . . . . . . . . . . . . . $4,800

Frederic March and Claudette Colbert

Note: The 1933 Movie Star cutouts shown here all vary in size, but all are approximately 28" x 36".

PCD085.000

1933 . . . . . . . . . . . . . . . . . . . . . . . . $4,500

Carole Lombard and Phillips Holmes

PCD086.000

1933 . . . . . . . . . . . . . . . . . . . . . . . . $4,500

Richard Arlen and Adrienne Ames

# CARDBOARD SIGNS (MOVIE STARS)

PCS087.000
1934  14" x 30"  . . . . . . . . $1,800
Wallace Beery

PCS088.000
1934  14" x 24"  . . . . . $1,300
Joan Crawford

PCS089.000
1934  14" x 30"  . . . . . . $3,300
Johnny Weissmuller and Maureen
O'Sullivan

PCD090.000
1935  31" x 41" . . . . . . . . . . . . . . . . . $4,000
Madge Evans, window display. Printed by
Snyder & Black

PCD091.000
1932  . . . . . $6,000
Jean Harlow

PCD092.000
1932  . . . . . . . . . $4,500
Lupe Velez

PCD093.000
1934  4 ¹/₂'  . . . . . . . . . . . . . . . . . . . $3,500
Wallace Beery and Jackie Cooper, window display

PCD094.000
1931  10" x 18 $^1/_2$"  . . . . . $2,000
Easel back. Printed by Snyder & Black

### The Pause That Refreshes

PCD096.000
1940  32 $^1/_2$" x 42 $^1/_2$"  . . . . . . . . . . $1,300
Window display. Printed by Niagara Litho Co., NY

PCD095.000
1938  15" x 20 $^1/_2$"  . . . . . . . $950
Hanging sign

PCD097.000
1931  31" x 43$^1/_2$"  . . . . . $2,200
Window display. Art by Haden Haden.

PCD098.000
1931  32" x 42 "  . . . . . . . . $1,300
Window display piece

PCD099.000

1938  22" . . . . . . . . . . . . . $2,800

Rare, Printed by Snyder & Black

PCD101.000

1927  12" x 13" . . . . . . . . . . $750

Rare, Printed by Snyder & Black

PCD100.000

1940  22" x 23" . . . . . . . $1,400

Rare, Printed by Snyder & Black

PCD102.000

1937  34" x 36" . . . . . . . . . . . . . . . . . $1,200

3-D

PCD103.001

1954  5' . . . . . . . . . . . . . . $2,000

Eddie Fisher, Easel back (folds in half)

PCD103.002

1954  19"  . . . $1,200

Eddie Fisher, Easel back

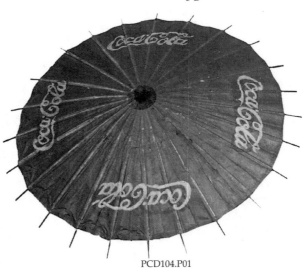

PCD104.P01

1920s . . . . . . . . . . . . . . . . . . . . . . . . $750

"Parasol", Paper and bamboo, This piece is actually part of a cardboard cutout display

# CARDBOARD CUTOUTS

PCD105.S01    PCD105.S02        PCD105.S03        PCD105.S04    PCD105.S05

1944  25" x 64" . . . . . . . . . . . . . . . . . . . . . . . . . . . . . . . . $1,100 Each
PCD105.S00 Complete set of 5 . . . . . . . . . . . . . . . . . . . . . . . . . . . $6,000
"Service Girls"

PCD106.S01  106.S02  106.S03  106.S04  106.S05
1944  17" . . . . . . . . . . . . . . . $500 Each
PCD106.S00 Complete set of 5 . . . $2,800
"Service Girls", small size

PCD107.000
1950  13" x 22" . . . . $500

PCD111.000
1950  24" x 35" . . . $300

PCD108.000
1926  15" x 20" . . . . . . . . $1,000
"Specials Today"

PCD109.S01
1948  . . . . . . . $200

PCD110.S01        PCD110.S02
1950s  16" x 24" . . . . . . . . . . . . . $185 Each

PCD112.000
1939  30" x 42" . . . . . . . . . . $350

PCD113.000

1931  12" x 14"  . . . . . . . . . . . . . . . . . $900

PCD114.000

1952  20" x 20"  . . . . . . . . . . . . . . . . . $425

3-D

PBD001.000

1927  . . . . . . . . . . . . . . . . $650

Bottle display

PCD115.000

1934  14" x 32"  . . . . . . . . $1000

Niagara Litho

PCD117.000

1960  . . . . . . . .$85

12oz. can display sign

PCD118.000

1950s  . . . . . . . . . . .$125

Bottle lighter carton display sign

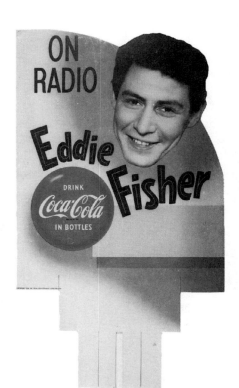

PCD116.000

1954  . . . . . . . . . . . . . . . . . . . . . . .$185

Eddie Fisher carton display sign

# CARDBOARD CUTOUTS

PCD119.000
1930s  20" x 34" . . . . . . . . . . . . . . $750

PCD120.002

PCD120.001
1944  Life size 62 $^1/_2$" . . . . . . . . $950
Miniature 17 $^1/_2$" . . . . . . . . . . . . .$450
"Woman Shopper" display

PCD121.000
1950  18" x 23" . . . . . . . . . $325
3-D

PCD122.000
1953  13 $^1/_2$" x 21" . . . . . . . $200

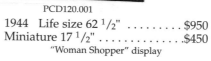

Note: Remember condition is the most
important factor when determining value.

PCD123.000
1936  24 $^1/_4$" x 47 $^1/_4$" . . . . . . . . . . $700

PCD124.S02

PCD124.S03
1935  10 $^1/_4$" x 18 $^1/_2$" . . . . . . . $250 Each

PCD125.000
1933   10" x 20" . . . . $650
3-D

PCD128.000
1933   10" x 20"  . . $850
3-D

PCD129.000
1933   10" x 20"  . . $750
3-D

PCD126.000
1931   10" x 20" . . . . . . . . . . . . . $800
3-D

PCD130.000
1932   14"   . . . . . . $385
Easel back

PCD131.000
1950s   18" . . . . . . $150
Easel back

PCD127.000
1932   10" x 20" . . . . . . . $650
3-D

Note: The 3-D Bottle Signs shown here were printed
and die-cut by Niagara Litho., Co., Buffalo, NY

PCD132.000
1930   10" x 20"   . . . . . $675
3-D

# CARDBOARD CUTOUTS

PCD133.S02
1927  5 $^1/_2$" x 13" . . . . . . . . . . . . . . . . $200
This is part of the 1927 "Toy Town" window display

PCD134.000
1957 . . . . . . . . . . . . . . . . . . . . . $150
3-D umbrella sign, heavy paper

PCD135.000
1960s 18" x 28" . . . . . . $185

PCD136.000
1960s  15" x 22"  . . . . . . . . . . . . . . . . $225
3-D

PCD137.000
1950s  12" x 23"  . . . . . $75
3-D bottle display

PCD138.000
1950s  15" x 24"  . . . . . . . . . . . . . $100
3-D hanging cutout

PCD139.000
1950  16" x 59"  . . . . . . $385

PCD140.000

1933   10" x 22"  . . . . . . . . . . . . . . . $1,100

3-D hanging sign, Printed by Niagara Litho

PCD141.000

1933   10" x 22"  . . . . . . . . . . . . . . . $1,200

3-D hanging sign, Printed by Niagara Litho

PCD142.000

1933   10" x 22"  . . . . . . . . . . . . . . . $1,000

3-D hanging sign, Printed by Niagara Litho

PCD143.S01

1924   11" x 24"  . . . . . . . . . . . . . . . $375

Flower box window display piece

PCD144.000

1937   13" x 34"  . . . . . . . . . . . . . . . $400

Hanging sign

PCD145.S03

1924   15" x 20"  . . . . . $350

"Flower Box"

PCD146.S02

Late 1930s  . . . $450

"Swan"

PCD145.S02

1924   15" x 20"  . . . . . $350

"Flower Box"

PCD147.000
1930s 8" . . . $385

PCD148.000
1930s 9" . . . $185

PCD149.000
1920s 7" x 12" . . . . . . . . . . . . . . . . . $550
One-sided

PCD150.000
1950s . . . . . . . . . . . . . . . . . $18

PCD151.000
1930s 7 1/2" x 12" . . . . $150

PCD153.000
1949 . . . . . . . $185

PCD154.000
1960s 10" . . . . . . . . . . . $70

PCD152.000
1920s 7 1/2" x 12" . . . . . . . . . . . . . . $550

PCD155.P01
1950s . . . . . . . . . . . . . . . $45

PCD156.000
1950s . . . . . . . . . . . . . . $75

PCD157.000
1920s 7 1/2" x 12" . . . . . . . . . $575

PCD158.000
1969 . . . . . . . . . . . . . . . . . $65
"Mobile"

TAKE ENOUGH HOME

PCD227.000
1950s . . . . . . . . . . . . . . . . . . . . . . . . . .$675
Point of purchase display, 12 bottle carton

BEVERAGE DEPT.

PCD228.000
1950s . . . . . . . . . . . . . . . . . . . . . . . . . .$675
Point of purchase display, 6 bottle carton

PCD230.000
1950s  7" x 7" . . . . . . . . . . . $50
Hanger

YOUR Coca-Cola BOTTLER OF DOTHAN BIDS YOU WELCOME

PCD229.000
1960s  18" . . . . . . . . . . . . . . . . . . . . . . . . . . $600
Easel back

Standard size

PCD231.000
1950s  7" x 7" . . . . . . . . . . . $30
Hanger

KING SIZE
puts you at your sparkling best

PCD233.000
1950s  7" . . . . . . . . . . . . . . . . . .$25
Hanger

ICE COLD
DRINK Coca-Cola

PCD234.000
1950s  7" x 7" . . . . . . . . . . . $100
Hanger

King size
puts you at your best!

PCD232.000
1950s  7" x 7" . . . . . . . . . . . $30
Hanger

# CARDBOARD CUTOUTS

PCD159.000

1960s . . . . . . . . . . . . . . . . . . . . . . . . $85

"Mobile" "King Size" bottle display

PCD160.000

1960s  36" . . . . . . . . . . . . . . . . . . . . . . $125

"Penguin"

PCD162.P01

1960s  8" x 10"  . . . . $50

"Diamond Can"

PCD161.000

1969 . . . . . . . . . . . . . . . . . $25

Vinyl

PCD163.000

1980s . . . . . . . . . . . . . . . . . . . . . . . . . $35

"Cabbage Patch Kids" cardboard cutouts

PCD164.000

c.1963 . . . . . . . . . . . . . . . . . . . . . $300

PCD168.000
1960s  17" x 19" . . . . . . . . . . . . . . $325
Two-Sided

PCD170.000
1941-48  14" x 25" . . . . . . . . . . . . . . $400
Canadian

PCD166.000
1942  16" x 21" . . . . . . . . . . . . . . . . $800
Snyder & Black

PCD167.000
1947  18" x 32" . . . . . . . . . . . . . . . . $1,200

PCD169.000
1944  14" x 32" . . . . . . . . . . . $1,000

PCD171.000
1941-48  11" . . . . . . . . . . . . . . . . . . $850
Two-Sided

PCD165.001                    PCD165.002
1947 . . . . . . . . . . . . . . . . . . . . . $125 Each
Display signs

# CARDBOARD CUTOUT BOTTLE DISPLAYS

PBD003.000
1927  8" x 10 1/2" . . . . . . . . . . . . . . $2,500
U.S. Printing & Litho Co.

PBD004.000
1930  8" x 11" . . . . . . . . . . . . . . . . $1,800

PBD008.001          PBD008.002          PBD008.003
1929  9 3/4" x 7" . . . . . . . . . . . . . . . . . $500 Each

PBD006.000
1930  8" x 11" . . . . . . . . . $1,800

PBD005.000
1930  8 1/2" x 11" . . . . . . . . . . . . . . $1,600

PBD007.000
1927 . . . . . . . . . . . . . . . . . . . . . . . . $2,200
Two bottle display

# CARDBOARD CUTOUT BOTTLE DISPLAYS

PBD009.S01            PBD009.S02
1939 . . . . . . . . . . . . . . . . . . . . . . . $325 Pair
German

PBD010.000
1926  11 ¹/₂" x 14"  . . . . . . $2,000
"Girl Holding Tray"

PBD011.000
1929  7" x 9 ³/₄"  . . . . . . . . . . $2,500
"Bathing Girl"

Note: Many collectors do shy away from foreign items, because of this even unusual pieces do not have the value of pieces produced for the U.S. market.

PBD012.000
Late 1920s  10" x 14"  . . . . . . . . . . $1,800
"Boy and Weiner"

PBD013.000
1930  9" x 17 ¹/₂"  . . . . . . . . . . . $1,600
"Girl in Swimsuit"

PBD014.000
c.1933  . . . . . $225
L.A. Bottling Co.

PBD015.000
1930s  7"  . . . . . . . . . . . . . . . . . $100
German

# FESTOONS

Festoons are cardboard displays that were hung above the soda fountain backbar. During the '20s and '30s they were changed with the seasons. Found in original envelope would certainly increase its value.

PFE012.000

c.1918 . . . . . . . . . . . . . . . . . . . . . . . . . $5,000

PFE013.000

1927 . . . . . . . . . . . . . . . . . . . . . . . . . $4,000

PFE014.000

1953 . . . . . . . . . . . . . . . . . . . . . . . . . $1,400

PFE015.000

1950s . . . . . . . . . . . . . . . . . . . . . . . . . $950

"State Birds"

PFE016.000

1951 . . . . . . . . . . . . . . . . . . . . . . . . . $900

PFE017.000

1958 . . . . . . . . . . . . . . . . . . . . . . . . . $650

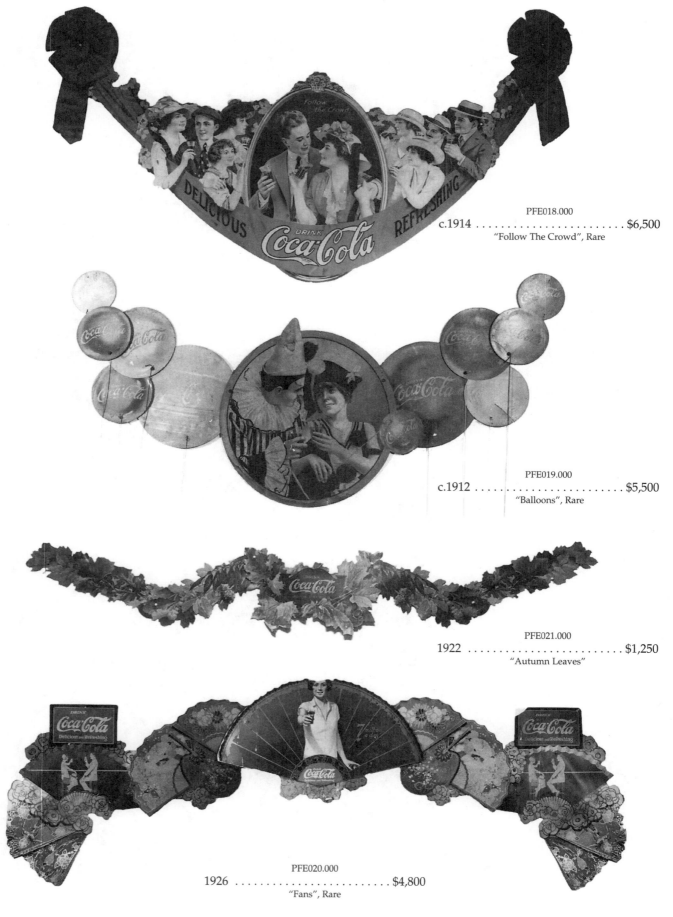

PFE018.000
c.1914 . . . . . . . . . . . . . . . . . . . . . . . $6,500
"Follow The Crowd", Rare

PFE019.000
c.1912 . . . . . . . . . . . . . . . . . . . . . $5,500
"Balloons", Rare

PFE021.000
1922 . . . . . . . . . . . . . . . . . . . . . . . $1,250
"Autumn Leaves"

PFE020.000
1926 . . . . . . . . . . . . . . . . . . . . $4,800
"Fans", Rare

# FESTOONS

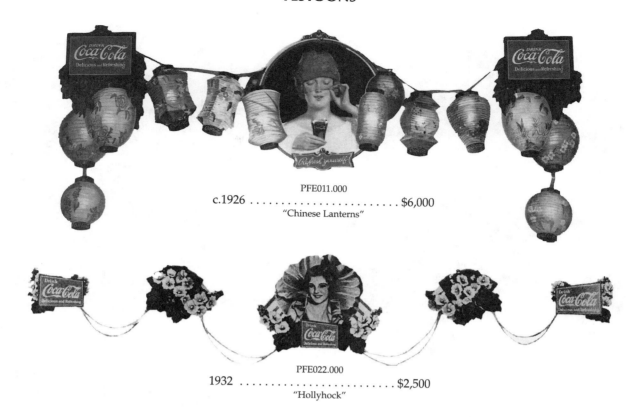

PFE011.000

c.1926 . . . . . . . . . . . . . . . . . . . . . $6,000

"Chinese Lanterns"

PFE022.000

1932 . . . . . . . . . . . . . . . . . . . . . . $2,500

"Hollyhock"

PFE023.000

1932 . . . . . . . . . . . . . . . . . . . . . . $2,500

"Verbena"

PFE024.000

1932 . . . . . . . . . . . . . . . . . . . . . . $4,000

"Morning Glory"

PFE025.000

1932 . . . . . . . . . . . . . . . . . . . . . . $3,500

"Corn Flower"

# FESTOONS (BACKBAR DISPLAYS)

PFE032.000

1950 . . . . . . . . . . . . . . . . . . . . . . . . $750

PFE033.000

1950s . . . . . . . . . . . . . . . . . . . . . . . $1,300

"Coke Club"

PFE026.000

1931 . . . . . . . . . . . . . . . . . . . . . . . . $2,200

"Pointsettia"

PFE027.000

1939 . . . . . . . . . . . . . $1,300

"Petunia"

PFE029.000

1939 . . . . . . . . . . . . . . . . . . . . . . . . $1,000

PFE030.000

Late 1930s . . . . . . . . . . . . . . . . . . . . $1,000

"Swans"

PFE028.000

1939 . . . . . . . $1,500

"Locket"

PFE031.000

1950s . . . . . . . . . . . . . . . . . . . . . . . . $950

"Host to Thirsty Main Street"

> *Note: The prices on these Festoons and Backbar Displays are for complete examples. It's always nice to have the original envelope, and I'm sure it would enhance the value.*

PFE043.000

c.1937 . . . . . . . . . . . . . . . . . . . . . . . . . . . . . . . . . . . . . . . . . . . . . . . . $3,600

Fish Festoon (Kay Displays), Rare. Note: This Kay display festoon is very unusual. End pieces are stamped tin with wood end logos, six fish are all detachable stamped tin. Center piece is stamped tin over wood backing, logo is cutout wood, canvas straps and rope connectors. When found complete with all nine pieces this festoon is considered rare.

PFE044.000

1953 . . . . . . . . . . . . . . . . . . . . . . . . $3,000

"Fan" Festoon, 3-D center

PFE045.000

1954 . . . . . . . . . . . . . . . . . . . . . . . . $1,600

School Kids Festoon, 3-D

# FESTOONS

PFE034.000

1930s . . . . . . . . . . . . . . . . . . . . . . . . . . . $900

"Icicles"

PFE035.000

1950s . . . . . . . . . . . . . . . . . . . . . . . . . $550

"State Tree"

PFE036.000

1950s . . . . . . . . . . . . . . . . . . . . . . . . . . . $650

"Antique Cars"

PFE037.000

1950s . . . . . . . . . . . . . . . . . . . . . . . . . $650

"Square Dance"

PFE038.000

1951 . . . . . . . . . . . . . . . . . . . . . . . . . $1,200

"Girls Heads"

PCD172.000
1936   36" x 40"  . . . . . . . . . . . . . . . $1,000
Cardboard cutout window display piece

PCD173.000
1931  10" x 20"  . . . . . . . . . . . . . $900
Cardboard cutout hanging sign

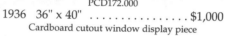

PCD174.S00
1932 . . . . . . . . . . . . . . . . . . . . . . . . . . . . . . . . . . . . . . . . $4,000
Window display, 5 pieces

PCD224.000

1934  3 ¹/₂' x 4' . . . . . . . . . . . . . . . $4,000
Santa window display, 3-D , Rare when found
complete

PCD225.000

1950s  36" . . . . . . . . . . . . . . . . . $225
Santa

PCD226.000

1947  26" x 54" . . . . . . . . . . . . $425
Santa, folds in center

PCS397.000

1949  11" x 17" . . . . . . . . . . . . . . . . $200
Canada, (French)

PCD175.001
1953   28" x 42" . . . . . . . . . . . . . $300

PCD176.001
1962   32" x 47" . . . . . . . . . . . . . . . . . $400
Also made in a smaller size 15 1/2" x 24"

PCD177.001
1953   29" x 42" . . . . . . . . $300
3-D display

PCD178.000
1949   15" . . . . . . . . . . . . . . . $350
Easel back display

PCD179.000
1950s   18" x 27" . . . . . . . . . . . . . $200
3-D

PCD180.001
1954   31" x 45" . . . . . . . . . . . . . . . . $300
3-D display

PCD183.000
1952  13 $\frac{1}{4}$" x 24 $\frac{1}{4}$" . . . . $150
Display hanger

PCD182.001
1948  5' . . . . . . . . . . . . . . . $475
Easel back, folds in center

PCD181.000
1952  13 $\frac{1}{4}$" x 24 $\frac{1}{4}$" . . . $150
"Carton case card"

PCD184.001 26" x 56 $\frac{1}{2}$" . . . . . . . $300
PCD184.002 8" x 17 $\frac{1}{2}$" . . . . . . . . $350
1952 Santa/Tree display, two sizes

PCD185.000
1960s  13 $\frac{1}{2}$" x 16" . . . . . . . . . . . $60
Hanging sign, two-sided

PCD186.001 27 $\frac{1}{2}$" x 52" . . . . . . . . . . . $550
PCD186.002 10 $\frac{3}{4}$" x 17 $\frac{3}{4}$" . . . . . . . . $600
1940s Santa display, two sizes

A Merry Christmas calls for Coke

Coca-Cola

Stock up for the Holidays

PCS366.000
1960  16" x 27" . . . . . . . . . . . . $65

When Friends drop in

ENJOY
Coca-Cola

Stock up for the Holidays

PCS367.000
1960s  16" x 27" . . . . . . . . . . . $65

Extra-Bright Refreshment

You trust in Quality

Stock up for the Holidays

KING SIZE
6 BOTTLE CARTON

STANDARD
6 BOTTLE CARTON

Coca-Cola

2 convenient sizes

PCS368.000
1955  16" x 27" . . . . . . . . . . . . $75

*Note: Many of theses cutout Santa display pieces were made in a number of different sizes. Generally, the smaller sizes are more desirable to collectors.*

SANTA GLASSES ARE HERE!

Buy a large size Coke $. & get a glass.

Collect a Set.

Today's Glass.

PCD189.000
1970s . . . . . . . . . . . . . . . . . . . $30
"Santa Glasses" cardboard display

Greetings from Coca-Cola

PCD187.000
1946  6" x 12" . . . . . . . . $300

Coca-Cola

Greetings

PCD188.000
1945  48" . . . . . . . . . . . . . . . . . . . $550
Santa Display, easel back, folds in center

Host for the Holidays

Take enough home

Coca-Cola

PPS077.000
1952 . . . . . . . . . . . . . . . $40
Paper sign

# SANTAS
Cardboard display pieces

PCD190.000
1950   9" x 14 $^1\!/_2$" . . . . . . . . . . . $300

PCD177.002
1953   9" x 18 $^1\!/_2$" . . . . . . . . . . . . . . $300
3-D

PCD180.002
1954  10 $^1\!/_2$" x 19" . . . . . . . . . . . $300

PCD175.002
1953  9" x 18" . . . . . . . . . . . . . . $325

PCD191.000
1956  14" x 28" . . . . . . . . . $225

PCD182.001
1948  7 $^1\!/_2$" x 13 $^1\!/_2$" . . . . . . . $425

# SANTAS

PPS078.000
c.1952  11" x 22" . . . . . . . . . . . . . . . . . $50
Paper banner

PCD192.000
1955  19"  . . . . . . . . . . . $85
Easel back display

PCD194.000
1957  13" x 33"  . . . . . . . . . . . $400
3-D Rocket ship display

PCD193.000
1958 . . . . . . . . . . . . . . . . . . . . . . $25
Hanger

PCD195.000
1960  16" x 24"  . . . . . . . . $75

PCD196.001                    PCD196.002
1970s  36"  . . . . . . . . . . . . . . . . . . . $20 Each
English and French

PCD197.000
1960s . . . . . . . . . $15
Hanger

PCD198.000
1958 . . . . . . . . . . . . . . . . . . . . . $40
Cardboard display

PCD203.000
1950s  36" . . . . . . $45

PCD200.000
1940s . . . . . . . . . . . . . . . . . $650
Window display

PCD202.000
1958 . . . . . . . . $30
Cutout hanger

PCD209.001     PCD209.002
1950s . . . . . . . . . . . . . . . . $12 Each
Carton inserts

PCS371.000
1960s  16" x 24"  . . $35

Santa's Helpers

PCS369.000
1970s  16" x 24"  . . $15

PCD207.000
1953  12" x 20"  . . . . . $85
Cutout

PCD199.000
1946  6" x 12"  $200
Stand up

PCD201.000
1959  . . . . . $25
Cutout hanger

PCS372.000
1953  14" x 18"  . . . $85

PCD208.000
1959  . . . . . $25
Cutout hanger

PCS381.000
1964  16" x 27"  . . $35

PCD204.000          PCD205.000
1960s  36" . . . . . . . . . . . . . . . . $40 Each
Cutouts

PCD206.000

PCS370.000
1958  16" x 27"  . . . . $85

PRC006.000
1880s   8" x 13"  . . . . . . . . . . . . . . . $2,000
"French Wine Coca", hanging sign, cardboard

PCS009.000
1896   6 1/2" x 10 1/2"  . . . . . . . . . . $15,000
Hanging sign, cardboard,
Photo Courtesy: Scott Rosenman

PCS010.000
1897   6 1/2" x 10 1/2"  . . . . . . . . . . $15,000
"Victorian Girl", hanging sign, cardboard

PCS012.000
1905  8 ¹/₂" x 11" . . . . . . . . . . . $8,500
"Lillian Nordica", hanging sign, celluloid with
metal frame, Rare. Photo Courtesy: Joe Happle

PCS011.000
1905  26" x 46" . . . . . . . . . . . . . $12,000
"Lillian Nordica", Rare.
Photo Courtesy: The Brinker Collection

PCS013.000
1905  19" x 25"  . . . . . . . . . . . . . $12,000
"Lillian Nordica", celluloid covered cardboard cameo
sign, Rare. Photo Courtesy: Author's Collection

PCS390.000
1909  28 $^1/_2$" x 45"  . . . . . . . . . . . .$13,000
Cardboard Sign, Rare.
Photo Courtesy: Author's Collection

PCD218.000
c.1890s  5 $^1/_2$" x 8 $^1/_2$"  . . . . . . . . . .$5,000
Display Piece, cardboard cutout, easel back, Rare
Wolf & Co., Phila., PA
Photo Courtesy: Author's Collection

PCD219.000
c.1912  . . . . . . . . . . . . . . . . . . . . .$3,000
Display, cardboard cutout (only part), Rare.
Photo Courtesy: Joe Happle

PFE010.000

c.1907 . . . . . . . . . . . . . . . . . . . . . .$6,000

"Roses" festoon,
Printed by Wolf & Co., Philadelphia, PA

PCD010.000

c.1909  5' x 6' . . . . . . . . . . . . . . . . . . . . .$12,000

Foldout window display,
Very Rare when found complete

PCD009.000
c.1912  30" x 46"  . . . . . . . . . . . . . . .$8,500
"Soda Fountain",
Window display, cardboard cutout

# CARDBOARD CUTOUTS

PCD014.000

1910  28 $^1/_2$" x 39 $^1/_2$" . . . . . . . . . . . $6,000

"Man in the Grass" (with glass),
printed by American Lithography,
(This cutout also exists in a bottle version)

PCD015.000

1913  30" x 35" . . . . . . . . . . . . . . . . $6,800

"Couple at the Beach" (with glasses)
(This cutout also exists in a bottle version)

PPA112.001

1913 . . . . . . . . . . . . . . . . . . . . . .$50

Magazine ad showing "Couple At Beach",
bottle version

# CARDBOARD CUTOUTS

PCD011.000

1902 8" . . . . . . . . . . . . . . . . . $6,500

Hanging Sign. Photo Courtesy: Author's Collection

PCD012.000

1901 8" . . . . . . . . . . . . . . $6,500

Hanging Sign.
Photo Courtesy: Chris Daniel, Pinehurst, NC

PCD020.000

1926 18" x 32" . . . . . . . . . . . . . . . . . $2,500

"Umbrella Girl", with bottle

PCD013.000

1908 14 3/4" . . . . . . . . . . . . . . . . . $5,000

"Cherub"

# CARDBOARD CUTOUTS

PFE011.000
1920s ........................ $5,000
"Lantern" festoon, Rare

PCD021.000
1922  19" x 19 $1/2$" .............. $5,000

PCD022.000
1924  36" x 40" ................. $5,000
Window display

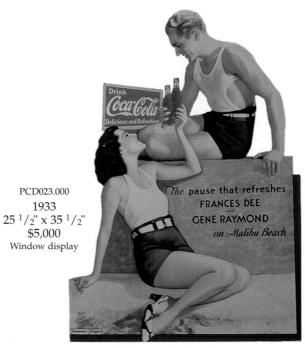

PCD023.000
1933
25 $1/2$" x 35 $1/2$"
$5,000
Window display

*Note: Some of the pieces shown on this color page can also be found in the black and white section.*

# CARDBOARD CUTOUTS

PCD019.S01

1932 . . . . . . . . . . . . . . . . . . $1,300

Dorothy Mackaill, easel back,
Niagara Litho Co.

PCD018.000

c. 1918

18" x 27" . . . . $6,000

Printed by Ketterlinus
Philadelphia, PA

PCD019.S02

1932 . . . . . . . . . . . . . . . . . $1,300

Loretta Young, easel back
Niagara Litho Co.

PCD017.000

c.1912  29" x 38"  . . . . . . . . . . . . . . $7,500

"All the World"
Photo Courtesy: Gordon Jakway

PCD016.000

c.1911  29" x 36"  . . . . . . . . . . . . . . $7,500

"Sundial"

PCD024.S00

1931 . . . . . . . . . . . . . . . . . . . . . . . . . . . . . . . . . . . . . . . . . . . . . . . . . . . . . . . . $8,000

"Uncle Remus and the Happy Animals," printed by Snyder & Black, NY. Complete window display consists of: Center piece—3-D 26" x 38 $^1/_2$"; Right side—Tiger, Camel, Elephant (all attached) 20" x 22"; Left side—Zebra, Lion, Giraffe (all attached) 21 $^1/_2$" x 22"; Tar Baby and Brer Rabbit 12" x 10"; Brer Rabbit and Brer Fox 9" x 15"; Bull Frog 5" x 8 $^1/_2$"; Brer Coon 6" x 9 $^1/_2$"; Brer Bear, Brer Terrapin (two pieces attached by string) 8" x 14 $^1/_2$", 10 $^1/_2$" x 13 $^1/_2$". Note: This display also has a place in back of the center piece for a light bulb. When lit, it gives the fireplace a lighted effect.

PCD025.S00

1930-31 . . . . . . . . . . . . . . . . . . . . . . . . . . . . . . . . . . . . . . . . . . . . . . . . . . . . $5,000

"Toonerville Town", Complete window display consists of eleven pieces, including track and Toonerville Trolley (all cardboard cutouts).

# CARDBOARD CUTOUTS

Note: Condition on these cardboard cutouts and festoons is very important. Values shown are based on complete examples in 8.5 or better condition.

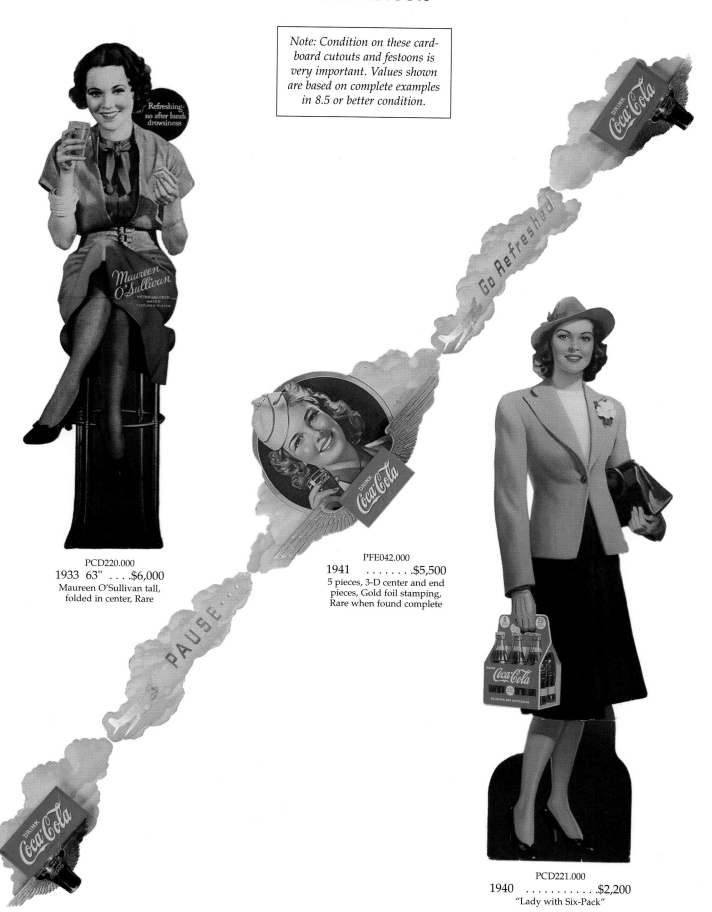

PCD220.000
1933  63"  . . . .$6,000
Maureen O'Sullivan tall,
folded in center, Rare

PFE042.000
1941  . . . . . . .$5,500
5 pieces, 3-D center and end
pieces, Gold foil stamping,
Rare when found complete

PCD221.000
1940  . . . . . . . . . . .$2,200
"Lady with Six-Pack"

# BOTTLES AND BOTTLE DISPLAYS

PBH010.000
Hutchinson Bottle . . .$2,800
Property of Coca-Cola (Script)

PBD016.000
1929 7" x 9 ³/₄" . . . . . . . . . . . . . .$2,500
"Winter Girl" Bottle Topper. Rare.

PBA047.000
Lexington, KY . .$450
Amber Bottle with Original
(Red Logo) Paper Label,
Very Rare

PBD017.000
1930s . . . . .$375
Masonite Bottle
Stacker. Another large
one was used under
this one

PBD018.000
1950s . . . . . .$35
Cardboard Fold-up
Bottle Display

PBG021.000
Enid, OK . . . . .$125

PBT028.000
1920s . . . . . . . . . .$3,000
Export Bottle, paper label, Rare.

Coca-Cola
for Export
in bottles!

This delicious and refreshing
beverage—pure and sparkling,
ready to drink—is now prepared especially for export. In
standard split bottles, hand-
somely labeled and decorated,
packed in substantial cases, five
dozen bottles to the case. Shipping weight, 85 lbs.

PPA377.000
1920s . . . . . . . . . . . . . . . . . .$45
Magazine ad, featuring the export bottle

PCD211.S01
"Refresh Your Guests" . . . .$500

Note: The late 1930s cardboard cutout carton display shown above is one of a set of four. Size is 8" x 11" and it slides onto actual six-pack as shown.

PCD210.000
1940 21" x 40" . . . . . . . . . . . . . . . .$1,000
Carton display, 3-D cutout, actual six-pack slides under hand

PCD211.S02
"Easy to Serve" . . . . . . . . . . .$500

PCD211.S03
"Good with Food" . . .$500

PCD212.000
1936 . . . . . . . . . . .$750
Six-pack display

PCD211.S04
"6 for 25¢" . . . . . . . . . .$500

PCD213.000

1937  8 ¹/₂" x 14"  . . . . . . . . . . .$800

Canada

PCD214.000

1939  12" x 16"  . . . . . . . . . . . . .$325

(French) Canada

PCD215.000

1937  29" across  . . . . . . . . . . . . . . . .$2,200

Rare

PCD216.000

1941  12 ¹/₂" x 17"  . . . . . . . . . . . . . . . . .$700

(French) Canada

PCD107.000

1950  13" x 22"  . . . . . . . . . . . . . . . . .$500

PCD399.S00

1946 . . . . . . . . . . . . . . . . . . . . . . .$1,500

"Sprite Boy" large 3-Piece Display

Note: Set-up options and
different end pieces were
available for the Sprite Boy
display shown above.
Another has three six-packs
on each side.

PCD056.000

1944  15" x 19"  . . . . . . . . . . . . . . . .$2,500

Cardboard Cutout Display (Niagara Litho) 3-D
hanging or stand-up (another Sprite Boy version
exists), Rare

PCD400.S00

c.1948 . . . . . . . . . . . . . . . . . . . . . . .$1,200

"Party Lady" large 3-piece display

# CARDBOARD CUTOUTS

Note: The condition of these cardboard cutouts is very important. When attempting to evaluate them, take into consideration bent corners, wear, and fading. The values shown are based in examples in 8.5 condition or better. 9.5 to Mint will be more, and in Poor condition values will be much less.

PCD222.001
1949  10 $^3/_4$" x 18 $^1/_2$"  . . .$500
Canada

PCD222.002
1949  10 $^3/_4$" x 18 $^1/_2$"  . . .$350
(French) Canada

Photos courtesy Scott Rosenman

PCD054.000
1956  18" x 19" . . . . . . . . . . . . . .$375

PCD057.S02
1951  14 $^1/_2$" x 17" . . . . . . . . . . . . .$375.00
Snyder & Black

PCS359.000
1950s  10" x 12" . . . . . . . . . . . . . .$850
Phil Rizzuto

PCD 223.000
1934  6" x 10" . . . . . . . . . . . . . . . . .$200
Billboard, cardboard, cutout easel back

PCD011.000
1902   8" . . . . . . . . . . . . . . . . . . . . . . . . . . . . . . . . . . . . . . . . . . $6,500
Hanging sign, photo shows both sides, Printed by Wolf & Co., Rare

PCS039.000
1914   30" x 38" . . . . . . . . . . . . . . $3,000
"Betty", with wood frame. This sign is rarely found
in the original wood frame.

PCS040.000
1923   14" x 24" . . . . . . . . . . . . . . . $2,200

# CARDBOARD SIGNS

PCS041.001

1928  21 1/2" x 32" . . . . . . . . . . . . . . $2,000

With bottle

PCS041.002

1928  21 1/2" x 32" . . . . . . . . . . . . . $2,000

With glass

PCS042.000

1940  21" x 42" . . . . . . . . . . . . . . . . $1,100

Snyder & Black

PCS043.000

1935  13" x 21" . . . . . . . . . . . . . . . . $650

Two-sided

PCS044.000

1945  10" x 26" . . . . . . . . . . . . . . . . $425

PCS045.000

1948  31" x 45" . . . . . . $700

PCS047.001            PCS047.002
1924   20" x 35 $^{1}/_{2}$" each . . . . . . . . . . . . . . . $1,500 Each
Two Poster panoramic

PCS046.000
1907   16" x 22" As shown . . $2,200
Complete . . . . . . . . . . . . . . . $8,000
Rare

PCS049.000
1931   21" x 38" . . . $1,300
Printed by Niagara Litho

PCS050.000
1931   10" x 20" . . $1,500
Printed by Niagara Litho

PCS051.000
1937   14" x 30"   . . . . $700

PCS048.000
1940s   16" x 27"   . . . . $700
With wood frame

PCS052.000
1950s   16" x 27"   . . . . . . . . $385
With wood frame

PCS053.000
1936   14" x 30"   . . . . . . . $1,500

PCS054.000
1943   16" x 27"   . . . . . . . . . . . . . $650
With wood frame

# CARDBOARD SIGNS

PCS061.000
c.1920s  21" x 60" . . . . . . . . . . . . . $2,000
Cardboard with metal frame showing two 1916 bottles.

PCS062.000
1937  22" x 43" . . . $800
Art by L. Wilbur

PCS058.000
1938  21" x 44" . . . $375

PCS055.000
c.1920s  8" x 11" . . . . . . . . . . . . . . . $1,200
3-D hanging sign

PCS059.000
1938  14 1/2" x 32"  . . $550

PCS063.000
1957  12" x 14" . . . . . . . . . . . . . . $225

PCS060.000
Late 1930s  14" x 22" . . . . . $600

PCS078.S02

THIS ENVELOPE CONTAINS
BOTTLE RATION MATERIAL—
1-FRAME DISPLAY
1-WINDOW BANNER

The FRAME DISPLAY should be placed in a preferred inside store position. It is equipped to hang with cord or stand with easel.

The Window Banner should be applied to the inside of the window. Remove Kleen-Stik tape and press banner against the glass. It should be placed about eye-level height from sidewalk.

PCS078.S03

PCS078.S01
1942  22" x 15"
Cardboard display sign only  . . . . . . . . . . . . . . . . . . . . . . $425
Paper window banner only  . . . . . . . . . . . . . . . . . . . . . . $85
(PCS078.S00) Complete set in envelope . . . . . . . . . . . . . . . . . $600
Self-framed display, Printed by Snyder & Black

PCS056.000
1934
14" x 30" . . . . .$400

PCS057.000
1935
14" x 30" . . . $1,200
Florine McKinney

# CARDBOARD SIGNS

PCS398.000
1936  29" x 50" . . . . . . . . . . $1,500

PCS399.000
1940  29" x 50" . . . . . . . . . . . . . $950

PCS400.000
1940s  29" x 50" . . . . . . . . . . . $650

PCS401.000
1943  29" x 50" . . . . . . . . $700

PCS402.000
1943  27" x 56" . . . . . . . . . . . . . . . . . $750

Note: Values shown reflect examples in 8.5 or better condition—every tear, scratch, and imperfection will affect that value.

PCS403.000
1944  27" x 56" . . . . . . . . . . . . . . . . $600

PCS404.000
1943  27" x 56" . . . . . . . . . . . . . . . . $600

# CARDBOARD SIGNS

PCS405.000
1940  16" x 27"  . . . . . . . . . . . . . . . $550

PCS406.000
1940  16" x 27"  . . . . . . . . . . . . . $600

PCS407.000
1943  16" x 27"  . . . . . . . . . . . . . . . $650

PCS409.000
1944  20" x 36"  . . . . . . . . . . . . . . . . . $850

PCS410.000
1950s  20" x 36"  . . . . . . . . . . . . . . . $400
Canada

PCS408.000
1943  16" x 27"  . . . . . . . . . . . . . . . $600

PCS064.000
1944  16" x 27" . . . . . . . . . . . . . $900
With gold wood frame

PCS065.000
1942  16" x 27" . . . . . . . . . . . . . . . . . $850
With  gold wood frame

PCS066.000
1955  20" x 36" . . . . . . . . . . . . . . . . $425

PCS067.000
1920s . . . . . . . . . . . . . . . . . . . . . . . . $575
Score board, cardboard

PCS068.000
1948  20" x 36" . . . . . . . . . . . . . . . . $325
Snyder & Black

PCS069.000
1964  20" x 36" . . . . . . . . . . . . . . . . $150

# CARDBOARD SIGNS

PCS070.000
1952  20" x 36"  . . . . . . . . . . . . . . . . . $275

PCS071.000
1948  20" x 36"  . . . . . . . . . . . . . . . . . $375

PCS072.000
1948  20" x 36"  . . . . . . . . . . . . . . . . . $375

PCS074.000
1944  16" x 27"  . . . . . . . . . . . . . . . . . $950
With gold wood frame. Note: There is a variation of
this same artwork, without cooler.

PCS073.000
1947  20" x 36"  . . . . . . . . . . . . . . . . . $375
Forbes-Boston

PCS075.000
1942  27" x 56"  . . . . . . . . . . . . . . . . . $750

PCS076.000
1942  29" x 50"  . . . . . . . . $750
"Snowman"

# CARDBOARD SIGNS

PCS077.000
1943  20" x 36" . . . . . . . . . . . . . . . . . $650

PCS079.000
1943  20" x 36" . . . . . . . . . . . . . . . . . $600

PCS080.000
1946  27" x 56" . . . . . . . . . . . . . . . . . $550

PCS082.000
1948  29" x 50" . . . . . . . . . . . . $550

PCS081.000
1943  20" x 36" . . . . . . . . . . . . . . . . . $1,200
Rare

PCS083.000
1942  27" x 56" . . . . . . . . . . . . . . . . . $1,000
With gold wood frame

PCS084.000
1948  29" x 50" . . . . . . . . $550

— 137 —

PCS423.000
1949  11" x 13"  . . . . . . . . . . . . . . . . . $550

PCS094.000
1937  14" x 31 $\frac{1}{2}$"  . . . . . . . . . $1,600

PCS095.000
1939  14" x 30"  . . . . . . . . . . $1,000

PCS424.000
1956  15" x 16"  . . . . . . . . . . . . . . . . .$300
Two sided

PCS096.000
c.1939  11" x 21"  . . . . . . . . . . . . . . . . $950

Reverse side of sign shown above.

PCS097.000
1930s  20" x 39 $\frac{1}{2}$"  . . . . . . . . . . . . $1,600

# CARDBOARD SIGNS

PCS106.000
c.1930s  29" x 50" . . $1,800

PCS107.000
1936  29" x 50" . . . . $2,500

PCS108.000
1942  29" x 50" . . . . $1,000

PCS109.000
c.1940s  29" x 50"  . . . $650

PCS110.000
1941  29" x 50"  . . . . . $1,000

PCS111.000
1943  29" x 50"  . . . . . . $500

PCS112.000
c.1940s  29" x 50" . . . . $550

PCS113.000
c.1940s  29" x 50" . . . . $550

PCS114.000
c.1940s  27" x 56"  . . . . . . . . . . . . . . $550

PCS115.000
c.1940s  20" x 36"  . . . . . . . . $600

PCS116.000
1953  20" x 36"  . . . . . . . $275

PCS117.000
1944  20" x 36"  . . . . . . . $500

PCS118.000
1949  20" x 36"  . . . . . . . $300

# CARDBOARD SIGNS
Many of the signs shown were offered in two different sizes.

PCS 138.000

1944  27" x 56"  . . . . . . . . . . . . . . . . . $900

With gold wood frame

PCS 139.000

1946  27" x 56"  . . . . . . . . . . . . . . . . . $1,000

With gold wood frame

PCS140.000

1949  27" x 56"  . . . . . . . . . . . . . . . . . $700

Notes: Prices shown for cardboard signs are based on original size. Pieces that have been trimmed from their original size are worth less.

PCS141.000

1944  20" x 36"  . . . . . . . . . . . . . . . . . $500

PCS142.000

1945  20" x 36"  . . . . . . . . . . . . . . . . . $500

PCS143.000

1945  27" x 56"  . . . . . . . . . . . . . . . . . $450

PCS144.000

1946  27" x 56"  . . . . . . . . . . . . . . . . . $450

# CARDBOARD SIGNS
Many of these signs were offered in two different sizes.

PCS145.000
1945  27" x 56" . . . . . . . . . . . . . . . . . .$450

PCS146.000
1945  20" x 36"  . . . . . . . . . . . . . . . . . $650
With gold wood frame

PCS122.000
1942  16" x 27"  . . . . . . . . . . . . . . . . . $550

*Note: Prices shown on many of these litho inserts (cardboard signs), are based on the subject matter of the artwork and visual appeal, as well as rarity and condition. Women in bathing suits, for example, tend to be more popular and worth more. Signs in the same condition from the same year can be priced quite differently.*

PCS147.000
1940s  16" x 27" . . . . . . . . . . . . . . . $700
With gold wood frame

PCS148.000
1945  20" x 36"  . . . . . . . . . . . . . . . . . $475

PCS149.000
1944  20" x 36"  . . . . . . . . . . . . . . . . . $475

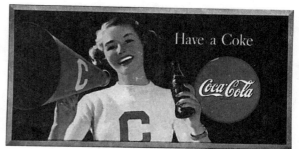

PCS150.000
1945  20" x 36"  . . . . . . . . . . . . . . . . . $450

# WOOD FRAMES

These litho insert frames, called "Gold Wood Frames" by collectors, are wood with metal rods on either side, a metal bottle emblem at bottom, and completely painted gold. This particular style was used mainly during the 1940s. There was another style of frame used during the 1950s into the early 1960s. These frames held litho inserts (cardboard signs), which slid into slots on the back of the frame and were held in place with clips. These litho inserts were changed periodically by the salesman, and the frames were used for many years. The prices shown are for examples in near perfect condition, and may only be worth this to a collector in need of one to display a cardboard insert. The value of cardboard signs go up when displayed with one of these gold wood frames; values drop considerably when rods or bottle emblems are missing.

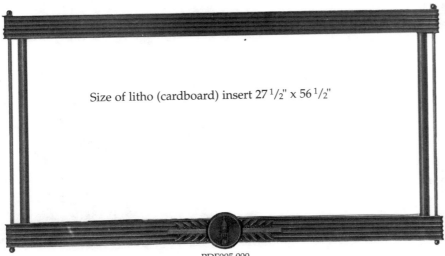

Size of litho (cardboard) insert 27 $1/2$" x 56 $1/2$"

PDF005.000
62 $3/8$" x 33 $1/4$" . . . . . . . . . . . . . . . . $250
Large horizontal size of frame

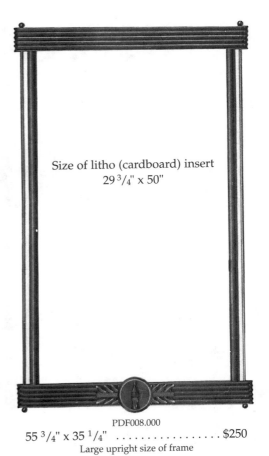

Size of litho (cardboard) insert
29 $3/4$" x 50"

PDF008.000
55 $3/4$" x 35 $1/4$" . . . . . . . . . . . . . . . . $250
Large upright size of frame

Note: I've seen these Wood Frames used for a number of different uses. Bulletin Boards, Mirrors, Etc. In some cases the company suggested their use for things other than for displaying Litho (cardboard) Inserts, but basically this was their main use.

Size of litho
(cardboard)
insert 16" x 27"

PDF006.000
31 $1/2$" x 20 $7/8$" . . . . $250
Small upright size of frame

PDF009.P00
Bag Holder attachment for back of wood Frame.

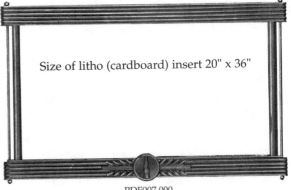

Size of litho (cardboard) insert 20" x 36"

PDF007.000
25" x 40 $7/8$" . . . . . . . . . . . . . . . . . . . . $250
Small horizontal size of frame

# CARDBOARD SIGNS

PCS188.000

1938  29" x 50"  . . . . . $1,800

Sundblum Art

PCS191.000

1944  16" x 27"  . . $400

PCS189.000

1942  20" x 36"  . . . . . . . . . . . . . . . $450

PCS193.000

1942  16" x 27"  . . $450

PCS190.000

1938  34" x 50"  . . . . . . . . . . . . . . . $2,800

"Girl with Roses", inside store display

PCS194.000

1950  16" x 27"  . . . . $300

PCS192.000

1929  19" x 31"  . . . . . . . . . $1,800

> Note: Remember, condition of these cardboard signs is
> very important. Fading, creases, and tears are common
> and certainly effect value.

PCS196.000

1937  29" x 50"  . . . . $600

PCS195.000

1941  29" x 50"  . . . . $550

PCS197.000

1940  29" x 50"  . . . . . $800

PCS198.000

1940s  29" x 50"  . . . $575

# CARDBOARD SIGNS

PCS199.001
1946  20" x 36" . . . . . . . . . . . . . . . . . . . . . . $450

PCS199.002
1946  27" x 56" . . . . . . . . . . . . . . . . . $750
With gold wood frame

PCS200.000
1944  29" x 50" . . . . . . . . $850
With gold wood frame

PCS129.001
1956  20" x 36" . . . . . . . . . . . . . . . . . $400

> *Note: Prices shown for paper and cardboard signs are based on original size. Pieces that have been trimmed from their original size are worth less.*

PCS201.000
1936  29" x 50" . . . . . . $2,000

PCS202.000
1930  29" x 50" . . . . $1,800

PCS203.000
1930s  29" x 50" . . $2,100

PCS204.000
1939  29" x 50" . . . . $1,100

# CARDBOARD SIGNS

Many of the signs shown were offered in two different sizes.

Note: Prices shown for paper and cardboard signs are based on original size. Pieces that have been trimmed from their original size are worth less.

PCS181.000
1945  16" x 27"  . . . . . . .  $425

PCS182.000
1946  16" x 27"  . . . . . .  $400

PCS183.000
1944  16" x 27"  . . . . . . . .  $475

PCS184.000
1953  27" x 56"  . . . . . . . . . . . . . . . . .  $800
Signed Elvgren

PCS185.000
1945  29" x 50"  . . . . . .  $400

Note: Original gold wood frames certainly enhance the value of any cardboard sign.

PCS186.000
1944  27" x 56"  . . . . . . . . . . . . . . . .  $875
With gold wood frame

PCS187.000
1945  27" x 56"  . . . . . . . . . . . . . . . .  $685
With gold wood frame

PCS159.000
1945  16" x 27"  . . . . . . . . .$485

PCS121.000
1941  16" x 27"  . . . . . . . . $550

PCS120.000
1942  16" x 27"  . . . . . . . . . . .$550

PCS160.000
1950s  16" x 27"  . . . $225

PCS161.000
c.1946  16" x 27"  . . . . . . . . . . $300

PCS162.000
1939 . . . . . . . . . . . . . . . . . . . . . . $650
Lillian Nordica

PCS163.000
1950s  16" x 27"  . . . . . . . . . . $250

PCS164.000
1958  20" x 36"  . . . . . . . . . . . . . . . .$175

# CARDBOARD SIGNS

PCS151.000
1950  16" x 27" . . . . . . . . . . $450

PCS152.000
1949  16" x 27" . . . . . . . . $500

PCS153.000
1952  16" x 27" . . . . . . . . . $375

PCS154.000
1952  16" x 27" . . . . . . . . . $325

PCS155.000
1941  16" x 27" . . . . . . . . . . . . . . $1,000
With gold wood frame

PCS156.000
1952  16" x 27" . . . . . . . . $325

PCS157.000
1942  27" x 56" . . . . . . . . . . . . . . . . $700

PCS158.000
1952  20" x 36" . . . . . . . . . . . . . . . $550

# CARDBOARD SIGNS
Many of the signs shown were offered in two different sizes.

PCS165.000
1954  16" x 27" . . . . . . . . $675
Signed "Elvgren". Printed by Edwards
& Deutsch Litho Co., Chicago.

PCS166.000
1947  16" x 27" . . . . . $425

PCS167.000
1946  16" x 27" . . . . . . $450

PCS168.000
1958  16" x 27" . . . . . . . $200

Note: Remember, condition is the
most important factor when
determining value.

PCS136.000
1939  16" x 27" . . . . . . . . . . . . . . . . . $1,100
1939 "Through The Years" campaign, with gold
wood frame

PCS170.000
1948  16" x 27" . . . . . . . . $325

Note: Additional cardboard
signs can be found on color
plate pages 182-189.

PCS171.000
1944  20" x 36" . . . . . . . . . . . . . . . $450

PCS172.000
1945  20" x 36" . . . . . . . . . . . . . . . . $475

PCS173.000
1940s  16" x 27"  . . . . . $375

PCS174.000
1944   27" x 56"  . . . . . . . . . . . . . . . . . $450

PCS175.000
1958  16" x 27"  . . . . . . . . . $225

PCS176.000
1955  16" x 27"  . . . . . . . . $285

PCS177.000
1940s  16" x 27"  . . . . . . . . . . . . . . . . . $650
With gold wood frame

PCS178.000
1944  16" x 27"  . . . $325

PCS074.001
1944  29" x 50"  . . . . . . $1,000
With gold wood frame

PCS179.000
1944  27" x 56"  . . . . . . . . . . . . . . . . . $400

PCS180.000
1950s  29" x 50"  . . . . . . . . . $500
With gold wood frame

# CARDBOARD SIGNS

Many of the signs shown were offered in two different sizes.

PCS229.001
1949  27" x 56"  . . . . . . . . . . . . . . . . . $950

PCS229.002
1949  16" x 27"  . . $600

PCS230.000
1952  16" x 27"  . . . . $350
With gold wood frames

---

*Note: Some images are rarer than others. Values shown reflect that rarity.*

---

PCS130.000
1954  20" x 36"  . . . . . . . . . . . . . . . . . $750
"Baseball Game", with gold wood frame

PCS231.001
1951  29" x 50"  . . . . . . . . $385

PCS231.002
1951  20" x 36"  . . . . . . . . . . . . . . . . $285

PCS132.000
1957  20" x 36"  . . . . . . . . . . . . . . . . $600
With aluminum frame

PCS232.000
1951  20" x 36"  . . . . . . . . . . . . . . . . . $225

PCS241.000

1946  20" x 36"  ................. $700

With gold wood frame

PCS242.000

1935  13" x 21"  ................. $650

Two-sided

PCS243.000

1955  16" x 27"  ................. $225

PCS244.000

1936  12 $^1/_2$" x 33"  ....... $625

Litho in Canada

PCS135.000

1956  16" x 27"  ........ $350

PCS169.000

1920s  11" x 17"  ......... $200

PCS245.000

1926  15" x 24"  ................. $750

This sign was also made in tin

PCS246.000

1920s  15" x 25"  ................. $525

PCS233.000
1952  29" x 50" . . . . . . . . . . . $950
With gold wood frame

PCS234.000
1949  29" x 50" . . . . . . . . . $600

PCS235.000
1952  29" x 50" . . . . . . . . . . $450

PCS236.000
1950  20" x 36" . . . . . . . . . . . . . . . . . $875
Niagara Litho, with gold wood frame

PCS237.000
1952  29" x 50" . . . . . . . . $450

PCS238.000
1940s 20" x 36" . . . . . . . . . . . . . . . . $450

PCS239.000
1950 16" x 27" . . . . . $425

PCS240.000
1950 16" x 27" . . . . $350

# CARDBOARD SIGNS

PCS411.000
1950s  20" x 36"  . . . . . . . . . . . . . . . . $600
In original aluminum frame

PCS412.000
1957  20" x 36"  . . . . . . . . . . . . . . . . $200

PCS413.000
1950  16" x 27"  . . . . . . $150
Canada

PCS414.000
1950s  29" x 50"  . . . . . . . . . . . . . . . . $650
"Baseball Game"

PCS415.000
1955  16" x 27"  . . . . . . . . $425
"Coke Time", in original gold
wood frame

*Note: Values shown are based on examples in
very nice condition of 8.5 or better. Every
imperfection will affect the value.*

PCS416.000
1951  20" x 36"  . . . . . . . . . . . . . . . . $350
In original aluminum frame

PCS205.000
1952  27" x 56"  . . . . . . . . . . . . . . . . . $285

PCS206.000
1948  16" x 27"  . . $400

PCS207.000
1947  20" x 36"  . . . . . . . . . . . . . . . . . $425

PCS208.000
1940s  20" x 36"  . . . . . . . . . . . . . . . $400

PCS209.000
1947  20" x 36"  . . . . . . . . . . . . . . . . . $450

PCS210.000
1956  20" x 36"  . . . . . . . . . . . . . . . . . $385

PCS211.000
1957  20" x 36"  . . . . . . . . . . . . . . . . . $175

# CARDBOARD SIGNS

PCS212.000
1952  20" x 36"  . . . . . . . . . . . . . . . . . $500

PCS214.000
1952  20" x 36"  . . . . . . . . . . . . . . . . . $400

PCS215.000
1949  20" x 36"  . . . . . . . . . . . . . . . . . $450
Niagara Litho

PCS217.000
1943  27" x 56"  . . . . . . . . . . . . . . . . . $550

PCS213.000
1952  16" x 27"  . . . . . . . . . $500

PCS216.000
1952  20" x 36"  . . . . . . . . . . . . . . . . . $385

PCS218.000
1952  20" x 36"  . . . . . . . . . . . . . . . . . $325
"Tables"

PCS219.000
1952  16" x 27"  . . $285

— 155 —

PCS220.000
1952  27" x 56"  . . . . . . . . . . . . . . . . . $385

PCS221.000
1952  20" x 36"  . . . . . . . . . . . . . . . . . $300

PCS222.000
1952  27" x 56"  . . . . . . . . . . . . . . . $675
Signed Bill Gregg

PCS223.000
1952  16" x 27"  . . . . . . . . . . . . . $400

PCS224.000
1952  20" x 36"  . . . . . . . . . . . . . . . . . $325

PCS225.000
1952  20" x 36"  . . . . . . . . . . . . . . . . . $325

PCS226.000
1955  20" x 36"  . . . . . . . . . . . . . . . . . $325

PCS227.000
1952  16" x 27"  . . $225

PCS228.000
1952  16" x 27"  . . $225

PCS247.000

1941  20" x 36" . . . . . . . . . . . . . . . . . $800

With gold wood frame

PCS248.001

1959  20" x 36" . . . . . . . . . . . . . . . . . $385

PCS249.000

1940s  16" x 27"  . . $425

PCS250.000

1950s  20" x 36" . . . . . . . $400

With wood frame

PCS251.000

1952  20" x 36" . . . . . . . $385

PCS252.000

1940s 20" x 36" . . . . . . . $500

PCS253.000

1942  20" x 36" . . . . . . . . $500

PCS254.000

1952  20" x 36" . . . . . . . $400

PCS255.000

1946  20" x 36" . . . . . . . $450

PCS256.000

1953  20" x 36" . . . . . . . . $450

PCS098.000
1957 16" x 27" ....... $285

Note: The value of these cardboard insert signs is as much dependent on the image depicted as on the sign's condition. Some images are just more desirable than others.

PCS099.000
1948 20" x 36" .................. $900
With gold wood frame

PCS100.000
1954 20" x 36" .................. $350
Edwards & Deutsch Litho, Chicago

PCS101.000
1948 16" x 27" ............. $385

Note: Many of the signs shown were offered in two different sizes.

PCS102.000
1941 16" x 27" ....... $550

PCS103.000
1952 16" x 27" ... $275

PCS104.000
1948 20" x 36". .................. $400
McCandlish Litho

# CARDBOARD SIGNS

PCS257.000
1953  16" x 27" . . . . . . . . . . . $425
With gold wood frame

PCS129.000
1956  29" x 50"  . . . . . . . . . . . . . . . . . $450
"Travel Girl"

PCS126.000
1957  16" x 27"  . . . . . . . . . . . . . . . $450
With gold wood frame

PCS258.000
1946  20" x 36"  . . . . . . . . $900
With gold wood frame

PCS259.000
1945  11" x 28"  . . . . . . . . . . . . . . . . . $375

PCS260.001
1945  12" x 18"  . . . . . . . . $285

PCS261.000
1955  20" x 36"  . . . . . . . . . . . . . . . . . $425
With gold wood frame

PCS262.000
1950s  20" x 36"  . . . . . . . . . . . . . . . . . $450
With gold wood frame

PCS263.000
1941 20" x 36" . . . . . . . . . . . . . . . $950

PCS264.000
1956 20" x 36" . . . . . . . . $350

PCS425.000
1955 16" x 27"... $100

PCS265.000
1930s 12" x 18" . . . . . . . . . . $150

### PICNIC PARTNERS

PCS266.000
1953 22" x 45" . . . . . . . . . . . . . . . . . $325

PCS268.000
1946 16" x 27" . . . $350

PCS267.000
1957 16" x 27" . . . $185

PCS269.000
1946 16" x 27" . . . $350

PCS155.001
1940s 27" x 56" . . . . . . . . . . . . . . . . $800

PCS270.000
1940s 27" x 56" . . . . . . . . . . . . . . . . $585

# CARDBOARD SIGNS

PCS248.002

1954 20" x 36" . . . . . . . . . . . . . . . . . . $785
With gold wood frame. Printed by Niagara Litho
Co. Note: There is another version of this sign
using a variation of the same artwork and
dated 1959.

PCS271.000

1952 20" x 36" . . . . . . . . . . . . . . . . . $1,100
Alice Coachman and Jesse Owens, Olympic Track
and Field Champions, with gold wood frame, Rare.

PCS272.000

1951 20" x 36" . . . . . . . . . . . . . . . . . $785
With gold wood frame. Printed by Edwards &
Deutsch Litho Co., Chicago.

PCS273.000

1954 20" x 36" . . . . . . . . . . . . . . . . . $600
With gold wood frame. Printed by Niagara Litho Co.

*Note: Remember, condition is the most important factor when determining value.*

PCS274.000

1955 20" x 36" . . . . . . . . . . . . . . . . . $625
With gold wood frame. Printed by Edwards &
Deutsch Litho Co., Chicago.

PCS105.P05

1950s 24" x 38" (Size of Frame) . . . . $150
Horizontal gold wood frame. Two types: hinged end
or screw in back bracket.

— 161 —

# CARDBOARD SIGNS

PCS275.000

1935  10" x 15"  . . . . . . . . . . . . . . . . . .$475

Hanging Sign

PCS276.000

1950s  20" x 36"  . . . . . . . . $325

PCS277.000

1950s  18" x 24"  . . . . . . . . . . . . . . . . . $285

Rand McNally Transcontinental Mileage
and Driving Time Chart

PCS278.000

1942  20" x 36"  . . . . . . . . . . . . . . . . . $385

PCS283.000

1950s  20" x 36"  . . . . . . . $185

PCS279.000

1948  16" x 27"

$325

PCS280.000

1959  20" x 36"

$150

PCS281.000

1960s  16" x 27"

$100

PCS282.000

1940s  20" x 36"

$450

PCS284.000

1960s  20" x 36"  . . . . . . . $125

# CARDBOARD SIGNS

PCS286.000

1953  16" x 27" . . . . $350

PCS287.000

1950s  16" x 27"  . . $285

PCS285.000

1930s  9" x 12"  . . . . . . . . . . . . . . . . $600

PCS139.001

1946  11" x 28"  . . . . . . . . . . . . . . . . . $450

PCS289.000

1950s  16" x 16"  . . . . . . . . $125

PCS139.002

1946  20" x 36"  . . . . . . . . . . . . . . . . . $700

"Outstanding Poster Award"

PCS288.000

1940  14 $^{1}/_{2}$" x 31 $^{1}/_{2}$"  . . . . . . $325

PCS291.000

1936  14" x 30"  . . . . . . . . . . . . $450

PCS290.000

1939  27 $^{1}/_{2}$" x 56"  . . . . . . . . . . . . . . . $550

"The Girl in the Calendar - Through the Years"

# CARDBOARD SIGNS

PCS292.000
1957  20" x 36"  . . . . . . . . . . . . . . . . . $275

PCS293.000
1957  20" x 36"  . . . . . . . . . . . . . . . . . $275

Note: Remember, condition is
very important when attempting
to determine value. Values
shown reflect average price for
Average condition.

PCS294.000
1953  16" x 27"  . . . . . . . $300
McCandlish Litho

PCS295.000
1940  16" x 27"  . . . . . . . . . . . . . . . . . $385
Canada

PCS296.000
1959  20" x 36"  . . . . . . . $200

PCS294.001
1953  20" x 36"  . . . . . . . . . . . . . . . . . $300

PCS297.000
1957  20" x 36"  . . . . . . . . . . . . . . . . . $385

# CARDBOARD SIGNS

PCS291.001
1936  14" x 30" . . . . $300
Canada

PCS298.000
1930s  14" x 30" . . . $300
Canada

PCS299.000
1930s  14" x 30"  . . $300
Canada

PCS300.000
1930s  14" x 30" . . . $300

PCS301.001
1. Cheese

PCS301.002
2. Fruits

PCS301.003
3. Cold Cuts

PCS301.004
4. Picnic

PCS301.005
5. Appetizers

PCS301.006
6. Sandwiches

PCS301.007
7. Vegetables

PCS301.008
8. Hot Dog

PCS301.009
9. Ham

PCS301.010
10. Market Basket

1952  22" x 45" . . . . . . . . . . . . . . . . . . . . . . . . . . . . . . . . . . . . . . . . . . . . . . . . $175 to $250 each

"Coke & Food" cardboard display signs

PCS085.000
1959  20" x 36"  . . . . . . . . . . . . . . . . . $365
The McGuire Sisters

PCS086.000
1950s  19" x 27"  . . . . . . . . . . . . . . . . . $150
Tony Bennett

PCS090.001

PCS090.002

1959-60  16 1/2" x 21 1/2"  . . . . . . . . . . . $225 Each
The McGuire Sisters, two different examples

PCS091.000
1959-60  14" x 18 1/2"  . . . $600
Ricky Nelson, Rare

PCS092.000
1950s  11" x 28"  . . . . . . . . . . . . . . . . . $600
The Nelsons, Rare

PCS093.000
1950s  8" x 20"  . . . . . . . . . . . . . . . . . $185

# CARDBOARD SIGNS

PCS302.000

1950s  14" x 22" . . . . . . . $75

PCS303.000

1950s  14" x 22" . . . . . . . . $85

PCS304.000

1956  29 1/2" x 30" . . . . . . . . . . . . . . $250

Simulated "Oil Painting" (back of frame stamped property of the Coca-Cola Co. Picture "A" unit.)

PCS305.001

PCS305.002

1950s  14" x 22" . . . . . . . . . . . . . $100 Each

Note: The Sprite Boy signs shown above are silk screened signs done by local bottlers.

PCS306.000

1960s  16" x 27" . . . . . $30

PCS307.000

1964  16" x 27" . . . . . . . $25

PCS308.000

1957  27" x 56" . . . . . . . . . . . . . . . . . $200

Signed Charles Heizerling

PCS309.000

1959  20" x 38" . . . . . . $185

PCS310.000

1960s  20" x 36"  . . . . . . . . . . . . . . . . $200

PCS311.000

1930s  12" x 18"  . . $125

PCS312.000

1960s  20" x 36"  . . . . . . . . . . . . . . $175

PCS313.000

1960s  16" x 27"  . . $125

PCS316.000

1958  20" x 36"  . . . $100

PCS319.000

1938 12" x 18"  . . . $50

PCS318.000

1952  22" x 45"  . . . . . . . . . . . . . . . . $300

PCS320.000

1950s  20" x 36"  . . . $385

PCS321.000

1940s  20" x 36"  . . . . . $400

PCS314.000

1950s  15" x 18"  . . . . $185

3-D

PCS315.000

1950s  16" x 27"  . . $225

PCS317.000

1958  16" x 27"  . .$100

PCS322.000

1958  20" x 36"  . . . . . . . . . . . . . . . . $150

# CARDBOARD SIGNS

PCS323.000
1950s  16" x 27"  . . . . . . . . . . . . . . . $175

PCS327.000
1960s  20" x 36"  . . . . . . . $125

PCS324.000
1960s  16" x 27"  . . $125

PCS325.000
1960s  16" x 27"  . . $125

PCS326.000
1959  16" x 27"  . . . . . . . . . . . . . . . . . $125

PCS329.000
1960s  16" x 27"  . . . . . $100

PCS330.000
1960s  20" x 36"  . . . . . . . . . . . . . . . $125

PCS328.000
1969  14" x 14"  . . . . . . . . . . . . . $20

PCS331.000
1960s  20" x 36"  . . . . . . . . . . . . . . . $125

PCS332.000
1970s  16" x 27"  . . . . . . $20

PCS333.000
1950s  20" x 36"  . . . . . . . . . . . . . . . . . . . $65

PCS334.000
1960s  19" x 27"  . . . . . . . . . . $100

PCS335.000
1970s 16" x 26" . . . . . . . . $25

PCS336.000
1976 20" x 29" . . . . . . . . . . . $20

PCS337.001
1960s 16" x 27" . . . . . . . . . $100

PCS338.000
1959 16" x 26" . . . . . . . $65

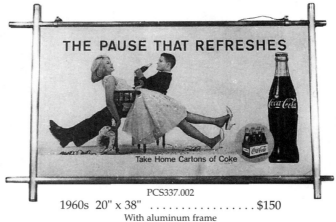

PCS337.002
1960s 20" x 38" . . . . . . . . . . . . . . . . $150
With aluminum frame

PCS339.000
1950s 14" x 24" . . . . . $50

PCS340.000
1959 20" x 38" . . . . . . . . . . . . . . . . $150
With aluminum frame

PCS341.000
1959 16" x 26" . . . . . . . . . $65

PCS342.000
1979 21" x 39" . . . . . . . . . . . . . . . . $35

PCS343.000
1970s . . . . . . . . . . . . . . . . . . $25
Repro tray offer

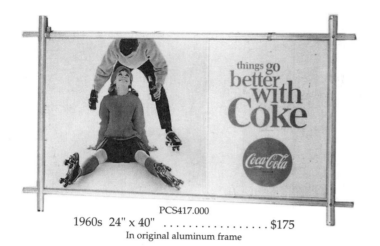

PCS417.000
1960s  24" x 40"  ................ $175
In original aluminum frame

PCS418.000
1960s  24" x 40"  ................ $175
In original aluminum frame

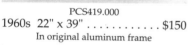

PCS419.000
1960s  22" x 39"  ........... $150
In original aluminum frame

PCS420.000
1950s  20" x 36"  ................ $300
Canada, (French)

PCS421.000
1950s  20" x 36"  ................ $250

PCS422.000
1970s  16" x 27"  .......... $75

PCS344.000
1959  20" x 36" . . . . . . . . . . . . . . . . . $250
With aluminum frame

PCS345.000
1964  16" x 27" . . . . . . $125

PCS346.000
1964  16" x 27" . . . . . . . $125

PCS347.000
1960s  20" x 36" . . . . . . . . . . . . . . . . . $185
With aluminum frame

PCS348.000
1964  16" x 27" . . . . . . . $125

PCS349.000
1960s  16" x 27" . . . . . $125

PCS350.000
1960s  20" x 36" . . . . . . . . . . . . . . . . . $185
With aluminum frame

PCS351.000
1960s  20" x 36" . . . . . . . . . . . . . . . . . $200
With aluminum frame

PCS352.000
1950s  16" x 27" . . . . . . $125

PCS353.000
1960s  16" x 27" . . . . . . $125

# AIRPLANE HANGERS

Beginning in 1941 and continuing until the end of the war, The Coca-Cola Company produced sets of "Airplane Hangers"—cardboard sign showing American War Planes winning the war. The Snyder and Black Advertising Agency hired the well-known artist and authority on aircraft, William Heaslip, who created all four sets. His fabulous paintings were well detailed and these sets were hung on soda fountain walls all over the country. Plain paper presentation sets were also produced by Snyder and Black; these sets were framed and hung in bottling plant lobbies and other locations.

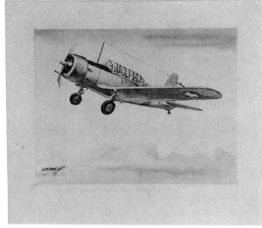

POA002.000
Original piece of rough art . . . . . . . . $225
Pencil sketch/water colors, signed by Heaslip

PCS354.S00

Set No. 1  1941-1942
Set consists of 12

PCS355.S00

Set No. 2  1943
Set consists of 20

PCS356.S00

Set No. 3  1944
Set consists of 20

PCS357.S00

Set No. 4  1945
Set consists of 20
(complete set not shown)

*Note: Complete sets shown on following pages*

PPM132.BS0
1943 . . . . . . . . . . . . . . . . . . . . . . . $275
"Fighting Airplanes" paper presentation set (without logos), compliments of "The Coca-Cola Co", complete set of 13 planes with envelope

PPM133.000
1944  17" x 22" . . . . . . . . . . $50
Catalog Sheet, showing complete set of airplane hangers

# AIRPLANE HANGERS

PCS354.S01
1-Grumman F4F-3

PCS354.S02
2-Ryan Low-Wing Trainer PT-21

PCS354.S03
3-Curtis P-40

PCS354.S04
4-Vultee Vengence

PCS354.S05
5-Bell Airacobra

PCS354.S06
6-North American B-25

PCS354.S07
7-Consolidated PBY

PCS354.S08
8-Boeing Flying Fortress B-17D

PCS354.S09
9-Glenn L. Martin B-26

PCS354.S10
10-Lockhead P-38

PCS354.S11
11-Vought F4U-1

PCS354.S12
12-Douglass A-20-A

# AIRPLANE HANGERS

PCS355.S01
1-Douglas B-19

PCS355.S02
2-Consolidated PBY2Y-2

PCS355.S03
3-Consolidated PBY-5

PCS355.S04
4-Vought-Sikorsky

PCS355.S05
5-Boeing B-17E

PCS355.S06
6-Consolidated B-24

PCS355.S07
7-North American B-25

PCS355.S08
8-Douglas SBD

PCS355.S09
9-Grumman F4-4

PCS355.S10
10-Brewster SB2A-1

PCS355.S11
11-Curtiss C-1

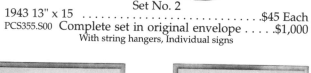

Set No. 2

1943 13" x 15 . . . . . . . . . . . . . . . . . . . . . . . . . . . .$45 Each
PCS355.S00  Complete set in original envelope . . . . .$1,000
With string hangers, Individual signs

PCS355.S12
12-Grumman TBF-1

PCS355.S13
13 Republic P-47

PCS355.S14
14-Douglas A-20

PCS355.S15
15-Martin B-26

PCS355.S16
16-Lockheed P-38

PCS355.S17
17-Waco Clider CG-4A

PCS355.S18
18-Bell P-39

PCS355.S19
19-Curtiss P40-F

PCS355.S20
20-Vultee Trainer

— 175 —

PCS356.S01

1-North American A-36 'Invader'

PCS356.S02

2-Lockheed P-38 'Lightning'

PCS356.S03

3-Republic P-47 'Thunderbolt'

PCS356.S04

4-Bell P-39 'Airacobra'

PCS356.S05

5-Curtiss P-40 'Warhawk'

PCS356.S06

6-Douglass P-70 'Havoc'

PCS356.S07

7-Boeing B-17 'Fortress'

PCS356.S08

8-Consolidated B-24 'Liberator'

PCS356.S09

9-North American B-25 'Mitchell'

THIS ENVELOPE CONTAINS—
**AMERICA'S FIGHTING PLANES**
*in action*
A NEW SERIES OF 20 HANGERS

NORTH AMERICAN-A-36 'Invader'
LOCKHEED-P-38 'Lightning'
REPUBLIC-P-47 'Thunderbolt'
BELL-P-39 'Airacobra'
CURTISS-P-40 'Warhawk'
DOUGLAS-P-70 'Havoc'
BOEING-B-17 'Fortress'
CONSOLIDATED-B-24 'Liberator'
NORTH AMERICAN-B-25 'Mitchell'
MARTIN-B-26 'Marauder'

GRUMMAN-F6F 'Hellcat'
GRUMMAN-F4F 'Wildcat'
VOUGHT-SIKORSKY-F4U 'Corsair'
CURTISS-SB2C 'Helldiver'
GRUMMAN-TBF 'Avenger'
MARTIN-PBM 'Mariner'
CONSOLIDATED-PBY 'Catalina'
VOUGHT-SIKORSKY-OS2U 'King...'
VOUGHT-SIKORSKY-YR4 'Helicop...'
LOCKHEED-C-69 'Constellation'

1944 set No. 3  13" x 15"  . . . . . . $45 Each
Individual signs with string hangers
PCS356.SB0  Complete set . . . . . . . . . $1,000
In original envelope

PCS356.S10

10-Martin B-26 'Marauder'

PCS356.S11

11-Grumman F6F 'Hellcat'

PCS356.S12

12-Grumman F4F 'Wildcat'

PCS356.S13

13-Vought-Sikorsky F4U 'Corsair'

PCS356.S14

14-Curtiss SB2C 'Helldiver'

PCS356.S15

15-Grumman TBF 'Avenger'

PCS356.S16

16-Martin PBM 'Mariner'

PCS356.S17

17-Consolidated PBY 'Catalina'

PCS356.S18

18-Vought-Sikorsky OS2U 'Kingfisher'

PCS356.S19

19-Vought-Sikorsky YR4 'Helicopter' YR-4

PCS356.S20

20-Lockheed C-69 'Constellation'

# CARDBOARD CUTOUT SANTAS

PCD176.001
1962  32" x 47"  . . . . . . . . .$400

PCD187.000
1946  6" x 12"  . . . .$300

PCD179.000
1950s  18" x 27"  . . . . . . .$200
3-D

PCD194.000
1957  13" x 33"  . . . . . . . .$400
3-D

PCD180.002
1954  10 $^{1}/_{2}$" x 19"  . . . . . . .$300

PCD175.002
1953  9" x 18"  . . . . .$325

PCD178.000
1949  15"  . . . . . . .$350
Easel back

PCD191.000
1956  14" x 28"  . . .$225

# TROLLEY SIGNS
## 11" x 20½" Cardboard

PCS035.000

1914 . . . . . . . . . . . . . . . . . . . . . . . . $6,000

PCS036.000

c.1912 . . . . . . . . . . . . . . . . . . . . . . . . $3,500

# TROLLEY SIGNS
11" x 20 ½" Cardboard

PCS032.000
1912 . . . . . . . . . . . . . . . . . . . . . . . . $6,000

PCS033.000
c.1918 . . . . . . . . . . . . . . . . . . . . . . . $3,500

PCS034.000
c.1927 . . . . . . . . . . . . . . . . . . . . . . . $2,500

PCS037.000

1923 . . . . . . . . . . . . . . . . . . . . . . . . . $3,000

"Flapper Girl"

PCS038.000

1923 . . . . . . . . . . . . . . . . . . . . . . . . $2,000

"The Four Seasons"

Note: Original artwork used by The Coca-Cola Company is very rare and valuable. The "Rip Van Winkle" piece shown at right is from the Snyder and Black Advertising Company. This is a piece of rough artwork, presented to the company and rejected in favor of another piece of art, which was then done in final form.

POA001.000
1930s . . . . . . . . . . . . . . . . . . . . . . . $3,000
"Rip Van Winkle", original (rough) presentation artwork, Rare

PBD002.S01    PBD002.S02    PBD002.S03    PBD002.S04

1923 . . . . . . . . . . . . . . . . . . . . . . . .$600 Each
PBD002.S00 **Complete set of four** . . . . . . $3,500
"Bottle Displays" cardboard cutouts, American Litho, NY

PCS029.000
c.1913  11" x 20 $\frac{1}{2}$" . . . . . . . . . . . . $3,500
Trolley sign

Note: Prices shown for paper and cardboard signs are based on original size. Pieces that have been trimmed from their original size are worth less.

PCS030.000
1914  11" x 20 $\frac{1}{2}$" . . . . . . . . . . . . . $3,500
Trolley sign

PCS391.000
1920s  10" x 14"  . . . . . . .$2,000
"Hot Dog", Rare

PCS050.000
1931  10" x 20"  . . . . . . . .$1,500
(Printed by Niagara Litho)

PCS107.000
1936  29" x 50"  . . . . . . . . . . . . . . . .$2,500
50th Anniversary

PCS087.000
1934  14" x 30"  . . . . .$1,600
Wallace Beery

NOTE: Values shown on these signs are based
on very nice condition of 8.5 or better.

PCS192.000
1929  19" x 31"  . . . . . . .$1,800

# CARDBOARD SIGNS

PCS125.001
1928  21 1/2" x 32" . . . . . . . . . . . $2,000
"Girl with Glass"

PCS125.002
1928  21 1/2" x 32" . . . . . . . . . . . $2,000
"Girl with Bottle"

PCS126.000
1957  16" x 27" . . . . . . . . . . . . . . . $450
"Snowman", with gold wood frame

PCS127.000
1944 . . . . . . . . . . . . . . . . . . . . . . . . . $750
With gold wood frame

PCS129.000
1956  29" x 50" . . . . . . . . . . . . . . . $450
"Travel Girl"

PCS128.000
1942  27" x 56" . . . . . . . . . . . . . . . . . . . . . $600
McCandlish, Litho

# CARDBOARD SIGNS

PCS119.000
1924  16" x 27" . . . . . $700
"Girl in Rain", Snyder & Black

PCS120.000
1942  16" x 27"  . . . . .$550
"Umbrella Girl", Snyder & Black

PCS121.000
1941  16" x 27" . . . . . .$550
"Girl Skater", Niagara Litho Co.

PCS122.000
1942  16" x 27" . . . . .$550
"Young Couple", McCandlish Litho

PCS123.000
1942  27" x 56" . . . . . . . . . . . . . . . . . $700
"Picnic Grill", Snyder & Black

PCS108.000
1942  29" x 50" . . . . . . . . . . . . . . $950
"Two Girls at Car", Edwards & Deutsch Litho

Note: The prices shown on these litho insert signs will certainly be higher for examples in Mint condition, or in original gold wood frame. Examples that are in Below Average condition will be worth less.

PCS076.000
1942  29" x 50" . . . . . . . . . $750
"Snowman", Niagara Litho

PCS124.000
1942  27" x 56" . . . . . . . . . . . . . . . . . . $750
"The Fireplace", McCandlish Litho

# CARDBOARD SIGNS

PCS392.000

1936  27" x 56"  . . . . . . . . . . . . . . . .$2,500

Rare

PCS393.000

1948  29" x 50"  . . . . . . . . . . . . . . . . .$750

PCS190.000

1938  34" x 50"  . . . . . . . . . . . . . . . .$2,800

"Girl with Roses", inside store display

PCS394.000

1956  20" x 36"  . . . . . . . . . . . . . . . .$550

With gold wood frame

PCS 424.000

1956  15" x 16"  . . . . . . . . . . . . . . . . .$300

2-Sided

— 185 —

# CARDBOARD SIGNS

PCS130.000

1954   20" x 36" . . . . . . . . . . . . . . . . . $750

"Baseball Game", with gold wood frame

PCS068.000

1948   20" x 36" . . . . . . . . . . . . . . . . . $700

With gold wood frame

PCS074.000

1944   16" x 27" . . . . . . . . . $1,000

With gold wood frame

PCS131.000

1938   29" x 50" . . . . . . . . . . . . . . . . $2,000

Signed Sundblom, printed by Niagara Litho,
Buffalo, NY.

PCS132.000

1957   20" x 36" . . . . . . . . . . . . . . $600

"Me Too", with aluminum frame

PCS133.000

1950   20" x 36" . . . . . . . . . . . . . . . . . $700

With gold wood frame

# CARDBOARD SIGNS

PCS134.000
1944  16" x 27"  . . . . . . . . . . . . $750
With gold wood frame

PCS135.000
1956  16" x 27"  . . . . . . . . $350

PCS136.000
1939  16" x 27"  . . . . . . . . . . . . $1,200
With gold wood frame

PCS137.000
1950s 11" x 14"  . . . . . . . . $600
Sugar Ray Robinson

Note: Some of
these pieces shown
on this color page
can also be found
in the black and
white section.

Note: In 1939, the advertising campaign
"Through The Years" featured reprints of vintage
Coca-Cola advertising pieces.

PCS115.000
1940s  20" x 36"  . . . . . . . . . . . . . . . $850
With gold wood frame

PCS091.000
1959-1960  14" x 18 1/2"  . . . . . . . . . . $600
Ricky Nelson

# ALL TIME SPORTS FAVORITE
# (CARDBOARD SIGNS)

PCS358.S01

1. Ty Cobb—Baseball
$250

PCS358.S02

2. Willie Hoppe—Billiards
$150

PCS358.S03

3. Red Grange—Football
$200

PCS358.S05

5. Man O' War—Horse Racing
$100

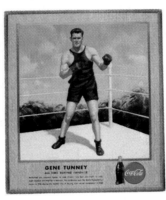

PCS358.S06

6. Gene Tunney—Boxing
$200

PCS358.S04

4. Ned Day—Bowling
$100

PCS358.S08

8. Colonial Lady M—Field Trial
$100

PCS358.S09

9. Bobby Jones—Golf
$300

PCS358.S07

7. Helene Madison—Swimming
$125

PCS358.S10

10. Don Budge—Tennis
$125

NOTE: *I have seen individual "All Time Sports Favorite" signs sell for higher than my estimated value shown above. The Ty Cobb and Bobby Jones signs have always been the most difficult to find. Higher prices will also be paid by a person attempting to complete the set, as well as by sports collectors.*

PCS358.S00

1947 Hanging Cardboard Signs, 13" x 15", printed by Snyder and Black, the complete set consists of 10 signs: Ty Cobb, Willie Hoppe, Red Grange, Man O' War, Gene Tunney, Ned Day, Colonial Lady M, Bobby Jones, Helene Madison, Don Budge.

Complete Set of 10 . . . . . . . . . . . . . . . . . . . . . . . . . . . . . . . . . . . . . . . . . . . . . . .$2,500

# CARDBOARD SIGNS

All of the signs shown here are 11" x 13" lightweight cardboard in
aluminum frame. Values could be slightly less without frame.

PCS382.000

1949 . . . . . . . . . . . . . . . . . . . . . . . . . .$550

PCS383.000

1951 . . . . . . . . . . . . . . . . . . . . . . . . . .$450

PCS384.000

1949 . . . . . . . . . . . . . . . . . . . . . . . .$450

PCS385.000

1949 . . . . . . . . . . . . . . . . . . . . . . . .$400

PCS386.000

1949 . . . . . . . . . . . . . . . . . . . . . . . .$400

PCS387.000

1949 . . . . . . . . . . . . . . . . . . . . . . . .$400

PCS388.000

1949 . . . . . . . . . . . . . . . . . . . . . . . .$350

PCS389.000

1949 . . . . . . . . . . . . . . . . . . . . . . . .$350

PTN018.004
c.1908  12" x 36" . . . . . . . . . . . . . . $1,300
Spanish

PTN012.000
1903  6" . . . . . . . . . . . . . $9,000
Hanging sign, Rare,
Chas. W. Shonk Co. Litho, Chicago, IL

PTN006.000
1895-1898  19 1/2" x 27" . . . . . . . . . $10,000
Rare, Ronemous & Co., Baltimore, MD

PTN009.000
c.1899-1900  19 1/2" x 27" . . . . . $6,500
Rare, Standard Advertising Co., Coshocton, OH

PTN023.000
1947  12 3/4" . . . . . . . . . . . . . . . . $850
Embossed edge, used for the export market

PTN022.002
1926  13" x 19" . . . . . . . . . . . . . . . . $7,500
Large oval

PTN014.000

1905  23" x 33" . . . . . . . . . . . . . . . .$12,000
Lillian Nordica, self-framed tin sign
(rare in this condition).
Photo Courtesty: James D. Julia, Inc.

PTN015.000

1914  31" x 41" . . . . . . . . . . . . . . . .$6,000
"Betty" self-framed tin sign

PTN016.000

1916  20" x 30 1/2" . . . . . . . . . . . . .$5,000
Self-framed tin sign

Note: The values shown on these signs are based on
examples in very nice conditon of 8.5 or better.  Signs in
Poor conditon, or even less than average, will have much
less value, especially the better signs.

PTN142.000

1920s  . . . . . . . . . . . . . . . . . . . . . .$2,200
Tin diecut sign, Rare

PTN060.000

1931 10" x 28" . . . . . . . . . . . . . . . . . . .$700
Embossed tin

PTN059.000

1934 12" x 34 1/2" . . . . . . . . . . . . . . .$600
Embossed tin

PTN028.000

1934 20" . . . . . . . . . . . . . . . . . . . . . .$650
Embossed tin

PTN058.001

1931 20" x 27" . . . . . . . . . . . . . . . .$800
Embossed tin (in bottles variation)

PTN026.000

1929 20" x 28" . . . . . . . . . . . . . . . .$1,800
"Gas Today" embossed tin

# BASEBALL PLAYERS (CARDBOARD SIGNS)

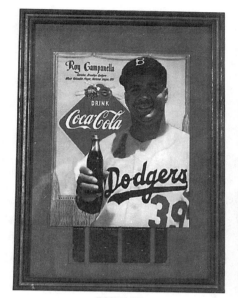

PCS360.000

12" x 17 ¹/₂" . . . . . . . . . . . . . . . . . . . $700

Roy Campanella

PCS359.000

1950s  10" x 12"  . . . . . . . . . . . . . . . . $850

Phil Rizzuto

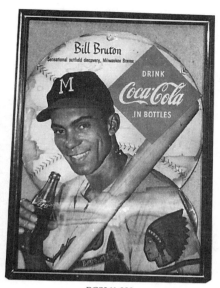

PCS361.000

11" x 14" . . . . . . . . . . . . . . . . . . . . $700

Bill Bruton

---

Note: These baseball player cutout signs are also very desirable to sports collectors.
Individual players may be more valuable to a baseball collector than a Coke collector.

---

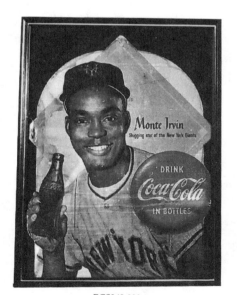

PCS362.000

11" x 14" . . . . . . . . . . . . . . . . . . . . $700

Monte Irvin

PCS363.000

11" x 14" . . . . . . . . . . . . . . . . . . . . $700

Larry Doby

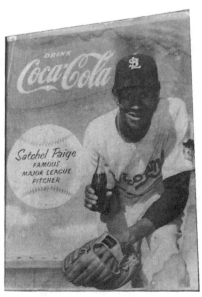

PCS364.000

11" x 14" . . . . . . . . . . . . . . . . . . $800

Satchel Paige

Note: Movie star, sports star and celebrity advertising pieces are always very popular among collectors.

PCH004.S02

1953 . . . . . . . . . . . $45

Mailer card for
Kit Carson kerchief

PCD398.000

11" x 14" . . . . . . . . . . . . . . . . . . . $385

Lionel Hampton

PCS365.000

1953 16" x 24" . . . . . . . . . . . . . . . . . . $225

Kit Carson, cardboard sign

PCH005.000

1955 . . . . . . . . . . . $60

Kit Carson "Rodeo Tie"

PPS079.000

1953 16" x 24" . . . . . . . . . . . . . . . . . . $150

Kit Carson, paper sign

PPS085.000

1953 16" x 24" . . . . . . . . . . . . . . . . . . $125

Kit Carson, paper window banner

PPS086.000

1951 11" x 22" . . . . . . . . . . . . . . . . . . $125

Mario Lanza paper window banner

PCH004.S01

1953 20" x 22" . . . . . . . . . . . . . . . . . . $60

Kit Carson kerchief

PCC001.000 c.1911 Canvas banner, 16" x 11' . . . . . . . . $2,500

PCC002.000 c.1914 Canvas banner, 10" x 72" . . . . . $2,000

PCC003.000 c.1910 Canvas banner, 9" x 48" . . . . . . $2,800
Note: Banners showing the straight side bottle are more desirable than without.

PCC005.000
1920s Umbrella . . . . $900
Note: Earlier Umbrellas
showing the straight side bottle
would certainly be worth more.
$1,200 - $1,600

PCC004.000 c.1911 Canvas banner, 9" x 48" . . . . . . $2,200

PCC006.000 1950 Cloth banner, 18 1/2" x 56" . . . . . . . $425

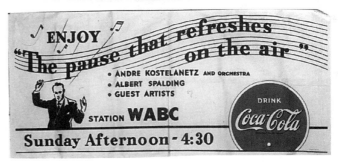

PCC008.000
1948 Canvas awning . . . . . . . . . . . . .$600
Part of inside store display

PCC009.000
c.1936 . . . . . . . . . . . . $125
Truck flag

PCC007.000 1950s Canvas truck banner, 48" x 64" . . . . . $385

PCC010.000 1950s Canvas truck banner, 64" x 44" . . . . $650

PCC011.000 c. 1939 Canvas truck banner, 24" x 50" . . . $400

PGS010.000
1904 8 1/2" x 11", as shown . . . . . . . . $4,500
Near mint . . . . . . . . . . . . . . . . . . . . . . $7,500
Lillian Nordica, glass covered, paper on cardboard,
metal frame with chain hange,
back of sign printed in reverse.

PGS012.000
1920s 10 1/2" x 20" . . . . . . . . . . . . . .$800
Reverse glass

PGS011.000
1939 11" x 21" . . . . . . . . . . . . . . .$2,500
Reverse glass, (red, white, black) chrome bands
and chain hanger, made by Brunhoff Mfg.

PGS013.000
1930s 9" x 13" . . . . . . . . . . . . . . . $1,600
This is a reverse glass, metal frame, shadow box
sign, light bulb could be put in back to illuminate.

PGS014.000
1920s  6" x 10" . . . . . . . . . . . . .$900
Reverse glass, black and silver, Rare

PGS015.000
1960s 6 1/2" x 12" . . . . . . . . . . . . . $60
Reverse glass

PGS035.000
1939-1941  8" x 16"  . . . . . . . . . . . . . . $800
Reverse glass, mirrored sign

PGS036.000
c.1902  5"  . . . . . . . . . . . . . . . . . . . $2,500
Reverse glass sign with chain trim and hanger, Rare

PGS016.003
1948  . . . . . . . . . . . . . . . . . . . . . . . $750
Glass with wood base. Note: This sign can be found
with two different plastic top pieces; glass or bottle,
as well as without, as shown above.

PGS016.004
1948  . . . . . . . . . . . . . . . . . . . . . . . $900
Glass with wood base, plastic top, (bottle version)

PGS037.000
c.1937  10" x 12"  . . . . . . . . . . . . . . $4,000
Glass sign, reverse glass, foil back, metal frame

PGS038.000
1950s  10"  . . . . . . . . . . . . . . . . . . . $300
Reverse glass

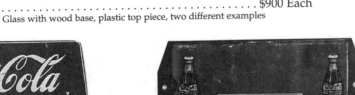

PGS016.001

PGS016.002

1948 . . . . . . . . . . . . . . . . . . . . . . . . . . . . . . . . . . . . . . . . . . . . . $900 Each
Glass with wood base, plastic top piece, two different examples

PGS017.000
1930s 10" x 14 1/4" . . $600
Metal framed

PGS018.000

1950s 11" . . . . . . . . . . . . . . . . . $450
"Cash Register Topper", glass on wood base,
enameled "Coke" plate on wood. (This sign
was also made with a plastic base.)

PGS019.000
1930s 3" x 7" . . . . . . . . . . . . . . . $325
Two bottle mirror

PGS020.000
Late 1930s 10 1/4" x 14 1/4" . . . $450
Metal framed

PGS021.000
1937 10" x 12" . . . . . . . . . . . . . . . . $4,000
Glass sign, reverse glass, foil back, metal frame.

PGS022.000
Late 1920s 8" x 17 3/4" . . $500
Beware of reproduction

PGS023.000
1920s to Mid 1930s
11 1/4" dia. . . . . . . . . . . . . . . $550
Reverse glass, mirror sign

PGS024.000
c.1939 10 1/4" x 14 1/4" . . . $600
With thermometer

PGS025.000
c.1940 5" x 15" . . . . . . . . . . . . $650
Reverse glass

PGS026.000
1930s 8 1/4" x 18 1/4" . . $550
Metal framed

# GLASS SIGNS

PGS027.000

1948 . . . . . . . . . . . . . . . . . . . . . . . . $850

Hanging sign, glass and plastic

PGS028.000

1950s . . . . . . . . . . . . . . . . . . . . . . . . $575

Counter sign, glass and plastic

PGS029.000

c.1940s . . . . . . . . . . . . . . . . . . . . . . . $400

Decal and etched glass

PGS030.001

1932  10" x 22" . . . . . . . . . . . . . . . . $2,800

PGS030.002

1932  6" x 12" . . . . . . . . . . . $2,500

PGS032.000

1930s  6" x 9¹/₂" . . . . $450

PGS031.001

1932  12" oval . . . . . . . . $3,500

PGS031.002

1932  12" x 20" . . . . . . . . . . . . . . . . $3,800

Black version, Manufactured by "The Brunhoff Mfg.
Co." Display Advertising Specialists.

PGS033.001

1932  24" . . . . . . . . . . . . . . . . . . . . . $5,500

"Stand up "Fan" sign

PGS033.002

1932 24" . . . . . . . . . . . . . . . . . . . . $5,500

Hanging "Fan" sign

# TIN SIGNS

PTN011.000
1903-1912  8¹/₂" x 10"  . . . . . . . . . . .$9,000
Printed by Chas. W. Shonk Co., Chicago, Rare

PTN007.000
1898  20" x 28"  . . . . . . . . . . . . . $15,000
Rare

PTN009.000
c.1899-1900  19 ¹/₂" x 27"  . . . . . . . . $6,500
Printed by Standard Advertising Co., Coshocton, OH, Rare

Note: The condition of these early and rare tin signs is very important. The signs shown on this page are Average condition and prices are based on that condition. Examples in Poor condition will be worth much less and those in Mint condition could command higher prices.

PTN008.000
1899  20" x 28"  . . . . . . . . . . $1,500
Hilda Clark, Rare

PTN010.000
c.1902  9 ¹/₂" x 13 ¹/₂"  . . . . . . . . . . .$4,800
Printed by Chas. W. Shonk Co., Chicago.

PTN003.000

c.1890  5" x 14"  . . . . . . . . . . . . . . $8,000
Tin, embossed, black and silver (This is quite
possibly the first production tin sign used
by Coca-Cola), Very Rare

PTN004.000

1880s  . . . . . . . . . . . . . . . . . . . . . . $6,000
French Wine Coca, Rare

PTN013.000

1907  18 1/2" x 27"  . . . . . . . . . . . . . $10,000
"Relieves Fatigue", self-framed, tin

PTN017.001

c.1914  19" x 27"  . . . . . . . . . . . . . . $2,200
Bottle sign, straight sided (variation), bolder logo
with no black outline around lettering

PTN143.000

1920s  12" x 35 1/2"  . . . . . . . . . . . . . $850
Showing 1916 bottle

PTN017.000

c.1914  19" x 27"  . . . . . . . . . . . . $1,500
Tin

PCS378.000

c.1914 18" x 30"  . . . . . . . . . . . . $2,000
Cardboard

Note: The straight-sided Coca-Cola bottle signs are certainly the most sought after Coca-Cola signs. The values shown are for examples in clean presentable condition. Signs in poor or less-than-excellent condition would be priced considerably lower. Examples in Near Mint to Mint condition would be higher.

PTN018.001

c.1908 12" x 36"  . . . . . . . . . . . . . . $2,000
Tin

PRE001.000

1970s 19" x 27"  . . . . . . . . . . . $375
Tin, reproduction, Note: "Trade Mark Registered" appears under the logo on the reproduction but in the tail of the "C" on the original.

PTN018.002

c.1908 12" x 36"  . . . . . . . . . . . . . . $1,600
Tin

PTN019.000

c.1914 14" x 39"  . . . . . . . . . . . . . $2,000
Tin, Rare

PTN018.003

c.1908 12" x 36"  . . . . . . . . . . . . . . $1,600
Tin, French

PTN018.004

c.1908 12" x 36"  . . . . . . . . . . . . . . $1,600
Tin, Spanish

PTN020.001

1927  20" x 15" . . . . . . . . . . . . . . . $5,000
Embossed tin

PTN021.000

1927  8 1/2" x 11" . . . . . . . . . . . . . . $2,400

PTN020.002

1929  20" x 15" . . . . . . . . . . . . . . . $3,500
Embossed tin

PTN020.003

1920s  20" x 15" . . . . . . . . . . . . . . . $3,700
Embossed tin

PTN021.001

1927  8 1/2" x 11" . . . . $900

PTN022.001

1926  8" x 11" . . . . . . . . . . . . . . . $2,600
Small oval

PTN022.002

1926  13" x 19" . . . . . . . . . . . . . . . $7,500
Large oval

PTN021.002

1926  8 1/2" x 11" . . . . . . . . . . . . . . $2,600

# TIN SIGNS

PTN024.001

PTN025.000
1931  18" x 54" . . . . $1,200

PTN026.000
1930s  20" x 28" . . . . . . . . . . . . . . . $2,500
"Gas Today", Rare

PTN024.002
1922  4" x 8" . . . . . . . . . . . . . . . $650 Each
Two different examples

PPC005.000
1920s  12" x 36" . . . . . . . . . . . . . . . $900
Porcelain

PTN027.000
1930  20" x 15" . . . . . . . . . . . . . . . . $750

PTN028.000
1934  20" . . . . . . . . . . $650

PTN029.000
1927  28" x 29" . . . . . . . . . . . . . . . $725

PTN030.000
c.1910  24" x 58" . . . . . . . . . . . . . . . . $650
Cross Press & Sign Co., Chicago

# TIN SIGNS

DRINK
*Coca-Cola*
"Delicious & refreshing"

PTN031.000
1941  19" x 54" . . $600

PTN032.000
1941  11" x 35" . . . . . . . . . . . . . . . . . $600

PTN033.000
1941  11" x 35" . . . . . . . . . . . . . . . $600

Note:  Many of these 1941 signs were made in both tin and masonite.

PTN034.000
1941  20" x 28" . . . . . . . $550

PTN035.000
1941  20" x 28" . . . . . . . . $550

PTN036.000
1941  19" x 54" . . . $600

PTN037.000

PTN038.000

1930s  14" x 16" . . . . . . . . . . . . . . . . . . . . . . . . . . . . . . . . . . . . . . . $700 Each
String Holders, showing two different examples, plus (reverse side) instructions

PTN039.000
1930s  20" x 28" . . $500

PTN040.000
1950s  20" x 28" . . . $350

PTN042.000
1930s  19" x 54" . . $500

PTN043.000
1950  18" x 54" . . $450

PTN078.P01
1950s  16" x 40" . . $350

PTN041.000
1930s  19" x 54" . . . . . . . . . . . . . . $500

PTN045.001
1934  19" x 28"  . . . . . . . . . . . . . $650
Green background

PTN045.002
1934  19" x 28"  . . . . . . . . . $650
White background

PTN046.000
1934 . . . . $1,600
Two-sided hanging sign
Enameled  . . . . . . . . .$2,000
Porcelain  . . . . . . . . . .$3,000

PTN047.000
1950s  12" x 25"  . . . . . . . . . . $300

PTN048.000
1950s  10" x 28"  . . . . . . $275

PTN049.000
1937  19" x 28" . . . $450

PTN050.000
1934  45 $\frac{1}{2}$"  . . . . . . . . . . . . . . . . . . . $850

PTN051.000
1940  19" x 54"  . . . $500

PTN052.000
1930s  19" x 54"  . . $650

PTN053.000
1948
16" x 40" . . . . $325

PTN056.001
$700
1930s  19" x 54"
Two different examples

PTN056.002
$325

PTN054.000
1930s
19" x 54" . . . . $550

PTN055.000
1920s
19" x 54" . . . . $950

PTN057.000

1938  18" x 54" . . . . . . . . . . . . . . . . . . $600

PTN058.000

1930  20" x 27" . . . . . . . . . . $750

PTN059.000

1934  12" x 36" . . . . . . . . . . . . . . . $600

DRINK Coca-Cola

PTN059.001

1934  12" x 36" . . . . . . . . . . . . . $600

PTN060.000

1931  10" x 28" . . . . . . . . $700

PTN061.000

1940s  12" x 36" . . . . . . . . . . . . . $425

PTN063.000

1931  9" x 12" . . . . . . . . . . . $600

PTN064.000

1948  16" x 32" . . . . . . . . $550

PTN062.000

1930s  20" x 28" . . . . . . . $650

PTN065.000

1930s  19" x 54" . . . . . . . . . . . . . . . . . $475

PTN066.000

1940s  20" x 28" . . $375
Also made in masonite.
Beware of masonite reproduction.

PTN067.000

1920s  12" x 17" wood base  . . . . $450
This is a top sign for an Icy-O cooler, reverse
has instructions on how to use the cooler.

PTN068.000

c.1936  19" x 54" . . . . . . . . . . . . . . . $600

PTN069.000

1940s  19" x 54" . . . . . . . . . . . . . . . . . $385

PTN144.000
1948  18" x 54"  . . . . $550

PTN146.000
1950s  16" x 40"  . . . . . . . . . . . . . . . . $550
Bag holder

PTN145.000
1948  18" x 54" . . . $650

PTN147.000
1932  19 1/2"  . . . . . . . . . . . . . . . . $750
American Art Works, Coshocton, OH

PFS016.000
c.1938  18" x 20"  . . . . . . . . . . . . . . $675
Flange, porcelain, Canada

PFS017.000
c.1938  18" x 20"  . . . . . . . . . . . . . . $650
Flange, porcelain, Canada

# TIN SIGNS

PTN070.000

1950s  16" x 50" . . . . . . . . . . . . . . . . . $400

PTN071.000

1940s  22" x 32" . . . . . . . . . . . $500

PTN072.000

1963  32" x 46" . . . . . . . . . . . . . . . . . $275

PTN073.000

1963  12" x 27" . . . . . . . . . . . . . . $185

PDR004.P01

1930s  8" x 16" . . . . . . . . . . . $350
Rack sign

PTN075.000

1960s  18" x 54" . . . . . . . . . . . . . . . . . $225

PTN076.000

1953  16¹/₄" . . . . . . . . . . . . . . . . . . . $650

PTN077.000

1952  20" x 28"  . . $325

PTN078.000  PTN079.000

1950s  16" x 40"  . . . . . $750 Each
Plus button sign, complete

PTN080.000
1948
18" x 54" . . . $500

PTN081.000
1964
18" x 54" . . . $325

PTN082.000
1950s
18" x 36" . . . . . $325

PTN083.000
1963
18" x 54" . . . $325

PTN148.000

1950s  18" x 54" . . . . . . . . . . . . . . . . . $275

PTN150.000

1950s  10" x 28" . . . . . . . . . . . . . . . . . $200

PTN149.000

1950s  18" x 54" . . . . . . $325

PTN040.000

1952  20" x 28" . . . . . . $350
Carton insert

*Note: These 20" x 28" tin signs were used as inserts for the sidewalk sign, as well as independently.*

PTN152.000

1950s  20" x 28" . . . . . . . . $350
Carton insert

PTN097.000

1950s . . . . . . . . $200
Bottle insert

PTN153.000

Value . . . . . . . . . . . . . . . . . . . . . . . .$150
Frame for sidewalk sign, steel frame only,
without insert

PMB012.001

1952  20" x 28" . . . . . . $125
Menu board insert

PTN077.000

1952  20" x 28" . . . . . $325
Case insert

# TIN SIGNS

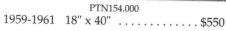

PTN154.000
1959-1961   18" x 40"  . . . . . . . . . . . . $550

PTN086.003
1963  20" x 28"  . . . . . . . . . . . . . . . . $200

PMS111.000
1950s  . . . . . . . . . . . . . . . . . . . . . . . $425
Door push bar, aluminum

PTN155.000
1960s  20" x 28"  . . . . . . . . . . . . . . . $150

PTN156.000
1950s  20" x 28"  . . . . . . . . . . . . . . . $200

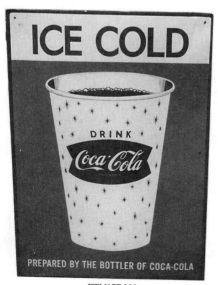

PTN157.000
1963  20" x 28"  . . . . . . . . . . . . $250

PTN158.000
1960s  24" x 66"  . . . . . . . . . . . . . . . $500
Dimensional sign, porcelain

PTN084.001

PTN085.000

20" x 28" . . . . . . . . . . . $300

PTN086.001

20" x 28" . . . . . . . . . . . . . . . . . . . . . $200

PTN084.002

20" x 28" . . . . . . . . . . . . . . . . . $200 Each
"King Size", two different versions

PTN088.000

1963 . . . . . . . . . . $375
Calendar Sign

PTN087.002

11" x 28" . . . . . . . . . . . . . . . . . . $325

PTN087.001

11" x 28" . . . . . . . . . . . . . . . . . . . . . . $200

PTN089.000

PTN090.000

20" x 28" . . . . . . . . . . . . . . . . . . . . . . . . . . . . . . . . . . . . . . $225 Each
Three different versions

PTN091.000

PTN087.003

18" x 54" . . . . . . . . . . . . . . . . . . $225

PTN087.004

18" x 54" . . . . . . . . . . . . . . . . $225

# TIN SIGNS

PTN086.002
1963  20" x 28"  . . . . . . . . $200

PTN092.000
1964  20" x 28"  . . . . . . . $300

PTN093.001
1964  20" x 28"  . . . . . . . . . . $250

PTN094.000
1948  19" x 28"  . . . . . . $185

PTN095.000
1950  19" x 28"  . . $325

PTN093.002
1964  19" x 28"  . . $250

PTN096.000
1960s  11" x 28"  . . . . $200

PDR005.P01
1949  . . . . . . . . . . $200
Sprite Boy Rack Sign

PTN097.000
1950s  19" x 28"  . . $200

PTN098.000
1964  24" x 24"  . . $185

PTN087.006
1963  18" x 54"  . . $300

PTN097.001
1950s  20" x 28"  . . . . . . . . . . . . $200

PTN093.003
1964  11" x 28"  . . . . . . . . . . . . . . . . . $225

PTN087.005
1963  11" x 28"  . . . . . . . . . . . . . . . . . $200

PTNO99.000
1980s  24" x 24"  . . . . . . . . . . . . . $30 Each

PTN100.000

PTN101.000
1930s 5 3/4" x 17 3/4" . . . . . . . . . . . . . $300
Dasco

PTN102.000
1922 6" x 23" . . . . . . . . . . . . . . . . . $325

PTN103.000
1926 10 1/2" x 31" . . . . . . . . . . . . . . . $525

PTN105.000
1939 19" x 28" . . $400

PTN106.002
1934 19" x 28" . . . $550

PTN106.001
1934 19" x 28" . . $600

PTN104.000
1950s 10" x 24" . . . . . . . . . . . . . . . $125

PTN107.000
1950s-60s 14" x 53" . . . . . . . . . . . . . $425
Menu board

PTN108.000
1950s 10" x 24" . . . . . $125

PTN109.000
1940s 16" x 36" . . . . . . . . . $135
Canada

PTN110.000
1950s . . . . . . . . $300
Calendar holder

PTN111.000
1960s . . . . . . . . . . . . . . . . $450
Tire rack sign

PTN112.000
1950s 36" x 36" . . . . . . . . . . . . . $175

PPC006.000
Late 1930s 22" x 26" .... $1,200

PPC007.000
1938-1939 24" x 26" ..... $1,800

PPC008.000
c.1950s 28" x 28" ............ $950
Made in one-sided and two-sided

PPC035.000
1934 14" x 27" ................. $800

*Note: Porcelain signs very often have scrapes or rub marks. This should be considered when determining value.*

PPC011.000
c.1950s 12" x 28" ............ $525

PPC009.000
c.1930s 10" x 28" ............... $550

PPC010.001
c.1950s 12" x 28" .............. $475

PPC012.000
Late 1930s 14" x 27" ........ $1,000
PPC012.001 Masonite Version .....$750

PPC010.002
c.1950s 12" x 28" ............... $475

PPC013.000
c.1950s 16" x 24" ... $375

PPC014.000
1960s 28" x 28" .... $375

PPC011.001
1950s 28" x 32" .... $600

PPC015.000
1949 12" x 29" .................. $400

PPC016.000
Late 1930s 4' x 5' ........ $850
Tenn. Enamel Mfg. Co.

PPC017.000
1950s 24" x 24" ........ $225

*Note: Many porcelain signs were produced in Canada for the Canadian market, both in French and English. The English versions have more value.*

PPC036.000
1940s 36" ................... $225
Canadian (French)

PPC026.P01
1930s 18" x 24" .............. $300

PPC019.000
1950s 12" x 28" ................. $500

PPC020.000
1952  12" x 29" . . . . . . . . . . . . . . . . . .$300
Canada

PPC021.000
1939  12" x 31" . . . . . . . . . . . . . . . . . . $625

PPC022.000
1949  17" x 19" . . . . . . . . . . . . . . . . . . $700
Canadian Flange

PPC023.000
1939-1941  $17\frac{1}{2}$" x 54" . . $850
Canadian

PPC024.000
1952  18" x 20"  . . . . . . . . . . . . . . . . . . $700
Canadian Flange

PPC025.000
1950s  26" x 36" . . . . . . . . $325

Certainly the most difficult pieces to evaluate in a book such as this are large signs. As in most cases with signs, the smaller versions have more appeal to collectors than large examples, not because they do not like the larger signs, but because limited display space is very common among most collectors. These large signs are often overlooked by many of today's collectors because "displayability" is usually the number one priority. Collectors feel the space a large sign takes can be better used to display a number of smaller signs. Because of this the values on large signs will vary much more than their smaller counterparts, not only based on condition, but also on the collector's ability to display the sign. From a personal standpoint, 5-foot, 6-foot and 8-foot signs are of no interest to me at any price. I do not collect them, nor do I have a good market for selling them. On the other hand, dealers and collectors who supply restaurants and taverns with these signs for decoration have a good market and will pay well for them. So, unless you can find the right buyer, selling these larger signs is sometimes a real problem. I have received many letters and calls over the years from frustrated collectors who cannot understand why they cannot find a buyer for their 6- or 8-foot porcelain sign. Therefore, before buying such a sign ask yourself a few questions: Do I have the space to display this piece? Do I have the patience to find the right buyer? Do I also realize this sign will not appreciate in value as the smaller signs? Also keep in mind that the values shown are based on collector desirability for such signs.

PPC031.000
1935  5' . . . . . . . . . . . . . . . . . . . . . . $850
Outdoor sign, porcelain, Tenn. Enamel, Co.

PPC032.000
1934  4 1/2 x 8' . . . . . . . . . . . . . . . . . $600
Porcelain

PPC033.000
1934  3' x 5' . . . . . . . . . . . $700
Porcelain

PTN160.000
1940s  3' x 6' . . . . . . . . . . . . . . . . . $650
Outdoor sign, tin

PTN161.000
1940s  3' x 6' . . . . . . . . . . . . . . . . . $700
Outdoor sign, tin

# LARGE SIGNS

PTN113.000

1952 43" x 108" . . . . . . . . . . . . . . . . . $375
Stamped frame tin

PTN114.000

1952 43" x 108" . . . . . . . . . . . . . . . . . $450
Stamped frame tin, with privilege panel

PTN113.001

1952 3' x 6' . . . . . . . . . . . . . . . $400
Stamped frame tin

PTN116.000

1948-52 48 3/4" x 48 3/4" . . . . . . . . . $500
Diamond sign with wood frame (other similar
versions exist of this sign)

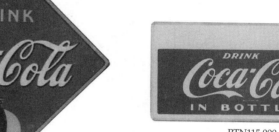

PTN115.000

1952 3' x 6' . . . . . . . . . . . . . . . $300
Stamped frame tin, with privilege panel

PTN113.002

1952 2' x 5' . . . . . . . . . . . $425
Stamped frame tin

PPC026.000

1948-52 36" x 52" . . . . $1,000
Silhouette porcelain

PTN118.000

1952 18" x 3' . . . $300
Tin with wood frame

Note: "Stamped Frame" is a tin
sign stamped out of a single sheet
of metal, giving a raised edge or
self-framed effect.

PTN117.001

1952 32" x 67 1/2" . . . . . . . . . $400
Dimensional bulletin sign, tin

PTN117.002

1952 40" x 108" . . . . . . . . . . . . . . . $400
Dimensional bulletin sign, tin

PPC027.000

1948-52 49" x 58" . . . . . . . . . . $800
Colonial porcelain, with privilege panel

PTN119.000

1952 18" x 36" . . . $300
Stamped frame tin

Note: Most of the signs shown on
this page were offered from 1948
through 1952.

PTN120.000

1952 2' x 5' . . . . . . . . . . . . . . . . . $425
Tin with wood frame

# LARGE SIGNS

PMS005.001

1952  10" x 78" . . . . . . . . . . . . . . . . . . . . . . . . . . . $700-$1,000
Wood and masonite with 12" discs, one-sided or two-sided

PMS005.002

1950s  10" x 78" . . . . . . . . . . . . . . . . . . . . . . . . . . . $950
Wood and masonite with clock, one-sided

PMS005.003

1950s  14" x 12' . . . . . . . . . . . . . . . . . . . . . . . . . . . $1,200
Tin, with clock or white disc with Sprite Boy

PTN121.001

1952  14" x 62" . . . . . . . . . . . . . . . . . . . . . . . . . . . $750
Tin with 12" disc

PTN122.000

1960s  24" . . . . . . . . . . . . . . . . . . . . . $325
Tin. Note: This tin fishtail sign was produced in
many different sizes ranging from 12" to over 6'.

*Note: There are many
different examples of the
large signs shown above.
This is only a small
sampling of the many
seen over the years.*

PPC028.000

1950s  5' high . . . . . . . . . . . . . .$600
Service Station Sign,  24" porcelain disc
and 5" x 28" privilege panels.

PTN123.000

c.1949  16" x 40" . . . . . . . . . . . . . . . . . . . . . . . . . . . $650
Bag Holder. There is another version of this Bag Holder without
the Sprite Boy on it. Approx. same value.

PDR004.P01
1930s  8 1/2" x 16" . . . . . . . . . . $350

PDR006.P01
1933  8 1/2" x 18" . . . . . . . . . . . . . . . $375

PDR007.P01
1950s  8 1/2" x 11" . . . . . . . $40

PDR008.P01
1930s  11" x 15 1/2" . . $450
(Unusually early "Enjoy" sign)

Note: These 1949 Display Racks were used into the 1950s and show up in bottlers catalog as late as 1952.

PDR005.P01
1949 . . . . . . . . . $200
Sprite Boy rack sign

PDR005.000
1949 . . . . . . . . .$385
Display rack with sign

PDR011.001
1949 . . . . . . . . . . . $225
Display rack (54 cartons)

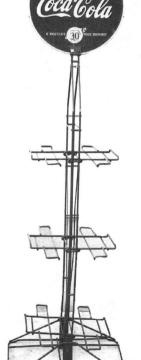

PDR009.001
Late 1930s-early 1940s . . . $350
Display rack

PDR010.000
1938 . . . . . . . . .$450
Display rack

PDR008.000
1930s . . . . . . . .$600
Display rack, Canada

PDR011.002
1949 . . . . . . . . . . . .$225
Display rack (26 cartons)

PFS007.000

c.1948 . . . . . . . . . . . . . . . . . . . . . . .$1,200

"Enjoy", Rare

PFS008.000

c.1948-50 . . . . . . . . $700

PFS009.000

1950 . . . . . . . . . . $700

PFS010.000

1950s with Bottle . . . . . . . . . . . . . . . . . . . . . $500
PFS010.001 1950s with Glass (not shown) . . . $700

> *Note: A flange sign is a sign with a metal flange at a right angle to the sign allowing it to be attached to the side of a building and be seen from both sides.*

PFS011.000

1950 . . . . . . . . . . . . . . . . . . . . . . . .$1,000
Wood-grain tin (showing both sides)

PFS005.000

1930s  12" x 16" . . . . . . . . . . . . . . $700

PFS006.000

Early 1930s  12" x 16" . . . . $750

PFS012.000

1940s . . . . . . . . . . . . . . . . . . . . . . . . . $550

PFS015.002

1960s . . . . . . . . . . . . . . . . . . . . . . . $225 Each
Two different examples

PFS015.001

PFS014.000

1938  18" x 20"  . .$475
Canada

PFS013.000

1934 . . . . . . . . . . . . . . . . . . . . . . $600

PTN127.001
1950s Tin . . . . . . . . . $200
PTN127.002 Porcelain . . .$300

PTN129.000
1959  11" x 12" . . . $625

PTN124.000
1933-34  3' . . . . . . . $1,000
Embossed

PTN128.001
1960s  3' . . . . . . $425
This sign was offered in a
number of different sizes.

PTN130.000
1951  11" x 12" . . . $700

PTN125.000
Early 1950s  3' . . . . $700
Embossed

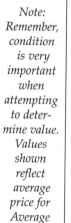

PTN126.000
1950s  3' . . . . . . . . . $500
Flat

*Note:
Remember,
condition
is very
important
when
attempting
to deter-
mine value.
Values
shown
reflect
average
price for
Average
condition.*

PTN131.000
1960s  30" x 35" . . . . $750

PTN132.000
1963  30" x 36" . . . . . . . . . . . . . . $850

PTN133.000
c.1955  13" x 20" . . . . . . . . $725

PTN134.000
1950s  11" x 12" . . . . . . . $700

# ARROW SIGNS

PMS006.000

c.1939 . . . . . . . . . . . . . . . . . . . . . . . $800
Wood and aluminum

PMS007.000

1939-41 . . . . . . . . . . . . . . . . $750
Masonite and aluminum

PMS008.001

1933 . . . . . $900
Plywood with applied
cardboard bottle, one-sided

PMS008.002

1933 . . . . . $1000
Plywood with applied
cardboard bottle, two-sided

PMS010.001

c.1940  Masonite . . . . . . . . . . . . . . . . $700
PMS010.002  Aluminum . . . . . . . . . . . $750

PMS009.000

1940s  30" . . . . . . . . . . . . . $1,300
Masonite

PMS011.000

c. 1940 . . . . . . . . . . . . . . . . . . . . $700
Masonite and aluminum

PTN135.000

1927-1929 7 3/4" x 30" . . . . . . . . . . . . . . . . . . . . . $800
Two-sided, I have seen at least two different types of these arrows.

— 224 —

# 1950s DISC (BUTTON) SIGNS

PMS012.001

24" . . . . . . . . . . . $650

With bottle

PMS014.000

18" . . . . . . . . . . . . . . . . . . . . . . . . . . . $850

With arrow

PMS013.001

24" . . . . . . . . . . $700

Bottle only

PMS013.002

36" . . . . . . . . . . . . . $550

Bottle only

Note: I have seen many different versions and sizes of these signs; this is just a sampling. Many were made in both regular and porcelain finish. They were used in the late 1950s and 1960s and many are still displayed on buildings today.

PMS017.001

36" . . . . . . . . . . . . . $325

PMS012.002

36" . . . . . . . . . . . . . . . . . . . . . $550

With bottle

PMS015.000

36" . . . . . . . . . . . . . $350

PMS016.002

24" . . . . . . . . . . $375

PMS017.002

24" . . . . . . . . . . $350

PMS074.000

18" . . . . . . . . . . . . . . . . . . . . . . $500

PMS016.001

36" . . . . . . . . . . . . . . . $350

Note: The prices shown here are for signs in Average condition. Porcelain versions are considered more valuable.

PMS017.003

12" . . . . . . . . . . $350

PMS016.003

12" . . . . . . . . . . $350

PMS017.004

16" . . . . . . . . . . $400

PMB005.000

1939 . . . . . . . . . . . . . $650

Wood and masonite

PMB006.000

1939 . . . . . . . . . . . . . . $650

Wood and masonite

PMB007.000

Late 1950s . . . . . . . . . . . $150

Wood

PMB009.000

1939 . . . . . . . . . . . . . $300

Tin

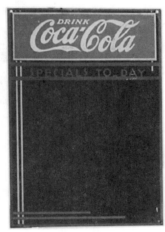

PMB008.000

1934 . . . . . . . . . . . . . . $250

Tin

PMB010.000

c.1960 . . . . . . . . . . . . . $175

Tin

PMB011.000

c.1960s . . . . . . . . . . . . $200

Tin

PMB012.000

c.1950s . . . . . . . . . . . . $125

Tin

PMB013.000

1970s . . . . . . . . . . . . . . $40

Tin

# MENU BOARDS

PMB014.000
1940s . . . . . . . . . . . $600
Wood with metal trim

PMB015.000
1950 . . . . . . . . . $325
Reverse Glass, metal frame

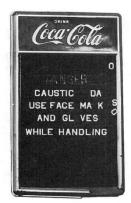

PMB016.000
1950s . . . . . . . . $125
Plastic

PMB017.000
1950s . . . . . . . . . . . $200
Cardboard

PMB018.000
1948 . . . . . . . . . $250
Cardboard

PMB019.000
1950s . . . . . . . . . $250
Cardboard

PMB020.000
1948 . . . . . . $250
Cardboard

PMB021.000
c.1960 . . . . . . $135

PMB022.000
1960s . . . . . . $200

PMB023.000
1960s . . . . . . . . . . $200
Plastic with clock

PMB024.000
1950s . . . . . . . . . $325
Enameled, Canada

PMB025.000
1960s . . . . . $300

PMB026.000
1950s . . . . $225

PMB027.000
1970s . . . . . . . . . . $35
Tin

PMB028.000
1929 . . . . . . . . . . . . . $600
Tin

# MENU BOARDS

PMB029.000

Late 1930s . . . . . . . . . . . . . . . . . . $675

Wood

PMB030.000

1960s . . . . . . . . . . . . . . . . . . . . . . . $285

Plastic and metal

PMB031.000

1970s . . . . . . . . . . . . . . . . . . . . . $45

Plastic

PMB032.000

1960s . . . . . . . . . . . . . . . . . . . . . . . . $150

Plastic

PMB033.000

c.1964 . . . . . . . . . . $175

PMB034.000

1960s . . . . . . . . . . . $150

PMB035.000

1950s . . . . . . . . $125

Enameled, Canada

PMB036.000

1970s . . . . . . . . . . . . . $25

Plastic

PMB037.000

1980s . . . . . . . . . . . . . . $15

Plastic and Cork Message Center

PMB038.001

1940s . . . . . . . . $100

French

(Canada)

PMB038.002

1940s . . . . . . . . $200

English

Note: Another version of this sign was used in the 1960s with the "Fishtail" logo.

PMS019.000

1939 . . . . . . . . . . . . . . . $800
Pedestal Sign, (has been dubbed "Lollipop" sign by some collectors). This is only an average price for this sign. They are often found rough and would be worth much less. (different versions used into the 1950s).

PMS018.000

1950s . . . . . . . . . . . . . . . . . . . .$1,300
"Policeman" crossing guard sign (showing both sides) with cast iron base. The price shown on this sign is an average price for a sign in Excellent condition. The sign in Near Mint to Mint condition could bring $1,800. I have heard of them selling for $2,500 and more. I personally feel this is too much. Without base deduct $100.

PMS020.000

1950s . . . . . . . . . . . . . . . . . . . . . . . . $750
School Zone Pedestal Sign 30", 2-sided porcelain on 5' high pedestal

PMS021.000

1950s-60s . . . . . . . . . . . . . . . . . . . . . $700
School Crossing Sign, wood with metal base

The name Kay Displays has become part of the every day vocabulary of today's Coca-Cola Collectors. The distinctive look of the signs produced by this company make them instantly recognizable by collectors. This unique look, and the quality that went into the production, have made the advertising pieces produced by Kay displays, Inc. among the most sought after of all Coca-Cola memorabilia.

Beginning in 1934 Kay Displays, Inc., a New York Company, produced signs and advertising displays for The Coca-Cola Company. While the stamping on the back of many of these signs state "Designed & Manufactured by Kay Displays, Inc." the company only designed these displays and did not do any actual manufacturing. The owner and president of the company, Mr. Kallenberg, (from which the company name derived) would supply manufacturers with designs and specifications for bids. Although a number of companies bid on and produced a portion of this material, Kallenberg had a good working relationship with a Grand Rapids manufacturer, American Seating Co., which eventually produced more and more of his designs. American Seating's Michigan plant manufactured school and church furniture as well as seating for auditoriums, stadiums and transportation. The company was perfect for the production of the designs submitted by Kallenberg, with large manufacturing facilities and high standards of quality which were essential for the quantity and quality required by The Coca-Cola Company. The relationship between Kallenberg's Kay Displays and American Seating obviously tightened in the mid-1930s with Kay Displays actually listing their manufacturing address as 901 Broadway Ave., N.W., Grand Rapids, Michigan, which is the address of American Seating Co. From 1934 to 1945 the Company name was "Kay Displays, Inc., and changed in 1945 to "Kay Inc." A number of addresses for Kay Displays, Inc., and Kay, Inc., executive and sales offices in New York are shown as 230 Park Ave., 119 W. 40th St., as well as 9 East 40th St., which seems to be the last New York address.

Prior to WWII the signs and displays designed by Kay and produced by American Seating Company seemed to run the gambit of material commonly used: embossed lithographed tin, stamped metal, ornate cutout tin, wood, cardboard, as well as composition material. With the approach of the war and constant demand for metal, for a country preparing to arm itself like it's never been armed before, the production of display advertising was limited to material that would not interfere with this buildup of arms.

The creative use of wood, cardboard, masonite, and composition by Kay Displays not only continued the high standards of past advertising that The Coca-Cola Company demanded, but actually improved the look of it, widening the possibilities for more elaborate designs. With the total elimination of the use of metal during the war for signs, and serving trays, the Kay Company and American Seating flourished with The Coca-Cola Company's need for advertising at an all time high. Many of the Kay Designs produced from December 7, 1941 to the end of the war reflected the patriotism and unity that swept the country. A pair of spread wings with a raised hand and bottle emblazoned many of the signs of this period, and are among the most desirable of all Kay creations. With the war over and the regained use of metal, the specialty signs of Kay Inc., slowly took a back seat to the quickly produced, inexpensive, and long-lasting tin signs that The Coca-Cola Company was now again using by the millions. In 1951 Kallenberg dissolved his company and ended his seventeen year relationship with American Seating Company, which by the way is still in business today.

But the Kay Company will live on forever in the hearts and collections of individuals who appreciate Coca-Cola Company advertising. Many of these beautiful and elaborate designs were contributed by the Kay Company. Throughout this book you will see many examples of Kay Displays' work, and even though not in their own section, there are probably more examples here than have ever been shown before.

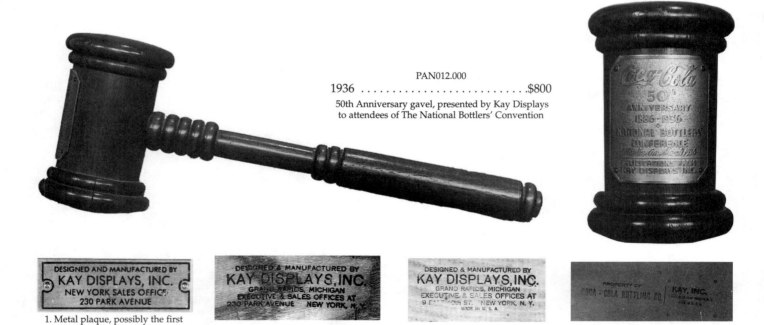

PAN012.000

1936 . . . . . . . . . . . . . . . . . . . . . . . . .$800

50th Anniversary gavel, presented by Kay Displays to attendees of The National Bottlers' Convention

1. Metal plaque, possibly the first Kay Display mark

2. 1934-1938, Stamped back

3. 1939-1945, Stamped back

4. 1945-1951, Stamped back

These four examples are marks used by Kay Displays from 1934 to 1951. These marks are either stamped on the back of the finished product, or a small metal plaque attached to the back. Take note that not all Kay signs are identified as such.

PMS023.P01

PMS023.P02

PMS023.P03

PMS023.S00

1930s . . . . . . . . . . . . . . . . . . . . . . . . $2500
Three-piece display, wood with metal trim

PMS084.000

Late 1930s  19" x 20"  . . . . . . . . . . . $1500
Wood with metal trim and bottle

PMS085.000

1940s  13"  . . . . . . . . . . . . . . . . . . . . $1300
Composition

PMS086.000

1930s  17" x 30"  . . . . . . . . . . . . . . . . $900
Wood with metal trim (logo is wood cutout)

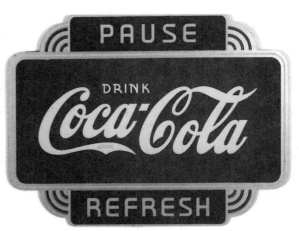

PMS087.000

Late 30s-early 40s  10 1/2" x 14"  . . . . $750
Wood

**PMS022.P01**
1930s   12" x 32" . . . . . . . . . . . . . . $1,200
Kay Displays, wood with metal trim

**PMS089.000**
1940s   14" x 18" . . . . . . . . . . . . . $1,500
Kay Displays, wood with metal trim

**PMS024.000**
1950s   15" x 19" . . . . . . . . . . . . . . . $475
Kay Displays, wood with rope trim

**PMS025.000**
1939-40   14 1/2" x 19" . . . . . . . . $650
Kay Displays, wood and tin

**PMS023.P02**
1930s   9" x 11" . . . . . . . . $600
Kay Displays, wood with metal trim,
part of three-piece display

**PMS026.000**
1940s   15 1/2" x 16" . . . . . . $750
Kay Displays, wood with metal emblem

| PMS026.S01 | PMS026.S02 | PMS026.S03 | PMS026.S04 | PMS026.S05 |

**PMS026.S00 Complete set 1950s** . . . . . . . . . . . . . . . . . . . . . . . . . . . . . . . . . . . . . . . . $1,100
Sports Festoon, five pieces, cardboard and foil paper

| PMS027.S01 | PMS027.S02 | PMS027.S03 |

| PMS027.S04 | PMS027.S05 | |

**PMS027.S00** 1940s Masonite, connected together with rope . . . $2,000
Individual pieces . . . . . . . . . . . . . . . . . . . . . . . . . . . . . $275 Each
Airplane Display (festoon) 5 pieces, 3-D

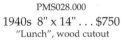

PMS029.000
Late 1930s  11" x 39"  . . . . . . . . . . . .  $750
Kay Displays, wood cutout

PMS028.000
1940s  8" x 14" . . . $750
"Lunch", wood cutout

PMB039.000
Late 1930s  20" x 39"  . . . . . . . . . . . .  $850
Wood menu board

PMS030.000
Late 1930s  19" x 20"  . . . . . . . . . . . .  $1,500
Wood with metal trim

e who enter here on refreshment bent — shall welcome be and forth with blessings sent •

PMS031.000
c.1940s  11" x 39"  . . . .  $1,000
Wood and masonite with gold trim

PMS033.000
1940s  12" x 16 1/2"  . . .  $600
Wood and metal

PMS032.000
Late 1930s  19" x 19"  . . . . . . . . .  $2,000
Wood with metal trim, Rare

PMS034.000
1940s  12"  . . . . . . .  $500
Wood

PMS035.000
1940s  13"  . . . . . . . .  $800
Composition

PMS036.S01

PMS036.S02

PMS036.S03

PMS036.S04

PMS036.S05

PMS036.S06

1940s . . . . . . . . . . . . . . . . . . $350 Each    PMS036.S00  Complete set . . . . . . . . . . . . . . . . . . . $2,500

Masonite and wood signs

Note: During the late 1930s and 1940s, masonite and wood were used on many signs to advertise Coca-Cola. Kay Displays was one of the major manufacturers of these speciality signs. You will find their name stamped on the back of many wood, masonite, and fiberboard signs of this period.

PMS037.000

1930s . . . . . . . . . . . . . . . . . . . . . . . . . . $425

Wood with metal brackets delivery truck roof sign

PMS038.000

1950s-1960s . . . . . . . . . . . . . . . . . . . $425

Wood and metal, two-sided

PMS039.000

Late 1930s  36"   . . . . . . . . . . . . . . . . $550

Wood

PMS040.000

1941  14" x 36"  . . . . . . . . . . . . . . . . . . $800

Wood and masonite

PMS041.P01

1960s  7" x 16"  . . . . . . . . . . . . . . . . . $250

Masonite and plastic with rope, (this in only part of a larger piece)

# MISCELLANEOUS SMALL SIGNS

PTN136.000

Late 1930s 8" . . . $525

Tin (with ribbon) hanging sign

PTN137.000

Late 1930s 10" . . . . . . . . $750

Embossed tin, cardboard back
(bottle in circle, decal)

PMS090.000

1940s 11" x 11" . . . $225

Masonite

PCS379.000

1921 6" x 11 1/4" . . . . . . . . . . . $2,000

Celluloid, black with gold trim, mfg. by
Whitehead & Hoag Co., Newark, NJ

PTN101.001                    PTN101.000

1930s 5 3/4" x 17 3/4" . . . . . . . $300 Each

Embossed tin, two different examples

PTN023.000

1947 12 3/4" . . . . . . . . . . . . . . . . . $1,000

Tin, embossed edge, Coca-Cola Export

PTN138.000

Late 1930s 10" . . . . . . . . . . . . . . . . $625

Embossed tin, cardboard back (bottle in circle, decal)
Note: Decal must be nice to warrant this price.

PMS091.000

1950s 6" x 6" . . . $65

PTN139.001
1931
4 1/2" x 12 1/2" . . . $550

Embossed tin

PMS088.000

1934 15" x 20" . . . . . . $650

Wood, Kay Displays, (National
Recovery Administration)

PMS022.000

1950s 6 1/2" x 16" . . . . $275

Paper over cardboard, German

PTN139.002
1931
6" x 13 1/2" . . . . . . $625

Embossed tin

— 235 —

PTN110.001      PTN110.000      PTN110.0002

1950s ..................... $300 each

Button calendar signs, three different examples

PTN088.000

1963 ...................... $375

Calendar sign

PMS108.000

1950s  6" x 11 3/4" .............. $125

License plate, red and white

PMS109.000

1950s  5 1/2" x 13 1/4" ............. $225

Tin sign, embossed, red and white

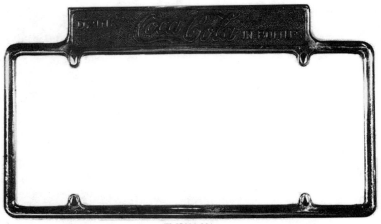

PMS099.001

1940s-1950s ................... $425

License plate holder, Dura Products Mfg. Co.,
Canton, OH

PMS110.000

1930s  5" x 5" ................... $275

License plate reflector sign

PMS092.000

1930s . . . . . . . . . . . . . . . . . . . . . . . $850

Cooler sign, white porcelain with black trim

PMS093.000

1920s  17" . . . . . . . . . . . . . . . . . . . . . $585

"Radiator Plate", chrome

PMS094.000

1950s . . . . . . . . . . . . . . . . . . . . . . . $850

"Spinner" Note: This is a top sign for vending machines, note four suction cups on base.

PMS096.000
1950s-1960s . . . $250
Parking meter sign

PMS095.000

1930s . . . . . . . . . . . . . . . . . . . . . . . $600

USA wire and wood, Kay Displays

*Note: Many of the special signs produced during the late 1930s and 1940s were made by Kay Displays. You will find their name stamped on the back of many wood, masonite, and fiberboard signs of this period.*

PMS097.P01

1930s . . . . . . . . . . . . . . . . . . . . . . $225

Tin and wood, Kay Displays

PMS098.001          PMS098.002          PMS098.003

1960s-70s . . . . . . . . . . . . . . . . . . $40 Each

License plates, three different examples

PMS099.002

1940s-1950s . . . . . . . . . . . . . . . . . . . . . $425

License plate holder

PMS100.000

1940s-50s . . . . . . . . . . . . . . . . . . . . $185

License plate sign

PMS101.S02                    PMS101.S01                    PMS101.S03

1932  Small size . . . . . $450 Each    Large size . . . . . $750    PMS101.S00 Complete set as shown . . . . . $2,000

Floral boxes, pressed paper and cardboard

Note: The bottle version of these signs is certainly the best looking, but also the most common.

PMS102.B00
c.1950s 9" . . . . . . . . . . . . . . . . . . . . . $350
Sign, celluloid, mint in original instruction envelope

PMS102.000
c.1950s . . . . . . . . . . . . . . $225
Sign only

PMS103.000
c.1940s . . . . . . . . . . . $275

PMS104.000
c.1940s . . . . . . . . . . . . $325

PMS107.000
1950s . . . . . . . . . . . . . $750
Plastic "Bottle Topper".
The two small gold bottles on this piece are original and must be attached to be complete.

PMS105.000
c.1950s . . . . . . . . . . . . $800

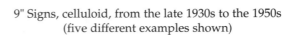
9" Signs, celluloid, from the late 1930s to the 1950s
(five different examples shown)

PMS106.000
1938 . . . . . . . . . . . $325

PMS042.S01

PMS042.S02

PMS042.S03

PMS042.S04

1960s . . . . . . . . . . . $100 Each      PMS042.S00 Complete set of 4 . . . . . . . . . . . . . . . $500

3-D cutout "Race Cars"

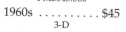

PMS043.000

1950  12" x 14" . . . . . . . . $125

PMS045.000

1960s . . . . . . . . . . $45

3-D

PMS047.000

1950s-60s  5'7" . . . . . . . . . . . . . . . . . $350

Plastic with raised letters and aluminum ring

PMS044.000

1960s . . . . . . . . . . . . . . . . . . $45

3-D

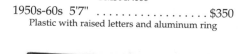

PMS046.000

1970s . . . . . . . . . . . . . $18

3-D

PMS048.000

1960s  10" x 18" . . . . . . . . . . . . . $20

PMS049.000

1960s  9" x 32" . . . . . . . . . . . . . . . . . $175

"Pop Corn"

PMS050.001              PMS050.002

1960s . . . . . . . . . . . . . . . . . . . . . . $40 Each

3-D cutout

PMS051.000

1960s  14" x 20" . . . . . . . . . . . . . . . . $20

# DOOR PUSH BARS

PMS052.000 1930s . . . . .$475    PMBS052.P01 Porcelain center piece only . . . . .$285

Porcelain (complete with wrought iron end pieces) Note: This porcelain push bar is very rarely found complete with wrought iron end pieces.

PMS053.002

1939-41  Tin, short version  . . . . . . . . . .$525

PMS059.000

1950s  Porcelain . . . . . . . . . . . . . . . . . . . .$200

PMS053.001

1939-41  Tin, long version . . . . . . . . . . .$500

PMS054.000

1950s  Porcelain . . . . . . . . . . . . . . . . . . . .$450

PMS055.000

1950s  Porcelain . . . . . . . . . . . . . . . . . . . .$425

PMS056.000

c.1960  Porcelain  . . . . . . . . . . . . . . . . . .$350

PMS057.000

c.1959  Porcelain  . . . . . . . . . . . . . . . . . .$375

PMS058.000

1950s  Porcelain . . . . . . . . . . . . . . . . . . . .$400

PMS060.000

1950s-60s  Adjustable  . . . . . . . . . . . . . . .$175

PMS061.001

1950s  Porcelain . . . . . . . . . . . . . . . . . . . .$185

PMS061.002

1950s  Porcelain (French) Canada  . . . . . .$85

PMS062.000

1970s-80s  (French) Canada  . . . . . . . . . .$30

PPC029.000
Pre-1900  8" x 24" . . . . . . . . . . . .$10,000
Porcelain, Rare

PPC030.000
1920s  6" x 15" . . . . . . . . . . . . . . . .$1,800
Porcelain, Rare

PMS083.000
1950s  16" . . . . . . . . . . . . . . . . . . . .$1,600
Button sign with arrow, white , Rare

PCS396.000
1920s  6" x 12" . . . . . . . . . . . . . . . .$1,000
Hanging sign, celluloid.
Photo Courtesy: Larry Dikeman

PGS031.003

1932  12" x 20"  . . . . . . . . . . . . . . . . $4,000
Reverse glass sign, red version, with chrome frame
and chain, Rare, (Brunhoff Mfg.)
Note: There is also a black version of this sign.

PMS023.P02

1930s  9" x 11"  . . . . . . . . . . . . . . . . . $600
Wood with metal trim, Kay Displays

PTN022.001

1926  8" x 11"  . . . . . . . . . . . . . . . . . $2,600
Tin

PTN021.000

1927  8 1/2" x 11"  . . . . . . . . . . . . . . . $2,400
Tin

PTN024.002

1922  4" x 8"  . . . . . . . . . . . . . . . . . $650
Tin, embossed

PCD149.000

1920s  7" x 12"  . . . . . . . . . . . . . . . . $550
Cardboard

PGS034.000
1920s  13" x 19"  . . . . . . . . . . . . . . .$1,800
Diekman's reverse glass with metal frame

PLS014.000
Late 1930s  12" x 14"  . . . . . . . . . . . .$3,900
Reverse glass, "The Brunhoff Mfg. Co."

PCL026.000
1939/40  17 1/2"  . . . . . . . . . . . . . .$3,600
"Spinner" neon clock

PLS048.000
1939  15" x 20"  . . . . . . . . . . . . . . . .$3,600
Neon hanging sign, Rare

PTO011.001
1903  15" x 18 $^1/_2$" . . . . . . . . . . . . .$8,000
Hilda Clark serving tray

PTO011.002
1903  9 $^1/_4$" . . . . . . . . . . . . . . . . . . .$6,500
Hilda Clark serving tray

PTT011.001
1903  6" . . . . . . . . . . . . . . . . . . . . .$1,800
Hilda Clark change tray

PTN141.000
1903  15" x 18 $^1/_2$" . . . . . . . . . . . .$16,000
Hilda Clark sign, tin with embossed edge, Rare.
Photo Courtesy: James D. Julia, Inc.

# SERVING TRAYS/CHANGE TRAYS

*Note: The condition on these early trays is very important. Values shown are based on 8.5 or better. Every defect will effect the condition. Values will drop considerably as the condition goes down.*

PTO008.000
1900  9 1/4" . . . . . . . .$9,000
Hilda Clark

PTO009.000
1901  9 1/2" . . . . . . . . . . . .$7,500
Hilda Clark

PTT009.001
1901  6 1/4" . . . . . . . . . .$3,200
Hilda Clark change tray
(wide rim and deeper variation)

PTO016.001
1907  10 1/2" x 13 1/4" . . . . . .$3,800

PTT009.000
1901  6" . . . . . . . . . . . . . . . .$2,800
Hilda Clark change tray

PTT016.000
1907  4 1/4" x 6" . . . . .$850
Change tray

PTO015.000
1906  10 1/2" x 13 1/4"  . . .$3,500

# SERVING TRAYS/CHANGE TRAYS

★★★ Indicates this tray has been reproduced

PTR019.000
1910 . . . . . . . . . . . . . . .$1,600
★★★

PTT019.000
1910 . . . . . . . . .$750
Change tray

PTT024.000
1913 . . . . . . . . .$600
Change tray

PTR024.000
1913 . . . . . . . . . . . . . .$950
★★★

PTR027.000
1920 . . . . . . . . . . . .$1,100

PTT027.000
1920 . . . . . . . . . . . . . . .$475
Change tray

PTO027.000
1920 13 $^{1}/_{4}$" x 16 $^{1}/_{2}$" . . . . . . . . . . . . .$950

Note: Rectangular serving trays shown are all 10 $^{1}/_{2}$" x 13 $^{1}/_{4}$". Oval change trays are 4 $^{1}/_{4}$" x 6". Values shown are based on example in 8.5 condition or better. As condition drops, so does the value.

PTR026.000
1916 8 $^{1}/_{2}$" x 19" . . . .$500

PTT026.000
1916 . . . . . . . . . . . . .$275
Change tray

# SERVING TRAYS
★★★ indicates that this tray has been reproduced.

PTR028.000

1921 ........................$1,100

PTR029.000

1922 ........................$950

PTR033.000

1926 ........................$1,000
★★★

Note: All trays shown are 10 1/2" x 13 1/4". Values are based on example in 8.5 condition or better.

PTR034.000

1927 ........................$950

PTR039.000

1930 ........................$600
(Bottle sales)

PTR040.000

1931 ........................$1,000

PTR041.000

1932 ........................$900

# SERVING TRAYS
*** indicates that this tray has been reproduced.

PTR042.000

1933 . . . . . . . . . . . . . . . . . . . . . .$750

PTR044.000

1935 . . . . . . . . . . . . . . . . . . . . . .$475

PTR045.000

1936 . . . . . . . . . . . . . . . . . . . . . .$450

Note: All trays shown are 10 ½" x 13 ¼". Values are based on examples in 8.5 condition or better. Trays in lesser condition will be worth less.

PTR043.000

1934 . . . . . . . . . . . . . . . . . . . . . . . . .$1,000

***

PTR048.000

1939 . . . . . . . . . . . . . . . . . . . . . .$350

PTR050.000

1941 . . . . . . . . . . . . . . . . . . . . . .$385

PTR051.000

1942 . . . . . . . . . . . . . . . . . . . . . .$385

# SERVING TRAYS

All trays shown on this page are 10 $\frac{1}{2}$" x 13 $\frac{1}{4}$"
★★★ indicates that this tray has been reproduced

PTR052.000

1950-52 . . . . . . . . . . . . . . . . . . . . . . . .$75
★★★ (screened background)

PTR052.001

1950-52 . . . . . . . . . . . . . . . . . . . . . . .$225
(solid background)

PTR053.000

1953-60 . . . . . . . . . . . . . . . . . . . . . .$60

PTM012.000

1957 . . . . . . . . . . . . . . . . . . . . . . . . . .$150

PTM010.000

1957 . . . . . . . . . . . . . . . . . . . . . . . . .$300

PTM009.000

1957 . . . . . . . . . . . . . . . . . . . . . . . . .$175

PTM045.000

c.1940s . . . . . . . . . . . . . . . . . . . . . . .$600
Mexico

PCB013.000

c.1907  7" . . . . . . . . . . . . . . . .$1,500

Change receiver, glass, The Empire
Ornamental Glass Co., NY

PCB015.000

1931  7 $1/4$" . . . . . . . . . . . . . . . . . . . .$300

Sandwich plate, Mfg. by E. M. Knowles
China Co.

PMD013.001

1950s  . . . . . . . . . . . . . . . . . .$1,000

Sprite Boy napkin holder, Rare

PCB027.000

1930s  7 $1/4$" . . . . . . . . . . . . . . . . . . . .$900

Sandwich plate, Rare Variation

PCB023.000

1969  . . . . . . . . . . . . . . .$175

Frozen Coca-Cola change receiver,
plastic

PTY153.000

1969  14" . . . . . . . . . .$100

Frozen Coca-Cola stuffed doll

PSP044.B00

c.1930s  . . . . . . . . . . . . . . . . .$75

Door lock, in original box

PTC006.000

c.1932 . . . . . . . . . . . . . . . . . . . . . . . . .$975

No. 171 Metalcraft truck, with rubber wheels

PTC050.000

1949-50 . . . . . . . . . . . . . . . . . . . . . .$1,800

Goso tractor trailer, wind-up, Very Rare

PTC019.000

1950s  5 1/2" . . . . . . . . . . . . . . . . . . . .$1,000

GMC truck

PTC049.000

Early 1950s  7" . . . . . . . . . . . . . . . . . .$475

Marx truck

PSS011.000

1929 . . . . . . . . . . . .$5,500

Glascock salesman sample cooler.

1929 . . . . . . . . . . .$12,000

Mint in original carrying case

PTY160.000

1930s . . . . . . . .$650

Child's baseball glove,
"Drink Coca-Cola in
Bottles", Rare

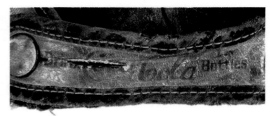

Close-up of baseball glove strap.

PTC008.000

1948 . . . . . . . . . . . . . . . . . . . . . . . . $3,500

Buddy-L, wood, Rare

PTC009.000

Early 1940s . . . . . . . . . . . . . . . . . .$1,600

Smith Miller, wood and metal, with wood blocks

PTC007.000

c.1934 . . . . . . . . . . . . . . . . . . . . . . . $2,500

Metalcraft, long front, rubber wheels, Rare

PTC016.000

c.1949 . . . . . . . . . . . . . . . . . . . . . . . $2,500

Goso, Rare

PTC075.000

1948-1950 . . . . . . . . . . . . . . . . . . . $2,900

Italian, wood, tin, and Bakelite, Very Rare

PTC056.000

1950s . . . . . . . . . . . . . . . . . . . . . . . $1,200

Marx No. 21 (Canadian version), Very Rare

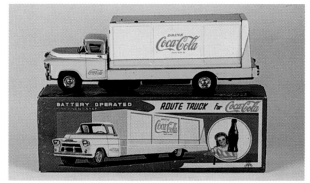

PTC041.B00

1950s-60s . . . . . . . . . . . . . . . . . . . . . $550

Battery operated, red and white

PTC042.B00

1950s-60s . . . . . . . . . . . . . . . . . . . . . $425

Battery operated, yellow and white

# TOY TRUCKS

PTC015.B00

1950s . . . . . . . . . . . . . . . . . . . . . . . $1,200
Marx

PTC035.B02

c.1954 . . . . . . . . . . . . . . . . . . . . . . . $550
Marx

PTC034.B00

1950s . . . . . . . . . . . . . . . . . . . . . . . $750
Marx, plastic

PTC013.B00

1950s . . . . . . . . . . . . . . . . . . . . . . . $825
Marx, Sprite Boy

PTC032.B00

1950s . . . . . . . . . . . . . . . . . . . . . . . $600
Marx, plastic

PTC031.B00

1950s . . . . . . . . . . . . . . . . . . . . . . . $675
Marx, plastic

PTC058.000

1959 . . . . . . . . . . . . . . . . . . . . . . . $725
Buddy-L, orange

PTC060.B00

1960s . . . . . . . . . . . . . . . . . . . . . . . $425
Buddy-L

Note: This Japanese R2-D2 radio is a rare, limited edition prize connected with collecting Coke bottle caps. The newspaper ad (shown below) which shows the offer would not have much value alone, but would certainly enhance the value of the radio.

**PTY158.B00**

1978 . . . . . . . . . . . . . . . . . . . . . .$1,500
Japanese R2-D2 Coca-Cola radio, in original box. Made by Fuji Electric, toy made by Takara, Rare

Japanese newspaper ad showing the radio offer.

**PTY133.001**

1950s 12" . . . . . . . . . . . . . . .$1,000
Buddy Lee Doll, plastic

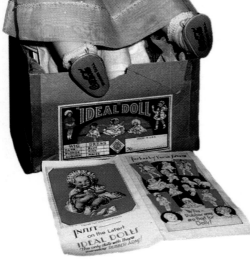

**PTY159.B00**

1930s . . . . . . . . . . . . . . . . . . . . . . .$3,000
Ideal "Wonder Doll" in original box and insert brochure. Coca-Cola on bottom of doll's shoes. This doll is rare, found with original box is very rare.

**PTY116.B00**

1980s . . . . . . . . . . . . . . . . . . . . . . . .$150
Cobot in original box

PMS065.000
1930s ...... $325
Bottle shaped,
aluminum

PMS066.001
1950s ...... $225
Bottle shaped,
plastic and metal

PMS067.000
1930s-40s ..... $275
Door handle,
metal and plastic

PMS063.S01          PMS063.S02

c.1905   3" x 8" Push .............. $650

2 1/4" x 8" Pull .................. $650

PMS063.S00 Push/Pull Set ........ $1,500

Aluminum Push/Pull Plates,
Mfg. by NJ Aluminum Co., Newark, NJ

*Note: Both of these door handles have been reproduced in cast iron. There is no known original cast iron door handle.*

PMS068.001
1930s ............ $200
Porcelain "Palm" press, Canada

PMS069.001
1940s-50s  4" x 6" ... $200
"Pull Plate", tin

PMS070.001
1940s-50s  4" x 8" ... $325
"Push Plate", flat, porcelain

PMS071.001
1960s  4" x 6" ... $135
"Pull Plate"

1930s Push Plates, porcelain, Canada

PMS072.001
$100

PMS073.004
$100

PMS073.003
$100

PMS073.002
$250

PMS073.001
$250

When I first started collecting memorabilia of The Coca-Cola Company, the serving tray was the main point of interest. It seemed that everyone's collection was judged by which trays you had and which trays you needed. There has been a fascination with the tin lithographed serving tray ever since the first day people became interested in collecting Coca-Cola, and early price guides on the subject reflect this fact. While other items were shown, of course, the most important subject was the serving tray. Even The Coca-Cola Company archives produced a book in 1970 called *Catalog of Metal Service Trays and Art Plates Since 1898*, which seems to be the first book on the subject, and in fact, on Coca-Cola collecting in general.

While much has been learned since the 1970 book and other early price guides and reference books, one thing remains the same: The serving tray is still king. While many collectors could care less, I find that the mainstream collector is still fascinated with the trays, and many are trying for the seemingly impossible feat of owning one of every tray known to exist.

While it is quite possible that earlier trays do exist, the so-called 1897 "Victorian Girl" tray has always been thought of as the first and certainly the most important and most difficult to find of the trays.

Because of the importance of the tray, I find collectors have placed more emphasis on the condition of trays, more so than other pieces. The typical tray collector considers every little scratch and dent on the tray. This is why it is so very hard for a book like this to place values on these trays, and I must stress, once again, that the prices you see here are just GUIDE prices. In other words, what I call the average price, considering a nice clean, presentable tray (excellent or better condition). If the tray is rough, the price will be lower, and in cases of the more common trays, much lower. If the tray is in mint condition, it certainly can be higher. Please don't forget that just because a tray might have sold for a "fortune" at an auction, that certainly doesn't mean that price is the true market value. It is very possible that two people just got carried away with the moment.

The earliest known trays were basically 9 1/4" round and made from 1897 through 1901. In 1903, there was also a 9 1/4" round tray, but another larger oval tray was used. In 1905, The Coca-Cola Company produced a smaller oval tray. This seemed to have continued until 1909 with a series of medium and larger oval trays. Tip or change trays vary in sizes from 4" to 6" circular types until 1907, when they became a standard 4 1/4" x 6" oval until 1920, after which they were no longer produced.

Beginning in 1910, a rectangular tray was produced, measuring 10 1/2" x 13 1/4", it became standard and was used right into the early 1960s. Between 1910 and 1919, only three of these rectangular trays were produced: in 1910, 1913, and 1914. In 1916, a completely different tray was produced measuring 8 1/2" x 19". Subsequently, no trays were made until after World War I. Then, in 1920, production resumed on a regular basis with at least one tray each year until 1942, and then not another until after World War II.

Most of these rectangular trays have turned up in sufficient numbers to keep collectors happy. However, most collectors strive for that mint or at least near mint example, which is not always that easy to find. I have always been one who believes in the "upgrade" system of collecting, which simply means that if you need a tray from a particular year, buy it even though it might not be in the most desirable condition. When you find one in better condition, you can sell the first one and eventually your collection will be fine tuned to your liking. Sometimes, waiting for that perfect example of a tray seems to take forever.

After World War II and into the 1950s and 1960s, the production of trays was, at best, spotty and irregular. TV trays, plastic, and commemorative trays replaced the popular and beautiful Coca-Cola girls of the 1920s and 1930s.

Displaying trays has always been a minor problem with collectors. Everything from magnets, plate hangers, and glue and string has been used, some successfully and others not. I personally think that the best method of display is a narrow shelf with an edge, simply leaning the tray on it. This works fine, with no chance of falling. But whichever way you decide to display your trays, remember that taking care of them is much more important. The first and the most important thing is humidity. Do not store or display your trays in a humid area. Over a period of time the trays will become slightly pitted, and this pitting will eventually get worse. This presents a special problem for Coke collectors, many of whom display their collection in game rooms or bars that are in the cellar. This could be a problem unless you have taken steps to reduce the humidity (a dehumidifier, for example). The other big problem with trays is dust. It always seems to accumulate on the bottom rim of the tray. If this dust is allowed to build up, it will be difficult to clean and could certainly detract from the tray. If trays are not cleaned and dusted properly, you will get a series of light scratches. With all of this warning, I am trying to stress the fact that you must take care of your trays if you want to retain their value. Also, remember that if you will be moving or storing trays, always put them into clear plastic bags. This is the best way to protect them from scratching.

So, whether you simply collect particular trays that strike your fancy, or you strive to own every example known, it is a fact that the serving tray is the classic Coca-Cola collectible.

# SERVING TRAYS

Note: Remember, the prices shown on these early trays are based on examples in Excellent or Better condition. Trays in Below Average condition, even rare examples, will not command a high price.

PTO005.000

1897  9 1/4" . . . . . . . . . . . . . . . . . . . $25,000

PTO007.000

1899  9 1/4" . . . . . . . . . . . . . . . . . . . $15,000

PTO011.001

1903  15" x 18 1/2" . . . . . . . . . . . . . . $8,500

PTO011.002

1903  9 1/4" . . . . . . . . . . . . . . . . . . . $7,000

PTO014.001

1905  10 1/2" x 13" . . . . . . . . . . $4,800

With glass

PTO014.002

1905  10 1/2" x 13" . . . . . . $4,800

With bottle

PTO008.000

1900 9 1/4" . . . . . . . . . . . . . . . . . . . $9,000

PTO009.000

1901 9 1/2" . . . . . . . . . . . . . . . . . . . $7,500

PTO012.000

1903  9 3/4" . . . . . . . . . . . . . . . . . . . $8,000
"Bottle Tray"

PTT012.000

1903  5 1/2" . . . . . . . . . . . . . . . . . $8,000
"Bottle Tray", Tip Tray

*Note: Both 1903 "Bottle Trays" are considered rare and sought after by collectors. However, to warrant the prices listed below they must be in similar condition. Both "Bottle Trays" produced by Chas. W. Shonk Co. Litho., Chicago, IL.*

PTO017.000

c.1908 . . . . . . . . . . . . . . . . . . . . . . $6,500
"Topless" Tray

PVA001.000

c.1908  In original gold frame . . . . . . $1,800

Without frame . . . . . . . . . . . . . . . . . $700

"Topless" Vienna Art Plate. This plate found in the original shadow box, could add as much as 50% to the value.

Reverse side of art plate imprinted in center.

# SERVING TRAYS

PTO016.001

1907  10 1/2" x 13 1/4"  . . . $3,800

PTO015.000

1906  10 1/2" x 13 1/4"  . . . . . $3,500

PTO018.001

1909  10 1/2" x 13 1/4"  . . . . . $2,800

PTO016.002

1907  13 1/2" x 16 1/2"  . . . . . . . . . . $6,000

PTR026.000

1916  8 1/2" x 19"  . . . . . $500

PTO018.002

1909  13 1/2" x 16 1/2"  . . . . . . . . . . $4,000

PTO024.000

1913  12 1/4" x 15 1/4"  . . . . . . . $800

PTO025.000

1914  12 1/2" x 15 1/4"  . . . . . $650

*Note: Beware of reproductions of both the 1916 and 1914 trays shown here. See the repro. section in the back of this book.*

PTO027.000

1920  13 1/4" x 16 1/2"  . . . . . . . $950

# VIENNA ART PLATES
## c.1908-1912

PVA002.000

Framed . . . . . . . . . . . . . . . . . . . . . . . $550
Without frame . . . . . . . . . . . . . . . . . $275

PVA004.000

Framed . . . . . . . . . . . . . . . . . . . . . . . $675
Without frame . . . . . . . . . . . . . . . . . $325

PVA007.000

Framed . . . . . . . . . . . . . . . . . . . . . . . $675
Without frame . . . . . . . . . . . . . . . . . $325

*Note: Framed price refers to original ornate gold frame. Plates found in original glass shadow box could add as much as 50% to the value.*

Reverse side of art plate
imprinted in center.

*Note: These prices are for plates in Excellent or Better condition. As that condition goes down, so does the value.*

PVA006.000

Framed . . . . . . . . . . . $950
Without frame . . . . . . $600
Rare

*Note: These plates can be found with other or no advertising on the back. These plates have much less value.*

PVA003.000

Framed . . . . . . . . . . . . . . . . . . . . . . . $675
Without frame . . . . . . . . . . . . . . . . . $325

PVA005.000

Framed . . . . . . . . . . . . . . . . . . . . . . . $675
Without frame . . . . . . . . . . . . . . . . . $325

PVA008.000

Framed . . . . . . . . . . . . . . . . . . . . . . . $950
Without frame . . . . . . . . . . . . . . . . . $600
Rare

# CHANGE TRAYS
Oval change trays are 4 1/4" x 6"

PTT008.000

1900  6" . . . . . . . . . . . . $4,500

PTT009.000

1901  6" . . . . . . . . . . . . $2,800

PTT011.001

1903  6" . . . . . . . . . . . $1,800

PTT011.002

1903  4" . . . . . . . . . . . $2,600

PTT015.000

1906  4" . . . . . . . . . . . . $900

PTT016.000

1907 . . . . . . . . . . $850

PTT018.000

1909 . . . . . . . . . . $650

PTT019.000

1910  . . . . . . . . . $750

PTT024.000

1913 . . . . . . . . . . . $600

PTT025.000

1914 . . . . . . . . . . . $325

PTT026.000

1916 . . . . . . . . . . . $275

PTT027.000

1920 . . . . . . . . . . . . $475

# SERVING TRAYS

All trays shown on this page are 10 1/2" x 13 1/4"   ★★★ Indicates that this tray has been reproduced.

PTR019.000

1910 . . . . . . . $1,600
★★★

PTR024.000

1913 . . . . . . . . $950
★★★

PTR025.000

1914 . . . . . . . . $900

PTR027.000

1920 . . . . . . . . . $1,100
★★★

PTR028.000

1921 . . . . . . . . $1,100

PTR029.000

1922 . . . . . . . . $950

PTR030.000

1923 . . . . . . . . $550

PTR031.001

1924 . . . . . . . . $1,200
Red (maroon) rim version

PTR031.002

1924 . . . . . . . . $800
Brown rim version

PTR032.000

1910 . . . . . . . $575
★★★

PTR033.000

1926 . . . . . . . . $1,000
★★★

Note: The copyright date on some Coca-Cola trays refers to the copyright date of the artwork, not the actual usage date which was usually the following year.

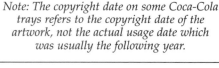

PTR034.000

1927 . . . . . . . . . . . . $950

PTR035.000

1928 . . . . . . . $900
Fountain sales

PTR036.000

1928 . . . . . . . . $900
Bottle sales

PTR037.001

1929 . . . . . . . $600
Fountain sales

PTR037.002

1929 . . . . . . . $750
Bottle sales

PTR038.000

1930 . . . . . . . $550
Fountain sales

PTR039.000

1930 . . . . . . . $600
Bottle sales

PTR040.000

1931 . . . . . . . $1,000

Note: Prices are based on trays in Excellent condition. Trays in Near Mint to Mint condition will be worth more and trays in Lesser condition will be worth less.

# SERVING TRAYS

All trays shown on this page are 10 ½" x 13 ¼"     ★★★ Indicates that this tray has been reproduced.

PTR041.000
1932 . . . . . . . . . $900

PTR042.000
1933 . . . . . . . . . $750

PTR043.000
1934 . . . . . . . . . . . . . . $1,000
★★★

PTR044.000
1935 . . . . . . . . . . $475

PTR045.000
1936 . . . . . . . . . . $450

PTR046.000
1937 . . . . . . . . . $350
★★★

PTR047.000
1938 . . . . . . . . . . $285

PTR048.000
1939 . . . . . . . . . $350

PTR049.000
1940 . . . . . . . . . . . $350

PTR050.000
1941 . . . . . . . . . $385

PTR051.000
1942 . . . . . . . . . $385

PTM012.000
1957 . . . . . . . . . . . $150

PTR053.000
1953-1960 . . . . . $60

PTM011.000
1957 . . . . . . . . $175

PTM010.000
1957 . . . . . . . . $300

PTR055.001
1961    . . . . . . . . . . .$30
There are at least three different
versions of this tray.

PTR054.000
1958 . . . . . . . . . . . .$40

PTR052.000
1950-1952
$75
★★★

Screened back-
ground Note: This
tray was the first
tray produced after
WWII and it has
been misdated 1943
and 1948.

PTR052.001
1950-1952
$225

Solid background

# TV TRAYS
$13^{1}/_{2}$" x $18^{1}/_{4}$"

PTM013.000

1956 . . . . . . . . . . . . . . . . . . . . . . . . $10

PTM014.000

1958 . . . . . . . . . . . . . . . . . . . . . . . $50

PTM015.000

1960 . . . . . . . . . . . . . . . . . . . . . . $100

PTM016.000

1961 . . . . . . . . . . . . . . . . . . . . . . $15

PTM017.000

1962 . . . . . . . . . . . . . . . . . . . . . . $15

PTM018.000

c.1963 . . . . . . . . . . . . . . . . . . . . . $85

PTM019.000

1969 . . . . . . . . . . . . . . . . . . . . . . $60

Mexican

PTM020.000

1968 . . . . . . . . . . . . . . . . . . . . . . $60

PTM021.000

1963 . . . . . . . . . . . . . . . . . . . . . . $50

PTM022.000

1970s . . . . . . . . . . . . . . . . . . . . . $20

Mexican

PTM023.000

1970s . . . . . . . . . . . . . . . . . . . . . $20

Mexican

PTM024.000

c.1959 . . . . . . . . . . . . . . . . . . . $125

"Drive In"

# MEXICAN TRAYS
Round Trays are 13 1/4"

**PTM025.000**

Pre-1920 4 1/2" . . . $700
Tip tray

**PTM026.000**

c.1940s . . . . . . . . $850

**PTM027.000**

c.1940s . . . . . . . . $800

**PTM028.000**

1953 . . . . . . . . . $225

**PTM029.000**

1954 . . . . . . . . . $185

**PTM030.000**

1959 . . . . . . . . . $200

**PTM031.000**

1961 . . . . . . . . . $150

**PTM032.000**

1961 . . . . . . . . . $125

**PTM033.000**

1963 . . . . . . . . . $200

**PTM034.000**

1965 . . . . . . . . . $125

**PTM035.000**

1965 . . . . . . . . . $125

**PTM036.000**

1966 . . . . . . . . . $125

**PTM037.000**

1968 . . . . . . . . . $50

**PTM038.000**

1969 . . . . . . . . . $45

**PTM039.000**

1970 . . . . . . . . . $15

**PTM040.000**

1971 . . . . . . . . . $15

**PTM041.000**

1972 . . . . . . . . . $15

**PTM042.000**

1973 . . . . . . . . . $15

**PTM043.000**

1974 . . . . . . . . . $15

**PTM044.000**

1976 . . . . . . . . . $15

PTM045.000

c.1940s . . . . . . . . . . . . . $750

PTM053.000

1939 . . . . . . . . . . . . . . $255

PTM054.000

1927 . . . . . . . . . . . . . . . . $675

PTM055.000

1950-1952 . . . . . . . . . . . $75

PTM046.000

1960s . . . . . . . . . . . . . . . . . . . . $150

PTM056.000

1953-1960 . . . . . . . . . . . $70

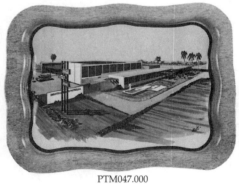

PTM047.000

1968 . . . . . . . . . . . . . . . . . . . . . . . . . $100

TV Tray

PTM048.000

1964 . . . . . . . . . . . . . $45

Tip Tray

PTM049.000

1964 . . . . . . . . . . . . . . . . $125

PTM050.000

1965 . . . . . . . . . . . . . . . . $55

Tip Tray

PTM051.000

1969 . . . . . . . . . . . . . . . . $35

Tip Tray

PTM052.000

1968 . . . . . . . . . . . . . . . $35

Tip Tray

PTM059.000

1938 . . . . . . . . . . . . . . . . . $160

PTM060.000

1940 . . . . . . . . . . . . . . . . . . . . $200

PTM010.001

1957 . . . . . . . . . . . . . . $200
French

PTM011.001

1957 . . . . . . . . . . . . . . $125
French

PTM061.000

1936 . . . . . . . . . . . . . . . . . . . . . . . . $225

PTM057.000

1953-1960 . . . . . . . . . . $45

PTM009.001

1957 . . . . . . . . . . . . . . $125
French

PTM012.001

1957 . . . . . . . . . . . . . . $125
French

PTM058.000

1950-1952 . . . . . . . . . . $75

PCB010.000

1890s 10 1/2" . . . . . . . . . . . . . . . . . . . $5,000
"The Ideal Brain Tonic"

PCB011.000

1901 8 1/4" . . . . . . . . . . . . . . . . . . . . $5,000
"Hilda Clark"

PCB013.000

c.1907 7" . . . . . . . . . . . . . . . . . . . . . $1,500
The Empire Ornamental Glass Co. NY

PCB012.000

c.1904 6" . . . . . . . . . . . . . . . . . . . . . $2,200

# SANDWICH PLATES

PCB015.000

1931 7 1/4" . . . . . . . . . . . . . . . . . . . . . $300
Manufactured by E.M. Knowles China Co.

Prior to 1930, The Coca-Cola Company very rarely showed the product associated with food. Beginning in the early 1930s, they decided to push the fact that Coca-Cola was great with food, especially hot dogs and other sandwiches. What better way to serve those hot dogs and sandwiches than on a "Sandwich Plate", designed and sold to soda fountains and drug stores by The Coca-Cola Company. Just when you were about to take a bite, there was that reminder to order a Coke. These plates are very collectible and sought after by collectors. While many styles have turned up over the years, the one shown to the left, manufactured by E.M. Knowles China Co., seems to be the most common. The cost of these plates to the store owner, along with the fact that they were easily damaged or broken, made their use impractical.

PCB018.000

1931 7 3/8" . . . . . . . . . . . . . . . . . . . . . $425
Manufactured by American Chinaware Corp.

PCB016.000

1930s 8 1/4" . . . . . . . . . . . . . . . . . . . . . $700
Rare

PCB017.000

1930s 7" . . . . . . . . . . . . . . . . . . . $800
Octagon, Rare, Manufactured by Thompson

PCB019.000

1940s-50s 6 1/2" . . . . . . . . . . . . . . . . $350
Mfg. Wellsville China Co., Wellsville, OH

PCB020.S01     PCB020.S02     PCB020.S03     PCB020.S04     PCB020.S05     PCB020.S06     PCB020.S07

c.1930s  Dinnerware individual pieces . . . . $250 Each     PCB020.S00 Complete place setting . . . . $2,000

PCB026.000

1970s  10 1/2" . . . . . . . . . . . . . . $175
Commemorative plate

PCB021.000

1950s  10 1/2" . . . . . . . . . . . . . . . . . $475
50th Anniversary, Lenox china plate

PCB024.000

1967  7 1/4" . . . . . . . . . . . . . . . $100
Glass, "World Dish"

PCB023.000

1930s  . . . . . . . . . . . . . . . . . . $225
Aluminum, "Pretzel Dish"

PCB025.000

1967  11 1/2" x 11 1/2" . . . . . . . . . . . . . $100
Glass, "World Dish"

PCB022.000

1930s  . . . . . . . . . . . . . . . . . . $425
Bowl, green glass

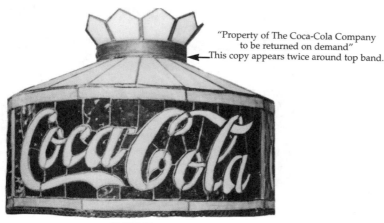

"Property of The Coca-Cola Company to be returned on demand"
← This copy appears twice around top band.

### PLS001.001
1920s 18" . . . . . . . . . . . . . . . . . . . . . . $5,000
"Chain Edge", Tiffany-type leaded glass shade, circular

Same copy as above must be on band. →

### PLS001.002
1920s 18" . . . . . . . . . . . . . . . . . . . . . $5,000
"Leaf Edge", Tiffany-type leaded glass shade, circular

*Note: The "Chain Edge" version of this shade originally had beaded fringe. They are rarely found with this original beading. Collectors have had this fringe restored or recreated. These shades look so much better with beads.*

*Note: Original beading, in tact, could raise the value by 50% or more.*

Close up of "Leaf Edge" leaded glass shade.

*Note: Beware of reproduction milk glass globes. See the Repro/Fantasy section of this book.*

### PLS002.000
With original hardware . . . . . . . . $2,500
Without or new hardware . . . . . . . $1,800
1930s milk glass globe with metal tassel

### PLS003.000
With original hardware . . . . . . . . $1,200
Without or with new hardware . . . . $850
1930s milk glass globe

PLS004.000

c.1936  12" x 23" . . . . . . . . . . . . . $3,000
Hanging neon sign, (Transformer marked: "Property
The Coca-Cola Co., 342 Madison Ave., NYC".)

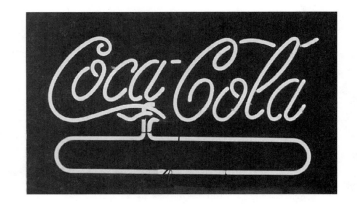

PLS005.000

1930s  12" x 24" . . . . . . . . . . . . . . . $1,400

Neon sign
PLS006.000

1989 . . . . . . . . . . . . . . . . . . . . . . . $1,000
Neon sign, three color. Note: Rarely will you find
items as recent as this neon in the book. However,
this sign is so outstanding I've decided to include it.

PLS007.000

1930s  15" x 24" . . . . . . . . . . . . . . . $5,000
"Drug Store" neon sign, chrome (boxed in) art deco,
Rare, Mfg. Electron Signs, Inc., Chicago

PLS008.000

Late 1940s  18" x 28" . . . . . . . . . . . $1,800
Neon sign

# LIGHT-UP SIGNS

PLS009.001
1948  12" x 20" . . . . . . . . . . . $750

PLS010.001
With clock . . . . . . . . . . . . . . . . . . $625

PLS011.001
Square clock . . . . . . . . . . . . . . . . . $625

PLS010.002
With clock . . . . . . . . . . . . . . . . . . $625

PLS010.003
With clock . . . . . . . . . . . . . . . . . . $625

PLS010.004
With clock . . . . . . . . . . . . . . . . . . $625

PLS009.002
1948  12" x 20" . . . . . . . . . . $900
Hanging sign

PLS009.004
1948  12" x 20" . . . . . . $750

## 1950s LIGHT-UP COUNTER SIGNS
### 9" x 20"

PLS011.002
Square clock . . . . . . . . . . . $625

PLS010.005
With clock . . . . . . . . . . . $625

> Note: Prices shown are average for signs in Excellent condition. Not working or Poor condition will be worth less and Near Mint to Mint condition would be worth more.

PLS010.006
With clock . . . . . . . . . . . $625

PLS009.003
1948  12" x 20" . . . . . . . . . . . . . . $750

> Note: The 1949 light-up sign was shown in the 1948 advertising manual and called an "Edgebrite." These signs were also available into the early 1950s. The lucite "Glass" ornament at top was also available in a "Bottle" version.

PLS012.001
Waterfalls (motion) . . . . . . . . . . . . $1,000

PLS012.002
Waterfalls (motion) . . . . . . . . . . . . $1,000

PLS013.001
Pause (motion) . . . . . . . . . . . . . . . $900

PLS010.007
With clock . . . . . . . . . . . . . . . . . . . $625

PLS014.000
Late 1930s 12" x 14" . . . . . . . . . . . $3,900
Reverse glass, "The Brunhoff Mfg. Co., Display
Advertising Specialities, Cinci., Ohio"

PLS017.000
1959 16" high . . . . . . . . . . . . . . . . . $1,200

PLS015.000
Late 1920s 7" x 15" x 5" . . . . . . . . $2,800
Reverse glass, "The Cincinnati Advertising Products
Company", Rare

PLS018.000
1960s 8" x 14" . . . . . . . . . . . . . . . . $100
Glass front, metal frame

PLS016.000
1939-1941 . . . . . . . . . . . . . . . . . . . $2,500
Reverse Glass, light-up, motion sign

PLS019.000
1950s 8" x 18" . . . . . . . . . . . . . . . . $385
Glass front, metal frame

PLS020.001          PLS020.002
1956 28" x 36" . . . . . . . . . . . . . $375 Each
Hanging signs, plastic, two different versions

# LIGHT-UP SIGNS

PLS021.001

1960s . . . . . . . . . . . . . . . . . . . . $700

Starburst (glass) sign

PLS021.002

1960s . . . . . . . . . . . . . . . . . . $650

Starburst (bottle) sign. Note: There is also a paper cup version of the "Starburst" sign (PLS021.003) This sign is made of plastic and tin.

PLS023.000

c.1960   18" x 32" . . . . . . . . . . . . . $700

Plastic, (should have plastic straw)

PLS022.000

1950s   12" x 18" . . . . . . . . . . . . . . . $650

PLS025.P02

Late 1940s . . . . . . . . . . . . . . . $600

Light-up shadow box display sign

PLS025.P01

Insert motion light-up

PLS024.000

1948-50s . . . . . . . . . . . . . . . . . . . . . . $475

Light-up cash register sign

PLS025.000

Shadow box sign with changeable inserts

PLS026.000

1960s . . . . . . . . . . . . . . . . . . . . $285

Plastic front

# LIGHT-UP SIGNS

1.

2.

3.

PLS027.000
c.1930s  12" x 20" . . . . . . . . . . . . . . . . . . . . . . . . . .$5,500

Light-up "Moving" sign, three photos shown: 1. "Drink Coca-Cola" 2. Changing 3. "The pause that Refreshes", wood box with cardboard slats that move and change messages. A very unusual and rare piece that very possibly could be a prototype and even a "One of a Kind"

PLS028.000
1960s  5" x 18" . . . . . . . . . . . . . . . . $65

PLS029.001
1950s  8" x 18" . . . . . . . . . $600
Glass front

PLS030.000
1950s  10" x 17" . . . . . . . . . . . . . . $575
Plastic front

PLS031.000
1950s  10" x 17" . . . . $575
Plastic front

PLS032.000
1950  10" x 17" . . . . . . . . . . . . . . $575
Plastic front

PLS029.002
1950s  8" x 18" . . . . . . . . . . . . . . $600
Glass front

PLS033.000
1960s  8" . . . . . . . . . $700
Plastic front

PLS034.000
1960s  8" x 18" . . . . . . . . . . . . . . $300
Plastic front

PLS020.003
1950s  28" x 36" . . . . . . . . . $375
Hanging sign, plastic front

PLS035.000
1960s  5" x 14" . . . $65
Plastic front

PLS036.000
1965  12" . . . . . . . . . . . . $225
Glass front

PLS037.000
1960s . . . . . . . . . . . . . . . . . . $425
Hanging sign, plastic, (2-sided)

PLS039.000
1960s . . . . . . . . . . . . . . . $425
Hanging sign, plastic, two-sided

PLS043.000
1960s  14" x 32" . . . . . . . . . . . . . . $200
Plastic front

PLS046.000
1960s  12" x 38" . . . . . . . . . . . . . . $185
Plastic front

PLS038.000
1950s . . . . . . . . . . . . . . $750
Stand-up sign, plastic, metal base

PLS042.000
1960s  18" x 18" . . . . . . . $185
Plastic

PLS044.000
1950s . . . . . . . . . . . . . $225
"Wall Basket" metal, light-up

PLS040.001
1950s  17" x 17" . . . . . . . . . . . . . . $425
Plastic, with cardboard inserts

PLS040.002
1950s  17" x 17" . . . . . . . . . . . . . . $425
Plastic, with cardboard inserts

PLS041.000
1960s  12" x 17" . . . . . . $225
Plastic front

PLS045.000
1970s  3" x 20" . . . . . . . . . . . . . . . . $55
Counter sign, glass front

PLS047.000
1960s . . . . . . . . . . . . . . . . . . . . $135 Each
Lantern signs, plastic and tin, showing both sides

PTH012.000
1915
5" x 21" . . . . . . $450
Wood

PTH010.000
1905
4" x 15" . . . . . . $425
Wood

PTH018.000
1944
7" x 17" . . . . . $385
Masonite

PTH017.000
1941   7" x 16"   . . . $385
Tin, can be found with
1942 date

PTH016.000
1939   6 1/2" x 16"   . . . $325
Tin, can be found with
1940 date

PTH015.000
1936
7" x 16" . . . . . . $325
Tin

PTH020.000
c.1950s
9" . . . . . . . . $200

PTH019.001          PTH019.002
1939   . . . . . . . . . . . $525 Each
Two different examples, Canada

PTH014.001
1929 . . . . . . $385
Canada

PTH013.000
1930s
17" . . . . . . $385
Tin

PTH021.000
1950s
17" . . . . . . $200
Tin

PTH022.000
1958
17" . . . . . . $125
Tin

PTH024.000
c.1948
9" . . . . . . . . . $200

PTH028.000
1960s
6" . . . . . . . . . $25

PTH025.000
c.1948
32" . . . . . . $1,600
Rare

PTH026.001          PTH026.002
1950s 30"   . . . . . . . . . $385 Each
Tin, two different examples

PTH023.000
1958   30" . . . . . . .$150
Tin

PTH027.000
1956
2 1/4" x 7 1/2" . . . . $20
Gold bottle

PTH029.000
1960s
7" . . . . . . . . $25
"Stick on"

PTH009.000
c.1905  5" x 21" .... $600
Rare

PTH011.000
c.1910  5" x 21" .... $450

PTH031.000
c.1950s  10" x 16 $^{1}/_{2}$" .. $1,200
Tin, Rare

PTH033.000
1950s  7"  ...... $65
Plastic

PTH032.000
Late 1930s  8 $^{1}/_{4}$" x 6 $^{1}/_{4}$"  ......... $650
Rare

PTH030.000
c.1939  9"  ................ $1,500
Tin, Rare

PTH052.000
1960s  3"  ......... $100
Honeywell

PTH034.000
1950s  4 $^{1}/_{2}$" x 5 $^{1}/_{4}$"  ....... $100
Plastic/metal base

PTH035.000
Late 1930s  10 $^{1}/_{4}$" x 14 $^{1}/_{4}$"  .. $600
Metal frame/mirror

# THERMOMETERS

PTH010.001

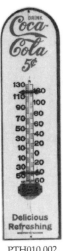

PTH010.002

c.1905  4" x 15"  . . . $425 Each
Wood, two different examples

PTH011.001
c.1905
5" x 21"  . . . . $475
Wood

PTH012.001
c.1915
5" x 21"  . . . . $450
Wood

PTH036.000
1930s  . . . . . . . . . . . . . . . $700
Desk thermometer, leather, Rare

PTH037.000
1950s  8" x 36"  . . . $950
Porcelain

PTH014.002
1929  . . . . . $185
(French) Canada

PTH022.001
1950s
17"  . . . . . . $65
Tin

PTH038.000
1950s
3 1/4" x 17"  . . . $650
Rare

PTH019.003

PTH019.004

c.1939  . . . . . . . . . . . . . . . . . . . $225 Each
Porcelain (French) Canada

PTH040.000
1960s  . . . . . . $30
Plastic

PTH039.000
1960s  . . . . . . $65
Plastic

Note: Prices shown are
based on thermometers in
working condition.
Examples with broken or
replaced glass would be
worth less.

PTH041.000
1980s  . . . . . . . . $25
Plastic

Note: Prices on these thermometers are based on working examples with glass. Thermometers found without glass front would be worth considerably less.

PTH043.001

1950s 12" . . . . . . . . . . . . . $200

PTH042.000

1948 12" . . . . . . . . . . . . . . . . . $550

PTH045.000

1964 18 1/4" . . . . . . . . . . $425

PTH048.000

1960s 18 1/4" . . . . . . . . . . . . . $300

PTH046.000

1964 12" . . . . . . . . . . . $300

PTH043.002

1950s 12" . . . . . . . . . $200

PTH047.000

Late 1940s 12" . . . . . . . . . . . . . . $750
Rare

PTH043.003

1957 12" . . . . . . . . . . . . . . $200

PTH050.000

1970s 12" . . . . . . . . . . . $50

PTH044.000

1959 12" . . . . . . . . . . . . . . . $450

PTH049.000

1960s 12" . . . . . . . . . . . $200

# CLOCKS

In the early days of Coca-Cola, the clock was certainly not considered an important advertising tool. Because of the cost, it would be impractical to justify its use in advertising Coca-Cola. This would soon change, and in the mid-1890s The Coca-Cola Company would not only use the clock to advertise, but it would also realize that it was a long-lasting, effective item that would more than justify the initial expense.

Because no evidence has proven otherwise, we do assume that the Baird Clock was the first to advertise the product. Edward Payson Baird was born in Philadelphia, on January 26, 1860. As a young man he worked for the William Torrey Co. The Torrey Co. made boxes for the Seth Thomas Clock Co. Baird became fascinated by the clock-making business and, in 1888, he started the Edward P. Baird and Co. Clock Manufacturers in Montreal, Canada. In 1890, he moved his company to Plattsburg, NY. It is here that he began to manufacture Coca-Cola advertising clocks. Baird is known to clock collectors mainly for his cases. In fact, his clocks were advertised as containing Seth Thomas movements. I have seen movements stamped "Seth Thomas" and "Baird Clock Co." Even movements stamped "Baird" were made by other clock makers, probably Seth Thomas. Baird's main contribution to clock making was the use of papier-mâché in mass-produced advertising clocks. They were produced easily and quickly at a low cost and, because of this, he was a leader in the field.

From 1893 to 1896, Baird produced many different versions of the wood case and papier-mâché (advertising portion) Coca-Cola clocks, most of which you will see on the following pages. Keep in mind that the advertising portion of these clocks (top and bottom rings) are made of molded papier-mâché, which is sometimes mistaken for wood, and can't be cleaned with solvent or any other solution. Solvent will dissolve the papier-mâché and, within minutes, you will own a completely worthless clock. During this "Plattsburg era," Baird produced two types of clocks for Coca-Cola: the "figure eight" and "gallery," both with papier-mâché. It seems that with every order for clocks, The Coca-Cola Company had the style and advertising message changed. It also seems that the molds for the papier-mâché didn't last very long, which accounts for the many different styles that have turned up over the years. The early "medicinal" claims predated some of the more toned-down "delicious and refreshing" versions.

In 1896, Baird moved his plant again, this time to Chicago, and with this move he changed his clocks completely. The "Chicago era" Baird clocks were now a wood case with tin embossed advertising and dial portion on top and a tin embossed bottom door outlined with wood. Personally, I believe that the Coca-Cola Chicago clock was made in 1889 or 1900. This clock has been shown in an earlier Coca-Cola price guide erroneously dated 1892. I also believe that this clock was made for a very short period of time and in very limited numbers, which would account for the fact that very few of these "Chicago era" clocks have turned up over the years. In

later years, Baird became famous for his inventions relating to telephone toll apparatus, locks and keys, but he will always be known to Coca-Cola collectors as the manufacturer of the first clock to advertise the product.

In 1901, The Coca-Cola Company used the Welch clock to advertise their product. The E.N. Welch Mfg. Co., of Forestville, CT, produced a well-made, dependable clock which I happen to think is the most beautiful and desirable Coca-Cola clock. It was basically an octagon school house regulator clock with a paper face printed with the Coca-Cola logo, brass bezel and a glass door. But what really makes this clock great was an advertising piece in the bottom door behind the pendulum. You will see two versions of this shown on the following pages. Between the years 1903 and 1907, Ingraham clocks were used to advertise Coca-Cola—both an octagon school house clock and a standard store regulator. These were both key wound, eight-day movements and are more common than the Welch clocks. Beginning in 1910, the Wm. L. Gilbert Clock Co., Winsted, CT, began producing clocks for Coca-Cola and they were the most common store regulators used by the company. They were used almost exclusively between 1910 and 1940, when the use of the eight-day regulator clock was discontinued.

The Gilbert clock was very dependable and well made, and seemed to run forever with very little care. These clocks all had "Coca-Cola" faces (Coca-Cola is printed in red), but they are very often found faded. There are a number of different types of faces, but all had standard Arabic numerals. They also had gold-painted glass bottom doors. This gold painting was done by stencil, which accounts for the fact that the lettering sometimes looked crude. Be very careful with these clocks— reproduction paper dials and new bottom glass are available and often put in old clocks and sold to the unsuspecting collector.

Prior to 1915, The Coca-Cola Company also used a number of small clocks in the form of celluloid-covered and gold-stamped leather clocks, some of which I have also shown in this section.

In the early 1930s, the company began using electric clocks, and in the late 1930s and into the early 1940s some of these clocks were the neon, light-up type, which are very popular among collectors and which bring premium prices today.

After World War II, the use of the advertising clock really took off, and the late 1950s saw a large variety of clocks in metal and glass, aluminum, plastic, and neon and other light-up clocks. Of course, the illuminated types are always more desirable and they became very popular in the late 1960s, both in glass and plastic. During the 1970s, The Coca-Cola Company still used a wide variety of clocks, both illuminated and not, most of which were made in plastic.

With all of the different types of clocks used by The Coca-Cola Company over the years, it is no wonder they have become a favorite item among collectors.

# BAIRD CLOCKS

PCL005.001

c.1891-1895 . . . . . . . . . . . . . . . $6,000
Upper and lower case letters, time only

BAIRD "GALLERY" CLOCK
Two different examples shown
The "Gallery" clock is considered much
more rare than the figure "8" versions.

PCL005.002

c.1891-1895 . . . . . . . . . . . . . . . $7,000
Upper case letters, time and strike, Very Rare

PCL006.001

PCL006.002

PCL006.003

PCL006.004

c.1891-1895 . . . . . . . . . . . . . . . . . . . . . . . . . . . . . . . . . . . . . . . . . . . $5,500
Baird clocks figure "8" versions (Plattsburg era) 4 different examples shown

PCL008.001

c.1896-1900 . . . . . . . . . . . . . . . $5,000
Eight-day movement, bottom door not original

Baird (Chicago Era) clock
Two different examples shown

PCL008.002

c.1896-1900 . . . . . . . . . . . . . . . $8,500
15-day movement, all original. Photo Courtesy: The
Rentzer Family Collection.

# BAIRD CLOCKS
## 5¢ Version 1894-1896

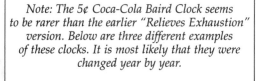

*Note: The 5¢ Coca-Cola Baird Clock seems to be rarer than the earlier "Relieves Exhaustion" version. Below are three different examples of these clocks. It is most likely that they were changed year by year.*

PCL007.001
$5,500

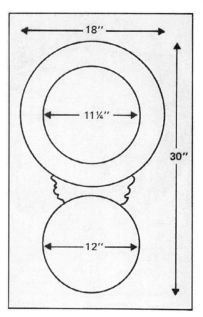

Dimensions of the Figure "8" clock.

PCL007.002
$5,500

PCL007.003
$5,500

*Note: Clocks are always more desirable when found with the original label. The label is pasted on the inside backboard of the clock and can be seen by opening the bottom door. The label shown is one example of the many different I've seen.*

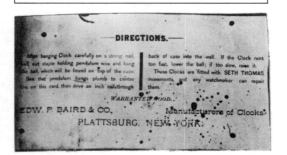

# CLOCKS

PCL010.002

**1901**

With insert . . . . . . . . . . . . . . . . . . . $5,500
Without insert . . . . . . . . . . . . . . . . $2,800

Welch octagon school house clock "E.N Welch Mfg.,
Co., Forestville, Conn. (2 different examples shown)
with "Hilda Clark" cardboard insert and 1901 calendar (top portion) insert. Rare when found complete.

PCL010.001

> *Note: Faded red ink is very common on these clock faces.*

> *Note: The Ingraham Clocks shown here have original bottom glass marked "Regulator." I have never seen these original clocks with any other glass.*

PCL011.000

**1903-1905** . . . . . . . . . . . . . . . . . . $2,600

Ingraham octagon school house, Mfg. by
The E. Ingraham Co. Bristol, Conn.

PCL012.000

**1905-1907** . . . . . . . . . . . . $2,400

Ingraham Store regulator, mfg. by the
Ingraham Co., Bristol, Conn.

# CLOCKS (STORE REGULATORS)

Note: These store regulators are the easiest clocks for the unsuspecting collector to get stuck with. Reproduction faces and bottom glass are easily available, especially among clock collectors and dealers. These faces can be put on legitimate old regulator clocks which are worth a couple of hundred dollars, turning them into the much sought after Coca-Cola clock. Remember, it is very common for the red printing on these faces to be faded. Dark red printed faces should be examined very carefully. The words "Trade Mark" or "Trade Mark Registered" should NOT be under the logo. The gold-painted bottom glass should look a little crude. If it is too perfect, be cautious.

PPM014.000

**1941 Postcard** . . . . . . . . . . . . . . . . . . . $65
Postcard from The Gilbert Clock Co. to Coca-Cola bottlers notifying them of the discontinued manufacturing of the No. 3022 8-day clock.

PCL014.000

**1916-1920** . . . . . . . . . . . . . . . . . $1,000
Gilbert

PCL013.000

**1910** . . . . . . . . . . . . . . . . . . . $5,000
Gilbert. The bottom of this clock is a decal on glass. The condition of that decal is most important when evaluating the clock. If the decal is poor the price will drop considerably.

PCL015.000

**1916-1920** . . . . . . . . . . . . . . . . $1,300
Gilbert

PPM015.000

**1931** . . . . . . . . . . . . . . . $50
Catalog sheet showing not only the electric clock but the regulator

PCL016.000

**Gilbert** . . . . . . . . . . . . . . . . . . $1,200
This clock was first offered in the late '20s and used through the 1930s and still available until 1941.

# CLOCKS

PCL017.000
c.1910  3" x 8"  . . . $1,800
Leather

PCL018.000
c.1910  4$^1$/$_2$" x 6"  . . . . $2,000
Leather

PCL046.000
1950s  6$^1$/$_2$" x 8$^1$/$_2$"  . . . $1,500
"Princess" Clock

PCL047.000
1950s  3$^1$/$_2$" x 5"  . . . . . . . . $750
"Contessa" Clock

PCL023.000
c.1939-41  16" x 16"  . . . $800
Wood frame

PCL024.000
c.1939-41  16" x 16"  . . . $1,100
Metal frame, light-up

PCL025.000
c.1942  16" x 16"  . . . . . $800
Metal frame, light-up

PCL030.000
1939  16" x 16"  . . . . . . $550
Wood frame

PCL031.000
1948  . . . . . . . . . . . $600

PCL032.000
1958  . . . . . . . . . . . $400

PCL033.000
1951  17$^1$/$_2$"  . . . . . . $150
Maroon

PCL034.000
1951  17$^1$/$_2$"  . . . . . $185
Silver

PCL035.000
c.1939-41  . . . . . . . . . . . . . . $675
Metal frame

PCL036.000
8"  . . . . . . . . . . . . . . . . $750
Early electric

PCL037.000
c.1948  19"  . . . . . . . . . . . $450

# CLOCKS

PCL038.000

1939-42 . . . . . . . . . . . . . . . . . . . . . $700
Reverse glass, metal frame

PCL039.000

c.1948  20" . . . . . . . . . . . . . . . . . . . $3,000
Neon light-up, bottle moves from 11 to 1,
Aluminum Frame, glass front, Swihart products, IN

PCL040.000

1950s . . . . . . . . . . . . . . . . . . . . $475
Glass front, light-up

PCL043.000

c.1969 . . . . . . . . . . . . . $100
Plastic

PCL026.000

1939-40  17 1/2" . . . . . . . . . . . . . $3,600
"Spinner" neon light-up

PCL041.000

1948-50 . . . . . . . . . . . . . . . . . $425
Glass front, metal frame

PCL027.000

1930s . . . . . . . . . . . . . . . . . . . . . . . $6,000
Neon light-up counter clock (Must be working
and 8 or better condition to warrant this price)

*Note: Prices shown are
based on clocks in
working order, in 8 or
better condition.
Examples not working or
in less than
Average condition, will
be worth less.*

PCL042.000

1960s . . . . . . . . . . . . . . . . . . $250
Plastic

PCL044.000

1964 . . . . . . . . . . . . . . . . . . . . . . . . $300
Plastic with metal frame, light-up

PCL028.000

c.1941  18"  . . . . . . . . . . . . . $2,800
Octagon, neon. Note: Beware of repros of
this clock.

PCL045.000

c.1942  14 1/2" x 14 1/2"  . . . . . . . . $725
Sessions

PCL029.000

1920s  . . . . . . . . . . . . . . . . . . . . . $1,600
Pocket watch.  Note: This is one of the very few
Coca-Cola pocket watches that I consider old and
completely original. Photo Courtesy: The Rentzer
Family Collection.

PCL049.000

1970s  . . . . . . . $85

PCL048.000

1980  . . . . . . . . . . . . . . . . . . . $650
Sessions. Numbered Limited Edition, time
and strike 8-day movement. Presented by
Coca-Cola USA for sales excellence.

PCL050.000

1950s  . . . . . . . . . . . . . . . . . . . . . $300

*Note: See the back of this book for
fantasy and recent pocket watches.*

PCL051.000

1981  12"  . . . . . . . . . . . . . . . . . . . . . $150
Ridgeway Anniversary Clock, battery operated

# CLOCKS

PCL019.000
c.1915   3 1/4" x 3 1/4" . . . $800
Leather

PCL021.000
c.1931   14" x 14" . . . . . . . . .$600
This is one of the first electric Coca-Cola Clocks

PCL020.000
c.1907   4 1/4" x 4 3/4" . . . . . . . . $1,800
Leather, brass corners, Rare

PCL052.000
1950s . . . . . . . . . . . . . . . . . . . . . $300
Plastic

Note: Remember condition is the most important factor when determining value.

PCL053.000
1950s . . . . . . . . . . . . . . . . . . . . . $550
Light-up, glass front

PCL056.000
1970s   3/4 size, 12" x 27" . . . $350
Battery operated

PCL054.000
1960s . . . . . . . . . . . . . . . $200
White/Red

PCL055.000
1960s . . . . . . . . . . . . . . . . . . . . . . . . $250
Plastic, light-up

PCL058.000
1960s . . . . . . . . . . . . . . .$75
Plastic

PCL057.000
1948  36" . . . . . . . . . . . . . . . . . . . . . $650

PCL086.000
1970s . . . . . . . . . $50
Plastic

# CLOCKS

During the 1950s, The Coca-Cola Company offered to bottlers three different Anniversary clocks, produced by the Forestville Clock Company. An Anniversary Clock is a key-wound mantel clock that, when wound, would run for a full year. The first was the "Contessa" (replica anniversary did not run for a full year) $3^1/_2$" x 5" with brass finish and glass dome, rotating pendulum consisted of three gold bottles. This was the least expensive at $6.00, and is most commonly found today. The next in the line was the "Princess." This $6^1/_2$" x $8^1/_2$" version had an enameled dial, adjustable leveling screws, glass dome with brass screw cap and rotating pendulum balls. The Princess is difficult to find today and originally sold to bottlers for $9. The top of the line was the "Cinderella." This Black Forest cottage-shaped clock had a brass finish and etched glass sides and was $5^1/_2$" x $7^1/_2$". Because of its very expensive price to bottlers of $11, the Cinderella is very rare today. The Contessa and Princess are also shown on another page.

Note: Values shown in this book for neon, spinner, or mechanical clocks are based on examples in working order with original parts. Others will be valued less.

PCL079.000
1950s  $5^1/_2$" x $7^1/_2$" . . . . . . . . $2,500
"Cinderella" Anniversary Clock, Rare

PCL079.001
Copy of catalog sheet from Forestville Clock Company showing the three Anniversary clocks

PCL081.000
c.1939  23" . . . . . . . . . . . . . $2,500
Spinner clock, neon (Electric Clock Co., Columbus, Oh)

PCL083.000
1950s  24" x 64" . . . . . . . . . . $200
Note: This clock was used by itself or with other parts for a larger display.

PCL082.000
1959-60s . . . . . . . . . . . . . . . . $600
Glass front

PCL084.000
1970s-80s . . . . . . . . . . . . . . . . . $35
Can clock

# CLOCKS

PCL022.000
1930s . . . . . . . . . . . . . . . . . . . . . $3,000
Light-up

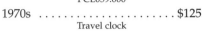

PCL059.000
1970s . . . . . . . . . . . . . . . . . . . . . $125
Travel clock

PCL060.000
1950s . . . . . . . . . . . $500
Glass front

Note: Prices shown are based on clocks in working order, in 8 or better condition. Examples not working or in less than Average condition, will be worth less.

PCL061.000
1960s . . . . . . . . 225.00
Glass/Metal

PCL065.000
1960s . . . . . . $100
Plastic

PCL064.000
1963 . . . . . . . . . . . . . . . $125
Plastic

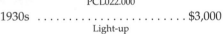

PCL062.000
1960s . . . . . . . . . . . . . . $175
Green, Red, White

PCL063.000
1960s . . . . . . . . $150
Glass

PCL066.000
1972 . . . . . . . . . . . . . $65
Plastic

PCL067.000
1974 . . . . . . . . . . . . . . . . $65
"Betty" plastic

PCL068.000
1970s . . . . . . . . $45
Plastic

PCL069.000
1970s . . . . . . . . $50
Plastic

PCL070.000

1950s . . . . . . . . . . . . . . $500

Dome clock, German

PCL071.000

1950s . . . . . . . . . . . . . . . . . . . . . . $275

Desk clock, German

PCL072.000

1970s . . . . . . . . . . . . . . $40

Plastic

PCL087.000

1960s . . . . . . . . . $150

Plastic

PCL073.000

1950s  15" x 24"  . . . . . . . . . . . . . . . . . $550

Metal and plastic

PCL074.000

1980s . . . . . . . . . . . . . . . . . . . . . . . . $25

Plastic

PCL075.000

1970s . . . . . . . . . . . $60

Plastic

PCL076.000

1970s . . . . . . . . . . . . . . $30

Tab, plastic

PCL077.000

1980s . . . . . . . . . . . . . . . . . . . . . $25

PCL078.000

1980s . . . . . . . . . . . . . . $35

# RADIOS

PRA011.000

1950  7" x 12" x 9 1/2"  . . . $750
Cooler radio. Note: The price shown
on the Cooler Radio is an average
price. I've seen this radio sell for $900
in Near Mint condition, and less than
$300 in Below Average condition.

PRA010.000

1933  24"  . . . . . . . . . . . . $6,000
Bottle radio. Note: The prices shown
on the bottle radio is based on radios
with original works, knobs, and no
repainting. These radios are notorious
for not working properly. Radios with
replaced works would be valued less. I
would rather have a non-working bottle radio, all original, than a working
one with all new works (interior).

PRA017.000

1970s Radio only . . . . . . . $135
PRA017.B00 In Box . . . . . . . $200
Vending machine-shaped

PRA013.000

c.1950s . . . . . . . . . . . . . . . . . $950
Radio in a case, Rare

PRA014.000

c.1960s  Small size . . . . . . . . . . . . . $285
PRA014.B00 In Box . . . . . . . . . . . . . . . $525
Vending machine-shaped

PRA015.000

1965  Large size . . . $200
Vending machine-shaped

PRA016.000

c.1963 . . . . . . . . . . . . . . $150
PRA016.B00 In Box . . . . . . .$200
Vending machine-shape

PRA011.000

1950s  7" x 12" x 9 ½" . . . . . . . . . . . $750
Cooler radio

PRA012.000

1950 . . . . . . . . . . . . . . . . . . . . . . . $1,800
Cooler clock/radio, Rare

PRA020.000

1950s . . . . . . . . . . . . . . $185
Music box, miniature. (Must be complete and working to warrant this price.)

PPM016.000

1950 . . . . . . . . . . . . . . . . . . . . . $50
Product book (showing cooler radio)

Bottom of cooler clock/radio showing instruction label

PRA018.001

1950s . . . . . . . . . . . . . . . . . . $2,000
Cooler music box, Rare (I've seen a number of different versions of this music box.)

PRA019.000

1950s . . . . . . . . $325
Crystal radio set, with instructions

PMI005.000

1950s . . . . . . . . . . . . . $125
Sales aid, miniature

# TOYS AND GAMES

For the first thirty years or so of The Coca-Cola Company's existence, the product was basically targeted to adults. One only has to examine the company's advertising to realize that this was an adult drink. For example, "Relieves Fatigue," "Restores Energy," "The Ideal Beverage for Discriminating People," and "For Shoppers and Businessmen" were all part of the extensive list of slogans used by the company in its early years. It wasn't until the late 1920s and early 1930s that The Coca-Cola Company considered youngsters as an important market for its popular drink. While this section includes toys and games, not all of these items were produced with children in mind. Playing cards, for example, have always been an important "give away" item for adults. A series of Milton Bradley games such as darts, bingo, checkers, and chess were also very popular games during the 1940s and '50s. They bore the Coca-Cola logo and were designed for adults. Without a doubt though, the most popular items in this section are the toy trucks and cars which were indeed produced with children in mind.

The 1930s Metalcraft truck is the first toy truck known to be used by The Coca-Cola Company to attract children. The Metalcraft Company produced a very well made and popular truck not only for Coca-Cola but for other companies to advertise their products as well. The Coca-Cola Company was, of course, a very important account for Metalcraft. These trucks were offered for a number of years, and while it is a very desirable truck, it has also turned up in large enough numbers over the years to keep collectors satisfied. Even with the number of Metalcraft trucks available, they still command a very respectable price. Examples in "mint in box" condition are still unobtainable for most collectors. The Metalcraft fleet basically consists of four versions. A metal wheel example is probably the earliest, followed by a rubber wheel truck and then a rubber wheel version with working headlights. Surely the rarest of the group is a long-front version which was obviously done in very small quantities or for a very short period of time. Many a collector is attempting to add this one to their collection.

The Smitty, Smith-Miller Company was one of the next trucks to carry the Coca-Cola logo. Starting in the 1940s and 1950s, these trucks began as all-wood models and evolved into wooden bodies with metal cabs; there were four different versions in all red. An all-metal Smith-Miller was manufactured later in the 1950s; this model was all yellow. Another Smith-Miller was produced in 1978 to 1980; this is an all-metal version in red and was done in limited quantities.

Buddy L should aptly be called the King of Coca-Cola trucks. They have been producing trucks since the 1940s. Their first truck was an all-wood example which is rare and sought after by collectors. The large yellow metal trucks produced during the 1950s and 1960s have turned up in many variations, including an orange example. The 1960s, '70s and '80s saw the Buddy L Company produce many different Coca-Cola trucks, including some boxed sets.

During the 1950s, the Marx Company made a number of quality trucks bearing the Coca-Cola logo, both in tin-litho and plastic. These trucks are very popular among collectors and are considered very valuable when found "mint in box."

Matchbox trucks produced during the 1950s and '60s are fairly common, but still popular, especially early examples found in the box. Dinky and Budgie also produced some trucks in the '50s and '60s. The Japanese manufactured tin-litho trucks began appearing in the 1950s and many examples were produced right into the '60s. While many are easy to find, some are quite rare. The 1960s Ford Station Wagon is certainly among the rarest. Other manufacturers since the '50s have included Solido (France), Yaxton (Italy), and Technofix (West Germany) as well as others from Argentina, Brazil, Mexico, Hong Kong, and Taiwan. All of these have produced trucks with the famous Coca-Cola logo. Most recently (1970s-1990s), Nostalgia Miniatures are producing many different models of vintage Coca-Cola trucks.

Many Coca-Cola collectors specialize in toys, especially toy trucks and cars. The ultimate find for these specialists is an example that is "mint in the box." Trucks found in the original box are so much more desirable and valuable. In this section you will see many trucks and cars with their boxes. Prices shown for examples without boxes are based on average condition of excellent or better. That same truck, however, found "mint in the box" could be worth considerably more.

This section is not limited to trucks. Also included are a number of items that were offered as premiums from local bottlers, including the American Flyer train set, Coca-Cola scooter and wagon, toy stoves, and baby dolls. Many of these items can be traced to The St. Louis Bottling Company. This bottler was very innovative in regard to offering premiums in return for bottle caps. A photo of their "premium room" can also be found in this section. Premiums, special offers and give-aways were among the many ways the company and bottlers gave these items to the kids. Yo-yos, marbles, jump ropes, kites, whistles, and cutouts are only a small sampling of the hundreds of items that carried the Coca-Cola logo and that were produced for children.

Beginning in 1927 and continuing into the early 1930s, The Coca-Cola Company produced a beautiful series of store window displays featuring Toonerville, Uncle Remus, The Circus, and The Olympics, among others. These were large, elaborate cardboard cutout window displays that also featured a small-size cutout for children. A window banner offered the cutout free inside the store. Some of these cutouts are rare; others are quite common and collecting the set is surely a challenge. All of these are shown in this section.

Schools are another place for the distribution of items targeted for children. Among the items geared toward school are rulers, pencil boxes, educational games, pencil sharpeners, pencils, baseball hats and other sports items. These are just some of the items given away by The Coca-Cola Company in hopes of reminding those kids to "Have a Coke."

Toys, games, and kid stuff have always been a favorite among many Coke collectors. This may be because they bring back memories of their youth, or maybe because they are just plain fun. These items can not only be found through the normal Coca-Cola sources (general antique shows and other collectors) but from the many toy shows that are held around the country as well. So whether you are a toy specialist or you have a few pieces in your collection, toys are a great source of enjoyment in the world of Coca-Cola collecting.

PTC005.B00

Mint in original box . . . . . . . . . . $2,800

Metalcraft No. 215 with rubber wheels and working headlight. Note: Beware of reproduction of this box.

PTC006.B00

Mint in original box . . . . . . . . . . $2,500

Metalcraft No. 171 with rubber wheels

---

*Note: 1930s Metalcraft trucks are 11" long and considered rare when found in original box. Keep in mind the prices listed here are for trucks in nice condition. Paint chips, pitting, and decal wear can effect the value drastically.*

---

PTC006.000

c.1932 . . . . . . . . . . . . . . . . . . . . . . . . $975

No. 171 with rubber wheels

PTC005.000

c.1933 . . . . . . . . . . . . . . . . . . . . . . . $1,100

No. 215 with rubber wheels with working headlights

PTC007.000

c.1934 . . . . . . . . . . . . . . . . . . . . . . $2,500

Long front with rubber wheels, Rare

PTC004.000

c.1931 . . . . . . . . . . . . . . . . . . . . . . . . $750

Metal wheels

# TOY TRUCKS

PTC008.000
1948  19" . . . . . . . . . . . . . . . . . . . . . $3,500
Buddy-L, wood, Very Rare

PTC022.B00
1960s  9" . . . . . . . . . . . . . . . . . . . . . $400
Ford Taxi "Taiyo", tin litho friction

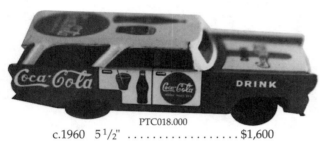

PTC018.000
c.1960  5 1/2" . . . . . . . . . . . . . . . . . . . $1,600
Ford station wagon, tin red and white, Very Rare

PTC023.B00
c.1960  MIB . . . . . . . . . . . . . . . . . . . . . $850
without box . . . . . . . . . . . . . . . . . . . . $500
"Soda Car" tin litho., wind-up, Ice Cream Truck

PTC019.000
1950s  5 1/2" . . . . . . . . . . . . . . . . . . . $1,000
GMC, green, yellow, white, Rare

PTC025.B00
c.1970  4 1/2" . . . . . . . . . . . . . . . . . . . $150
Europa VW pick up, battery operated

PTC020.000
1950s  5" . . . . . . . . . . . . . . . . . . . . . $500
Linemar, tin

PTC021.000
1980s  4" . . . . . . . . . . . . . . . . . . . . . $250
Micro Models (International), Rare

PTC024.000
c.1950s  4 1/4" . . . . . . . . . . . . . . . . . . $450
"HAJI" tin litho., made in Japan

PTC026.B00
1970s  4" . . . . . . . . . . . . . . . . . $275
Micro Models "Holden Van", plastic,
in box, Rare

PTC027.001           PTC027.002

c.1950s  4 1/2" . . . . . . . . . . . . $1,350 Each
AMBO (Italy) tin, Very Rare. Showing two different
versions, wheels and hood variations.

PTC082.BS0

c.1963

MIB (4 trucks) . . . . . . . . . . $275
PTC082.000 Coke truck only . . $85
Flip-O-Matic set

PTC028.B00

1960s  13" . . . . . . . . . . . . . . . . . . . . . $775
National (Italy) Fiat delivery truck in box, Rare

PTC029.000

c.1960s . . . . . . . . . . . . . . . . . . . $750
Japan, tin and plastic, Rare

PTC083.BS0

1950s . . . . . . . . . . . . . . . . . . . . . . $550
Tiny Giant set, tin and plastic, with Coke truck

PTC030.000

1950s  10 3/4" . . . . . . . . . . . . . . . . . . . $900
Marx (Canadian version), red plastic, Rare

PTC131.BS0

c.1980  1 3/4" . . . . . . . . . . . . . . . $175
Super-Mini set with Coca-Cola truck

PTC031.B00

1950s  10" . . . . . . . . . . . . . . . . . . . . $675
Marx, plastic, MIB, Rare

PTC033.B01

1950s  10 3/4", MIB . . . . . . . . . . . . . . $600

Marx, plastic, made with and
without doors.
PTC084.B00

1960s . . . . . . . . . . . $200
Blue Box, Rare

# TOY TRUCKS

PTC133.001     PTC133.002     PTC133.003         PTC133.004     PTC133.005     PTC133.006

PCT133.S00  1970s . . . . . . . . . . . . . . . . . . . . . . . . . . . . . . . . . . . . . . . $450 Set

Individual trucks . . . . . . . . . . . . . . . . . . . . . . . . . . . . . . . . . . . $60 Each

50th Anniversary Panama (set of 6) metal and plastic trucks

PTC049.000

Early 1950s  7" . . . . . . . . . . . . . . . . . . $475

Marx, red plastic, Rare

PTC009.000

Early 1940s . . . . . . . . . . . . . . . . . . . $1,600

Smith-Miller, wood and metal, with wood blocks,
Rare

PTC038.B00

1960 . . . . . . . . . . . . . . . . . . . . . . . $2,000

Corvair pick-up, MIB

PTC131.000

c.1980  1 3/4" . . . . . . . . . . . . . . . $20

Super-Mini

PTC050.000

1949-50 . . . . . . . . . . . . . . . . . . . . . $1,800

Goso tractor trailer, wind-up, Very Rare

PTC051.B00

1950s  4 3/4" . . . . . . . . . . . . . . . . . $1,100

Hubley (Canadian) die-cast, in original
package, Rare

PTCF132.000

1980s . . . . . . . . . . . . . . . . . . . . . . . . $25

Plastic and cardboard

# TOY TRUCKS

**PTC043.B00**

1950s . . . . . . . . . . . . . . . . . . . $250

Budgie, MIB

**PTC041.B00**          **PTC042.B00**

1950s Yellow/white . . . . . . . . . . . . . . . . . . . . . . . . . $425

1950s Red/white . . . . . . . . . . . . . . . . . . . . . . . . . $550

Battery operated, Two different examples, with original box

**PTC044.B00**

1950s  9"  . . . . . . . . . . . $650

Tippco, export version,
in original box

PTC033.000      PTC032.000
$475          $325

1950s Marx plastic (When complete with side doors)

PTC047.000    PTC046.000    PTC045.000

c.1965  . . . . . . . $160   1950s . . . . . . $150   1950s . . . . . . . . . . $185

Dinky       Friction       Linemar

**PTC138.000**

c.1960  . . . . . . . $100

Plastic

**PTC048.B00**

c.1960s . . . . . . . . . . . . . . . . . . $1,100

Plastic, French

**PTC038.000**

1960  . . . . . . . . . . . . . . . . . . . . . . . . . $950

Pick up with cardboard insert

**PTC064.B00**

c.1960  . . . . . $55

Matchbox

**PTC098.B01**

1973  . . . . . . . . . . . . . . . $85

Big Wheel, MIB
3 variations: 1. Atlanta, 2. New York,
3. Coca-Cola

**PTC097.000**

1970s . . . . . . . . . . . . . . . . . . $45

Plastic

**PTC099.B00**

1970s . . . . . . . . . . . . . . . . . . $60

Model T van kit

**PTC054.000**

1950s . . . . . . . . . . . . . . . . . . . . . . $85
Plastic, (two variations: plastic/rubber wheels)

**PTC055.000**

1960s  3 3/4" . . . . . . . . . . . . . . . . . . . . . . . . . . . . $600
AMBO (Italy), tin Litho-plastic wheels

**PTC064.000**

c.1960 . . . . . . . . . . . . . $45
Matchbox

**PTC085.000**

1960s . . . . . . . . . $185

**PTC052.000**

1950s 4" . . . . . . . . . . . . . . . . . . . . . . $150

**PTC053.000**

1950s . . . . . . . . . . . . . . . . . . . . . . . . $200
Linemar, three versions exist

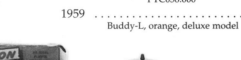

**PTC058.000**

1959 . . . . . . . . . . . . . . . . . . . . . . . . . . . $725
Buddy-L, orange, deluxe model

**PTY013.B00**

1960s . . . . . . . . . . . . . . . . . $50
Train car, in box

**PTC100.B00**

1970s . . . . . . . . . . . . . . . . . . . . . . . . . $350
Japan, double decker bus

**PTY015.B00**

1950s . . . . . . . . . . . . . . . . . . . . . . . . . $585
**PTY015.000** Without Box . . . . . . . . . . . . $375
Toy hot dog wagon

**PTY014.BS0**

1973-1974 . . . . . . . . . . . . . . . . . . . . . $400
Lionel train set, complete in box

**PTC015.B00**

1950s . . . . . . . . . . . . . . . . . . . . . . . $1,200
Marx, MIB

1940s . . . . . . . . . . . . . . . .$175 each

Set of 4 jigsaw puzzles, with original box.

PTY125.B02

Crossing the Equator

PTY125.B03

Teenage Party

PTY125.B01

Halloween Party

PTY125.B04

Hawaiian Beach

1952  12" x 18"

Puzzle (Bill Gregg Art) with original envelope

PTY060.B00

English . . . . . . . . . . . . . . .$385

PTY060.B01

French . . . . . . . . . . . . . . .$250

Canadian

PTY156.B00

"15" Puzzle . . . . . . . . . . . . . . . . . . . .$185

Wood

1940s-1950s Milton Bradley Games

PTY157.B00

Tick-Tac-Toe . . . . . . . . . . . . . . . . . . . .$185

PSM100.000
c.1908 . . . . . . . . . . . . . . . . . . . . . . .$3,000
Match safe, celluloid, made by Whitehead
and Hoag, showing both sides, Rare

PPJ008.000
c.1912 1 $^1/_2$" dia. . . . .$2,500
Watch fob, celluloid,
showing both sides

PMD032.000
1930s 6 $^1/_2$" tall . .$600
"Salesman of the Month"
statue

PMD033.000
1930s 6 $^1/_2$" tall .$600
"Salesman" statue (gold
dipped)

PPJ092.001          PPJ092.002          PPJ092.004

1920s . . . . . . . . . . . . . . . . . . . . . . . . . . . . . . . . . . . . . . . . . . . . . . . . .$350 each
"Safe Driving Award" pins, enameled, Rare

PSM070.001

1936 . . . . . . . . . . . . . . . . . . . . . .$700
50th Anniversary Ashtray, porcelain, Rare.
(Personally signed at the 1936 Convention)

PPM123.002

PPM123.001

1930s . . . . . . . . . .$175 Each
Cigar Bands (Glass & Bottle)

NOTE: *The top of this pullmatch is decaled on plastic. The condition of these decals is very important when determing value. Flaking or bad decals will drop this value considerably.*

PSM071.000

1930s . . . . . . . . . . . . . . . . . . . . . .$1,600
"Pullmatch" Ashtray

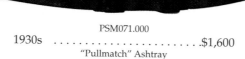

PSM015.000

1910 . . . . . . . . . . . . . . . . . . . . . . .$1,100
"The Coca-Cola Girl" matchbook,
showing both sides, Rare

PSM101.000

c.1914 . . . . . . . . .$750
Matchbook

PSM018.000

c.1913 . . . . . . . . .$650
Matchbook

PFN070.000
c.1894 . . . . . . . . . . . . . . . . .$3,000
Fan, showing both sides, Rare

PCT008.000
c.1892  3 1/2" x 5 1/2" . . . . . . . . . . .$1,700
Trade card, Rare

PCT048.002
1901  1 5/8" x 3 3/8" . . . . . . . . . . . . . .$700
Hilda Clark "Free Drink" coupon

PCT043.000
c.1907 . . . . . . . . . . . . . . . . . . . . .$850
Folding Trade Card, shown open and closed

PMC019.000
1900  1 1/2" x 2 1/2" . . . . . . . . . . . . . .$550
Stamp holder with calendar, celluloid

PBM007.000            PBM009.001
1898 and 1900   2" x 2 1/4" . . . . . . .$700-$600 Each
Bookmarks, celluloid

PBM013.000
c.1906   1 1/2" x 3 1/8" . . . . . . . . $800
"Owl" bookmark, celluloid

Note: Prices are based on items in
Excellent condition. Items in Near Mint
to Mint condition could be worth more
and in Poor condition that same item
would be worth far less.

Note: Some of the pieces shown
on this color page can also be found in
the black and white section.

PBM011.000
1904   2" x 6" . . . . . . . $325
Lillian Nordica bookmark

PMC021.000
1903   2 1/2" x 5" . . . . . . . $600
Hilda Clark note pad, celluloid

PBM010.000
1903   2" x 6" . . . . . . . . . . $375
Hilda Clark bookmark

PBM012.000
1905   2 1/4" x 5 1/4" . . . . . . . $700
Lillian Nordica bookmark

PPM011.000

1902  4 1/8" x 6 1/8" . . . .$800
Menu

PPM013.000

1904  4 1/8" x 6 1/2" . . . .$750
Lillian Nordica menu

Back of both menus

PCT015.000

1910  . . . . . . . . . . . . . . .$700
"The Coca-Cola Girl" post card,
Hamilton King Art

PPM348.000

c.1910  6" x 7" . . . . . . . . . . .$500
Sales folder, open, showing both sides

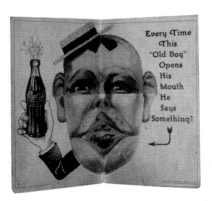

PCT044.002

c.1920s  . . . . . . . . . . . . . . . .$950
Mechanical folding card.
(NOTE: This card is a variation of the one
shown in the B&W section.)

PCT016.000

1911  . . . . . . . . . . . . . . . . . .$700
"Motor Girl" post card

NOTE: Both the 1910 and
1911 postcards shown
above must be in very nice
condition of 8.5 or better to
warrant the values shown.
Postmarked and written
cards do not detract from
the card, but cannot be
called mint.

PPM121.000
1914 . . . . . . . . . . . . . . . . . . . . . . . . .$650
"Verigraph" (Early 3-D) glasses, Rare

PCT052.000
1905  6 $^1/_2$" x 9 $^3/_4$" . . . . . . . . . . . . . . .$275
"Lillian Nordica" magazine ad with coupon,
beware of smaller size reproduction. See repro section of book.

PCA167.000
1911 . . . . . . . . . . . . . . . . . . . . . . . .$900
Lillian Nordica coupon card calendar, can also be
found from 1909, 1910

PCT053.000
1905  3 $^3/_4$" x 7" . . . . . . . . . . . . . . . . .$750
"Lillian Nordica" ad card with coupon,
(front and back shown).
Rare when found complete, coupon must be
attached to warrant this price.

# 1936 OLYMPIC FOLDERS

The following is a complete set of 1936 Olympic Games Schedules, showing front and back of each. Individual folders are Rare and the complete set is Very Rare.     Individuals . . . . . $250.00 each.     PPM347.S00 Complete set . . . . . $1,200.00

PPM347.S01

PPM347.S02

PPM347.S03

PPM347.S04

PTC010.000

Late 1940s . . . . . . . . . . . . . . . . . . . . . $725
With wood blocks . . . . . . . . . . . . $1,100

Smith-Miller, wood and metal

PTC036.000

1953 . . . . . . . . . . . . . . . . . . . . . . . . . $900

Smith-Miller

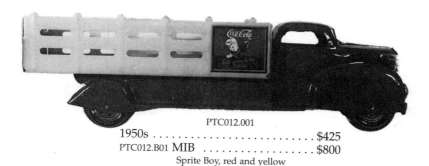

PTC012.001

1950s . . . . . . . . . . . . . . . . . . . . . . . $425
PTC012.B01 MIB . . . . . . . . . . . . . . . . $800

Sprite Boy, red and yellow

*Note: MIB = Mint in box*

PTC061.B00

1969 . . . . . . . . . . . . . . . . . . . . . . . . . $425

Buddy-L, MIB

*Note: Prices are based on items in Excellent condition. Items in Near Mint to Mint condition could be worth more and in Poor condition that same item would be worth far less.*

PTC013.000

1950s . . . . . . . . . . . . . . . . . . . . . . . $475

Marx Sprite Boy

PTC060.000

1960s . . . . . . . . . . . . . . . . . . . . . . . $200

Buddy-L

PTC130.000

1980s . . . . . . . . . . . . . . . . . . . . . . . $65

Nylint 18 wheeler

PTC086.000

1950s . . . . . . . . . . . . . . . . . . . . . . . $250

VW van

PTC087.000

1950s . . . . . . . . . . . . . . . $285

VW van, small size

PTC137.B01

1960s . . . . . . . . . . . . . . . . . . . . . . . $275

Car, tin friction, MIB

PTC035.B01    PTC035.B02

c.1954 . . . . . . . . . . . . . . . . . . . . . . . . $550 Each

Marx, MIB, two different examples

PTC037.B00

c.1950s  8" . . . . . . . . . . . . . . $485

Beverage truck, tin friction, made by Rosko

PTC032.B00

1950s . . . . . . . . . . . . . . . . . . . . . . . . $600

Marx plastic, MIB

PTC039.000

c.1956 . . . . . . . . . . . . . . . . . . . . . . . . $450

PTC039.B00 MIB . . . . . . . . . . . . . . . . . $800

Tin friction

PTC011.001

Late 1940s Red version . . . . . . . . . . . $900

PTC011.002 Gray version . . . . . . . . . . $1,000

Lincoln (Canada), Rare when found with original
wood cases

PTC038.P01

1950s . . . . . . . . . . . . . . . . . . . . . . . . $800

Pick up (without cardboard insert piece)

PTC014.000

c. 1956 . . . . . . . . . . . . . . . . . . . . . . . . $475

PTC014.B00 MIB . . . . . . . . . . . . . . . . . $800

Marx, Sprite Boy

Note: MIB = Mint in box

PTC015.000

c.1957 . . . . . . . . . . . . . . . . . . . . . . . . $750

Marx

PTC040.B00

1950s . . . . . . . . . . . . . . . . . . . . . . . . $375

Tin Wind-up double decker bus and terminal, in box

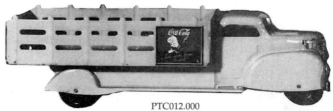

PTC012.000

Late 1940s  Without rear decal . . . . . $425

PTC012.002 With rear decal . . . . . . . . $500

PTC012.B00 MIB . . . . . . . . . . . . . . . . . $950

Marx, Sprite Boy, yellow

# TOY TRUCKS

PTC017.000
1950s  8 1/4" . . . . . . . . . . . . . . . . . . $1,850
GOSO, wind-up, Rare

PTC016.000
c.1949  8 1/4", Rare . . . . . . . . . . . . . $2,500
PTC016.B00 MIB, Very Rare . . . . . . . $3,500
GOSO, wind-up

PTC013.B00
1950s . . . . . . . . . . . . . . . . . . . . . . . . $825
Marx, Sprite Boy, MIB

PTC057.B00
c.1950 . . . . . . . . . . . . . . . . . . . . . . . $550
Buddy-L, MIB

PTC069.B00
c.1965 . . . . . . . . . . . . . . . . . . . . . . . $375
Dinky Toy, MIB

Note: MIB = Mint in box

PTC126.B00
1979 . . . . . . . . . . . . . . . . . . . . . . $1,000
Smith Miller, MIB (only 50 made) Rare

PTC067.000
1950s  8 1/2" . . . . . . . . . . . . . . . . . . $700
Rare

# TOY TRUCKS

PTC063.B00

c.1958 . . . . . . . . . . . . $125

Matchbox even load, gray wheels

PTC062.B00

c.1953 . . . . . . . . . . . . . $150

Matchbox staggered load

PTC064.B00

c.1960 . . . . . . . . . . . . . . $75

Matchbox, black wheels

PTC065.B00

c.1950 2 1/2" . . . . . $225

Bembrose U.K., Rare
(Matchbox copy)

PTC066.000

c.1960 2 1/4" . . . . . . $150

Barklay fishtail

PTC134.000

1970s 2" . . . . . . . . . $90

Nostalgic Miniature

PTC071.000

1960s 1 1/2" . . . . . . . . . . . . . $45

Roskopf (Germany), plastic

PTC055.001

1960s 3 3/4" . . . . . . . . . . . . . . . . . . $800

AMBO (Italy), tin litho., tin wheels, Rare

PTC068.000

c.1960 5" . . . . . . . . . . . . . . . . . . . . $875

Japan, tin litho., Very Rare

PTC070.000

1960s . . . . . . . . . . . . . . . . $275

Japan, tin/plastic, pink or red cab, Rare

PTC101.001

1970s 3 1/2" . . . . . . $15-$30

Tin/plastic, six different variations

PTC127.000

c.1983 4 1/4" . . . . . . . . . . . . . . . $60

Ralstoy

PTC128.000

1970s 4 3/4" . . . . . . . . . . . . . . . . $85

Portugal, plastic

PTC129.000

1970s 5 1/2" . . . . . . . . . . . . . . . . . . . . $55

Hong Kong, plastic friction

### PTC088.B00
c.1960s 4" . . . . . . . . $500
France Jouet, die cast, Berliet,
Very Rare

### PTC089.B00
c.1960s 4" . . . . . . . $385
France Jouet Stradair

### PTC090.000
c.1960s 10" . . . . . . . . . . . . . . . . . . . $425
Italy, Rare

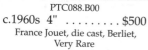

### PTC074.000
c.1960s 12" . . . . . . . . . . . . . . . . . . . $525
Buddy-L (USA), plastic, Rare, two different versions exist

### PTC120.B00
1970s 6 1/4" . . . . . . . . . . . . $275
Tranvia (Spain) trolley, tin and
plastic, MIB

### PTC140.B00
1960s 4" . . . . . . . . . . . . . . . $400
VW Van (Gama), Germany, die cast
and plastic

### PTY012.S00
c.1950s 14 3/4" . . . . . . . . . . . . . . . . . $550
West Germany, train, tin wind-up, Rare

### PTC121.000
c.1980s 11" . . . . . . . . . . . . $450
Ford Model T, Maxitoy (Austria)
Collectors market, all metal limited
edition, Rare

### PTC092.BS0
c.1970s . . . . . . . . . . . . . . . $300
Buddy-L (USA) "Pop Art" set, Rare
when found complete, MIB

*Note: MIB = Mint in box*

### PTC091.001        PTC091.002
1970s-1980s . . . . . . . . . . . . . . . . $45 Each
Flip-O-Matic, plastic, several color and bottle variations

### PTC122.B00
c.1980s 7 1/2" . . . . . . . . . . . . . . $150
"Cola Truck" (Hong Kong), plastic friction

### PTC094.000
c.1970s 3" . . . . . . . . . . . . $225
"Van Line" (Japan), tin wind-up, Rare

### PTC141.BS0
c.1960s . . . . . . . . . . . . . $975
Sesame (France) set with Coca-Cola
route truck, Rare, MIB

# TOY TRUCKS, ETC.

PTC056.000
1950s . . . . . . . . . . . . . . . . . . . . . . $1,200
Marx No. 21 (Canadian version), Very Rare

PTC072.B00
1960s . . . . . . . . . . . . . . . . . . . . . . $185
Milton, MIB, Rare

PTC123.000
1980s 3 1/2" . . . . . . . . . . . . . . . . . . . . . $40
Plastic

Note:
MIB = Mint in box

PTC073.B00
1960s 8 1/2" . . . . . . . . . . . . . . . . . . . $375
Van with moving eyes, MIB,
two versions: moving eyes and stationary eyes

PTC093.000
1970s . . . . . . . . . . . . . . . . . . . . . . . . $200
Japan, wind-up

PTC102.000
1970s 15" . . . . . . . . . . . . . . . . . . . . . . $125
Race car pillow

PTC120.000
1970s 6 1/4" . . . . . . . . . . . . . $150
Spain, trolley

PTC124.000                          PTC125.000
1980s 4 1/4" . . . . . . . . . . . . . . . . . . . $75 Each
VW bank and VW lighter

PTC075.000
1948-1950 . . . . . . . . . . . . . . . . . . . . . $2,900
Italian, wood, tin, and Bakelite, Very Rare

PTC076.000
1 1/2" . . . . . . . . . . . . . . . . . . $600
Date unknown tin litho., Rare

PTC080.001

PTC080.002
c.1960  4" . . . . . . . . $160 Each
Sesame (France), plastic and tin
friction, three different colors

PTC034.B00
1950s MIB . . . . . . . . . . . . . . . . . . . . . $750
PTC034.000 Without box . . . . . . . . . . . . $425
Marx, Plastic

Note:
MIB = Mint in box

PTC103.000
1970s . . . . . . . . . . . . . . . . . . . . . . . . . $55
Japan, plastic and tin friction

PTC092.000
1970s  2 1/2" . . . . . . . . . . . . . . . . . $35
Buddy-L racer

PTC119.000
1980s  12 1/2" . . . . . . . . . . . . . . . . . . . $175
Yaxon, Italian, die-cast, three color variations

PTC077.000

1950s 3 1/2" . . . . . . . . . . . . . . . .$125
Wiking (Germany), plastic

PTC116.B00

c.1980 4" . . . . . . . . . . . . . . . . . . . .$160
Tomica, Dandy, VW

PTC135.000

c.1980 4" . . . . . . . . . . . . . . . . .$100
M.T.I. Route Truck

PTC078.B00

c.1960 2 3/4" . . . . . . . . . . .$300
Spanish, plastic, Rare

PTC079.000

c.1970 6 1/2" . . . . . . . . . . . . . . .$85
Dinky (Hong Kong), plastic

PTC046.BS0

1950s . . . . . . . . . . . . . . . . . . . . . . .$700
Assorted van set, complete set of 12 vans in box, Rare

PTC117.000

c.1970 4" . . . . . . . . . . . . . . . . . . . . .$125
Mexico, van, plastic, Rare

PTY011.S00

1950s . . . . . . . . . . . . . . . . . . . . . .$450
Japan, train, tin wind-up, seven pieces, 14",
Very Rare

PTC136.000

1982 2 1/2" . . . . . . . . . . . . . . . . . . . .$80
Playart, recent Diet Coke, metal

PTC118.000

1980s 5" . . . . . . . . . . . . . . . . . . . . . . .$50
Scania (Brazil), plastic

PTC141.000

c.1960 6", part of set . . . . . . . . . . .$350
PTC141.BS0 Full set of 6 in box . . . . .$975
Sesame (France), Rare

# TOY TRUCKS

PTC106.001                               PTC106.002
1970s 4" . . . . . . . . . . . . . . . . . $250 Each
Peugot (France), Rare

PTC108.B00
c.1980  2 1/2" . . . . . . . . . . . . $75
Tomica (Japan)

PTC105.000
c.1969  7 1/4" . . . . . . . . . . . . . . . . . $275
GMC (Mexico), plastic, Rare

PTC107.000
c.1970 . . . . . . . . . . . . . . . . . . . . . . $50
Tente (Mexico)

PTC111.000
1980s  7" . . . . . . . . . . . . . . . . . . . . $50
Scania (Brazil), metal

PTC109.001

PTC112.000
c.1980s  5 1/4" . . . . . . . . . . . . . . . . . $25
Saurer (Germany), plastic

PTC109.002
c.1970s  4" . . . . . . . . . . . . . . . . . $45 Each
Solido (France) Renaults,
yellow and red versions

PTC113.000
1980  7 1/4" . . . . . . . . . . . . . . . . . $40
Jirapuru (Brazil) Ford route truck, plastic

PTC110.001                    PTC110.002
1980s . . . . . . . . . . . . . . . . . . . $35 Each
Renaults (France) metal and plastic versions

PTC096.000

VW Lemy . . . . . . . . . . . . . . . . . . . . . $175
PTC096.B00 MIB . . . . . . . . . . . . . . . . $275
Mexico

PTC143.000

1950s VW Tippco 9" . . . . . . . . . . . . $550
PTC143.B00 MIB . . . . . . . . . . . . . . . . $650
Germany

PTC095.000

c.1950 15 1/2" . . . . . . . . . . . . . . . . . . $450
Schildkroet (Germany), plastic, Rare

PTC104.000

1970 4 1/4" . . . . . . . . . . . . . . . $275
VW Gama (Germany)

PTC142.000

1960s 4" . . . . . . . . . . . . . . . $275
VW Gama (Germany)

PTC114.B00

1970s 16" . . . . . . . . . . . . . . . . . . . . . $225
Japan, jumbo trailer

PTC089.000

1960s 4" . . . . . . . . . . . . . . . . . . $300
PTC089.B00 MIB . . . . . . . . . . . . . $400
Stradair (France)

PTC115.B00

1980s 12" . . . . . . . . . . . . . . . . . . . . $185
Japan, plastic

PTC139.B00

1960s 13 3/4" . . . . . . . . . . . . . . . . . . . $350
Tigre 2000 (Spain)

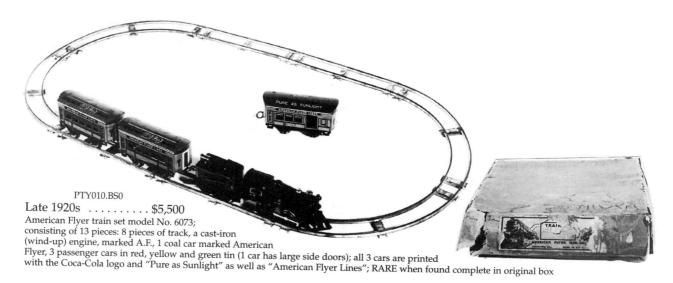

PTY010.BS0
Late 1920s . . . . . . . . . . $5,500
American Flyer train set model No. 6073;
consisting of 13 pieces: 8 pieces of track, a cast-iron
(wind-up) engine, marked A.F., 1 coal car marked American
Flyer, 3 passenger cars in red, yellow and green tin (1 car has large side doors); all 3 cars are printed
with the Coca-Cola logo and "Pure as Sunlight" as well as "American Flyer Lines"; RARE when found complete in original box

PTY010.PO1
Individual "American Flyer" Train Cars . . . . . . . . . . . . $1,500

PTY017.B00
1970s . . . . . . . . . . . . . . . . . . . . . . $25
Tyco kit (drug store) for train set

PTY016.B00
1970s . . . . . . . . . . . . . . . . . . . $18
Lima train car

PTY018.B00
1950s . . . . . . . . . . . . . . . . . . . . . . $275
"Playtown" Hamburger Stand

PTY019.BS0
1950s . . . . . . . . . . . . . . . . . . . . . . . . . . . . . . . . $125
"Railroad Set", cardboard set-up for train set with Coca-Cola billboard

PTY020.B00
1950s . . . . . . . . . . . . . . . $150
"Hamburger Stand"

PTY021.000
1950s . . . . . . . . . . . . . . . . . . . . . . . . . . . . $285
Toy shopping basket

PTY022.000
1960s . . . . . . . . . . . . . . . . . . . . . . . . . . $200
Rocking horse. Note: This was a giveaway item
from the Salem N.H. Coca-Cola Bottling Co. and
Rockingham Park (Racetrack).

PTY023.000
1970s . . . . . . . . . . . . . . . . . . $85
Kiddy-Car (plastic)

PTY024.000
1930-31 . . . . . . . . . . $2,500
"Coca-Cola Flyer", 3-wheel scooter, marked on front fork "Save
Coca-Cola crowns - get one", 36"
long, Rare. Photo Courtesy: Ron
Paradoski St. Louis, MO

> Note: Prices are based on items in Excellent condition. Items in Near
> Mint to Mint condition could be worth more and in Poor condition
> that same item would be worth far less.

PTY025.B00
c.1960  in box . . . . . . . . . . . . . . . . . $285
PTY025.000 Without box . . . . . . . . . . . $125
Bottle Case Wagon

PPH010.000
1930-31  8" x 10" . . . . . . . . . . . . . . . . . $35
Photo, St. Louis Bottling Plant "The Premium Room",
shows many Coca-Cola scooters, wagons, etc.

PTY026.B00
1930s . . . . . . . . . . . . . . . . . . . . . . . . . . $525
Toy plane, celluloid and wood, in original box

PTY027.BS0
1972 . . . . . . . . . . . . . . . . . . . . . . . . . . $125
"Sopwith Camel" Snoopy plane, complete in box,
with all parts and paperwork

PTY161.000
1930s . . . . . . . . . $400
Wood "top"

PTY028.000
Early 1930s  $8^{1}/_{2}$" x $4^{1}/_{4}$" x $8^{1}/_{2}$"  . . $1,800
Toy stove, green with red panels

PTY029.000
1950s . . . . . . . . . $185
Toy telescope

PTY030.S00
1930s . . . . . . . . . . . . . . . . . . . . . . . . . . $200
Golf tee set

PTY031.BS0
1960s . . . . . . . . . . . $225
Magic kit

# TOYS AND GAMES

PTY032.000

c.1950 . . . . . . . . . . . $60

"Paddle Ball" (local bottler)

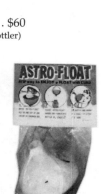

PTY036.B00

1950s . . . . . . . . . . . . . . . . . $6 Each

Astro-Float, showing both sides

PTY037.B00

1960s . . . . . . . . . . . . . . . . $300

Yo-Yo, complete box

PTY033.000

1930s . . . . . . . . . . . . . $325

American Flyer kite

PTY038.000

c.1950s . . . . . . . . . . . . . . . . . . . . $20

Golf ball

PTY040.S00

1930s . . . . . . . . . . . . . . . . . . . . . . . . . $125

Wooden "top" game

*Note: Many times local bottlers would give away items without using the standard "Coca-Cola" logo, but rather a different type style. These items are still collectible, but generally are not as desirable.*

PTY034.000

1950s . . . . . . . . $50

Marbles (Beware of reproductions)

PTY035.000

Late 1940s . . . . . . $50

Marbles

PTY039.000

1930s . . . . . . . $160

Yo-Yo

PTY041.000

1970s . . . . . . $6

Yo-Yo

PTY037.000

1960s . . . . . . $12

Yo-Yo

PTY043.000

1970s . . . . . . $30

Baseball

PTY042.000

1970s . . . . . . $6

Yo-Yo

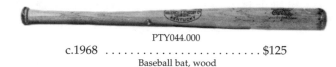

PTY045.000

1970s . . . . . . . . . . . . . . . . . . . . . . . $60

Baseball bat, aluminum

PTY044.000

c.1968 . . . . . . . . . . . . . . . . . . . . . . . $125

Baseball bat, wood

PTY046.B00

c.1927 . . . . . . . . . . . . . . . . . . . . . . $950
"Pure as Sunlight" puzzle, in original envelope,
Very Rare

PTY047.B00

c.1928 . . . . . . . . . . . . . . . . . . . . . . $650
Card game "Age Cards", in original envelope
six cards, Rare

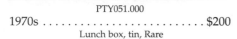

PTY049.B00

1950s . . . . . . . . . . . $285
Wall Quoits

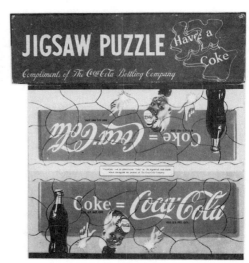

PTY048.B00

1950s . . . . . . . . . . . . . . . . . . . . . . $300
Sprite Boy, jigsaw puzzle

PTY051.000

1970s . . . . . . . . . . . . . . . . . . . . . . $200
Lunch box, tin, Rare

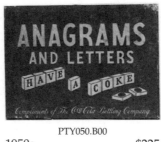

PTY050.B00

1950s . . . . . . . . . . . . . . . $225
Anagrams

PTY052.B00

1968 . . . . . . . . . . . . . . . . . . . . $55
Hemisfair kaleidoscope puppets,
Sid & Marty Kroft

PTY053.000

1950s . . . . . . . . $100
"Hi-Fi Club" record holder,
plastic

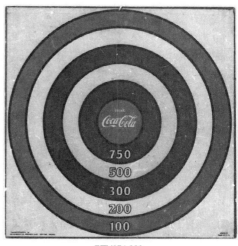

PTY054.000

1940s-50s . . . . . . . . . . . . . . . . . . . . . . $125
Dart board

PTY055.000

1930s  9 1/4" x 9 1/4" . . . . . . . . . . . . . $700
Punchboard

PTY058.BS0

c.1916 . . . . . . . . . . . . . . . . . . . . . . . . $160
"Household Words Game" card game 48 cards, each
with a different product on the face: Coke, Orange,
Crush, Wrigley's Gum, etc., Rare

PTY056.000

1930s  9 1/4" x 9 1/4" . . . . . . . . . . . . . $750
Punchboard

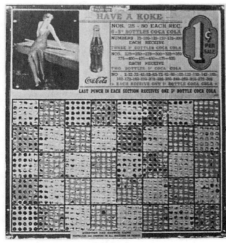

PTY057.000

1930s  9 1/4" x 9 1/4" . . . . . . . . . . . . $1,100
Punchboard

PTY059.000

1946 . . . . . . . . . . . . . . . . . . . . . . . . $185
"The Coke Crowd" paper dolls cutout book, printed
by Merrill Co., Publishers Chicago, IL

**PTY060.B00**

1952 . . . . . . . . . . . . . . . $385
Puzzle (Bill Gregg Art), 12" x 18",
with original envelope

**PTY061.000**

1940s-50s  7 1/4" . . . . . . . . $200
Christmas horn, cardboard,
Memphis, TN

**PTY062.001**

Late 1920s . . . . . . . . . . . . . . . . . . . . . $425
Jump rope with whistle, "Pure as Sunlight"

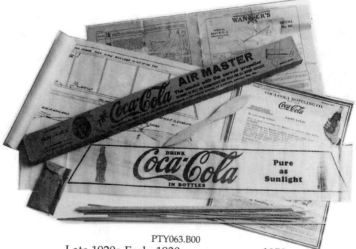

**PTY063.B00**

Late 1920s-Early 1930s . . . . . . . . . . . $850
Airplane model kit, Coca-Cola "Airmaster",
complete in box with instructions, Rare.
Photo Courtesy: Rudy LeCoadic.

**PTY062.002**

Late 1920s . . . . . . . . . . . . . . . . . . . . .$385
Jump rope, "Pure as Sunlight"

**PTY064.000**

1920s  2 3/4" . . . . . . . . . . . . . . . . . . . . $225
Whistle, cardboard

**PTY065.000**

1940s . . . . . . . . . . . . . . . . $125
Clicker, tin

**PTY066.000**

Late 1920s . . . . . . . . . . . . . $85

Bang gun

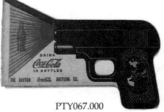

**PTY067.000**

1950s . . . . . . . . . . . . . . . $60

Bang gun

**PTY070.001**     **PTY070.002**

1950s . . . . . . . . . . . . . . . $65 Each

"Smile" game cards, Dayton

**PTY068.000**

1950s . . . . . . . . . . . . . . . . . $45

Clicker pistol

**PTY069.000**

1970s . . . . . . . . . . . . . . . $4

Bang gun

**PTY072.000**

1980s . . . . . $3

Santa "Ring Toss"

**PTY071.000**

1950s . . . . . . . . . . . . . . . . . . . . . . . . . $55

3-D glasses

**PTY076.000**

1960s . . . . . . . . . . . . . . $10

Pop corn box

**PTY073.000**

1960s . . . . . . $6

Pop corn bag

**PTY074.000**

1932 . . . . . . . $500

Puzzle, wood, Rare

**PTY075.S00**

1940s . . . . . . . . . . . . . . . . . . . $250

"Coca-Cola Commandos" cutouts

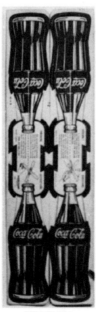

**PTY078.000**

c.1950 . . . . $20

Boomerang

**PTY079.B00**

1980s . . . . . . . . . . . $20

"Stunt Plane"

**PTY077.S01**   **PTY077.S02**   **PTY077.S03**   **PTY077.S04**

1950s . . . . . . . . . . . . . . . . . . . . . . . . $15 Each

PTY077.S00 . . . . . . . . . . . . . . . . . . . . $75 Set

"Rootie Kazootie" pop-out puppets carton stuffers

# GAMES

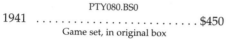

PTY080.BS0

1941 . . . . . . . . . . . . . . . . . . . . . . . . . . . $450

Game set, in original box

PTY084.B00

1950s . . . . . . $30

Shanghai game

PTY081.B00

1940s . . . . . . . . . . . . . . . . . . . . . . . . . . . $65

Cribbage board

PTY082.BS0

1940s-50s . . . . . . . . . . . . . . . . $50

Darts (darts not marked with logo)

PTY083.BS0

1940s . . . . . . . . . . . . . . . . . $60

Dominos

PTY085.BS0

1940s . . . . . . . . . . . . . . . . . $45

Checkers

PTY086.BS0

1930s . . . . . . . . . . . . . . . . . . . . . . . . . . . . . . . . . . . . . . . . . . . . . . . . . . . . . . $750

Coca-Cola punching ball game, complete in box with mask and ball, Rare

PTY087.000

1940s . . . . . . . . . . . . . . . . . $120

Dart Board

PTY088.000

1940s . . . . . . . . . . . . . . . . . $125

Chinese Checkers

PTY089.000

1940s-50s . . . . . . . . . . . . . . . $125

Parcheesi game

# TOYS AND GAMES

PTY090.000
c.1910-1916  6 1/4" . . . . . . . . . . . . . . . $750
Whistle, cardboard, shown open
(Inside of whistles shown at right)

PTY091.000
c.1916-1920  5 3/4" . . $650
Whistle, cardboard, shown
open

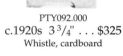

PTY092.000
c.1920s  3 3/4" . . . $325
Whistle, cardboard

PTY094.000
1920s . . . . . . . . . . $125
Whistle, tin

PTY096.000
1920s . . . . . . . . . . . . . . . . . . . . . . . . . $60
Whistle, wood

PTY097.000
1930s . . . $60
Siren whistle

PTY098.000
1930s . . . $150
Whistle, tin

PTY093.000
c.1920s . . . $225
Clicker, metal

PTY095.000
1930s . . . . . . . . $135
Clicker, metal

PTY099.000
c.1950 . . . . . . . . . . . . . . . $20
Whistle, plastic

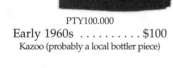

PTY100.000
Early 1960s . . . . . . . . . $100
Kazoo (probably a local bottler piece)

PTY103.000
c.1930s . . . . . . . . . . . . . . . . . . . . . $65
Play moustache, heavy paper cutout,
"Roanoake Coca-Cola Bott. Works, Inc."

PTY102.000
c.1930s . . . . . . . . . . . . . . . . . . . $300
"Machine Gun Bubble Blower", with
instructions, Rare

PTY104.000
c.1957 . . . . . . . . . . . . . . . . . . . . . . . $175
Eddie Fisher "Charm Bracelet"

PTY101.000
1920s . . . . . . $150
Whistle, wood

PTY105.BS0
c.1920 . . . . . . . . . . . . . . . . . . . . $325
Dice set (5) in leather case

PTY106.000

1970s . . . . . . . . . . . . . . . . . $15

Pillow

PTY107.000

c.1950 . . . . . . . . . . . $125

Pillow

PTY109.P01

1950s . . . . . . . . . . $3

Bingo card

PTY110.000

1930s . . . . . . . . . . . . $35

Bingo card

PTY113.BS0

1950s . . . . . . . . . . $60

Picnic set

PTY108.000

1960 . . . . . . . $20

Plastic (blow-up) can

PTY111.000

1940s . . . . . . . . . . . . . . $35

Bingo card

PTY112.000

1941 . . . . . . . . . . . . . $45

Bingo card

PTY114.BS0

1950s . . . . . . . . . . . . . $200

"Dolly Loves A Party" set

PTY115.BS0

1950s . . . . . . . . . . . . . . . . . . . . . . . $200

"Dolly Picnic Set"

PTY116.B00

1980s Cobot (in box) . . . . . . . . . . . . . $150

PTY116.000 Cobot only . . . . . . . . . . . . . .$85

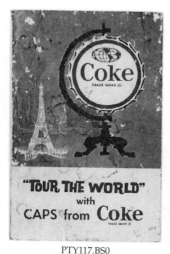

PTY117.BS0

1950s . . . . . . . . . . . . . $125

"Tour the World" Coke bottle cap set

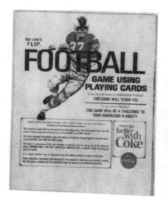

PTY118.000

c.1964 . . . . . . . . . . . . . . . . . . . . . . . . $25

"Bo-Lyn's Flip Football" game

# GAMES
## MILTON BRADLEY 1940s-50s

PTY119.BS0

Dominos . . . . . . . . . . . . . . . . . . . $50

PTY048.B00

Jigsaw puzzle . . . . . . . . . $300

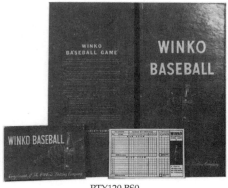

PTY120.BS0

Winko baseball . . . . . . . . . . . . . . . . $225

PTY121.BS0

Ring toss . . . $165

PTY109.BS0

Bingo set . . . . . . . . . . . . . . . . . . . . . $65

PTY122.BS0

Table tennis set . . . . . . $65
Paddles marked with logo

PTY123.BS0

Checkers . . . . . . . . . $45

PTY124.BS0

Darts . . . . . . . . . . . . . . $50
Darts not marked with logo

PTY125.B01

Jigsaw puzzle . . . $175

PTY126.BS0

Tower of Hannoi game . . . . . . . . . . . $200
Rare

PTY127.BS0

Game set . . . . . . . . . . $175

PTY129.BS0

Game set . . . . . $375
Two decks of cards, cribbage board, dominos, checkers

PTY128.000

Broadsides game . . . . . $65

PTY130.BS0

Checkers, backgammon . . . . . . . . . . $150

PTY131.BS0

Chess Set . . . . $85

PTY132.BS0

Horse race game . . . . . . . . . . . . . . . $300
Rare

— 334 —

# DOLLS

PTY133.000
**Buddy Lee Doll**
PTY133.000 c.1950s  12 1/2"
Composition . . . . . . . . . . . . . . $1,200
PTY133.001 Plastic . . . . . . . . . . . $1,000
Only when complete

1950s-1960s COCA-COLA
SANTA DOLLS

PTY134.001
White boots  . . . . . . . . $100

PTY134.002
Black Santa . . . . . . . . . . $85

*Note: These values are for dolls with original uniforms. Reproduction uniforms are common. Be Careful!*

PTY134.003
Black boots  . . . . $100

*Note: The "Santa Doll" quite frankly, has never been my favorite piece of Coca-Cola advertising. I have seen these dolls sell for more than my estimated values, however, I just don't feel they are worth it. I have also seen quite a few different variations and do consider some of them questionable.*

PTY135.000
1960s . . . . . . . . . . . . $35
Santa

PTY136.000
Santa with
Coca-Cola (label)
belt buckle,
questionable

PTY134.005
White boots . . . . . . . $85

PTY134.004
1960s . . . . . . . . . . . . $60
Santa (with caution tag)

# CUTOUTS FOR CHILDREN

** Very Common, have turned up in quantity over the years    * Common, turn up regularly

PTY137.000

1930s . . . . . . . . . . . . . . . . . . . . . . . . . $275

"Toonerville Town"

PTY138.000

1929 . . . . . . . . . . . . . . . . . . . . . . . . . $275

"Corner Store"

PTY139.000

1932 . . . . . . . . . . . . . . . . . . . . . . . . . $85**

"Olympics"

*Note: These cutouts are 10" x 15" printed on lightweight cardstock. They were given away to children, at the same time the corresponding window display was in the store window. There was also a window banner with each display informing the children of the free cutouts.*

PTY140.000

1927 . . . . . . . . . . . . . . . . . . . . . . . . . $125*

"Circus"

PTY141.001

1932 . . . . . . . . . . . . . . . . . . . . . . . . . $85**

"Circus" (with glass)

PTY141.002

1932 . . . . . . . . . . . . . . . . . . . . . . . . . $200

"Circus" (with bottle)

*Note: These cutouts have a history of turning up in quantity. When this happens, prices will drop like a rock.*

PTY142.000

1927 . . . . . . . . . . . . . . . . . . . . . . . . . $125*

"Toy Town"

PTY143.000

1931 . . . . . . . . . . . . . . . . . . . . . . . . . $325

"Uncle Remus"

The Hi-Fi Club was a very successful promotion sponsored by local radio stations and Coca-Cola bottlers. The club's initial intent was to sponsor school dances. Prizes were given away through drawings to eligible students who signed up for the club in their high school. Winners were announced at the club's weekly dances. Indianapolis, Indiana was chosen as the test city and the first dance was held there in the fall of 1958. The dances and club were a big hit, and in late 1958 "The Hi-Fi Club" went nationwide. Because of the popularity of the Hi-Fi Club and what it eventually led to, many advertising pieces, prizes, and promotional items exist today. Some of the prizes given away include portable radios, record players and racks, jewelry, pins, clothing and many other items. Club sponsored dances were held in school gyms decorated with Hi-Fi Club banners and signs. Students had to show their Hi-Fi Club Membership card to be admitted. With continued success throughout 1959 with 340 participating bottlers, the Club held a talent search. The 340 chapters throughout the country claimed a membership of over two million teenagers. The purpose of this talent search was to find young America's most talented new singers and musicians, with local contests for Hi-Fi Club Members. The local contest winner competed in fifteen area contests during the month of April. The two winners from each of the fifteen area contests received trophies and recordings of their winning performances. During the month of May they went on to compete in five division contests. The two winners from each division contest received trophies, five hundred dollar wardrobes, luggage sets and spent a week in June, 1960, at the Commondore Hotel in New York City to compete in one grand final contest for three five thousand dollar scholarships and guaranteed record releases. Anything related to the Hi-Fi Club is very collectible especially some of the better prizes like radios and record players. Shown here are just some of the pieces related to this program, others can be found throughout the book.

PPJ090.000

Tie clip . . . . . . . . . . . . . . . . . . $25

7' . . . . . . . . . . . . . . . . . . . . . . . . . . . $600
PCC012.000
Satin banner

PPJ077.000
Tin pinback button . . . . . . . . . . . . . . $25

PCH079.000
Vest . . . . . . . . . . . . . . . . . . . . . . . . . $100
Hi-Fi Club

No. 235530 C

1959    1960

No. 235530 C

Free prizes every week, nothing to buy. Your number may be drawn at any time. Listen to the Hi-Fi Club on the air every week, Radio Station WTSB. Saturday, 10:30 until 11:30 A.M. Winner's name announced on broadcast.

Lumberton Coca-Cola
Bottling Co.

**1959-1960**

PTY053.000
Record holder . . . . . . . . . . . . . . . . . $100
Plastic

**MEMBERSHIP CARD**
SPONSORED BY YOUR COCA-COLA BOTTLER

PPM333.000
Membership card . . . . . . . . . . . . . . . $25
Showing both sides

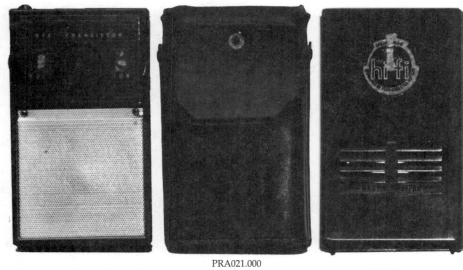

PRA021.000
Portable radio . . . . . . . . . . . . . . . . . . . . . . . . . . . . . . . . . . .$185
Hi-Fi Club, with carrying case, showing both sides

PDE032.000
Decal . . . . . . . . . . . . . . . . . . . . . $12

PSS010.000

1929  5 $^1/_2$" x 5 $^1/_2$" x 10 $^1/_2$" . . . . . . . . .$7,500

PSS010.B00  Mint in original
carrying case . . . . . . . . . . . . . . . . . . $12,500
Glascock "Junior", Rare

Note: 1929 Glascock Salesman Sample Coolers found with original carrying case are considered very rare.

PSS011.000

1929  8" x 10 $^1/_2$" x 13" . . . . . . . . . . $5,500

PSS011.B00  Mint in original
carrying case . . . . . . . . . . . . . . . . . .$12,000
Glascock "Standard"

PSS012.P02

1939  8 $^1/_2$"x 11" x 9"  . . . . . . . . . . . $2,800
"Closed Front"

Note: 1939 Salesman Sample Coolers came equipped with a group of pages entitled "A Business Builder", attached by a ring binder on the inside of lid. These pages show the different coolers available. The cooler is much more interesting and desirable when found with these pages. The "Closed Front" is actually a snap on piece that goes onto the "Open Front" cooler. Prices shown are based on examples complete with pages. Carring case will add to value

PSS012.P01
Carrying Case

Note: 1939 Salesman Sample Coolers found with original carrying case would certainly be worth more.

PSS012.000

1939  8 $^1/_2$" x 11 x 9"  . . . . . . . . . . . $2,500
"Open Front"

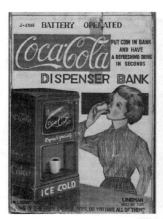

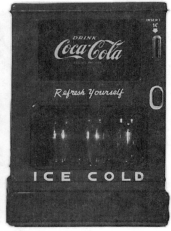

PTY144.000

1950s . . . . . . . . . . . . . . . . . . . . . . . . . $425
PTY144.B00 Near mint
in original box . . . . . . . . . . . . . . . . . .$750
Dispenser bank, (different script on Coca-Cola logo)

PTY145.000

1950s . . . . . . . . . . . . . . . . . . . . . . . . . . . . . . $400
PTY145.B00 Near Mint in original box . . . . . .$700
Dispenser bank

PRA020.000
1950s . . . . . . . . $185
Music box, working

PTY147.000

1950s . . . . . . . . . . . . . . . . . . . . . . . . . $125
PTY144.B00 Complete in Box . . . . . . . . $200
Vending machine bank, plastic, Beware of 1980s
reproductions of this bank.

PTY146.000

1950s 5 1/2" . . . . . . . . . . . . . $125
PTY146.B00 Complete in Box . . . . $225
Plastic, Vending machine bank

PTY148.000

1960s . . . . . . . . . . . . . . . . . . . . $100
PTY148.B00 Complete in Box . $175
Vending machine bank, plastic

PTY149.B00
1960s . . . . . . . . . . . . . . . . . . . . . . . . $65
Toy dispenser, plastic, in box

PTY150.B00
1970s . . . . . . . . . . . . . . . . . . . . . . $40
Toy dispenser, plastic, in box

PTY151.B00
1950s . . . . . . . . . . . . . . . . . . . . . . . . . $125
Toy dispenser, plastic, in box

# MINIATURES

PMI006.000

1950s . . . . . . . . . . . . . . . . . . . . . . . . $350

12-pack, tin, Rare

PMI007.000

1930s . . . . . . . . . . . . . . . . . . . . . . . . $165

Wood case

PMI015.000        PMI016.000

1950s . . . . . . . . . . . . . . . . . . . . . $125 Each

Two different examples

PMI021.000

1960s . . . . . . . . . . . . . . . . . . . . . . . . $125

Plastic case

PMI014.000

4" x 7" x 4 1/2" . . . . . . $225

Wood Cooler, this could have been
a salesmans sample

PTY151.S01

1950s . . . . . . . . . . . . . . . . . . . . . . $185

Plastic Mini picnic cooler with bottles

PMI019.000

1950s . . . . . . . . . . . . . . $75

PMI029.000

1970s As shown . . . . . . . . . . . . . $18
Red plastic case and green bottles
Yellow case w/green bottles . . $25
Yellow case w/gold bottles . . . $30

PMI013.000

1930s . . . . . . . $175

PMI017.B00

1950s . . . . . . . . . . . . . . $225

Plastic case, in original box

PMI018.000

1950s . . . . . . . . . . . . . $85

Carrier with embossed bottles,
tin, Mexico

PMI022.000

1960s . . . . . . . . . . . . . $30

PMI020.000

1950s . . . . . . . . . . . . . . $100

Plastic case

PMI027.000
1970s . . . . . . . . . . $16

PMI028.000
1970s . . . . . . . . . . . $16

PMI023.000
1960s . . . . . . . . . . $35

PMI024.000
1960s . . . . . . . . . . $35

PMI011.000
1930s . . . . . . . . . . . . . . . . . $50
Pure As Sunlight wood case

PMI012.000
c.1939 . . . . . . . . . . $200

PMI010.000
1930s . . . . . . . . . . . . . . $125
12 Bottle, with wood case

PMI030.000
1970s . . . . . . . . . . . . . $15
Salt and Pepper Cans

PTY152.000
c.1950  4" x 2 1/4" . . . . $125
Bank, tin

PMI008.000
1930s . . . . . . . . . . . . . . . . . . . . . . . . . . . $350
24 Bottle, with wood case

PMI009.000
1930s . . . . . . . . . . . . . . . . . . . . . . . . . . . $200
24 Bottle, with wood case

PMI025.000
1970s . . . . . . . . . . . . . . . . . . . . . . . . . . . . $60
24 Bottle, with wood case

PMI026.000
1970s . . . . . . . . . . . . . . . . . . . . . . . . . . . . $65
24 Bottle, with plastic case

# BOTTLES

ottles have long been a favorite among collectors of Coca-Cola memorabilia. A fascinating variety of styles, shapes, and colors were used through the years, although most collections seem to center around the different cities where Coca-Cola bottling franchises have existed.

The earliest bottles known to contain Coca-Cola were of the Hutchinson stoppered variety. The words Coca-Cola appear in either block print or script lettering on the bottles, and embossing usually designated the city where the bottle was originally filled as well. These Hutchinson bottles were used only briefly by fewer than a dozen bottling works just after the turn of the century. Relatively few have survived.

Crown-top, straight-sided bottles replaced the heavier, cruder Hutchinson bottles in the early 1900s. Literally millions of these crown-top bottles were used by the ever-increasing number of Coca-Cola franchises between 1902 and 1915. Few records were kept, however, and individualism was rampant. A given Coca-Cola bottling works might use bottles of several different styles and colors at various times. Some bottles had fancy designs such as rings, shields, or arrows embossed onto the glass; still others had slug plates identifying the then proprietor of the Coca-Cola franchise. All of these straight-sided bottles displayed a paper label identifying the product they contained, and bore the Coca-Cola trademark embossed in script lettering as well.

The early crown-top bottles were hand-blown in molds with their necks and lips finished-off by special hand-held tools. Such techniques often left rough seams, irregular patterns of thick and thin glass, numerous bubbles and imperfections in the glass itself, and sometimes crooked shapes. Machine-made crown-top bottles with fewer deficiencies and evenly formed seams began to replace the hand-tooled bottles after 1910. The variety of glass colors used ranged from clear and aqua to differing shades of blue, green, and amber. Even the amount of liquid a bottle contained varied considerably since 6, 6 $1/2$, 7 and up to quart-size 24 and 26 ounce bottles existed. The script writing Coca-Cola trademark sometimes appeared at the base of the bottle, sometimes in the center, and sometimes up on the shoulder. While this tremendous lack of uniformity makes for some interesting collections of straight-sided Coca-Cola bottles, the inevitable confusion generated by such diversity eventually led to the adoption of the now famous "hobbleskirt" or "Mae West" shaped bottle as the standard glass container for Coca-Cola shortly after 1915.

The first patent for these hobbleskirt bottles was issued on Nov. 16, 1915 to the Chapman Root Glass company of Terre Haute, Indiana. This patent was renewed on Dec. 25, 1923. Such "Thanksgiving" or "Christmas" Cokes, as they are sometimes called, have become quite popular among collectors because on the base plate most of these bottles bear the name of the city where they were first filled. Well over 2,000 cities are known to have existed as the Coca-Cola bottling network continued to expand. Several patent renewals of the classic shape have occurred since 1923. Hundreds of millions of hobbleskirt bottles were put into service over the years.

Many bottles can be found on which the words Coca-Cola or "property of Coca-Cola" appear in block letter print only. Although some of these bottles are of the older, hand-blown variety, most date from the 1920s or later. Collectors generally agree that these block letter bottles probably contained the various fruit flavored drinks that were handled by individual bottling franchises rather that the beverage Coca-Cola itself. Often these bottles had paper labels identifying the kind of soda water they contained. Larger, quart-size bottles were also used in this way. These "block letter" bottles come in a variety of colors and shapes, and make for an interesting collection in and of themselves. A surprising number have fancy embossings such as people or animals. But once again, it is important to remember that very few, if any, were ever used for Coca-Cola. Keep in mind that these "flavor bottles" generally do not have the value of bottles that actually contained Coca-Cola.

Two other types of bottles deserve mention when writing about Coca-Cola bottle collections. Syrup bottles did indeed contain genuine Coca-Cola syrup obtained from the parent company in Atlanta and were used at sit-down soda fountains to hand mix one's 5¢ drink with carbonated water. Many of these tall, clear glass bottles have the words Coca-Cola in acid-etched lettering or printed on paper labels sometimes sealed under glass. The trademark appears on such bottles in block lettering or in script.

Certain Coca-Cola franchises also bottled and sold seltzer water to local outlets such as bars, restaurants and soda fountains. This was done in a variety of beautifully colored or clear glass siphon bottles that had acid-etched lettering or applied color labeling. The words Coca-Cola are found on these bottles in both block letter or script writing styles, although such bottles were used for seltzer water only and never to dispense Coca-Cola itself.

The relative value placed upon Coca-Cola bottles is determined in great part by such factors as the age of the bottle (Hutchinson, straight-sided, hobbleskirt), its scarcity (small town versus franchise, for example), and also the color of the glass and condition of the bottle itself (free from chips, cracks, cloudiness, or considerable wear). An original metal crown or paper label would enhance the value of a Coca-Cola bottle appreciably.

# BOTTLES
## Hutchinsons c.1894-Early 1900s

The Hutchinsin stoppered bottles are rare; examples with script lettered logo's are more desirable and valued higher than the block lettered examples. These bottles are embossed glass. Beware of scratched in examples (see Repro and Fantasy section). Bottles that are worn, chipped or repaired will have less value.

PBH012.000
Script . . . . . . . $2,200
Jasper, AL

PBH010.000
Script . . . . . . . $2,800
Property of Coca-Cola

PBH011.000
Script . . . . . . . $2,000
Birmingham, AL

PBH013.000
Script . . . . . . . $3,000
Bessemer, AL

PBH019.000
Block type . . . $1,800
Brunswick, GA

---

Examples not shown: PBH009.000 Atlanta, GA /PBH015.000 Gadsden, AL/PBH016.001 Tuskegee, AL Bottling Co./PBH0017.000 Valdosta, GA/
PBH011.001 Birmingham, AL (variation—Root on Rev.) Shown is Doc. 13 on Rev.

---

PBH016.000
Block type . . . . $2,200
Tuskegee, AL Bottling works

PBH018.000
Block type . . . . $2,200
Talladega, AL

PBH014.000
Misspelled "Coco" . . $1,600
Chattanooga, TN

PBH020.000
No mention of
Coca Cola . . . . . . $250
Biedenharn Candy Co.

PBH021.000
1961 . . . . . . . . $375
Commemorative

# BOTTLES
### Amber c.1905-1916

PBA015.000
Greenwood, MS . . . $65
C.E. Wright

PBA016.000
Pittsburgh, PA . .$80
Light amber

PBA019.000
Akron, OH . . . . . $125
Straight arrow

PBA020.000
Cumberland, MD . . $175
Double diamond

PBA021.000
Huntsville, AL . . $65

PBA017.000
Dalton, GA. . . . $325
With original label

PBA018.000
Indiana, PA . . . . $65

PBA022.000
Bristol, VA. . . . $100

PBA023.000
Wheeling, WV . . $85

PBA024.000
Huntington, WV . . $85

PBA025.000
Louisville, KY. . $100
Circle arrow

PBA026.000
Toledo, OH . . . $175
Double diamond

PBA027.000
Painsville Mineral
Springs . . . . . . . $100

PBA048.000
Rochester, NY,
10oz. . . . . . . . . . $200

# BOTTLES
## Amber c.1905-1916

> *Note: Amber bottles, for the most part, are more desirable and valued higher than clear or light green straight side bottles.*

**PBA028.00**
Value . . . . . . . . $100
Toledo, OH

**PBA029.000**
Value . . . . . . . . . $125
Florence, AL

**PBA030.000**
Value . . . . . . . . $75
Huntsville, AL 7 oz.

**PBA031.000**
Value . . . . . . . . $285
Buchheit's Bottling Works,
New Decatur, AL

**PBA032.000**
Value . . . . . . . $150
Sheffield, AL

> *Note: Amber bottles can be found in a number of color variations from a light amber, or honey amber, to medium and dark.*

**PBA033.000**
Value . . . . . . . . $125
Murfreesboro, TN

**PBA034.000**
Value . . . . . . $125
Cleveland, OH

**PBA035.000**
Value . . . . . . . . $85
Wheeling, WV

Front                                    Rear

**PBA036.000**
Value . . . . . . . . . . . . . . . . . $150
Senate Bottle, Dayton, OH

# BOTTLES
### Amber c.1905-1916

PBA037.000
Value . . . . . . . $125
Jackson, TN

PBA038.000
Value . . . . . . . $100
Louisville, KY

PBA039.000
Value . . . . . . . $125
Greenville, MS

PBA040.000
Value . . . . . . . $175
Clarksdale, MS

PBA041.000
Value . . . . . . . $125
Cleveland, OH

PBA042.000
Value . . . . . . . $125
Memphis, TN
(Rare seam arrow)

PBA043.000
Value . . . . . . $200
Jellico, TN

PBA044.000
Value . . . . . . . $125
Cincinnati, OH

PBA045.000
Value . . . . . . . $125
Helena, AR

PBA046.000
Value . . . . . . $150
Knoxville, TN

# BOTTLE LABELS

Note: Drawing of label shown on left does not show background lines.

PPM355.001

**1. 1903-1908** . . . . . . . . . . . . . . . . . . . . $250
Atlanta label, red (logo) and blue printing. "Atlanta, GA," lower right border, "Trademark registered, Jan 31st, 1892" in tail of "C," Very Rare. Two variations may exist on this label (as depicted on various advertising materials from this period) one with "5¢" printed at left and right corners, and another with "Trade Mark" in block letters beneath logo. (I have not seen any actual labels with these variations)

PPM355.002

**2. 1907-1913** . . . . . . . . . . . . . . . . . . . . $75
Registered 1907 label, blue and black printing. "Asa G. Candler PT" signature on lower right border printing below logo reads "Registered Jan'y 1st 1907 No. 13298" "United States Patent Office". The #4 label shown below is the most common of the available original labels and most of the reproductions I have seen are of this label. I have on file five different recent reproductions of this label other than the #6 reproduction shown below.

PPM355.003

**3. 1913-1917** . . . . . . . . . . . . . . . . . . . . $75
Copyright 1907 label, blue and black printing, "Asa G. Candler PT" signature on lower right border, printing below logo reads "Reg. U.S. Pat. Off." "Copyright 1907, By Coca-Cola Co."

1903-1908 ATLANTA LABEL
Value (label only) . . . .$250
Actual example of #1 label shown on amber straight-sided bottle

PPM355.004

**4. 1915-1917** . . . . . . . . . . . . . . . . . . . . $40
Volume 6 1/2" oz. label, blue and black printing, identical to #3 label with added border on lower right, which reads "Minimum Volume 6 1/2" oz."

PPM355.005

**5. 1917-1919** . . . . . . . . . . . . . . . . . . . . $100
Contents 6 fluid oz. label, blue and black printing, identical to #3 label but with "Chas H. Candler PT" signature on right border, and added border reads "Contents 6 Fluid oz."

The label values apply to original labels. Many bottles show up in the marketplace with labels on them. My experience is the majority of these are reproduction labels. Most reproduction labels are heavier stock paper and background lines are more exact (uniform). Beware, know your seller, seek advice of advanced, knowledgeable collectors. (A special thanks to Thom Thompson of Versailles, KY for compiling this information.)

PRE051.000

**6. 1960s** . . . . . . . . . . . . . . . . . . . . . . . . $5
Reproduction label, blue and black printing, identical to the #4 1913-1917 label, except background lines are more uniform (unbroken) and printed on heavier stock paper. Printed by Coca-Cola Company for use on various advertising ads and promotional purposes in late 1960.

# BOTTLES
Clear/Light Green c.1905-1916

PBG015.000
Value . . . . . . . . $125
Springville, ME

PBG016.000
Value . . . . . . . . $125
Richmond, VA

PBG017.000
Value. . . . . . . . $285
Rochester, NY

PBG018.000
Value . . . . . . . . $100
Biedenharn

PBG019.000
Value . . . . . . . . . $65
Jackson, TN

> *Note: Values shown on these bottles are based on very nice condition of 8.5 or better.*

PBG020.000
Value . . . . . . . . $100
Kalamazoo, MI

PBG021.000
Value . . . . . . . . $125
Enid, OK

PBG022.000
Value . . . . . . . $145
Muskogee, OK

PBG023.000
Value . . . . . . . $225
Okmulgee, OK, Rare

PBG024.000
Value . . . . . . $100
Altus, OK

PBG025.000
Value . . . . . . . . $50
Charleston, SC

PBG026.000
Value . . . . . . . . $75
Collinsville, AL

PBG027.000
Value . . . . . . . . $50
Montgomery, AL

PBG028.000
Value . . . . . . . . $50
Atlanta, GA

PBG029.000
Value . . . . . . . . $150
Light Blue, Rochester, NY

*Note: The variations of the Coca-Cola bottles prior to the standard bottle change in 1916-1917, created a gold mine for today's collectors.*

PBG030.000
Value . . . . . . . . $225
DeRidder, LA

PBG031.000
Value . . . . . . . . . $200
The Vincent Co., Auburn, ME

PBG032.000
Value . . . . . . . . $140
Sheffield, AL

PBG033.000
Value . . . . . . . . $200
Notasulga, AL

PBG034.000
Value . . . . . . . . $100
Des Moines, IA

PBG035.000
Value . . . . . . . . . $45
Newbern, NC

PBG036.000
Value . . . . . . . . . $50
Logan, WV

PBG037.000
Value . . . . . . . . . $85
Talladega, AL

PBG038.000
Value . . . . . . . . . $75
Huntsville, AL

PBG039.000
Value . . . . . . . . . . $70
Verner Springs, Greenville, SC

---

*Note: The values shown on these bottles are based on very nice condition of 8.5 or better.*

---

PBG040.000
Value . . . . . . . . . $100
L.C. Heibel, Madison, WI

PBG041.000
Value . . . . . . . . . . . $75
A.L. Joyce, Traverse City, MI

PBG042.000
Value . . . . . . . . $200
E. Dannenberg, Wilson,
Goldsboro, NC

PBG043.000
Value . . . . . . . . . $75
Roanoke, AL

PBG044.000
Value . . . . . . . . $45
Selma, AL

# BOTTLES
Clear/Light Green c.1905-1916

---

*Note: Rare cities, unusual variation, can account for higher values of certain bottles.*

---

PBG045.000
Value . . . . . . . . $100
Denver, CO

PBG046.000
Value . . . . . . . $125
Dannenburg Bros.,
Goldsboro, NC

PBG047.000
Value . . . . . . . . $125
Thomasville, GA

PBG048.000
Value . . . . . . . $200
Peoria, IL

PBG049.000
Value . . . . . . . . . $50
Fort Valley, GA

PBG050.000
Value . . . . . . . $85
Youngstown, OH

PBG051.000
Value . . . . . . . . $125
Cordele, GA

PBG052.000
Value . . . . . . . . $60
Litchfield, IL

PBG053.000
Value . . . . . . . . . $65
Columbus Ice Co., MS

PBG054.000
Value . . . . . . $200
Lineville, AL

# BOTTLES

Clear/Light Green, c.1905-1916

PBG005.000
**Biedenharn Candy
Co.** . . . . . . . . .$165
Vicksburg, MS

PBG006.000
**Best By a
Dam Site** . . . . . $85
Las Vegas, NV

PBG007.000
**Petersburg, IL** . . . . . $225
With original paper label

PBG008.000
**R.J. Shine** . . . . . $100
Winchester, VA

PBG009.000
**Jewell Bottling
Works** . . . . . . . . $125
Jackson, GA, full with
original cap

PBG010.000
**Hygeia Bottling
Works** . . . . . . . . $75
Pensacola, FL

PBG011.000
**Nussbaum Bros.**
. . . . . . . . . . . . . $65
Bainbridge, GA

PBG014.000
**Macon, GA** . . . . . $60

PBG012.000
**Washington, D.C.** . $125

PBG013.000
**VR Electric Light &
Power Co.
Bottlers** . . . . . . . . $150
Villa Rica, GA

PBT025.000
**1965** . . . . . . . . . . . . . . . . . . . . . . . . .$165
PBT025.501 **With tag add** . . . . . . . . . . . .$25
PBT025.S00 **Complete in box** . . . . . . . .$500
Root Commemorative Bottle

*Note: Collecting the bottles of The Coca Cola Company is a hobby that is enjoyed by thousands of people today. The best part of collecting bottles is the wide range that is available and the fact that you can get started at any level. Items include rare Hutch bottles, straight sides, hobble skirt, commemorative and recent, with a large variety and variations available of each. Prior to standardization of the Coke bottle in 1916, bottlers basically came up with their own style of bottle. This huge number of different styles of bottles have proven to be a collector's dream. Rare cities, variations, misspellings, and imperfections have all led to a seemingly never-ending challenge to bottle collectors who are always striving to uncover that one example that no one has seen before. The condition of the bottle, like everything else, is very important. Cracks, chips, case wear, and bruises all add to the depreciation of values shown. Because of the popularity of bottle collecting, the values of these bottles has appreciated over the years making collecting them not only fun, but a good investment.*

PBT026.000
1916-1924 . . . $6 to $15
Embossed "Bottle Pat'd
Nov. 16, 1915"

PBT027.000
1924-1937 . . . $3 to $8
Embossed "Bottle Pat'd Dec.
1923" (Xmas Coke)

PBT028.000
Late 20s . . . . . . . . $3,000
Paper label's export
bottle, Rare

PBT029.000
1937-1948 . . . $1 to $3
Embossed "Bottle Pat.
D105529" 1951 changed to
"In U.S. Patent Office"

PBT030.000
1949 . . . . . . . $50 to $85
Embossed, gold dipped,
Anniversary bottle

> *Note: It is important to understand that embossed hobbleskirt bottles, were produced by the millions and readily available to today's collectors. Many collectors do collect them by cities, some cities are rarer than others. Condition is very important rare examples could be valued much higher than values shown. ACL Hobbleskirt bottles are very common.*

PBT031.000
1950s . . . . . . $1 to $2
ACL and embossed,
"Contents 6 1/2 Fluid Ozs."

PBT032.000
1960s . . . . . . $.50 to $1
ACL "Coke" on reverse side

PBT033.000
Mid-1960s . . . . $20
Diamond embossed,
10 oz., no return

PBT034.000
Mid-1960s . . . . $125
Diamond paper label,
Green glass, Rare

PBT035.000
Mid-1960s . . . . . . .$65
Diamond paper label,
clear glass

# BOTTLES

Large bottles generally called quart bottles, vary in size from 24oz. to 32oz. and were produced in a variety of colors.

PBQ010.000

30 oz. . . . . . . . . . . . . . . . $225
Script logo, Rochester, N.Y., light blue

PBQ011.000

Quart size . . . . . . . . . . $200
Script logo, Wyanoke Brand, light green

PBQ012.000

Quart size . . . . . . . . $125
Block-type logo, light green, The
Northern Coca-Cola Bott. Co.,
Kalamazoo, MI

PBQ013.000

24 oz. . . . . . . . . . . . . $125
Block-type logo, clear, Coca-Cola
Bottling Co., Westminster, MD

# FLAVOR BOTTLES

Coca-Cola Bottling Co.

Many different versions of these flavor bottles exist, most are very common. The flavor was usually printed on the cap. These bottles never held Coca-Cola.

PBF010.000

PBF011.000

6 oz. . . . . . . . . . . . . . . . . . . . . . . . . . $5
J.S. Francis, Avon Park FL, dark green and
light green examples

> *Notes: Flavor bottles did not hold Coca-Cola, but rather other flavors bottled by local bottlers.*

PBF012.000

Big Chief . . . . . . . . . $10
Embossed Indian head,
light green

PBF013.000

6 oz. . . . . . . . . . . . . . . $4
Quality Brand Soda Water,
Asheville, NC, light green

PBY013.000
c.1961 42" . . . . . $400
Styrofoam

PBY006.002
1929 26" . . . . . . . $7,500
Bottle lamp Note: This is
a variation glass bottle lamp;
the difference being size, style
of cap, a completely different
un-marked base, and no
marking under the logo.

PBY006.001
Late 20s 20" . . . . . . . . . . . $7,500
Bottle lamp

PBY005.000
c.1920s 36" . . . . . . . . . . . . . .$15,000
Leaded glass display bottle

<u>20" Glass Display Bottles (not shown)</u>
PBY010.000 Pat. D version . . . . . . . . .350
PBY009.000 ACL (applied color
lettering) . . . . . . . . . . . . . . . . . . . .175
PBY008.000 ACL Mexico . . . . . . . . . .100

Display bottles found with original cap would
certainly increase their value.

PBY007.000
1930s 20" . . . . . . . . . . . . . . $375
Glass (Christmas Coke) display bottle

PBY0012000
1953 20" . . . . . . $400
Plastic

PBY011.000
1948 4' . . . . . . .$1,000
Hard rubber

PBY014.000
c.1953   20" x 14" x 21" . . . . . . . . . . . . . . . . . . . . . . $3,000
Six-pack display, wood, complete with six (plastic) 20" metal cap bottles

PBY013.001
c.1961   5' . . . . . . . . $425
Styrofoam

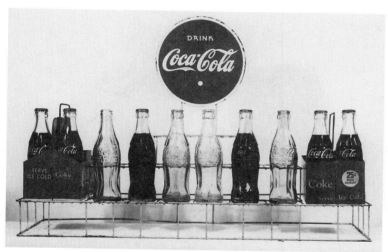

PDR012.000
1930s   . . . . . . . . . . . . . . . . . . . . . . .$1,200
Bottle display, metal, three tier, Rare

PBY015.000
1937 . . . . . . . . . . . . . $50
Display bottle, painted inside,
standard size, glass

PBY016.000
1955 . . . . . . . . . . . . . . $100
Display bottle, painted inside,
standard size, glass, Rare

PDR013.000
1950s . . . . . . . . . . . . . . . . . . . . . . $200
Six-pack display, cardboard

PDS005.S00

c. 1896 Ceramic Syrup Dispenser

Complete dispenser with base, bowl, lid, and spigot, all in Near Mint condition . . . . . . . . .$6,500
Complete dispenser without spigot, in Excellent to Near Mint condition . . . . . . . . . . . . . . .$5,500
Dispenser only (base and bowl) no lid or spigot, in Excellent to Near Mint condition . . . . .$3,500
PDS005.S03 Lid only . . . . . . . . . . . . . . . . . . . . . . . . . . . . . . . . . . . . . . . . . . . . . . . . . . . . . . . . .$1,200
PDS005.S02 Bowl only . . . . . . . . . . . . . . . . . . . . . . . . . . . . . . . . . . . . . . . . . . . . . . . . . . . . . . . . . .$800
PDS005.S01 Base only . . . . . . . . . . . . . . . . . . . . . . . . . . . . . . . . . . . . . . . . . . . . . . . . . . . . . . . . . .$500

Syrup dispenser, ceramic (Prices shown on individual pieces may only be worth that to a collector in need of the piece to upgrade or complete a dispenser.)

> *Note: This c. 1896 syrup dispenser is 18" high and consists of four pieces: lid, syrup bowl, base, and brass spigot. Base and bowl should be marked in a wreath "The Wheeling Pottery Co." These dispensers are not considered rare unless found complete and in Near Mint condition. The lid to the dispenser was very easily broken; it is very common to find this dispenser without the lid. Many collectors with dispensers are in need of a lid. When a lid is available, it certainly brings a premium price.*

"The Wheeling Pottery Co." (as shown) should be stamped on the bottom of both bowl and base.

PRE002.001

c.1950s . . . . . . . . . . . $600

Reproduction (hard rubber), used for display purposes, complete with lid

PSC005.000
Early 1900s . . . . . . . $2,000
Label under glass

PSC006.000
Early 1900s . . . . . $2,000

PSC012.000
1920s . . . . . . . . . $400
Label under glass

PSC008.000
Early 1900s . . . . $1,000
Label under glass

*Note: Syrup bottles are always desirable when found with original cap. Bottles with no caps will lower the value, but not by a large percentage.*

PSC010.000
1920s . . . . . . . . . . . $650
Foil label

PSC011.000
1920s . . . . . . . . . . $500

PSC007.000
Early 1900s . . . . . . $1,200
Label under glass

PSC009.000
c.1910 . . . . . . . . . $500

PBS005.000
$400

PBS006.000
$325

PBS007.000
$600

PBS008.000
Red ACL ......... $525

PBS009.000
Orange ACL .. $285

PBS010.000
Red ACL ..... $285

PBS011.000
$550

PBS012.000
$285

PBS013.000
Denver, CO . . . . . . $450
Blue

PBS014.000
Miles City, MT . . $425
Blue/white, ACL

PBS015.000
Monongahela, PA . . $200
ACL

PBS016.000
Fargo, ND . . . . . $250
ACL

PBS017.000
Champaign, IL . . $200
ACL

Note: ACL = Applied Color Labeling

PBS018.000
Billings, MT . . . . . . . $350
Red, ACL

PBS020.000
Ashtabula, OH . . . $185

PBS021.000
Denver, CO . . . . . $450
Clear

PBS019.000
Morgantown, WV . . . . . $450
Red, ACL

PBS022.000
$275

PBS023.000
$275

PBS024.000
$275

PBS025.000
$275

Note: ACL = Applied Color Labeling

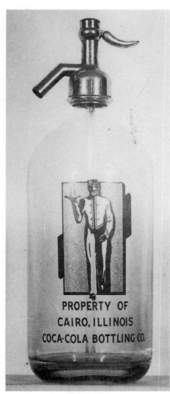

PBS026.000
$250

PBS027.000
$185

PBS028.000
$450

PBS029.000
$175

# SELTZER BOTTLES

PBS030.000
Billings, MT . . . . . $400
Clear

PBS031.000
Red ACL . . . . . . . $400

> Note: Dating these bottles is very difficult;
> most were in use for many years.

PBS032.000
$350

PBS033.000
$275

PBS034.000   PBS035.000   PBS036.000
$450          $285          $225

PBS037.000
1940s . . . . . . . $165

PBS038.000
1940s . . . . . . . . . $165

PBS039.000
$200

PBS040.000   PBS041.000
1930s-40s . . . . . . $150 Each

PBS042.001   PBS042.002
Chicago, IL . . . $385 Each
Clear

PBS043.000   PBS044.000
$150          $250

> Note: Seltzer bottles with script
> logos as opposed to block type
> have more value.

PBS045.000
$200

PSC013.000
Early 1900s . . . . . . . . . . . . . $2,000
Ceramic with paper label, Rare

PSC014.000
Early 1900s . . . . . . . . . . . . . $3,000
Embossed glass, Rare

PSC0015.000
Early 1900s As shown . . $325
Near mint label . . . . . .1,000
Ceramic with paper label

PSC016.000
1914-1919 . . . . . . . . . . . . . . . . . . . . $350
Glass jug, with two paper labels showing both sides

PSC017.000
1930s . . . . . . . . . . . . . . . . .$425
Glass jug, amber, with paper label

PSC018.000
1930s . . . . . . . . . . . $125
Glass jug with paper label

PSC020.000
1940s . . . . . . . . . . . $85

PSC021.000
1950s . . . . . . . . . . . $10

PSC024.000
1960s . . . . . . . . . . . $10

PSC019.001
1930s . . . . . . . . . . . . . . . . . $275
Wood syrup keg, five gallon

PSC025.000
1930s . . . . . . . . . . . . . . . . . . . . . . . . . . $125
Cardboard box for syrup jug

PSC019.002
1930s . . . . . . . . . . . . . . . . . . $275
Wood syrup keg, five gallon

PSC022.000
1950s . . . . . . . . . . . . . . . . . . . . . $8
PSC022.BS0  Full case of four  . . $40
Syrup jug

PSC026.000
Late 1940s . . . . . . . . . . . . . . . . . . . . . . $250
Syrup can, paper label on lid, five gallon

PSC023.000
1960s  . . . . . . . . . . . . . . . . . . $7
PSC023.BS0  Full case of 4  . . . $35
Syrup jug

# GLASSES

PGC005.000
1900-1904 . . . . . $1,000
Straight side

PGC006.000
1912-1913 . . . . . . . . . . . . $1,000
Small 5¢, flare

PGC007.000
1912 . . . . . . . . . . . . . . . . . $750
Large 5¢, flare

PGC010.000
c.1915 . . . . . . . . . . $1,000
Bottlers, flare, Rare

PGC011.000
c.1916 . . . . . . . . . . . . $650
"Bottle", flare

PGC009.000
1914-1918 . . . . . . . . . . . $450
"Drink", flare with syrup line.
Note: 1970s Reproduction of this
glass has an "F" in a shield on
bottom, Value $3

PGC008.000
1904 . . . . . . . . . . . . . . $450
Flare with syrup line

PGC016.000
1936 . . . . . . . . . . . . . $500
50th Anniversary dinner glass, Rare
Photo courtesy: John Morgerson,
Lexington, KY

PGC015.000
1927 . . . . . . . . . . . . . $125
Modified flare, trademark in
tail of "C"

PGC014.000
1923-1925 . . . . . . . . $125
Modified flare, no trademark in
tail of "C"

PGC018.000
1941-1946 . . . . . . . . . . . $15
Bell-shaped glass, trademark
under logo

PGC017.000
1929-1940 . . . . . . . . . . . $40
Bell-shaped glass, trademark in
tail of "C"

# GLASSES

PGC019.000
1940s . . . . . . . . . . . . . $10
Bell glass, Canadian

PGC020.000
1946-69 . . . . . . . . . . . . . $6
Bell glass with "Drink"

PGC022.000
1970 . . . . . . . . . . . . . . . . $2
Bell glass with "Enjoy"

PGC021.000
1950s . . . . . . . . . . . . . $3
Canadian (French)

PGC023.000
35th Anniversary . . . . . . $8
Cape Cod

PGC024.000
1976 . . . . . . . . . . . . . . . . $3
Olympics

PGC025.S00            PGC026.S00
1950s  8oz. and 6oz.  . . . . . . . . $150 Each
50th Anniversary, gold dipped, ACL,
with plastic stand

PGC027.000
1962 . . . . . . . . . . . . . . . . . . . . . . . . . . $15
25th Anniversary, Maine (showing both sides)

# GLASSES, MUGS, GLASS HOLDERS

PGC004.000

**Early 1900s** . . . . . . . . . . . . . . . . . . **$1,500**
Silver glass holder, take note the word "Drink"
does not appear on the original, Rare

PRE003.000

**1970s** . . . . . . . . . . . . . . . . . . . . . . . . . . **$5**
Reproduction (pewter-type material) glass holder,
take note the word "Drink" above Coca-Cola
appears only on the reproduction

> *Note: The Silver Glass Holder was made available to soda fountains from 1901 thru 1904. It is actually a triple plate silver over a German or nickel silver base metal. These were made to fit the straight sided glass of this period, many of which did not have the script Coca-Cola on the glass. This was a very elegant item, and shows up in some of the advertising artwork of this period. These were probably discontinued because the cost of 5¢ each was considered too expensive by the soda fountain operators.*

PGC013.000

**c.1920** . . . . . . . . . . . . . . . . **$1,000**
Coca-Cola mug, embossed ceramic, Rare

> *Note: Both of these mugs originated in West Virginia. The mug at right is an earthen color with blue logo and design; the handle is missing on this example. The mug at left is thought to be from the Dan Mercer Pottery and has a light green glaze. Whether these were ordered by bottlers for a specific occasion or usage or got more widespread distribution is unknown.*

PGC012.000

**c.1912** . . . . . . . . . . . . . **$1,000**
Coca-Cola 5¢ Arrow Mug, Very Rare

PGC028.S00

**c.1930s** . . . . . . . . . . . . . . . . . . . . . . . **$550**
With leather pouch, bell-shaped glass, pewter

PGC028.000 **Without leather pouch** . . . $225

PGC029.000

**1930s** . . . . . . . . . . . . . . . . . . . . . . . . . **$125**
Water cup, tin, (printing is in bottom of cup)

PGC038.000
1980s . . . . . . . . $6
Tab

PGC030.000
Akron . . . . . . . $150
Coca-Cola Soap Box
Derby glass

PGC035.000
1916-1966 . . . . . . . . . . . . . . . . . . . $45
50th Anniversary, gold, Sommersworth, N.H.

PGC036.000
1960 . . . . . . . . $5
Diamond

PGC037.BS0
Canada . . . . . . . . . . . . . . . $125
Set of eight Coca-Cola tumblers in box

PGC039.BS0
1970s . . . . . . . . . . . . . $25
Wine set

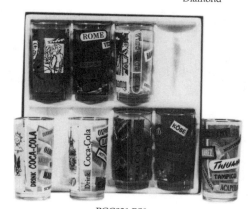

PGC031.BS0
1960s . . . . . . . . . . . . . . . . . . . . . . . . . . . $125
"Around the World" tumblers, complete set of eight in box

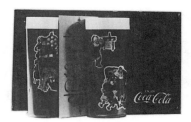

PGC040.BS0
1970s . . . . . . . . . . . . . . . . . . $25
Set of plastic tumblers, in box

PGC034.BS0          PGC033.BS0          PGC032.BS0
1950s-1960s . . . . . . . . . . . . . . . . . . . . . . $65 Each
Case of 12 glasses, in original box

PGC041.000
Cup holder . . . . . . . . . . $135
Wood

PGC042.000
1950s . . . . . . . . $2

PGC043.001    PGC043.002    PGC043.003    PGC043.004
1960s . . . . . . . . . . . . . . . . . . . . . . . . . . $1 Each
Paper cups

PGC045.000
c.1960 . . . . . . . . . . $12
Ice bucket

PGC046.000
1970s . . . . . . . . $2

PGC044.000
1960s . . . . . . . . $1

PGC047.001    PGC047.002    PGC047.003
1950s-70s . . . . . . . . . . $10 Each
Waxed cones

# STRAWS

PST006.BS0
c.1939 . . . . . . . . $250

PST007.BS0
1940 . . . . . . . . $225

PST008.BS0
1940 . . . . . . . . . . $185

PST009.BS0
Late 1940s-1950s . . . $165
Small size

PST009.BS1
Late 1940s-1950s . . $165
Large size

PST010.BS0
1060s . . . . . . . . . $75

*Note: Prices shown on these boxes of straws reflect full or near full boxes. Empty boxes would be worth considerably less.*

PST016.000
1948-1950s . . . . . . . . . . . . . . . $1-$2 Each
Single straw

PST015.000
1950s-60s . . . . . . . . . . . . . . 50¢ to $1 Each
Wrapped straw

PST013.BS0
c.1969 . . . . . . . $35

PST012.BS0
1964 . . . . . . . . $85

PST014.000
1950s . . . . . . . . . . . . . . . . . 50¢ to $1 Each
Wrapped straw

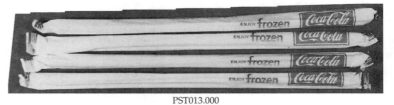

PST011.BS0
Early 1960s . . . . . . . . . . . . . . . . . $75
Showing both sides of box

PST013.000
c.1969 . . . . . . . . . . . . . . . . . . . . 25¢ Each
Wrapped straw

# CANS

PCN010.000
c.1960 . . . . . . . $175
Large diamond

PCN011.000
1960s . . . . . . . $200
Rare

PCN012.000
1960s . . . . . . . $150
Bottle diamond

PCN014.000
1960s . . . . . . . $25
Diamond

PCN014.001
1960s . . . . . . . $30
Diamond can lighter

PCN013.000
1960s . . . . . . . . . . . . . $200
With opener add . . . . . $75
Bottle diamond, Japan, Opener is
stamped Coca-Cola

PCN015.000
1960s . . . . . . . $25
Tab (Coca-Cola product)

PCN016.000
1960s . . . . . . . . . $12
Fresca (Coca-Cola product)

PCN017.000
1960s . . . . . . . . . . . $6
Fanta (Coca-Cola product)

PSC032.000
1970s . . . . . . . . . . . . . . . . . . . $10
Syrup cans, one gallon

PSC027.000
Late 1930s . . . $300
Syrup can with paper label

PSC031.000
1950s . . . . . . . . . . . . . . $85
Syrup can, export

PSC028.000
1930s . . . . . . . . $350
Syrup can

PSC029.000
1950s . . . . . . . . . . . . . $200
Syrup can, green/red paper label

PSC030.000
1950s . . . . . . . . . . . . . $250
Syrup can, white paper label

# BOTTLE CARRIERS

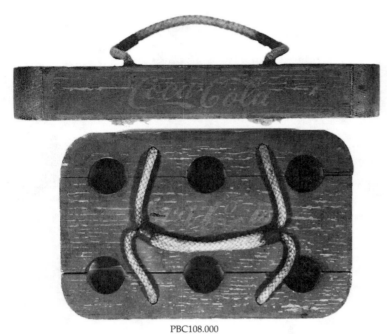

PBC108.000
1930s-1940s . . . . . . . . . . . . . . . . . . $400
Wood with rope handle, logo on side and top,
hanging bottle type, Rare

PBC109.000
1940s . . . . . . . . . . . . . . . . . . . . . . . . . $100
Wood with cutout handle

PBC110.000
Early 1940s . . . . . . . . . . . . . . . . . . $350
Wood, with bottle separators,
red with white lettering, Rare

PBC111.000
1940s . . . . . . . . . . . . . . . . . . . . . . . . . $225
Wood

PBC112.000
1940s . . . . . . . . . . . . . . . . . . . . . . . . $250
Wood with wire handle

PBC113.000
1940 . . . . . . . . . . . . . . . . . . . . . . . $150
Wood with cutout handle

PBC019.001

1941 . . . . . . . . . . . . . . . . . . . . . $250

Wood, with bottle separators, Rare

PBC013.000

1930s . . . . . . . . . . . . . . . . . . $285

Christmas

PBC019.002

1941 . . . . . . . . . . . . . . . . . . $130

Wood, wings on side

PBC071.000

1950s . . . . . . . . . . . . . . . . $25

PBC008.000

1920s . . . . . . . . . . . . . . . . . . . . . . . . . $450

Showing front and back, Rare

PBC070.000

1950s . . . . . . . . . . . . . . . $100

PBC067.000

1950s . . . . . . . . . $25

PBC088.000

1960s . . . . . . . . . $15

PBC068.000

1950s . . . . . . . . $20

PBC069.000

1950s . . . . . . . . $20

PBC012.000

1930s . . . . . . . . . . . . . . $250

4th of July, with paper wrapper, Rare

PBC036.000

Late 1950s . . . . $125

Plastic

PBC020.000

1940s . . . . . $125

PBC099.000

1970s . . . . . . . . . . . . . . . . . . . . . $8

PBC089.000

PBC090.000

1960s . . . . . . . . . . . . . . . . . . . . . . $8 Each

PBC114.000
1930s ...................... $350
Tin and wire, wood handle, Rare

PBC115.000
1950s .................... $100
Aluminum

PBC116.000
1950s ..................... $40
Two- bottle holder for shopping cart

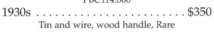

PBC117.000
1950s ......................... $185
Stamped aluminum

PBC118.000
1950s ......................... $100
Aluminum

PBC119.000
1950s ......................... $60
Aluminum

PBC120.000
1960s ........................ $45
Plastic, hanging bottle type

# BOTTLE CARRIERS

PBC025.000

c.1949 . . . . . . . . . . $200

Christmas

PBC015.000

1938 . . . . . . . . . . . . . . . $250

Christmas

PBC037.000

1950s . . . . . . . . . . . . . . . . . . . . . . . . . $200

12-bottle carrier, plastic

PBC072.000

1950s . . . . . . . . $18

PBC028.000

1940s-50s . . . . . . . . . . . . . . . . . . $285

12-bottle carrier, aluminum

PBC027.000

Late 1940s . . . . . . . . . . $150

Six-bottle carrier, aluminum

PBC026.000

1940s . . . . . . . . . . $100

Six-bottle carrier, wire with
stamped aluminum,
Oklahoma

PBC040.001

1950s . . . . . . . . . . . . . . $100

Aluminum (six bottles 25¢ plus deposit)

PBC040.000

1950s . . . . . . . . . . . . . $50

Aluminum
(Delicious and Refreshing)

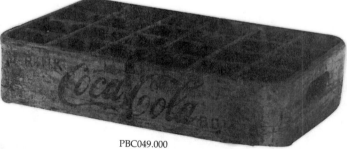

PBC049.000

1940 . . . . . . . . . . . . . . . . . . . . . . . . . $125

24-bottle carrier, plywood

PBC124.000

1940s . . . . . . . . . . . . . . . . . . . . . . . . . . . . . . $45

24-bottle carrier, wire with stamped aluminum. Note: This
24-bottle carrier did not come in chrome; however, I have
seen these chromed by dealers and sold for more than the
value shown. The chrome finish is not original.

PBC091.000

c.1960 . . . . . . . . . . . . . . . . . . . . . . . $185

Six-bottle carrier (large bottles), wire with
tin litho side plates

PBC005.000

c.1920 . . . . . . . . . . . . . . . . . . . . . . . . . $500

24-bottle carrier, cardboard

PBC007.002

1924 . . . . . . . . $300

Six-pack carrier, cardboard

PBC010.000

1930s . . . . . . . . $100

Six-pack carrier, cardboard

PBC011.000

1930s . . . . . . . . $85

Six-pack carrier, cardboard

PBC016.000      PBC017.000      PBC018.000

1930s . . . . . . . . . . . . . . . . . . . . . $50 Each

Six-pack carriers, cardboard

PBC021.000      PBC021.001

1940s . . . . . . . . . . . . . . . . . $65 Each

Six-pack carriers, wood

PBC038.000      PBC039.000

1950s . . . . . . . . . . . . . . $100 Each

Six-pack carriers, aluminum

PBC023.000

1940s . . . . . . . $175

Six-pack carrier, wood
and masonite

PBC040.000

1950s . . . . . . . . . . $50

Six-pack carrier, aluminum

PBC024.000

1940s . . . . . . . . $85

Six-bottle carrier, masonite

PBC073.000      PBC074.000

1950s . . . . . . . . . . . . . . . . . . . . . $25 Each

Twelve- and six-bottle carriers, cardboard

PBC075.000

1950s . . . . . . . . . . . . . . . $15

Eight-bottle carrier, plastic

PBC076.000

1950s . . . . . . . . $15

Six-bottle carrier, plastic

PBC082.000

1950s . . . . . . . . . . . . $12

Plastic

PBC081.000

1950s . . . . . . . . . . . . $15

Plastic

PBC080.000

1950s . . . . . . . . . . . $10

Plastic, French

PBC079.000

1950s . . . . . . . . . . .$15

Plastic

PBC006.000
1924 . . . . . . . . $400

PBC007.001
1924 . . . . . . . . $300

PBC009.000
1931 . . . . . . . . $600

PBC032.000
1949 . . . . . . . . . . . $50

PBC029.000
1940s . . . . . . . . . $50
Four bottle carrier

PBC014.000
1930s . . . . . . . $100

PBC018.000
1930s . . . . . . . . . $50

PBC030.000
1940s . . . . . . . . $75
Cardboard with
wire handle

PBC031.000
Late 1940s . . . . $200
Metal

PBC033.000
Late 1940s-Early
1950s . . . . . . . . . . . . $60
Cardboard with wire handle

PBC035.000
1950 . . . . . . . . . $85

PBC034.000
1949-1950 . . . . . $50

PBC022.000
1940s . . . . . . . . $50

PBC092.000
1960s . . . . . . . . . . . . $6

PBC077.000        PBC078.000
1950s . . . . . . . . . . . . . . . . . . . . . $15 Each
Twelve- and six-bottle carriers, plastic

PBC042.000
1917  9" x 18" x 25 1/2" . . . . . . . . . . $275
48-bottle shipping case, wood

PBC010.S00
1930s . . . . . . . . . . . . . . . . . . . . . . . $1,500
Six-pack display rack, metal, complete with
eight cartons

# BOTTLE CARRIERS

PDR009.002
Late 1930s . . . . . . . . . $400
Six-pack display rack

PBC069.001
1950s . . . . . . . . $20

PBC083.000
1950s . . . . . . . . . $15

PBC084.000
1950s . . . . . . . . $15

PBC093.000
1960s . . . . . . . . . $8

PBC085.000
1950s . . . . . . . . . . . . . . $20
12-pack carrier

PBC094.000
1960 . . . . . . . . $15

PBC095.001

PBC095.002
c.1963 . . . . . . . . . . . . . . . . . $8 Each

PBC096.001

PBC096.002
c.1963 . . . . . . . . . . . . . . . . . $6 Each

PBC086.000

PBC087.000
1950s . . . . . . . . . . . . . . . . . . $15
Plastic

PBC043.000
Early 1900s . . . . . . . $250
Syrup bottle case

PCP014.000
1956 . . . . . . . . . $100
Cooler bag

PCP015.001
1960 . . . . . . . . . . $85
Insulated cooler box

PBC048.000
c.1930s . . . . . . . . . . . . . $485
12-bottle case, tin/wood

PBC047.000
Early 1930s . . . . . . . . . . $125
24-bottle case

PBC044.000
c.1920s . . . . . . . . $425
Six-bottle carrier, dovetail,
wood, Rare

PBC041.000
1950s . . . . . . . . . . . . . . . . . $125
12-bottle carrier, aluminum

PBC045.000
Early 1900s . . . . . . . . . . . $425
Shipping case, wood, very unusual
example

PBC098.000
1975 . . . . . . . . . $5

PBC097.000
1950s . . . . . . . . . . . . . . . $125
Display stand, cardboard

— 378 —

PBC046.000
Early shipping case ...... $225
Wood, with lid

PBC054.000
1920s ..................... $70
Wood

PBC053.000
Pre-1920 ..................... $85
Wood

PBC059.000
1940s .................... $50
Wood

PBC057.000
1930s .......... $40
Wood (seltzer case)

PBC058.000
1930s .................... $45
Wood

PBC056.000
1930s ...................... $45
Wood

PBC065.000
1950s .......... $20
Wood

PBC052.000
Teens ....................... $100
Wood

PBC062.000
1940s-50s ...................... $10
Wood

PBC060.000
1940s .................... $45
Cardboard

PBC063.000
1950 ...................... $20
Wood

PBC064.000
1950s ...................... $15
Cardboard

PBC066.000
1970s ................. $8
Cardboard

PBC125.000
1950s-60s ...................... $18
Plastic

PBC051.000
1920s ............. $100
Wood

PBC050.000
Teens ......................... $185
Wood shipping case with lid

PBC055.000
1930s .......... $65
Board

PBC061.000
1940s .......... $40
Wood

Note: The vendor carrier shown here is shown in periodical advertising with straight-sided bottles as well as after the bottle change. It also shows up in photos in the 1930s.
This carrier is a stock piece, and can be found with other brand names such as Dr. Pepper, Whistle, and others.

PBC121.000
Mid-teens to 1930s . . . . . . . . . . . . . $600
Vendors carrier with straw holder, yellow
with red lettering

PCP028.000
Late 1940s to early 1950s . . . . . . . . $200
Picnic cooler

PBC122.B00
1940s-1950s . . . . . . . . . . . . . . . . . . . $500
Masonite vendors carrier in original box
PBC122.000 Without box . . . . . . . . . . $375

PCP029.B00
1950s . . . . . . . . . . . . $425
Acton picnic cooler in original box

PBC123.000
1930s . . . . . . . . . . . . . . . . . . . . . . . $100
Bottle case, wood with hinged lid

PCP030.000
1950s . . . . . . . . . . . . $300
Royal picnic cooler, red vinyl in
original box

PBC104.000

1950s . . . . . . . . . . . . . . . . . . $275

Metal

PBC103.000

1950s . . . . . . . . . . . . . . . . . . . . . $285

With strap and cup holder

PCI010.000

1920s . . . . . . . . . . . . . . . . . . . . . . . . . $550

Cooler box, wood

PCI011.000

1940s-50s . . . . . . . . . . . . . . . . . $450

Airline cooler

PBC102.000

1940s . . . . . . . . . . . . . . . . . . . $425

Metal

PBC100.000

1920s . . . . . . . . . . . . . . . . . . . . . $385

Wood

PBC101.000

1920s-30s . . . . . . . . . . . . . . . . . . . . . $400

Metal, yellow with red lettering,

PBC105.000

1930s-40s . . . . . . . . . . . . . . . . . . . $285

Metal/wire

PBC107.000

1950s-60s . . . . . . . . . . . . . . . . . . . . . . . . $85

Metal/wire

PBC106.000

1930s-40s . . . . . . . . . . . . . . . . . $150

Metal/wire, Canada

PCP006.000
1950s . . . . . . . . . . . $200
Red, vinyl

PCP012.000
1950s . . . . . . . . . . . $35
Cooler bag, small size, vinyl

PCP011.002
1950s . . . . . . . . . . . . $60
Cooler bag, vinyl, white with
red lettering

PCP013.000
1950 . . . . . . . . . . . . . . . . . $45
Cooler bag, vinyl, white

PCP011.001
1950s . . . . . . . . . . . . . . $60
Cooler bag, vinyl, red with
white lettering

PCP015.002
1964-65 . . . . . . . . . $100
Worlds Fair cooler box, vinyl

PCP018.000
1960s . . . . . . . . . . . . . . . $40
Cooler bag, vinyl, Foreign

PCP024.000
1964 . . . . . . . . . . . . . . . . . . $125

PCP005.000
1940s . . . . . . . . . . . . . . . . . . . . . $225

PCP023.000
1960s . . . . . . . . . . . . . . . . . . . . . $125

PCP010.002
1950s . . . . . . . . . . . . . . . . . $50
Cooler bag, vinyl, white

PCP007.B00
1950s . . . . . . . . . . . . . . $375
Large size, in original box

PCP020.B00
1960s . . . . . . . . . . . . . . . $325
In original box
PCP020.000 Without box . . $125

PCP009.000
1950s . . . . . . . . $165

PCP021.000
1960s . . . . . . . . $125

PCP007.000
1950s . . . . . . . . . . . $100
Large size

PCP008.000
1950s . . . . . . . . . . . . . . . $200
PCP008.B00 In original box . . $450
Small size

PCP025.000
c.1963 . . . . . . . . . . . . . . . . . . . . . . $250
"Picnic cooler seat", vinyl

PCP019.B00
c.1963 . . . . . . . . . . . . . . . . $220
In original box
PCP019.000 Without box . . . . $100

PCP016.000          PCP015.001
1960s . . . . . . . . . . . . . . . . . . $65 Each
Cooler boxes, vinyl

PCP010.001
1950s-60s . . . . . . . . . $35
Cooler bag, vinyl

PCP017.000
1960s . . . . . . . . . . . . $75
Cooler bag, vinyl

PCP006.001
1950s . . . . . . . . . . . . . . . . . . . . . . . . . . . $325
Vinyl, white, Mfg. Royal Mieco, Inc., Clinton, OK

PCP026.000
1970s . . . . . . . . . $35
Cooler bag, vinyl

PCP022.000
1960s . . . . . . . . . . . . . . . . . $175

# GLASCOCK COOLERS
## Standard Size

PCI012.000

c.1929 . . . . . . . . . . . . . . . . . . . . . . . $1,500

Single case, junior size

PCI013.000

1929-32 . . . . . . . . . . . . . . . . . . . . . . $1,000

Double case, full size

PCE005.000

1930s . . . . . . . . . . . . . . . . . . . . . . . . $2,500

Electric (vendor) cooler

*Note: These values are for coolers in choice condition. Coolers with repainted sides, and in rough condition would certainly be worth less. There have been times when the Junior size coolers have sold for a much higher price than the larger version because of their more desirable smaller size.*

PCI014.000

c.1929 . . . . . . . . . . . . . . . . . . . . . . . . $950

Table-top cooler. Note: Beware, the table-top cooler must be as shown. Junior size coolers with sawed off legs are NOT table-top coolers.

# COOLERS

Prices on electric coolers are based on working condition.

PCE006.000
1940s . . . . . . . . . . . . . . $475
Westinghouse 6-Case Master, electric,
140 bottles

PCI015.000
1940s . . . . . . . . . . . . . . . . . $2,000
Table-top vending machine, coin
operated, ice cooled (working), Rare

PCI019.000
1940s . . . . . . . . . . . . . . $500
Westinghouse 6-Case Master, ice
cooler, 144 bottles

PCE018.000
1940s . . . . . . . . . . . . $500
Westinghouse 3-Case Junior, ice
cooler, 80 bottles (also made in
electric)

PCI016.000
1939   24" x 30" x 34" . . . . . . . . . . . . . . $500
Westinghouse Ice Cooler

PCI017.000
1940s . . . . . . . . . . . . . . $425
Westinghouse Master Electric
Cooler, 140 bottles

Note: Prices shown are for coolers in Excellent
condition. Examples in Near Mint or unused condition
would certainly be worth more.

Note: Missing cap catchers on these 1939
Westinghouse coolers are very common. A good cap
catcher will add value to nice cooler.

PCE008.000
1940s . . . . . . . . . . . . . . . . . . . $475
Cavalier 10-Case Giant, electric,
240 bottles

PCE007.000
1940s . . . . . . . . . . . . . . . . . $500
Vendo V-59, vends 59 bottles
(coin mechanism top for open cooler)

PCI020.000
1940s . . . . . . . . . . . . . . . . . . . $400
Cavalier 10-Case Giant, ice cooler,
256 bottles

# SAMPLE COOLERS AND VENDING MACHINES
## Fold-up cardboard—Late 1940-1950s

PSS013.000
3" x 6" x 1 3/4"  .... $125
Vendo V-80,

PSS014.000
2 1/2" x 4" x 2"  .... $125
Vendo V-23

PSS015.000
4 1/4" x 4" x 3" .............. $125
Westinghouse WE-6

PSS016.000
2 1/4" x 5 1/2" x 2" .. $125
Vendorator VMC3D-33

PSS017.000
3 1/2" x 8" x 2"  .. $135
Vendo V-216

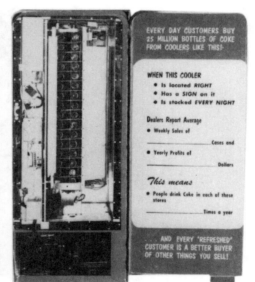

PSS018.000
3 1/2" x 3 1/2" x 8 3/4" ............. $125
Westinghouse BV-240

Note: These are small-size cardboard fold-up sample coolers, not standard-size coolers.

PSS019.000
2 3/4" x 7" x 2 1/4"  .... $130
Cavalier C-102

PSS020.000
8" x 4 1/4" x 3" .................. $150
Victor C-45A

PSS021.000
3 1/2" x 6 3/4" x 2"  .... $125
Vendo 6-Case Vertical

PSS022.B00

c.1960s  16 $1/2$" x 12"  . . . . . . . . . . . $2,500
Salesman's sample counter dispenser, all plastic
with heavy canvas padded carrying case, Rare

Ceramic, soda fountain (insert), syrup dispenser. Note: These
"Insert" syrup dispensers are considered common by collectors.
I've seen many different examples.

PDS006.001 Block lettering (as shown) . . . . . . . . . $75
PDS006.002 Script lettering (not shown) . . $85 to $100

PDS007.000

c.1950s . . . . . . . . . . . . . . . . . . . . . . . $650
Vendor dispenser

PDS009.000

Late 1930s . . . . . . . . . . . . . . . . . . . . . . $850
Double dispenser, stainless steel with enamel plates

PDS010.000

Late 1930s . . . . . . . . . . . . . . . . . . . . . . $550
Dispenser, red with chrome and enamel plates

PDS012.000

1950s . . . . . . . . . . . . . . . . . . . . . . . . . $500
Vendo coin changer, with "Have a Coke" insert.
Note: These machines were used in the late 1940s
into the 1950s. I have seen them with inserts other
than Coca-Cola.

PDS008.000

1930s . . . . . . . . . . . . . . . . . . . . . . . . $1,800
Art Deco, chrome and enamel, six sided, dispenser
mfg. by Multiplex Faucet Co., St. Louis, MO, Rare

PDS011.000

1950s-60s . . . . . . . . . . . . . . . . . . . $550
Barrel Dispenser

PMD011.S00

1963 . . . . . . . . . . . . . . . . . . $275
Bookends, bottle shaped, bronze

PMD012.000

1920s . . . . . . . . . . . . $250
Fire bucket

PMD010.000

1930s . . . . . . . . . . . . . . . . . . . . . . . $1,100
Without cord deduct . . . . . . . . . . . . . $100
PMD010.B00 In Original Box add . . . . . $500
Sandwich toaster. Note: Used in soda fountains,
this piece has erroneously been called a
"Krumkake Maker."

PMD013.001

1950s . . . . . . . . . . . . . . . . . . . . . . . $1000
Sprite Boy napkin holder, Rare. Note: These napkin
holders can be found with Coca-Cola on both sides,
or with different advertising on one side as shown.

PMD014.000

1930s-40s . . . . . . . . . . . . . . . . . . $1,500
Napkin holder, Mexican, Rare

PMD015.001                    PMD015.002

1950s . . . . . . . . . . . . . . . . . . . . . . . . $750 Each
Mileage table, plastic, two different examples shown

PMD016.B00
Coca-Cola barbecue grill . . . $85
In box

PMD017.B00
1970s . . . . . . . . . . . . . . . . . . . . . . . . . $85
Two-man boat kit, inflatable, in box

PCP027.000
c.1960 . . . . . . . . . . . . $65
Vinyl cooler bag

Note: Many collectors do shy away from anything with the so-called "New Logo"; however some of the more unusual pieces are very collectable.

PMD018.000
1970s . . . . . . . . . . . . . . . . . . . $12
Stadium seat cushion, plastic

PMD019.000
c.1960 . . . . . . . . $175
Folding chair

PMD020.000
1970s  4" x 6" . . . . . . . . . . . . . . . . . . . $350
Rug, red and white

PMD023.000
1970s . . . . . . . . . . . . . . $18
Waste paper basket

PMD022.000
1970s . . . . . . . . . . . . $20
Tennis racket cover

PMD021.000
1980s  4" x 6" . . . . . . . . . . . . . . . . . . . $150
Rug, red and white

# FROZEN COCA-COLA

In 1969, The Coca-Cola Company introduced "Frozen Coca-Cola" which was actually not another product, but rather the same product in a different form. A simple combination of Coca-Cola and chipped ice—sort of a Coca-Cola snow-cone. The campaign was short lived, but many items were used for the Frozen Coca-Cola campaign. You will find others throughout the book.

PCB023.000
Change receiver . . . . . . . . . . $175
Plastic

PTY153.000
14" . . . . . . . . . . . . . . . . . . . . . . . $100
Stuffed doll

PCH078.000
Uniform patch . . . . . . . . . . . . . $3

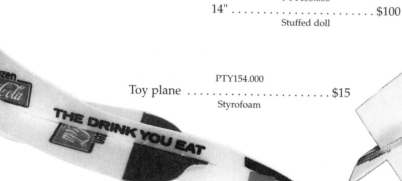

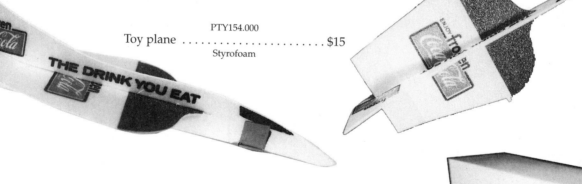

PTY154.000
Toy plane . . . . . . . . . . . . . . . . . . . . $15
Styrofoam

PCT084.000
Free (the drink you can eat) coupon  . . . . $2

PDS013.000
Frozen Coca-Cola dispenser  . . $700

# POCKET MIRRORS

1920 ← YEAR USED

← PHOTO
Actual Size 1³/₄" x 2³/₄"

PMC014.000 ← PETRETTI CODE

Bastian Bros. Co. ← COPY
Rochester, N.Y. Appearing on lower and side rims
$750 ← VALUE

*Note: All mirrors shown (except the two at right) are celluloid covered artwork, with a metal rim and glass mirror on back side.*

PMC022.001     PMC022.002
$100            $135
         1936
"Memos" pocket mirrors  different examples
shown,  in original package add $35

---

| 1906 | 1907 | 1908 | 1909 | 1910 |
|---|---|---|---|---|

| PMC005.000 | PMC006.000 | PMC007.000 | PMC008.000 | PMC009.000 |
|---|---|---|---|---|
| The Whitehead & Hoag Co., Newark, NJ, Duplicate Mirrors 5¢ Postage, Coca-Cola Company, Atlanta, GA $550 | From the Painting, copyright 1906, by Wolf & Co., Phila., Bastian Bros. Co., Roch, N.Y., Duplicate Mirrors 5¢ Postage, Coca-Cola Company, Atlanta, GA $550 | Bastian Bros. Co., Rochester, NY, Duplicate Mirrors 5¢ Postage, Coca-Cola Company, Atlanta, GA $925 | J.B. Carroll, Chicago, Duplicate Mirrors 5¢ Postage, Coca-Cola Company, Atlanta, GA $500 | J.B. Carroll, Chicago, Duplicate Mirrors 5¢ Postage, Coca-Cola Company, Atlanta, GA. $325 |

---

| 1911 | 1914 | 1916 | 1920 | 1922 |
|---|---|---|---|---|

| PMC010.000 | PMC012.000 | PMC013.000 | PMC014.000 | PMC015.000 |
|---|---|---|---|---|
| The Whitehead & Hoag Co., Newark, NJ, Duplicate Mirrors 5¢ Postage, Coca-Cola Company, Atlanta, GA $300 | The Whitehead & Hoag Co., Newark, NJ $575 | The Whitehead & Hoag Co., Newark, NJ $375 | Bastian Bros. Co., Rochester, NY $750 | The Whitehead & Hoag Co., Newark, NJ, Rare $3,500 |

PMC011.000
1911 . . . . . . . . . . . . . . . . . . . . . . $3,050

Not Pictured: "Motor Girl" (formally called "Duster Girl") pocket mirror, oval 1 ⁵/₈" x 2 ³/₈". This mirror was made available by "The Coca-Cola Bottling Company" of Atlanta, one of the parent bottlers (all of the above mirrors were issued through "The Coca-Cola Co."). The "Motor Girl" mirror, in addition to picturing the "Motor Girl" artwork, has the copy "Drink Coca-Cola In Bottles" at bottom and "Cruver Mfg. Co., Chicago" on left rim. Rare

# WATCH FOBS AND CONVENTION BADGES

Most, but not all, early fobs have the manufacturer's name stamped on them. A few of the fobs have been reproduced and there are a number of fantasy fobs on the market, so the novice collector should be cautious and ask the advice of advanced collectors on a questionable fob.

**PPJ009.000**
C.1913
1 3/4" Dia. . . $2,200
Celluloid

**PJ008.000**
c.1912
1 1/2" Dia. . .$2,500
Celluloid

**PPJ013.000**
c.1910 . . .$250
Showing both sides

**PPJ006.000**
c.1910 . . . $900
Celluloid, "Drink
Coca-Cola in Bottles,
5¢" on back

**PPJ007.000**
1911 . . . $800
Celluloid, "Drink
Coca-Cola in Bottles,
5¢" on back

**PPJ016.000**
c.1920s . . . $150
Brass with red enamel

**PPJ005.000**
c.1905 . . . $1,000
Celluloid, "Drink
Coca-Cola in Bottles,
5¢" on back

**PPJ015.000**
c.1915 . . .$200
"Drink Coca-Cola
in Bottles, 5¢" on
back (refer to
"Swastika" note
below right)

"Drink Coca-Cola
in Bottles 5¢"  "Drink Coca-
Cola Sold
Everywhere 5¢"

**PPJ017.002**
c.1920s
1 1/4" x 1 1/4" . . $150
Bulldogs, "Drink Coca-
Cola Delicious and
Refreshing 5¢" on back

**PPJ018.000**
c.1920s . . . . . $150
"Swastika", brass (showing
both sides)

**PPJ011.000**
1908 . . .$125
Keychain

**PPJ010.001   PPJ010.002**
c.1907 . . . . $150 Each
"Relieves Fatigue", brass with
either silver or gold wash
Sterling silver . . . . . . . $250
10K Gold . . . . . . . . $1,000

**PPJ012.000**
c.1909 . . . . $150
Brass with red
enamel

**PPJ014.000**
c.1912 . . . $175
Brass with
black enamel

**PPJ017.001**
c.1920s
1 1/2" x 1" . . .$200
Bulldogs

*Note: The Swastika was a Good Luck symbol in
the Old World and America and did not have
Nazi connotations until the 1930s.*

**PPJ019.000**
1909 . . . . . . . . . . $800
Convention token (First
Bottlers Convention),
Swastika on back, brass

**PPJ026.001**
c.1930 . . . $90
Convention badge

**PPJ027.000**
1936 . . . $200
Convention badge

**PPJ028.000**
1939 . . . $90
Convention badge

**PPJ031.000**
c.1950 . . . $65
Convention badge

**PPJ025.000**
1917 . . . $800
Convention medal
with ribbon

**PPJ022.000**
1911
1 1/4" dia. . . . $2,500
Convention badge, celluloid
"Motor Girl" Pin (with ribbon, (Hyatt Mfg. Co.,
Baltimore), Rare

**PPJ024.000**
1916 . . . $800
Convention medal,
porcelain inlay

**PPJ021.000**
1912 . . . . . . . . $700
Convention lapel button

**PPJ020.000**
1910 . . . $700
Convention lapel
button

**PPJ023.000**
1915 . . . . . . . . . . . . . $650
Convention medal, porcelain inlay

**PPJ030.000**
c.1947 . . . $65

**PPJ029.000**
c.1943 . . . $50
Convention badges.
Note: Other convention badges also shown
in "Miscellaneous" section of this book.

# POCKET KNIVES

An attempt is made to show mostly older knives, common and uncommon. Since the late 1960s literally hundreds of different knives marked Coca-Cola have been manufactured in all shapes, sizes, and materials. Many fantasy styles appear old and rare when "Aged"—BEWARE! Refer to the "Fantasy and Reproduction" pages of this book.

Knife photos courtesy of Thom Thompson.

**PKP005.000**

c.1905-1915 . . . . . . . . . . . . . . $450

Brass, 2 blade, marked "Kaster & Co." and "Coca-Cola Bottling Co., Germany", note opener on this original

**PKP006.000**

c.1905-1915 . . . . . . . . . . . . . . $400

Brass, 1 blade, marked "Kaster & Co." and "Coca-Cola Bottling Co., Germany", note opener on this original

**PKP007.000**

c.1905-1915 . . . . . . . . . . . . . . $500

Nickel silver, 4 blades including awl, can opener and screwdriver, marked "D. Peres Solingen Germany" and "Coca-Cola Bottling Co., Germany," another example: "Royal Brand, U.S.A."

**PKP008.000**

c.1910 . . . . . . . . . . . . . . . . . . . . . . . $250

Nickel silver, 1 blade and opener, marked "D. Peres, Solingen" and "Coca-Cola Bottling Co., Germany", another example marked "Kastor & Bros." and "Coca-Cola Bottling Co., Germany", (both sides shown)

**PKP011.000**

c.1915 . . . . . . . . . . . . . . . . . $250

Copper, 2 blades, marked "A. Kastor & Bros., N.Y." and "Coca-Cola Bottling Co., Germany"

**PKP009.000**

c.1910 . . . . . . . . . . . . . . . . . $350

Brass, 2 blade, marked "D. Peres, Solingen" and "Coca-Cola Bottling Co., Germany", also made in aluminum

**PKP012.000**

c.1915-1925 . . . . . . . . $125

Bone, one blade and opener, marked "A. Kastor & Bros., New York." and "Coca-Cola Bottling Co."

**PKP013.000**

c.1930 . . . . . . . . . $100

Celluloid, two blades, marked "Shapleigh HDW, Co."

**PKP015.000**

c.1930 . . . . . . . . . . . . . . . $125

Stainless, two blades, marked "Remington UMC" in circle, many stamped with bottlers name on back

**PKP053.000**

c.1940 . . . . . . . . . . . . . . . . . . . . $175

"Serve Coca-Cola", one blade and nail file, pearl handle, "Be Smart" in window when open, marked "Solingen Germany"

**PKP014.000**

c.1930 . . . . . . . . . . . $65

Celluloid, two blades, marked "Hammer Brand, USA"

**PKP016.000**

c.1930 . . . . . . . . . $125

Stainless, two blades, marked "Coca-Cola Co., Atlanta"

**PKP017.000**

c.1930 . . . . . . . . . $150

Stainless, two blades, marked "Remington" in circle.

**PKP018.000**

c.1930 . . . . . . . . . $150

Stainless, two blades, marked "Coca-Cola Co., Atlanta"

**PKP020.000**

c.1930-1950 . . . . . $40 to $85

Celluloid, many variations and manufactures, "Camco USA", "Clover Brand", etc.

**PKP019.000**

c.1930 . . . . . . . . . $75

Stainless, two blades, most marked "Coca-Cola Bottling Co., Germany"

**PKP025.000**

c.1940 . . . . . . . . . . . . . . .$60

Stainless, two blades (diff. mfgrs.) when marked "Remington" $100

**PKP036.002**

**PKP036.001**

**PKP030.000**

c.1950 . . . . . . . .$20

One blade, plastic

**PKP021.000**

1937 . . . . . . . . . . $275

Switch blade, blade marked "Remington Pat. 11-9-37"

**PKP022.000**

c.1935 . . . . . . . . . . . . . . $125

Celluloid, two blades, "Drink Coca-Cola in Bottles" on opposite side, blade marked "Remington"

**PKP035.000**

c.1950-1970 . . . . $35 to $50

Stainless, one blade and nail file, numerous logo designs and manufacturers.

**PKP031.000**

$150

**PKP032.000**

$200

**PKP023.000**

c.1935 . . . . . . . . . . $75

Pearl with corkscrew, blade marked "Colonial Prov. R.I."

**PKP024.000**

c.1930 . . . . . . . . . . . $125

Pearl with corkscrew, "Pure As Sunlight" on opposite side, blade marked "Imperial Prov. RI"

**PKP034.000**

c.1948 . . . . . . . . . . . . . $75

Stainless, two blades, "The Coca-Cola Bottling Co." opposite side

**PKP033.000**

$250♦

c.1930 Boy Scout style, bone and plastic handles, diff. shaped shields, most with blade marked "Coca-Cola Bottling Co.", three examples shown

*Note: Additional Knives can be found on page 398*

**PKP026.000**

c.1940 . . . . . . . . . . . . . $125

Pearl, two blades, "Westinghouse" on opposite side, blade marked "Made by Winchester Trademark" and "Quickpoint St. Louis"

**PKP037.000**

c.1960-1970 . . . . . . . $15

Two blades, gold colored plating

# OPENERS

The majority of the early openers were bought directly from the manufacturer by the bottlers. This accounts for a very large number of styles, types, and varieties of openers. We have tried to show a representative assortment here, but with an emphasis on the rare and unusual. Many of the earlier openers have a small square "Prestolite Key" hole, which served as a wrench to adjust the carbide gas for early automobile headlights (prior to widespread adoption of the battery and generator). This has erroneously been called a "skate key" hole. Some of the most sought after openers are the "Figural" styles shown on this page. Many openers are imprinted with bottler name and town.

All opener photos courtesy Thom Thompson, Versailles, KY

PP005.001

PP005.002

POP05.003

c.1912 to late 1920s . . $125

"Eagle Head", (three examples shown)

POP008.000

c.1914 to 1920s . . . . . $275

"Baseball Player", Very Scarce

POP014.000

c.1910-1930 . . . . . $125

"Lion Head", (one example with "Goldelle Ginger Ale" stamped on back)

POP025.000

POP025.001

c.1905-1910 . . . . . . . . . . $175

"Handy Pocket Companion", button hook, ruler and key ring combination (two examples shown)

POP027.000

c.1930 . . . . . . . . . $50

"End Formed"

POP006.000
"Early Morn" (nude)

POP007.000
"The Calendar Girl" (clothed)

c.1913-1930s . . . . . . . . . . . . . . . . . . . $175

"Girl" opener, three different reverse stampings shown and the two available obverses, Scarce

POP009.000

c.1920-1930 . . . . . $200

"Saber" or "Sword", example shown has "Purity is sealed in a bottle" on opposite side, Scarce

POP023.000

c.1905-1915 . . . . . . . . . . . . $50

"Key Ring" opener, has cigar box cutter and nail puller, plus square hole (both sides shown)

POP026.000

c.1930-1940 . . . . . $250

"Shoe Horn" opener

POP028.000

c.1930 . . . . . . . . . . . . $50

Cap lifter, opener end bent about 15° to handle

POP010.000

c.1910-1920 . . . . . . . . . . $75

Brass with red and black enamel value less with paint worn

POP011.000

c.1910-1920 . . . . . . $75

Steel with enamel, red background and red with green background

POP012.000

c.1930 . . . . . . . . . . . . . $100

Bottle shaped, Glascock

POP013.000

c.1911-1930 . . . . . . $175

"Spinner" fish shaped, marked "spin to see who wins" on back

POP024.001

POP024.002

c.1915-1930 . . . . . . $125

"Spinner" hand shaped, marked "spin to see who pays" on back (two examples shown)

POP029.000

c.1930 . . . . . . . . . . . $65

"Heavy Duty" (recent examples of this opener with "Enjoy"...etc. $3)

# OPENERS

Most opener styles were available for many years. The dates indicated in most instances are the patent date until probable discontinued use. When this information couldn't be verified, a probable circa date is shown, in most cases an educated guess, based on slogans, logo style, material, weight, etc.

POP030.000
c.1930-1940 . . . . . . . . . . . . . $50
"Improved Perfection", formed body

POP031.000
c.1900-1920 . . . . . . . . . . $100
"Cast Iron" (The cast iron openers are
some of the first patented openers)

POP032.000
c.1920-1930 . . . . . . . . $25
"Perfection", raised metal
reinforced

POP033.000
c.1908-1915 . . . . . . . . . . . $40
"When Thirsty", picnic style, also
available with figure-8 key hole and
square hole at opener end

POP034.000
c.1940 . . . . . . . . $45
"Ribbed" opener, stainless
steel by Dow

POP035.001

POP035.002

POP035.003
c.1905-1920 . . . . . . . . $40
"Outing Key Style" (three
examples shown)

POP038.001

POP038.002

POP038.003

POP038.004

POP038.005
c.1921-1940 . . . . . . . . . . . $40
"Over The Top" opener, (five
examples shown)

POP037.001

POP037.002

POP037.003

POP037.004

POP037.005

POP037.006
c.1930-1940s . . . . . . . . . . . . . . . . . $40
"Never Slip" opener (six examples shown)

POP036.000
c.1901-1915 . . . . . . . . . $50
"Picnic" opener, Dated 1901

POP039.001

POP039.002

POP039.003

POP039.004

POP039.005

POP039.006
c.1920-1950s . . . . . . . . $20 to $25
"Vaughan's Special", most common of the
pocket openers (six examples shown)
Marked "In Bottles" or bottlers name in
block letters, value to $30

POP041.001

POP041.002

POP041.003

POP041.004
c.1909-1950s . . . . . . $10 to $20
"Formed" hand opener, many variations, earlier ones marked "Sesco" or
"Sealtite" and dated 1909, later ones
marked "Consolidated Cork Corp."

POP040.000
c.1950s . . . . . . . . . . . . . $35
"Walden" cap lifter, concave handle

POP042.000
c.1919-1930 . . . . . . . . . . . $100
"Bottle Stopper" opener (also example
with Glascock Cooler advertising)

# OPENERS

Many openers are still being produced, some advertising 75th Anniversary celebrations, many in combination with other novelties. Most current openers can be purchased for $1 to $5 depending on quality and supply. There are many foreign openers in the market place, which we have not attempted to show.

POP043.000
c.1960-1970 . . . . . . . $20
"Folding" can piercer/opener

POP044.000
c.1960-1970 . . . . . . . $25
"Ribbed" can piercer/opener

POP045.000
c. 1963 . . . . . . . . . . . . . $65
"Handy Walden" can piercer/opener, painted on logo, Scarce

POP046.000
c.1960-1980 . . . $2 to $4
Can piercer/opener, many variations in size, length, logo, mfg., etc.

POP051.000
c.1948 . . . . . . . . . $250
"Muddler" opener, heavy brass, Scarce

POP052.000
c.1930-1940 . . . . . . . $35
"Bone Handle" wire opener

POP072.000
c.1950-1970 . . . . . . . . $10
"Plastic Handle" can piercer, bottle opener,

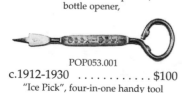

POP053.001
c.1912-1930 . . . . . . . . . . . $100
"Ice Pick", four-in-one handy tool

POP053.002
c.1915-1940 . . . . . . . . . $100
"Ice Pick, Bottle Opener"

POP048.000
1952 . . . . . . . . . . $75
"Nashville 50th Anniversary", gold plated

POP055.000
c.1928-mid 1940s . . . . . . $4
"Drink" wire opener  Earlier variations can have "Delicious & Refreshing" on opposite side $20

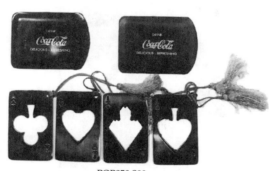

POP050.S00
c.1970 . . . . . . . . . . . . . . $20 Each
"Card Suit Openers", stainless steel, only sleeves are marked

POP058.000
c.1948-1950 . . . . . $65
"Formed Metal" wall-mount opener, red enamel logo

POP061.000
c.1950 . . . . . . . . . $100
"Bottle Cap" opener, with actual bottle cap attached to wall-mount opener

POP054.000
c.1930 . . . . . . . . . . . . . . . . . $100
"Spoon Opener", there are many variations of the spoon with handle-style opener available

POP049.000
c.1950 . . . . . . . $200
Bottle shaped

POP047.001        POP047.002
1950 and 1952 . . . . . . . . . . . . $100
POP047.B00  With presentation box
"Bottle Cap" design, 50th Anniversary

POP056.000
late 1940s-1960 . . . . . $1
"Have A Coke" wire opener, common Later variations with current slogans $1 Each

POP057.000
c.1940s . . . . . . . . . . . . . $35
"Syrup Can" opener

POP059.000
c.1920-1950 . . . . . . . $75
"Never Chip" wall opener

POP060.000
c.1930 . . . . . . . . $125
"Toothed" wall opener,
The Protector Mfg. Co.

POP062.001        POP062.002
c.1929-1940 . . . . . . . . . $75
"Wall Mount", bent plate opener,
(two examples shown)

**POP015.000**

c.1910-1930 . . . . . . . . . . . . . . . . . $225

"Horse Head", Very Scarce

**POP020.001**

**POP020.002**

c.1916-1940 . . . . . . . . . . . . . . . . . $75

"Nifty", combination bottle opener and corkscrew (two examples shown)

**PKP028.000**

c.1940 . . . . . . . . . . . . . . . $125

Key-shaped pocket knife, celluloid face, "Kent U.S.A." stamped on back. "Kent" and "Patent Applied for" stamped on blade

**PKP027.000**

c.1940 . . . . . . . . . . . . . . . . . . . . . $200

Single blade with opener, ebony handle, "Be Smart" and "Sell Coca-Cola" in window, "Solingen Germany" and "Pat. Pend." stamped on blade

**POP066.001**

c.1929-1942 . . . . . . . . . . . . . . . . $2 to $3
**POP066.B01** Mint in Original Box . . . . . $8
Starr "X" wall-mount cast opener, dated Apr. 1925

**POP066.002**

c.1940s-1980s . . . . . . . . . . . . . .$1 to $2
**POP066.B02** Mint in Original Box . . . $5
Starr "X" wall-mount cast opener, Patent 2,033,088 (issued 1943), (still being made by "Brown Mfg., Co.")

**POP016.000** "Bathing Girl"(clothed)
**POP017.000** "Mermaid"(nude)

c.1915-1930s . . . . . . . . . . . $225

"Mermaid" opener, two available obverse stampings shown, Rare

**POP021.000**

c.1920 . . . . . . . . . . . . . . . . . . $350

"Boot" bone handle opener, pocket knife, "Henry Sears & Son, 1865, Solingen" stamped on both blades

**POP022.000**

c.1920 . . . . . . . . $300

"Jim Dandy" combination button hook, bottle opener, screwdriver, cigar cutter, Very Scarce

**POP064.001**

c.1920 . . . $100

Cast wall opener, corkscrew and hook, dated Apr. 1925

**POP063.000**

c.1932 . . . . $50

Wall opener cast "Hoof shaped"

**PKP018.000**

1920 . . . . . . . . . . . . . . . . . . . . . . $200

"Dancer", legs with ballet slippers and garter

**PKP019.000**

c.1915 . . . . . . . . . . . . . . . . . . . $200

"Legs", bare legs with garter, with square gas hole

**PKP010.000**

c.1920 . . . . . . . . . . . . . . . . . . . . . . . $500

Two bladed pocket knife, nickler panels, "Coca-Cola Bottling Co. Germany" and "D. Peres, Solingen Germany" stamped on blade

**POP065.000**
c.1925 . . . $30
"Starr" cast wall opener, dated April 1925

**POP064.003**
c.1950-1960s
$40
Cast wall opener, chromed, corkscrew

**POP064.002**
c.1940 . . $100
Cast wall opener, chromed, corkscrew and hook (hook was for attachment of cap catcher)

**PKP038.000**

**PKP039.000**

Top: c.1930s . . . . . . . . . . . . . . . . . . . . . . . . . . . . $150
Combination measuring spoon and wire handled cap lifter or opener
Bottom: c.1930s . . . . . . . . . . . . . . . . . . . . . . . . . . $150
Wire handled meat fork.
Note: Similar pieces exist with "Slotted Ladle", "Cake Server", "Pancake Turner", "Spatula", etc., most with openers or cap lifters at end of handle.

POP067.000

1930s ........ $150

Opener, cast, wall-mount

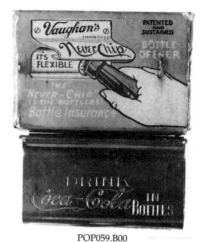

POP059.B00

c.1920 ............... $150

Opener, wall-mount, Vaughan's "Never Chip", in original box

POP068.000

c.1925 ................ $85

Opener, cast, wall-mount, Star "X", speciality use with side holes, Rare (Common examples with mounting holes at top and bottom are valued at $1 to $3.)

POP069.000

1950s-60s ....... $20

Opener, wall-mount

*Note: These street markers were used near schools to mark crosswalks. Used in the late 1930s and again after the war. A number of variations and manufacturers exist. Cast metal with short stem on back that anchors into asphalt.*

POP070.B00

1950s ........... $50

"Can Punch", Topmaster, Coca-Cola logo stamped on top, in original package

POP071.B00

1960s ...... $150

Bottle opener and cap catcher, "Akbilt", in original box

PMD030.000          PMD029.000

1930s thru postwar ................... $200

Street markers, two different examples, near mint to mint condition

Good to poor condition, worn ..... $75 to $100

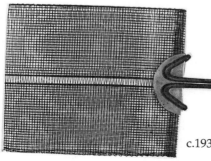

PKP054.000

c.1930s ......................... $175

Fly swatter, wire handle

Close up of handle

PKP040.000

1920s . . . . . . . . . . . . . . . . . . . . . . . . . . . .$40

With corkscrew and bottle opener

PKP041.000

1920s . . . . . . . . . . . . . . . . . . . . $50

PKP042.000

1920-30s . . . . . . . . . . . . . . . . . . . . . . $25

With bottle opener

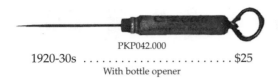

PKP043.000

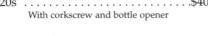

PKP043.B00

1930s Ice pick only . . . . . . . . . . . . . . . .$25
With bottle opener in box . . . . . . . . . . $40

PKP044.B00

1940s-50s . . . . . . . . . . . . . . . . . . . . . . . $30

in box

PKP047.000

1920s . . . . . . . . . . . . . . . . . . . . . . . . . . . $350

Ice tongs

PKP045.000

1960s . . . . . . . . . . . . . . . . . . . . . $10

PKP050.000

1920s . . . . . . . . . . . . . . . . . . . . . . . . . $100

Fly swatter (showing both sides)

PKP046.000

1960s . . . . . . . . . . . . . . . . . . $8

PKP051.000

1950s . . . . . . . . . . . . . . . . . . . . . . . .$20

Helena, AK

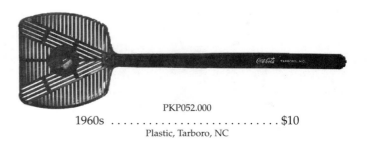

PKP052.000

1960s . . . . . . . . . . . . . . . . . . . . . . . . . $10

Plastic, Tarboro, NC

PKP029.000
c.1932 . . . . . . . . . . . . . . . . . . . . . . . . . $350
Carving knife, "Pure as Sunlight"

PMD026.000
1950s  10" High  . . . . . . . . . . . . . . . . $400
Ice bucket, brass finish

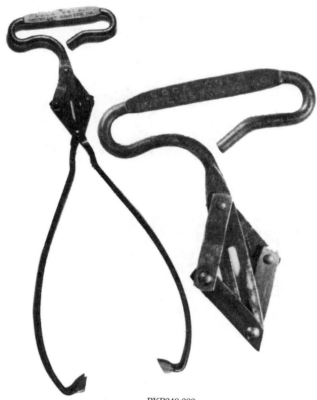

PKP049.000
1940s  9"  . . . . . . . . . . . . . . . . . . . . . $250
Ice tongs, aluminum

PKP048.000
1940s . . . . . . . . . . . . . . . . . . . . . . . . $375
Ice tongs

PMD028.000
1930s  2" x 4" x 1" . . . . . . . . . . . . . . $150
Brick (Help Build Lamar Community House)

PMD027.000
c1929  12 $1/2$" long  . . . . . . . . . . . . $1,100
Axe, "For Sportsmen", red, green, yellow paint inlay,
(head only 2" x 5")

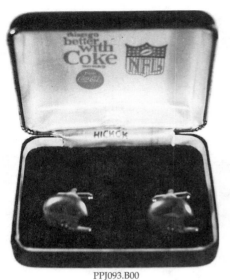

PPJ093.B00

1960s . . . . . . . . . . . . . . . . . . . . . . . . $50
Cufflinks (NFL football helmets) in original box

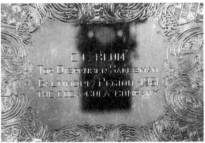

PMD034.S00

1961 . . . . . . . . . . . . . . . . . . . . . . $275
Tea set, silver plated, engraved tray, five
pieces, presented to "Top dispenser salesman"

PSP051.000

1930s-40s . . . . . . . . . . . . . . . . . . . $175
Paperweight, glass, Beeville Coca-Cola Bottling
Company, Beeville, TX

PSP050.B00

1970s . . . . . . . . . . . . . . . . . . . . . . . . $100
Camera, "Micro 110", complete with box and
instructions

PSP052.B00

Value . . . . . . . . . . . . . . . . . . . .$20
Hi-Jacs (sleeves) for Coke bottles, cloth,
complete set of six, in box

PSP053.000

c.1948  11" long  . . . . . . . . . . . . . $200
Pencil box (showing both sides), Memphis Bottling
Co., cork end piece comes off to insert pencils

# MISCELLANEOUS ANNIVERSARY ITEMS

PAN009.000

1957  12 ½" x 17 ½" . . . . . . . . . . . . .$450
50th Anniversary, embossed metal plaque, mounted
on wood

PAN010.000

1979  15" x 18" . . . . . . . . . . . . . . . . $225
75th Anniversary, embossed metal plaque, mounted
on wood

PAN006.BS0

1950s  . . . . . . . . . . . $250
50th Anniversary, "Promotional
Material" boxed kit
PAN006.001    Tablet
PAN006.002    Billfold
PAN006.003    Patch
PAN006.004    Key Chain

PAN005.000

1936  16" . . . . . . . . . . . . . . . . . . . $1,250
50th Anniversary, pressed metal plaque, red, gold,
and white with chain hanger,

PAN008.000

1950 . . . . . . . . . . . . . . . . . . . . . . . . $50
50th Anniversary, postcard Louisville, KY

PAN007.000

1950s . . . . . . . . . . . . . . . . . . . . . $35
50th Anniversary, coaster, silk-screened cork

**PSP010.000**

c.1950s . . . . . . . . . . . . . . . . . . . . . . $150

Hohner Harmonica (miniature) Key Ring, in leather case, German

**PSP011.000**

c.1930  3 1/4" high . . . $350

Bell, stamped metal, front and back same

**PSP012.000**

c.1920  3 1/4" high . . . . . . . . . . . . . . . $425

Bell, stamped metal, brass plated steel, front and back shown

**PSP014.000**

c.1930  2 3/4" . . . . . . . . . . . $55

Equipment tag or key tag, brass

**PSP013.000**

c.1920s  2 1/4" high . . . . . . . . . . . . . . . $350

Bell, enameled printing, (not stamped), front and back shown

**PSP017.000**

c.1910  3/4" . . . . $125

Uniform Button

**PSP015.000**

c.1950s . . . . . $100

Key ring, Nashville, TN

**PSP016.000**

c.1930  2 1/2" . . $150

Routemans pin, brass, Indianapolis Bottling Co.

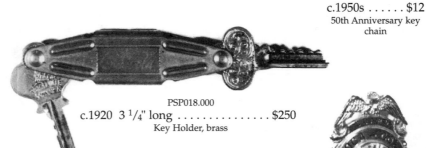

**PSP018.000**

c.1920  3 1/4" long . . . . . . . . . . . . . . $250

Key Holder, brass

**PAN006.004**

c.1950s . . . . . $12

50th Anniversary key chain

**PSP020.000**

c.1930s  1 1/2" x 2" . . . . $350

Hat pin, "cloisonne"

**PSP021.000**

c.1920  4" . . . . . . . . . . . . . . . . . . . $225

Hat pin, chromed

**PSP019.000**

c.1920  2 1/2" . . . . $275

Security guard badge, chromed, Coca-Cola Bottling Co., IN

**PSP022.000**

c.1959 . . . . . $50

Car key, in original package add $15

# MISCELLANEOUS

PKP055.000

1930s . . . . . . . . . . . . . . . . . . . . . . . . . $400
Gravity knife, blue with black lettering (cap is removed, with flick of wrist, blade is released and locked. Turned upward with button pressed, blade drops back into shaft)

PTY155.000

1920s-30s . . . . . . . . . . . . . . . . . . . . $200
Whistle, tin, Raleigh Coca-Cola Bottling Works

PSP046.000

c.1920s 3 1/4" high . . . . . . . . $500
Bell, stamped metal

PSP049.000

1940s . . . . . . . . . . . . . . . . . . . . . . . . $100
Wartime medallion, Shelbyville, KY

PSP047.000          PSP048.000

1940s-50s . . . . . . . . . . . . . . . . . . $35 Each
"Paper Clips", metal, San Marcos
Coca-Cola Bottling Co.

PPJ091.S00

c.1943 . . . . . . . . . . . . . . . . . . . . . . . . . . . . . . . . . $35 Each
Pinbacks, celluloid, WWII squadron insignias (Parisian Nov. Co. Chicago)
(thought to be 25 in set)

PSP023.000
1920s . . . . . . . . . . . . . . . . $300
Note pad holder, for candlestick phone

PSP024.000
1940s . . . . . . . . $300
Driver's badge

PSP025.BS0
1930s . . . . . . . . . . . $3,000
Salt and pepper set, sterling silver,
in box, Rare when found complete

PPJ035.000
1950s . . . . . . . . . . . . $65
50th Anniversary Convention
Badge

PSP026.001

PSP026.002

PSP026.003

PSP026.004

1920s . . . . . . . . $165 Each piece
Silverware, 4 different pieces shown
Not shown items:
PSP026.005    knife
PSP026.006    dinner fork
PSP026.007    teaspoon

PSP027.000
1950s . . . . . . . . $200
Tap knob, enameled

PSP028.001          PSP028.002
1960s-70s . . . . . . . . . . . $20 Each
Tap knobs

PSP029.001          PSP029.002          PSP029.003
1960s-70s . . . . . . . . . . . . $10 Each
Tap knobs

PSP030.B00
1920s-30s . . . . . . . . . . . . . . . . . . . $300
Ice pick holder, with box (this is a stock item)

PSP031.000
1940s . . . . . . . . . . . . . . . . . . . . . . . . $300
"Sun Dial" paperweight, The Coca-Cola Co., of
Miami, Inc., "The Best Refreshment Under The Sun"

PSP032.001

1920 . . . . . . . . . . $35

Thimble, many varieties of
these aluminum thimbles
exist, both red (above) and
blue (PSP032.002) enamel
inlay

PPJ051.S01

c.1920s Red . . . . . . . $75

PPJ051.S02 Blue . . . . . . $120

Cufflinks, celluloid

PSP033.000

c.1920s . . . . . . . . . . . . . . . $375

PSP033.B00 In original box . . $450

Salt and pepper shakers, aluminum
with enamel inlay

PSP034.000

c.1920s . . . . . $200

Puzzle, metal

PMC016.000

c.1920s 2 $^1/_2$" x 2 $^1/_2$" . . . . . . . $500

Pocket mirror, "Cat", cardboard, Rare

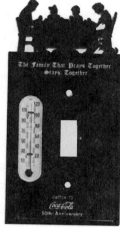

PSP035.000

c.1950s . . . . . . . . . $250

Plastic switch plate cover with
thermometer, (bottler item)

PPJ052.000

c.1912 . . . . . $375

Lapel pin,
Whitehead and Hoag

PPJ053.S00

c.1960s . . . . . . . $35

Bottle earrings, sterling
silver

PSP036.S00

c.1913-1915 . . . . . . . . . . . $500 Each

Door knobs, in both brass and steel, two different sizes available. Used in the Coca-Cola
buildings in Kansas City, MO, and Baltimore,
MD, built by Asa Candler in 1913 and 1915.

PSP037.000

c.1960 . . . . . . $400

Perfume bottle, sterling
silver case with applied
sterling bottle

PSP039.000

c.1950 . . . . . . . . $525

Bottle stopper, Sprite Boy
head with cork neck,
enameled plaster

PSP054.B00

c.1950 . . . . . $35

Garment hanger, plastic,
in original package

PSP038.000

c.1920s 2 $^1/_4$" . . . . . . . . . . . . . . . . . $600

Compact with powder puff, celluloid, "Parisian Nov.
Co., Chicago"

PSP055.001

1940s . . . . . . . . . . . . . . . . . . . . . . . . . . . . . . . . . $50 Each

Sewing kits, U.S. Marines, U.S. Army, (not shown: U.S. Navy and Coast Guard)

PSP040.000

c.1960s . . . . . . . $45

Money clip knife

PSP041.000

c.1960s . . . . . . . $45

Money clip knife

# SERVICE EMBLEMS

PPJ036.000
$35
Pledge pin

PPJ037.000
1 Year . . . . . . . . $35
No stones (non-Booker)

PPJ038.000
3 Year . . . . . . . $40
No stones (non-Booker)

PPJ039.000
5 Year . . . . . . . . $85
1932 Booker design

PPJ040.00
5 Year . . . . . . . . . $60
1945 Booker design (no stones)

PPJ041.000
10 Year . . . . . $75

PPJ042.000
15 Year . . . . . $85

PPJ043.000
20 Year . . . . $100

PPJ044.000
25 Year . . . . $100

The above pins are 1945 Booker design with stones

Note: *Service emblems were originally designed in 1932 by Roy G. Booker. They didn't change until 1945. The earlier versions were larger than the new "Streamlined" service pins of 1945. Also available from Booker in 1945 was a less expensive pin without stones. The 1945 design stayed intact for many years. Available from Booker were a Pledge Pin and Service Emblems for 5, 10, 15, 20, 25, 30, 35, 40, 45, and 50 years. Over 50 years were custom ordered. Other Service Pins were used over the years. 1, 2, 3, and 4 year versions were available from other companies, but the Booker emblems were the most popular.*

PPJ045.000
30 Year . . . . . . . $35
Tie clip

PPJ046.000
20 Year . . . . . . . . . $65
Tie bar

PPJ048.001       PPJ048.002       PPJ048.003       PPJ048.004

Enameled service pins
1950s . . . . . . . .$35 Each

PPJ047.000
1945 . . . . . . . . . . . . . . . . . . . . . . . . . . . . $100
Color brochure from Roy G. Booker, Atlanta, GA, showing and pricing service emblems, both with and without stones. Not Shown:
30-35 and 40 years . . . $110 Each (with stones)
45 and 50 years . . . . . $125 Each (with stones)

Note: **CAUTION:** *Do not over pay for these Service Emblems—they are very common. Some unknowledgeable dealers may overrate these. However, keep in mind that after 1945 the same emblems were in use for many years, and are readily available to collectors.*

PPJ049.000
1961 . . . . . . . . . $1,000
100,000 Gallon Club Gold
Medallion, Rare

PPJ050.001
1930s . . . $50
Driver's tie tack

PPJ050.002
1930s . . . $100
Driver's lapel pin,
sterling silver

PSP042.000
1930s . . . . . . . . . . . . . . . . . . . . . . $85
Bookmark, enameled, metal

PPJ054.000
1930s . . . . . . . . . . . . . . . . $100
Driver's belt buckle

PPJ055.S00
1970s . . . . . . . . . . . $30
Earrings, bottle cap

PPJ056.S00
$18
All Star Dealer Campaign
Award cufflinks

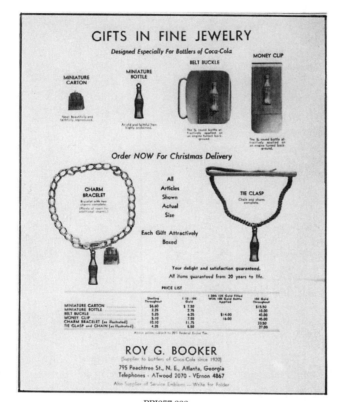

PPJ057.000
1940 . . . . . . . . . . . . . . . . . . . . . . . . $50
Catalog sheet from Roy G. Booker showing and
pricing jewelry

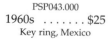

PSP043.000
1960s . . . . . . $25
Key ring, Mexico

PPJ058.000
1950s-60s . . . . . . $30
Safe driver pin

PPJ060.000
1960s . . . . . . . . . . . . . . . . . . . . . . $55
NFL Football charm bracelets

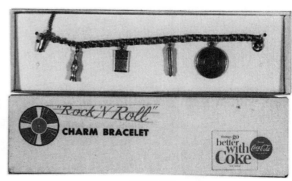

PPJ059.B00
1964 . . . . . . . . . . . . . . . . . . . . . . . . $65
Rock n' roll charm bracelet with box

PPJ061.000
Late 1930s . . . $65

PPJ062.000
1950s . . . $15

PPJ063.000
1977 . . . $5

PPJ064.000
1976 . . . $4

PPJ065.000
1960s . . . $6

PPJ066.000
1960s . . . $15

PPJ068.000
1970s . . . $3

PPJ069.000
1970s . . . $3

PPJ070.000
1980s . . . $3

PPJ071.000
1980s . . . $3

PPJ067.000
1960s . . . $10

PPJ072.000
1980s . . . $5

PPJ073.000
1970s . . . $3

PPJ074.000
1980s . . . $3

PPJ075.000
1980s . . . $3

PPJ076.000
1970s . . . $2

PPJ077.000
1950s . . $25

PPJ078.001, 002, 003
1950s . . . $8 Each

PPJ079.000
1977 . . . $3

PPJ080.000
1980s . . . $2

PPJ081.000
1970s . . . $3

PPJ082.000
1980s . . . $1

PPJ081.001
1970s . . . . . . . . $3

PPJ083.000
1980s . . . . . . . . . $2

PPJ084.000
1970 . . . . . . . . . . $3

PPJ085.000
1980s . . . . . . . . . $5

PPJ086.000
1983 . . . . . . . . . . . $2

PPJ087.000
1981 . . . . . . . . . $2

PPJ088.000
1980s . . . . . . . . . $4

PPJ089.000
1976 . . . . . . . . . . . $4

# WALLETS AND CHANGE PURSES

PWC008.000
c.1912 . . . . . . . . . . . . . . . . . . . . . . . . . $275
Change purse

PWC007.000
c.1910 . . . . . . . . . $175
Change purse

PWC005.000
c.1908 . . . . . . . . . . . . . . $250

PWC006.000
c.1907 . . . . . . . $145

PWC010.000
c.1907 . . . $100

PWC016.000
c.1920s . . . . $35

PWC011.00
1918 . . . . . . . . . $75
With calendar

PWC012.B00
c.1920s . . . . . . . . . . . . . . . . . . . . . . . $220
With envelope

PWC023.B00
1950s . . . . . . . . . . . . . . . . . . . . . . . . $25
With box

PWC018.000
1928 . . . . . . $25
Billfold

PWC017.000
c.1920s . . . . . . . $25
With embossed 1916 bottle

*Note: Wallets and Change Purses are difficult to date. In most cases, the dates are just good estimates. I have seen many different examples of Wallets and Change Purses. This is just a small sampling of the many different types that have been given away by The Coca-Cola Company over the years.*

PWC024.000
1920s . . . . . . $25

PWC023.001
1950s . . . . . $15

PWC025.000
1950s . . . $15

PWC009.000
c.1919 . . . . . . . $100
Change purse

PWC019.000
1930s . . . . . . . . . $25

PWC022.000
1936 . . . . . . . $125
50th Anniversary, pocket
secretary, leather, Rare

PWC027.000
1950s . . . . . . . . . . . . . . . . . . $30
Pocket secretary

PWC020.000
1930s . . . . . . $25

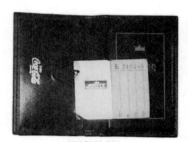

PWC034.000
1960s . . . . . . . . . . . . . . . . $10

PWC033.000
1960s . . . . . . . . . . . . . $10
Key case

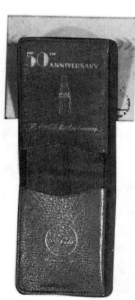

PWC026.B00
1950s . . . . . . . . $55
50th Anniversary, Coca-
Cola Bottling Co., with box

PWC035.000
1970s . . . . . . . . . . . . . . . . $6

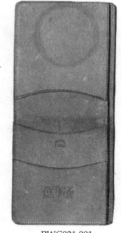

PWC021.001        PWC021.002
1920s . . . . . . . . . . . . . . . . . . . . . $25 Each
Wallet, pigskin, two different examples

PWC036.000
1970s . . . . . . . . . . . . . . . . . . $5
Tab

PWC039.000
1970s-1980s . . . . . . . . . . . . . . . . . . . . $10

PWC038.000
1960s . . . . . . . $10
Telephone book

PWC037.000
1960s . . . . . . . . $15

# WALLETS, KEY CASES, ETC.

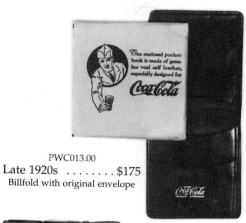

PWC013.00
Late 1920s ........ $175
Billfold with original envelope

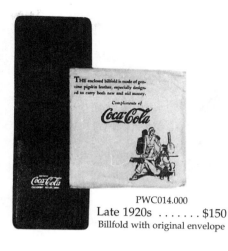

PWC014.000
Late 1920s ....... $150
Billfold with original envelope

PWC015.000
1920s ............. $60
Change purse

PWC045.000
1960s ........ $15
Wallet, ladies

PWC028.000
1950s ................. $25
Key case

PWC029.000
1950s .......... $15
Key case with gold bottle

PWC044.000
1970s ........ $5
Pocket secretary

PWC032.000
1950s ........................ $25
Pocket secretary

PWC031.000
1950s ........................ $25
Pocket secretary

PWC040.000
1960s ............ $8
Note pad pocket protector

PWC043.000
1960s ...................... $6
Wallet

PWC042.000
1960s ...................... $5
Billfold

PWC041.000
1960s .......... $6
Note pad holder

# MATCHBOOKS AND MATCH HOLDERS

PSM013.000
1910 . . . . $325
Matchbook holder

PSM012.000
1907 . . . $375
Matchbook holder

PSM014.000
1911 . . $1,200
Match safe

PSM011.000
c.1908 . . $675

PSM016.000
c.1912 . . $800

PSM020.000
1922 . . . . . . . . . . $135

PSM017.000
1912 . . . . . . . . . . . . . . $900

PSM010.000
1908 . . . $1,000
Rare

PSM018.000
c.1913 . . . . . . . . . . . . . . . . . . $650

PSM019.001
c.1914 . . . $750
With bottle

(Same back)

PSM019.002
c.1914 . . . . $750
With glass

PSM022.000
1930s . . . $20

PSM023.000
1929-1935. . $12

PSM024.000
1930s . . . $8

PSM026.000
1937-1943 . . . $6

PSM025.000
1936 . . . $7

PSM028.000
1944 . . . $6

PSM030.000
1952 . . . $12

PSM029.000
1940s . . . $5

PSM031.001
1950s . . . $25

PSM037.000
1945-1950s . . $4

PSM038.000
1959 . . . $5

PSM039.000
1950s . . . $5

PSM040.000
1963 . . . $5

PSM041.000
1963 . . . $6

PSM042.000
1964 . . . $4

PSM044.000
1963 . . . $3

PSM048.000
1960s . . . $3

PSM045.000
1958 . . . . . . $12

PSM043.000
1964 . . . . . . . . $8

PSM046.000
1959 . . . $3

PSM049.000
1963 . . . $3

PSM047.001
1959 . . . $3

PSM047.002
1959 . . . $3

PSM111.000
1970s . . . 50¢

PSM050.000
1970s . . . 75¢

PSM015.000

1910 . . . . . . . . . . . . . . . . . . . $1,100
"The Coca-Cola Girl" matchbook, Rare

PSM036.000

1930s . . . . . . . . . . . . . . $285
Matchbook holder brass

PSM055.000

1940s . . . . . . . . $400
Match holder, tin

PSM057.000

Late 1940s . . . . $425
Lighter, Rare

PSM058.000

c.1950 . . . . . . . . . . . . . . $50
Lighter

PSM053.000

1933 . . . . . . . . . . . . . . . . . . . . . . $5,500
Countertop, stick match dispenser, bakelite, Rare
(Showing front and side view)

PSM031.002

1950s . . . . . . . . $30
Large size

PSM021.000

Late 1920s . . $35

PSM035.000

1948 . . .$30

PSM110.000

1930s . . . . $40

PSM027.000

1930s . . . $35

PSM032.000

1948-1950 . .$20
Mexico

PSM033.000

1950s . . . . . . . . . . . . . . . $30

PSM034.00

1950s . . $12

# CIGARETTE LIGHTERS, ETC.

**PSM052.000**
1930s . . . . . . . . . . . . . . . . . . . . . . . . . $350
Match holder (stick-match), celluloid

**PSM051.000**
Individual packs . . . . . . $6 Each

**PSM051.BS0**
Complete set in box . . . . . . $85

1965 Match books, "Miami Convention" commemorative, box of ten

**PSM054.S00**
c.1959 . . . . . . . . . . . . . $165
Matchbook holder, metal, complete

**PSM056.000**
1939 . . . . . . . . . . . . . $375
Match striker, porcelain,
Canada

**PSM059.000**
1950s . . . . . . . . . . . . . . $25 Each
Miniature bottle lighter Note: This bottle
lighter is a very common piece. Without
lighter it is sometimes called a "Pill Box."

**PSM060.001    PSM060.002**
1963 . . . . . . . . . . . . . . . . . $125 Each
Musical lighter, red and white, different tunes
**PSM060.B00**
In Original Box . . . . . . . . . . . . . . . . $175

**PSM061.000**
1960s . . . . . . $30

**PSM062.000**
1950s . . . . . . $50

**PSM063.000**
1960s . . . . . . $20

**PSM064.000**
1960s . . . . . . $75
Mini lighter

**PSM065.000**
1960 . . . . . . $60
Mini can

**PSM066.000**
1950s . . . . . $85

**PSM067.000**
1960s . . . . . . $40

**PSM068.000**
1964 . . . . $35

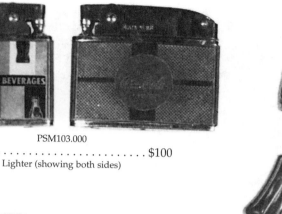

PSM103.000
1950s . . . . . . . . . . . . . . . . . . . . . . . . . $100
Lighter (showing both sides)

PSM102.000
1960s . . . . . . . . . . . . . . . . . . . $60
Lighter

PSM059.001
1950s . . . . . . . $45
Lighter, miniature gold
bottle

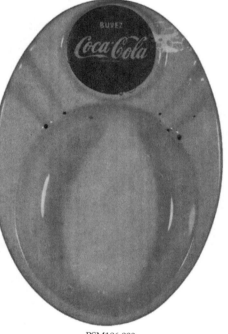

PSM104.000
Late 1950s . . . . $50
Lighter

PSM106.000
1940s-50s . . . . . . . . . . . . . . . . . . . . . $50
Ashtray, ceramic, Canada

PSM105.000
1980s . . . . . . .$12
Scripto lighter

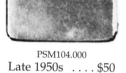

PSM108.000
Value . . . . . . . . . . . . . . .$25
Color flyer (small), for
"Pullmatch" dispenser

PSM107.000
1940s . . . . . . . . . . . . . . . . . . . $60
Bakelite ashtray

PSM109.000
Value . . . . . . . . . . . . . . . . . . . . . . . .$125
Refill roll of matches for "Pullmatch" dispenser, complete. Note: I've seen these refills sell for more than
price shown to collectors who need one for a dispenser.

PSM069.000

1936 . . . . . . . . . . . . . . . . . . . . . . . . . $700
Cigarette box, frosted glass, "50th Anniversary"

PSM072.000

1950s . . . . . . . . . . . . . . . . . . . . . . . . $150
Glass with wood base, "Silver Beach Park"

PSM070.001

1936 . . . . . . . . . . . . . . . . . . . . . . . $700
Ashtray, porcelain, 50th Anniversary, Rare
(personally signed at the 1936 convention)

PSM071.000

1930s-1940s . . . . . . . . $1,600
"Pullmatch" ashtray

PSM073.000

1940s . . . . . . . . . $40

PSM074.000

1950s . . . . . . . . . . . . . . . .$185
Ceramic

PSM075.BS0

In original box . . . . . . . . . . . . . . . . . . $600
PSM075.S00  Without box . . . . . . . . . . . $325
1950s Ashtray set, ruby glass

PSM076.000

1950s . . . . . . . . . $20
Tin

PSM077.000

1950s . . . . . . . . . $20

PSM078.000

1950 . . . . . . . . . $15

PSM079.000
$65
Ashtray, Shelbyville, IN,
New Plant

PSM080.000

1950s . . . . . . . . . $20

PSM081.000

1964 . . . . . . . . . $15
Tin

# ASHTRAYS

PSM082.S00

1950s . . . . . . . . . . . . . . . . . . . . $200

Ashtray with bottle lighter

PSM059.000 Bottle lighter only . . . $25

PSM083.000

Late 1920s . . . . . . . . . $225

PSM084.000

1950s . . . . . . . . . . . . $100

PSM085.000

1966 . . . . . . . . . . . . . . . . . . . . . . . $75

"World Press Institute Dinner",
showing Coke caps from around the world

PSM086.000

1960s . . . . . . . . . $8

Mexico

PSM087.000

1950s . . . . . . . . . $8

PSM088.000

1970s . . . . . . . . . $4

Mexico

PSM089.000

1940s . . . . . . . . $50

Glass

PSM090.001          PSM090.002

1958 . . . . . . . . . . . . . . . . . . . . . $85 Each

"Historic Series"

PSM096.000

1970s . . . . . . . . . . . . . . $4

PSM091.000

1940s . . . . . . . . . . . . $60

Bakelite

PSM095.000

1960s . . . . . . . . . $10

Aluminum

PSM098.000

1974 . . . . . . . . . . $10

PSM092.000

1940s . . . . . . . . . . . . . $35

Glass

PSM097.000

1970s . . . . . . . . $3

Glass

PSM094.000

1969 . . . . . . . . . . $8

Aluminum

PSM093.000

1950s . . . . . $8

Aluminum

PSM099.000

1970s . . . . . . . . . $4

Mexico

PFN071.BS0

1970s . . . . . . . . . . . . . . . . . . . . . . . $200
Coaster set in original box
PFN071.000 Individual coasters . . . . . . $30

PFN040.002

PFN040.003

PFN040.004

PFN040.005

1940s . . . . . . . . . . . . . . . . . . . . $18 each
Cardboard

PFN072.000

1950s . . . . . . . . . . . . . . . . . . . . . . . $45
12-Bottle carton coaster, aluminum

PFN073.000

1950s . . . . . . . . . . . . . . . . . . . . . . . $45
Six-Bottle carton coaster, aluminum

PFN074.000

1940s . . . . . . . . . . . . . . . . . . . . . . . $125
Foil covered stamped cardboard, Rare

# COASTERS

PFN037.000

1940s . . . . . . . . . . . . $25

PFN041.BS0
Complete set in envelope . . . . . . . . . . $35
PFN041.000 Individual coasters . . . . . . . . $5
1940s Coasters, rubber

PFN042.006

1950s . . . . . . . . . . $5

PFN043.000

1950s . . . . . . $15

PFN039.000

1939 . . . . . . . $16

PFN040.001

PFN040.002

1940s . . . . . . . . . . . . . . . . . . . . . $18 Each

PFN052.000

1960s . . . . . . $4

PFN044.000

1950s . . . . . . . $10

PFN045.000

c.1950 . . . . . . . . $3

PFN046.000

1950s . . . . . . . . $4

PFN047.000

1950s . . . . . . . . $3

PFN053.000

1960s . . . . . . $2

PFN054.000

1960s . . . . . . . . . . $2

PFN060.000

1970s . . . . . . $1

PFN062.000

PFN063.000

1970s . . . . . . . . . . . . . . . . $2 Each
Foreign

PFN064.000

1970s . . . . . . . . . $1

PFN061.000

1970s . . . . . . $1

PFN065.000

1970s . . . . . . $1

PFN057.000

1950s . . . . . . $20
Metal

PFN059.000

1960s . . . . . $10
Metal Sales Award

PFN058.000

1960s . . . . . . . $5
Aluminum

PFN056.000

1950s . . . . . $10
Foreign

# COASTERS

PFN049.000

1950s . . . . . . . . . . . . . . . . . . . . $8 Each

German

PFN068.S00

1970s-80s . . . . . . . . . . . $16

Set of coasters, ceramic in wood base

PFN069.000

1980s 75th . . . . . $3

Anniversary coaster

PFN067.001

Each . . . . . . . . . . . . . . . . $3

PFN067.S00 Set of 6 . . . . . $25

1980s Set of six coasters, "History of Coca-Cola"

PFN038.000

1937 . . . . . . . . . . . . . . . . . . . . . . . . . . . .$375

Nazi Germany coaster, showing both sides, Rare

Note: Pre-War Coca-Cola German items showing the "Swastika" are rare. Very little of this material exists today.

PFN051.001          PFN051.002

1950s . . . . . . . . . . . . . . . . . . . $6 Each

Canadian

PFN048.000

1950s . . . . . . . . . . $25

Coaster/Ashtray, foil, Russellville, KY

PFN050.001          PFN050.002

PFN050.003

1950s . . . . . . . . . . . . . . . . . . . . $5 Each

Foil Coasters

PFN055.BS0

1966 . . . . . . . . . . . . . . . . . . . . . $30

Coasters, plastic, Fountain Sales Dept., Sales Meeting, in box, set of eight

PFN066.000

1980s . . . . . . . . . . . . . $4

Jumbo coaster

# STAMP HOLDERS AND NOTE PADS

PMC017.000
1902  1 1/2" x 2 1/2" . . . . . . . . . . . . . . . $550
Postage stamp carrier, celluloid

PMC018.000
1910  1 3/4" x 2" . . . $500
Stamp holder, celluloid, with
pullout calendar and tissue
stamp pages

PMC019.000
1900  1 1/2" x 2 1/2" . . . $550
Stamp holder with Calendar,
celluloid

PMC020.000
1902  2 1/2" x 5" . . . . . . . . . . . . . . . . . . $650
Note pad, celluloid

PMC021.000
1903  2 1/2" x 5" . . . . . . . . . . . . . . . . . . . . $600
Note pad, celluloid

PBN006.000
1905  2 3/4" x 4 1/2" . . . . . . . . . . . . . . . . $200
Note book

PBN005.000
1903  2 3/4" x 5 3/4" . . . . . . . . . . . . . . . $275
Note book, brown leather with gold embossing,
(This book also put out in 1904, 1905 and 1906 listing
all syrup sales.)

PPM013.000
1904   4 $^1/_8$" x 6 $^1/_2$" . . . . . . . . . . . . . $750
Lillian Nordica

PPM012.000
1903   4 $^1/_8$" x 6 $^1/_8$" . . . . . . . . . . . . . $750
Hilda Clark

PPM011.000
1902   4 $^1/_8$" x 6 $^1/_8$" . . . . $800

*Note: The back of these menus are very interesting. When framing make sure the back is displayed.*

Back of Menus

PPM010.000
1901   11 $^3/_4$" x 4" . . . . . . . . . . . . . $1,600
Hilda Clark (shown open)

PBM005.000
1896  2 ³/₈" x 2 ³/₄"  . . . . . $1,500
Celluloid, Rare

PBM006.000
1896  2" x 2 ¹/₄"  . . . . . . . . . . . . . . . $1,200
Celluloid, two-sided, Rare

PBM007.000
1898  2" x 2 ¹/₄"  . . . . . $700
Celluloid

PBM008.000
1899  2" x 2 ¹/₄"  . . . . . $550
Celluloid

PBM009.001

PBM009.002

1900  2" x 2 ¹/₄"  . . . . . . . . . . . . . $600 Each
Celluloid, (two examples shown)

---

*Note: Prices are based on items in Excellent condition. Items in Near Mint to Mint condition could be worth more, and in Poor condition, that same item would be worth far less.*

---

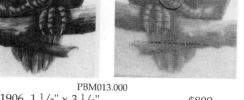

PBM010.000
1903
2" x 6"  . . . . . $375

PBM011.000
1904
2" x 6"  . . . . . $325

PBM012.000
1905
2 ¹/₄" x 5 ¹/₄"  . . . $700

PBM013.000
c.1906  1 ¹/₂" x 3 ¹/₈"  . . . . . . . . . . . . $800
"Owl", celluloid

PRC005.000
c. 1900 . . . . . . . . . . . $185
Botanic Blood Balm Trade Card

PCT008.000
c.1892
3 1/2" x 5 1/2" . . . . $1,700
Trade Card, Rare

PCT007.000
1891 3 3/4" x 5" . . . . . . . . . . . . . . $1,600
Trade Card

PCT006.000
1891 3 3/4" x 5" . . . . . . . . . . . . . . . $1,600
Trade Card

PRC006.000
1880s . . . . . . . . . . . . . . . . . . . . . . $2,000
French Wine Coca Diecut Hanging Sign

*Note: Dr. John Pemberton, inventor of Coca-Cola, as well as Asa Candler, to whom he sold it, were both druggists. Any products associated with either of these two men are of interest to many Coca-Cola Collectors. Some of these products include: French Wine Coca, Extract of Stillingia, Globe Flower Cough Syrup, Indian Queen Hair Dye, Triplex Liver Pills, Botanic Blood Balm (B.B.B.) Electric Bitters, Everlasting Cologne, Bucklen's Arnica Salve, King's New Discovery, Cheney's Expectorant, and De-Lec Ta-Lave. Trade Cards, signs, letterhead, etc., mentioning any of these products, especially if Pemberton or Chandler's name is associated with it, would certainly be collectible.*

PRC007.000
1889 . . . . . . . . . . . . . . . . . $175
B.B.B. Botanic Blood Balm Letter with
Asa Candler & Co. envelope

PCT009.000

1892  3 1/2" x 5 1/4" .......................................... $2,000
Trade Card shows Machinery Hall of the upcoming 1893 World's Columbian Exposition,
Chicago, IL, back shows 1890 and 1891 fountain sales, Rare.  Photo courtesy: Thom Thompson

PCT011.000
1902  4 1/8" x 6 1/8" .............. $800
Trade Card, Rare

PCT010.000
1902  2 1/4" x 3 7/8" .............. $1,000
Trade Card, Rare

PRC008.00
c.1877  4" x 5" ................. $500
A.G. Candler Trade Card

PCT012.000
c.1908  2" x 3 1/2" ................ $30
Business Card

# 1892 DEALER MAILING PIECE

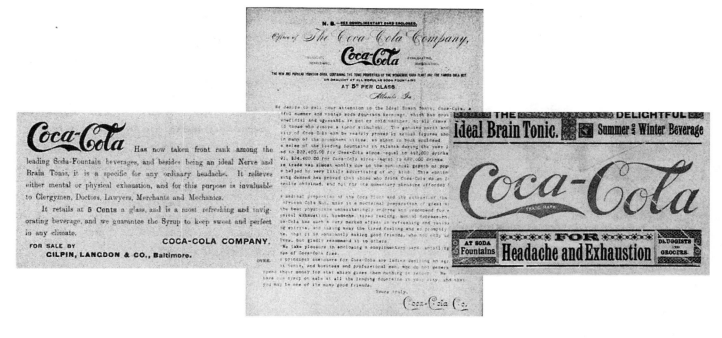

PPM332.S00

Value . . . . . . . . . . . . . . . . . . . . . . . . . . . $2,800

During the early years, The Coca-Cola Company used direct mail as an effective sales tool. To consumers went a letter and "Free Drink Tickets." To pharmacies, soda fountains, and any prospective dealers that would dispense Coca-Cola, dealer "sales packages" were sent. This 1892 set (shown) consists of a letter introducing the product, a two-sided statement card showing gallons used in 40 cities around the country for 1890 and 1891, a very elaborate envelope (printed both sides) and a 16-page booklet (all pages shown) which includes an ad for botanic blood balm (B.B.B.), sales records and testimonials from various druggist extolling the advantages of selling Coca-Cola. These early mailing pieces are rare and especially desirable when complete like this set.

# THE COCA-COLA NEWS

PPM314.000

Feb. 1896 .... $800

Vol. 1, No. 1

PPM315.000

March 1896 ... $700

Vol. 1, No. 2

NOTE: In 1892, The Coca-Cola Company granted a contract to Seth Fowle and Sons, of Boston, Mass., for sales rights to six New England states for a period of 20 years. The contract ran its course and expired in 1912. It was not renewed. Seth Fowle was very active in promoting Coca-Cola within his territory. In addition to advertising material being supplied by Atlanta, Fowle produced much of his own. On January 15, 1896 he began publication of The Coca-Cola News. It was targeted to pharmacies, soda fountains, and outlets that would dispense Coca-Cola. This four-page 6" x 8" paper sported a banner below the masthead which read "Sheds Light On Subject's Peculiar To The Soda Fountain." While these issues of The Coca-Cola News do not contain a wealth of information for today's collectors, they are early, unusual, and rare. Remember, pre-1900s or turn-of-the-century pieces are always very desirable. Values shown reflect outstanding condition; worn or in poor condition would be worth considerably less.

PPM316.000

April 1896 ... $700

Vol. 1, No. 3

PPM317.000

May 1896 ..... $700

Vol. 1, No. 4

PPM318.000

June 1896 ...... $700

Vol. 1, No. 5

PPM319.000

July 1896 ...... $700

Vol. 1, No. 6

PPM320.000

Feb. 1897 ..... $600

Vol. 2, No. 1

PPM321.000

March 1897 .... $600

Vol. 2, No. 2

PPM322.000

April 1897 .... $600

Vol. 2, No. 3

PPM323.000

May 1897 ..... $600

Vol. 2, No. 4

PPM324.000

June 1897 ..... $600

Vol. 2, No. 5

PPM325.000

Feb. 1900 ..... $500

Vol. V, No. 1

PPM326.000

Feb. 1900 ...... $500

Vol. V, No. 2

PPM327.000

Feb. 1900 ..... $500

Vol. V, No.3

PPM328.000

Feb. 1900 ...... $500

Vol. V, No.4

PPM329.000

Feb. 1901 ..... $500

Vol. VI, No.1

PPM330.000

Feb. 1901 ..... $500

Vol. VI, No.2

PPM331.000

Feb. 1901 ...... $500

Vol. VI, No.3

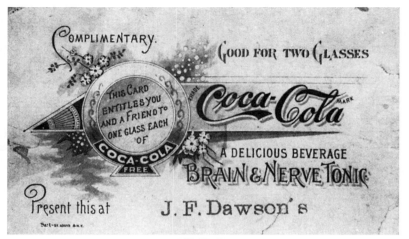

PCT085.000

1890s  3" x 5"  . . . . . . . . . . . . . . . . . $3,500
Complimentary ticket, "Good for two glasses of
Coca-Cola", Rare

PBN030.000

1913 . . . . . . . . . . . . . . . . . . . . . . . $325
Booklet "Truth Justice and Coca-Cola", 20 pages

PCT086.000

c.1910  . . . . . . . . . . . . . . . . . . . . . . . . . . . . . . . . . . . . $850
Folding advertising card (sent out monthly to prospective dealers of Coca-Cola)

PPM348.000

c.1907  6" x 7"  . . . . . . . . . . . . . . . . . . . . . . . . . . . $500
Folder (open) showing front and back, promoting Coca-Cola by the case

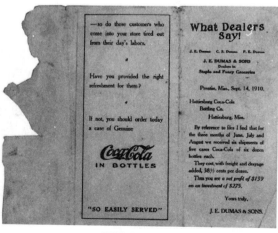

PCT043.000

c.1907 . . . . . . . . . . . . . . . . . . . . . . . $850
Folding Trade Card, shown open and closed

PCT044.001

c.1920s . . . . . . . . . . . . . . . . . . . . . $950
Mechanical Folding Card. Note: There are
other variations of this 1920s mechanical
folding card

PCT045.000

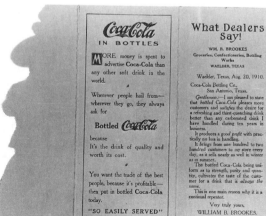

PCT046.000

c.1910 . . . . . . . . . . . . . . . . . . . . . . . . . . . . . . . . . . . . . . . . . . . . . . . . . . . . . . $850 Each
Folding Advertising Cards (these cards were sent out on a monthly basis to prospective dealers of Coca-Cola)

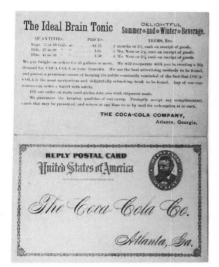

PCT013.000

1893 . . . . . . . . . . . . . . . . . . . . . $850

Double Postal Card  Note: Pieces this early
are Very Rare. Photo courtesy: Thom
Thompson.

PCT015.000

1910 . . . . . . . . . . . . . . . . . . . . . . . . $700

"The Coca-Cola Girl", Hamilton King Artwork

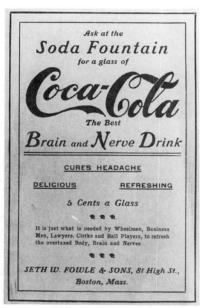

Note: Although an unused
postcard in flawless condition
would be very desirable, I personally prefer
a used "postmarked" card,
which I find so much more
interesting.

PCT014.000

c.1898 . . . . . . . . . . . . . . . . . . . $450

PCT016.000

1911 . . . . . . . . . . . . . . . . . $700

"Motor Girl" (Formally called the
"Duster Girl")

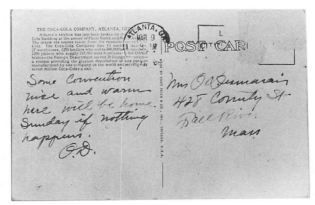

PCT017.000

c.1920s . . . . . . . . . . . . . . . . . . . . . . . . . . . . . . . $135

"The Home of Coca-Cola" in Atlanta

# POSTCARDS

PCT018.000

c.1906 . . . . . . . . . . . . . . . . . . . . . . . . $125
Soda Fountain Photo Card

*Note: Pre-1920 Soda Fountain cards showing Coke advertising especially photo cards, are always very desirable.*

PCT020.000

1910 . . . . . . . . . . . . . . . . . . . . . . . . . $85
"Reminder" Card

PCT019.000

1912 . . . . . . . . . . . . . . . . . . . . . . . . $50
Brown's Pharmacy, Ozark, AL

PCT022.000

1930s . . . . . . . . . . . . . . . . . . . . . . . $45
Atlantic, IA Bottling Plant

PCT021.000

1936 . . . . . . . . . . . . . . . . . . . . . $30
"Free Calendar" Postcard

30 Caliber Machine Gun, Water Cooled

PCT022.001

Back of card

1944 . . . . . . . . . . . . . . . . . . . . . . . . . . . . . . . . $12 Each
Army Exhibit Post Card, two different fronts shown, same back

50 Caliber Machine Gun Trainer

PCT022.002

PCT023.S01    PCT023.S02    PCT.023.S03    PCT023.S04    PCT023.S05

1940s . . . . . . . . . . . . . . . . . . . . . . . . . . . . . . . . . . . . . . . . . . . . . . . . . . . . $85 Set
Individual cards . . . . . . . . . . . . . . . . . . . . . . . . . . . . . . . . . . . . . . . . . . . $5 Each
"Cartoon" Postcard Sets (four cards to a set) five different sets shown Complete set in wrapper

PCT024.000

International Truck Post Card ...... $12

PCT027.000          PCT028.000

1906 and 1909 ...... $20 Each
Candler Building Atlanta, GA

PCT025.000

1930s . . . . . . . . . . . . . . . $10
Richfield Oil

PCT026.000

1930s . . . . . . . . . . . . . . $25
Weldmech Truck

PCT029.000          PCT030.00

Early 1900s . . $12     1916 . . . . . . . . $12
Candler Building     Coca-Cola Building,
Atlanta, GA          Kansas City, MO

PCT031.000

1920s . . . . . . . . . . . . . $25
Coca-Cola Building, Baltimore, MD

PCT032.000

1930s . . . . . . . . . . . . . . $30
Coca-Cola Bottling Co., Little
Rock, AR

PCT039.000

1940s . . . . . . $12
Free Bottle Opener

PCT035.000

1940s . . . . . . . . . . . . . . . . $5
Bakersfield, CA

PCT033.000

c.1907 . . . . . . . . . . . . $25

PCT034.000

c.1907 . . . . . . . . . . . . $10
Atlantic City

PCT036.000

Early 1920s . . . . . . . . $60
Ad Agency Post Card

PCT037.001          PCT037.002

1940s . . . . . . . . . . . . . . . . . . . . $6 Each
Christmas "May We Suggest" Post Card (two examples shown)

PCT038.000

1920s . . . . . . . . . . . . . . . . $25
Brown Mfg., Co. Order Post Card

PCT040.000

1968 . . . . . . . . . . . . . . . . . $5
Coke Pavilion World's Fair

PCT041.000

1964 . . . . . . . . . . . . . . . . . $5
Coke Pavilion World's Fair

PCT042.001          PCT042.002

1970s . . . . . . . . . . . . . . . . . . . . $5 Each
Bobby Allison Coke Race Car

PCT048.001

1901  1 5/8" x 3 3/8" ....... $700

Hilda Clark

PCT050.001

c.1908  1 5/8" x 3 3/8" ....... $200

Purple

PCT047.001

Pre-1900  1 1/2" x 3 3/8" ........ $275

Seth W. Fowle & Sons

PCT048.002

1901  1 5/8" x 3 3/8" ........ $700

Hilda Clark, different back

PCT050.002

c.1908  1 5/8" x 3 3/8" ....... $300

Red and Green

PCT047.002

Pre-1900  1 1/2" x 3 3/8" ........ $275

"The Coca-Cola Company"

---

*Note: These early coupons were called "Complimentary Tickets" by The Coca-Cola Company.*

---

PCT052.000

1905  6 1/2" x 9 3/4" ...... $275

"Lillian Nordica" magazine ad with
coupon, placed in 9 different magazines
in the summer of 1905 (back similar to
that at right).

PCT053.000

1905  3 3/4" x 7" .................. $750

"Lillian Nordica" Ad Card with coupon (front and
back shown). Rare when found complete, coupon
must be attached to warrant this price.

PCA167.000

1909, 1910,
1911 .......... $900

Calendar

---

*Note: A large quantity of these "Ad Cards" (PCA167.000) were converted to a small size calendar by "Wolf & Co." in the above years. The coupon was removed and a metal grommet added for hanging. This calendar is old and original. Why this art work was used again, so many years after its first 1905 usage, is really not known. This calendar was pictured in the April 1949 Coca-Cola Bottler magazine, which disputes speculation by some that this was a piece fabricated in the 1970s.*

---

PCT049.000

c.1903  1 5/8" x 3 3/8"  . . . . . . . $400

Purple and green

PCT047.003

Pre-1900  1 1/2" x 3 3/8"  . . . . $275

"The Coca-Cola Company"

PCT059.000

c.1930

2" x 2 1/2"  . . . . . $7

PCT060.000

c.1930s  1 1/2" x 2 3/4" . . $8

Box carton on back

PCT057.000

c.1920s

1 1/8" x 2"  . . . . $8

PCT054.000

c.1927  2 1/4" x 4"  . . . $50

"Soda Jerk (front and back)"

PCT064.000

1934  2" x 4"  . . . . . . . . . . $20

PCT056.000

Late 1920s  2" x 5"  . . . . . . . $20

Coupon Book

PCT051.000

c.1906  2 3/4" x 5 1/8"  . . $175

PCT058.000

c.1930

2 1/2" x 4"  . . . $10

PCT068.000

1950s

2 7/8" x 4"  . . . . . . . $3

PCT069.000

c.1950  2 3/8" x 4 3/8"  . . . . . . $5

PCT066.000

1939  2 3/8" x 4 3/8"  . . . . $10

PCT061.000

2 1/2" x 3 1/2"  . . . . . . $30

Late 1920s

PCT067.000

c. 1939  2 1/2" x 4"  . . . . . . . $7

PCT055.000

c.1929  2 3/8" x 3 5/8"  . . . . . . . . . $65

PCT065.000

1930s  1 3/4" x 6"  . . . . $8

Bottle Shaped

PCT063.000

Late 1920s  2" x 2 3/4"  . . $3

"Thomas Coupon"

PCT062.S00

Late 1920s  2 1/2" x 3 1/2"  . . . . . . $40

Three coupons in envelope

PCT062.000  . . . . . . . . . . . . . . $5 Each

Individual coupons

# COUPONS

Below are fourteen different examples of "Complimentary" six-bottle coupon cards. They were used during the late 1930s.

PCT070.000
$15

PCT071.000
$18

PCT072.000
$18

PCT073.000
$15

PCT074.000
$15

PCT075.000
$15

PCT076.000
$20

PCT077.000
$10

PCT078.000
$15

PCT079.000
$15

PCT080.000
$12

PCT081.000
$12

PCT082.000
$20

PCT083.000
Early 1950s . . . . . . . . . . . $8

# BLOTTERS

Shown on the following pages is the most complete and accurately dated collection of Coca-Cola blotters ever illustrated. My special thanks to Thom Thompson of Versailles, KY for his extensive research and collaboration on this section. Blotters from 1904 through 1923 were issued advertising either "Bottled" (B) sales or Advertising "Fountain" (F) sales. After c.1923, they all advertised bottled sales.

PBL005.000
c.1904 (B) . . . $1,000
"Atlanta Litho. &
Print Co."

PBL007.001
c.1904 (F) . . . . . . . . . . . $125
"Edwards Deutsch & Heitmann,
Chicago"

PBL008.00
c.1905 (B) . . . . . . . . . . $150

PBL006.001
c.1904 (B) . . . . $450
"Edwards Deutsch
& Heitmann
Chicago"

PBL007.002
1904 (F) . . . . . . . . . . . . .$500
"Atlanta Litho & Printing, Co."

PBL009.000
1906 (B) . . . . . . . . . . . . $150

PBL006.002
c.1904 (B) . . .$450
No Litho Co.

PBL010.000
c.1906 (F) . . . . . . . . . $125

PBL011.000
1909 (B) . . . . . . . . . . . . . $225

PBL012.000
c.1909 (F) . . . . . . . . . . . $125

PBL014.000
1911 (B) . . . . . .$900
Blue and Pink Backs
"Motor Girl" (previously
called "Duster Girl")

PBL013.000
1910 (B) . . . . . . . . . . . . $350

PBL015.000
c.1912 (F) . . . . . . . . . . . $125

PBL016.000
c.1913 (F) . . . . . . . . . . . $30

PBL027.000
c.1915 . . . . . $1,500
"Chewing Gum"

PBL017.000
c.1913 (B) . . . . . . . . . . . $40

PBL018.000
c.1915 (B) . . . . . . . . . . . $75

PBL019.000
c.1915 (F) . . . . . . . . . . . $225

PBL020.000
c.1916 (B) . . . . . . . . . . . $30

PBL021.000
c.1920 (F) . . . . . . . . . . . $125

PBL022.000
c.1920 (B) . . . . . . . . . . . $40

PBL023.000
c.1923 (B) . . . . . . . . . . . $30

PBL024.000
c.1923 (F) . . . . . . . . . . . $400

PBL028.000
c.1916 . . . . . . . . . . . . . . $800
"Chewing Gum"

PBL025.000
c.1924 (B) . . . . . . . . . . . $400

PBL026.000
c.1926 (B) . . . . . . . . . . . $20

# BLOTTERS

PBL029.000

1927 . . . . . . . . $60

PBL030.000

1928 . . . . . . . $75

PBL031.000

1929 . . . . . . $225

PBL032.000

1929 . . . . . . $100

PBL033.000

1929 . . . . . . $150

PBL034.000

1929 . . . . . . $125

PBL035.000

1930 . . . . . . . $75

PBL036.000

1930 . . . . . . . $75

PBL037.000

1930 . . . . . . $175

PBL038.000

1930 . . . . . . $125

PBL039.000

1931 . . . . . . $150

PBL040.000

1931 . . . . . . $225

PBL041.000

1931 . . . . . . $125

PBL042.000

1931 . . . . . . $100

PBL043.000

1932-33 . . . . . $75

PBL044.000

1932-33 . . . . . $125

PBL045.000

1932-33 . . . . . $225

PBL046.000

1932-33 . . . . . $225

PBL047.000

1934 . . . . . . . $100

PBL048.000

1934 . . . . . . . $100

PBL049.000

1934 . . . . . . . $100

PBL050.000

1934 . . . . . . . $100

PBL051.001  PBL051.002

1935 . . . . . . . . . . $60

(dated and undated)

PBL052.001  PBL052.002

1935 . . . . . . . . . . $35

(dated and undated)

PBL053.001  PBL053.002

1935 . . . . . . . . . . $35

(dated and undated)

PBL054.001  PBL054.002

1935 . . . . . . . . . . $35

(dated and undated)

PBL055.000

1936 . . . . . . . $50

PBL056.000

1937 . . . . . . . $30

PBL057.000

1938 . . . . . . . $20

PBL058.000

1939 . . . . . . . $20

PBL059.000

1940 . . . . . . . $65

PBL060.001  PBL060.002

1941 . . . . . . . . . . $15

(TM in tail and without)

PBL061.000

1942 . . . . . . . . $6

PBL062.000

1942 . . . . . . . . $6

PBL063.000

1944 . . . . . . . . $6

PBL064.000

1947 . . . . . . . . $6

PBL065.000

1951 . . . . . . . . $4

PBL066.000

1952 . . . . . . . $125

PBL067.000

1953 . . . . . . . . $4

PBL068.000

1956 . . . . . . . . $4

PBL069.000

1957 . . . . . . . . $5

PBL070.000

1960 . . . . . . . . $4

PBL071.000

1942 . . . . . . . $15

PBL072.000

1942 . . . . . . . $15

PBL073.000

c.1950 . . . . . . $15

# BLOTTERS

The following are miscellaneous blotters not used by "The Coca-Cola Co.": stock blotters used by individual bottlers as well as pencil box blotters.

## Pencil box blotters issued by The Coca-Cola Co.

PBL075.000
c.1907 . . $150

PBL074,000
c.1911 . . . . . . . . . . . . . $135
"Western"

PBL079.000
1906 . . . . . . . . . . . . . . $250
"Western" (Shown trimmed down)

PBL078.00
1905 . . . . . . . . . . . . . $300
"Palatka"

PBL080.00
1935 or 1937 . . . $10

*Pencil box blotters used by the Coca-Cola Co.*

PBL081.000
1935 or 1937 . . . $10

PBL076.000
1944 . . . . . . . . . . . . . . . $125
Dispensers (Coca-Cola Machine on right)

PBL077.000
1931 . . . . . . . . . . . $125

## The following are foreign blotters.

PBL200.F00
c.1904 . . . . . . . . . . . . . $300
Cuba

PBL201.F00
c.1909 . . . . . . . . . . . . . $300
Cuba

PBL206.F00
1947 . . . . . . . . . . . $100
"Export Corp"

PBL202.F00
c.1935 . . . . . . . . . . $225
German

PBL204.F00
1942 . . . . . . . . . . . $10
Mexico

PBL207.F00
c.1947 . . . . . . . . . $100
Belgium

PBL203.F00
c.1935 . . . . . $275
Canada

*Almost all Canadian blotters have been printed in both French and English. Some of these variations are shown here.*

PBL205.F00
1939 . . . . . . . . . . $50
Canada

PBL208.F00
1938 . . . . . . . . . . . .$50
Canada

PBL212.F00
1947 . . . . . . . . $40
Canada

PBL209.F00
1940 . . . . . . . . . . . $50
Canada (French)

PBL211.F00
1946 . . . . . . . . . . $35
Canada

PBL219.F00
1953 . . . . . . . . . . . $35
Canada

PBL213.F00
1948 . . . . . . . . . . . $20
Canada

PBL210.F00
1945 . . . . . . . . . . . $60
Canada

PBL215.F00
1950 . . . . . . . . . . $35
Canada

PBL216.F01
1951 . . . . . . . . . $40
Canada, English

PBL216.F02
1951 . . . . . . . . . $40
Canada, French

*Note: There have been times when a good blotter has turned up in quantity. If and when this happens, a $100 blotter could become a $20 blotter.*

PBL217.F01
1954 . . . $20
Canada (Fr.)

PBL217.F02
1954 . . . $20
Canada (Eng.)

PBL214.F00
1949 . . . . . . . . . . $40
Canada

PBL218.F00
1952 . . . . . . . . . . $40
Canada

PBL220.F00
1955 . . . . . . . . . $25
Canada

# PLAYING CARDS

PPL005.000
1909
$4,000

PPL006.000
1915
$2,800

PPL007.000
1928
$750

PPL030.000
1937
$275

PPL031.000
1939
$175

PPL032.000
1939
$275

PPL033.000
1939
$300

PPL034.000
1939
$475

PPL035.000
1943
$100

PPL036.000
1943
$100

PPL037.000
1943
$100

PPL038.000
1943
$100

PPL039.001
1943
$300

PPL040.000
1943
$300

PPL041.000
1951
$85

PPL042.000
1951
$85

PPL043.000
1956
$85

PPL044.000
1956
$85

PPL045.000
1958
$100

PPL046.000
1958
$85

PPL047.000
1959
$85

PPL048.000
1959
$85

PPL049.000
1960
$75

PPL050.000
1960
$125

PPL051.000
1961
$75

PPL052.000
1961
$75

PPL053.000
1963
$85

PPL054.000
1963
$75

PPL055.000
1963
$65

PPL056.000
1963
$65

PPL057.000
1971 . . . . . . . . . . . . . .$250
Boy Scouts Jamboree

PPL058.000
1971
$15

PPL059.000
1971
$15

PPL060.000
1971
$30
Mexico

PPL061.000
1974
$10

PPL062.000
1976
$10

PPL063.000
1976
$8

PPL064.000
1970s . . . . . . . . . . . . . . . . . . . . . . . . .$175
"Bucks"

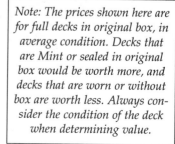

> *Note: The prices shown here are for full decks in original box, in average condition. Decks that are Mint or sealed in original box would be worth more, and decks that are worn or without box are worth less. Always consider the condition of the deck when determining value.*

# CARD TABLES

During the 1930s and 40s, the card game of "Bridge" was a national craze. It seemed that everyone was playing bridge—at home, in groups—there were bridge clubs popping up everywhere, as well as tournaments. The Coca-Cola Company and its local bottlers felt the home market was very important and took advantage of the national fascination with bridge. Playing cards, score pads, tally cards, card cases, and instruction booklets were used consistently and effectively to get the message across to the card players that with their refreshments they needed an ice cold Coke. One of the more expensive items made available was a card table. Because of the cost it wasn't given away but rather sold at cost. Tables have never been considered rare, and aside from being an interesting novelty piece they have never been a collector favorite.

PMD024.000

1930s . . . . . . . . . . . . . . . . . . . . . . . . $100
Card table with pre-sold advertising corners.
Note: This table was not done by Coca-Cola but was just advertising space sold to a local bottler.

Close up of paper label on bottom of table. I've seen other versions of this label.

Close up of corner showing bottle. I've seen other variations of the trim lines, with solid or multiple stripes. Bottle and trim printed in gold, red or green. Top is black cardboard with a simulated leather look.

PMD025.000

1930s . . . . . . . . . . . . . . . . . . . . . . . . $200
Card table, cardboard top with wood legs

# PLAYING CARDS, BRIDGE, ETC.

PPL065.S00

1950 . . . . . . . . . . . . . $325
NAPL Convention
Bridge set

PPL066.000

1950s . . . . . . . . . . . . . . . $10
Bridge tally card

PPL067.000

1950s . . . . . . . . . . $10 Each
Bridge tally cards

PPL070.S00

1940s . . . . . . . . .$12
Bridge score pad and
tally card

PPL068.000

1960s . . . . . . . . . . . . . . .$30
Bridge set (case)

PCS319.000

1938  12" x 18" . . . . . . . . . . . . . . . $45
Sign, cardboard

PPL071.000

1943 . . . . . . . . . $12
Score pad

PPL073.000

1930s-40s . . . . . . . $5
Score pad (Canada)

PPL075.001

1950s . . . . . . . . . . . . . . . . . . . . . . . $12
Bridge tally card

PPL072.000

1980s . . . . . . . $3
Bridge score pad

PPL074.000

1950s . . . . . . . . . . . . . . . . . . . . . $12
Bridge Digest booklet

# SHEET MUSIC

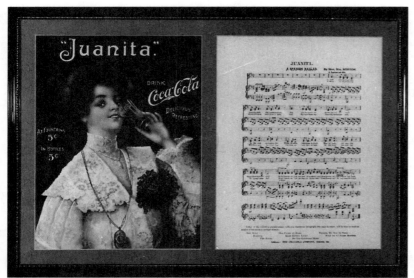

PMU005.001

1906 . . . . . . . . . . . . . . . . . . . . . . . . . . $1,200
"Juanita"

PMU005.002

1906 . . . . . . . . . . . . . . . . . . . . . . . . . . . $800
"We Found That He'd Been Drinking Coca-Cola"

PMU005.003

1906 . . . . . . . . . . . . . . . . . $800
"The Palms"

ADDITIONAL TITLES OF 1906
"Juanita" sheet music not shown
PMU005.005—Ben Bolt
PMU005.006—My Old Kentucky Home
PMU005.007—Rock Me To Sleep Mother
PMU005.008—Old Folks At Home
PMU005.009—Lead Kindly Light
PMU005.010—Nearer, My God To Thee

PMU005.004

1906 . . . . . . . . . . . . . . . . . . . . . $800
"My Coca-Cola Bride"

# SHEET MUSIC

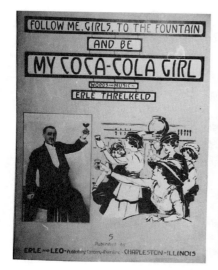

PMU006.000

1915   10 ³/₄" x 13 ³/₄" . . . . . . . . . . . $650
"Follow Me Girls to the Fountain and Be My Coca-
Cola Girl" (amusing compliments to Coca-Cola Co.,
by author), Rare

PMU007.000

1913   10 ¹/₂" x 13 ¹/₂" . . . . . . . $375
"My Coco-Cola Belle", pictures Fannie Brice
(misspelled "Coco-Cola" on cover, inside
title and lyrics spelled "Coca-Cola".)

PMU008.000

1927   9 ¹/₂" x 12 ¹/₂" . . . . . . . . . . . $225
"The Coca-Cola Girl" (This piece of sheet music is
not too difficult to find, therefore it must be Mint to
warrant this price.)

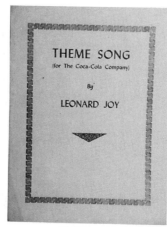

PMU009.000

1942   9" x 12" . . . . . . . . . . $65
"Theme Song for The Coca-Cola
Company"

PMU010.001

1944   10 ¹/₂" x 13" . . . . . . . . . . . $50
"Rum and Coca-Cola"(French printed version)

PMU011.000

1955 . . . . . . . . . . . . . . . . . . . . . . .$85
"50 Million Times A Day"

PMU043.000

c.1912 . . . . . . . . . . . . . . . . . . . . . . $400
"When The Do-Do Bird Is Singing In The Coca-Cola Tree"

PMU014.000

1970s . . . . . . . . . . . . . . . $12
"Look upAmerica"

PMU012.000

1941 . . . . . . . . . . . . . . . . . . . $35
"We Stand United"

PMU010.002

1940s . . . . . . . . . . . . . . . $25
"Rum and Coca-Cola"
Jeri Sullavan

PMU010.003

1940s . . . . . . . . . . . . . $18
"Rum and Coca-Cola"
The Andrew Sisters

PMU013.000

1941 . . . . . . . . . . . . . . . . . . . . . . . $35
"Favorite American Songs"
Music Book

PMU015.000

1970 . . . . . . . . . . . . . . . . . . . . . . . . . . $20
"I'd Like To Buy The World A Coke"

PMU016.000

1972 . . . . . . . . . . . . . $6
"Country Sunshine"

PMU017.000

1970s . . . . . . . . . . . . . $6
"I'd Like To Buy The World A Coke"

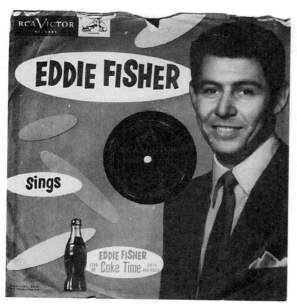

PMU018.000

1950s . . . . . . . . . . . . . . . . . . . . . . . . $35
Eddie Fisher, 78 record with original sleeve

PMU019.000

1950s . . . . . . . . . . . . . . . . . . . . . . . . $200
Eddie Fisher cardboard poster record offer

PMU024.001

1960s  33 1/3 . . . . . . . . . . . . . . . . . $12
Salesman's training record

PMU023.000

1960s . . . . . . . . . . . . . . . $30
"Swing The Jingle", 45 record, with
sleeve

PMU025.001

1940s  33 1/3 . . . . . . . . . . . . . . . $15
Salesman's training record

PMU036.000

1970s . . . . . . . . . . . . . . . . . $3
"It's The Real Thing", 45 record

# RECORDS

PMU020.001

1953-1957 . . . . . . . . $15
Eddie Fisher 45 rpm record
and sleeve

PMU033.000

1968 . . . . . . . . . . . . . . $8
"Camelot", Los Angeles
Bottling Co., 45 rpm

PMU029.000

1965 . . . . . . . . . . . . . . . . . . . $35
"Sue Thompson Swings The Jingle",
33 1/3 rpm record and sleeve (Canada)

PMU028.000

1963 . . . . . . . . . . . . . $15
"Here and Now" songs
from 1963 Convention, with
folder insert, 45 rpm

PMU031.000

1962 . . . . . . . . . . . $30
"Anita Bryant Refreshing New
Feeling" radio spots
33 1/3 rpm

PMU022.000

c.1950 . . . . . . . . . . $25
"Rum and Coca-Cola"
45 rpm, sleeve only (foreign)

PMU020.003

1953-1957 . . . . . . . . . . . $15
Back of Eddie Fisher sleeve,
Eddie Fisher bottle hanger
record offer for 25¢

PMU035.000

1970s . . . . . . . . . . . . . . $20
"I'd Like to Teach the World to
Sing", 45 rpm record and sleeve
(Canada)

PMU021.000

1958 . . . . . . . . . . . $30
"Theme Music" 45 rpm
record and sleeve

PMU026.000

1950s . . . . . . . . . . . . $12
"Rum and Coca-Cola"
Andrew Sisters, 45 rpm

PMU034.000

1967 . . . . . . . . . . $12
"Trini Lopez", 45 rpm
record and sleeve
advertising "Fresca"

PMU027.000

c.1950 . . . . . . . . . . . . . $6
"Learn to Dance at Home"
by Andy Capps, 45 rpm

PMU032.000

1960s . . . . . . . . . . . $12
Cardboard Sleeve with Coca-
Cola advertising, contained
top hit 45 rpm (Canada)

PMU030.000

1965 . . . . . . . . . . . . .$20
"Petula Clark Swings The
Jingle" radio spots,
33 1/3 rpm record

# RECORDS

PMU037.000

PMU037.001

PMU025.002
Late 1940s-Early 1950s . . . . . . . .$15 Each
Salesman's training records, 33 1/3 rpm

PMU037.002

PMU037.004          PMU037.005
1970s . . . . . . . . . . . . . . . . . . . . . . $20 Each
Original radio broadcast albums

PMU037.003

PMU040.000
1982 . . . . . . . . . $15
Penn State "Coke Is It"
45 rpm

PMU039.000
1960s . . . . . . . . . . $30
"12 Top Hits" album

PMU041.000          PMU042.000
1960s-1970s . . . . . . . . . . . . . . . . $15 Each
"Radio Spots" tape

PMU038.000
1951 . . . . . . . . . . . $12
Tony Bennett, 45 rpm with
sleeve

# FANS

PFN005.000
1890s   7" x 12 ¼" . . . . . . . . . . . . . $6,000
Very Rare

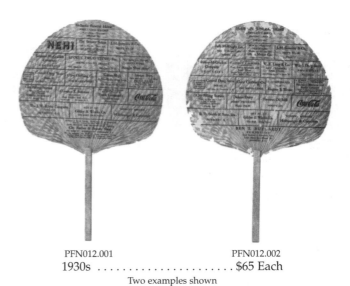

PFN012.001                                    PFN012.002
1930s . . . . . . . . . . . . . . . . . . . . . $65 Each
Two examples shown

PFN008.000                          PFN009.000
c.1911 . . . . . . . . . . . . . . . . . . . . . $200 Each
Showing front and two different backs

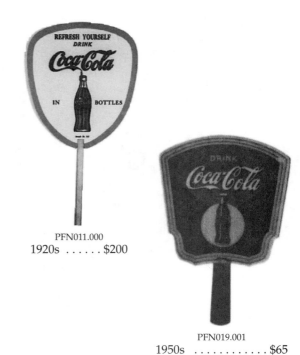

PFN011.000
1920s . . . . . . $200

PFN019.001
1950s . . . . . . . . . . . $65

PFN021.001
1950s . . . . . . . . . . . . . . . . . . . . . . $50

PFN020.001
1930s . . . . . . . . . . . . . . . . . . . . . . $85

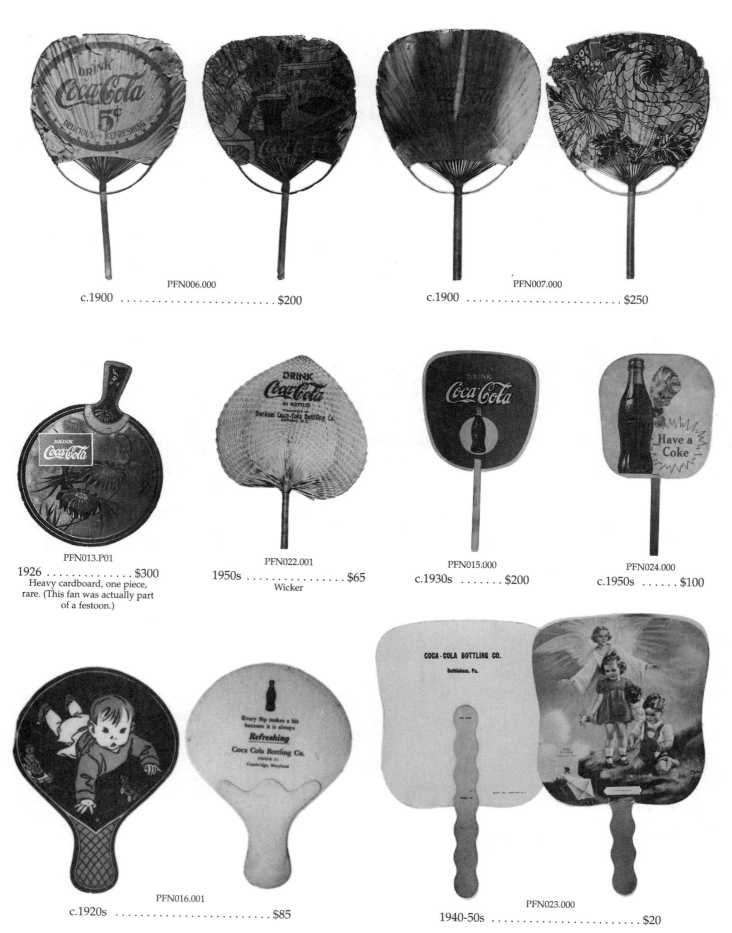

PFN006.000

c.1900 . . . . . . . . . . . . . . . . . . . . . . . . . $200

PFN007.000

c.1900 . . . . . . . . . . . . . . . . . . . . . . . . $250

PFN013.P01

1926 . . . . . . . . . . . . . . . $300
Heavy cardboard, one piece,
rare. (This fan was actually part
of a festoon.)

PFN022.001

1950s . . . . . . . . . . . . . . . . $65
Wicker

PFN015.000

c.1930s . . . . . . $200

PFN024.000

c.1950s . . . . . . $100

PFN016.001

c.1920s . . . . . . . . . . . . . . . . . . . . . . . $85

PFN023.000

1940-50s . . . . . . . . . . . . . . . . . . . . . . . $20

# FANS

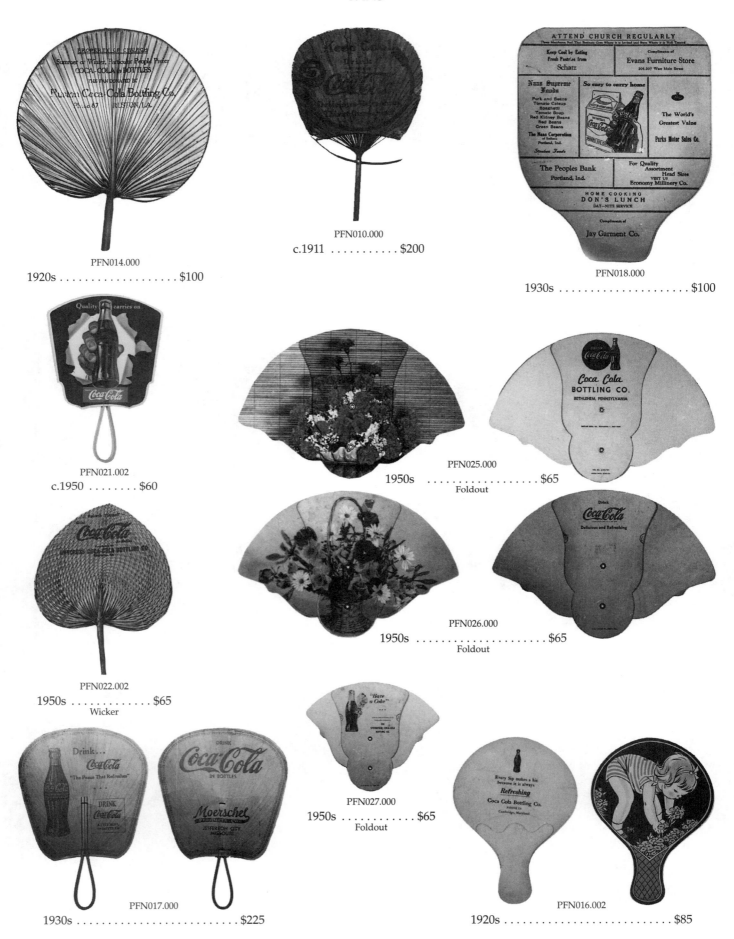

PFN014.000

1920s . . . . . . . . . . . . . . . . . . $100

PFN010.000

c.1911 . . . . . . . . . . $200

PFN018.000

1930s . . . . . . . . . . . . . . . . . . . . . $100

PFN021.002

c.1950 . . . . . . . . $60

PFN025.000

1950s . . . . . . . . . . . . . . . . . $65

Foldout

PFN022.002

1950s . . . . . . . . . . . . . $65

Wicker

PFN026.000

1950s . . . . . . . . . . . . . . . . . . . . . $65

Foldout

PFN017.000

1930s . . . . . . . . . . . . . . . . . . . . . . . . $225

PFN027.000

1950s . . . . . . . . . . . $65

Foldout

PFN016.002

1920s . . . . . . . . . . . . . . . . . . . . . . . . $85

PFN028.000

Pre-1900 . . . . . . . . . . . . . . . $650
Rare

PFN033.000

1912 . . . . . . . . . . . . . . . . . .$100

PFN032.000

c.1911 . . . . . . . . . . . $60

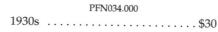

PFN034.000

1930s . . . . . . . . . . . . . . . . . . . . . . . $30

PFN035.000

1950s . . . . . . . . . . . . . . . . . . $8

PFN036.000

1960s . . . . . . . . . . . . . . . $4

> Note: The printing quality on many of these napkins is certainly not a work of art, but early ones are rare and all are very collectible.

PFN030.000

Early 1900s . . . . . . . . . . . . . $100

PFN029.000

Pre-1900 . . . . . . . . . . . . . . . . . . . . $375
4th of July

PFN031.000

c.1911 . . . . . . . . . . . . . . . . . . . . . $40

# PHOTOS
8" x 10" Originals  Only (reprints have very little value)

PPH011.000
$35
Ireland's Drug Store, Portland, OR

PPH012.000
1923 . . . . . . . . . . . . . . . . . .$45
McAlpine Hotel, NY

PPH013.000
1935 . . . . . . . . . . . . . . . . .$40
Display, Rochester, NY

PPH014.000
1925 . . . . . . . . . . . . . . . . .$50
Ohio Food Show Toledo, OH

PPH015.000
1923 . . . . . . . . . . . . . . . .$60
Walgreen drug store, Chicago

PPH016.000
1930 . . . . . . . . . . . . . . . . . $35
Wisconsin Food Show

PPH017.000
$30
The Empire Luncheonette,Denver, CO

PPH018.00
1923 . . . . . . . . . . . . . . . . $75
Moberly Ice Cream Co., MO

PPH019.000
1922 . . . . . . . . . . . . . . . . $45
Mother Goose Shop, St. Louis, MO

PPH020.000
1924 . . . . . . . . . . . . . . . . .$45
Food Show, Albany, NY

PPH021.000
1920s . . . . . . . . . . . . . . . . $30
Billboard, Flint, MI

PPH022.000
1923 . . . . . . . . . . . . . . . .$45
Liggetts, New York City

PPH023.000
1920s . . . . . . . . . . . . . . .$40
Santa Display

PPH025.000
1924 . . . . . . . . . . . . . . . . .$45
Pure Food Show, Albany, NY

PPH024.000
1923 . . . . . . . . . . . . . . . . $45
Wilder Drug Store Boston, MA

# PHOTOS

The following is a group of 8" x 10" publicity photos.  Originals only, reprints have very little value.

PPH026.000
1933 . . . . . . . . . . . . . . . . .$325
Johnny Weissmuller and Maureen
O'Sullivan

PPH027.000
1932 . . . . . . . . . . . . . . . . $100
Sue Carol

PPH028.000
1930s . . . . . . . . . . . . . . . $50

PPH029.000
1932 . . . . . . . . . . . . . . $250
Jean Harlow and Clark Gable

PPH030.000
1932 . . . . . . . . . . . . $200
Jean Harlow

PPH031.000
1932 . . . . . . . . . . . $200
Jean Harlow

PPH032.000
1933 . . . . . . . . . $100
Maureen O'Sullivan

PPH033.000
1933 . . . . . . . . . . .$100
Joan Crawford

PPH034.000
1930s . . . . . . . . . . . $50

PPH035.001        PPH035.002        PPH035.003
1950s . . . . . . . . . . . . . . . . . . . . . . . . . .$35 Each
Eddie Fisher (Inscription and signature printed not signed)

PPH036.000        PPH037.000
1932   5" x 7" . . . . . . . . . . . . . .$175 Each
Jean Harlow

# PHOTOS AND CATALOG SHEETS

Photo prices listed below are for original photos, reprints have very little value.

PPH038.000
1907  5" x 7"  . . . . . . . . . . . $150
Washington, DC

PPH039.000
$150
Early Horse-drawn delivery wagon
Norton, VA

PPH040.000
1908  8" x 10"  . . . . . . . . $150
Coca-Cola Delivery Truck

PPH041.000
5" x 7"  . . . . . . . . . . . . . . . . $125
Early salesman's horse-drawn wagon,
St. Louis, MO

PPM017.000
1929  . . . . . . . . . . . . . . . . . . . . . . . $400
Standard painting system chart, showing paint
colors by Sherwin Williams Co.

PPM018.000
1940s  . . . . . . . . . . . $20
Truck catalog sheet

PPH042.000
Late 30s  8" x 10"  . . . . . . . $15
Drug store photo

PPH043.000
8" x 10"  . . . . . . . . . . . . . . . . .$30
1938  Truck photo

PPM019.000
1940s  . . . . . . . . . . . $20
Truck catalog sheet

PPH044.000
Late 1930s  8" x 10"  . . . . . . . $15

PPH045.000
1920s  8" x 10"  . . . . . . . . . . . . . . . . . . $45
Delivery truck photo

# JOHN S. PEMBERTON LETTER

On Sunday, October 2, 1887, Dr. John S. Pemberton placed an ad in the Atlanta Constitution for "An acceptable party with two thousand dollars to purchase one half interest in a very profitable and well established manufacturing business." Although not mentioned in the ad, his business was "The Pemberton Chemical Co," which manufactured, among other things, the six month old product he called Coca-Cola, which was listed along with other products on his letterhead. His ad was responded to by one A.O. Murphy of Barnesville, GA. Murphy's inquiry was answered by Pemberton with a ten-page letter dated October 4, 1887 (shown below). This letter, along with other pieces of evidence, was used in a lawsuit filed by The Coca-Cola Company on January 22, 1917 against A.O. Murphy and his partner J.C. Mayfield, of the Koke Co. of America. Signed Pemberton letters are very desirable, this one, because of its length, information and historical significance is valued at $5,000.

PLE176.000

# LETTERS WITH ENVELOPES

PLE011.S00

1912 . . . . . . . . . . . . . . . . $175
Handwritten and signed by Howard Candler

PLE008.S00

1892 . . . . . . . . . . . . . . . . . . . . . . $1200
Typed and signed by "Asa G. Candler", Very Rare

PLE009.S00

1889 . . . . . . . . . . $350
Asa G. Candler & Co.
Atlanta, GA

PLE013.S00

1919 . . . . . . . . . . . . . . . . $150
With newspaper stock listing showing
Coca-Cola stock, by Howard Candler

PLE012.S00

1915 . . . . . . . . . . . . . . . . . $100
Handwritten and signed by Howard Candler

PLE014.S00

1924 . . . . . . . . . . . . . . . . $175
Handwritten by "Asa G. Candler"

PLE010.S00

1905 . . . . . . . . . . . . . . . . . . . . . . . . $300
From Asa Candler to his son Walter

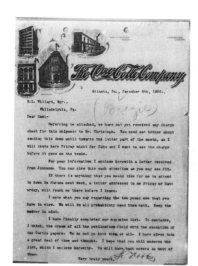

PLE019.000

1903 . . . . . . . . . . . . . . . . . . . . . . . . . . $35

Macon, GA

PLE018.000

1916 . . . . . . . . . . . . . . . . . . . . . $20

So. Pittsburgh, TN

PLE017.000

1906 . . . . . . . . . . . . . . . . . $100

Atlanta, GA

*Note: Many of these letterheads were used for years after the bottle change.*

PLE020.000

c.1910 . . . . . . . . . . . . . . . . . . . . . . . $15

Waycross, GA

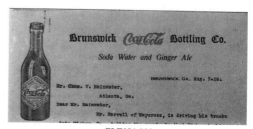

PLE021.000

1916 . . . . . . . . . . . . . . . . . . . . . . . . . $20

Brunswick, GA

PLE016.S00

1889 . . . . . . . . . . . . . . . . . . . . . . . . $350

Two-page letter and envelope Asa G. Candler &
W. Atlanta

PLE022.000

1923 . . . . . . . . . . . . . . . . . . . . . . . . . $25

Cuthbert, GA

PLE023.000

1915 . . . . . . . . . . . . . . . . . . . . . . . . . $20

Valdosta, GA

PLE015.S00

Early 1900s . . . . . . . . . . . . . . . . . . . . $200

Includes two page letter and envelope,
Indianapolis, IN

PLE024.000

1918 . . . . . . . . . . . . . . . . . . . . . . . . . $15

Douglas, GA

# LETTERHEAD

PLE025.000

1908 . . . . . . . . . . . . . . . . . . . . . . . . . . $125

PLE026.000

1906 . . . . . . . . . . . . . . . . . . . . . . . . . . $100

PLE027.000

1903 . . . . . . . . . . . . . . . . . . . . . . . . . . $100

PLE028.000

1909 . . . . . . . . . . . . . . . . . . . . . . . . . . $30

PLE029.000

1911 . . . . . . . . . . . . . . . . . . . . . . . . . . $100

PLE030.000

1912 . . . . . . . . . . . . . . . . . . . . . . . . . . $30

PLE031.000

1909 . . . . . . . . . . . . . . . . . . . . . . . . . . $85

PLE032.000

1903 . . . . . . . . . . . . . . . . . . . . . . . . . . $40

PLE033.000

1911 . . . . . . . . . . . . . . . . . . . . . . . . . . $30

PLE177.000

1931 . . . . . . . . . . . . . . . . . . . . . . . . . . $15

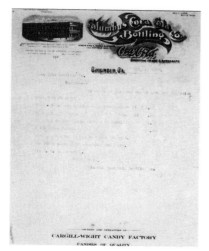

PLE034.000

1910 . . . . . . . . . . . . . . . . . . . . . $75

Columbus, GA

PLE035.000

1913 . . . . . . . . . . . . . . . . . . . . . $135

Memphis, TN

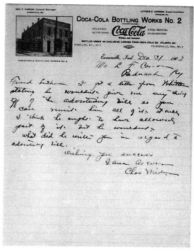

PLE036.000

1907 . . . . . . . . . . . . . . . . . . . . . $40

Evansville, IN

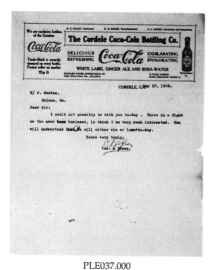

PLE037.000

1908 . . . . . . . . . . . . . . . . . . . . . $30

Cordele, GA

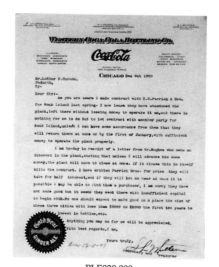

PLE038.000

1909 . . . . . . . . . . . . . . . . . . . . . $20

Western Coca-Cola, Chicago, IL

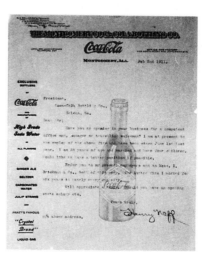

PLE039.000

1911 . . . . . . . . . . . . . . . . . . . . . $65

Montgomery, AL

PLE040.000

1914 . . . . . . . . . . . . . . . . . . . . . $25

McRae Coca-Cola, Helena, GA

PLE041.000

1920 . . . . . . . . . . . . . . . . . . . . . $120

Rockwood, IL

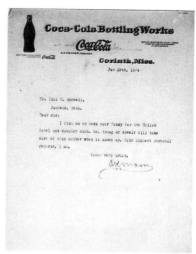

PLE042.000

1924 . . . . . . . . . . . . . . . . . . . . . $25

Corinth, MS

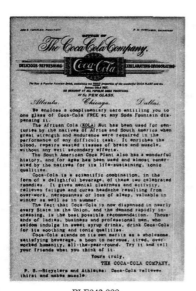

PLE043.000

1900 . . . . . . . . . . . . . . . . . . $100

"Complimentary Card" letter, Rare

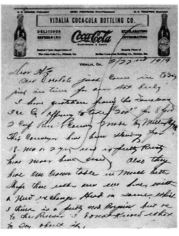

PLE044.000

1919 . . . . . . . . . . . . . . . . . . $25

Vidalia, GA

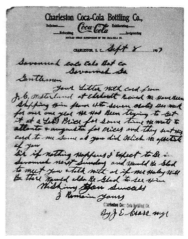

PLE045.000

1903 . . . . . . . . . . . . . . . . . . $30

Charleston, SC

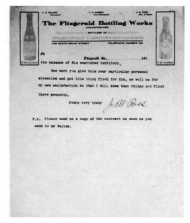

PLE046.000

1911 . . . . . . . . . . . . . . . . . . $30

Fitzgerald, GA

PLE047.000

1909 . . . . . . . . . . . . . . . . . . $15

Chattanooga, TN

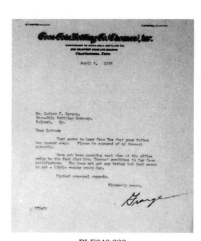

PLE048.000

1938 . . . . . . . . . . . . . . . . . . $25

Coca-Cola Bottling Co. (Thomas) Inc.,
Chattanooga, TN

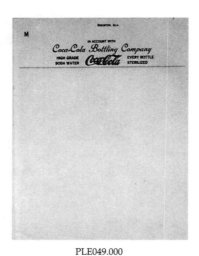

PLE049.000

1920 . . . . . . . . . . . . . . . . . . $15

Brenton, AL

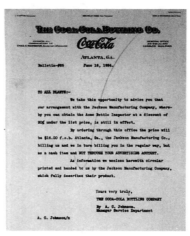

PLE050.000

1924 . . . . . . . . . . . . . . . . . . $20

Atlanta, GA

PLE051.000

1935 . . . . . . . . . . . . . . . . . . $12

Danville, VA

# LETTERHEAD

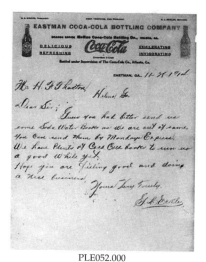

PLE052.000

1914 . . . . . . . . . . . . . . . . . . . . . . $25

Eastman, GA

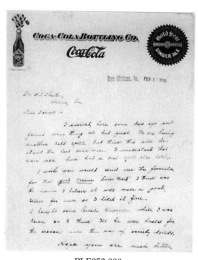

PLE053.000

1910 . . . . . . . . . . . . . . . . . . . . . . $25

Western Coca-Cola Bottling Co.

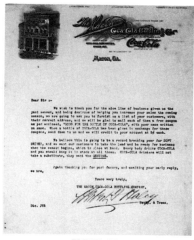

PLE054.000

1908 . . . . . . . . . . . . . . . . . . . . . . $50

Macon, GA

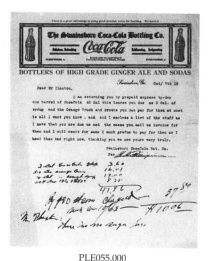

PLE055.000

1919 . . . . . . . . . . . . . . . . . . . . . . $15

Swainsboro, GA

PLE056.000

1929 . . . . . . . . . . . . . . . . . . . . . . $15

Swainsboro, GA

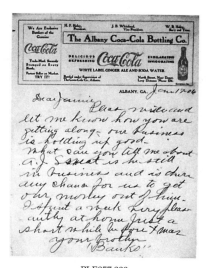

PLE057.000

1906 . . . . . . . . . . . . . . . . . . . . . . $30

Albany, GA

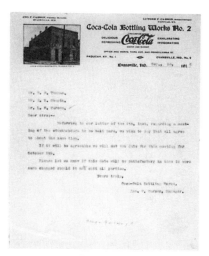

PLE058.000

1910 . . . . . . . . . . . . . . . . . . . . . . $25

Evansville, IN

PLE059.000

1906 . . . . . . . . . . . . . . . . . . . . . . $25

Cline & Ludwig, Brunswick, GA

PLE060.000

1923 . . . . . . . . . . . . . . . . . . . . . . $20

Wilcox Bottling Company, Rochelle, GA

PLE116.000

1913 . . . . . . . . . . . . . . . . . . . . . . . . . . . $30

Augusta, GA

PLE117.000

1916 . . . . . . . . . . . . . . . . . . . . . . . . . . . $25

Danville, VA

PLE118.000

1913 . . . . . . . . . . . . . . . . . . . . . . . . . . . $25

Live Oak, FL

PLE119.000

1913 . . . . . . . . . . . . . . . . . . . . . . . . . . . $40

Dayton, OH

PLE120.000

1910 . . . . . . . . . . . . . . . . . . . . . . . . . . . $25

Cleveland, OH

PLE121.000

1916 . . . . . . . . . . . . . . . . . . . . . . . . . . . $25

Huntsville, AL

PLE122.000

1917 . . . . . . . . . . . . . . . . . . . . . . . . . . . $50

Statesville, NC

PLE123.000

1917 . . . . . . . . . . . . . . . . . . . . . . . . . . . $20

Alabama Coca-Cola

PLE124.000

1914 . . . . . . . . . . . . . . . . . . . . . . . . . . . $25

Baton Rouge, LA

PLE125.000

1913 . . . . . . . . . . . . . . . . . . . . . . . . . . . $30

Monroe, GA

PLE126.000

1918 . . . . . . . . . . . . . . . . . . . . . . . . . . . $25

St. George, SC

PLE127.000

1913 . . . . . . . . . . . . . . . . . . . . . . . . . . . $35

Hutchinson, KS

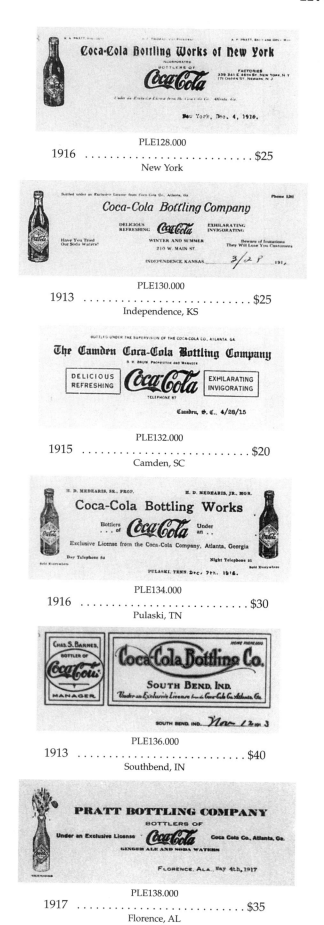

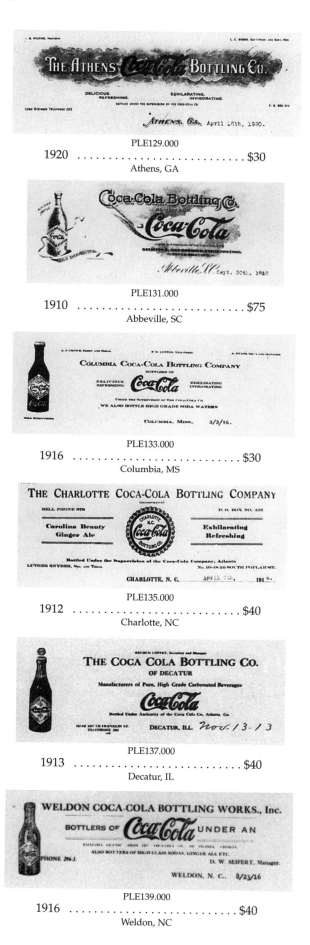

PLE128.000

1916 . . . . . . . . . . . . . . . . . . . . . . . . . . $25

New York

PLE129.000

1920 . . . . . . . . . . . . . . . . . . . . . . . . . . $30

Athens, GA

PLE130.000

1913 . . . . . . . . . . . . . . . . . . . . . . . . . . $25

Independence, KS

PLE131.000

1910 . . . . . . . . . . . . . . . . . . . . . . . . . . $75

Abbeville, SC

PLE132.000

1915 . . . . . . . . . . . . . . . . . . . . . . . . . . $20

Camden, SC

PLE133.000

1916 . . . . . . . . . . . . . . . . . . . . . . . . . . $30

Columbia, MS

PLE134.000

1916 . . . . . . . . . . . . . . . . . . . . . . . . . . $30

Pulaski, TN

PLE135.000

1912 . . . . . . . . . . . . . . . . . . . . . . . . . . $40

Charlotte, NC

PLE136.000

1913 . . . . . . . . . . . . . . . . . . . . . . . . . . $40

Southbend, IN

PLE137.000

1913 . . . . . . . . . . . . . . . . . . . . . . . . . . $40

Decatur, IL

PLE138.000

1917 . . . . . . . . . . . . . . . . . . . . . . . . . . $35

Florence, AL

PLE139.000

1916 . . . . . . . . . . . . . . . . . . . . . . . . . . $40

Weldon, NC

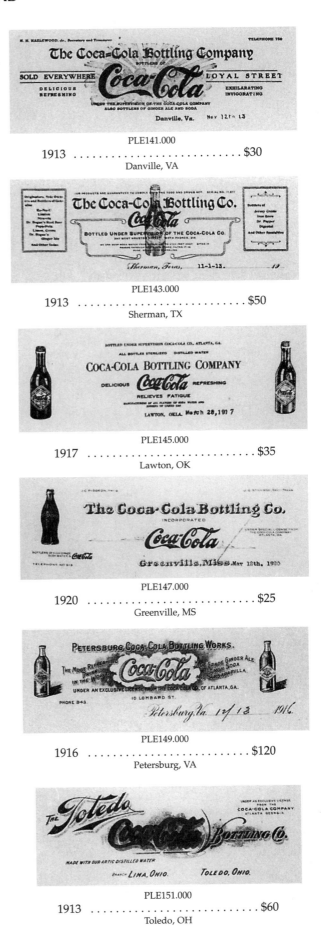

PLE140.000

1920 . . . . . . . . . . . . . . . . . . . . . . . $75

El Paso, TX

PLE141.000

1913 . . . . . . . . . . . . . . . . . . . . . . . $30

Danville, VA

PLE142.000

1920 . . . . . . . . . . . . . . . . . . . . . . . $25

Baton Rouge, LA

PLE143.000

1913 . . . . . . . . . . . . . . . . . . . . . . . $50

Sherman, TX

PLE144.00

1915 . . . . . . . . . . . . . . . . . . . . . . . $200

Atlanta, GA

PLE145.000

1917 . . . . . . . . . . . . . . . . . . . . . . . $35

Lawton, OK

PLE146.000

1913 . . . . . . . . . . . . . . . . . . . . . . . $60

Rome, GA

PLE147.000

1920 . . . . . . . . . . . . . . . . . . . . . . . $25

Greenville, MS

PLE148.000

1916 . . . . . . . . . . . . . . . . . . . . . . . $50

Statesville, GA

PLE149.000

1916 . . . . . . . . . . . . . . . . . . . . . . . $120

Petersburg, VA

PLE150.000

1916 . . . . . . . . . . . . . . . . . . . . . . . $65

Asheville, NC

PLE151.000

1913 . . . . . . . . . . . . . . . . . . . . . . . $60

Toledo, OH

PLE152.000

1913 . . . . . . . . . . . . . . . . . . . . . . . . . . . . $35

Quincy, FL

PLE153.000

1913 . . . . . . . . . . . . . . . . . . . . . . . . . . . . $35

Washington, GA

PLE154.000

1916 . . . . . . . . . . . . . . . . . . . . . . . . $30

CORDELE, GA

PLE155.000

1913 . . . . . . . . . . . . . . . . . . . . . . . . . . . . $45

Palatka, FL

PLE156.000

1914 . . . . . . . . . . . . . . . . . . . . . . . . $35

Tulsa, OK

PLE157.000

1914 . . . . . . . . . . . . . . . . . . . . . . . $30

Hickory, NC

PLE158.000

1913 . . . . . . . . . . . . . . . . . . . . . . $40

New Bern, NC

PLE159.000

1914 . . . . . . . . . . . . . . . . . . . . . . . . $35

Thomson, GA

PLE160.000

1918 . . . . . . . . . . . . . . . . . . . . . . . . $25

Washington, GA

PLE161.000

1917 . . . . . . . . . . . . . . . . . . . . . . . $60

Carrollton, KY

PLE162.000

1920 . . . . . . . . . . . . . . . . . . . . . . . . $25

Lumberton, NC

PLE163.000

1918 . . . . . . . . . . . . . . . . . . . . . . . $30

Grand Rapids, MI

# LETTERHEAD

PLE164.000

1913 . . . . . . . . . . . . . . . . . . . . . . . . . $25

Olney, IL

PLE165.000

1913 . . . . . . . . . . . . . . . . . . . . . . . . . $60

Spartanburg, SC

PLE166.000

1913 . . . . . . . . . . . . . . . . . . . . . . . . . $25

Beaumont, TX

PLE167.000

1916 . . . . . . . . . . . . . . . . . . . . . . . . . $30

Waco, TX

PLE168.000

1915 . . . . . . . . . . . . . . . . . . . . . . . . . $40

Pensacola, FL

PLE169.000

1915 . . . . . . . . . . . . . . . . . . . . . . . . . $40

Hampton, SC

PLE170.000

1916 . . . . . . . . . . . . . . . . . . . . . . . . . $25

Charlotte, NC

PLE171.000

1913 . . . . . . . . . . . . . . . . . . . . . . . . . $50

Alexandria, LA

PLE172.000

1916 . . . . . . . . . . . . . . . . . . . . . . . . . $100

Charleston, SC

PLE173.000

1912 . . . . . . . . . . . . . . . . . . . . . . . . . $25

Greenville, MS

PLE174.000

1913 . . . . . . . . . . . . . . . . . . . . . . . . . $35

McComb, MS

PLE175.000

1917 . . . . . . . . . . . . . . . . . . . . . . . . . $30

Wadesboro, NC

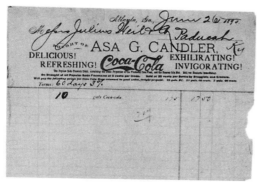

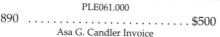

PLE061.000

1890 . . . . . . . . . . . . . . . . . . . . . . . $500

Asa G. Candler Invoice

PLE062.000

1892 . . . . . . . . . . . . . . . . . . . . . . . $125

Invoice, Atlanta, GA

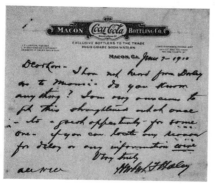

PLE063.000

1910 . . . . . . . . . . . . . . . . . . . $35

Macon, GA

PLE064.000

1908 . . . . . . . . . . . . . . . . . . . $35

Invoice and envelope, Richmond, VA

PLE065.000

1910 . . . . . . . . . . . . . . . . . . . $12

Waycross Receipt

PLE066.000

1910 . . . . . . . . . . . . . . $25

Invoice, Jacksonville, FL

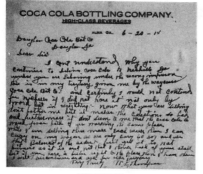

PLE067.000

1914 . . . . . . . . . . . . . . . . . . . $12

Alma, GA

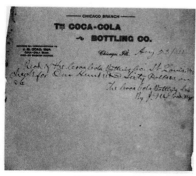

PLE068.000

1904 . . . . . . . . . . . . . . . . . . . $15

Chicago, IL

PLE069.000

1915 . . . . . . . . . . . . . . . . . . . $20

Eastman, GA

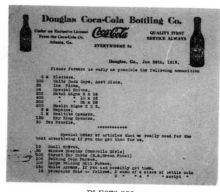

PLE070.000

1919 . . . . . . . . . . . . . . . . . . . $15

Douglas, GA

PLE071.000

1888 . . . . . . . . . . . . . . . . . . . . . . . . . $150

Invoice, Asa G. Candler & Co.

PLE073.000

1902 . . . . . . . . .$125

Invoice, Atlanta, GA

PLE074.000

1905 . . . . . . . . . . . . . . . . . . . . . . . $125

Invoice, Atlanta, GA

PLE080.000

1916 . . . . . . . . . . . . . . . . . . . . . . . $20

Invoice, Florida Coca-Cola

PLE077.000

1909 . . . . . . . . . . . . . . . . . . . . . . $100

Invoice, Atlanta, GA

PLE072.000

1888 . . . . . . . . . . . . . . . . . . . . . . $300

Receipt, Asa G. Candler & Co., signed by
Asa G. Candler

PLE076.000

1903 . . . . . . . . . . . . . . . . . . . . . . $125

Invoice, Atlanta, GA

PLE079.000

1908 . . . . . . . . . . . . . . . . . . . . . . $50

Invoice, Macon, GA

PLE075.000

Early 1900s . . . . . . . . . . . . . . . . . . . $10

Receipt, Paducah, KY

PLE078.000

1900 . . . . . . . . . . . . . . . . . . . . . . $135

Invoice, Atlanta, GA

# ENVELOPES

PLE081.000

1897 . . . . . . . . . . . . . . . . . . . . . . . . . . $75

Boston

PLE082.000

1898 . . . . . . . . . . . . . . . . . . . . . . . . . . $100

Coca-Cola Company

PLE083.000

1898 . . . . . . . . . . . . . . . . . . . . . . . . . . $75

Complimentary ticket envelope

PLE084.000

1904 . . . . . . . . . . . . . . . . . . . . . . . . . . $25

Richmond, VA

PLE085.000

1905 . . . . . . . . . . . . . . . . . . . . . . . . . . $30

The Coca-Cola Co.

PLE086.000

1913 . . . . . . . . . . . . . . . . . . . . . . . . . . $30

Sanford, NC
(Hires Rootbeer printing on flap)

PLE087.000

Early 1900s . . . . . . . . . . . . . . . . . . . . . . $85

Waycross, GA (printed on both sides)

PLE088.000

1918 . . . . . . . . . . . . . . . . . . . . . . . . . . $15

The Coca-Cola Company

*Note: Those envelopes with postmarks and stamps (generally called "Covers") are more desirable. Some would command a higher value because of the rarity of a stamp.*

PLE089.000

1923 . . . . . . . . . . . . . . . . . . . . . . . . . . $15

Zanesville, OH

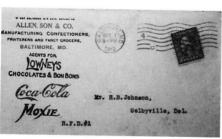

PLE090.000

1912 . . . . . . . . . . . . . . . . . . . . . . . . . . $30

Baltimore, MD

PLE091.000

1921 . . . . . . . . . . . . . . . . . . . . . . . . . . $30

Baltimore, MD

# ENVELOPES

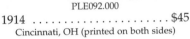

PLE092.000

1914 . . . . . . . . . . . . . . . . . . . . . $45

Cincinnati, OH (printed on both sides)

PLE093.000

1917 . . . . . . . . . . . . . . . . . $125

Montgomery, AL (very desirable back of envelope printing)

PLE094.000

1903 . . . . . . . . . . . . . . . . . . . . . . . . . . . $25

Jacksonville, FL

PLE095.000

c.1912 . . . . . . . . . . . . . . . . . . . . . . . . . $20

Anniston, AL

PLE096.000

1907 . . . . . . . . . . . . . . . . . . . . . . . . $25

Hattiesburg, MS

PLE097.000

Early 1900 . . . . . . . . . . . . . . . . . . . . . $20

Waycross, GA, return postcard

PLE098.000

1904 . . . . . . . . . . . . . . . . . . . . . . . . . $25

Montgomery, AL

PLE099.000

1919 . . . . . . . . . . . . . . . . . . . $60

Camden, AR (very unusual, showing both bottles. Note misspelled "Coco-Cola")

PLE100.000

1937 . . . . . . . . . . . . . . . . . . . . . . . . $10

Holdrege, NE (unusual, non-standard hand and bottle design)

PLE101.000

1927 . . . . . . . . . . . . . . . . . . . . . . . . . . $5

Piqua, OH (standard hand and bottle design)

PLE102.000

1931 . . . . . . . . . . . . . . . . . . . . . . . . . . . $5

St. Louis, MO (standard hand and bottle design)

PLE103.000

1936 . . . . . . . . . . . . . . . . . . . . . . . $15

Buffalo, NY (standard hand and bottle, 50th Ann.)

# ENVELOPES

PLE104.000

1924 . . . . . . . . . . . . . . . . . . . . . . . . . . . $40

Asa Candler

PLE105.000

1918 . . . . . . . . . . . . . . . $15

Lexington, KY

PLE106.000

c.1915 . . . . . . . . . . . . . . . . . . . . . . . . . $30

Indianapolis, IN

PLE109.000

c.1920s . . . . . . . . . . . . . . . . . . . . . . . .$25

Indianapolis, IN (back of envelope)

PLE108.000

1920 . . . . . . . . . . . . . . . . . . . . . . . . . . . $10

The Coca-Cola Company

PLE110.000

1919 . . . . . . . . . . . . . . . . . . . . . . . . . . . $10

The Coca-Cola Company, New York

PLE111.000

1943 . . . . . . . . . . . . . . . . . . . . . . . $5

Fayetteville, NC

PLE113.000

1950s . . . . . . . . . . . . . . . . . . . . . . $3

Mexico

PLE107.000

1908 . . . . . . . . . . . . . . . . . . . . . . . $25

Danville, VA

PLE114.000

1940s . . . . . . . . . . . . . . . . . . . . . $5

Standard design

PLE112.000

c.1908 . . . . . . . . . . . . . . . . . . . . . . $10

New York

PLE115.000

c.1930s . . . . . . . . . . . . . . . . . . . . . . $5

Palmerton, PA (standard hand and
bottle design)

# CHECKS

PPM020.000

1962 . . . . . . . . . . . . . . . . . . . . . . . . . . . . . $2

New Castle, IN

PPM021.000

1927 . . . . . . . . . . . . . . . . . . . . . . . . . . . $5

Jackson, TN

PPM028.000

1946 . . . . . . . . . . . . . . . . . . . . . . . . $3

Dickson, TN

PPM030.000

1937 . . . . . . . . . . . . . . . . . . . . . . . . $3

Dickson, TN

PPM031.000

1928 . . . . . . . . . . . . . . . . . . . . . . . . . $4

Dickson, TN

PPM022.000

1948 . . . . . . . . . . . . . . . . . . . . . . . . . . . $2

New Castle, IN

PPM023.000

1917 . . . . . . . . . . . . . . . . . . . . . . . . . . $4

Dickson, TN

*Note: These checks are all common with low values, because they have turned up in large quantities over the years.*

PPM025.000

1919 . . . . . . . . . . . . . . . . . . . . . . . . . . $4

Dickson, TN

PPM024.000

1939 . . . . . . . . . . . . . . . . . . . . . . . . . . . $3

Piqua, OH

PPM027.000

1958 . . . . . . . . . . . . . . . . . . . . . . . . . $2

Dickson, TN

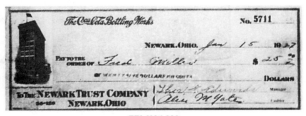

PPM026.000

1927 . . . . . . . . . . . . . . . . . . . . . . . . . . . $4

Newark, OH

PPM029.000

1923 . . . . . . . . . . . . . . . . . . . . . . . . . . $4

Dickson, TN

# STOCK CERTIFICATES

PPM032.000

1934 . . . . . . . . . . . . . . . . . . . . . . . . $125

Coca-Cola Bottling Sales Co.

PPM033.000

1929 . . . . . . . . . . . . . . . . . . . . . . . $125

10 shares

PPM034.000

1930s . . . . . . . . . . . . . . . . . . . . . . . $40

Blank certificate

PPM037.000

1923 . . . . . . . . . . . . . . . . . . . . . . . $125

Atlanta Stock Yards Stock Certificate with
Asa Candler signature

PPM035.000

1958 . . . . . . . . . . . . . . . . . . . . . . . $40

10 Shares

PPM036.000

1958 . . . . . . . . . . . . . . . . . . . . . . . $40

100 Shares

# MISCELLANEOUS

PPM038.000
Early 1930s 16" x 22" . . . . . . $375
Poster

PPM041.000
1930s . . . . . . . . . . . . . . . . . . . . . . $45
Matchbook order form and sample cover

PPM039.000
Early 1930s 12 1/2" x 19" . . . . . . . $400
Poster

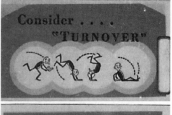

PPM040.000
1930s . . . . . . . . . . . . . . . . . $50
Folder, "Rapid Turnover"

PPM043.000
Late 1920s . . . . . . . . . . . . . . . . . . . . . $60
"Keep It Cold" Folder

PPM045.000
Late 1920s . . . . . . . . . . . . . . . . . . . . . .$35
Folder

PPM044.000
1930s 4" x 10" . . . . . . . . . . . . . . . . $175
Metalcraft truck brochure

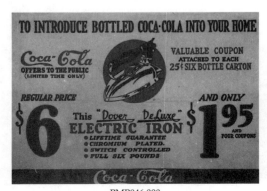

PMP046.000
Early 1930s 15" x 22" . . . . . . . . . . $250
Poster

PPM042.000
Early 1930s . . . . . . . $60
Glascock Cooler Folder

PPM047.000
Early 1930s 6 1/2" x 16" . . . . . . . . . . $200
Banner

— 476 —

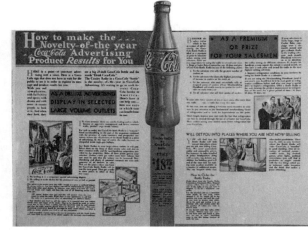

PPM048.000

1933 . . . . . . . . . . . . . . . . . . . . . . . . . . . . . . . . . . . . $450
Crosley Radio folder for Coca-Cola Bottle Radio, die-cut, pop-out

PPM049.000

1933 . . . . . . . . $275
Crosley Radio folder for
Coca-Cola Bottle Radio

PPM050.000

1930s . . . . . . . . . . . . . $25
Handbill

PPM051.000

Early 1930s 17" x 22" . . . . . $350
Poster

PPM052.001

Late 1920s . . . . . . . . . . . . . . . . $35
Folder

PPM053.000

Early 1930s 5" x 8" . . $65
Handbill

PPM054.000

Early 1930s 17" x 22" . . . . . . . . . . . $375
Poster

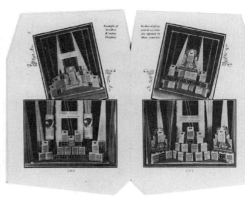

PPM055.000

1930  7 1/2" x 11"  . . . . . . . . . . . . . . . . . . . . . . . . . . . . $475
Six-pack book, die-cut, 24 pages (shown open and closed)

PPM056.000

1920s  . . . . . . . . . . . . . . . . . . . . . . . . $225
"Drink It In Your Office" folder (signed Norman
Rockwell art)

PPM057.000

1930  3" x 5 1/2"  . . $100
"Magic Card"

PPM058.000

Four pages . . . . . . . . . . . . . . . . . . . $20
German Folder

PPM059.000

1931  . . . . . . . . . . . . . . . . . . . . . . . . . . $45
Booklet, promoting Glascock Coolers, 16 pages

PPM060.000

1930s  . . . . . . . . . . . . . . . . . . . . . . . $125
Folder, promoting Glascock Coolers

PPM061.000

Late 1920s  . . . . . . . . . . . . . . . . $40
Folder

PPM062.000

1929  . . . . . . . $40
Dealer help folder

PPM065.000
1940  6" x 9"  . . . . . . . . . . . . . . . . . . . $65
Frigidaire electric cooler, closed

PPM063.000
Late 1940s  5 $1/2$" x 7"  . . . . . . . $100
Vendo brochure, 14 pages

PPM064.000
1950  3" x 6"  . . . . . $50
Westinghouse WC-42T

PPM068.000
c.1940  6" x 9"  . . . . . . . . . . . . . . . . . . . $85
Westinghouse electric coolers

PPM066.000
1960s  5" x 5"  . . . . . . . . . . . . . . $55
Westinghouse WH-12T

PPM067.000
1950s  3 $1/4$" x 6"  . . $45
Vendo six case vertical

PPM069.000
1956  3 $3/4$" x 7"  . . . . $50
Vendo V-23

PPM070.000
1960s  3" x 6"  . . . . . $50
Westinghouse WC-42T

PPM071.000
1950s  3 $1/2$" x 7"  . . . . $40
Cooler booklet, 15 pages

PPM072.000
1950s  4" x 8"  . . . . . . $50
Cavalier C-51

PPM074.000

1930 . . . . . . . . . . . . . . . . . . . . . . . . . $125
Brochure showing different coolers

PPM073.000

1930 . . . . . . . . . . . . . . . . . . . . . . . $200
Brochure showing coolers and prices, six pages

PPM076.000

1938 . . . . . . . . . . . . . . . . . . . . . . . . . $40
"Cooler" brochure

PPM075.000

1938 . . . . . . . . . . . . . . . . $50
"Coolers" brochure and price list

*Note: Prices shown are only guide prices
and will vary depending on conditions.*

PPM077.000

1930s . . . . . . . . . . . . . . . $45
Glascock counter cooler, price card

PPM078.000

1936 . . . . . . . . . . . . . . . . . . . . . . . . . $40
Frigidaire electric coolers brochure

PPM079.00

c.1960 . . . . . . . . . . . . . . $15
"Starlet" bottle vendor catalog sheet

PPM080.000

Mills letter and foldout brochure . . . . $65
Showing new machine

# VENDING MACHINE BROCHURES

The following are 1960 folders showing and describing vending machines and their features.

PPM081.000
3 3/4" x 9" . . . . . $15
Cavalier CS-96C

PPM082.000
3 3/4" x 9" . . . . . $15
Cavalier CS-244C

PPM083.000
3 3/4" x 9" . . . . . $15
Cavalier CS-124

PPM084.000
3 3/4" x 9" . . . . . $15
Cavalier CS-148C

PPM085.000
4" x 9" . . . . . . . . $15
Cavalier CS-80C

PPM086.000
4" x 9" . . . . . . . . $15
Cavalier CS-64C

PPM087.000
3 3/4" x 9" . . . $15
Cavalier CS-72

PPM088.000
3 1/2" x 9" . . . . $25
Westinghouse Select-o-
matic WC-102-MD

PPM089.000
1964  7 1/2" x 4 1/4"  . . $20

PPM090.000
4" x 7" . . . . . . . . $18
Westinghouse WC-174-4

PPM091.000
3 1/4" x 7 1/4" . . . $18
Westinghouse WC-160T

PPM092.000
WC-240T . . . . . . . $18
Westinghouse

# SALESMAN'S RECORD FOLDERS

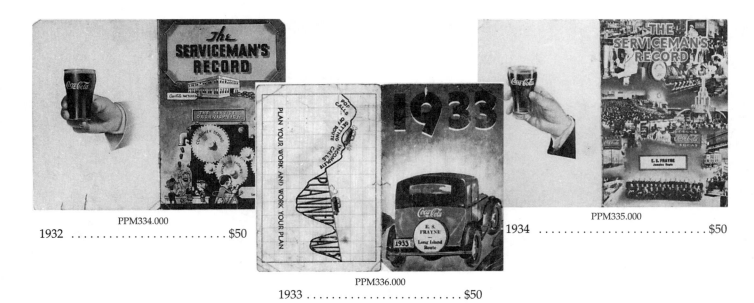

PPM334.000
1932 . . . . . . . . . . . . . . . . . . . . . . . . $50

PPM336.000
1933 . . . . . . . . . . . . . . . . . . . . . . . . $50

PPM335.000
1934 . . . . . . . . . . . . . . . . . . . . . . . . $50

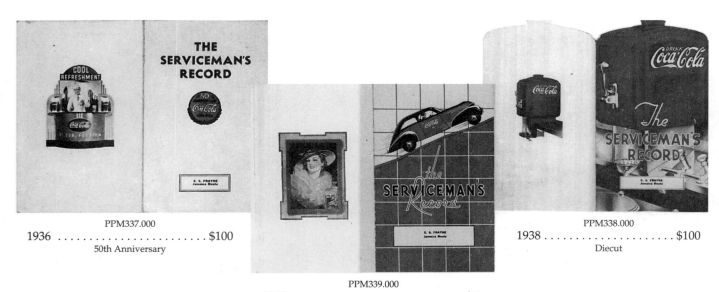

PPM337.000
1936 . . . . . . . . . . . . . . . . . . . . . . . . $100
50th Anniversary

PPM339.000
1937 . . . . . . . . . . . . . . . . . . . . . . . . $40

PPM338.000
1938 . . . . . . . . . . . . . . . . . . . . . . . . $100
Diecut

PPM340.000
1943 . . . . . . . . . . . . . . . . . . . . . . . . $40

PPM341.000
1944 . . . . . . . . . . . . . . . . . . . . . . . . $50
Diecut

PPM342.000
1945 . . . . . . . . . . . . . . . . . . . . . . . . $40

# TOONERVILLE CONTEST

The 1930-1931 Coca-Cola Toonerville Contest was a sales incentive contest for Coca-Cola salesman. Shown below are many of the paper items associated with that contest. The small folders, nine of which are shown below, are surely the highlight of this campaign. These folders are very colorful and nicely illustrated, showing Mickey McGuire and the Toonerville gang. Some are very rare.

PPM093.001
$60

PPM093.002
$45

PPM093.003
$30

PPM093.004
$45

PPM093.005
$30

PPM093.006
$30

PPM093.007
$20

PPM093.008
$45

PPM093.009
$50

PPM094.000
Postcard . . . . . . . . . . $5

Note: When and if any of these folders turn up in quantities over ten, these prices will drop like a rock.

PPM095.000
Contest details brochure . . $35

PPM098.003
PPM098.001
Toonerville Topics . . . . . . . . . . $35 Each
Newsletter

PPM098.004
PPM098.002

PPM096.000
1930 . . . . . . . . . . . . . $15
Letter

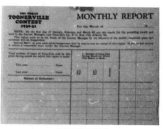

PPM097.000
Report form . . . . . . . . . . $5

# MISCELLANEOUS

PPM099.000
1939 . . . . . . . . . . . . . . . . . . . . . . . . . $125
Dutch calendar card

PPM100.000
1920s . . . . . . . . . . . . . . . . . . . . $150
Booklet showing right way to advertise
(showing many past mistakes)

PPM101.000
1940s . . . . . . . . . . . . . . . . . . . . . . . . . $85
Christmas carols songbook, Coca-Cola Bottling
Company, Asheville, NC

PPM102.000
1948-50 . . . . . . . . . . $40
Bookmark, Arabic on reverse

PPM103.000
1937 . . . . . . . . . . . . . . . . . . . . . . . . . $100
The Mystic Oracle sales aid folder, Williams
Ice-O-Matic coin controlled dispenser

PPM104.001
1927  3 1/2" x 6" . . . . . . . . . . . . . . $15 Each
The Five Star Contest pamphlets

— 484 —

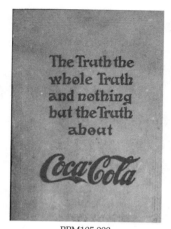

PPM105.000

1913 . . . . . . . . . . . . . . $125

The Truth Booklet

PBN007.S01    PBN007.S02    PBN007.S03

1923-1938 . . . . . . . . . . . . . $1,500

Hardcover books regarding trademark
infringements, Vol. 1-3, set

PPM106.000

1930s . . . . . . . . . . . . . . . . . . . . . . $400

Catalog Dura-Products Mfg. Canton, OH, Specialty
Sign Mfg.

PPM107.000

1941 . . . . . . . . . . . . . . . . . . . . . . . $175

Tournament of Roses souvenir folder, "Pandas Are
Very Rare, Coca-Cola is Everywhere"

PPM108.S00

1964-65 . . . . . . . . . . . . . . $100

NY Worlds Fair, The Coca-Cola
Pavilion Presskit

PPM109.000

1913 . . . . . . . . . . . . . . . . . . . . . . $100

"The Coca-Cola Controversy" by Harold Hirsh

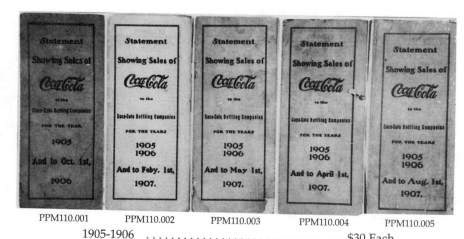

PPM110.001    PPM110.002    PPM110.003    PPM110.004    PPM110.005

1905-1906 . . . . . . . . . . . . . . . . . . . . . . . . . . . $30 Each

Coca-Cola Bottling Company Sales Statements

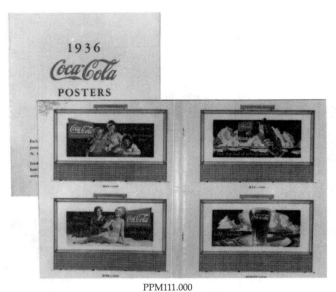

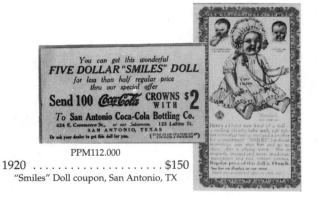

PPM112.000

1920 . . . . . . . . . . . . . . . . . . . . . $150
"Smiles" Doll coupon, San Antonio, TX

PPM111.000

1936 . . . . . . . . . . . . . . . . . . . . . . . . . $75
Catalog sheet, showing billboards for 1936

PPM113.000

1920s . . . . . . . . $150
"Tickletoes" The Wonder
Doll coupon

PPM114.000

1950s . . . . . . . . . . . . . $175
Catalog sheet for Buddy Lee doll

PPM115.000

1934 . . . . . . . . . . . . . . . . . . . . . . . $45
Catalog sheet, showing Jackie Cooper display

PPM116.000

1950s . . . . . . . . . . . . . . . . $12
Catalog sheet, showing picnic cooler

PPM117.S00

1950s . . . . . . . . . . . . . . . . . . . . . . . . . $75
Bottlers' information kit for picnic coolers

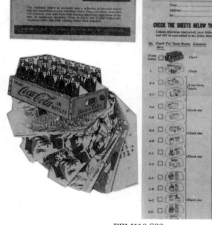

PPM118.S00

1960s . . . . . . . . . . . . . . . . . . . . . . . . . . . . . $75
Plant tour fan souvenir, with order form in original envelope

PPM120.000

c.1908 . . . . . . . . . . . . . . . . . . $55
Goldelle Ginger Ale label, Coca-Cola
Bottling Co.

PPM123.001

PPM123.002

1930s . . . . . . . . . $175 Each
Cigar bands (glass and bottle)

PPM127.000

1934 . . . . . . . . . . . . . . . . . . . . . $50
Century of Progress ticket, free Coke offer
on reverse

PPM130.000

1925 . . . . . . . . . . . . . . . . . . $75
Needle case

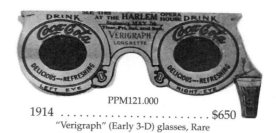

PPM121.000

1914 . . . . . . . . . . . . . . . . . . . . . $650
"Verigraph" (Early 3-D) glasses, Rare

PPM124.000

March 13, 1929 . . . . . . . . . . . . . . . $250
*Sioux City Tribune* (complete newspaper)
announcing death of Asa G. Candler

PPM129.000

4" x 9 1/2" . . . . . . . . . . . . . . . . . . . . $350
Cutout, cardboard, "Coca-Cola Baby Doll"

Inside of needle case folder, same on both 1924 and 1925

PPM122.000

c.1898-1901 . . . . . . . . . . $275
U.S. proprietary revenue stamp with
Coca-Cola cancellation

PPM126.000

1941 . . . . . . $20
Bottlers' Conference
program, San
Antonio, TX

PPM125.000

1930 . . . . . . . $20
Bottlers' Conference
program, Atlanta, GA

PPM128.000

c.1929 . . . . . . . . . . . . . . . . . . . . $4
Trolley transfer

PPM131.000

1924 . . . . . . . . . . . . . . . . . . . . . $75
Needle case

PPM345.000

1940s ......................... $500

Cardboard needle holder, diecut, Bogalusia, LA

PCT087.000

1930s ................... $185

Free bottle card

PBN033.000

1940 ............. $25

Fountain Sales Division
Convention program

PPM346.000

1930s ........................... $75

United States at a Glance, wheel

PBN034.000

1936 ................. $85

50th Anniversary Fountain Sales
Convention program

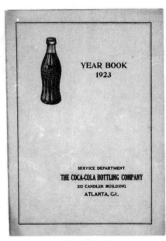

PBN035.000

1923 ................. $20

Service Department Year Book

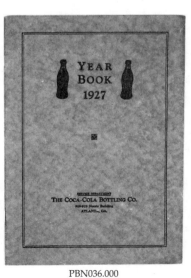

PBN036.000

1927 ................... $20

Service Deptartment Year Book

PPM343.000

1941 . . . . . . . . . . . . . . . . . . . . . . . . $350
Catalog sheets from Neon Products, Inc. Lima, OH,
with photos and prices for Coca-Cola clocks and
light-up signs

PBN031.000

1930s . . . . . . . . . . . . . . . . . . . . . . . $100
Soda Fountain Operation and Maintenance manual

PBN032.000

1940 . . . . . . . . . . . . . . . . . . . . . . . . $300
Photo album from the Golden Gate International
Exposition, showing Coca-Cola exhibit

PPM344.000

1950s . . . . . . . . . . . . . . . . . . . . . . $150
Brochure for the Coca-Cola bottle door handle

# MISCELLANEOUS

PPM132.BS0

1943 . . . . . . . . . . . . . . . . . . . . . . . $250

"Fighting Airplanes" paper presentation set (without logos), compliments of "The Coca-Cola Co", complete set of 13 planes with envelope

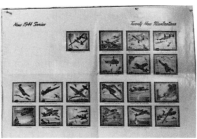

PPM133.000

1944  17" x 22" . . . . . . . . . . . . . . $50

Poster or Catalog Sheet, showing complete set of airplane hangers

PPM134.BS0

1943  2" x 3¹/₂" . . . . . . . $65

"America's Fighting Planes", set of 20 cards in envelope

PPM135.000

1943 . . . . . . . . . . . . . . $50

B&W photo showing "Service Women" display

PPM136.001        PPM136.002

1943 . . . . . . . . . . . . . . . . . . . . . $85 Each

Photo and letter to the Snyder & Black Co., from the War Dept. approving proposed artwork

PPM137.000

1929 . . . . . . . . . . . . . . . . . $200

"Aviation News" showing airport window display and famous planes, eight-page sepia-tone newspaper

PPM138.000

1929 . . . . . . . . . . . . . . . $85

"The Story of Achievement In Aviation"

PPM139.000

1920 . . . . . . . . . . . . . . . . . . . . $125

"The Langley Field Times", with Coke ad on back cover

PPM140.000

1940s . . . . . . . . . . . . . . . $45

World atlas

PPM141.000

1943 . . . . . . . . . . $50

"Know Your War Planes"

PPM142.000

1943 . . . . . . . . . . . . . . $45

B&W photo (proposed artwork)

# "FIGHTING PLANES" CARDS

PPM134.S01
Consolidated
"Catalina" U.S.Navy

PPM134.S02
Boeing B-17
"Fortress" U.S. Army
Air Force

PPM134.S03
Republic P-47
"Thunderbolt U.S.
Army Air Force

PPM134.S04
Martin PBM
"Mariner" U.S. Navy

PPM134.S05
Grumman TBF
"Avenger" U.S. Navy

PPM134.S06
Vought-Sikorsky
"Helicopter" U.S.
Army Air Force

PPM134.S07
Curtiss "Helldiver"
U.S. Navy

PPM134.S08
Lockheed
"Constellation" U.S.
Army Air Force

PPM134.S09
Grumman F4F
"Wildcat" U.S. Navy

Envelope

Reverse side of cards

PPM134.S10
Grumman F6F
"Hellcat" U.S. Navy

PPM134.S11
North American A-36
"Invader"

PPM134.BS0
1943  2" x 3 ¹/₂" Complete set . . . . . . .$65
Individual cards . . . . . . . . . . . . . .$2 each
"America's Fighting Planes", complete set of 20 cards
(actually medium weight paper), in original envelope.
Note: Do not confuse these small cards with the larger
"Airlane Hangers" cardboard signs.

PPM134.S12
Martin B-26
"Maurauder" U.S.
Army Airforce

PPM134.S13
Bell "Airocobra" P-39
U.S. Army Air Force

PPM134.S14
Lockheed P-38
"Lightning" U.S.
Army Air Force

PPM134.S15
Consolidated B-24
"Liberator" U.S.
Army Air Force

PPM134.S16
Curtiss P-40
"Warhawk" U.S.
Army Air Force

PPM134.S17
North American B-25
"Mitchell" U.S. Army
Air Force

PPM134.S18
Vought-Sikorsky
"Corsair" U.S. Navy

PPM134.S19
Douglas P-70 "Havoc"
U.S. Army Air Force

PPM134.S20
Vought-Sikorsky
"Kingfisher" U.S.
Navy

PSP045.001    PSP045.002

1920s . . . . . . . . . . . . . . . . . . . $125 Each

Glass advertising slides, hand colored

PMS093.000

1920s 17" . . . . . . . . . . . . . . . . . . . $585

"Radiator Plate", chrome.
Note: The back of this plate is stamped "Brown Mfg.,
Co." Beware of reproduction, not stamped.

PPM143.000

Early 1930s . . . . . . . . . . . . . . . . . . . $150

Folder and order form from Kansas City Slide Co.,
showing Coca-Cola and other advertising slides

**1911**

**List of Bottler's Advertising Matter**

**The Coca-Cola Bottling Co.**

233 CANDLER BUILDING

**Atlanta, Ga.**

PPM145.000

1911 . . . . . . . . . . . . . . . . . . . $125

Price List of bottlers advertising matter

PPM146.000

1920s . . . . . . . . . . . . . . . . . . . $150

Advertising and testimonial sheet from
Brown Mfg., regarding "Radiator Plates"

PPM147.S00

1920s . . . . . . . . . . . . . $60

Profit sharing poster and coupons

PPM144.000

1928 . . . . . . . . . . . . . . . . $65

Icy-O Cooler sheet showing different
coolers

*Note: Pre-1920 bottlers' price lists are
very interesting and useful for dating and
identifying pieces. The 1911 price list shown
above is particularly interesting because it
identifies the so called "Duster Girl" as the
"Motor Girl". These early price lists are rare.*

# MISCELLANEOUS

PPM148.000

1898 . . . . . . . . . . . . . . . . . . . . . . . . . . . . . . . . . . . . $350

Track field day program and paper folder, with "Imperial Cafe" of
Atlanta, and "Coco-Cola" (note misspelling) advertising on back

PPM149.S00

1929 . . . . . . . . . . . . $75

Letter and folder showing
six bottle carrier

PPM150.000

1913 . . . . . . . . . . . $35

Ringling Bros. Circus program

PPM151.000

1920s . . . . . . . . . . . . . . . . . $75

Token holder

PPM152.000

1920s . . . . . . . . . . . . . . . $25

Handbill

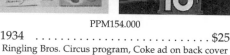

PPM154.000

1934 . . . . . . . . . . . . . . . . . . . . . . . . . . . $25

Ringling Bros. Circus program, Coke ad on back cover

PPM153.000

1930s . . . . . . . . . . . . . . . . . . . $20

"Cooler" sales folder

PPM352.000

PPM353.000

PPM354.000

1930s to 1950s . . . . . . . . . . . . . . . . . . . . . . . . . . . . . . . . . . . . . .$6 Each

Menu sheets (I've seen many variations of these sheets)

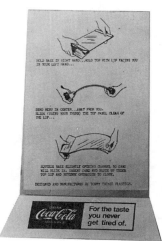

PMD031.000

1960s . . . . . . . . . . . . . . . .$15

Menu holder, plastic

PPM155.000

1930s . . . . . . . . . . . . . . . . . . . . . . . . . . $30

Bridge score pad

PPM156.000

1940s . . . . . . . . . . . . . . . . . . . . . . . $12

Roller derby ticket

PPM158.000

1930s . . . . . . . . . . . . . . . . . . . $45

Bridge score card

PPM159.000

1930s . . . . . . . . . . . $5

Bridge score sheet

PPM157.000

1950s . . . . . . . . . . . . . . . . . $15

Golf score card

PPM160.000

1955 . . . . . . . . . . . . . . . . . $35

American Legion program

PPM161.000

1950s . . . . . . . . . . . . . . . . . . . . . . $25

"Free Bottle" birthday card

PPM162.000

1931 . . . . . . . . . . . . . . . . . . $85

Toonerville contest folder (shown open and closed) Note: Beware of reproduction of this piece. See the"Repro" section of this book for more information.

# MISCELLANEOUS

PPM163.000

c.1915 . . . . . . . . . . . . . . . . . . . . . . . . . . $200
"Accept No Imitations", Confederate souvenir bill

PPM164.000

c.1920 . . . . . . . . . . . . . . . . . . . . . . . . $125
"Accept No Imitations", Confederate souvenir bill

PPM165.000

1931 . . . . . . . . . . . . . . . . . . . . . . . . . $85
"Accept No Imitations", Confederate souvenir bill
(United Confederate Veterans Reunion)

## BOTTLE SHIPPING CASE ADDRESS TAGS

PPM166.000

c.1910 . . . . . . . . . . . . . . . . . $18
Waycross case tag

PPM167.000

c.1910 . . . . . . . . . . . . . . . . . $18
Panama City case tag

PPM168.000

c.1920 . . . . . . . . . . . . . . . . . $6
Bogalusa case tag

PPM171.000     PPM169.000

c.1920s . . . . . . . . . . . . . $3    c.1920s . . . . . . . . . . . . . . $5
Ronceverte case tag     Owensboro case tag

PPM170.000

c.1920 . . . . . . . . . . . . . . . . . $5
Lexington case tag

## PLANT TOUR SOUVENIRS

PPM118.000

1960s   3 1/2" x 6" . . . $15
Case

PPM172.000    PPM173.000    PPM174.000

1930s-40s . . . . . . . . . . . . . . . . . . . . $6 Each
Drivers license holders, three different examples,
showing both sides of each

*Both of these are fan-out paper tour guides.*

PPM119.000

1950s   6 1/2" . . $10
Bottle

PPM176.000
1964 ....... $6
World's Fair folder

PPM177.000
1968 ......................... $5
"Coca-Cola Day" ticket

PPM175.000
1964 ........................... $25
Christmas party poem folder

PCT063.000
Late 1920s .......... $3
"Thomas" free bottle coupon

PPM180.000
1940s ..... $3
"Safety Rules"
sheet (Canada)

PPM178.000
1940s .................. $15
Edgar Bergen (Canada) free bottles offer

PPM179.000
1950s ............... $18
"Birthday Card" free drink offer

PPM181.S00
1964 ..................... $20
World's Fair Pavilion cards

PPM185.BS0
1930s Complete set ............. $55
"Nature Study Cards" in box
PPM185.001 Individual packs ...... $6
with wrapper
PPM185.000 Individual cards .. 85¢ Each

PPM182.000
1950s ...... $12
"Coke Caps" envelope

PPM183.000
1941 ....... $25
Cavalier Coolers folder

PPM184.000
1940s ......... $45
"Birthday Card" free
drink offer

**CONVENTION
BADGES**

PPJ026.002
c.1930 ......... $100

PPJ034.000
1961 .......... $45

PPJ033.000
1959 ......... $65

PPJ032.000
1955 ......... $50

PPM187.S01
## 1. Ropin' a Steer

PPM187.S02
## 2. The Chuck Wagon

PPM187.S03
## 3. They Caught the Hombre

PPM187.S04
## 4. The Hayloft

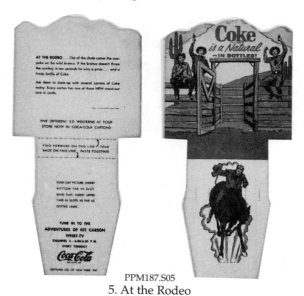

PPM187.S05
## 5. At the Rodeo

Individual Cards . . . . . . . . . . . . . . . . . . . . . . . . . . $25
PPM187.S00  Complete Set . . . . . . . . . . . . . . . . . . . . . $175

"The Adventures of Kit Carson" was a very popular TV series from 1951-1956. The show starred Bill Williams as Kit Carson and his sidekick "El Toro," played by Don Diamond. The show was sponsored by local Coca-Cola Bottlers. Many premiums were made available to viewers by the bottlers including The Kit Carson Kerchief, which is probably the most common premium. Additional items were "Bola Tie;" cardboard and paper signs; Kit Carson stagecoach and others many of which can be found in this book. The carton stuffers shown are 3-D punch-out and consist of five cards to the set.

PPM188.S01
1. Secret Camp Code

PPM188.S02
2. Easy-to-Make Tents

PPM188.S03
3. Coke-Cap Feeding Station for Birds

PPM188.S04
4. Tin-Can Wood's Lantern

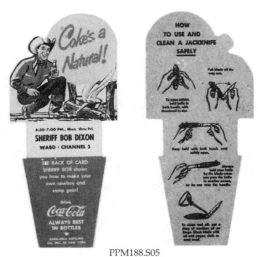

PPM188.S05
5. How to Use and Clean a Jackknife Safely

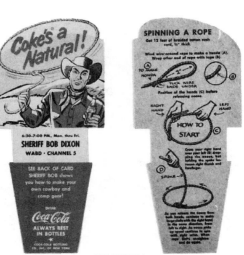

PPM188.S06
6. Spinning a Rope

Individual cards . . . . . . . . . . . . . . . . . . . . . . . . . . . . . . $15
PPM188.S00  Complete set of six cards . . . . . . . . . . . . . $150
1950s Sheriff Bob Dixon carton inserts, six different inserts

# CARTON INSERTS

PPM349.S01

1950s  Individual cards . . . . . . . . . . . . . $8
PPM349.S00  Complete set . . . . . . . . . . $50
Thanksgiving (punchout) place card carton stuffers.
Complete set of five showing front and back of each.

PPM349.S02

PPM349.S03

PPM349.S04

PPM349.S05

PPM350.S01

Reverse side

PPM350.S02

1960s  Individual cards . . . . . . . . . . . . . . . . . . . . . . . . . . . . . $5
Set of two . . . . . . . . . . . . . . . . . . . . . . . . . . . . . . . . . . . . . . . $15
Thanksgiving (punchout) place card, carton stuffers, set consists of two, with
three place cards on each.

PPM351.S01

PPM351.S02

PPM351.S03

PPM351.S04

Reverse side

1960s Individual cards . . . . . . . . . . . . . . . . . . . . . . . . . . . . . . . . . . . . . . . . . . . . . $10 each
PPM.351.S00  Complete set . . . . . . . . . . . . . . . . . . . . . . . . . . . . . . . . . . . . . . . . . . . . $50
Halloween (punchout) masks, carton inserts, set consists of four

PPM189.000
1970 . . . . . . . . . . . . . $3
Santa

PPM190.000
1950s . . . . . . . . . . . $10
Santa, cutout

PPM191.000
1970 . . . . . . . . . . . . . . $3
Santa

PPM192.001
1950s . . . . . . . . $5
Cutout

PPM193.000
1960s . . . . . . $3

PPM194.000
1950s . . . . . . . $3
"T'was The Night
Before Christmas",
foldout

PPM196.000
1950s . . . . . . . . . . . . . . . . . . . . . . . . . $15
"Twas The Night Before Christmas", foldout

PPM195.000
1950s . . . . . . . $3
"T'was The Night
Before Christmas",
foldout

PPM197.000
1950s . . . . . . . . . $8
"Party Time"

PPM198.000
1950s . . . . . . . . . . . $10
"Balance Clown"

PPM199.001   PPM199.002   PPM199.003
1950s . . . . . . . . . . . . . . . . $10 Each

PPM200.000
1950s . . . . . . . . . . . $1

# NO-DRIP BOTTLE PROTECTORS

The "No-Drip Bottle Protector" or "Dry Server" is a paper sleeve that would fit over an iced bottle to keep your hand dry. These were used from the late 1920s up into the 1940s. Electric coolers eliminated the need for the "Bottle Bags" (as they are sometimes called). All pictured are 3 7/8" x 6 3/4", unless noted. An attempt has been made to put these in chronological order and to note the advertising slogan, for reference purposes. Of course, any design might be used over several years, but I believe these dates would be approximately correct. I have seen other designs not shown below. These may often be bought for 25¢ to $1 each, as they have a tendency to turn up in large quantities.

Photos Courtesy: Thom Thompson, Versailles, KY

"In Bottles"
PPM201.001
c.1929  2 7/8" x 6"... $10

"Pause That Refreshes"
PPM201.002
c.1929  2 3/4" x 6"... $7

PPM201.003
c.1930 . . . . .$5

PPM201.004
c.1931 . . . . . . . . . . . .$7
"Our Sandwiches Delicious with Ice Cold"

PPM201.005
c.1934 . . . . . . . . . . . .$7
"Good Things To Eat" (A)

PPM201.006
c.1934 . . . . . . . . . . . $7
"Good Things To Eat" (B)

PPM201.007
c.1936 . . . . . . . . . . . .$6
"Pause That Refreshes"

PPM201.008
c.1936 . . . . . . . . . . $6
"And Now. . . The Pause That Refreshes"

PPM201.009
c.1938 . . . . . . . . . . .$6
"A Great Drink With Good Things To Eat"

PPM202.000

PPM203.000
c.1930s . . . . . . . . . . . . . . . . . . . . . . . . . . . . . . . .$45 and $65
2 different dispensers for the "No-Drip Protectors", would fasten to the side of coolers, these are NOT marked "Coca-Cola"

PPM201.010
c.1938 . . . . . . . . . . . . .$6
"So Refreshing With Food"

PPM201.011
c.1940 . . . . . . . . . . . . . .$6
"The Drink Everybody Knows" (A)

PPM201.012
c.1940 . . . . . . . . . . . $6
"The Drink Everybody Knows"(B)

PPM201.013
c.1942 . . . . . . . . . . . $6
"So Easy To Serve At Home"

PPM201.014
c.1942 . . . . . . . . . . . $8
"When You Entertain"

PPM201.015
c.1942 . . . . . . . . . . . $6
"Thirst Asks Nothing More"

PPM201.016
c.1944 . . . . . . . . . . . $3
"Makes A Light Lunch Refreshing"

PPM201.017
c.1944 . . . . . . . . . . . $4
"Home Refreshment"

PPM201.018
c.1946 . . . . . . . . . . . .$4
"Take A Minute To Refresh" (A)

PPM201.019
c.1946 . . . . . . . . . . . $4
"Take A Minute To Refresh" (B)

PPM201.020
c.1946 . . . . . . . . . . . $4
"A Great Drink With Lunch"

PPM201.021
c.1946 . . . . . . . . . . . $7
"The Taste That Always Charms"

PPM201.22
c.1946 . . . . . . . . . . . $6
"Take Off Refreshed"

PPM201.023
c.1948 . . . . . . . . . . . $6
"It's The Real Thing"

PPM201.024
c.1948 . . . . . . . . . . . .$6
"Refreshment Right Out Of The Bottle"

PPM201.025
c.1948 . . . . . . . . . . . $6
"Every Bottle Refreshes"

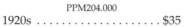

PPM205.000

1920s . . . . . . . . . . . . . $35

PPM206.000

Late 1920s . . . . . . . . . . . . . $50

PPM204.000

1920s . . . . . . . . . . . . . . . . . . . $35

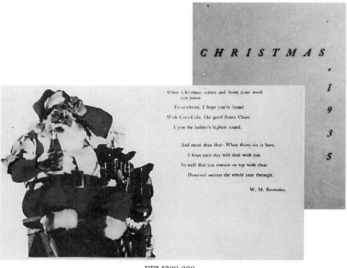

PPM209.000

1935 . . . . . . . . . . . . . . . . . . . . . . . . . . $18

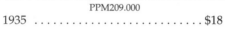

PPM208.000

Early 1940s . . . . . . . . . . . . . . . . . . . . . $25

PPM211.000

Early 1940s . . . . . . . . . . . . . . . . . . . . . $12

PPM210.000

1936 . . . . . . . . . . . . . . . . $18

PPM207.000

c.1935 . . . . . . . . . . . . . . . . . $25

# COCA-COLA AND SPORTS

PSR010.000
1940  17" x 31" . . . . . . . . $575
Poster, paper, metal strips top and
bottom, recaps 1939 baseball season,
pictures 1939 All Stars, with additional records and historical data, shows
1940 schedule, printed both sides

PSR012.000
1915 . . . . . . . . . . . . . . . . . . . . . . . . $200
Glass advertising slide, Lew McCarty,
Brooklyn Dodgers

PSR011.000
1939  21" x 28" . . . . . . . . . $575
"100 Years of Baseball" poster, paper,
metal strips top and bottom, history of
baseball, records, pictures hall of fame
players, shows 1939 schedule printed
both sides

PSR015.000
1920s . . . . . . . . . . . . . . . . . . . . . . $75
Coca-Cola baseball team photo

PSR014.000
1933 . . . . . . . . . . . . . . . . . . . . . . . . $40
St. Petersburg, FL , photo,
Softball Team with Buster Keaton in center

PSR017.000          PSR017.001
1938 and 1940  . . . . . $35 Each
Horse racing programs with Coke ads

PSR013.000
1910  . . . . . . . . $325
Baseball record book

PSR019.000
1936-37 . . . . . . . . . . . . . . . . . $40
Basketball score book

PSR016.000
1926 . . . . . . . . . . . . . . . . . . . . . . $50
Coca-Cola Canada, photo, local hockey team

PSR018.000
1932  . . . . . . . . . . . . . . . . . $65
"Boston Garden News" ad

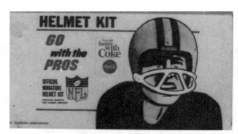

PSR021.000

1964 . . . . . . . . . . . . . . . . . . . . . . . . . . . $85
Football helmet kit, seven plastic helmets in box
Note: This set can be found without Coca-Cola on box.

PSR020.000

1937 . . . . . . . . . . . . . . . . . . . . . . . . . . . .$55
Cricket Scorecard (England) Surrey vs. New Zealand

PSR022.000

1949 . . . . . . . . . . . . . . . . . . . . $40
Program, Army All Stars vs. Air Force All Stars, showing center page score-card

PSR023.000

1930-40s . . . . . . . . . . . . . . . . . . . . . $8
Bowling score sheet

PSR024.000

1948-50 . . . . . . . . . . . . . . . . $6
Bowling score sheet

PSR025.000

1948-50 . . . . . . . . . . . . . . . . . . . $6
Bowling Score sheet

PSR026.001

PSR026.002

PSR027.001

PSR027.002

1960 . . . . . . . . . . . . . . . . . . . . . . . . . .$65
"Hall of Fame Records" showing both sides,
American and National leagues

$150

$275

1932 "Olympic Record Indicator" showing both sides of two
different examples.

PSR032.000

1930 . . . . . . . . . . . . . .$25
Jersey City, N.J. Baseball
Program

PSR028.000

1960s . . . . . . . . . . . . . . . . . . . .$6
Boating guide

PSR031.000

1949 . . . . . . . . . . . . . . . . . . . . . .$5
"Baseball Rules" booklet

PSR030.000

1907 . . . . . . . . . . . . . . . . . .$100
Baseball scorekeeper

PSR033.000

1970s . . . . . . . . . . . . . . . . . . . . . . .$25
Coca-Cola USA "Great Olympics Moments"
coin set

PSR034.001

PSR034.004

PSR034.003

PSR034.002

1950s . . . . . . . . . . . . . . . . . . . . . . . .$6 each
Sports Programs

PSR029.000

1980 . . . . . . . . .$15
Topps, set of 11
Champion Phillies

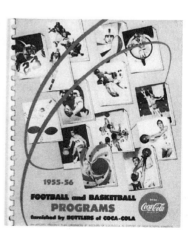
PSR035.000

1955-56 . . . . . . . . . . . . . . . . . . . .$35
"Sports Programs", catalog of samples
and prices

# BASEBALL CARDS

1952 Coca-Cola baseball card carton inserts.

Individual cards . . . . . . $85 Each      PSR036.S00 Complete set of 10 . . . . . .$1,000

PSR036.S01
Wes Westrum
Giants

PSR036.S02
Bobby Thomson
Giants

PSR036.S03
Gil McDougal
Yankees

PSR036.S04
Gil Hodgers
Dodgers

PSR036.S05
Hank Bauer
Yankees

PSR036.S06
Ed Lopat
Yankees

PSR036.S07
Bobby Thomson
Giants

PSR036.S08
Carl Furillo
Dodgers

PSR036.S09
Don Mueller
Giants

PSR036.S10
Peewee Reese
Dodgers

# BASEBALL SCORE CARDS

PSR037.000

1916 . . . . . . . . . . . . . . . . . . . . . . $250

Chicago and St. Louis

PSR038.000

1957 . . . . . . . . . . . . . . . . . . . . . . . $15

Dodgers

PSR039.000

1946 . . . . . . . . . . . . . . . . . . . . . $25

Athletics

PSR040.000

1944 . . . . . . . . . . . . . . . . . . . . $25

Athletics

> Note: These score cards are very collectible and interesting. Keep in mind that some may be worth more to a baseball collector than to a Coke collector. A World Series card would be a good example.

PSR041.000

1942 . . . . . . . . . . . $25

St. Louis Cards

PSR042.000

1942 . . . . . . . . . . . $30

St. Louis Browns

PRSR043.000

1947 . . . . . . . . . . . . . . . . . . . . . . . . . . . . . . . . $25

Athletics

PSR044.000

1964 . . . . . . . . . . . . . . . . . . . . . . . $10

Red Sox

PSR045.000

1949 . . . . . . . . . . . . . . . . . . . . . . $20

Cardinals

PSR046.000

1942 . . . . . . . . . . . . . . . . . . . . . . $25

Athletics

# BASEBALL SCORE CARDS

PSR047.000

1961 . . . . . . . . . . . . . . . . . . . . . . . . . . . $15

Red Sox

PSR051.000

1951 . . . . . . . . . . . . . . . . . . . . . . . . . . . $20

Athletics

PSR049.000

1960 . . . . . . . . . . . . . . . . . . . . . . . . . . . $10

Orioles

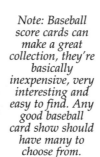

*Note: Baseball score cards can make a great collection, they're basically inexpensive, very interesting and easy to find. Any good baseball card show should have many to choose from.*

PSR048.000

1963 . . . . . . . . . . . . . . . . . . . . . . . . . . . $25

Yankees

PSR052.000

1952 . . . . . . . . . . . . . . . . . . . . . . . . . . . $12

Pittsburgh Pirates

PSR053.000

1952 . . . . . . . . . . . . . . . . . . . . . . . . . . . $12

Athletics

PSR054.000

1966 . . . . . . . . . . . . . . . . . . . . . . . . . . . $10

Red Sox

PSR050.000

1963 . . . . . . . . . . . . . . . . . . . . . . . . . . . $10

Mets

PSR055.000

1950 . . . . . . . . . . . . . . . . . . . . . . . . . . . $10

Chicago Cubs

# BOTTLERS ADVERTISING PRICE BOOKS
Values on these books vary depending on contents and condition.

PPM212.000

1927 . . . . . . . . . . . . . . . . . . . . . . . . . . $200

PPM213.000

1928 . . . . . . . . . . . . . . . . . . . . . . . . . . $200

PPM214.000

1928 . . . . . . . . . . . . . . . . . . . . . . . . . . $200

PPM215.000

1929 . . . . . . . . . . . . . . . . . . . . . . . . . . $200

PPM216.000

1929 . . . . . . . . . . . . . . . . . . . . . . . . . . $200

PPM217.000

1931 . . . . . . . . . . . . . . . . . . . . . . . . . . $200

PPM218.000

1932 . . . . . . . . . . . . . . . . . . . . . . . . . . $225

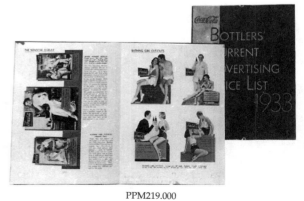

PPM219.000

1933 . . . . . . . . . . . . . . . . . . . . . . . . . . $225

# BOTTLERS ADVERTISING PRICE BOOKS
Values on these books vary depending on contents and condition.

PPM220.000

1936 . . . . . . . . . . . . . . . . . . . . . . . . . . . $325

PPM221.000

1937 . . . . . . . . . . . . . . . . . . . . . . . . . . . $175

PPM222.000

1938 . . . . . . . . . . . . . . . . . . . . . . . . . . . $150

PPM223.000

1939 . . . . . . . . . . . . . . . . . . . . . . . . . . . $150

PPM224.000

1939 . . . . . . . . . . . . . . . . . . . . . . . . . . . $125

PPM225.000

1940 . . . . . . . . . . . . . . . . . . . . . . . . . . . $110

PPM226.000

1943 . . . . . . . . . . . . . . . . . . . . . . . . . . . $110

PPM227.000

1944 . . . . . . . . . . . . . . . . . . . . . . . . . . . $110

PPM228.000

1944 . . . . . . . . . . . . . . . . . . . . . . . . . . . $110

PPM229.000

1946 . . . . . . . . . . . . . . . . . . . . . . . . . . . $110

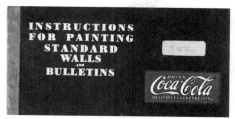

PPM230.000

Late 1920s . . . . . . . . . . . . . . . . . . . . $135

Instruction book for painting standardization
(showing layouts and paint samples)

PPM231.000

Late 1920s . . . . . . . . . . . . . . . . . . . . $135

Coca-Cola Trade Mark standardization book
(showing different logo layouts and color samples)

PPM232.000

1950s . . . . . . . . . . . . . . . . $200

1950s Advertising price list
(price based on near complete book)

PPM233.000

1934 . . . . . . . . . . . . . . . . . . . . . . . . . . . . . . . . . . . . . . . $300

Bottler price list

*Note: Prices on these books
and manuals vary
depending on contents.*

PPM234.000

1940s . . . . . . . . . . . . . . . . . . . . . . . $375

Advertising manual

PPM235.000

1920s . . . . . . . . . . . . . . . . . . . $200

Bottler's price list

PPM236.000

1938 . . . . . . . . . . . . . . . . . . . . . . . . . . . . . . . . . . . . . . . $225

Advertising manual, (price based on near complete book)

PPM237.000

1960s . . . . . . . . . . . . . . . . . . . . . . . . . . . . $200

Advertising manual, (price based on near complete book)

PPM238.000
1928 . . . . . . . . . . . . . . . . . . . . . . $75
Summer display

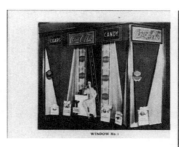

PPM239.000
1929 . . . . . . . . . . . . . . . . . $75
Orchid display

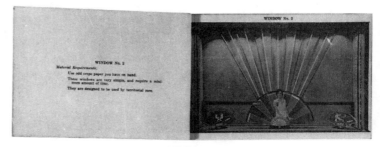

PPM240.000
1926 . . . . . . . . . . . . . . . . . . . . . . . . . $75
Fan display

PPM241.000
1926 . . . . . . . . . . . . . . . . . . $100
Window displays

PPM242.000
1927 . . . . . . . . . . . . . . . . . . . . . . . . . $75
Fan display

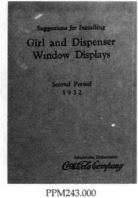

PPM243.000
1932 . . . . . . . . . . . . . . . . . . . . $75
Girl and Dispenser

PPM244.000
1928 . . . . . . . . . . . . . . . . . . . . . . . . $75
Bench display

PPM245.000
1932 . . . . . . . . . . . . . . . . . . . . . $75
Olympic display

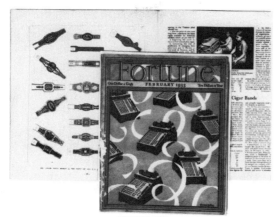

PPM246.S00

Feb. 1933 . . . . . . . . . . . . . . . . . . . . . . $75

*Fortune* magazine with cigar band insert page,
featuring a Coca-Cola cigar band

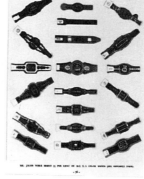

PPM246.S01
$50
Cigar band page only

PPM247.000

1927 . . . . . . . . . . . . . . . $40

Newspaper advertising tear sheet

PPM248.S00

1928 . . . . . . . . . . . . . . . . . . . . . . . $225

"A Letter" booklet and insert pieces
concerning the new six-pack box

PPM249.000

1950 . . . . . . . . . . . . . . . . . . . . . . . . . $35

Newspaper advertising book

PPM250.000

1950s . . . . . . . . . $20

Westinghouse Coolers
catalog

PPM251.001          PPM251.002

Early 1900s . . . . . . . . . . . . . . . $35 Each

*Pharmaceutical Era* magazine with Coke ads

PPM252.000

1928 . . . . . . . . . . . . . . . . . . . . . $30

Outdoor sign painting specification catalog

PPM253.000

1950s . . . . . . . . . $25

Coolers sales tips

PPM254.000

1927 . . . . . . . . . . . . $50

PPM255.000

1926 . . . . . . . . . . . . $45

PPM256.000

1939 . . . . . . . . . . . . . . . . . . $20

Rand McNally road maps

PPM257.000

1928 . . . . $30

PPM259.000

1930s . . . . . . . . . . . . . . . . . . . . . . . . . . $40

Folder showing display pieces available

PPM260.000

1936 . . . . . . . . . . . . . . . . . . . . . . . $45

Window display instruction folder

PPM261.000

1935 . . . . . . . . . . . . . . . . . . . . . . . . . . $75

Advertising catalog sheet

PPM264.000

1930 . . . . . . . . . . . . . . . . . . . . $60

"Telephone Window Displays" instruction booklet

PPM258.000

1931 . . . . . . . . . . . . . . . . . . . . . . .$225

Standardized delivery equipment booklet

PPM262.000          PPM263.000

1932 and 1933 . . . . . . . . . . . . . . .$50 Each

Window display instruction folders

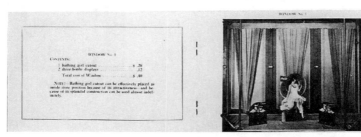

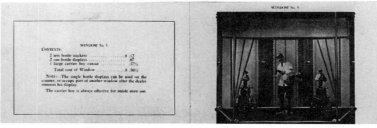

PPM265.000

1926 . . . . . . . . . . . . . . . . . . . . . . . . . . . . . . . . . $125

Booklet showing window displays, description, prices, and layouts

PPM266.000

c.1909 . . . . . . . . . . . . $50

"Window Displays for Druggists" book showing store window displays (not a Coca-Cola publication)

# STANDARDIZATION BOOK (TRUCK PAINTING)

Over the years the Coca-Cola Company published books on standardization for all its bottlers. In an attempt to keep everything uniform, these books dealt with everything from plant design, sign painting, stationary, uniforms, and of course truck painting. These books are very interesting, and prices will vary depending on contents.

PPM267.P01

PPM267.P02

PPM267.P03

PPM267.P04

PPM267.P05

PPM267.P06

PPM267.P07

PPM267.P08

PPM267.P09

PPM267.P10

PPM267.P11

PPM267.P12

Individual pages . . . . . . . . . . $40 Each     PPM267.000  Complete book . . . . . . . . . $375
Pages shown are not a complete book

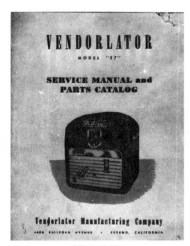

PPM268.000
Vendorlator Model 27 . . . . . $65

PPM269.000
Vendo Parts and Service Manual . . $45

PPM270.000

PPM271.000
1939 and 1940 . . . . . . . . . . . . . . $30 Each
Vendo Parts and Service Manuals

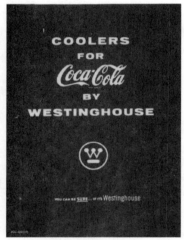

PPM274.000
Westinghouse Coolers . . . . $30

PPM272.000

PPM273.000
1936 and 1941 . . . . . . . $12-$16 Each
Cavalier Parts Catalog

PPM275.000
Vendo V-83 . . . . . . . . . . . $30

---

*Note: These manuals are especially interesting and sought after by collectors who specialize in vending machines, and often pay premium prices for particular manuals.*

---

PPM276.000
Mills Model 45 . . . . . . $25

PPM277.000
Cavalier C-51 . . . . . . $15

PPM278.000
1940 Mills . . . . . . . . $25

PPM279.000
Vendo V-39 . . . . . . . . $30

PPM280.000

1936 . . . . . . . . . . . . . $45
"What Happened In Atlanta"
bottlers' conference material

PPM281.000        PPM282.000        PPM283.000

1912-1915 . . . . . . . . . . . . . . . $6-$30 Each
"Dime Novels", with color Coca-Cola ads on back
covers (Price depends on ad and condition of book)

PPM284.000

1960s . . . . . . . . . . . $30
"Truck Decals", brochure

Note: Many of these Dime Novels have copyright dates much
earlier than the actual printing of the book. This date refers to
the copyright of the story, not the book or ad.

PPM285.000
Late 1960s-Early 1970s . . $3 Each
*Golden Legacy* magazines

PPM286.000

1940s . . . . . . . . $10
U.S. Army note pad

PPM287.S00

1958-1961 . . . . . . . $12
"Pause for Living", bound volume

PPM288.000

1940s . . . . . . . . . . . . . . $18
"Radio Material" booklet

PPM289.000

1930s . . . . . . . . . . . $25
"These Changing Times",
Soda fountain book

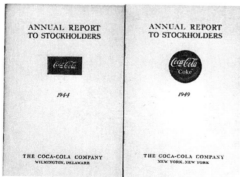

PPM290.000        PPM291.000
1940s . . . . . . . . . . . . . . . . . . . . . $10 Each
"Annual Report to stockholders"

PPM292.000

1934 . . . . . . . . . . . . . . . . . . $18
Western Bottlers Conference program

PPM293.000

1959 . . . . . . . . . . . . . . $6
Coca-Cola "Overseas"

# THE COCA-COLA BOTTLER AND RED BARREL MAGAZINE

Both *The Coca-Cola Bottler* and *Red Barrel* are company publications, directed to bottlers, company employees, and executives. All of these publications are very difficult to price because the contents vary so much. If the magazine shows a lot of interesting advertising, it could be worth more than my estimate.

PPM294.S00
1934 . . . . . . . . . $250
Complete year, bound

PPM294.266
March 1945 . . . $30

PPM294.124
May 1933 . . . . $35

PPM294.247
Aug. 1943 . . . . $25

PPM294.136
May 1934 . . . . . . . . . . . . . . $60
With envelope

PPM294.215
Dec. 1940 . . . . . $30

PPM294.227
Dec. 1941 . . . . . $25

PPM294.224
Sept. 1941 . . . . $25

PPM294.241
Feb. 1943 . . . . . $25

PPM294.239
Dec. 1942 . . . . . $25

PPM295.020
1949 . . . . . . . . . . . . . . . . . $18

PPM295.P21
1909 . . . . . . . . . $10
Reprint, This was an
insert in the *Coca-Cola
Bottler* magazine (1959)
shown below.

PPM295.010
Oct. 1938 . . . . . $30

PPM295.008
Jan. 1928 . . . . . . $30

PPM295.022
1959 . . . . . . . . . . $85
50th Anniversary Issue

PPM295.021
1949 . . . . . . . . . . . . . . $75
40th Anniversary Issue

*Note: Both* The Coca-Cola Bottler *and* Red Barrel *have a wealth
of information for the collector. Much of the information that we
have, as far as dating and identifying advertising and production
materials, has come from these publications.*

# THE RED BARREL MAGAZINE

PPM294.072
January 1929 . . . . $35

PPM294.074
March 1929 . . . . . $75

*Note:* The Red Barrel *magazine was first published in Jan. 1924 as the company's in-house publication, available to all employees. From 1924 to 1950* The Red Barrel *was published monthly. In 1951 it went out bi-monthly and eventually quarterly, until its final issue in 1953. These magazines contain a wealth of information for today's collectors.*

PPM294.099
April 1931 . . . . . $30

PPM294.111
April 1932 . . . . . $40

PPM294.163
August 1936 . . . . $25

PPM294.165
October 1936 . . . . $25

PPM294.166
November 1936 . . . $25

PPM294.170
March 1937 . . . . . $25

PPM294.171
April 1937 . . . . . . $25

PPM294.172
May 1937 . . . . . . . $25

PPM294.173
June 1937 . . . . . . $25

PPM294.174
July 1937 . . . . . . . $25

PPM294.177
October 1937 . . . . $25

PPM294.178
November 1937 . . $25

PPM294.179
December 1937 . . $25

PPM294.185
June 1938 . . . . . . . $25

PPM294.180
Jan. 1938 . . . . . . $35

PPM294.184
May 1938 . . . . . . $25

PPM294.186
July 1938 . . . . . . . $25

# THE RED BARREL MAGAZINE

PPM294.188
September 1938 . . . $25

PPM294.189
October 1938 . . . $25

Note: The value on these magazines depend on condition. Worn or separated covers will lower the value. Content that includes lots of photos, good information, or movie stars will certainly increase values. Good cover shots are also more valuable as are special editions.

PPM294.191
December 1938 . . . $25

PPM294.195
April 1939 . . . . $25

PPM294.198
July 1939 . . . . . $25

PPM294.202
November 1939 . . $25

PPM294.204
1940 . . . . . . . . $40
Convention issue

PPM294.287
December 1946 . . . $25

PPM294.300
January 1948 . . . $25

PPM294.301
February 1948 . . . $25

PPM294.303
April 1948 . . . . $25

PPM294.304
May 1948 . . . . . $25

PPM294.314
March 1949 . . . $25

PPM294.326
March 1950 . . . $20

PPM294.333
October 1950 . . $20

PPM294.348
1st Quarter 1952 . . . $15

PPM294.351
2nd Quarter 1952 . . . $15

PPM294.354
3rd Quarter 1952 . . . $15

PPM294.357
4th Quarter 1953 . . . $15

# BOOKS AND SCORE PADS

PPM296.000
1951 . . . . . . . . . . . . . $7
Easy Hospitality

PPM297.000
1944 . . . . . . . . . . . . . . . . . . . . . . . . $20
Boy Scouts Handbook

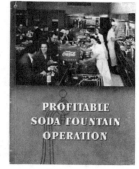

PPM298.000
1950 . . . . . . . . . . $18
"Profitable Soda Fountain
Operation"

PPM299.000
1960s . . . . . . . . . . . . . . $7
Touch Football Rules Book

PES075.B00
1930s . . . . . . . . . . . . . . . . . . . . . $15
"Visual Instruction in Nature Study", with
envelope

PPM301.000
1950s . . . . . . . . . . . . . . . . . . . . .$6
"Old Chips and Charlie" comic

PPM302.000
1940s . . . . . . . . $6
"Our American
Neighbors"

PES071.000
1925 . . . . . . . . $50
"Websters Little Gem
Dictionary"

PPM300.000
1950s . . . . . . . . $5
Comic Book

PPM306.000
Score pad . . . . $5
Canada

PPM307.000
c.1920s . . . . . . . $35
"The Charm of Purity"

PPM309.001
1941 . . . . . . . . . . . . . . . . . . $12
"Pause Prints"(In-house publication)

PPM310.000
"The Romance of Coca-Cola" . . $18

PPM305.000
1946 . . . . . . . . $6
"Group Life Insurance
Plan" booklet

PPM308.000
1915 . . . . . . . . . . . . . . . . . . . . . . . . $350
"Coca-Cola The Universal Beverage"

# BOOKS, NOTE, AND SCORE PADS

PPM356.000

c.1912 . . . . . . . . . . . . . . . . . . . . . . . . $35

"The Truth about Coca-Cola", 16-page booklet

PPM357.000

1916 . . . . . . . . . . . . . . $85

"The Romance of Coca-Cola"

PPM311.000

1928 . . . . . . . . . . . . . . . . . . $60

"Alphabet Book of Coca-Cola"

PBN008.000

1932 . . . . . . . . . . $8

"When You Entertain", by
Ida Bailey Allen

PPM141.000

1943 . . . . . . . . . . $50

"Know Your War Planes"

PPM312.000

1923 . . . . . . $50

"Facts" book

PPM313.000

1939 . . . . . . . . . . . . . . . . . . . . . . . . $15

"My Daily Reminder" booklet

PSR056.0000

1950s . . . . . . $5

"Sports Manual"

PBN009.000      PBN010.000      PBN011.000

1940s . . . . . . . . . . . . . . . . . . . . . . . . . . . . . . . . $5 Each

Flower arranging books, Volumes 1, 2, and 3, by Laura Lee Burrough

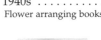

PBN013.000

1943-44 . . . . . . $5

Notebook

PPL071.000      PPL076.000

1940s . . . . . . . . . . . . . . $12 Each

Score pads

PBN012.000

1957 . . . . . . . . . . . . . . $35

Book listing bottlers, commem-
orating their 50th Anniversary

PPL074.000

1950s . . . . . . . . . . $12

"Bridge Digest" booklet

# NOTEBOOKS AND TABLETS

PBN014.000

1940 . . . . . . . . . . . . . . . . . . . . . . . . . . . $65

School notebook, embossed cover

PBN015.000

1931 . . . . . . . . $50

Note pad, Norman
Rockwell Art

PBN016.000

1937-1939 . . . . . $8

PBN018.000

1936 . . . . . . . $15

50th Anniversary

PBN020.000

1949-1950s . . . $4

PBN017.000

1932-1935 . . . . . . . . . $12

PBN019.000

c.1940-1945 . . . $6

PBN021.000

Late 1950s . . $3

PSP023.000

c.1920s . . . . . . . . . . . . . . . . . . . . . $300

Note pad holder for candlestick phone, this piece
always looks nice when displayed on a phone
Price shown is for note pad holder only.

PBN022.000

Early 1960s . . . . . . . $4

Atlanta Bottling Co.

PBN025.000

Late 1960s . . . . . . . . $3

PBN024.000

Late 1960s . . . . $3

PBN023.000

c.1960 . . . . . . . . $3

PBN027.000

Mid-1970s . . . . $3

PAN006.001

1950s . . . . . $35

Bottlers' 50th
Anniversary, Scarce

PBN026.000

Early 1970s . . . $2

PBN028.000

Late 1970s . . . . . . . . $2

PES010.000

1960s . . . . . . . . . . . . . . . . . . . . . . . . . . $250

Pencil Holder, ceramic. Note: A reproduction of this pencil holder was produced in the 1980s to commemorate the 75th Anniversary of the New York Bottling Co.; it is so marked and worth approximately $75.

PES011.000

1942 . . . . . . . . . . . . . . . . . . . . . . . . . . $30

All Star mechanical pencil catalog sheet showing Coca-Cola pencil

PE012.000

PES019.BS0

Early 1940s 12-pack . . . . . . $25

PES019.000 Single pencil . . . . . $2

Plastic ferrules used during WW II

1940s-1960s Mechanical pencil . . . . . . $20

PES012.B00 With box . . . . . . . . . . . . . . $35

PES013.000

c.1942 . . . . . . . . . . . . . . . . . . . . . . . . $50

Mechanical pencil with bottle on end

PES020.BS0

1938-40s and 50s 12-pack . . . . $20

PES020.000 Single pencil . . . . . . . . $1

Except WW II

PES014.000

PES015.000

PES021.BS0

1960s 12-Pack . . . . . . . . . . $15

PES021.000 Single pencil . . . . $1

PES016.000

1940s . . . . . . . . . . . . . . . . . . . . . $45 Each

Mechanical pencils, tortoise shell, local bottlers

PES022.BS0

1970s 12 Pack . . . . . . . . . . . . . . . . . . . . $3

PES022.000 Single pencil . . . . . . . . . . . 25¢

PES017.000

1930s . . . . . . . . . . . . . . . . . . . . . . . . . . $35

Pencil with opener

PES023.BS0

1970s 12 Pack . . . . . . . . . . $3

PES023.000 Single pencil . . . 25¢

PES018.000

c.1940s-1950s . . . . . . . . . . . . . . . . . . $50

Pen/Pencil

# RULERS

PES086.000
Western Coca-Cola . . . . . . . . . . . . . . $25

PES087.000
1950s . . . . . . . . . . . . . . . . . . . . . . . $12
"Fishing Ruler"

PES089.000
"Golden Rule" . . . . . . . . . . . . . . . . . . . $1
PES089.001 If dated . . . . . . . . . . . . . . . . $2
Showing both sides, This is the most common ruler,
produced from the late 1920s into the 1960s.

PES088.000
1940s . . . . . . . . . . . . . . . . . . . . . . . $8

PES024.000
1950s . . . . . . . . . . . . . . . . . . . . . . . $5

PES025.000
1950s-60s . . . . . . . . . . . . . . . . . . . . . $3
Mexico

PES026.000
1970s . . . . . . . . . . . . . . . . . . . . . . . $3

PES027.000
1980 . . . . . . . . . . . . . . . . . . . . . . . . $3
Jackson, TN

PES028.000
Late 1950s English . . . . . . . . . . . . . . . $10

PES029.000
1973 . . . . . . . . . . . . . . . . . . . . . . . $10
Houston Astros, plastic

PES030.001
Pencil box ruler . . . . . . . . . . . . . . . . . $3

PES032.000
1980s . . . . . . . . . . . . . . . . . . . . . . . $1
Plastic

PES031.000
1970s . . . . . . . . . . . . . . . . . . . . . . . $3
Plastic

PES034.000
1982 . . . . . . . . . . . . . . . . . . . . . . . . $2
Corinth, MS

PES033.000
1970s . . . . . . . . . . . . . . . . . . . . . . . $3
Plastic

PES036.000
"Golden Rule" yard stick . . . . . $10

PES035.000
1967 . . . . . . . . . . . . . . . . . . . . . . . . $4
Piqua, OH, plastic

*Note: Rulers were produced and given away in such
large quantities that most are very common.*

PES036.001
1950s . . . . . . . . . . . . . . . . . . . . . . . $10
Yard stick

PES030.BS0

c.1930s . . . . . . . . . . . . . . . . . $55
Pencil box (complete with 10 pieces)

PES037.000 Envelope only . . . . . . . .$15
PES037.BS0 Complete package . . . . $85
1937 school package

PES038.000 Envelope only . . . . . . . . $8
PES038.BS0 Complete package . . . . $50
1940s school package

PES039.BS0

1950s . . . . . . . . . . . . . . . . . . . . . . . . . . . . . . . $45
School package, complete with four pieces including envelope

PES040.000 c.1929 Envelope only . . $20
PES040.B50 Complete package . . . .$125
School package

PES042.000 Envelope only . . . . . $10
PES042.BS0 Complete package . $50
School package

PES043.000
1930s
$35 Each
Pencil sharpeners

PES043.BS0
Box of 12 . . . . . $500
Complete

PES045.000

1930s . . . . . . . . . . . . . . . . . . . . . . . . $135
Game of "Safety and Danger", Canada, showing
both sides

PES041.000

1930s Envelope only . . . . . . . . $8
PES041.BS0 Complete package . . $65
1930s School package

PES044.000

1938 . . . . . . . . . . . . . . . . . . . . . . . . $135
Game of "Steps to Health", Canada, This game came
in an unmarked envelope, along with game piece
and die.

# BOOK COVERS

PES046.000

1930-31 . . . . . . . . . . . . . . . . . . . . . . . $6

PES048.000

1931 . . . . . . . . . . . . . . . . . . . . . . . . . $12

Rockwell Art

PES050.000

1950s . . . . . . . . . . . . . . . . . . . . . . . . $6

PES052.000

1939-40 . . . . . . . . . . . . . . . . . . . . . . . $6

PES054.000

c.1937 . . . . . . . . . . . . . . . . . . . . . . . $6

PES047.000

1950s . . . . . . . . . . . . . . . . . . . . . . . . $6

PES049.000

1960s . . . . . . . . . . . . . . . . . . . . . . . . $5

PES051.000

1950s . . . . . . . . . . . . . . . . . $10

PES053.000

1950s . . . . . . . . . . . . . . . . . . $2

Canada

PES055.000

1950s . . . . . . . . . . . . . . . . . . $2

Canada

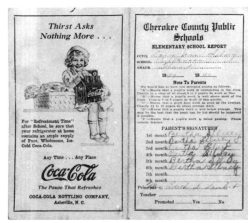

PES056.000

1939-1940 . . . . . . . . . . . . . . . . . . . . . . .75

Report card

PES057.000

1939-1940 . . . . . . . . . . . . . . . . . . . . . $135

"Teacher's Record" book

PES058.000

1932-1933 . . . . . . . . . . . . . . . . . . . . . . $125

Report card holder

PES059.000

1945-1946 . . . . . . . . . . . . . . . . . . . . . . $40

Report card

PES060.000

1949-1950 . . . . . . . . . . . . . . . . . . . . . . $40

Report card

PES061.000

1933-1934 . . . . . . . . . . . . . . . . . . . . . . $75

Report card holder

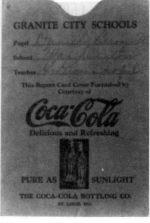   

| PES062.000 | PES063.000 | PES064.000 |
|---|---|---|
| 1940-1941 . . $40 | 1942-1943 . . $40 | 1939-1940 . . . $40 |
| Report card | Report card | Report card |

PES065.000

1940  26" x 32"  . . . . . $35

Declaration of Independence,
Coca-Cola Bottling Co.

PES066.000

1970s  . . . . . . . . . . . . . . $25

"Black Guardians of Freedom",
in box

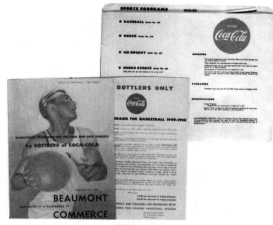

PES067.BS0

1950s . . . . . . . . . . . . . . . . . . . . . . . . . $40

Sports program kit, complete

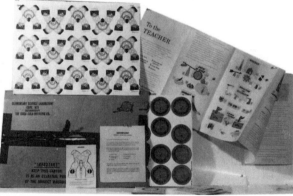

PES068.BS0

1940s  . . . . . . . . . . . . . . . . . . . . . . . $200

"Elementary Science Lab", complete set in box

PES069.S00

1969  . . . . . . . . . . . . . . . . . . . $50

"Trip to the Moon", poster and record

PES071.000

1925  . . . . . . $50

"Webster's Little
Gem Dictionary"

PES072.S00

Complete set  . . . . . . . . . . . . . . . . . . $200

1932 Famous Doctors Series, set consists of six heavy
paper folders (12" x 17" open, 8 1/2" x 12" closed)

Individual folders  . . . . . . . . . . . $35 Each

| PES072.S01 | Hippocrates |
| PES072.S02 | William Harvey |
| PES072.S03 | Louis Pasteur |
| PES072.S04 | Lord Lister |
| PES072.S05 | W.C. Rontgen |
| PES072.S06 | Walter Reed |

PES070.S00

1940s  . . . . . . . . . . . . . . . . . . . . . . . $65

"Terrestrial Globe" index and information kit

# EDUCATIONAL MATERIAL
## "Nature Study Series" 1929-1934

PES073.BS0

Complete set in box (96 cards) . . . . . . . . . . . . . . . . . . $55
PES073.001  Individual series (12 cards) with wrapper . . $6
PES073.000  Individual cards . . . . . . . . . . . . . . . . . 75¢ Each
Nature Study Cards, complete set consists of eight series of 12 cards each, card size 2 1/2" x 4". Note: Nature Study Cards were used for a number of years, and given away in large quantities. They are very common.

PES075.000  Book only, 6" x 9"  . . . . . . . . $10
PES075.B00  Book and envelope  . . . . . . $15
*Visual Instruction in Nature Study,*
by Dr. E.L. Crandall

| PES074.S03 | PES074.S04 | PES074.S02 | PES074.S01 |
| Series 3 & 6 | Series 7 & 8 | Series 4 & 5 | Series 1 & 2 |

2 1/2" x 4" (Card size) . . . . . . . . . . . . . . . . . . . . . . . . . $18 Each
Nature Study Cards (small set) each set consists of two series of 12 cards each,
in separate envelopes

# WILD FLOWER CARDS

1923 Wild Flowers of America Cards. Set consists of 20 cards (1 3/4" x 2 3/4"). Each card is full color from a painting by M.E. Eaton. The back of each card is a full description of the flower followed by "Do Not Pick the Wild Flowers Leave Them For All To Enjoy." Cards were individually numbered 1-20 and were available by sending 2¢ postage to the advertising department of The Coca-Cola Company, Atlanta, GA.

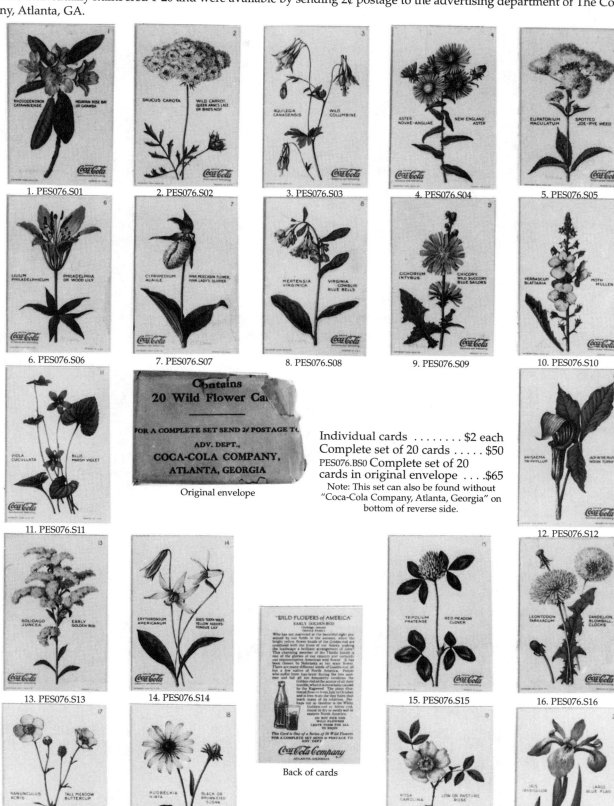

1. PES076.S01   2. PES076.S02   3. PES076.S03   4. PES076.S04   5. PES076.S05

6. PES076.S06   7. PES076.S07   8. PES076.S08   9. PES076.S09   10. PES076.S10

Original envelope

Individual cards . . . . . . . $2 each
Complete set of 20 cards . . . . . $50
PES076.BS0 Complete set of 20 cards in original envelope . . . .$65
Note: This set can also be found without "Coca-Cola Company, Atlanta, Georgia" on bottom of reverse side.

11. PES076.S11   12. PES076.S12

13. PES076.S13   14. PES076.S14

Back of cards

15. PES076.S15   16. PES076.S16

17. PES076.S17   18. PES076.S18   19. PES076.S19   20. PES076.S20

# EDUCATIONAL MATERIAL

PES077.000

1940s  30 x 36 . . . . . . . . . . . . . . . . . . . $50

"Map of North America"

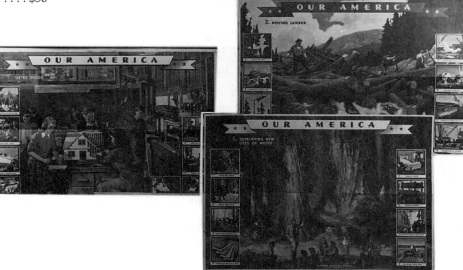

PES081.S01

1946 . . . . . . . . . . . . . . . . . . . . . . . $15 Each

"Our America" posters

PES078.S04

PES083.S04

PES079.S04

PES080.S04

PES084.S04

1946 . . . . . . . . . . . . . . . . . . . . . . . . . . . . . . . . . . . . . . . . . . . . . . . . . . . . . $6 Each

Complete with unused stamps . . . . . . . . . . . . . . . . . . . . . . . . . . . . . . $10 Each

"Our America" booklets. Note: These "Our America" booklets came with sets of stamps that were to be glued into position. They are often found without them.

# EDUCATIONAL MATERIAL
## "Our America Series"

1946 "Our America" series (teachers kit) consists of 8 complete sets—all are shown. Each set contained a set of four large (foldout) posters (1 thru 4); one small poster; one "Visual Instruction" book, and one Stamp book (with four rows of stamps). Each set was enclosed in an envelope. Everything in the "Our America" series has turned up in sufficient quantities over the years to keep collectors satisfied. Educational material in general has never been the most sought after Coca-Cola items. In turn, low values reflect that lack of interest.

PES078.BS0
1. Cotton

PES079.BS0
2. Oil

PES080.BS0
3. Steel

PES081.BS0
4. Lumber

PES082.BS0
5. Electricity

PES083.BS0
6. Transportation

PES084.BS0
7. Motion Pictures

PES085.BS0
8. Glass

Complete "Our America" teacher's kit, 11 pieces, in original envelope . . . . . . . . . . . . . . . . . . . . . . . . . $50 Each
Individual pieces from "Our America" series:    Large posters . . . . . $10 Each    Small posters . . . . . $5 Each
Visual Instruction book . . . . . . . . . . . . . . . . . . . . . . . . . . . . . . . . . . . . . . . . . . . . . . . . . . . . . . . . . . $5 Each
Stamp book, with stamps . . . . . . . . . . . . . . . . . . . . . . . . . . . . . . . . . . . . . . . . . . . . . . . . . . . . . . $10 Each

PCH029.000
1969 . . . . . . $18

PCH028.000
1970s . . . . . . $10

PCH026.000
1953 . . . . . . . $45

PCH025.000
1950s-60s . . . . $30

PCH024.000
Early 1950s . . . . . $45

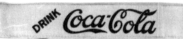

PCH034.000
c.1920s . . . . . . . . . . . . . . . . . . . $20
Soda jerk cap, cloth

PCH037.000
1950s . . . . . . . . . . . . . . . . . . . . . $12
Paper hat, Sprite Boy

PCH035.000
1940s . . . . . . . . . . . . . . . . . . . . $15
Soda jerk cap, cloth

PCH036.000
1950s . . . . . . . . . . . . . . . . . . . . $10
Visor cap, cardboard

PCH041.000
1959 . . . . . . . $30
Beanie

PCH042.000
1950 . . . . . . . $10
Baseball cap

PCH039.000
1940s . . . . . . $15
Beanie

PCPH040.000
1930s . . . . . . . . . . . . . $35
Baseball cap

PCH043.000
1930s . . . . . . . . . . $30
Beanie

PCH038.000
1960s . . . . . . . . $8
Visor cap, cardboard

PCH044.000
1960s-70s . . . . . . . $10
String tie

PCH045.000
1970s . . . . . . $10

PCH046.000
1960s . . . . . . . . . . . . . . . . $12
Western-type bow tie

PCH047.000
1950s . . . . $250

PCH048.000
1940s . . . . $60

PCH049.000
1960s . . . $40

PCH031.S01

1940s . . . . . . . . . . . . . . . . . . . $185

Baseball Shirt

PCH030.S00

1940s . . . . . . . . . . . . . . . . . . . $450

Baseball Uniform

PCH032.000

1950s . . . . . . . . . . . . . . . . . . . . . . $250

Sweater "Storer Nanigans". Note: The "Storer
Nanigans" were a small group of teenagers, who
toured and entertained around the world, (goodwill ambassadors of sorts). They were
sponsored in part by The Coca-Cola Company.
Each sweater was personalized.

PCH023.000

1950s . . . . . . . . . . . . . . $30

PCH033.000

1930s . . . . . . . . . . . . . . . . . . . . $175

Change apron

PCH021.000

1940s-50s . . . . . $35

PCH020.000

1920s . . . . . . . . . . . . . . . . . . . $110

PCH027.000

1960s . . . . . . . . . . . . . $30

PCH022.000

1950s . . . . . . . . . . $30

PCH050.000

1950s . . . . . . . . . . . . . . . . . . . . . . . . . $135

"Coke and Cowboys" boys shirt

PCH052.000

1970s . . . . . . . . . . . . $12

Shorts

PCH053.000

1970s . . . . . . . . . . . . . . $12

Pants

PCH004.S01

1953   20" x 22" . . . . . . . . . . . . . . $60

Kit Carson kerchief

PCH051.000

1948  32" x 34"  . . . . . . . . . . . . . . . . . $100

Scarf

PCH057.000

c.1939 . . . . . . . . . . . . . . $75

Driver's cap

PCH054.000

c.1939 . . . . . . . . . . . $125

Driver's vest, knit sleeves

PCH055.000

c.1939 . . . . . . . . . . . $65

Driver's shirt, winter

PCH056.000

c.1939 . . . . . . . . . . . . . . . . $75

Driver's coat, winter

# UNIFORM PATCHES

PCH061.000
1950s . . . . . . $15

PCH059.000

PCH060.000
1920s . . . . . . . . . . . . . . . . $65 Each

PCH069.000
1960s . . . . . . $7

PCH063.000
1950s . . . . . . . $8

PCH062.000
1950s . . . . . . $10

> Note: Early uniforms, patches,
> and drivers caps are very collectable,
> and often difficult to find.

PCH067.000
1960s . . . . . $6

PCH068.000
1960s . . . . . . $6

PCH070.000
1960s . . . . . . . $6

PCH058.000
1950s . . . . . . . . . . . . . . . . . . . . . . . . $50
Driver's shirt

PCH071.000
1960s . . . . . . . . . . $10

PCH072.000
1960s . . . . . . . . . . $10

PCH073.000
1960s . . . . . .$8

PCH074.000
1960s . . . . . . . $3

PCH075.000
1970s . . . . . . $4

PCH076.000
1976 . . . . . .$3

PCH064.000      PCH065.000      PCH066.000
1950s-1960s . . . . . . . . . . . . . . . . . . .$15 Each
Large back patches

PCH077.000
1970 . . . . .$5

— 537 —

PDE010.001

PDE010.002

1929-1930  7 1/4" x 9 1/4" . . . . . . . $135 Each
Window decals

## Come In-
## Have a Coke

PDE012.000

c.1948 . . . . . . . . . . . . . . . $85
Window sticker

PDE011.001

PDE011.002

PDE013.000

1941  12" . . . . . . . . . . . . . . . . . . . . . . $135
Decal

PDE026.000

1960s  . . . . . . . . . $30
Door sticker

1930s  3" x 11" . . . . . . . . . . . . . . $150 Each
Decals, two different examples

PDE025.000

1960s  . . . . . . . . . $25
Door sticker, foil

PDE022.000

1947  12" . . . . . . . . . . . . . . . . . . . . . .$45
Bottle decal, circular

PDE023.000

1950s  16" . . . . . . . . . . . . . . . . . . . . $30
Sticker

# DECALS AND STICKERS

PDE014.000
1950s   10" x 10" . . . . . . . . . $40
Decal

PDE015.000
1930s . . . . . . $30
Menu label

PDE017.000          PDE018.000
1950s-1960s  8" x 11" . . . . . . . . . $15 Each

PDE019.000
1950s . . . . . . . . . . . . . . . . . $7
Decal

PDE016.000
1950s . . . . . . . . . . . . . . . . . . . . . . . . . $25
Decal

PDE024.000
Early 1960s . . . . . . . $20
Door decal

PDE029.000
Early 1970s . . . . . . . . . . . . . $5
Tab, foil

PDE030.000
1970s . . . . . . . . . . . . . . . . . . . . . . . . . $2
Bumper sticker

PDE031.000
1970s . . . . . . . . . . . $1
Sticker

PDE021.000
1950s . . . . . . . . . . . . . . . . . . . . . $6
Coke "King Size" sticker

PDE020.000
1950s . . . . . . . . . . . . . . . . . . . . . $7
Decal

PDE028.000
1970s . . . . . . . . . . . . . . . . $8
Foil

PDE027.000
1960s . . . . . . . . . . . . . . . . . . . . $10
Foil

# PERIODICAL ADVERTISING

Periodical ads are surely the easiest, most interesting and least expensive area of Coca-Cola collecting. Because of the vast amount of periodical advertising used by The Coca-Cola Company, this section of the book only scratches the surface of the literally thousands and thousands of ads available. I've tried to only show early and interesting examples. Periodical advertising is broken down into three categories: newspaper ads, magazine ads, and miscellaneous ads. The last category covers a wide range of baseball and sports programs, theater and circus programs, journal and catalog ads, school programs, report cards, and lots of other items. Anything the company could buy advertising space on become an ad. Newspapers were the first form of periodical advertising done by The Coca-

Cola Company. John S. Pemberton placed an ad in the May 29, 1886 issue of the Atlanta Daily Journal and for well over 100 years, The Coca-Cola Company has never stopped using this most important form of advertising. Newspaper ads are also the hardest to find and most difficult to store and display.

Because most newspapers were just thrown away, most of the early unusual examples will never be seen. These early ads are so unusual because most layout and typesetting was done by the newspaper staff rather than an advertising agency. This makes for some interesting collecting, including mistakes and misspelling. Most of this advertising was done by local bottlers, some introducing plant openings, others celebrating the 4th of July and other holidays. In 1906, the D'arcy Company began to produce advertising copy for The Coca-Cola Company, and it was at that point that newspaper ads became more standardized and mistake free. Among the most popular and sought after newspaper ads is a series of baseball player ads produced for Coca-Cola by the D'arcy Company. These baseball player ads started around 1906 and continued into the mid-teens. Many of these ads show the familiar "circle arrow" and the great ballplayers of the day including: Ty Cobb, Napoleon Lajoie, Skeets Dunleavy, Brainy Collins, and many others. Some were testimonial-type ads, many of them are shown in this section, and collecting a complete set of them is truly a challenge.

Magazine ads are the most common of all periodical advertising simply because of the fact that so many magazines were saved. The Coca-Cola Company advertised in so many of America's most popular magazines such as the

Saturday Evening Post, Collier's, The Literary Digest, Liberty, Life, and many others. These ads are so abundant in fact that, in any stack of old magazines, one would have difficulty finding one without a Coke ad in it. The Messengle Advertising Agency and the D'arcy Company produced most of the early magazine ads which were done in one color, two colors, or full color. The most popular magazine ads belong to a series from *The Theater Magazine* and like the sports series, collecting the entire set has been a challenge for many a Coke collector. Probably the most common ads of all are the ads placed on the back covers of *National Geographic* magazine. Beginning in the 1930s, these ads graced the magazine right through the 1960s. While these ads are very easy to find—most for only a dollar or two—many collectors attempt to collect the complete set.

The miscellaneous area of ads can be found in other sections of this book. For example, ads placed by The Coca-Cola Company in baseball score cards and programs can be found in the sports section, while ads on the back of dime novels and in boy scout handbooks can be found in the book section.

Preserving and displaying ads is usually very easy. Most collectors keep their ads in plastic sleeves in three ring binders, and frame some of the more desirable examples. Newspaper ads require more care and should be matted on acid free board.

Collecting and cataloging Coca-Cola periodical advertising can be very rewarding, and viewing them is like reviewing the history of America for the last 110 years through the styles and fashions, the wars, the sports and the entertainment. Coca-Cola is part of America and Americana like baseball, apple pie and all of the things that we remember most in growing up. The best thing about collecting Coca-Cola ads is that you can create your own history book of this country without a large investment. To the collectors who say to me "I buy newer items because the old stuff is so expensive," I say "Why not collect ads? They are so challenging, fun, and inexpensive." The sources of ads are just about endless. Fellow collectors, antique publications, outdated book stores, box lots of magazines at auction, sports shows and any good antique show or flea market are just some of the many sources of ads. I hope everyone will enjoy viewing and collecting these ads as much as I do.

# NEWSPAPER AND MAGAZINE ADS

(N) Newspaper (M) Magazine

PPA053.000

1907 . . . . . . . . . . . . . $18

Black & white (M)

PPA054.000

1906 . . . . . . . . $25

Black & white (M)

PPA055.000

c.1905 . . . . . . . . . . . . . $25

Program (back cover)

PPA050.000

1885 . . . . . . . . $185

"Pemberton's French Wine
Coca" (N), Rare

PPA051.000

1905 . . . . . . . . . . . . . $20

Black & white (N)

PPA056.000

1906 . . . . . . . . . . . . . . . . . . . . . . . $150

*Scientific American*, full page, Rare (M)

PPA057.000

1907 . . . . . . . . . . . . . . . $18

Black & white (M)

PPA052.000

1907 . . . . . . . . . . . . . . . . $35

Black & white (M)

PPA058.000

1913 . . . . . . . . . . . . . . . . . . . . . . . . $175

4th of July, color newspaper ad, Rare

# MAGAZINE ADS

The following ads are color Massengale. (The Massengale Company was an advertising agency which produced many ads for The Coca-Cola Company.)

PPA059.000
1906 ....... $100

PPA060.000
1907 ......... $100

PPA061.000
1907 .......... $75

PPA062.000
1906 ........... $65

PPA063.000
1906 .......... $100

PPA064.000
1906 .......... $85

PPA065.000
1907 ............. $75

PPA066.000
1906 ........... $85

PPA067.000
1906 ......... $65

PPA068.000
1906 ......... $75

PPA069.000
1907 ........... $65

PPA070.000
1907 ......... $45

PPA071.000
1905 .................. $225

PPA072.000
1905 .................. $125

PPA073.000
1905 ................... $150

# MAGAZINE ADS
The following are black & white Massengale ads.

PPA074.000

1905 . . . . . . . . . . . . . . . . . $75

PPA075.00

1905 . . . . . . . . . . . . . $15

PPA076.000

1904 . . . . . . . . . . . . $20

PPA077.000

1905 . . . . . . . . . . . . . . $12

PPA078.000

1905 . . . . . . . . . . . $18

PPA079.000

1905 . . . . . . . . . $12

PPA080.000

1906 . . . . . . . . . . . $15

PPA081.000

1905 . . . . . . . . . . . . . $20

PPA082.000

1906 . . . . . . . . . $50

PPA083.000

1906 . . . . . . . . . . . . . . . . . $25

PPA084.000

1906 . . . . . . . . . . . . . . . . . $25

PPA085.000

1906 . . . . . . . . . . . . . . . . . $25

PPA086.000

1906 . . . . . . $50

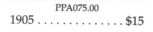

# MAGAZINE ADS
The following are black & white Massengale ads.

PPA087.000
1907 . . . . . . . . . . . . . . . . . . . . . $45

PPA088.000
1907 . . . . . . . . . . . . . . . . . . . . . $40

PPA090.000
1907 . . . . . . . . . . . $40

PPA089.000
1907 . . . . . . . . . . . . . $35

PPA092.000
1907 . . . . . . . . . . . $30

PPA093.000
1907 . . . . . . . . . . . . . . . $60

PPA094.000
1907 . . . . . . . . . . . $25

PPA091.000
1907 . . . . . . . . . . . $30

PPA095.000
1907 . . . . . . . . . $25

PPA096.000
1907 . . . . . . . . . $25

PPA097.000
1907 . . . . . . . . $60

PPA098.000
1907 . . . . . . . . . . . . . . . . . . . . . $35

PPA099.000
1907 . . . . . . $18

PPA100.000

1910   5" x 8" . . . . . . . . . . . . . . . $35

(N)

PPA101.000

1910   2 1/2" x 3"  . . . . . . $35

(N)

PPA102.000

1911   2 1/2" x 3" . . . $35

(N)

PPA103.000

1910   . . . . . . . . $30

(N)

PPA104.000

1907   5" x 7"  . . . . . . . . . . $15

Juanita, (M)

PPA105.000

1919   6" x 9" . . . . . . . . . . . . . . . . . . . . $20

Sepia, (M)

PPA106.000

1912   2 1/2" x 3 1/2"  . . $35

(N)

PPA107.000

1915   2 1/2" x 3"  . . . . . . $35

(N)

PPA108.000

1914   2 1/2" x 3 1/2"  . . $30

(N)

# MAGAZINE ADS

The following ads are color, front and back covers, from *Housewife, Household,* and *The People's Popular Monthly.*

PPA109.000

June 1910 . . . . . . . . . . . . . . . . . . $200

PPA110.000

August 1911 . . . . . . . . . . . . . . . $135

PPA111.000

August 1912 . . . . . . . . . . . . . . . . . . $135

PPA112.000

July 1913 . . . . . . . . . . . . . . . . . . . . . $150

PPA113.000

August 1913 . . . . . . . . . . . . . . . . . . . $135

PPA114.000

June 1914 . . . . . . . . . . . . . . . . . . $145

PPA115.000

July 1914 . . . . . . . . . . . . . . . . . . . $135

PPA116.000

May 1915 . . . . . . . . . . . . . . . . . $135

PPA117.000

July 1916 . . . . . . . . . . . . . . . . . . $135

PPA118.000

July 1917 . . . . . . . . . . . . . . . . . . $135

# MAGAZINE ADS
The following ads are two color or full color.

PPA128.000

1907 . . . . . . . . . . . . . $25

PPA129.000

1912 . . . . . . . . . . . . . . $12

PPA130.000

1920 . . . . . . . . . . . . . $20

PPA131.000

1912 . . . . . . . . . . . $18

PPA132.000

1914 . . . . . . . . . . . . . $15

PPA133.000

1915 . . . . . . . . . . . . . $15

PPA134.000

1915 . . . . . . . . . . . . $15

PPA135.000

1917 . . . . . . . . . . . $10

PPA136.000

1917 . . . . . . . . . . . $12

PPA137.000

1915 . . . . . . . . . . . $15

PPA138.000

1916 . . . . . . . . . . . . . $15

PPA139.000

1916 . . . . . . . . . . . . . $15

PPA140.000

1917 . . . . . . . . . . . . . $12

PPA141.000

1917 . . . . . . . . . . . . . $12

PPA142.000

1915 . . . . . . . . . . . . . $20

PPA143.000

1915 . . . . . . . . . . . . . $15

PPA144.000

1909 . . . . . . . . . . . . . . . . . . . . . $20

Two color

PPA145.000

May 1913 . . . . . . . . . . . . . . . . $35

*Bulletin of Pharmacy*, B&W

PPA146.000

1912 . . . . . . . . . . . . . . . . . . . . . $15

Two color

PPA147.000

June 1913 . . . . . . . . . . . . . . $30

*Bulletin of Pharmacy*, B&W

PPA148.000

June 1909 . . . . . . . . . . . . . . . . $35

*Bulletin of Pharmacy*, B&W

PPA149.000

1907 . . . . . . . . . . . . . . . . . . . . $20

Black & white

PPA150.000

1909 . . . . . . . . . . . . . . . . . . . . . $20

Two color

PPA151.000

1909 . . . . . . . . . . . . . . . . . . . . $20

Full color

PPA152.000

1908 . . . . . . . . . . . . . . . . . . . .$18

Two color

# MAGAZINE ADS
The following ads are two color or full color

PPA162.000

1912 . . . . . . . . . . $35

PPA163.000

1916 . . . . . . . . . . $35

PPA164.000

1909 . . . . . . . . . . $45

PPA165.000

1908 . . . . . . . . . . $25

PPA166.000

1914 . . . . . . . . . . $35

PPA167.000

1912 . . . . . . . . . . $20

PPA168.000

1908 . . . . . . . . . . $35

PPA169.000

1908 . . . . . . . . . . $25

PPA170.000

1914 . . . . . . . . . . $15

PPA171.000

1914 . . . . . . . . . . $15

PPA172.000

1913 . . . . . . . . . . $15

PPA173.000

1914 . . . . . . . . . . $15

PPA174.000

1908 . . . . . . . . . . $15

PPA175.000

1914 . . . . . . . . . . $15

PPA176.000

1913 . . . . . . . . . . $15

PPA177.000

1909 . . . . . . . . . . $25

# MAGAZINE ADS

The following are two color, split column ads from *Mother's Magazine*.

PPA178.000

1913 . . . . . . . . . . . . . . . . . . . . . . . . . . . $15

PPA179.000

May 1915 . . . . . . . . . . . . . $18

PPA180.000

May 1914 . . . . . . . . . . . . . . $18

PPA181.000

1913 . . . . . . . . . . . . . . . . . $18

PPA182.000

June 1915 . . . . . . . . . . . . . $18

PPA183.000

June 1913 . . . . . . . . . . . . . . . . . . . . . $18

PPA184.000

June 1914 . . . . . . . . . . . . $18

PPA185.000

July 1915 . . . . . . . . . . . . $18

PPA186.000

May 1916 . . . . . . . . . . . . $18

PPA187.000

1912 . . . . . . . . . . . . . . . . . . . . . . . . . . . $15

Black & white

PPA188.000

1909 . . . . . . . . . . . . . . . . . . . . . . $18

Two color

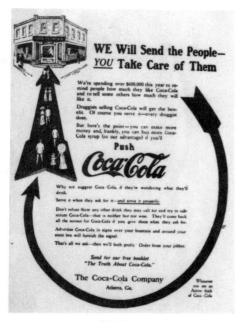

PPA189.000

1908 . . . . . . . . . . . . . . . . . . . . . . . . . $25

Black & white

PPA190.000

1912 . . . . . . . . . . . .$15

Black & white

PPA191.000

1914 . . . . . . . . . . . . . . . . . . . $18

Black & white

PPA192.000

1913 . . . . . . . . . . . . . . . $20

Black & white

PPA193.000

1913 . . . . . . . . . . . $20

Two color

PPA194.000

1913 . . . . . . . . . . . . . $20

Two color

PPA195.000

1913 . . . . . . . . . . . . $25

Full color

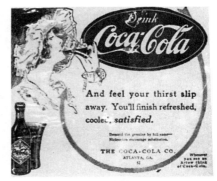

PPA196.000

1914 . . . . . . . . . . . . $15

Chicago

PPA197.000

1914 . . . . . . . . . . $15

Cleveland

PPA198.000

1914 . . . . . . . . . . . . . . $15

Richmond

PPA199.000

1914 . . . . . . . . . . . . . . . . . . . . . . . $18

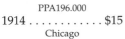

PPA200.000

1908 . . . . . . . . . . . . . . . . . . . . . . . . . $20

PPA201.000

1913 . . . . . . . . . . . . $20

PPA202.000

1914 . . . . . . . . . . . . . . . . . . . . . $15

PPA203.000

1910 . . . . . . . . $15

PPA204.000

1913 . . . . . . . . . . $15

PPA205.000

1914 . . . . . . . . . . . . . $15

PPA206.000

1913 . . . . . . . . . . $15

# MAGAZINE ADS
The following are two color and black & white baseball player ads from *American Boy* magazine.

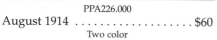

PPA226.000
August 1914 . . . . . . . . . . . . . . . . . . $60
Two color

PPA228.000
July 1914 . . . . $25

PPA229.000
June 1914 . . . $25

PPA227.000
1916 . . . . . . . . . . . . . . . . . . . . . $30
Two color

PPA230.000
May 1914 . . . $25

PPA231.000
Sept. 1914 . . . . $25

PPA232.000
Sept. 1916 . . . $25

PPA233.000
June 1916 . . . $25

PPA234.000
May 1916 . . . $25

PPA235.000
July 1916 . . . $25

# NEWSPAPER ADS
The following are black & white newspaper ads.

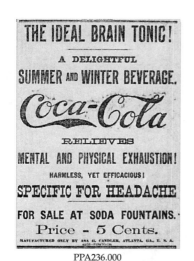

PPA236.000
1891  4 1/2" x 6"  . . . . . . $275
Pre-1900 ads are rare

PPA237.000
1907 . . . . . . . . . . . . . . . . . . . . . . . . . $30

PPA240.000
1907 . . . . . . . . . . . $35

PPA238.000
1906 . . . . . . . . . . . . . . . . . . . . . . . $30

PPA239.000
1906 . . . . . . . . . . . . . . . . . . . . . . . . . $20

PPA241.000
1915  11" x 11"  . . . . . . . . . . . . . . . . $35

PPA242.000
1910 . . . . . . . . . . . . . . . . . . . . . . . $20

PPA243.000
1910  7" x 9"  . . . . . . . . . . . $65

PPA244.000
1903  2" x 4"  . . . . . . $35

PPA245.000
1906 . . . . . . . . . . . . . . . . . . . . . . . $30

PPA246.000
1904 . . . . . . . . . . . . . . . . . . . . . . . $30

# NEWSPAPER ADS
The following are black & white newspaper ads.

PPA247.000

1906 . . . . . . . . . . . . . . . . . . . . $20

PPA248.000

1906 . . . . . . . . . . . . . . . $18

PPA249.000

1906 . . . . . . . . . . . . . . . . . . . . . . . $20

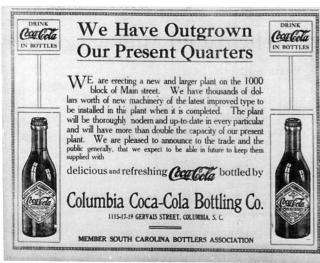

PPA250.000

1907  10" x 15" . . . . . . . . . . . . . . . . . $30

PPA251.000

1907  10" x 15" . . . . . . . . . . . . . . . . . $30

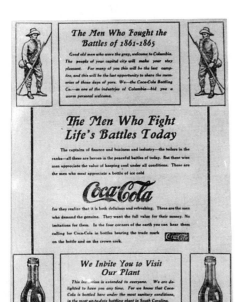

PPA254.000

1915  9" x 13" . . . . . . . . . . . . . . . . . $150

"Reunion of Confederate Soldiers", Rare

PPA252.000

1906 . . . . . . . . . . . . . . . . . $20

PPA255.000

1911 . . . . . . . . . . $20

PPA253.000

1915 . . . . . . . . . . . . . . . $25

PPA256.000

1915 . . . . . . . . . . . . . . . $12

Autocar trucks

# NEWSPAPER ADS

The following black & white baseball player ads are approx. 5" x 7". Take note that generally newspaper ads, because of brittleness and quality of printing, are not worth as much as magazine ads.

PPA257.000

1911 . . . . . . . . . . . . . . . . . . . . . . . $20

Hugh Jennings, Tigers

PPA258.000

1911 . . . . . . . . . . . . . . . . . . . . . . . $20

Hans Wagner, Pittsburgh Pirates

PPA259.000

1910 . . . . . . . . . . . . . . . . . . . . . . . $20

George Mullin, Detroit

PPA260.000

1911 . . . . . . . . . . . . . . . . . . . . . . . $20

Fred Merkle

PPA261.000

1910 . . . . . . . . . . . . . . . . . . . . . . . $20

George Gibson, Pittsburgh Nationals

PPA262.000

1910 . . . . . . . . . . . . . . . . . . . . . . . $20

Jack O'Connor, Mgr., St. Louis Americans

PPA263.000

1910 . . . . . . . . . . . . . . . . . . . . . . . $20

Frank Chance, Cubs

PPA264.000

1911 . . . . . . . . . . . . . . . . . . . . . . . $20

Del Howard, Louisville

PPA265.000

1910 . . . . . . . . . . . . . . . . . . . . . . . $20

Konetchy, St. Louis Cardinals

PPA266.000

1914 . . . . . . . . . . . . . . . . . . . . . . . $20

John Daubert, Brooklyn

PPA267.000

1914 . . . . . . . . . . . . . . . . . . . . . . . $20

John J. Evers, Boston Braves

PPA268.000

1906 . . . . . . . . . . . . . . . . . . . . . . . $20

Lajoie, Cleveland

# NEWSPAPER ADS
The following black and white baseball player ads are approximately 5" x 7".

PPA269.000

1911 . . . . . . . . . . . . . . . . . . . . . . . $20

Charlie Dooin

PPA270.000

1911 . . . . . . . . . . . . . . . . . . . . . . $20

Hugh Jennings

PPA271.000

1910 . . . . . . . . . . . . . . . . . . . . . . $20

Fred Merkle

PPA272.000

1914 . . . . . . . . . . . . . . . . . . . . . . . $20

J. J. Callahan, Chicago White Sox

PPA274.000

1913 . . . . . . . . . . . . . . . . . . . . . . $20

Walter Johnson, Washington

PPA275.000

1915 . . . . . . . . . . . . . . . . . . . . . . .$20

Rabbit Maranville

PPA273.000

1914 . . . . . . . . . . . . . . . . . . . . . . $20

H.F. Sallee "The Coca-Cola Kid", St. Louis

PPA276.000

1910 . . . . . . . . . . . . . . . . . . . . . . $20

Owen Bush

PPA277.000

1911 . . . . . . . . . . . . . . . . . . . . . . $20

Owen Bush

PPA278.000

1907 . . . . . . . . . . . . . . . . . . . . . . $20

Lajoie, Cleveland

# NEWSPAPER ADS

The following black & white baseball player ads are approx. 5" x 7". Take note that generally newspaper ads, because of brittleness and quality of printing, are not worth as much as magazine ads.

PPA291.000

1913 . . . . . . . . . . $20

Callahan, White Sox

PPA292.000

1916 . . . . . . . . . . . . $20

Fred Luderus, Philadelphia A's

PPA293.000

1913 . . . . . . . . . . . . $20

"Slim" Sallee, Cardinals

PPA294.000

1915 . . . . . . . . . . $20

"Rabbit" Maranville, Boston Braves

PPA295.000

1916 . . . . . . . . . . . . $20

Grover Cleveland Alexander, Philadelphia Nationals

PPA296.000

1916 . . . . . . . . . . . . $20

Joe Tinker, Cubs

PPA297.000

1916 . . . . . . . . . . $20

Larry Doyle, Cubs

PPA298.000

1909 . . . . . . . . . . . . $25

Connie Mack, Philadelphia A's

PPA299.000

1916 . . . . . . . . . . . . $20

Heine Zimmerman, Cubs

PPA300.000

1915 . . . . . . . . . . . . . . $20

Fireball Johnson, Washington. Nationals

PPA301.000

1916 . . . . . . . . . . . . $20

Fielder Jones Browns

PPA302.000

1916 . . . . . . . . . . $20

Carl Weilman, St. Louis Browns

# NEWSPAPER ADS

The following black and white baseball player ads are approximately 5" x 7".

PPA279.000

1913 . . . . . . . . . . . . . $20

Walter Johnson, Washington Nationals

PPA280.000

1912 . . . . . . . . . . . . . $20

George Stovall, St. Louis Browns

PPA281.000

1913 . . . . . . . . . . . . . $20

Miller Huggins, Cardinals

PPA282.000

1915 . . . . . . . . . . . . . $20

Eddie Collins, White Sox

PPA283.000

1916 . . . . . . . . . . . . . $20

Prince Henry Schaefer, NY Americans

PPS284.000

1913 . . . . . . . . . . . . . $20

"Koney" Konetchy, Cardinals

PPA285.000

1913 . . . . . . . . . . . . . $20

Slim Sallee, St. Louis Cardinals

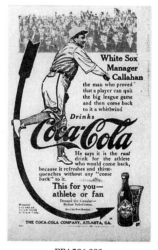

PPA286.000

1914 . . . . . . . . . . . . . $20

Callahan, White Sox

PPA287.000

1912 . . . . . . . . . . . . . $20

Charlie Dooin, Phillies

PPA 288.000

1916 . . . . . . . . . . . $20

Del Pratt, St. Louis Browns

PPA289.000

1912 . . . . . . . . . . . $20

Owen Bush

PPA290.000

1913 . . . . . . . . . . . $20

Joe Tinker, Cincinnati Reds

# NEWSPAPER ADS

The following black & white baseball player ads are approx. 5" x 7". Take note that generally newspaper ads, because of brittleness and quality of printing, are not worth as much as magazine ads.

PPA303.000
1910 . . . . . . . . . . . . . . $20
Johnny Evers, Cubs

PPA304.000
1912 . . . . . . . . . . . $20
Konetchy, St. Louis Cards.

PPA305.000
1912 . . . . . . . . . . . . . $20
Brainy Collins, Philadelphia A's

PPA306.000
1909 . . . . . . . . . . . . . $20
Harry David, Philadelphia A's

PPA307.000
1910 . . . . . . . . . . . . . . . . $35
Skeets Dunleavy, Louisville

PPA308.000
1911 9" x 11" . . . . . . . . . . . . . . . $40
Dell Howard, Louisville

PPA309.000
1915 . . . . . . . . . . . . . . . . . . $25
Cozy Dolan, St. Louis Browns

PPA310.000
1906 . . . . . . . . . . . . . . . . . . . . $20
"Athletes" coupon ad

PPA311.000
1914 . . . . . . . . . . . . . . . . . . $20
Walter Johnson, Washington Senators

PPA312.000
1914 . . . . . . . . . . . . . . . . . . . . . $20
Collins, Philadelphia A's

# NEWSPAPER ADS

The following are full-page (16" x 22") full-color newspaper ads. Color newspaper ads are somewhat rare.

PPA341.000

1931 . . . . . . . . . . . . . . . . . . $40

PPA342.000

1933 . . . . . . . . . . . . . . . . . . $50

Joan Crawford

PPA343.000

1931 . . . . . . . . . . . . . . . . . . $20

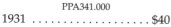

PPA344.000

1936 . . . . . . . . . . . . . . . . . . $35

PPA345.000

1936 . . . . . . . . . . . . . . . . . . $35

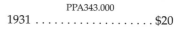
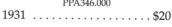

PPA346.000

1931 . . . . . . . . . . . . . . . . . . $20

PPA347.000

1935 . . . . . . . . . . . . . . . . . . $30

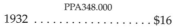

PPA348.000

1932 . . . . . . . . . . . . . . . . . . $16

PPA349.000

1931 . . . . . . . . . . . . . . . . . . $18

# RECENT, REPRODUCTION, AND FANTASY

This section is the only part of this book that I truly dislike, and it is a section that I wish I did not have to include. It's also the most incomplete section in the book; incomplete because it's virtually impossible to keep up with all the recent, reproduction, phony, or misrepresented junk that is often attempted to be passed off as authentic, old, and original Coca-Cola advertising. At this point, let me make it perfectly clear that I have absolutely no problem with pieces that are produced by, or for, The Coca-Cola Company with their permission, and that are so marked or dated so the buyer knows without any doubt that he or she is buying a new item and not an old one. My problem is with pieces that are produced—sometimes very innocently by the way—that are not marked or dated, attempting to make these pieces look old. Manufacturers of these items create big problems, especially with new collectors who are anxious to find a great piece. These rip-off items go on forever, and the longer they are around the harder it is to convince dealers and collectors that they are not old. The "Nude Nun" belt buckle is a perfect example of this. This is an item that has been around for almost as long as organized Coke collecting, and no matter how often this piece is shown as a fantasy item, there are people who insist that they have the original. There are actually some pieces that have been around so long that they have become legitimate to many.

The number of Coca-Cola collectors grows daily, and as this group gets larger there is more and more money being spent on Coca-Cola items. This growth, along with the belief that anything with the Coca-Cola logo on it has value, brings out both the best and worst in people. The best will search out and buy legitimate original Coca-Cola items to collect or resell at a profit—in some cases to help finance their own collection. The worst will attempt to rip-off people by creating or reproducing items to sell as old. Unfortunately, even if these items were not produced with that intent, it usually ends up that they are resold by others for a quick buck.

I really wish that in this section I could show every new, repro, and fantasy item produced, but it's just not possible. In fact there is so much of this stuff around that I don't even scratch the surface. I am able, however, to give some basic information that may help identify many of these items. Besides the pieces shown in this section, I've indicated which trays have been reproduced. There are also some other things to watch out for. The first is "decals." Over the past few years, decals featuring the Coca-Cola logo, hand with bottle, and the Sprite boy with bottle, have been produced in various sizes. These decals are being put on anything and everything from trash cans, wagons, ice boxes, coolers, cash registers, clocks—you name it and someone will smack a decal on it. These decals are inexpensive and readily available, so be very careful of "decaled" items.

Cast-iron toys are another group of items you should be aware of. You will find a couple of examples of these in this section, but many others have been produced. I know of no original cast-iron Coca-Cola toy. Speaking of cast iron, there is also a recent Taiwan import, which is a bottle-shaped doorpull made of cast iron. I have seen some of them painted or rusted-over to look older.

Belt buckles and metal stamped tokens and letter openers are another group of items you should be very wary of. With all the examples shown, there are still many others. There are also some "warning words" which appear on many of these items which you should be aware of. Creators of these pieces, in an effort to further enhance them, have used a number of words or phrases which you will not find on old, original Coca-Cola items. "Tiffany Studios," "1904 Trans Pan Expo," "St. Louis Worlds Fair 1904," "Worlds Fair," "Pan American Exposition 1915" are just a few of these. People have actually said to me, "The piece has to be good because it is stamped 'Tiffany Studios'." The manufacturers of this stuff will put anything on these items to make the unsuspecting believe it's original.

It is very important to understand the difference between the three types of items that you will find in this section: Recent, Reproduction, and Fantasy. First, a recent item is something that has been produced from the early 1970s to the present, such as special event items, anniversary, or commemorative items. A 1976 Olympic tray is a good example of a recent item. I don't consider these pieces objectionable because they usually don't fool anyone, but they are certainly not a good investment. Next comes a reproduction item which very simply is a copy of an original Coca-Cola item—in some cases an exact copy, while others have slight differences, enabling us to (hopefully) detect the original from the copy. The 1914 "Betty" calendar top is a good example of a "reproduction." These items are especially objectionable to me when they are not easily identified as reproductions. Finally, a fantasy item is an item that is actually created, with no original piece just like it. These pieces are made usually with only one thing in mind: that is, to deceive the collector. Remember, items that are produced with the approval of The Coca-Cola Company and are so marked are the exception to all these rules. Coca-Cola is collecting memorabilia of The Coca-Cola Company!!!! The key is: know what you are buying.

Recent, Repro, and Fantasy items can be found everywhere; at antique shows, shops, and through antique publications. Often dealers are not aware that they are selling a phony. But, without a doubt, the biggest dumping ground for this material are the auction houses. It is easy, anonymous, and there is always the possibility that these items can go for many times the normal selling price. Many auctioneers will allow these items to go through their sale with a "play dumb" attitude. When questioned, the stock line is usually: "I don't know anything, I just sell it." The decaled items thrive in auctions and sometimes the auctioneer will attempt to sell them by calling them "decorator items." Please be extra careful at auctions.

It is unfortunate that this type of material has infested The Coca-Cola collecting market. But keep in mind that it is found in all other areas of collecting and it is your responsibility as a collector to make yourself and others aware of these items. Point them out to antique dealers and remind auctioneers that they really shouldn't sell this type of material. And, for the newer collectors, if you haven't been taken for a large amount of money, don't get too upset over getting stuck with one of these items—chalk it up to experience, learn from your mistakes, be extra careful especially with the obvious items, and tell others so they don't get ripped-off. Over the years, I've heard of many horror stories about people paying hundreds of dollars for items that are basically worthless. It is very upsetting, but with the proper information, you won't suffer from the same experience.

# FANTASY AND REPRODUCTION

In 1974, The Coca-Cola Company produced a multiple page calendar that featured 1920s calendar girls. This was a seven-image calendar which included Santa Clause on the December 1973 cover sheet. The piece was well done, colorful and soon became a favorite among the group of recently produced items. Unfortunately, it has also become a favorite among the "Rip-Off" artists. Thankfully, The Coca-Cola Company has made enough alterations to the original art to make detection easy. Never-the-less hundreds of collectors get stuck every year with this revised art. Below you will find photos of the complete calendar; take note of the differences between them and the orig-inal art. This artwork has been misused. Unscrupulous dealers will frame individual pages, cutting off the 1974 calendar portion. The use of old frames, rusty nails, and sometimes old newspaper backing finish off the scam. The second problem is that most, if not all, of these images have been reproduced in various sizes, some made into repro calendars, larger posters, etc. Hopefully this information will save some of you. Note: This 1974 calendar (shown) has not been reproduced. Individual pages, however, are being passed off as old, and the art itself has been reproduced. Beware!

Cover sheet of 1974 calendar showing December 1973 page.

Artwork of 1927 calendar. Notice different border from original and the model is facing right, instead of left as on the original.

Artwork of 1924 calendar. Notice ornate border that does not appear on original, and the model is facing right instead of left as on the original.

Artwork of 1925 calendar. Notice ornate border that does not appear on the original.

Artwork of 1928 calendar. The ornate border on this art is the same as original; however the model is facing right instead of left as on the original.

Artwork of 1923 calendar. Notice bottom of art has been cropped and ornate border does not appear on the original.

Artwork of 1921 calendar. Notice bottom of art has been cut off just below the knee. Also, ornate border does not appear on the original.

PRE046.000

Value . . . . . . . . Worthless

Reproduction 1928 calendar. This art was copied from the 1974 calendar. Notice the model facing right instead of left, and phony pad. Also notice bogus brown aging marks on the edge.

# FANTASY AND REPRODUCTION

In 1991, The Coca-Cola Company produced a re-issue of the 1935 (Normal Rockwell Art) calendar. 1935 and 1991 are identical; the idea and the finished products are fine; however, the results have proven disastrous to collectors. The top two sheets of this new calendar explained that it is a reproduction, however, after they were removed the calendar appears to be an exact copy. Since then the calendar has been reproduced again, fortunately from the reproduction and not an original. This second repro was done illegally, by the way. Some of the second reproductions have grommet holes at top instead of a metal strip, others have metal strips. Because of the problems with this calendar, I've decided to show both the original and the reproduction side-by-side, showing the differences so you will never be fooled again.

REPRODUCTION          ORIGINAL

PRE010.000

PCA059.000

Two top sheets of first reproduction from The Coca-Cola Company. The second reproduction did not have these.

Two top sheets of original
1. Poem cover sheet
2. December 1934

# FANTASY AND REPRODUCTION

PRE011.000
Note: Model facing right

← **REPRODUCTIONS** →

1. SIZE: 11" x 21 ¹/₂" (including pad)

2. PAD: White paper with black lettering
(No mention of Coca-Cola on any sheet)

3. HANGER: Metal strip and hanger

4. BORDER: Ornate orange and brown border
around print with logo at bottom

5. QUALITY: Printing is fuzzy/dull with
muted colors

6. VALUE: Worthless

PRE012.000

---

Note: **WARNING** It is illegal to produce
anything with the Coca-Cola logo, or any
artwork belonging to The Coca-Cola Company,
without written permission, or being
licensed by the company.

---

PCA048.000
1924—Note: Model facing left

← **ORIGINALS** →

1. SIZE: 12" x 24" (including pad)

2. PAD: Reverse brown printing with white
lettering. (Coca-Cola mentioned on pad)

3. HANGER: Metal strip and hanger.

4. BORDER: Small white border around print.
No logo at bottom

5. QUALITY: Printing is sharp with bright colors

$1,500 ← VALUE → $1,200

PCA049.000

## 1914 CALENDAR TOP

ORIGINAL

PCA035.P01

Value . . . . . . . . . . . .$350 Top only
1. Size: 13" x 27"
2. Printed on a textured paper (because of the texture many people have mistakenly confused it with canvas)
3. Printed at bottom: at left—"Copyright the Coca-Cola Co." in center—"BETTY"

REPRODUCTION

PRE013.000

Value: . . . . . . . . . . . . . . . . . . . .$5
1. Size: 11 1/4" x 23 3/4"
2. Printed on a smooth finish ivory heavy paper
3. No printing at bottom
4. Printed stain (obviously on original that this was photographed from) that covers the bottom right-hand corner. (see photo right)
5. Printed crease across bottom

REPRODUCTION

*Note: Often times when reproducing something ,the reproduction is reduced in size, (as is the 1914 calendar top by 87%) to sharpen up the quality. In this case, as in most cases, it didn't work. The quality is poor; however, it's very difficult to tell that unless you've seen the original. I know of many cases of this reproduction selling for hundreds of dollars. When it first appeared in the marketplace in the mid-1970s, they sold for $2 each. I have given this piece a value of $5 very hesitantly as I do consider this piece worthless.*

PFA007.000

c.1970s  9 1/8" x 13 3/4" . . . . . Worthless
Fantasy (heavy paper) sign, Copy in lower left: "Copyright 1911 Coca-Cola Atlanta, GA" Copy in lower right: "Printed in U.S.A." Note: This piece came on the market at the same time as the repro "BETTY" calendar top. I suspect it was done by the same person. They originally sold for $2. I consider this piece worthless.

PFA005.000

1980s . . . . . . . . . . . . . $2
Fantasy metal coaster

PFA006.000

1980s 3/4" . . . . . . . . . $3
Change purse

# FANTASY AND REPRODUCTION

### ORIGINAL

PTR043.000

1934 . . . . . . . . . . . . . . . . . . . . $1,000
  1. Back of tray black/very dark green
  2. Gold trim—metallic and bright gold
  3. Printing sharp and clear

### REPRODUCTION

1980s . . . . . . . . . . . . . . . . . . . . . $5
  1. Back of tray white, ivory, light gray, red
     (four different versions)
  2. Gold trim—flat, greenish gold
  3. Printing fuzzy and blotchy

PRE014.000

### ORIGINAL

PTC005.P01

Value: . . . . . . . . . . . . . . . . $400  Box only
  1. No. 215 Metalcraft (above "Bottling Truck")
  2. "Electric Headlights" (listed at left)
  3. "Demountable, Goodrich Silvertown Rubber
     Wheels" (listed at left)

### REPRODUCTION

PRE015.000

Value: . . . . . . . . . . . . . . . . $10 Box only
  1. Metalcraft only (above "Bottling Truck")
  2.. No mention of "Electric Headlights" (even
     though picture shows truck with headlights)
  3. No mention of "Rubber Wheels" (even though
     picture shows truck with rubber wheels)

PCL004.S01

1953  20" x 22"  . . . . . . . . . . . . . . . . $60
Original, red, white, and green

PRE016.000

1990  14" x 14 1/2"  . . . . . Worthless
Reproduction, White and red
(have seen other colors)

### ORIGINAL          REPRODUCTION

PTY101.000                PRE017.000

1920s . . . . . . $150    1990 . . . . . . . . . . $5
Original, yellow with      Reproduction, red with
red lettering              white or yellow lettering
Whiste, wood               Whistle, wood

# TRAYS (RECENT, REPRO, & FANTASY)

PRE018.000

1980s . . . . . . . . . . . . . . . . . . . . $5 Each

PFA008.000

PFA009.000

1973 . . . . . . . . $35

PFA010.000

1974 . . . . . . . . $35

PFA011.001

1969 . . . . . . . . $85

PFA011.002

1975 . . . . . . . . . $12

PFA012.000

1980s . . . . . . . . $12

PFA013.000

1980s . . . . . . . . $25

PFA014.000

1980s . . . . . . . . $10

PFA015.000

1980s . . . . . . . $10

PFA016.000

1978 . . . . . . . . $100

PFA017.000

1981 . . . . . . . . . . $8

PFA018.000

1982 . . . . . . . . $8

PFA019.000

PFA020.000

1980s . . . . . . . . . . . . . . . . . . $25 Each

PFA021.000

PFA022.000

1980s . . . . . . . . . . . . . . . . . . . . . $6 Each

PFA023.000

1975 . . . . . . . . . . . . . $15

PFA024.001

1970s . . . . . . . . . . . . . . $18

PFA025.000

1980s . . . . . . . . . . . $10

PFA026.000

1980s . . . . . . . . . $15

PFA027.000

1975 . . . . . . . . . $8

PFA028.000

1976 . . . . . . . . . . $8

PFA029.000

PFA030.000

PFA031.000

PFA032.000

1980s . . . . . . . . . . . . . . . . . . . . . . . . . . . . . . . . . . . . . $2 Each

Fantasy, made in Taiwan

1986 . . . . . . . . . . . $6

PRE019.000

1970s-80s . . . . . . . $10

Repro

PFA033.000

1980s . . . . . . . . . . . . $5

PFA034.000

PFA035.000

1980s . . . . . . . . . . . . . . . . . . . . . . $5 Each

"The Romance of Coca-Cola", Fantasy
unauthorized

PRE020.000

1978 . . . . . . . . . . $10

Repro

PFA036.000

1983 . . . . . . . . . . . $5

PFA037.000

1980s . . . . . . . $20

Plastic tray and coasters

PFA038.000

1979 . . . . . . . . $6

PFA039.000

1977 . . . . . . . . . . $35

PFA040.000

1976 . . . . . . . . . . $6

PFA041.000

1982 . . . . . . . . . . $8

PAN011.000

1977 . . . . . . . . . . . . . . . . . . . . . . . . . . . . $50

75th Anniversary tray in box

PFA042.001

PFA042.000

PFA043.000

PFA044.000

1980s . . . . . . . . . . . . . . . . . . . . . . . . . . . . . . . . . . . . . . . . . . . $8 Each

Oval tray (four different versions)

# FANTASY AND REPRODUCTION

ORIGINAL

PTR052.000

1950-1952 ........... $75

1. Border (rim): Silver
2. Under Logo: Reg. U.S. Pat. Off.
3. Back (color): Dark gray
4. Under logo on bottle: "RK Registered"
5. Rim: Nothing printed on rim

REPRODUCTION

PRE021.000

1980s ................... $5

1. Border (rim): White
2. Under Logo: REG.D TRADEMARK
3. Back (color): Gold or mustard yellow
4. Under logo on bottle: Nothing legible
5. Rim: printed on left side—"1943 Girl with Wind in her Hair/The design of this tray is for memorabilia purposes, taken from a 1943 advertisement." "Coca-Cola is the registered trademark of The Coca-Cola Company".

PRE022.000

1970s 12" dia ................. $100
Victorian Girl, maroon or dark red rim and back, 1 1/4" deep lip

PRE023.000

4 1/4" x 8 1/4" ...Worthless
Repro bottle bag, red on white

PRE024.00

Value ............. Worthless
Tell City bookmark, recent reproduction
Original: Sharp and Clear
Repro: Fuzzy with muted colors

PFA045.000

1980s-90s .................... $1

PFA046.000

1970s ......................... $50
Truck, wood, in box

PFA047.000

1970s ............. $50
Truck, wood/tin, in box

PRE025.000

1980s-90s ........ $100
Repro Marx truck, plastic, logos are stickers, with marked box

— 570 —

# TRAYS (RECENT, REPRO, & FANTASY)

PCS343.000

1970s ...... $25 Each

Signs, "Tray Offer", cardboard, showing repro and fantasy trays. Note: These two signs are not reproductions

PCS380.000

PTR024.000

1913 ............... $950

1. "Trademark Registered" in tail of "C"
2. Large "5" on glass

PRE026.000

1970s ................. $25

1. "Reg. U.S. Pat. Off" under logo
2. "Drink Coca-Cola" logo on glass

PRE028.000

1970s ........... $15

1916 reproduction
(reg U.S. Pat Off. under logo)

ORIGINAL

PTR032.000

1925 ................... $575

1. "Trademark Registered" in tail of "C"
2. No bottle in lower right-hand corner

REPRODUCTION

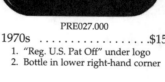

PRE027.000

1970s ................. $15

1. "Reg. U.S. Pat Off" under logo
2. Bottle in lower right-hand corner

PFA048.000

1970s ............. $10

Fantasy

PFA049.000

1969 ........... $35

Fantasy

PFA050.000

1970s ........... $10

Fantasy

PRE029.000

1970s ............. $20

1914 reproduction,
(reg. U.S. Pat. Off. under logo)

PRE018.001

1971 .......... $20

Repro flat

# FANTASY AND REPRODUCTION

ORIGINAL

REPRODUCTION

PRE048.000

1990s Repro Buddy Lee doll, molded, 11 $^{1}/_{2}$" tall. Plain
white material. Note soda jerk type hat instead of billed
cap unauthorized. No value as a Coca-Cola item
Selling for $250 to $350

PTY133.001

1950s 12 $^{1}/_{2}$" tall . . . . . . . $1,000
Buddy Lee doll, plastic. "Buddy Lee"
embossed on back between shoulders.
Green striped material. Lee label
sewn on waistband

PFA190.000

Value . . . . . . . . . . . . . . . . . . . . . . . . .$2.
Horse-drawn delivery wagon, cast-iron, Fantasy

*Note: It is sometimes difficult for
collectors to understand that these cast iron
toys are not old. Rusting, wear, and
that aged look will fool many into believing
they have age. There is no known original
Coca-Cola cast-iron toy.*

PFA191.000

Value . . . . . . . . . . . . . . . . . . . . . . . . .$10
Pocket watch, Fantasy , one of many versions, watch
may be old, but phony Coke faces replace original face

# FANTASY AND REPRODUCTION

PFA061.000

Value . . . . . . . . . . . . . . . . .$10-$25
Recent pocket watch, (new face on old
watch). This is a Fantasy item that's worth
nothing as a Coca-Cola item, but rather
what the watch is worth

PFA064.000

Value . . . . . . . . . . . . . . . .$1
Recent "Sprite Boy" sewing kit

PFA062.000          PFA063.000

Value . . . . . . . . .Less than $10 Each
Pocket watches (watch could be old but
dials are new)

PFA065.000

Reproduction clock face on old clock. I've seen this
face on many different types of clocks. Worth only
what the clock is worth, not as a Coke item.

PFA066.000

Value . . . . . . . . . . .Worthless
Fantasy glass door knobs,
outline-type logo

PFA067.000

1970-80s . . . . . . . . . . . . . . .Worthless
Glass dish, clear glass with white lettering

PFA068.000

Value . . . . . . . . . . . . . . . . . . . . .$25
"Owl" coin in a box, stamped in gold "1915
Convention", not old

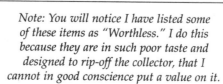

*Note: You will notice I have listed some
of these items as "Worthless." I do this
because they are in such poor taste and
designed to rip-off the collector, that I
cannot in good conscience put a value on it.*

PFA069.000

1980s . . . . . . . . . . . . . . .$5
"MSR Imports", plastic, stamped
on back "made in Hong Kong"

# FANTASY AND REPRODUCTION POCKET KNIVES

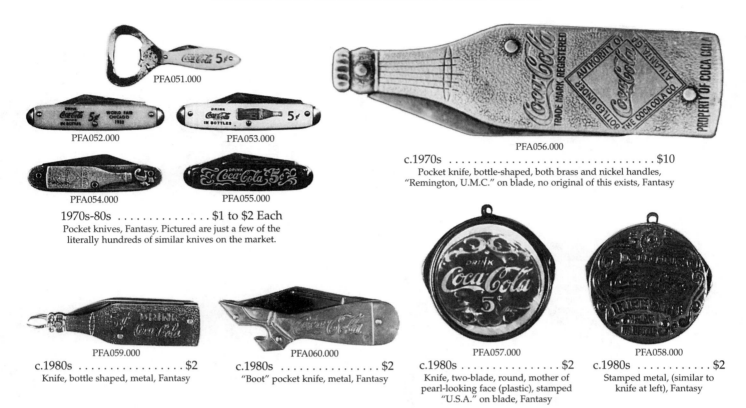

PFA051.000

PFA052.000

PFA053.000

PFA054.000

PFA055.000

**1970s-80s** . . . . . . . . . . . . . . . **$1 to $2 Each**
Pocket knives, Fantasy. Pictured are just a few of the
literally hundreds of similar knives on the market.

PFA056.000

**c.1970s** . . . . . . . . . . . . . . . . . . . . . . . . . . . . . . **$10**
Pocket knife, bottle-shaped, both brass and nickel handles,
"Remington, U.M.C." on blade, no original of this exists, Fantasy

PFA059.000

**c.1980s** . . . . . . . . . . . . . . . . **$2**
Knife, bottle shaped, metal, Fantasy

PFA060.000

**c.1980s** . . . . . . . . . . . . . . . **$2**
"Boot" pocket knife, metal, Fantasy

PFA057.000

**c.1980s** . . . . . . . . . . . . . . . **$2**
Knife, two-blade, round, mother of
pearl-looking face (plastic), stamped
"U.S.A." on blade, Fantasy

PFA058.000

**c.1980s** . . . . . . . . . . . . **$2**
Stamped metal, (similar to
knife at left), Fantasy

The following five knives (four pictured) are all recent reproductions of the 1905-1915 corkscrew pocket knives. The dates are approximate for the item's first appearance in the market place.

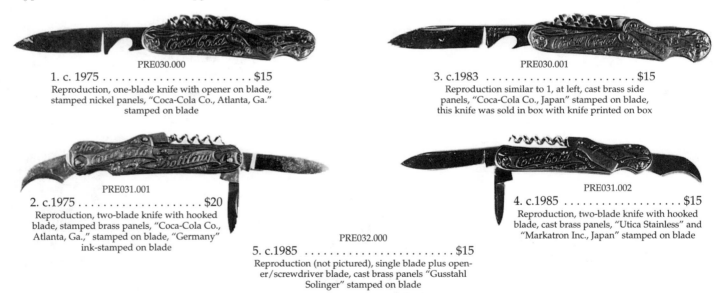

PRE030.000

**1. c. 1975** . . . . . . . . . . . . . . . . . . . . . . **$15**
Reproduction, one-blade knife with opener on blade,
stamped nickel panels, "Coca-Cola Co., Atlanta, Ga."
stamped on blade

PRE030.001

**3. c.1983** . . . . . . . . . . . . . . . . . . . . . . . **$15**
Reproduction similar to 1, at left, cast brass side
panels, "Coca-Cola Co., Japan" stamped on blade,
this knife was sold in box with knife printed on box

PRE031.001

**2. c.1975** . . . . . . . . . . . . . . . . . . . **$20**
Reproduction, two-blade knife with hooked
blade, stamped brass panels, "Coca-Cola Co.,
Atlanta, Ga.," stamped on blade, "Germany"
ink-stamped on blade

PRE031.002

**4. c.1985** . . . . . . . . . . . . . . . . . . . **$15**
Reproduction, two-blade knife with hooked
blade, cast brass panels, "Utica Stainless" and
"Markatron Inc., Japan" stamped on blade

PRE032.000

**5. c.1985** . . . . . . . . . . . . . . . . . . . . . . . **$15**
Reproduction (not pictured), single blade plus open-
er/screwdriver blade, cast brass panels "Gusstahl
Solinger" stamped on blade

*Note: Knives 1 and 2 were first to appear in the 1970s; their side panels were stamped with newly cut dies patterned after the
original knives. There are many very minor variations in the leaf and vine designs when compared to the original knives.
Knives 3, 4, and 5 are actually reproductions of knives 1 and 2, showing the same minor variations. Knives 3, 4, and 5 appear to have
cast side panels, and are not as sharp in detail as knives 1 and 2.
Through the years, many collectors have been fooled by these knives, including myself. A little wear or simulated aging and rust
can be deceiving. But knowing what is stamped on these blades and what is stamped on the originals, plus knowing the type of
opener blades on the originals, you should be able to determine whether a knife is an original or reproduction. Refer to the "Pocket Knife"
section of this book for blade stamping of original knives. A special thanks to Thom Thompson of Versailles, KY for his research
on this topic and for providing the photos and text.*

# FANTASY AND REPRODUCTION

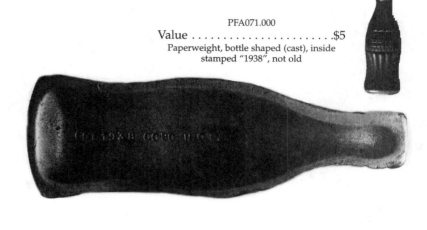

PFA071.000

Value ............................$5

Paperweight, bottle shaped (cast), inside
stamped "1938", not old

PFA070.000

Original and old National Cash Register
with (Fantasy) Coca-Cola top and face
plates. Made in two sizes for large and
small registers. These plates add nothing to
the value of an original register.

PFA072.000

Value ..............................$2

Letter opener, stamped metal, Fantasy

PFA073.000

1970s-80s  1" x 2 $^{1}/_{2}$" ...............$5

Money clip, stamped copper-colored metal, back is
stamped "Tiffany Studios, St Louis World's Fair, 1904
Patent Pending" (Fantasy). Can also be found without "Tiffany Studios" on the back

PFA074.000

Value ...........................$5

Straight razor, etched blade

PFA076.001    PFA076.002    PFA076.003

PFA078.000

Value .............................$2

Letter opener, knife

PFA075.000

Value .........$3

Vendors badge, stamped
metal, not old

PFA076.004    PFA076.005    PFA076.006

Value .................Worthless

Free drink tokens, stamped metal, not old,
some have bottle stamped on reverse (Fantasy)

PFA077.S00

PFA079.000

PFA079.S00

PFA079.004

PFA079.005

PFA079.001

PFA079.002

PFA079.003

Value ...................................................................Worthless

Silverware with Bakelite handles stamped "Drink Coca-Cola", outline-type logo.  Note: This stuff is old,
but "Drink Coca-Cola" has been added.  I've seen everything imaginable: silverware, carving sets, button
hooks, hair receivers, hair brush and mirror sets—anything that can be stamped.  This is real Junk.

# FANTASY AND REPRODUCTION POCKET MIRRORS

All mirrors shown on this page (except oval reproductions) are "Fantasy Mirrors." This is only a small sampling of the many I've seen over the years. Keep in mind these mirrors are very easy to make and I consider them all worthless junk.

PFA080.000

PFA081.000

PFA082.000

PRE033.S00

1973 . . . . . . . . . . . . . . . . . . . . . . . . . . . . . $2 Each

Reproduction pocket mirrors, oval, These were distributed by The Coca-Cola Co. There is a lesser quality copy of these that I consider worthless. See pocket mirror page in this book on how to identify originals.

PFA083.000

1970s . . . . . . . . . . . . . . $10

"Betty" mirror, Fantasy

PFA084.000

PFA085.000

PFA090.000

PFA086.000

PFA087.000

PFA089.000

PFA091.000

PFA092.000

PFA088.000

PFA093.000

PFA094.000

PFA095.000

PFA096.000

PFA097.000

PFA098.000

PFA099.000

PFA100.000

PFA101.000

PFA102.000

# FANTASY AND REPRODUCTION

PFA103.000

1980s . . . . . . . . . . . . . . . . . . . Worthless
Cast aluminum horse on Coca-Cola base, made in
Mexico, this is real junk

PFA104.000

1980s . . . . . . . . . . . . . $2
Coke bottle brass pipe (India)

PFA105.000

1970s . . . . . . . . . . . . . under $5
Push plate, tin or brass. Note: This is a
"Fantasy" item, not a reproduction.
There is no original item like this piece.

PFA106.000

1980s . . . . . . . . . . . . . . . . . . . . . . . . . $5
Knife, plastic handle, in sheath, Fantasy

PFA107.000

1970s-80s . . . . . . . . . . . . . . . . . . . . . . . $5
Hunting knife, etched blade, Fantasy

ORIGINAL            REPRODUCTION

PBL067.000              PRE034.000

1953  3 3/8" x 7 7/16" . . . . . . . . . . . $4
1. Blotter printed on vellum (blotter) paper
2. Printing is sharp and clear
3. Dated 1953

1980s 3 3/8" x 7 7/16" . . . . . .Worthless
1. Blotter printed on cardboard (white front,
   gray back)
2. Printing is blurry
3. Two versions, dated 1953 and no date

PFA110.000

PFA108.000        PFA109.000

1970s . . . . . . . . . . . . . . . . . . . . Worthless
Matchsafes, three examples. Note: These matchsafes
are old but Coca-Cola pieces have been added. These
are not embossed with the Coca-Cola logo.

> *Note: I personally find all (unauthorized) Fantasy items very objectionable. Many collectors have paid a lot of money for these items that are basically worthless. The prices you see on these items are token prices. In most cases I hesitate to assign any value at all.*

# FANTASY AND REPRODUCTION

PFA111.000

1970s  14" x 21"  . . . . . . . . . . . . . . . $50
"Gypsy Girl" paper sign, Lower right: "67003
Copyright, 1904 by Detroit Photographic Co."
Note: This is an old print, however the
"Drink Coca-Cola" and "5¢" was
overprinted in white much later.

PFA113.000

1980s . . . . . . . . . . . . . . . . . . . . . $5
Blotter. Note: This blotter could be old,
however the Coca-Cola advertising has
recently been added.

PFA114.000

1990s . . . . . . . . . . . . . . . . . . . . . . $1
Punch-out paper doll, Coca-Cola has been added

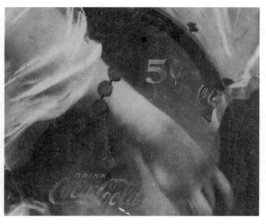

Detail of overprinted areas

PFA112.000

1980s . . . . . . . . . . . . . . . . . . . . . . $5
Blotter. Note: This blotter could be old, however the
Coca-Cola advertising has recently been added.

ORIGINAL

PPM162.000

REPRODUCTION

PRE035.000

Size (both same): 6 1/2" x 6 1/2" (Closed), 10" x 12 1/4" (Open)

| 1931 . . . . . . . . . . . . . . . . . . . . . $85 | 1980s . . . . . . . . . . . . . . . . . . . . . .$5 |
|---|---|
| 1. Off white/tan lightweight cardstock | 1. White medium-weight cardstock |
| 2. No color or "Dots" behind "More Business" at top | 2. Tone "Dots" behind "More Business" at top |
| 3. No "Dots" in "More Business" at bottom | 3. Tone "Dots" in "More Business" at bottom |

# FANTASY AND REPRODUCTION

PRE036.S01

PRE036.S02

PRE036.S03

PRE036.S04

Individual signs . . . . . . . . . . . $75 Each          Complete set of 5 . . . . . . . . . . . . . $450

Reproduction Signs (date unknown) overall size including matting 20" x 26"; size of print only approx. 13 ³/₄" x 19 ¹/₂".
These signs were framed and used in lobbies of bottling plants. Each sign has a small gold label under print identifying
the model. These reproduction signs are one of the very few repro. items that I do approve of. They are very well done and
collectible. Produced by The Coca-Cola Co. (Not shown Lillian Nordica, Green Artwork.)

PFA115.S01

PFA115.S02

PFA115.S03

PFA115.S04

1970s . . . . . . . . . . . . . . . . . . . . . $3 Each

Placemats, plastic coated, (set consists of five
placemats, only four shown— "Motor Girl" missing). Note: Be very careful of these placemats. I
have seen them cut down and framed and they
have fooled the unsuspecting.

PFA116.000

Mid- to Late 1970s . . . . . . . . . $100 Each

Ice cream chairs, wire back, embossed metal seat,
made in Mexico. Note: Many people think these chairs
are old. I'm sorry to say they are NOT. I remember
them coming into the market around the mid-1970s
offered in set of two and sold for $50 per set.

PFA117.BS0

1980s . . . . . . . . . . . . . . . . . . . . Worthless

Playing cards (double deck), in tin and cardboard
box. I've seen a few different versions of these.
cards. This is a Fantasy item at its worst.

# FANTASY AND REPRODUCTION

PRE037.000

1976  26" x 40" . . . . . . . . . . . . . . . . . . . . . . . . . . . . $750

"Meisel Print", in 1975-76 The Meisel Company was authorized to photograph art from The Coca-Cola Company Archives, 30 images were available to bottlers through a brochure called "50 Years of Nostalgia." Each image varied in size and were either mounted on artboard or bonded to canvas and mounted on stretcher frame. Note: I consider these "Meisel Prints" desirable, and very collectible.

PRE038.000

1917  8" x 19 $^1/_2$" . . . . . . . . . . . . . . . . . . . . $200

Reprint, Constance calendar. This calendar was thought to be old and original by me and others for many years. After close examination by experts in paper and printing it is conclusive that this piece could not have been printed in 1917. Actual printing date or usage date is still unknown. Many were examined.

PRE039.000

1990s . . . . . . . . . . . . . . . . $35

Die-cut, mounted on foamcore

PRE040.000

1990s . . . . . . . . . . . . . . $35

Die-cut, mounted on foamcore

PRE041.000

1990s  22" x 23" . . . . . . . . . . . . . . . . $35

Die-cut, mounted on foamcore

PFA118.000

1976 . . . . . . . . . . . . . . $10

Olympics tray

PFA119.000

1980s . . . . . . . . . . . . . . . . $2

3-D coaster, Fantasy, not old

— 580 —

# FANTASY AND REPRODUCTION

PFA120.000

1970s . . . . . . . . . . . . . . . . . $10

Paperweight, glass, Fantasy

PFA121.000

Value . . . . . . . . . . . . . . . . . . . . .$20
Paperweight, glass, date unknown. Note: The
"Coke is Coca-Cola" glass paperweights, as
far as I'm concerned, is a very questionable
item. Firsthand information on when and by
whom this piece was produced is not available. As long as it remains questionable, I will
keep it in this section.

PFA122.000

1970s . . . . . . . . . . . . . . . $10

Paperweight, glass, Fantasy

PFA123.000

1970s . . . . . . . . . . . . . . . . . . . . . . . . . $5
Paperweight, glass, Fantasy. This piece has been
shown in another price guide as 1916, it's NOT old.

Note: BEWARE of cast-iron,
bottle-shaped door handle.
Photo not available. This
is a recent Taiwan
import. It is worthless.

Note: BEWARE of all Coca-Cola
cast-iron toys. I don't know
of any such originals.

PFA124.000

1980s . . . . . . . . . . . . . . . . . . . . . . . . . $10

Truck, cast iron, Fantasy

PFA125.000

1980s . . . . . . . . . . . . . . . . . . . . . . . . . $10

Truck, cast iron, Fantasy

# BELT BUCKLES (RECENT & FANTASY)

PFA126.001

PFA126.002

PFA126.003

PFA127.000

> *Note: I personally object to all (unauthorized) "Fantasy" items, but these "nude" belt buckles are especially objectionable and I consider them worthless.*

PFA128.000

PFA129.000

Value . . . . . Worthless
The Famous Nude Nun
(slides up to reveal nude nun), tasteless

PFA130.000

PFA131.000

PFA132.000

PFA133.000

PFA134.000

PFA135.000

PFA136.000

PFA137.000

PFA138.000

PFA139.000

PFA140.000

PFA141.000

PFA142.000

PFA143.000

PFA144.000

PFA145.000

PFA146.000

PFA147.000

Shown above are 24 examples of Fantasy, Recent, and 75th Anniversary belt buckles. Keep in mind these are NOT reproductions, meaning they were not copied from originals, but rather created for the collectibles market. I have seen many other examples, and I consider them all worth about the same, between $5 and $10 each. I have never seen any of these belt buckles that I consider old and original.

PFA184.000

Value . . . . . . . . . . . . . . . . . . . . .Worthless

Glass sign, red and yellow. Note: These Coke 5¢
glass signs are being produced in many sizes and
variations; they're all recently produced junk.
Fantasy

PFA185.000

Value . . . . . . . .Worthless

Coca-Cola Chewing Gum jar,
milk glass, wood lid, applied
color lettering. Fantasy

Note: These rip-off
glass pieces are produced
without permission from
The Coca-Cola Co. They
have no part in the
history of The Coca-Cola
Company.

PFA186.000

Value . . . . . . . . . . . . . . . . . . . . .Worthless

Pitcher, applied lettering, I've seen these
in different colors. Fantasy

Note: This seltzer bottle, glass globe
and pitcher is obviously produced by
the same person. I've seen different
versions. Many styles of the milk glass
globe were produced. Notice the logo,
word "Drink" and "glass or bottle"
are all the same.

PFA187.000

Value . . . . . . . . . . . . . .Worthless

Seltzer bottle, green and red
applied lettering

PFA188.000

Value . . . . . . . . . . . . . . .Worthless

Milk glass globe, green and red
applied lettering

Note: Keep in mind these fantasy glass pieces were
created for no other reason than to rip-off the collector.
I cannot give these pieces any value.

PFA189.000

Value . . . . . . . . . . . . . . . . . . . . .Worthless

Glass sign, red and white. Fantasy

PFA194.000

Value . . . . . . . . . . . . .Worthless
Fountain glass, engraved, Fantasy. I've
seen other types.

PFA192.000

Value . . . . . . . . . . . . . .$2
China plate, Fantasy. Can be
found with gold or black lettering. Back of some marked
"Buffalo China USA"

PFA193.000

6 $1/2$" x 9" . . . . . . . . . . . . . . . . . . . . . . . . $2
Candy dish, milk glass, Fantasy

PRE049.000

Value . . . . . . . . . . . . . .Worthless
Repro Jasper, AL. Hutch bottle,
original is embossed. Phony is
scratched or engraved into glass, then
filled in with white paint

PFA195.000

28" x 40" . . . . . . . . . . . . . . . . . . . . . . . .$50
Pub mirror, wood frame, Fantasy, many variations
exist. Note that slogans are from different years.
Early and original reverse glass mirrors with girls or
are otherwise similar to this, do not exist.

# FANTASY AND REPRODUCTION

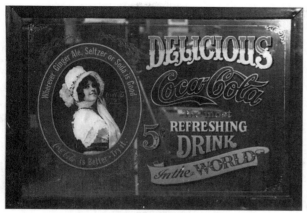

PFA148.000

1970s  28" x 40"  . . . . . . . . . . . . . . . . . $50

"Betty" pub mirror, wood frame, Fantasy

PFA149.000

1970s  12" x 18"  . . . . . . . . . . . . . . . . . $10

Pub mirror, wood frame, Fantasy

PFA150.000

1980s  14" x 16"  . . . . . . . . . . . . . . . . . $10

Pub mirror, wood frame, Fantasy

PFA152.000

1977  . . . . . . . . . . . . . . . . . . . . . . . . . $350

Pemberton/Candler commemorative mirror

PFA151.000

1970s-80s  12" x 18"  . . . . . . . . . . $25

Pub mirror, wood frame, Fantasy

PRE042.000

1970s-80s  . . . . . . . . . . . . . . . . . . . . . $75

Repro festoon (all one piece), framed

PFA153.000

1970s  . . . . . . . . $5

"Betty" push plate, glass, Fantasy

PFA154.000

1980s  . . . . . . . . . . . . . . $25

75th Anniversary pub mirror

PFA155.000

1970s  . . . . . . . . . . . . . . . . . . . . . . . $25

Sign, glass, oval, (two different versions), Fantasy

# FANTASY AND REPRODUCTION

PFA156.000

1970s  22 ¹/₂" x 28 ¹/₂" . . . . . . . . . . . $200

PFA157.000

1970s  29" x 48" . . . . . . . . . . . . . . . . . $25

Wood frame

PFA159.000

PFA161.000

PFA160.000

1980s-90s  12" . . . . . . . . . . . . . . . . . . . . . . . . . . . . . . . . . . . . . . . . . . . . . . . . . . . . . . . . $12.50 Each

Thermometer, still available

PFA158.000

1980s . . . . . . . . . . . . . . . . . . . . . . . $5

Miniature pub mirror, metal frame

PFA162.000

1970s-80 . . . . . . . . . . . . . . . . . . . . . $50

"Spinner" clock, reverse glass,
Fantasy, (I hesitate to give any value)

PFA212.000

1990s . . . . . . . . . . . . . . . . . . . . . . . $5

Light switch plate, plastic

# FANTASY AND REPRODUCTION

ORIGINAL (front and back)

PCT052.000

1905   6 1/2" x 9 3/4"   . . . . . . . . . . . . . $275

Lillian Nordica magazine ad with coupon. Printing
is high quality with sharp image and vibrant colors.
Small type is sharp and clear. Gloss finish

REPRODUCTION (front and back)

PRE050.000

5" x 7 1/2"   . . . . . . . . . . . . . . . . Worthless

Lillian Nordica magazine ad with coupon. Poor
printing quality, dull and muted colors. Small type is
blurry. Under a magnifying glass a dot pattern can be
seen. From the screen printing process not used in 1905

Fantasy and reproduction pieces are being produced today in record numbers. It is very important for you to understand that with all this phony material on the market it is virtually impossible to show it all or even close. Don't assume for one minute that a piece you are suspicious of is old and original because it is not shown in this section. With todays continual hot market for Coca-Cola Collectibles the thieves and rip-off artists are flourishing. Please try to understand that when you see "worthless" under one of the photos in this section, it is there because the piece was created for only one reason, to fool and cheat you out of money. These pieces have nothing to do with the history of The Coca-Cola Company nor do they have any place in our collections. One of the biggest problems we have today is with "color copiers." With more and more sophisticated equipment that is less expensive to buy or use, the sale of phony color copied material is flourishing. The problem is actually two fold, first of all we have your basic uncreative thieves. These are the individuals who blatantly take photos from this book and color copy them, usually to the size indicated in my description. These color copies are usually framed in early or worn frames, often early newspaper is used to back the frame, as well as rusted or old nails. These inexpensive copies are sold to the unsuspecting collectors at record numbers today and for many times their cost of less than $10. Remember it is illegal to copy anything from this book or any other book that is copyrighted. Then we have what I call the "creative thieves". These are the people who design artwork using existing Coca-Cola advertising like magazine art to create a totally new piece than have it color copied. Sometimes mounted on cardboard or on the photo side of dated and postmarked postcards. These "creative thieves" may indeed be creative but they are also "Dumb." Their work is sloppy, unbelievable, and done with no knowledge of Coca-Cola history. As a result their work is amateurish and obvious fakes. In some cases to additionally enhance the popularity of Coca-Cola collectibles these thieves will combine Coca-Cola art with the image of black memorabilia, famous people like Will Rogers, Hopalong Cassidy, Roy Rogers, Mickey Mouse and others, as well as such unique pieces as soap, scales, games and many others. For those of us who are familiar with the printing process, color copies and what to look for when identifying created artwork is easier than the unfamiliar and that is exactly who these "rip-off" artists target. There are a number of things you can do to make yourself more aware of these phony pieces. First of all become suspicious of pieces that seem to be "too good to be true," especially when the Coca-Cola advertising is added to other collectible themes, for instance movie stars, black memorabilia, TV stars, Disney,

Value . . . . . . .Worthless
Fan, Fantasy, color copied art
work glued to cardboard, with
wood handle

cowboys, etc. Second become familiar with the color copy process, have something color copied and compare it to the original, notice the color differences, type of finish, the paper, the feel, get to know a color copy from something that has been printed. Thirdly, don't be fooled by paper, glass, old frames or newspaper backing that is old. Buying old paper, and windows to take out old irregular glass is easy, any flea market will have an abundance of old frames. Remember framing hides a multiple of sins. If you are not sure, tell the dealer you want to take it out of the frame and you will put it back, if you do not purchase it. If they decline, keep on walking.

**Remember** it is illegal to create or manufacture items using the Coca-Cola name, logos or trademark without written permission or licensing from The Coca-Cola Company. This is a very serious trademark law that The Coca-Cola Company does not take lightly.

The following is only a partial list of the many repro, fantasy and phony Coca-Cola pieces not shown in this section. (F) fantasy with no such original.

Cast-Iron bottle shaped door handle (F)

Cast-Iron toys, cars, trucks (F)

Scales—painted postal scales with color copy Coke art on round dial, some have color copies glued on sides and back. (F) I know of no original, Coca-Cola scale, I have also seen store scales with decals or painted with Coke logos.

Hoppy Pieces—Hopalong Cassidy signs, displays and games with Coke logos (F)

Mickey Mouse—Mickey Mouse or any other Disney characters with Coke logos on cardboard or wood, some are cutout. (F)

Post Cards—created art is glued to existing cards that are dated and post marked, corners are usually crudely rounded to hide the fact that something has been added. (F)

Cash Registers—Cheap cash registers painted red (or other colors) Coca-Cola decals or painting applied. (F)

Porcelain Signs—Many recently produced versions including an oval made in different colors, red, blue, green, black, etc. (F)

Pedal Cars—Restored pedal cars with added Coca-Cola logos are pure fantasy, no such originals. (F)

# FANTASY AND REPRODUCTION

The pieces shown on this page are only a small sampling of the work done by one individual cutting and pasting Coca-Cola bottles, logos, dates, and other information onto signs and postcards and then reproducing them on a color copier. Glued to cardboard, some are cut out to appear to be die-cut; others have rounded corners and string hangers are attached to the back. This stuff is pure rip-off junk and totally worthless as Coca-Cola collectibles.

*Note: Sizes are all approximate. This is only a small sampling of these illegal signs.*

PFA163.000
Postcard (Cincinnati Reds)
There maybe a whole series of these postcards.
Most are pasted on the back of actual postcards.

PFA164.000
Cutout 10 $^1$/$_2$" x 15 $^3$/$_4$"

Back of some signs

PFA165.000
9 $^1$/$_2$" x 12 $^1$/$_4$"

PFA166.000
Cutout 10" x 15"

---

**WARNING!**
*It is illegal to produce or copy anything with the Coca-Cola logo on it without permission from The Coca-Cola Company.*

PFA167.000
9 x 14 $^1$/$_2$"

PFA168.000
7 $^1$/$_4$" x 12 $^3$/$_4$"
Showing both sides

PFA169.000
10 $^3$/$_4$" x 14 $^3$/$_4$"

PFA170.000
9" x 14"
Color copy of magazine ad

# FANTASY AND REPRODUCTION

PFA196.000

Value . . . . . . . . . . . . . . . . .Worthless junk

Bar of soap (showing front, back and side), Fantasy, other variations exist, This is a color copy wrapper, using phony artwork—no such original exists.

PFA197.000

Value . . . . . . . . . . . . . . . . . . . . .Worthless

Fishing lure on card (color copy), Fantasy. I've seen other variations. No original Coca-Cola fishing lure exists.

> Note: It is illegal to produce anything using the Coca-Cola logo without permission from the company.

PFA198.000

Value . . . . . . . . .Worthless

Checker set, Fantasy, in Poor quality stamped box, checkers not marked

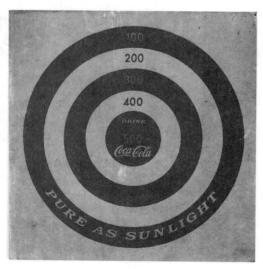

PFA199.000

Value . . . . . . . . . . . . . . . . . . . . . . . . . . . .$2

"Pure as Sunlight" dartboard, Fantasy

> Note: Make yourself aware of what color copies look like. The person reproducing this junk is ripping off collectors with all these phony color copy creations. Beware!

PFA200.000

Value . . . . . . . . .Worthless

BB-game, Fantasy. Inside is a color copy using created phony artwork and bogus copyright dates. Other versions exist.

PFA206.000                    PFA207.000

1980s-1990s . . . . . . . . . . . . . . . Worthless

Punch cards, small and large size, Fantasy,
no such originals

PFA208.000

Value . . . . . . . . . . . . . . . . . . . . . . . . . . .$5

Coca-Cola cigar box label, white and red, Fantasy,
cheaply printed, no such original exists

PFA209.000

Value . . . . . . . . . . . . . . . . . . . . . . . . . .$1

Recent paper sign, red printing on tan or
off-white paper

PFA210.000

She was working for you in '99.
That girl of ours upon our sign—
We hope she's still your Valentine.

Thanks for helping us keep our
love affair with America going
for 87 years.

Coca-Cola USA

Reverse side of
valentine calendar

PRE052.000

11 1/2" x 21 1/2" . . . . . . . . . . . . . . . . . . $35

Reproduction 1899 calendar. In 1973 Coca-Cola
produced this large size reprint to honor the
87th year of serving their customers. This is called
the Valentine calendar. Beware: this calendar is
sometimes framed and sold to unsuspecting
collectors for many times its value.

PFA211.000

Value . . . . . . . . . . . . . . . . . . . . . . . . .25¢

Post cards, printed on old card stock, Fantasy. These
cards have been around for quite a few years

# FANTASY AND REPRODUCTION

PRE043.000

1970s-80 . . . . . . . . . . . . . . $25

Canvas sign

PRE044.000

1980s 20" x 28" . . . . . . . . . . . . . . . . $25

Masonite

*Note: BEWARE of cast iron bottle-shaped door handle. Photo is not available, this is a recent Taiwan import. Worthless*

PFA171.000

1980s . . . . . . . . . . . . . . . . . . $50

Sign, tin, Fantasy

PRE045.000

1980s 10 $^1/_4$" x 16 $^1/_2$" . . . . . . . . . . . . $10

Sign, tin, embossed

PFA172.000

1970s . . . . . . . . . . . . . . . . . . . . . . . . . $25

Sign, light-up, plastic and wood

PFA173.000

1980s . . . . . . . . . . . . . . . . . . . . . . . . . $10

Street sign, Fantasy

PFA174.000

1975 17" x 24" . . . . . . . . . . . . . . . . $8

Poster, paper (c.1975 Portal Pub in lower left corner is easily removed, one of a set)

PFA175.000

1980s . . . . . . . $15

Thermometer

PPA176.001        PFA176.002

1980s 18 $^3/_4$" x 24" . . . . . . . . . . . . . . . $10 Each

Reproduction paper posters, (glued on wood slats, to look old; I've seen horizontal and vertical slats). There are at least four different versions, only two are shown.

# FANTASY AND REPRODUCTIONS

PFA177.000

PFA178.000

**1980s-1990s** ........ $15 to $25 Each
Straw holders, glass. I've seen other examples, no
such original straw holders are known to exist

PFA179.000

This example was made in two
different sizes—small and large

PFA180.000
**1970s** .......... $10
Bottle, brass, made in India

---

> **WARNING!**
> *It is illegal to produce or copy anything with the Coca-Cola logo
> on it without permission from The Coca-Cola Company.*

---

PFA182.000
**1980s-90s** ........... $125
"Hutch" display bottle, glass, no original "Hutch" display bottle exists

PFA181.S01    PFA181.S02    PFA181.S03    PFA181.S04

**1972 7"** .................... $20 Each
PFA181.S00 **Set of four** ............. $100
Poor quality fantasy pieces

PFA183.001                    PFA183.002
**1970s** ..................... $20 Each
Chinese lanterns, paper, Fantasy, (I have seen other
variations, no other such original exists)

# FANTASY AND REPRODUCTION

PFA203.000

PFA201.000          PFA202.000

1990s . . . . . . . . . . . . . . . . . . . . Worthless
Porcelain signs (small size), Fantasy. I've seen other
variations. These signs look old and original and
have fooled many. They were made for only one
reason, to rip-off collectors.

PFA204.000

1980s-90s . . . . . . . . . . . . . . . . . Worthless
Porcelain sign (small size), Fantasy. Part of a number
of porcelain signs produced without permission of
The Coca-Cola Company.

PFA206.S01          PFA206.S02          PFA206.S03          PFA206.S04

PFA206.S00  1970s-80s complete set . . . . . . . . . . . . . . . . . . . . . . . . . . . . . . . . . . . . . . $4
Individual trays . . . . . . . . . . . . . . . . . . . . . . . . . . . . . . . . . . . . . . . . . . . . . . . . $1 Each
Set of tip trays (rip-off), Fantasy, redesign of existing Coke girls, Poor quality, cheap looking

PFA205.000

Coca-Cola bicycle with cooler, Fantasy. This piece has been totally created.
No such original exists. Basically a "made-up" item. I have seen these
"creations" being offered and sold for thousands of dollars, for what is
basically a fraud. I find this very offensive.

# REPRODUCTION BOTTLE RADIO

ORIGINAL      REPRODUCTION

PRA010.000      PRE047.000

Both original and reproduction are the same size—24". However, repro is much lighter in weight than original. Note: This reproduction bottle radio is an obvious phony—poor quality and cheaply made. However, for those who have not seen an original, it is understandable how they could be duped.

ORIGINAL          REPRODUCTION

Notice the difference between the two caps; original. is split in two parts (front and back). Repro cap is one piece, glued on top.

ORIGINAL          REPRODUCTION

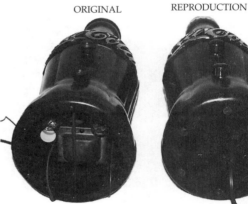

Original has full open bottom with six (round) pieces on edge. Interior of radio is fully visible. Notice metal bar that runs across inside bottom, which connects with screw from back. Repro has a closed bottom, with six plastic (flat) pieces. Interior of radio is concealed. Cord exits from bottom center.

*Note: There are many differences between the original and repro I'm showing only the basic standouts. This radio was created as a rip-off item, to fool the buying public. It is not a licensed piece, and I consider it worthless. Many have been duped into paying a lot of money for a bogus radio.*

Special Thanks to
Dave Goddard for his work on this radio.

ORIGINAL          REPRODUCTION

Notice the difference in the two dials and knobs

# CONDITION GUIDES

The condition of any Coca-Cola collectible is the most important factor in determining its value. There are two types of grading systems used by collectors. The "Poor" to "Mint" system seems to be used less nowadays in favor of the "1" to "10" method of grading. Described below are both methods not only in relationship to each other but also with a photographic example of the range "1" to "10" and "Poor" to "Mint". This example is in the form of a 1934 tray, but basically will hold true with any form of collectible. Please keep in mind when grading an item that it is not in anyone's best interest to overgrade that item.

| | | |
|---|---|---|
| 10 | | **MINT** |
| 9.5 | | New condition, unused, flawless, no visible marks or scratches. There is no middle ground in this category; it's either perfect or it's not. You can't say "it's Mint but it has a scratch." Mint = Perfect. |
| 9 | | **NEAR MINT** |
| 8.5 | | Very minor or slight marks, chips, or scratches, a minor tear (on paper). Nothing serious that would detract from the color or beauty of the piece. This is the category that is most often misused. |
| 8 | | **EXCELLENT +** |
| 7.5 | | Visible minor scratches, perhaps minor chips, minor tears or peeling of paper items. The Excellent category is the area that most pieces fall into, and the area that prices in this book are based on. |
| 7 | | **EXCELLENT** |
| 6.5 | | Just a few more minor chips than normal, scratches, minor marks, but still not serious, a repairable tear on paper items. Still a very good looking piece, and very collectible. |
| 6 | | **VERY GOOD** |
| 5.5 | | This is the extreme low end of Excellent condition. Still collectible, but a few more problems, perhaps a white spot on a tray, slight pitting, edge chips and rubs, a few tears, or a small piece out of edge of paper items. |
| 5 | | **GOOD** |
| 4.5 | | Scratches, minor flaking, possibly minor dent and rust or pitting, serious tears, or portion missing on paper items. An OK item. This is the point when it becomes questionable whether the piece is collectible or not. |
| 4 | | **FAIR** |
| 3.5 | | More than minor pitting and flaking, dents, trimmed or torn paper, fading or bad color. Collectible only if it's a rare piece; a good filler item. |
| 3 | | **POOR** |
| 2.5 | | In worn state, rusted, dents, or pitting. A paper item that has been torn and repaired, possibly restored; generally not very collectible. |
| 2 | | **POOR** |
| 1.5 | | Extensive pitting and rust areas, extensive fading and wear, dents and bends, restoration work that has been done poorly. This would be an item that would not be collectible or have much value at all. |
| 1 | | **WORTHLESS** |
| 0 | | An item that has no redeemable qualities, something that you would not display regardless of rarity; something you didn't have to pay for. |

## COLLECTING COCA COLA—GENERAL OR SPECIALIZED

There seem to be many reasons why people enjoy collecting Coca-Cola memorabilia. Surely one of the greatest attractions is the wide range of collectibles available. There are many different areas of collecting, but most collectors will collect anything with the famous Coca-Cola logo. Others are specialized collectors. Because of the expense involved, it may be difficult for one collector to amass a great collection encompassing all areas. But, that same collector could have a fantastic collection in one specific area. Collecting only Coca-Cola bottles, for example, is a hobby enjoyed by many. Others may have set a goal to have every tray or calendar the company has produced. But when trying to track down items from the early or pre-1900s, they suddenly realize that it is quite a task.

One of my favorite specialized areas of collecting, and one that even the new collector can get into without spending a fortune, is postcards. Any postcard showing a nice Coca-Cola sign is a very good item. Postcards are easy to find and early ones are very desirable. But whether you collect anything and everything, or choose to specialize, you always have a good feeling when you add a nice piece to your collection.

## KEEP A RECORD

It is extremely important to keep an accurate and up-to-date record of each and every piece in your collection. Many people do not realize that you're not just collecting, but also investing. Every piece that you spend money on or trade for is an investment that must be recorded. Could you imagine putting money in a bank without having a bank book recording the date, amount, and interest? Well, the same holds true with money spent on your collection. If you have a computer, like so many people do, it is a terrific way to store all of this information. If a computer is not available to you, go to your stationary store and buy a good hardbound record book. In it, list every piece, the date of purchase, amount paid, the condition, and any other information you may want about the piece. You may want to keep things such as trays, calendars, toys, etc., separate so you can find them more easily. If you sell or trade a piece, take note of the amount that you received for it.

If you have been collecting for some time and haven't done this, do so as quickly as possible. Listing each and every item is a big job, I grant you, but believe me it should be done. This is very important also if you decide to sell your collection or perhaps leave it to a spouse or children. Remember, an up-to-date recording is the backbone of every collection.

## INSURANCE

Not being an insurance agent or knowing your collection, I could not begin to tell you how to insure it. But I can give you some hints. One thing to remember is that you should not assume that your collection is covered on your homeowners policy. Don't assume anything when it comes to insurance. Call your agent, invite him into your home or apartment, show him what you collect, and get his advice. If you are not happy with what your agent tells you, call another and then another if necessary until you find a policy that you feel comfortable with.

There seems to be a number of ways to insure a collection, but whichever of these you choose, be sure that it is insured some way. The agent may recommend that you increase your homeowners policy by adding a rider which will include the collection. Also inquire about a "Fine Arts" policy to cover some of the more expensive items.

You may be required to keep a photographic record of your collection for your insurance company. This, by the way, is something that I recommend whether it is required or not. Try to set a minimum value for the items which are to be photographed.

## FAKES AND REPRODUCTIONS

It's unfortunate but true: fakes and repros are a part of collecting. Whether it be Coca-Cola, Ming vases or teddy bears, reproductions are everywhere. The trick is to keep your mistakes to a minimum, and the best way to do that is plain and simple "education." Read everything you can get your hands on and ask questions. Put your mistakes behind you and learn from them. Also, tell other collectors about items that you know are phony.

In this book you will find a number of pages devoted to fakes and repros. Remember, even with the many pieces shown it is still only a small sampling of the new, repro, and just plain junk that is passed off as old and original. Finding out if a piece is original or reproduction is important, but questioning the dealer is not always the answer. They all seem to say the same thing, "We got this from a woman who had it in a trunk for the last fifty years." Don't be fooled by appearance. Many pieces can be instantly aged by unscrupulous dealers who are looking to make a buck from the collector who is anxious to make a major find.

I wish that there was some perfect way to know the repro from the original, but there isn't. I suggest seeing the original, holding it in your hands and feeling it. In many cases this is the best and surest method of not getting burnt.

## RESTORING, CLEANING AND PRESERVING

Of all the tips one can give to the collector, this is certainly the most delicate. Can you imagine someone telling you how to clean and polish a tray, then trying it only to find that you have totally destroyed the item. Well, believe me, it's happened many times—especially with trays and metal signs.

My rule of thumb is: Outside of simple dusting, leave the piece alone unless you know exactly what you are doing. Some collectors have been very successful with dirt removal, cleaning, and polishing, but many of them have learned through trial and error. This is certainly another area where education and asking questions is very important.

Touching up trays or signs is also a very sticky subject. It should never be done without complete knowledge of what you are doing. Keep in mind that a tray that has been touched up, whether or not it is a good job, does not have the same value as a piece which has not been touched up. Many times a touched up piece is difficult to sell.

As far as paper is concerned, the same rules apply. Do not do anything unless you know what you are doing. I do strongly recommend protecting those paper items in an album or in a frame, especially calendars. And finally, always choose a frame shop that is knowledgeable in paper preservation and uses acid free mat board.

## BUYING AT AN AUCTION

Auctions are great sources of Coca-Cola collectibles because they display some excellent artwork. Many pieces were saved and do turn up at house sales and auctions. Be sure to subscribe to mail auctions and antique publications, and make sure that you are aware of sales in and out of your area. Many auction houses will accept absentee bids, so don't be afraid to ask and to use your phone. It can save you a lot of wasted time. I can't tell you how many miles I have traveled to auctions because a creative auctioneer listed in his advertisement "very rare Coke tray" only to find a 1950 tray that looked as if it had been run over by a truck. On the other hand though, I took a six-hour trip to an auction that listed a Coke sign which turned out to be one of the most important pieces that I have ever purchased. Those pieces are the ones that make it all worthwhile.

Get to know your local auctioneers. If you feel that you trust them, let them know what your interests are. Believe me, the next time that they have a Coke piece, they will let you know about it. If a piece is listed in the advertisement, make a call, asking for a description and the condition. Go to the sale preview, but don't run up to the piece. Look at other items first and try not to be over anxious. Another tip, as difficult as it may be, is to try to set a limit on what you will spend. Many great Coke pieces have sold at auctions far below their value because they just didn't have the right audience. Yet, many pieces have sold far above their value because the right group of people were in the room.

## CONSIDER CONDITION

As I have mentioned many times before, condition is the most important factor in determining the value of an item. That is why it is so difficult to put a value on an item in a book such as this. People very often do not consider condition. This is a major mistake. The prices that you see in this book are what I call "average prices," considering the item is in nice condition. If the piece is in mint condition the value is obviously higher, and if it is in poor condition the price is of course lower. The price should always reflect the piece's condition.

It would be an error to purchase a piece for, let's say, $50, because it is in the price guide for $50 but the condition is poor. You should point out to the dealer any flaws in the piece and the price should be adjusted accordingly.

I, personally, have always been in favor of the "up-grade" system of collecting. This is, basically, buying a piece and when you find the same piece in better condition, up-grade and sell the lesser of the two. Keep in mind that selling pieces in poor condition is not easy in many cases. So, before you turn your money over to a dealer, ask yourself this important question: "Am I considering condition in the purchase of this piece?"

## GET INVOLVED

Join national and/or international clubs and local chapters of those clubs, and become acquainted with other collectors and dealers. Read books, go to shows and auctions, and, of course, ask questions. Find out what pieces were recently found and how much they sold for. Know the market and remember that an informed and knowledgeable collector is a good collector. It is he or she who will eventually end up with a good collection, I can't tell you how many times I've heard things like "I've, been collecting for years and I thought I was the only one" and "I had no idea that this stuff was worth this much." The more you know about the subject, the better off you will be.

I feel that it is so important to join a group such as the "Coca-Cola Collectors Club International" (an application can be found at the back of this book) not only because it's a great group of people with a common interest, but it is a great source of information to help you and your collection. Coca-Cola collectors have what many others don't. That is the tremendous support system of the Club. So, take advantage of it. Find out who specializes in a particular area and ask questions if you need to. You will be surprised at how many collectors are willing to help. And, if at all possible, try to attend at least one of the national conventions held by the Club. Getting to meet and talk to some knowledgeable collectors is a wonderful experience that you will never forget.

## HELP FINANCE YOUR COLLECTION

Over the past ten or twelve years, I've seen the prices of Coca-Cola collectibles rise constantly, and unless you have just hit the lottery or are independently wealthy, it can be very difficult to amass a nice collection. But there are ways to finance your collection as long as you are willing to spend some money.

I have heard many people say that they have passed up worthwhile pieces because they have the item in their collection. This is a mistake. If you are at a show and see an item that you feel is priced right, you should buy it, even if you have it or if it is in a different area than your collection. You can sell it for a profit or use it for trade.

Another good way to make money is to put out a list of items for sale, up-grade items or duplicates. Advertise in the club newsletter. Let other collectors know that you have a list of items for sale. (Remember to keep close track of what you pay for items and what you sell them for.) Soon you will have a little nest egg for use when you want to purchase that piece for your collection that always seemed to cost a fortune.

## COCA-COLA COLLECTING AS AN INVESTMENT

Many collectors of Coca-Cola memorabilia only consider themselves collectors and not investors. This, in my opinion, is a big mistake. Different people collect for different reasons— they enjoy the hunt, they are taken by the visual appeal, or perhaps it is the owning of a piece of the history of The Coca-Cola Company that makes them feel a part of it. Every dime that one spends on a collection is money that had to be earned, and that collection is an investment. In the case of most collectors, this investment is a major one. Taking this into consideration, one may ask if one would invest in the stock market or buy a C.D. if the investor knew it would never appreciate in value? I doubt it! The same rules apply with buying collectibles as with any other investment. Most important is to know the market in which you are dealing, getting as much information about Coca-Cola collectibles as possible. People who invest in the stock market try to get information on how the market works, how to avoid losses, and as much information as they can get about the company that they are about to invest in. The same thing that has to be done when buying a piece for a collection. I am sure that you are buying a piece because you've always wanted it or it is beautiful or rare, but you must also consider if it is a good investment. To answer that question, there are some simple rules to follow.

The first is a very touchy one and I'm sure to get lots of "flack" over it, but I suppose that I'm just a Coca-Cola "purist." I really believe that buying newer items is not a very good investment. I have been buying and selling Coca-Cola for a long time, and prices have risen year after year, but not on the repro, fantasy and newer collectible items. Many think the size of a collection is very important. I've heard many boast of having thousands of pieces in their collection, and to accomplish this they will buy anything and everything bearing the Coca-Cola logo. Please don't fall into this trap! Many of the recently produced items for the collectibles market that sell for five to ten dollars today may not even be worth what you paid for them in ten to fifteen years from now. If you ask anyone who has tried to sell a collection loaded with commemorative and newer items, you will find that it is not easy. If the collection is sold, the collector usually ends up taking a loss. On the other hand, collectors who have sold their collections consisting of original advertising pieces not only find it easy, but they also make large profits. I personally would rather have a smaller collection consisting of quality, older items, rather than newer items. When I say "older," I don't mean collect items from the '30s rather than the '50s, but rather avoid items that are being produced for today's collectible market. Because they are made in huge quantities, these pieces will not appreciate in value and do not make good investments. So, whether you collect any age Coca-Cola items or are specific about a particular era, you cannot go wrong with original quality items.

This brings us to the next point: condition. If you're investing in a piece that you're going to bring home and hang on your wall, why not make sure that the item is in the best possible condition. Sometimes it is best to wait to find a particular item in better condition rather than buying one in poor condition just because you "must" have it. It is true my "up-grade" method of collecting applies here. By this I mean that you can always buy a better example and sell off the poorer one. But, before you turn your money over, make sure the condition of the piece is acceptable to you personally, and the condition won't be a big problem if you should want to upgrade. However, a piece that you have purchased at a very reasonable price can always be sold in poor condition even if you make just a few dollars on it. I know that most collectors never think about selling their collection. We all believe that we will be collecting forever, but this is not always true. Whether it be changing interests, financial problems, marital problems, or a host of others, some day your collection may have to be sold. It is better to be certain that if and when a collection is sold, it is for lots more than what was paid for it. Remember: Know the market, buy old instead of new, and buy the best quality you can find. This is how investing works and this is how to assure that your collection will grow in quality and value.

## WHERE TO FIND COCA-COLA COLLECTIBLES

When people see my collection, one of the first things they ask is: "Where do you find all of this stuff?" Well, as many of you long time collectors know, it is not easy and it takes a lot of time and hard work to build a collection. Collections are not made overnight, and even if you have a fortune to spend, it is not always that easy to find quality pieces. For this reason alone, Coca-Cola collecting is such a challenge, and adding a beautiful piece to your collection becomes so exciting. It is very important to let collectors know who and where you are and what your interest is. The Coca-Cola Collectors Club International is a great place to start. Buying and selling through ads in the classified section of that group's publication is certainly a good source. One must also keep abreast of what is happening in the field of antiques and collectibles, subscribing to publications such as the *Antique Trader Weekly*, P.O Box 1050, Dubuque, IA 52001, and many other newspapers and magazines devoted to collectors is one of the most important link-ups with people who have pieces for sale, and an excellent medium to let people know your wants. These publications also list antique shows and auctions in and out of your area. I have a good friend who travels often, and he never leaves home without checking the *Antique Trader* to see what shows will be taking place in the area he will be traveling to.

Check out auction listings in antique and other publications as well. Many good Coke pieces have been hidden away in a "general" auction with no competition from other collectors. Subscribe to auctions and try to get on mailing lists of auction houses even if they don't specialize in Coke or advertising items. Coca-Cola pieces turn up in most auctions eventually. Stay alert, don't assume that because it is an all furniture auction, for example, that there are no Coke items in it. Ask questions to be sure. Large antique shows all over the country sell anything and everything in antiques and collectibles, while many other shows specialize in advertising, coin-op, paper items, toys, etc. All of these are good sources of Coca-Cola memorabilia. Know when and where they are, and then be there. The annual convention of the Coca-Cola Collectors Club International is certainly one of the best places to buy, and if you can get to one, do so. Some collectors find placing inexpensive "want ads" in local papers to be a great source of items right in your own backyard. Local antique shops are another important stop. Go to the ones in your area on a regular basis, leave your card, let them know your interests, and ask them to give you a call if anything should turn up. Many towns have areas heavy with antique shops or malls that specialize in antiques and collectibles. Year-round, weekend antique shows are also very popular. Find out where they are and visit them, perhaps as part of a day trip or a long weekend with the family. Buying nice stuff and building a good collection takes work. Coca-Cola pieces don't come to you— you have to go out and find them. Good Luck!

## BUYING THROUGH THE MAIL

Buying a Coke piece by mail is not always as easy as going to a shop, looking at the piece, and deciding whether or not to buy it. A great number of collectibles are offered for sale in antique publications, and the entire transaction takes place through the mail. Many collectors have been quite successful both buying and selling through the mail, while others have found it to be a complete nightmare. There are some simple rules which, when followed, should minimize your problems.

First, the ideal situation is to get a photo of the piece prior to making a decision on buying or not. The photo accomplishes two things. First, it lets you know that the seller actually has the item, and second, it helps in determining the condition of the piece. However, getting a photo is not always possible. If a good item is advertised in a popular antique publication, chances are that the seller will get many calls and, if the item is priced right, will have little problem selling the piece. Sometimes a decision must be made quickly whether to buy or not to buy. If a caller requests a photo first, the seller may just sell the item to another caller not requesting a photo. At this point, your decision has to be made based on the seller's opinion of the item's condition. If the piece is in mint condition, this obviously makes your decision much easier. However, there are not many good pieces out there in mint condition. Very often, people tend to overgrade an item to make it more appealing, or conveniently leave out some important information like the tray has a hole drilled in the center of it. Because of this it is very important to ask some relevant questions. For example, if it is a tray or a tin sign, is it dented? Is there any pitting? Does it have a nice shine? Is the color good, or is it faded? Ask as many questions as you feel necessary, and don't assume the seller uses the same keen eye for condition that you do. I'm always amused by "the condition is great considering it's age" or "the piece was used but not abused." Don't let the seller give you these vague, meaningless descriptions; get specific details and make sure you can return the piece if it was not correctly described. If you still feel comfortable after these questions, buy the piece.

This step brings on more questions. If you and the seller are not acquainted, it would be foolish to assume he or she will send you the piece for your inspection. In most of these transactions, the buyer takes all of the risks—be aware of this. Also, you must send a check along with postage and insurance costs. Some sellers often request a cashier's check or money order. Still others will not ship the item until your check clears, and understandably so. Remember, they have no idea who you are. The buyer also takes the risk of loss or damage in shipping. Be sure that the seller has properly insured the piece. Also, keep in mind that the seller is not required to refund shipping costs. That part of the deal is usually lost. Buying from fellow club members through the club publication will certainly lessen these risks. However, the problem of overgrading is always going to be present. A reminder to you sellers: Overgrading accomplishes nothing. The buyer usually gets upset and wants to return the item. If he or she does, please have the good sense to send a refund. I am not trying to discourage making purchases through the mail, but you must be aware of some of the problems that I and many other collectors have had over the years in hopes that you might overcome them. Good luck!

## TRACKING THE MARKET

Tracking the Coca-Cola collectibles market is no different than tracking the stocks and bonds market, the real estate market, mutual funds, or any other form of investing. When tracking Coca-Cola memorabilia, however, it is very important to focus on particular areas within Coca-Cola memorabilia as a whole. It is true, and easy to say, that Coca-Cola collectibles as a whole are a good investment and have appreciated well over the years, in turn, that it is a good market to invest in. I am sorry to tell you that things are just not that simple. While it is true that the overview of collecting Coca-Cola is very positive as an investment, not all areas of collecting are worth investing in. In fact, many areas are just bad investments. That is why tracking the market on a more individual basis is very important in determining what is a good investment and what is a bad one. Some dealers with their sky high prices on anything Coca-Cola would have you believe that everything is worth a fortune and will be worth twice as much next year. This could not be further from the truth. So what is the catch? How could the market be great, but certain areas be so bad? Well, it is just like the stock market. If you invest your money on good solid companies with a good track record, a good present value, and a solid-looking future, even though the stock is expensive, it should give you good growth and a good return. On the other hand, the "flash in the pan" stock that is selling cheap and shoots up fast probably won't even get you your money back.

Collecting Coca-Cola memorabilia is exactly the same— stick with the old tried-and-true pieces and you can never go wrong. Which pieces are the tried-and-true ones? Well, that is exactly what tracking the market will tell you. But very simply, the tried-and-true pieces are the ones that, year after year, are being sold for record-breaking prices and are continually in demand by collectors. Display pieces are always on the high end of collectors' lists of desirable pieces. Display items include trays (in above average condition); calendars; signs in cardboard, tin, and porcelain; toy trucks; clocks; light-ups; and anything early, original, and in high quality condition. Tracking the market will show that other areas of collecting are also on the rise, like bottles, blotters, magazine ads, cards, games, and many others. But, in general, the area with the most impressive growth is the display pieces.

Now, what does this all mean to the collector? Well, if you just collect and really don't care about growth, it means nothing. However, if you are like most collectors who not only enjoy collecting, but want to know that your collection is appreciating in value, it should give you a good indication of how to direct your collection so that it is not overloaded with items that do not have good growth potential or that have a track record of not appreciating. For example, collections loaded with newer items or 75th Anniversary pieces or commemorative items will not appreciate in value or sell as quickly in today's market as will a collection heavy in original quality trays, signs, cutouts, and a nice selection of above average condition items. But, most of all, if one tracks prices

over the years and takes note of the condition of those pieces, one will certainly come to the conclusion that the best investment and, in turn, the best collection, will be those with pieces in excellent (8) or better condition. Keep in mind that prices shown in this book are based on the "excellent" condition. To illustrate this point, I have tracked two 1934 Weismuller trays; one in near mint condition (9+) and the other in fair condition. Tracking these trays for the past twenty-four years will clearly show that condition has to be one of, if not the, most important factor in making a purchase. Tracking the market is a very simple process. It is basically just being aware of the market in which you are investing. Take note of those items you see changing hands around you in antique publications, through word of mouth, auction results, convention prices, and your own purchases. Do not forget to take note of the condition as well as the price of the piece. Remember that educated collectors have the best collections.

## VALUE—AUCTIONS VS REALITY

Without fail, collectors and dealers will look at auction prices realized and will mistakenly accept those prices as current market value. One only needs to analyze this to understand that current market value is certainly not set by what a piece sells for in one particular auction. It is much more complicated than that, and I personally have a problem with price guide authors who use the latest auction price as new current value. I feel it is taking the easy way out and certainly does not reflect reality. If an auction price is the yard stick by which we now measure current value, which auction should we use as this yard stick? If we took two identical highly desirable Coca-Cola pieces worth, let us say, $3,000 and put one in an auction that

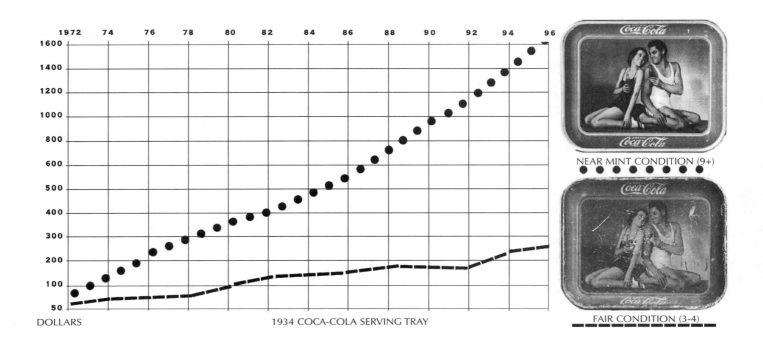

DOLLARS · 1934 COCA-COLA SERVING TRAY · NEAR MINT CONDITION (9+) · FAIR CONDITION (3-4)

is advertised for three weeks in the *Antique Trader* with beautiful photographs of the piece and it sells for $6,500, and the other piece in an auction that uses very little, if any, advertising, and realizes a final hammer price of $500, which is, by the way, very possible, which of these two auction prices do we now use as the new market value? I say neither! I certainly use auction prices realized when I track current value. I record the prices paid at both extremes; however, these prices paid are only one ingredient that goes into the mix that will eventually give us something close to what we think of as current market value. Traditionally auctions have always been the best way to sell in a "Hot" market and a bad choice in a "Cold" market. The hype and "feeding frenzy" mentality associated with a "Hot" market can do unbelievable things to a piece in a well-advertised sale. This type of auction does funny things to people, sometimes things they regret for years to come. When the auctioneer introduces that one piece they have been waiting for, the adrenaline starts to flow, the heart starts to pound, and the paddle starts moving and sometimes not in conjunction with the brain. What these people do not understand is that these same feelings are being felt by others in the room who are bidding against them. What started out as a simple procedure of adding a piece to your collection has turned out to be a challenge, a duel, a threat to the seriousness of the person's collection, and often goes way beyond the piece itself. Quickly the field of seven or eight contenders is three or four, then two, and finally it is over. They have the piece, but for how much? Two, three, four times what they would have paid in a shop or at a show. Are we now to believe that this procedure is how we determine value. I hope not; at least, it is not the way I determine value. Now, please don't get me wrong, I love auctions. I attend as many as I can. They are fun, exciting, interesting and it happens to be the way I sell the majority of pieces that go through my hands. However, I try to be realistic enough to understand that auction prices must be more closely scrutinized before we use them as current market value.

We talked about auctions being properly advertised, about two people getting swept up in the moment, but we must also discuss the "hype job." Smart and successful auctioneers are masters of hype. If any of you doubt this, just get a copy of the Jackie O, JFK sale and tell me that hype had nothing to do with the "way beyond" reality prices realized. There are many ways to hype a sale and I am sure that most of us have used them or fallen into the trap at one time or another. The practice of making something bigger than it is or expanding reality has been used by auctioneers since the first auction took place. That is part of the fun and excitement. So what do these crazy auction prices mean?—and, by the way, you only hear about the "crazy" high prices, not the low or "just right" prices. Was the sale advertised or not? If so, how much advertising? Was the piece rare? What condition was the piece in? Where and when did the sale take place? How much time and hype was used prior to the auction? Not long ago, a clock that should have sold in the "under $10,000" range went for $25,000. For the next two weeks, I heard, "Weren't you shocked?" or "Boy, are you off on your book price of that clock?" I can honestly tell you that the prices realized from any auction never shocks me. I am perfectly prepared for these "beyond belief" prices because I understand how and why they happen. But, at the same time, I am realistic enough to understand that for whatever reason a $3,000 item sells for $6,500, that the rest of the collecting community be saddled with that standard is ridiculous.

## DISPLAYING AND STORING

One of the greatest attractions of collecting antique advertising and Coca-Cola collectibles in particular are the colors and wonderful graphics used to promote the product. I find that the most important factor that goes into the collector's decision to buy or not to buy is how will this piece display in my collection? I call this "displayability." This "displayability" directly affects the value of the piece. If the condition is great, the piece will display well. If it displays well, it will be highly desirable. If it is highly desirable, it will be valued high. So, it is easy to see how important this "displayability" is on one's collection, not only to have a quality collection, but a quality investment as well.

I have always felt that collecting is an investment and it is very important to maintain that investment by keeping pieces in your collection in the same condition as the day you purchased them. Displaying and storing your collection properly is an important factor in protecting that investment. When a piece is purchased for your collection, you must determine if it will be displayed or stored. For display purposes of paper or cardboard signs, calendars, or posters, proper framing is very important. Make sure the person doing the framing uses the proper paper conservation methods and is aware of the value and importance of the piece you are about to leave in their care. It is very important that the framer does not do anything to the piece that you have not discussed, such as gluing, trimming, or removing anything from it, such as a metal strip or calendar page. Also make sure the framer is insured to cover your piece while it is in his possession and put that on your receipt with the value. Point out the importance of using acid free mats and backing as well as using a spacer such as a mat so the printed piece does not touch the glass. If the edges of the piece are nice and sharp with no tears or edgewear, do not cover the edge with a mat, so if you should ever decide to sell it, the potential buyer can see that nothing is being hidden. When mounting framed pieces on the wall, be sure they do not get constant sunlight. Framed pieces in a high humidity room such as a bathroom or basement could create problems with moisture. Creative lighting is also very important when displaying framed pieces. Hooded frame lights are nice on small quality pieces and add a rich feeling to the piece. Today wide varieties of track lighting are available and it is always the best type of lighting for areas with many framed pieces. The ability to move individual lights to eliminate glare is a big advantage, but remember, eliminating all glare from a room with many framed pieces is just not possible. The use of non-glare glass when framing has become a solution for some, however, I personally don't use it because it is not complimentary to the wonderful colors used on this advertising.

Paper signs, calendars and cardboard pieces that are not going to be framed and displayed require proper care for storage and handling. I find the best way to protect these pieces is to go to an art supply store and purchase foamcore and a roll of thin, clear acetate. Measure the piece and allow an extra quarter of an inch all around. Cut the foamcore to this size. Do not attach the piece to the foamcore with any tape or glue, simply put the piece face up on the foamcore, then lay face down on a rolled-out section of acetate. Cut the sheet with plenty of excess and pull tightly across the back of the foamcore and tape the acetate. Cut the ends and again pull tightly and tape. This stiff foamcore back and tight acetate seal accomplish a lot. Besides the obvious protection factor, the piece is kept flat, helps eliminate slight creasing or rolling, allows stacking and transports easily as well as allowing the piece to be seen and handled. Foamcore and acetate are not cheap, but the cost is well worth the protection you will have achieved.

Serving trays and tin signs require a lot more attention and should be checked periodically when being displayed. Some people do frame certain trays and tin signs, and that is fine, but make sure that a sealed, framed piece can breathe, meaning it is not air tight. If you are not framing a tray or sign, be careful where the piece is being displayed. High humidity is always a problem with tin. Light pitting can be prevented with a nice mild car wax once a year or every other year. The best possible place to display tin is in an area where there is a fairly constant temperature. Continual temperature changes is not a good environment for tin lithographed pieces.

Small collectibles, such as pocket mirrors, watch fobs, knives and celluloid pieces, display well and are protected nicely in showcases. If you do not have room for a large showcase, many small flat ones are available that allow these pieces the best possible protection as well as display.

Flat paper items like blotters, coupons, magazine ads, letterheads and other paper collectibles are always best kept in the plastic sleeves that are now available in so many sizes and filed in a three-ring binder for easy access. Storage of books, paper items, and other collectibles are best kept in corrugated file boxes that are readily available and inexpensive from the large chain stationery supply stores. Pack the items, label the outside of the box, and store off the ground in a dry area.

When displaying your collection, try to be creative and do not take it too seriously. Remember why you collect it—because it is attractive and it is fun. Move things around until you find that perfect spot for your favorite piece. Personally, I find it difficult to have high quality pieces that are not displayed. I collect it because I enjoy it, and I cannot enjoy it if I cannot see it.

## MADE FOR THE COLLECTOR'S MARKET

The one question I am asked more often than any other about Coca-Cola collecting is "How long is this interest, fascination and continual price increases going to last?" Since the mid-1970s I have listened to the dooms dayers who insisted the Coca-Cola collecting boom is coming to an end and prices will never be higher. Well, I told them then, and I will tell you now, over 20 years later, No Way! Traditionally collectibles go through hot and cold phases. I have watched beer cans go through the roof then drop almost out of sight. Baseball cards, slot machines, toys and hundreds of other collectibles will rise and fall as interest wanes. In all the years I have been collecting and dealing in Coca-Cola memorabilia, I have never experienced this problem. Of course, particular areas of collecting within Coca-Cola will cool off at times, like toys, cards, and magazine ads, but Coca-Cola collecting on the whole has been on a consistent upward trend. What I find so good about this trend, and the reason why I have always been so positive is that this continual increase is not that "flash-in-the-pan," high rising, latest hot collectible, but, rather, a consistent and steady increase that is gaining not only in value, but collector interest year by year. Some of the reasons for this nice steady growth are obvious and others a bit more difficult to understand. The obvious, of course, are the things I have been repeating throughout the book: the beauty and quality of this advertising captivates us as collectors and takes us on a tour of the history of our country, and, no matter how old you are, brings back fond memories of a more simple time. To put it in real simple terms, it is just plain "fun." The other reason that I have such a positive outlook on the future of our favorite collectible is the wonderful support we get from The Coca-Cola Company. This support may not be the type of support you are thinking of. However, The Coca-Cola Company has always known how good their product is and obviously how to sell it. They have also added products and companies to The Coca-Cola family which have also been very successful, but it has only been within the last few years that it has realized how important and profitable it is to sell itself, and that is exactly what it is doing.

You would have to live on Mars not to realize that marketing and merchandising of new Coca-Cola collectibles are everywhere, from the corner store to the home shopping network and everywhere in between. This merchandising of everything from pens to music boxes to clothing and jewelry have created a whole new division within the company. Marketing and licensing the most recognizable trademark on earth has become big business. Thousands and thousands of potential collectors are buying this merchandise every day and building collections around their latest purchase. Traditional collectors, especially the purest type of collectors, frown on these "made for the collector's market" products. How could these recently produced pieces capture the quality and appeal that original advertising did? Well, the fact is that it can't, but that is no reason to have disdain for it. Besides making a lot of money for The Coca-Cola Company, these recently produced pieces serve a purpose for not only the new buyers of it, but for long time traditional collectors as well. That is what brings me back to the reason why I have such a positive outlook on the future. Coca-Cola collectors have what most other collectibles do not have: this constant merchandising support that brings to the public eye on a regular basis a look at the history that has created this interest to such a large number of collectors. While these people are buying new items, a percentage of them are trickling down into traditional collecting of original vintage advertising. This continual influx of new blood is what keeps me so positive and bullish on the future.

The people who buy the recent collectibles do find it difficult to understand why these items cannot be found in this book or other price guides. This is where the reality of buying new as opposed to old comes in. It is obvious that buying good original vintage Coca-Cola advertising is good investment that will appreciate nicely. On the other hand, buying new "made for the collector's market" merchandise can be fun, and makes a nice collection. However, I personally do not see any positive long-term investment growth on this type of collectible. Even with the high quality standards The Coca-Cola Company demands for licensed products, the facts are simply that new collectibles are not a great investment. So, if you buy new pieces, buy them because you like them, you like the way they look and will enjoy them. But please do not be fooled into believing you are building a major investment-based collection. There is a phrase that I happen to like. It is not mine, but I do use it all the time and I think it fits perfectly here: "If it was not meant to be collected.......collect it."

## STORIES

How many times have you heard people say, "Oh! . . . I could write a book." Well get ready to hear it again, because I could write a book and I would like to title it "The Stories People Tell . . . and The People Who Believe Those Stories."

It seems that people who deal in antiques and collectibles find it necessary not only to sell the piece, but to attempt to enhance it with some sort of history or story to add to the mystique of such a rare treasure. The problem is that many of these stories are true or have some basis of truth to them, and it is always important to get any available information about a piece. In fact, I always ask if the dealer has any information such as where it came from and was there anything else with it. These questions will sometimes offer leads to future finds.

The main problem is determining the fact from the fiction, and basically learning about what you collect is the best way to separate one from the other. The people who make up these stories usually do not have the correct facts to back up the fantasy they have created or are passing on. It is your job as a knowledgeable collector to get as much information as you can and then analyze it and try to separate the truth from the fiction. I just wish that after every "fantastic" story I have been told about a Coke piece, that I would have recorded or written it down. They would really make great reading. If you have been collecting for more than two months, you must have already heard many of them: warehouse find, bought out of an old bottling plant, found in the rafters of an old house, bought out of an old woman's trunk that has never been opened, and my personal favorite: "bought out of an old store that has been boarded up since 1920."

Hopefully the information found in this book should help you as a collector make the correct decisions on buying a particular piece, without relying on a fantastic story by the dealer. Unfortunately most of these old stories are used to enhance a phony piece rather than an original piece. Try to use some common sense and do not rely on the story to make the decision to buy or not. I can tell you many times people have told me "the piece cannot be a phony because the dealer told me he bought it from a woman who had it for fifty years." Do your homework, study the logos on pieces used over the years and how they have changed. So, if a piece is presented to you as early 1900s and found in a treasure chest that has been buried since 1905, and the logo is of 1950s vintage, you will be able to better understand the type of story you are dealing with.

One of my pet peeves is the misuse of words or phrases by dealers or auction houses in this same attempt to enhance a particular piece. You know the words and phrases because you have heard them hundreds of times, and that is the problem, the over-use will dilute the meaning to the point that when it is truly called for, it is not believed. Rare, very rare, only one known to exist, never seen before, the only one I have ever seen, only one of three known—the list goes on, but you get the idea. Through this book, you will see a number of pieces that I have marked as rare or very rare. I do so because they are rare and I feel confident that the piece is scarce enough to be called rare. I get a real kick out of auction ads or dealers who claim the piece they have is very rare or the only one known to exist when I have sold a number of them over the years. Try to take these stories and over-used phrases with a grain of salt and try to realize that it is part of the nature of dealing in antiques and collectibles.

## RESTORATION

There does not seem to be a general consensus among Coke collectors regarding restoration. Some feel very strongly against having any restored pieces in their collection. Others seem to have more of an open mind about it. Traditionally, certain areas of collecting have an almost complete acceptance for restoration—vending machines are a perfect example. Personally, I have very strong feelings about restoration, and I would like to share them with you. Keep in mind that this acceptance level that I have is my own, and does vary from other collectors you may talk with. My feelings on restoration, what is acceptable and what is not acceptable are based on years of selling this memorabilia and realizing what the majority of the collecting community finds tolerable with restorations.

I am very much against any restoration other than cleaning and polishing on metal or porcelain, signs, trays, etc. I do not have a single piece of metal in my collection that has been touched up or restored in any way. Some find this perfectly acceptable, however I find it very difficult to sell trays, metal or porcelain signs that have been touched up. Of course, every rule has its exceptions, and this exception is the rare or super rare pieces. For example, I would have no problem owning a "Victorian Girl" tray that had been touched up. But for most collectors, including myself, metal, tin and porcelain restoration is not acceptable.

On the other hand, I find it perfectly acceptable to have major cleaning, buffing, touchup and restoration, and in some cases re-creation of parts of cardboard and paper pieces, especially rare cardboard cutouts. I have many paper signs, cardboard cutouts and early calendars in my collection that have had work done to them. Of course, I am talking about moderately rare to rare pieces and better. I would not consider restoration on common cardboard signs. Because of the cost of restoration, there has to be a cutoff or dividing point between what is worth restoring and what is not. I do not recommend using a particular date as a guide line. Rather, decide if the piece is rare or very rare. If it is, restore it. If it is common, do not restore it, but, rather, wait to find a better example, then sell off the other.

Restoration of clocks is also acceptable, but only on certain areas of the clock. Regulator clocks and other wood framed clocks can and should be refinished (if necessary). Have the wood case stripped and refinished. Of course, the proper procedure of removing movement, glass, face, and hinges prior to stripping and refinishing is important. Repair and reconditioning of clock movements should also be done on non-working examples. Movements that cannot be repaired should be replaced, mainly because a working clock is more desirable and valuable than a non-working clock. Please keep in mind, however, if it is possible, try to replace the movement with the same or similar movement from another clock. New movements are acceptable, but it is important to keep the old movement with the clock, as well as any repair bill or any other information regarding work that has been performed on the clock. The ability to show this information some time in the future to a potential buyer is certainly an advantage. There are a number of things that should not be done to clocks. Repainting or reproduction bottom glass is certainly a problem as well as replacing pendulums or ornate woodwork that is not original should also not be done. But the worst possible thing you can do to a clock is repaint, touch-up, or replace the face (dial) with a reproduction. This is certainly the "Kiss of Death," as far as value of any clock goes.

Bottles also have a minor acceptance level of restoration, but only on very rare examples. Repaired or replaced tops of Hutchinson bottles have been done successfully to improve the "displayability" of the bottle, however, the value of these repaired Hutch bottles is certainly lower.

I have two other areas of restoration that I personally find acceptable. First is the base of pedestal signs or the policeman crossing guard sign. These cast bases and poles can and should be repainted to enhance the overall look of the sign. Strip down old paint and spray with silver paint. The Coca-Cola logo in relief should be painted red. The second thing concerns gold wood frames for "litho insert." These gold wood frames and metal trim work can and should be repainted. Use a high quality gold spray paint. Remove the cardboard insert sign, and tin bottle emblem on the front (if it has one) and give only the front two coats. Be sure to turn the metal rods on each side between coats. Spray the tin emblem separately. Do not repaint the back of the frame. Most are stamped with the "Kay Display" information and you do not want to cover this up.

When buying a piece for resale or for your collection, it is important to know if it has been restored. Ask the seller what has been done, examine the piece carefully, looking for breaks in the paper or uneven color. If the piece is framed, ask if you may take it out to be examined. Do not forget that framing and matting can hide a multitude of sins. If the dealer will not let you take it out of the frame, be very skeptical. Also be sure when buying a piece that it can be returned if you become aware it has been restored if you were told otherwise. From a collector's stand point, you would like everything in your collection to be in mint, original condition, however this is just not reality, especially with something as delicate, and rare, as early paper. Most collectors find the need to display their collection, especially those rare pieces, in the best possible way—very important— and restoration certainly is an option in the "displayability" of the piece.

If you decide on restoration, please keep a few things in mind. Make sure that you find someone you feel comfortable with. Get recommendations or see samples of his or her work. Sometimes calling museums in your area and asking if they can make recommendations might be helpful. Also it is very important to photograph the piece prior to any restoration, attach an envelope to the back of the frame when it is done to keep these photos and receipts, dates, and the name of the person who restored it. It is always nice to show a future buyer of the piece a before photo as well as any other restoration information you have. Most importantly, you must realize that a piece of restored advertising, no matter how rare or how well that restoration was done, cannot be called mint and should always be hyphenated "restored" prior to condition. A restored piece will never have the value of a non-restored piece, even if they both appear to be of equal condition.

What this all comes down to is that restoration is a personal issue and, as a collector, you must decide if it is acceptable to you and how limited or extensive that restoration will be. The fluctuation of standards as far as restoration goes among collectors will always be there and setting standards for your collection is your choice, not mine or any other collector's. However, when setting your acceptance level, try to keep in mind not only what is best for your collection, but the appreciation and future potential value and resale-ability of the collection, and, finally, do not forget that some of the greatest works of art have been restored.

Certainly one of the main reasons why collectors are drawn to the advertising of The Coca-Cola Company is the beautiful artwork produced by some of the countries top artists working for the best advertising agencies. For the most part these artists remain un-named, sort of the "un-sung" heroes of Coca-Cola collectors. Of course the big names that we are all familiar with like Rockwell, Sundblum, Wyeth, and Stanley have become part of the vocabulary of collectors. Most of the other artists who produced this beautiful art are unfamiliar to the majority of the collecting community.

I believe it is very important for collectors to understand the process that went into the production of this art. The first and most important thing that has been misunderstood by most collectors is that this art was not produced by The Coca-Cola Company in Atlanta, but rather by advertising agencies from around the country who produced the art, hired models, put complete campaigns together, contracted with printing companies for production, and in many cases actually shipped advertising material to local bottlers. This misconception by many collectors that artists and their models were hired by The Coca-Cola Company is just not true. The models who appear on this beautiful art were hired by, and worked for, the artist or advertising company. The complete process of an advertising campaign and the art needed to accomplish it was basically very simple.

Account executives from an advertising company like Synder & Black, who produced for many years the quality pieces that we all search for, would travel to Atlanta to meet with the advertising department. These meetings would result in ideas from both sides, outlining the campaign or needs for the following year's advertising. With this outline in hand the agency would direct artists as to what was needed. Copywriters would fill in the blank spaces and create slogans, newspaper and magazine ad copy, billboards—whatever needed words. In some cases the advertising for a campaign revolved around a particular piece of art or a slogan. The image of the Sprite Boy or the slogan "Refresh Yourself" is a perfect example. The art itself was not done at first in its finished form. Rough or conceptual art was first created, some rejected, some accepted, or changed to meet the requirements of this particular campaign.

With rough art and strategy complete, artists would then create composition art or "comps." This was basically a refined piece of rough art, usually pencil drawings and watercolor. This composition art, along with copy, slogans and campaign strategy was then taken back to Atlanta for another meeting. Approvals, rejections and changes to numerous pieces of art and copy resulted in a fine tuning of the campaign. The approved comps were then returned to the artists for the creation of original art. In many cases artists were chosen for their particular specialty. The importance of the distinctive bottle and how it appeared on the final piece of art was of the utmost importance. Often the bottle or six-pack carton was added afterwards by another artist who specialized in this area of art.

One page from 1952 Elvgren calendar featuring TV stars of the day and a great Coke bottle

Close-up of Elvgren signature

Over the years The Coca-Cola Company became interested in particular artists and requested their work. Many were the obvious names previously mentioned--favorites like Norman Rockwell, N. C. Wyeth, Fred Mizen, Fredric Stanley and others who were in demand to produce artwork that The Coca-Cola Company felt best captured the image or look that they wanted presented to the buying public.

One of these artists, probably the best known to all Coca-Cola collectors, was Haddon Sundblum. His art, whether it be man, woman, or child, or the legendary image of Santa Claus, was the epitome of what The Coca-Cola Company felt their product stood for—that wholesome all-American, just-plain-folks look that made people feel good. Sundblum had a special relationship with the company that seemed to go way beyond the advertising agency, as letters and records between Sundblum and The Coca-Cola Company indicate. And, for good reason, Sundblum's images on the beautiful advertising that The Coca-Cola Company used not only impresses us as collectors, but in many cases was the model for advertising used throughout America during that period.

How is this artwork identified to a particular artist? Well, it is not easy, as many of you already know. Most of this art was not signed, or the signature does not appear on the finished (printed) piece. The reason for this is very simple. Producing advertising art by most if not all of these artists was not necessarily their intended advocation. It was, however, a dependable and reliable source of income, much more reliable than, lets say, painting a beautiful portrait of a woman and selling it through a gallery. In simple terms "It was a paycheck," and if you were good and could produce, it was usually a very nice paycheck. Most artists were not completely thrilled with working on a schedule or painting an image that was required and not "created." As with most of the creative community, deadlines, pre-arranged work, daily work schedules and constant changes does not fit well with the lifestyle of artists. Signing a piece of art was not that important to them, or in many cases just did not fit in with the image, and it was removed during the printing process. Obviously, a visual signature by a well-known artist like Norman Rockwell would not be removed; however, even Rockwell produced art for Coca-Cola can be found unsigned.

Gillett (Gil) Elvgren is one of my favorite artists who produced many pieces of art for Coca-Cola. With very few exceptions, his signature does not appear on finished pieces. He is also almost unknown in the Coca-Cola collectors community, while remaining one of the most well-known and accomplished pinup artists of all time, with his signature appearing on almost 100% of the pinup art he produced. Elvgren's first love was pinup art—that slightly naughty, beautiful girl next door art work that adorned calendars that were mainly seen in bars, auto supply stores, and gas stations. This was artwork that you would not associate with The Coca-Cola Company. Elvgren was actually a student of Sundblum. He admired him, worked with him, and actually copied his style—so much so, in fact that for reasons that I will not go into here, he used to complete unfinished paintings produced by Sundblum.

Elvgren's style made a complete change in the late 1940s. The style was not a subtle change, but rather a dramatic one that also included a change in his signature. Elvgren was one of the main pinup artists for the Brown & Bigelow Company and with his style change, in my opinion, became one of the greatest "pinup" artists of all time. Elvgren also worked for Snyder & Black with some of his best work being done during the 1950s with only a few pieces actually showing his signature. It has become a real challenge for myself and others to distinguish an unsigned piece of Coca-Cola art as an Elvgren or a Sundblum. Gil Elvgren died in 1980, but he will live forever through the beautiful artwork he produced over the years. Unfortunately, he is among the group of un-sung heroes of the wonderful world of collecting Coca-Cola memorabilia, and the history of this great company.

Original artwork, including sketches, comps, rough art and original oil paintings are among the most desirable and prestigious of all Coca-Cola memorabilia—as well as being the most valuable—with paintings by Rockwell, Sundblum, Wyeth and others going for hundreds of thousands of dollars. But those are the exceptions, not the rule. Quality original art has changed hands for hundreds of dollars and in the thousands for original paintings.

Values on original art are based on the individual piece, but I can give you some guidelines regarding how valuable a particular piece may be. The first and most important piece would be an original oil painting of a "recognizable" image, signed by a well-known artist. Less value is given if the artist is unknown, much less if it is an unheard of artist. "Recognizable" art is an image that was actually used as an advertising piece, and can be identified, like a cardboard sign or calendar. Next would be a recognizable piece of art that remains unsigned (the difference between signed and unsigned art could be thousands of dollars.) And, finally, a piece that is not recognizable and is unsigned would certainly be desirable, but not in the high dollar range. Sketches or rough art and comps are much more common, but are still prized pieces in any collection. For the most part, however, original art, and in particular an original painting, remains only a "dream piece" for even the most advanced Coca-Cola collector.

The following is only a partial list of the many talented artists who created the advertising art of The Coca-Cola Company. Because so much of this art remains unsigned, and the names of most were only known by the advertising agencies that hired them, this list will never be complete.

| | | | |
|---|---|---|---|
| Harry Anderson | James Montgomery Flagg | Gerald Keane | Lyman Simpson |
| McClelland Barclay | Frank Godwin | Hamilton King | Robert Skemp |
| Lester Beall | Bill Gregg | B. Lichtman | Ben Stahl |
| Joseph Binder | Hananiah Harari | Victor Livoti | Frederic Stanley |
| Al Buell | Hayden Hayden (Howard Renwick) | Andrew Loomis | Haddon Sundblum |
| Pruet Carter | | Lougheed | Kenneth Thompson |
| Dean Cornwell | Heaslip | Athos Menaboni | Larry Tisdale |
| Bradshaw Crandall | Charles Heizerling | Fred Mizen | Thorton Utz |
| Stevan Dohanoe | John Held, Jr. | Norman Price | L. Wilbur |
| Albert Dorne | Everett Henry | George Rapp | Mortimer Wilson |
| Harvey Dunn | John Howard | Redoute | Jack Witrup |
| Gillett Elvgren | John Newton Howitt | Norman Rockwell | N. C. Wyeth |
| A. T. Farrell | Nick Hufford | Virgil Ross | |
| Fred Fixler | Lynn Bogue Hunt | George Schreiber | |

# COCA-COLA AND THE COMPETITION

When a new product hits the market that is accepted and enjoyed by the buying public, it stands to reason that competitors and imitators will soon follow. Some of this competition comes in the form of a similar product with its own look, style and advertising program that is new and fresh. The company will honestly make attempts to create its own look and style, and capture its own niche in the market—that is the American way. Others, attempting to quickly cash in on a hot new product's success, will unfairly use the name, goodwill and hard work of a successful company to promote a product that is only an imitation of the "Real Thing." This attempt to deceive the consumer was usually at the expense of The Coca-Cola Company, either with the manipulation of the name, nickname or slang term, or creating the appearance of a similar trademark, labeling or packaging. This, of course, is illegal today, but much of the trademark law that is in use today was written from cases brought against the "imitators" of The Coca-Cola Company.

The hoards of imitators began jumping on the bandwagon as soon as they realized how much the public enjoyed this new cola drink. The problem The Coca-Cola Company had with these new companies was two fold. First, the infringement of The Coca-Cola Trademark, and secondly, the deception and misleading of the public by substituting a less expensive or poorer quality syrup when Coca-Cola was requested. In either case, this growing problem was dealt with by the legal department of The Coca-Cola Company, headed by a young new Columbia Law School Graduate named Harold Hirsch. In 1909, Hirsch declared war on the "imitators," filing suit against any individual or company that used the company's trademarks, symbols, name or packaging, no matter how flagrant or subtle that use was. Hirsch's pursuit of these so-called "fake cola's" was unparalleled. He actually hired Pinkerton Detectives for undercover missions into soda fountains. After asking for a Coca-Cola, the sleuth would take samples for chemical analysis. With proof in hand, Hirsch filed lawsuits in record numbers, at one point actually filing an average of one per week.

To back up Hirsch's fervent pursuit to crush the "imitators," The Coca-Cola Company launched an all-out campaign to inform the public of the problem. "Call for it by full name…nicknames encourage substitution" was a typical slogan incorporated in the company advertising in 1914 in the hope that popular nicknames like "Dope" and "Koke" would not become the norm. The most important of all trademark infringement cases was brought by The Coca-Cola Company against "The Koke Company of America" in 1912. Finally settled and won by The Coca-Cola Company in 1920, a decree was handed down by the U.S. Supreme Court. The decree, written by Associate Justice Oliver Wendell Holmes, recognized that the word "Koke" was an abbreviation for "Coca-Cola," and declared that Coca-Cola meant "a single thing from a single source, and well known to the community." This historical decision in American trademark law strengthened Harold Hirsch and The Coca-Cola Company's position on its trademark, packaging, and even the color of the product. With precedent-setting decisions and stacks of cases won, Hirsch cataloged three volumes of Coca-Cola Law. The first of these was published in 1923: *Opinions, Orders, Injunctions and Decrees Relating to Unfair Competition and Infringement of Trade-Mark.* This hardbound 650-page law book was distributed by The Coca-Cola Company to lawyers and libraries. Volume #2 covers 1923 to 1930, followed by Volume #3, which includes 1931 to 1938. Any of these three volumes are sought after by Coca-Cola collectors and historians. The complete set is a real prize. While these books are very technical and may only be totally understood by an attorney, the cases, decisions and decrees are very interesting. The books contain many interesting photos of defendants, trademarks, labels and crowns, some of which are in color. I think the dedication in Volume One really sums up the reason for, and results of, this entire program: "Respectfully dedicated to the patrons of Coca-Cola. The protection given by law to trademarks had for it's object the protection of the owner in his property and the protection of the public from deception."

Collecting the advertising of these imitators or (sometimes called) "rip-off" brands has eluded all but the true diehard collectors, which I feel is a big mistake. Because these brands are such an important part of the history of The Coca-Cola Company, they do indeed have a place in any Coke collection.

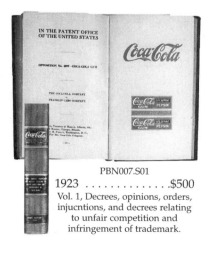

PBN007.S01
1923 . . . . . . . . . . . . .$500
Vol. 1, Decrees, opinions, orders, injucntions, and decrees relating to unfair competition and infringement of trademark.

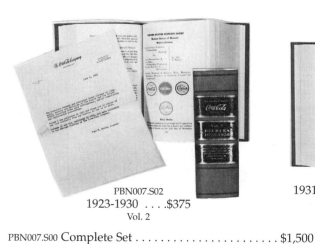

PBN007.S02
1923-1930 . . . .$375
Vol. 2

PBN007.S03
1931-1938 . . . .$350
Vol. 3

PBN007.S00 Complete Set . . . . . . . . . . . . . . . . . . . . . . $1,500

# COCA-COLA AND THE COMPETITION

While most of these products were short lived because of a law suit, the threat of a lawsuit, or just plain "heat" by The Coca-Cola Company, most of the advertising associated with these products is very rare—possibly much more rare than the equivalent Coca-Cola piece. Locating, collecting and displaying this material should certainly be of interest to today's Coca-Cola collectors. Naturally, the most blatant or obvious illegal use of the Coca-Cola name or trademark would be most collectible and, in turn, most valuable. "Koke," "Koka-Nola," "Coca-Kola," among others, would be highly desirable. On the following pages you will find a group of very interesting examples of advertising associated with some of these brands, as well as an extensive but in no way complete list of brand names which The Coca-Cola Company felt were

illegally using their name, trademark, or packaging in such a way as to deceive the buying public.

Many of these brands caused concern to The Coca-Cola Company, and the list includes products that the company sued, threatened to sue, or that simply died of natural causes from the pressure. After reviewing this list you will notice that very few of these brand names are familiar, even to the most advanced and long time soda-pop collector. Many of these brands were produced by companies that were so small, under financed, or the product was so locally distributed that any suit or threat of suit would quickly do them in. Remember, this list is by no means complete. In fact, it has been said (unofficially) that by 1926 The Coca-Cola Company could account for thousands of so-called "fake colas" being eliminated from the market.

The following is an extensive, but certainly not complete, list of brands that The Coca-Cola Company felt were illegally using their name, trademark, or packaging in such a way as to deceive the buying public.

| | | | | |
|---|---|---|---|---|
| Acme Kola | Coke | Hayo-Kola | Kos-Kola | Rox-Kola |
| Afri-Kola | Coke-Ola | Heck's Cola | Kos-Kolo | Rye-Ola |
| Apola Cola | Coke Extract | Hi-Peak Cola | Krinkly-Kola | Schokakola |
| Arkola | Cola | High Grade Cola | Lemo-Kok | Setzler's Cola |
| Ayers Cola | Cola-Nip | Hunt's Cola | Lemon Kola | Sheri-Cola |
| Bolama-Cola | Cola Coke | Hunt's Koke | Lime Cola | Sherry-Coke |
| Buster Kola | Cola Hiball | Hy-Po | Loco-Kola | Silver-Cola |
| C-Co | Cola Soda | Iceola | Luck-Ola | Smoke |
| Cafa-Cola | Cola-Rica | Jacob's Kola | Mellow-Nip | Sod-Ola |
| Cafe-Cola | Cold-Cola | John D. Fletcher's Coca- | Mexicola | Sola-Cola |
| Candy-Cola | COQ | and-Cola | Mi-Ola | Standard Cola |
| Capa Cola | Cream-Cola | Joyola | Mil-Coa | Star-Cola |
| Carbo-Cola | Cremo-Cola | Judge & Jerry | Mint-ett Kola | Star Coke |
| Caro-Cola | Cresent Coca-Cola | Julo Cola | Mint-Ola | Taka-Kola |
| Celery-Cola | Cresta Cola | K-O-K | Mint Cola | Takola |
| Celro-Kola | Crisola | Kal-Kola | Mitch-O-Cola | Taxi-Cola |
| Chapion Cola | Crown Cola | Kalinola | Mixo-Cola | Temptation Coke |
| Charcola | Curo-Cola | Kaola | My Coca | Tenn-Cola |
| Checkola | Curo-Kola | Kaw-Kola | Nerv-Ola | Texo-Cola |
| Cheriola | Derr's Coke | Kaye-Ola | Nifti-Cola | Toca-Coca |
| Chero-Cola | Derr's Cola | Keen Kola | Norka-Cola | Tona-Tona |
| Cherre Kola | Dextra Cola | Kel-Kola | Nova Kola | Top Cola |
| Cherri-Coke | Dixi-Cola | King Kola | O-Kola | Trico |
| Cherry-Kola | Dope | King-Cola | Okay Cocke | Tripure |
| Cherry and Coke | Drinkola | Kirk's Koke | Okla-Cola | True-Cola |
| Cherry Coke | Eastside Cola | Klu-Ko Kola | Ora-Ola | Twin Cola |
| Chocola | El-Cola | Ko-Co-Lem-A | Osce-Kola | Uneeda Cola |
| Choctaw Cola | Eli-Cola | Ko-Kola | Osce-Y-Ola | Vaco-Kola |
| Citra-Cola | Espo-Cola | Ko-Lo | Pat-Ra-Cola | Vani-Kola |
| Clove Cola | Extract of Coca-Cola | Ko-Nut | Pau-Pau Cola | Vera-Coca |
| Club Cola | Fairmont Kola | Koala | Penn Cola | Veri-Best Cola |
| Co-Club-Cola | Farri-Cola | Koca-Nola | Pepsi-Cola | Vimola |
| Co-Co-Cola | Fig-Cola | Koka Nova | Pepsi Nola | Vine-Cola |
| Co-Kola | Fletcher's Coca-Cola | Koke | Pillsbury's Coke | Vita-Cola |
| Coca-Beta | Four-Kola | Kokelo | Prima Cola | Vogel's Cola |
| Coca-Kola | French Wine Coca | Koko | Prince Cola | Wine-Cola |
| Coco-Lett | Frigola | Kokokola | Pure Cola | Wise-Cola |
| Coca and Cola | Gay-Ola | Kola | Qua-Kola | Yes, It's A Cola |
| Coca-Cola (Startup | Gerst's Cola | Kola-Ade | Quakola | Zippi-Cola |
| Candy Co.) | Glee-Nol | Kola-Kola | Reisch's Cola | |
| Cocasane | Hanne's Coca and Kola | Kola-Mist | Revive-Ola | |
| Coca-Lime | Hav-A-Dope | Kola-Vena | Rock & Rye | |
| Coffee Cola | Hava-Kola | KoLoKo | Roco Cola | |

PRB010.000
c.1915   4" x 8"  . . . . . . . . . . . . . . . . . $650
Koke stamped celluloid sign

PRB011.000
c.1914   5" x 10"  . . . . . . . . . . . . . . . . . $600
Dope celluloid sign

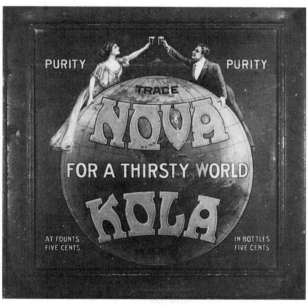

PRB012.000
c.1913   14" x 14"  . . . . . . . . . . . . . . . . . $600
Nova Kola self-framed tin sign

PRB015.000
Early 1900s  . . . $600
Koca-Nola wood
thermometer, Rare

PRB013.000
c.1902  . . . . . . . . . . . . . . . . . . $250
Koca-Nola celluloid watch fob

PRB014.000
c.1915   5" x 7"  . . . . . . . . . . . . . . . $650
Koke celluloid sign

PRB016.000
c.1902  . . . . . . . . . . . . . . . . . . . . . . $350
Koca-Nola match safe, Rare

PRB017.000

1915 . . . . . . . . . . . . . . . . . . . . . . . . $400

Koke calendar

Note: Keep in mind
most of this stuff is
considered rare. As
collector interest grows,
values will rise.

PRB018.000

1914 . . . . . . . . . . . . . . . . . . . . . . . . $400

Dope calendar

PRB019.000

1914 . . . . . . . . . . . . . . . . . . . . $500

Koke calendar

PRB021.000

1914 . . . . . . . . . . . . . . . . . . . . . . . . $50

My-Cola letter

We Guarantee the Contents of this Package to
Comply with the Requirements of the Pure Food
and Drugs Act. June 30. 1906.    KOKE CO.

BURNT SUGAR COLOR ADDED

DRINK
DELICIOUS
AND
REFRESHING    Koke    AT
FOUNTAINS
AND IN
BOTTLES

TRADE        MARK

ABSOLUTELY FREE FROM COCAINE

OR OTHER DELETERIOUS DRUGS PROSCRIBED
UNDER PURE FOOD AND DRUG LAWS
MANUFACTURED AND    KOKE CO.    SHREVEPORT
GUARANTEED BY    LOUISIANA

PRB020.000

1910 . . . . . . . . . . . . . . . . . . . . . . . . $125

Koke syrup keg label

Note: Part of the logo
of the My-Cola Co. was the
slogan "Manufactured
from the original
Coca-Cola formula."

# THE COCA-COLA SCRIPT TRADEMARK

The story or legend surrounding the naming and creating of that now well-known script trademark for Coca-Cola is an interesting one, and since it has never been disputed, the legend lives on. Frank Robinson, Pemberton's associate, named the product by using two of its ingredients, and changing the "K" in "Kola" to a "C." It was also Robinson, as the legend goes, who penned the famous script lettering that we are so familiar with. However, this early script version of the trademark was probably not used until 1887. Pemberton did apply for the registration of a trademark which was granted in June of 1887. However, this was for the words "Coca-Cola" in block letters, and not the script lettering. This script lettering, or "logo," has changed and has seen many variations over the years. Shown below are many of those variations. Study them, because knowing these logos and when they were used can be very helpful in determining age, as well as detecting a counterfeit piece. Keep in mind that many of the companies producing advertising for The Coca-Cola Company and especially local Coca-Cola Bottlers took liberties with the logo, in some cases altering or misusing—or even using—an out-dated logo, especially in the earlier years.

PLO-1        1880s-1892
Early script variation with diamonds

PLO-2        1890-1891
Unusual typestyle used on a number of calendars

PLO-3        1887-1890
Early script with line extending from first "O"
"Trade Mark" in tail; also no trademark in tail.

PLO-4        1893-1901
Crude script with "Trade-Mark" in tail, under tail or
no trademark with "Trade Mark Registered" in tail
1901-1903

PLO-5        1898-1902
Custom script with "Trade-Mark" in tail; note open
"O's", and unusual tails on "C's"

PLO-6        1903
Misused script "Trade-Mark Registered" in tail; used
on some 1903 calendars.

PLO-7        1903-1931
Traditional script "Trade-Mark Registered" in tail

PLO-8        1930-1941
Traditional script "Trade-Mark Reg. U.S. Pat. Off."
in tail

PLO-9        1941-1962
Traditional script "Reg. U.S. Pat. Off." under script

PLO-10        1950-Present
Traditional script "Trade Mark ®" under script

PLO-11        1958-1963
"Arciform" logo also called "Fishtail" logo by
collectors

PLO-12        1970-Present
"Dynamic Ribbon" also called "Wave"
logo; actually introduced in late 1969

# SLOGANS

Listed on the following pages is an extensive list of slogans used by The Coca-Cola Company from 1886 to the 1980s. Keep in mind that with all the slogans shown, this is still not a complete list. I have tried to date these slogans based on the starting year. However, because many of these slogans were used for a number of years, in some cases dates shown may be within the slogans time span rather than the starting year. It is also important to understand some of these slogans were used for many consecutive years. "Delicious and Refreshing" is a perfect example. Other slogans were used for a very short period, or possibly only for one particular piece of advertising. Collectors should find this list helpful in dating pieces in their collection, or researching potential new pieces. Dating by slogan is not absolute, but it is one more element that should help.

Accepted home refreshment. . . . . . . .1942
Adds a refreshing relish to every
    form of exercise. . . . . . . . . . . . . . .1906
Add zest to the hour. . . . . . . . . . . . . .1951
After the day's shopping, rest and
    relief in Coca-Cola. . . . . . . . . . . . . .1909
After the day's journey drink a glass
    of delicious, refreshing, Coca-Cola.
    It satisfies the thirst and pleases the
    palate. It relieves fatigue and
    imparts new vigor and new energy.
    Cooling, Refreshing. Delicious. . . . .1909
All-American choice for "time-out." . .1937
All roads lead by Coca-Cola signs. . .1925
All the world loves a Coca-Cola. . . . .1912
All the year round. . . . . . . . . . . . . . . .1923
All trails lead to ice-cold Coca-Cola. . .1935
Almost everyone appreciates the best. 1955
Along the highway to anywhere. . . . .1949
Always a delightful surprise. . . . . . . .1924
Always a fresh delight. . . . . . . . . . . . .1954
Always delightful. . . . . . . . . . . . . . . . .1923
America, give me your tired, your hot,
    your thirsty, your weary, your
    parched, your worn-out, etc. . . . . . .1969
America's family fun drink. . . . . . . . .1956
America's favorite moment. . . . . . . . .1937
America's preferred taste. . . . . . . . . . .1955
America's year-round answer to
    thirst. . . . . . . . . . . . . . . . . . . . . . . .1940
An ice cold with a red hot. . . . . . . . . .1929
And the same to you. . . . . . . . . . . . . .1940
The answer to thirst. . . . . . . . . . . . . . .1922
Any time, everywhere, the favorite
    beverage. . . . . . . . . . . . . . . . . . . . . .1918
Any time is the right time to pause
    and refresh. . . . . . . . . . . . . . . . . . . .1938
Appearances are sometimes deceiving
    but Coca-Cola can always be relied
    on as nourishing, refreshing and
    exhilarating. . . . . . . . . . . . . . . . . . .1908
Around the corner from anywhere. . . .1927
As American as Independence Day. . .1946
Ask for a bottle . . . sold everywhere. .1908
Ask for it by its full name–then you
    will get the genuine. . . . . . . . . . . . .1913
Ask for it either way. . . . . . . . . . . . . .1959
Ask for it . . . we serve the genuine. . .1912
At all Soda Fountains . . . . . . . . . . . . .1898
At ease . . . for refreshment. . . . . . . . .1942
At the little red sign. . . . . . . . . . . . . . .1927
At the red cooler. . . . . . . . . . . . . . . . . .1938
The ballplayers' one best beverage. . . .1914
Be really refreshed. . . . . . . . . . . . . . . .1959
Be refreshed. . . . . . . . . . . . . . . . . . . . .1952
The best beverage under the sun. . . . .1913
The best brain and nerve drink. . . . . .1898
The best drink anyone can buy. . . . . .1913

The best friend thirst ever had. . . . . .1938
The best is always the better buy. . . . .1942
The best of taste. . . . . . . . . . . . . . . . . .1956
The best served drink in the world. . .1929
Best loved sparkling drink in all the
    world. . . . . . . . . . . . . . . . . . . . . . . .1957
Between bites. . . . . . . . . . . . . . . . . . . .1933
Big bold taste that's always just
    right. . . . . . . . . . . . . . . . . . . . . . . . .1963
A big, bold unmistakable taste. . . . . .1965
Biggest catch—Ice Cold Coca-Cola. . . .1968
The bold taste of Coke lifts your
    spirits, boosts energy. . . . . . . . . . . .1965
Both—Delicious & Refreshing. . . . . . .1912
Bottle that launched 100 summers. . . .1969
Bounce back to normal. . . . . . . . . . . . .1933
Bright and bracing as sunshine. . . . . .1955
Bright, right taste. . . . . . . . . . . . . . . . .1955
Brighten every bite with Coke. . . . . . .1959
Brighten your meals with Coke. . . . . .1955
Bring home the Coke . . . . . . . . . . . . . .1956
Bring home the Coke today. . . . . . . . .1956
Bring in your thirst and go away
    without it. . . . . . . . . . . . . . . . . . . . .1940
The busiest man in the world
    (Santa Claus) . . . . . . . . . . . . . . . . . .1930
Buy someone you love a Coke. . . . . . .1972
By the way—refresh yourself. . . . . . . .1928
Call for Coke. . . . . . . . . . . . . . . . . . . . .1953
Call for it by full name, nicknames
    encourage substitution. . . . . . . . . . .1914
Carbonated in bottles 5c . . . . . . . . . . .1905
Carry a smile back to work. . . . . . . . .1934
A casual symbol of pleasant things. . . .1943
Cheerful lift of Coke. . . . . . . . . . . . . . .1958
Cheerful lift that's bright and lively. . .1959
A cheerful place to refresh! . . . . . . . . .1952
A chore's best friend. . . . . . . . . . . . . . .1963
Christmas calls for cartons of Coke. . .1958
Christmas without Coca-Cola—Bah,
    humbug! . . . . . . . . . . . . . . . . . . . . .1966
The classes and masses all enjoy Coca-
    Cola. . . . . . . . . . . . . . . . . . . . . . . . .1907
Coca-Cola—along the highway to any-
    where. . . . . . . . . . . . . . . . . . . . . . . .1949
Coca-Cola—a pure drink of natural
    flavors. . . . . . . . . . . . . . . . . . . . . . .1928
Coca-Cola belongs. . . . . . . . . . . . . . . .1941
Coca-Cola—continuous quality. . . . . .1947
Coca-Cola gives a touch of hospitality
    to sociable moments. . . . . . . . . . . . .1946
Coca-Cola gives that special zing—
    refreshes best. . . . . . . . . . . . . . . . . .1964
Coca-Cola goes along. . . . . . . . . . . . . .1939
Coca-Cola has that extra something. . .1942
Coca-Cola has the taste thirst goes for. 1939
Coca-Cola has the taste you never get
    tired of. . . . . . . . . . . . . . . . . . . . . . .1966

Coca-Cola helps show the world the
    friendliness of American ways. . . . .1945
Coca-Cola—High Balls—Gin Rickies .1906
Coca-Cola invites you to lunch. . . . . .1937
Coca-Cola is a delightful, palatable,
    healthful beverage. . . . . . . . . . . . . .1904
Coca-Cola is a perfect answer to
    thirst that no imitation can satisfy. .1919
Coca-Cola is an all year round must. . .1943
Coca-Cola is better, try it. Wherever
    ginger ale, seltzer or soda is good,
    Coca-Cola is better, try it. . . . . . . . .1908
Coca-Cola is full of vim, vigor and
    go—is a snappy drink. . . . . . . . . . .1907
Coca-Cola is good. . . . . . . . . . . . . . . . .1943
Coca-Cola is the shortest distance
    between thirst and refreshment. . . .1926
Coca-Cola lightens worries. . . . . . . . .1907
Coca-Cola makes flow of thought more
    easy and reasoning power more
    vigorous. . . . . . . . . . . . . . . . . . . . . .1899
Coca-Cola—makes good things taste
    better. . . . . . . . . . . . . . . . . . . . . . . .1956
Coca-Cola puts you at your sparkling
    best. . . . . . . . . . . . . . . . . . . . . . . . . .1956
Coca-Cola refreshes you best. . . . . . . .1962
Coca-Cola revives and sustains. . . . . .1905
Coca-Cola—satisfies. . . . . . . . . . . . . . .1904
The Coca-Cola Sprite. . . . . . . . . . . . . .1942
Coca-Cola—the great temperance
    beverage—it has none of the ill
    effects or "let down" qualities of
    alcoholic stimulants. . . . . . . . . . . . .1907
Coca-Cola—the pause that brings
    friends together. . . . . . . . . . . . . . . .1935
Coke . . . . . . . . . . . . . . . . . . . . . . . . . . .1941
Coke Adds Life . . . . . . . . . . . . . . . . . .1976
Coke adds life to everything nice. . . . .1970
Coke Adds Zest. . . . . . . . . . . . . . . . . . .1952
Coke—after Coke—after Coke. . . . . . .1966
Coke and food—refreshing new
    feeling. . . . . . . . . . . . . . . . . . . . . . .1961
Coke belongs. . . . . . . . . . . . . . . . . . . . .1948
Coke follows thirst everywhere. . . . . .1952
Coke . . . for hospitality. . . . . . . . . . . .1948
Coke for me too. . . . . . . . . . . . . . . . . .1945
Coke is the taste you never get tired
    of. . . . . . . . . . . . . . . . . . . . . . . . . . .1967
Coke headquarters. . . . . . . . . . . . . . . .1942
Coke is a natural. . . . . . . . . . . . . . . . . .1952
Coke is best in bottle naturally. . . . . .1952
Coke is just right. . . . . . . . . . . . . . . . . .1957
Coke is it. . . . . . . . . . . . . . . . . . . . . . . .1980
Coke means Coca-Cola. . . . . . . . . . . . .1945
Coke on-the-job keeps workers
    refreshed. . . . . . . . . . . . . . . . . . . . .1959
Coke party. . . . . . . . . . . . . . . . . . . . . . .1942
Coke refreshes you best. . . . . . . . . . . .1960

# SLOGANS

Coke time. .......................1954
Coke time . . . join the friendly circle. .1955
Coke with food. ..................1937
Cold, crisp, refreshing. ...........1958
Cold, crisp taste of coke. .........1958
Cold, crisp taste that deeply satisfies. .1959
Come in . . . We have Coca-Cola. .....1951
Come over for a Coke. ............1947
Come up smiling for a fresh start. ....1931
Completely refreshing. ............1941
Continuous quality is quality you
    trust. ........................1947
Cool off with coke. ...............1960
Cool refreshment. ................1952
Cooling lift. .....................1958
Cooling refreshment. ..............1935
Cooling—refreshing—delicious. ....1907
Cures Headache. ..................1898
Cures headache, Relieves exhaustion. .1896
Delicious and refreshing. ..........1904
Delicious and refreshing all the year
    'round. .......................1923
Delicious Coca-Cola, sustains,
    refreshes, invigorates. ..........1907
Delicious! Refreshing! Exhilarating!
    Invigorating! ..................1886
Delicious refreshing invigorating. ....1886
Delicious—Refreshing—Thirst
    Quenching ....................1909
Delicious, sparkling, always
    refreshing. ....................1953
Delicious, wholesome, refreshing. ...1909
Delicious, wholesome, thirst-
    quenching. ....................1909
Deliciously refreshing. ............1900
Deliciousness belongs to Coca-Cola. ..1910
Delightful beverage. ..............1893
Delightful? Healthful? Refreshing? ...1907
Delightful summer and winter
    beverage. .....................1896
Delightful summer and winter drink. .1891
Delightfully carbonated and so easily
    served. .......................1911
Demand the genuine by full name. ...1913
Demand the genuine—refuse
    substitutes. ...................1912
Dependable as sunrise. ............1953
A distinctive drink in a distinctive
    bottle. .......................1922
Don't wear a tired thirst face. .......1953
Drink a bottle of carbonated
    Coca-Cola. ....................1905
Drink a bottle of Coca-Cola. ........1913
Drink bottled Coca-Cola—so easily
    served. .......................1910
Drink carbonated Coca-Cola in bottles.1902
Drink Coca-Cola ..................1886
Drink Coca-Cola all the year 'round. ..1924
Drink Coca-Cola, anywhere, anytime. .1933
Drink Coca-Cola at soda fountains. ...1905
Drink Coca-Cola Highballs (the
    morning after). ................1921
Drink Coca-Cola in bottles. ........1910
Drink Coca-Cola with soda. ........1920
Drink delicious Coca-Cola. .........1909
Drink it—you'll enjoy it! ...........1910
Drink the drink the Nation drinks. ...1913
The drink everybody knows. .......1939
The drink everybody remembers. ....1943
The drink you eat. ................1969

A drink of all the year. ............1917
The drink of hospitality. ...........1935
The drink of quality. ..............1906
The drink that adds life and sparkle
    to living. .....................1945
The drink that awakens energy. ......1934
The drink that cheers but does not
    inebriate. .....................1908
The drink that has outgrown the
    seasons. ......................1928
The drink that keeps you feeling fit. ..1934
The drink that makes the pause
    refreshing. ....................1932
The drink they all expect. ..........1942
Drive refreshed. ..................1952
Drive safely—drive refreshed. .......1953
Enjoy a glass of liquid laughter. ......1911
Enjoy Coca-Cola. .................1965
Enjoy Coca-Cola with ice cream. ....1964
Enjoy for it's purity and
    wholesomeness. ................1927
Enjoy frozen Coca-Cola. ...........1969
Enjoy refreshment and be refreshed
    for enjoyment. ................1929
Enjoy that refreshing new feeling. ....1962
Enjoy the lively life of Coke. ........1962
Enjoy the real great taste. ..........1957
Enjoy the sociable drink. ...........1925
Enjoy the quality taste. ............1956
Enjoy thirst—Drink Coca-Cola. .....1924
Enjoy thirst through all four seasons. .1923
Entertain your Thirst. .............1941
Even the bubbles taste better. .......1956
Every bottle refreshes. ............1948
Every bottle sterilized. ............1931
Every day is election day for
    Coca-Cola. ....................1936
Every delicious sip has the flavor of
    refreshment. ..................1941
Every glass holds the answer to thirst. 1922
Everybody drinks Coca-Cola—it answers
    every beverage requirement—vim,
    vigor, refreshment, wholesomeness.1913
Everybody likes it. ................1925
Everybody likes to work refreshed. ...1948
Everybody welcomes Coca-Cola—
    it's the real thing. ...............1942
Everybody's club. .................1947
Everything your thirst could ask for. ..1941
Everywhere the pause that refreshes
    has become symbol of good will. ..1945
Exhilarating, Invigorating. .........1886
Experience proves that nothing takes
    the place of quality. .............1941
Extra-bright. ....................1955
Extra bright refreshment. ..........1953
Face the day refreshed. ............1939
Face the sun refreshed. ............1941
Face Uncle Sam with a Coke in your
    hand. ........................1969
Fagged? Follow the arrow. .........1908
Familiar refreshment. .............1940
Favored above all others for
    refreshment. ..................1953
The favorite drink for ladies when
    thirsty, weary and despondent. ...1905
Feel fit for what's ahead. ...........1934
Feel the difference. ...............1956
Flows from every fountain. .........1905
Follow the crowd. ................1914

For everybody everywhere. ........1913
For extra fun . . . Take more than
    one. .........................1963
For extra fun—take more than one!
    Take an extra carton of Coke. .....1965
For headache and exhaustion, drink
    Coca-Cola. ....................1893
For headache or tired feeling. .......1891
For headache or tired feeling summer
    or winter. .....................1890
For home and hospitality. ..........1951
For people on the go. ..............1954
For the taste you never get tired of. ...1963
For that tired, discouraged feeling,
    drink Coca-Cola. ...............1927
For tired nerves and brain. ..........1893
For extra fun . . . take more than one. .1963
Foul-weather friend. ..............1969
The friendliest club in the world. .....1946
The friendliest drink on earth. .......1956
Friendliness and Coca-Cola go
    together, like bread and butter. ....1946
A friendly hand r.o matter where
    you are. ......................1920
Friendly pause. ..................1948
A friendly place to meet. ...........1952
Friendly refreshment. .............1952
Friends for life. ..................1935
From a bottle through a straw. ......1909
Fun gets better when you have a
    Coke. ........................1957
Fun to be thirsty. ................1916
Get it here ice cold. ...............1931
Get that look alive, be alive sparkle. ..1962
Get the feel of wholesome
    refreshment. ..................1936
Get the genuine. .................1906
Get the zest that refreshes best. ......1960
Get together club. ................1947
Get together with refreshment. ......1941
Get value, lift, and good taste, too! ...1958
Get what you ask for and see that
    you get it. ....................1910
The gift for thirst. ................1952
Give a bright little lift. ............1956
Gives so much and asks so little. .....1937
A glass of Coke, a pair of straws
    and thou. .....................1969
A great combination. ..............1929
A great drink . . . with good things
    to eat. .......................1938
The glass of fashion. ..............1926
The glass that answers that call of
    millions. ......................1919
The gift for thirst. ................1953
The global high sign. ..............1944
Go better refreshed. ..............1963
Go refreshed. ....................1952
Go with Coke. ...................1969
Good all the way down. ...........1905
Good company. ..................1927
Good food and Coca-Cola just
    naturally go together. ...........1951
Good taste. .....................1957
Good taste and refreshing. .........1928
Good taste for all. ................1955
Good taste is in fashion. ...........1957
Good to the last drop. .............1908
Good with food. .................1950
Good with snacks. ................1959

# SLOGANS

Good with so many good things......1951
Got enough Coke on Ice?..........1945
Got a long thirst, get a long king!....1959
A gracious place in daily living......1957
Graduate to Coke.................1963
A great combination...............1929
A great drink with food...........1942
The great national drink..........1907
The great temperance beverage—a
   liquid food for brain, body and
   nerves......................1906
Great together....................1932
Great to have on ice at home.......1922
The greatest pause on earth........1940
Greetings from Coca-Cola..........1946
Guaranteed under the Pure food
   and Drug Act, June 30th, 1906,
   Serial #3324..................1906
Halloween treat'em right with Coke..1955
A happy answer to thirst..........1932
Happy ending to thirst............1942
A happy thought..................1927
A happy thought "Refresh Yourself"..1926
Happy Days.....................1910
Happy Days drink Coca-Cola.......1910
Happy days—Good company.......1926
Happy hour—have a Coke.........1947
Happy moment of hospitality.......1946
Happy pause for the youth of all ages.1958
Happy sparkle of coke............1955
The happy symbol of a friendly way
   of life......................1945
Have a Coke and a smile..........1979
Have a Coke and be happy.........1954
"Have a Coke" means............1943
Have a Coke with us.............1956
Have a float with Coke...........1964
Have a large Coke...............1958
Have a large Coke at our fountain...1956
Have an ice cold Coke right now....1950
Have Fun! Have a Coke!..........1957
Heart's desire..................1916
Heed the little thirst—the big one
   surely takes care of itself.......1926
Hello Coke.....................1944
Help yourself to refreshment.......1950
Here's a Coke for you............1961
Here's what you want—Coca-Cola....1913
High sign of friendship...........1944
The high sign of refreshment.......1929
The hit that saves the day.........1920
Home refreshment...............1937
Home refreshment on the way......1945
Hospitality at its best............1953
Hospitality is in your hands........1947
Host for the holidays.............1952
Host of the Highways............1950
Host to thirsty Main Street........1952
Hot foods call for ice cold Coke!....1962
Hot? Tired? Thirsty?.............1908
Ice-cold Coca-Cola has that taste that
   charms, and never cloys.........1940
Ice-cold Coca-Cola is everywhere else
   —it ought to be in your family
   refrigerator..................1934
Ice-cold Sunshine—Thirst come, thirst
   served......................1932
The ideal beverage for discriminating
   people......................1906
The ideal brain tonic.............1893

I'd like to buy the world a Coke......1971
I love its flavor.................1902
I'll bring the Coke...............1946
Imitations are made to fool you, not to
   please you...................1906
In wintertime too...............1935
The inspiring alliance—Coca-Cola,
   delicious, refreshing, and thirst
   quenching...................1918
An international passport to
   refreshment.................1945
In sterilized bottles.............1926
In the distinctive bottle..........1924
Invitation to be happy...........1954
Invitation to pause—refresh!.......1939
Is a delightful, palatable and healthful
   beverage....................1905
It answers every beverage requirement—
   vim, vigor, refreshment,
   wholesomeness...............1913
It cools you...................1936
It had to be good to get where it is...1925
It has the charm of purity.........1925
It invites a pause...............1933
It is a charming—healthful drink....1906
It is always nourishing, refreshing,
   invigorating. More than 250 million
   bottles (glasses) used last year. For
   sale everywhere...............1908
It is the ideal beverage...........1906
It means so much—cost so little.....1932
It never fails to please...........1942
It satisfies....................1910
It satisfies the thirsty and helps the
   weary......................1905
It satisfies thirst..............1919
It sustains because it is a true food. It
   refreshes because it has a slightly
   tonic effect on the system. It
   invigorates because it supplies the
   elements for physical and mental
   exertion....................1907
It will satisfy you..............1913
It's a date at the fountain.........1944
It's a family affair..............1942
It's a lucky thirst that meets an ice-cold
   Coca-Cola...................1939
It's a natural..................1953
It's a refreshing little minute that's long
   enough for a big rest...........1940
It's always summer to your thirst....1938
It's clean and pure, That's Sure!.....1909
It's easy to relax with the pause that
   refreshes...................1947
It's fun to be thirsty when you can get
   a Coca-Cola.................1916
It's great to be thirsty when you know
   the answer..................1922
Its life and sparkle fit any occasion...1939
It's part of the game to take "time
   out".......................1938
Its taste holds the answer.........1939
It's the real thing. (First used this
   year).......................1948
It's the real thing. (Used with
   "Everybody Welcomes
   Coca-Cola").................1970
It's the refreshing thing to do.......1936
It's time to drink Coca-Cola........1911
It's twice time.................1968

I've been thirsty, and I've been refreshed,
   and believe me refreshed is better..1969
Join the club...................1952
Just a drink—but what a drink!......1928
Just one glass will tell you.........1916
Keep at home for all occasions......1962
Keep cool—Drink Coca-Cola........1911
Life, liberty, and the pursuit of thirst..1926
A liquid food for brain, body and
   nerves......................1907
A little minute—a big rest.........1952
A little minute is long enough for a
   big rest.....................1929
The little red sign at a cool and
   cheerful place................1927
Look up America................1975
Lunch refreshed................1948
Make it a real meal.............1959
Make lunch time refreshment time...1939
Make mine a Coke..............1941
Make refreshment complete.......1956
Makes a little moment long enough
   for a big rest................1929
Makes good things taste better......1956
Makes travel more pleasant........1939
March goes better with Coke.......1969
Matchless flavor................1954
Matchless—that's Coke—matchless...1954
Meet me at the sofa fountain.......1930
A Merry Christmas calls for Coke....1960
Midsummer magic..............1953
7 million drinks a day............1926
A moment on the sunnyside.......1944
More than just a drink...........1933
The most asked for soft drink for 75
   years......................1980
The most asked for soft drink in the
   world.....................1954
The most delicious and refreshing of
   all summer drinks. Eminent
   scientists in every section of the
   country declare it to be no more
   harmful than tea or coffee......1910
The most refreshing drink in the
   world.....................1902
The most refreshing drink on earth...1911
My hat's off to the pause that
   refreshes...................1931
The national beverage—and yours...1914
The national family drink.........1927
The national drink at the great
   national game...............1907
National thirst eliminator..........1969
A natural drink of natural flavors....1926
A natural drink that answers natural
   thirst......................1919
A natural partner of good things to
   eat.......................1934
Nature's purest and most wholesome
   drink......................1926
Nicknames encourage substitutions..1913
No. 1 in the sun................1969
No wonder Coke refreshes you best..1960
Nothing like that great taste of Coke!.1956
Nothing refreshes like a Coke......1943
Nothing soft about the taste of
   Coca-Cola..................1965
Now King Size too!.............1955
Now! 12 oz. cans too!...........1960
Off to a fresh start..............1930

# SLOGANS

Old Santa says: "Me Too." . . . . . . . . . .1930
One little minute that's long enough
    for a big rest. . . . . . . . . . . . . . . . .1927
One of the simple things that make
    living pleasant. . . . . . . . . . . . . . . .1941
Only Coca-Cola refreshes you best. . . .1962
Only Coke gives you that refreshing
    new feeling. . . . . . . . . . . . . . . . . .1962
The official soft drink of summer. . . . .1989
The only thing like Coca-Cola is
    Coca-Cola itself. . . . . . . . . . . . . . .1941
The package that gets a welcome
    at home. . . . . . . . . . . . . . . . . . . . .1940
Ours is ice cold. . . . . . . . . . . . . . . . . .1929
Palate pleasing. . . . . . . . . . . . . . . . . .1908
Park your thirst at the familiar red
    cooler. . . . . . . . . . . . . . . . . . . . . . .1941
Part of every day. . . . . . . . . . . . . . . . .1942
Part of the game. . . . . . . . . . . . . . . . .1936
Passport to refreshment . . . . . . . . . . .1945
Pass-words to a delightful experience. 1942
Pause a minute—Refresh yourself. . . .1926
Pause and refresh yourself. . . . . . . . .1924
Pause—Go Refreshed. . . . . . . . . . . . .1944
Pause often, and always drink Coke. .1959
Pause Refresh . . . . . . . . . . . . . . . . . . .1954
Pause refresh yourself. . . . . . . . . . . . .1952
The pause that brings friends together. 1935
The pause that keeps you going. . . . .1934
The pause that refreshes. . . . . . . . . . .1929
People go better refreshed. . . . . . . . . .1964
People on the go—go for Coke. . . . . .1954
A perfect blend on many flavors—
    has a flavor all its own. . . . . . . . . .1929
A perfect blend of pure products from
    nature. . . . . . . . . . . . . . . . . . . . . . .1923
A perfect drink—both nourishing and
    refreshing. . . . . . . . . . . . . . . . . . . .1907
The perfect gift for thirst. . . . . . . . . . .1954
The perfect way to climax a happy
    occasion—to make any occasion
    happy. . . . . . . . . . . . . . . . . . . . . . .1946
Physically sustaining, good to the taste,
    and an aid to the digestion. . . . . . .1907
Pick up 6 for home refreshment. . . . .1952
Picnic partners. . . . . . . . . . . . . . . . . .1952
Planning Hospitality. . . . . . . . . . . . . .1952
Play host to thirst. . . . . . . . . . . . . . . .1952
Play refreshed. . . . . . . . . . . . . . . . . . .1949
Pleasure all the way. . . . . . . . . . . . . .1952
Pre-eminently the drink of quality. . . .1906
Proves big help for tired housewives. .1909
Pure and healthful. . . . . . . . . . . . . . .1904
Pure and wholesome. . . . . . . . . . . . . .1914
Pure and wholesome it is tempting. . .1912
Pure as sunlight. . . . . . . . . . . . . . . . .1927
A pure drink of natural flavors. . . . . . .1929
Purity and flavor sealed in a bottle. . . .1928
Puts vim and go into tired brains and
    bodies. . . . . . . . . . . . . . . . . . . . . . .1907
Puts you at your sparkling best. . . . . .1953
A quality drink. . . . . . . . . . . . . . . . . .1906
Quality carries on. . . . . . . . . . . . . . . .1942
Quality is the reason millions have
    made it theirs. . . . . . . . . . . . . . . . .1919
The quality of Coca-Cola is a friendly
    quality you can always trust. . . . . .1947
The quantity only is cut, by keeping
    up it's quality. Coca-Cola keeps faith
    with it's friends. . . . . . . . . . . . . . . .1918

Quality tells the difference. . . . . . . . . .1919
Quality you can trust. . . . . . . . . . . . . .1942
Quenches the thirst as nothing else
    can. . . . . . . . . . . . . . . . . . . . . . . . .1910
Quenching thirst everywhere. . . . . . . .1922
Real holidays call for the real thing. . .1970
Real satisfaction in every glass. . . . . .1911
Refresh and add zest to the hour. . . .1950
Refresh at our fountain. . . . . . . . . . . .1937
Refresh yourself. . . . . . . . . . . . . . . . .1923
Refresh your guests. . . . . . . . . . . . . . .1934
Refresh yourself while shopping. . . . .1933
Refreshes the weary, brightens the
    intellect, clears the brain. . . . . . . . .1905
Refreshes you best. . . . . . . . . . . . . . .1959
Refreshing anytime—anywhere. . . . . .1953
Refreshing as a morning breeze. . . . .1935
Refreshing as a morning dip. . . . . . . .1935
Refreshing as a summer breeze—
    Invigorating as a dip in the sea. . . .1907
Refreshing surprise. . . . . . . . . . . . . . .1953
The refreshing custom. . . . . . . . . . . . .1939
The refreshment of friends. . . . . . . . .1953
The rest—pause that refreshes. . . . . .1943
Refreshment for shopping days. . . . . .1929
Refreshment right out of the bottle. . . .1948
Refreshment that can't be duplicated. .1942
Refreshment the whole world prefers. 1958
Refreshment through the years. . . . . .1951
Refreshment through 70 years. . . . . . .1955
Refreshment time. . . . . . . . . . . . . . . .1925
Refreshment with the lively going
    taste. . . . . . . . . . . . . . . . . . . . . . . .1962
Refreshment you go for. . . . . . . . . . . .1944
Refuse imitations. . . . . . . . . . . . . . . .1918
Relax refreshed. . . . . . . . . . . . . . . . . .1959
Relax with Coke. . . . . . . . . . . . . . . . .1960
Relax with the pause that refreshes. . .1947
Relieves fatigue. . . . . . . . . . . . . . . . . .1906
Relieves fatigue and calms over-
    wrought nerves without undue
    stimulation. . . . . . . . . . . . . . . . . . .1907
Relieves fatigue and is indispensable
    for business and professional men,
    students, wheelmen and athletes. . .1905
Relieves fatigue of brain, body and
    nerves. . . . . . . . . . . . . . . . . . . . . . .1909
Relieves fatigue . . . quenches thirst. . .1910
Relieves mental and physical
    exhaustion. . . . . . . . . . . . . . . . . . .1891
Relieves spring fever. . . . . . . . . . . . . .1969
Restful and bracing. . . . . . . . . . . . . . .1906
Rests the tired nerves and brain. . . . .1898
Restores energy. . . . . . . . . . . . . . . . . .1906
Restores energy—strengthens the
    nerves. . . . . . . . . . . . . . . . . . . . . . .1906
Revive with Coke. . . . . . . . . . . . . . . .1960
Right off the ice—Coca-Cola. . . . . . . .1910
Right through the year the best
    beverage. . . . . . . . . . . . . . . . . . . . .1911
The satisfactory beverage. . . . . . . . . .1908
Satisfied. . . . . . . . . . . . . . . . . . . . . . .1906
Satisfies the thirst and pleases the
    palate. . . . . . . . . . . . . . . . . . . . . . .1907
Satisfies the thirsty and helps the
    weary. . . . . . . . . . . . . . . . . . . . . . .1905
The Satisfying Beverage. . . . . . . . . . .1912
See you at the beach. . . . . . . . . . . . . .1969
Serve Coca-Cola & add punch to
    your holidays. . . . . . . . . . . . . . . . .1958

Serve ice cold. . . . . . . . . . . . . . . . . . .1953
Serve Ice Cold with sandwiches,
    cookies, cheese and crackers, and
    with your meals. . . . . . . . . . . . . . .1931
Serve it to your guests. . . . . . . . . . . .1935
Served all over the world. . . . . . . . . . .1932
Served here . . . Ice Cold. . . . . . . . . . .1937
Served right below 40 degrees. . . . . . .1936
Serving Coca-Cola says you do things
    right. . . . . . . . . . . . . . . . . . . . . . . .1956
Serving Coca-Cola serves hospitality. .1947
Shoppers and Business Men—tired
    people and thirsty people—nerve
    worn and brain weary people
    —people who just like to tickle the
    palate occasionally with a delicious
    beverage—all classes, ages and
    sexes—Drink Coca-Cola. . . . . . . . .1909
Shop refreshed. . . . . . . . . . . . . . . . . .1963
Sign of good taste. . . . . . . . . . . . . . . .1957
Simply Delicious. . . . . . . . . . . . . . . . .1909
Sip and see: Coke refreshes you best! .1962
Sip and Zip! . . . . . . . . . . . . . . . . . . .1962
Six keys to the popularity of Coca-Cola:
    Taste, Purity, Refreshing, Sociability,
    the Nickel, Thirst. . . . . . . . . . . . . .1927
Smart birds go for Coke. . . . . . . . . . .1964
So easily served. . . . . . . . . . . . . . . . .1910
So easy, so welcome. . . . . . . . . . . . . .1952
So easy to carry home. . . . . . . . . . . . .1942
So easy to serve—and so inexpensive. 1937
So easy to take home—the six bottle
    carton. . . . . . . . . . . . . . . . . . . . . . .1938
So good in taste, in such good taste. . .1957
So refreshing. . . . . . . . . . . . . . . . . . . .1930
So refreshing with lunch. . . . . . . . . . .1939
So refreshing with food. . . . . . . . . . . .1938
So right, so bright. . . . . . . . . . . . . . . .1962
The sociability of thirst. . . . . . . . . . . .1925
The sociable drink. . . . . . . . . . . . . . . .1925
Sold everywhere—5c . . . . . . . . . . . . .1907
Sold in bottles. . . . . . . . . . . . . . . . . . .1905
Solutions go better refreshed. . . . . . . .1964
Some treat. . . . . . . . . . . . . . . . . . . . . .1933
Something more than a soft drink. . . .1965
Something more than mere thirst-
    slaking. . . . . . . . . . . . . . . . . . . . . .1906
Sparkling—harmless as water, and
    crisp as frost. . . . . . . . . . . . . . . . . .1908
Specific for Headache. . . . . . . . . . . . .1893
The spirit of hospitality is in the life
    and sparkle of ice-cold Coca-Cola. .1948
The standard beverage. . . . . . . . . . . . .1915
A star drink, Morning, Evening, Night.
    At home or Abroad, Traveling or
    Resting. Working or Recreating. . . .1904
Stay merry—refresh with Coke. . . . . .1964
Step into the nearest place and ask for
    a Coca-Cola. . . . . . . . . . . . . . . . . .1907
Stock up for the holidays. . . . . . . . . . .1953
Stop at the red sign. . . . . . . . . . . . . . .1926
Stop at the red sign and refresh
    yourself. . . . . . . . . . . . . . . . . . . . . .1925
Stop for a pause—go refreshed. . . . . .1937
A stop that belongs on your daily
    time-table. . . . . . . . . . . . . . . . . . . .1941
Strengthens the nerves. . . . . . . . . . . .1906
Summer goes better with Coke. . . . . .1969
Summertime goodness for winter
    thirst. . . . . . . . . . . . . . . . . . . . . . . .1925

Sure way to get a big smile—get Coke in the picture. . . . . . . . . . . . . . . . . .1964
Take Coke along. . . . . . . . . . . . . . . . .1952
Take home a carton. . . . . . . . . . . . . . .1958
Take home a few bottles. . . . . . . . . . . .1933
Take home several cartons. . . . . . . . . .1955
Take some home today! . . . . . . . . . . . .1952
Talk about refreshing. . . . . . . . . . . . . .1943
A taste all its own. . . . . . . . . . . . . . . . .1943
Taste is the lure in ice-cold Coca-Cola. . . . . . . . . . . . . . . . . . . . .1935
That taste-good feeling. . . . . . . . . . . . .1926
The taste is the test. . . . . . . . . . . . . . . .1919
The taste is the test of the Coca-Cola quality. . . . . . . . . . . . . . . . . . . . . . . .1917
The taste of victory. . . . . . . . . . . . . . . .1984
The true spirit of hospitality. . . . . . . .1933
The year round drink. . . . . . . . . . . . . .1921
They go together. . . . . . . . . . . . . . . . . .1942
Things go better with the taste of Coke. . . . . . . . . . . . . . . . . . . . . . . . .1963
Through the years. . . . . . . . . . . . . . . . .1939
Taste the difference. . . . . . . . . . . . . . .1956
A taste thrill. . . . . . . . . . . . . . . . . . . . .1932
Taste Treat. . . . . . . . . . . . . . . . . . . . . .1955
Tells your taste to go fly a kite. . . . . . .1968
That extra something. . . . . . . . . . . . . .1943
That extra something—you can spot it every time. . . . . . . . . . . . . . . . . . . .1943
That taste good feeling. . . . . . . . . . . . .1939
That's for me. . . . . . . . . . . . . . . . . . . . .1945
There never was a thirst that Coca-Cola couldn't satisfy. . . . . . . .1912
There's a delicious freshness to the flavor of Coca-Cola. . . . . . . . . . . . .1917
There's a refreshing little minute on the sunny side of things. . . . . . . . .1942
There's money in it. . . . . . . . . . . . . . . .1909
There's no drink so easy to get . . . . . .1930
There's nothing like a Coke. . . . . . . . .1957
There's nothing like it when you're thirsty. . . . . . . . . . . . . . . . . . . . . . . .1923
There's nothing like that great taste of Coke. . . . . . . . . . . . . . . . . . . . . . . . .1956
There's this about Coke. . . . . . . . . . . .1954
Things go better with Coke. . . . . . . . .1963
Things would have gone better with Coke. . . . . . . . . . . . . . . . . . . . . . . . .1969
Think of lunchtime as refreshment time. . . . . . . . . . . . . . . . . . . . . . . . .1948
Thirst and taste for Coca-Cola are the same thing. . . . . . . . . . . . . . . . .1926
Thirst asks nothing more. . . . . . . . . . .1938
Thirst can't be denied. . . . . . . . . . . . . .1922
Thirst come—thirst served. . . . . . . . .1932
Thirst is a touch of nature which makes the whole world kin. . . . . . .1924
Thirst is discriminating. . . . . . . . . . . .1925
Thirst knows no seasons. . . . . . . . . . . .1922
Thirst quencher. . . . . . . . . . . . . . . . . . .1950
Thirst-quenching—delicious and refreshing. . . . . . . . . . . . . . . . . . . . .1906
Thirst reminds you—drink Coca-Cola. 1922
Thirst stops here. . . . . . . . . . . . . . . . . .1939
Thirst tells you when. . . . . . . . . . . . . .1938
Thirst—the natural call for refreshment. . . . . . . . . . . . . . . . . . .1925
Thirst, too, seeks quality. . . . . . . . . . .1950

The thirsty one's best beverage. . . . . . .1914
This is the time for real refreshment. . .1965
This is when you want something more than a soft drink. Nothing soft about the taste of Coca-Cola—lifts your spirits—boosts your energy. . . . . . .1965
365 shopping days. . . . . . . . . . . . . . . . .1926
Three million a day. . . . . . . . . . . . . . . .1917
Through all the years since 1886. . . . . .1936
Through 50 years. . . . The pause that refreshes. . . . . . . . . . . . . . . . . . . . . .1936
Time for a pause—have a Coca-Cola. .1947
Time for coke. . . . . . . . . . . . . . . . . . . . .1952
Time out for Coke. . . . . . . . . . . . . . . . .1950
Time out for food and drink. . . . . . . . .1938
Tingling refreshment. . . . . . . . . . . . . .1931
A toast to health and happiness. . . . . .1906
Travel where you may, they (Coca-Colas) are never more than a thirst apart. . . . . . . . . . . . . . . . . . . .1925
Treat yourself right. . . . . . . . . . . . . . . .1926
Treat yourself to a Coke. . . . . . . . . . . .1952
Try it just once and you will know why. . . . . . . . . . . . . . . . . . . . . . . . . .1940
Universal symbol of the American way of life. . . . . . . . . . . . . . . . . . . . .1943
Universally popular, always reliable, tested by time and proved good. . .1914
Unmatched sparkling taste. . . . . . . . .1965
Unmistakably Coke. . . . . . . . . . . . . . . .1956
Unvarying quality. . . . . . . . . . . . . . . . .1954
The upper hand on thirst. . . . . . . . . . .1952
Visit our fountain. . . . . . . . . . . . . . . . .1954
Water when boiled and filtered will do to bathe in or even drink if it costs nothing, but if you have to buy it, get a drink which has something to it more than mere dampness. Get Coca-Cola. . . . . . . . . . . . . . . . . . . . . .1906
Wave after wave—drink after drink. . .1968
A welcome addition to any party—any time—anyplace. . . . . . . . . . . . . . . . .1913
Welcome as springtime. . . . . . . . . . . . .1959
Welcome Friend. . . . . . . . . . . . . . . . . . .1944
What a refreshing new feeling you get from Coke. . . . . . . . . . . . . . . . . . . . .1960
What refreshment ought to be. . . . . . .1936
What you want is a Coke. . . . . . . . . . . .1952
When it's hard to get started, start with a Coca-Cola. . . . . . . . . . . . . . .1934
When thirst comes home to you. . . . . .1922
When thirsty, tired or headachy, or after a night out try a Coca-Cola High Ball. It hits the spot. . . . . . . .1906
When Thirsty try a bottle. . . . . . . . . . .1907
When tired Coca-Cola will refresh you: Headachy, help you; Nervous, relieve you; Thirsty, fill you. . . . . . .1906
When you feel all hot and sticky and tired and "headachy" when the life and energy seems to be oozing out of your pores with each drop of perspiration and it just seems you can't go a step further or do a lick more of work, step into any place and Drink a Bottle of Coca-Cola. You'll wonder first thing who turned on the cool wave, your

headache will disappear, that nervous, exhausted feeling will be replaced by a general all 'round "brace up," the rough spots will be smoothed out of your temper and you'll feel refreshed and exhilarated. The great temperance, tonic beverage for men, women and children, now try a bottle today. . . .1910
When you get a good thirst—treat it right. . . . . . . . . . . . . . . . . . . . . . . . .1923
When you need something more than a soft drink—Coca-Cola. . . . . . . . . .1965
Whenever you hear "Have A Coke" you hear the voice of America. . . . .1945
Whenever you see an arrow think of Coca-Cola. . . . . . . . . . . . . . . . . . . . .1909
Where there's Coca-Cola there's hospitality. . . . . . . . . . . . . . . . . . . . .1948
Wherever Ginger ale, Seltzer or Soda is Good—Coca-Cola is Better— Try it. . . . . . . . . . . . . . . . . . . . . . . . .1908
Wherever thirst goes. . . . . . . . . . . . . .1942
Wherever you go, north, east, south, or west, you will find Coca-Cola. . .1911
Wherever you go . . . Pause Refresh. . .1960
Wherever you go you'll find Coca-Cola. . . . . . . . . . . . . . . . . . . . .1905
Which? Coca-Cola or Goldelle Ginger Ale. . . . . . . . . . . . . . . . . . . . . . . . . . .1903
Whoever you are, whatever you do, wherever you may be, when you think of refreshment think of ice-cold Coca-Cola. . . . . . . . . . . . . .1939
Wholesome. . . . . . . . . . . . . . . . . . . . . .1937
Wholesome and refreshing. . . . . . . . . .1952
Wholesome bit of energy. . . . . . . . . . .1955
Why Grow Thirsty. . . . . . . . . . . . . . . .1945
With a drink so good—'tis folly to be thirsty. . . . . . . . . . . . . . . . . . . . . . . .1925
With a taste all its own—It's the Real Thing. . . . . . . . . . . . . . . . . . . . . . . . .1942
With good things to eat. . . . . . . . . . . .1937
Within easy reach of your thirst. . . . . .1940
The wonderful nerve and brain tonic and remarkable therapeutic agent. . . . . . . . . . . . . . . . . . . . . . . . .1890
Work better refreshed. . . . . . . . . . . . . .1953
Work refreshed. . . . . . . . . . . . . . . . . . .1948
The world's friendliest club. . . . . . . . .1946
The year-round answer to thirst. . . . . .1941
Yes. . . . . . . . . . . . . . . . . . . . . . . . . . . . .1946
You can't think of "delicious" or "refreshing" without thinking of Coca-Cola. . . . . . . . . . . . . . . . . . . . .1919
You come up smiling for a fresh start. . . . . . . . . . . . . . . . . . . . . . . . .1931
You taste its quality. . . . . . . . . . . . . . .1951
You taste the quality. . . . . . . . . . . . . . .1941
You trust it's quality. . . . . . . . . . . . . . .1965
You work better refreshed. . . . . . . . . .1943
You'll enjoy it too. . . . . . . . . . . . . . . . .1923
You'll go better refreshed. . . . . . . . . . .1964
Young America loves it. . . . . . . . . . . . .1954
Your thirst takes wings. . . . . . . . . . . . .1941
Your thirst takes wings when you treat it to an ice-cold Coca-Cola. . . .1940
Zing! Refreshing New Feeling. . . . . . . .1962

# IMPORTANT YEARS IN THE HISTORY OF THE COCA-COLA COMPANY AND ORGANIZED COCA-COLA COLLECTING

1831—John S. Pemberton born in Knoxville, Georgia

1851—Asa Candler born in Villa Rica, Georgia

1869—John S. Pemberton moves to Atlanta

1873—Asa Candler comes to Atlanta

1878—Asa Candler marries Lucy E. Howard

1881—John S. Pemberton sells a product called Ginger and Coca Tonic

1882—John S. Pemberton develops French Wine Coca

1882—Asa Candler buys out partners and becomes sole proprietor of Asa Candler & Company

1885—Frank Robinson arrives in Atlanta in hopes of starting an advertising business

1885—Pemberton Chemical Co. Incorporated

1886—Coca-Cola invented by John S. Pemberton

1886—The Pemberton Chemical Company is incorporated

1886—May 29, the first Coca-Cola newspaper ad in *The Atlanta Journal*

1886—May 8th, Coca-Cola is first sold at Jacobs' Pharmacy, Atlanta

1887—John S. Pemberton registers his label for "Coca-Cola Syrup & Extract with the U.S. Patent Office

1887—Pemberton sells two thirds interest in Coca-Cola to G.S. Lowndes & Willis Venable

1888—April 14th, remaining one third interest is sold by Pemberton

1888—April 17th, Asa Candler buys half interest owned by Dozier & Walker

1888—August 16th, John S. Pemberton dies

1888—August 30th, Asa Candler purchases remaining 1/3 interest from Dozier & Walker

1889—Dec. 6th, Robert W. Woodruff, future president of The Coca-Cola Company, is born

1890—Annual sales reaches nine thousand gallons

1891—First known Coca-Cola calendar

1891—April 22nd, Asa Candler takes over all remaining interest in Coca-Cola

1892—January 29th, The Coca-Cola Company Incorporated

1892—First recorded annual advertising budget, $11,401

1892—Rights for sale of Coca-Cola is given to Seth W. Fowle and Sons for six New England states.

1893—January 31st, Coca-Cola registered in the U.S. Patent Office

1894—First manufacturing plant outside of Atlanta is in operation in Dallas, Texas

1894—J. A. Biedenharn begins bottling Coca-Cola without formal contract

1896—*The Coca-Cola News* is first published

1897—First known Coca-Cola serving tray

1899—July 21st, contract signed with Thomas and Whitehead to bottle and distribute Coca-Cola in that package

1899—Hilda Clark (singer/actress) first used on Coca-Cola advertising

1900—Annual Sales 370,877 gallons

1900—Joseph Whitehead receives permit to open bottling plant in Atlanta

1901—The Coca-Cola Company introduces the silver plated glass holder, for use with a straight-sided glass

1903—First convention for fountain sales is held in Atlanta

1903—March 17, The Coca-Cola Gum Co., is chartered in Atlanta, GA.

1904—Opera star Lillian Nordica first appears on Coca-Cola advertising

1904—The Coca-Cola flare fountain glass is first used

1904—Annual gallon sales exceed one million

1905—Western Coca-Cola Bottling Company is formed

1906—The first "Arrow" magazine ad is used

1906—The first bottling plants outside the continental United States established in Cuba and Panama

1906—Asa Candler establishes a separate sales department headed by his nephew, Samuel C. Dobbs

1906—The first bottling operations in Canada

1907—Slogan "Good To The Last Drop" first used by The Coca-Cola Company

1907—Diamond-shaped paper label is registered

1907—The image of baseball great Ty Cobb is first used in Coca-Cola advertising

1909—The Associated Advertising Clubs of America elects Coca-Cola the "Best Advertising product In America"

1909—January, first convention of bottling plant owners and managers held in Atlanta

1909—*The Coca-Cola Bottler* magazine first introduced

1910—First rectangle Coca-Cola serving tray is used

1912—Annual sales exceed 12 million gallons

1913—Harold Hirsch, General Counsel for The Coca-Cola Company, urges parent bottlers to develop a uniform and distinctive package for Coca-Cola

1915—November, a contoured shape bottle concept is patented to Alexander Samuelson

1915—The Hobbleskirt (contoured) bottle is patented for the first time

1916—Asa Candler retires as president to seek position as mayor of Atlanta

1916—July, a modified version of the contoured bottle is introduced into the market

1917—April 17th, sugar, the main ingredient in Coca-Cola, is rationed because of the American war effort

1919—September 12, The Coca-Cola Company is sold for $25,000,000

1919—Annual gallon sales reaches almost 19 million

1919—Individual bottlers number well over one thousand

1920—October, Justice Oliver Wendell Homes hands down the decision of Supreme Court, which upholds trademark violations for The Coca-Cola Company against "The Koke Company of America"

1922—Harrison Jones, Vice President in charge of sales, initiates research of the six-bottle carton

1923—The first Coca-Cola six-bottle carton is manufactured by the Empire Printing & Box Co., in Atlanta

1923—April 28th, Robert Winship Woodruff takes over as President of Coca-Cola

1923—The Coca-Cola modified flare glass is introduced

1923—First billboard poster made available to Bottlers

1924—January, *The Red Barrel* magazine begins publication

1924—A Standardization Committee is formed by The Coca-Cola Company

1925—First billboard advertising done by The Coca-Cola Company

1926—October 23rd, "Export Bottle" label registered as a trademark

1927—"Five Star Dealer" sales contest starts

1927—"Six Keys" $30,000 contest begins

1927—The Coca-Cola Company first uses commercial radio broadcasting to advertise their product

1927—The Coca-Cola "Export Bottle" is first introduced

1928—"Nature Study" cards are copyrighted

1929—The Coca-Cola "Bell" fountain glass is first used

1929—Asa Candler dies

1929—The first "Big City" spectacular electric sign advertising Coca-Cola was put to use in Times Square, New York

1930—Artist Fred Mizen painted the first Santa Claus used in a magazine ad

1930—The first mechanically refrigerated coolers are offered to bottlers

1930—Formation of The Coca-Cola Export Corporation

1931—December, the first Haddon Sundblum Santa Clause appears

1932—May, The Coca-Cola "When You Entertain" advertising campaign begins

1931—The automatic fountain dispenser is developed by The Coca-Cola Company and the Dole Valve Company

1933—The Dole Automatic Fountain Dispenser for Coca-Cola is introduced in Chicago at The Century of Progress Exposition

1934—January, The Westinghouse Cooler is shown at Bottlers convention

1934—Coca-Cola first bottled in the United Kingdom by R. Fry and Company

# IMPORTANT YEARS IN THE HISTORY OF THE COCA-COLA COMPANY AND ORGANIZED COCA-COLA COLLECTING

1935—December 12th, Coca-Cola acquires parent bottler Western Coca-Cola Bottling Co.

1936—Coca-Cola celebrated its 50th Anniversary

1939—First one gallon metal syrup can is produced

1940—Program introduced to prevent incorrect use of Coke and Coca-Cola by press

1941—The Coca-Cola Company first used "Coke" in its advertising

1941—First "Multiple" page calendar used by The Coca-Cola Company

1941—First (standard design) paper cup is introduced by The Coca-Cola Company

1941—Kay Kyser's "Spotlight Bands" debutes on radio

1942—"The Little Sprite" (Sprite Boy) figure is conceived by Archie Lee and delineated by Haddon Sundblom

1943—June 29th, General Eisenhower requests ten Coca-Cola Bottling Plants in operation for the troops overseas

1943—The debut of "Songs By Morton Downey" radio show

1945—"Coke" is registered in the U.S. Patent Office

1946—July, the Award Winning "Yes" poster debut

1946—The Coca-Cola Export Corp. acquires the trade mark "Fanta"

1947—First Coca-Cola clothing is sold in stores

1948—First Coca-Cola Cooler radio is produced

1950—November, Coca-Cola sponsors it's first television program starring Edgar Bergen and Charlie McCarthy

1950—Coca-Cola sponsors Walt Disney's first television show

1950—The French Government threatens to outlaw the sale of Coca-Cola

1951—June 10th, Coca-Cola sponsored "The Mario Lanza Show" on radio

1951—Coca-Cola sponsors "The Adventures of Kit Carson" television show

1953—April 29th "Coke Time" with Eddie Fisher debuted on the NBC television network

1953—*Red Barrel* magazine stops publication

1953—*The Refresher Magazine* first published

1953—Annual sales well over 151 million gallons

1954—First *Pause For Living* booklet is published

1954—First family size (King Size) bottle introduced

1955—January 1st, Robert W. Woodruff retires as an officer of The Coca-Cola Company

1955—Initial use of cans of Coke, confined to U.S. Military in Far East

1955—10-ounce and 12-ounce bottles test marketed in Ohio

1955—First eight bottle carton is test marketed

1955—"Coca-Cola Refreshment Center" opens at Disneyland

1955—Coca-Cola starts sponsorship of "The Mickey Mouse Club" television show

1956—Following the death of Archie Lee in 1950 of the D'arcy Company, The Coca-Cola Company ends its relationship with The D'arcy Advertising Company

1956—First Santa Clause doll used by Coca-Cola

1958—Coke's "HiFi Club" concept is tested in Indianapolis

1958—Coca-Cola introduces the "Arciform" (Fishtail) logo

1959—Test marketing of 12-ounce flat top cans in several U.S. areas

1959—E. J. Kahn's book, *The Big Drink—The Story of Coca-Cola* is published by Random House

1960—April 12th, the famous Coca-Cola Hobbleskirt Bottle, is registered as a trademark, only the second package to become a registered trademark in this country

1960—First 16-ounce bottle is test marketed

1960—The Coca-Cola Company purchases The Minute Maid Corporation

1961—February 1st, Sprite, a lemon-lime drink, is made available to bottlers

1961—Test marketed 12- and 16-ounce one-way, no return bottles

1961—October 9th, 75th Anniversary Convention for Coca-Cola begins

1962—John Paul Austin moves up to the presidency of The Coca-Cola Company

1963—McCann Erickson develops Advertising and Marketing

1963—Coca-Cola Company's first low-calorie sugarless soft drink, Tab, is introduced

1963—"Things Go Better With Coke" slogan is first used in magazine ads

1963—The Coca-Cola Company manufactures its 4,000,000,000th gallon of syrup

1964—May 8th, the merger of The Coca-Cola Company and Duncan Food Company becomes effective

1966—Coca-Cola sponsors "A Charlie Brown Christmas"

1966—Fresca, a citrus flavored sugar free soft drink, made available to bottlers

1967—August 7th, The Coca-Cola Company Foods Division is formed

1968—March 1st, Coca-Cola USA, a division of The Coca-Cola Company, is organized

1968—May, "Frozen Coca-Cola" first introduced

1969—The Coca-Cola Company manufacturers its 6,000,000,000th gallon of syrup

1969—The Coca-Cola Company introduces a new logo

1969—Prototype of the first plastic bottle, one way, contoured design is tested

1969—October 14th, the "Dynamic Ribbon Device" introduced at the Bottlers Convention

1970—J. Paul Austin becomes Board Chairman of The Coca-Cola Company

1970—Santiba made available to bottlers, following test marketing

1971—The Coca-Cola Company manufactures its 7,000,000,000th gallon of syrup

1971—Coca-Cola is the most widely distributed trademarked product in the history of the world

1972—*The Illustrated Guide To The Collectibles of Coca-Cola* written by Cecil Munsey is published

1972—Mr. Pipp is introduced

1973—Lawrence Dietz's *Soda Pop* book is published by Simon and Schuster

1974—The Cola Clan (later to be known as The Coca-Cola Collectors Club) is established in Memphis by Bob Buffaloe

1974—Worldwide Sales for Coca-Cola is more than 165 million drinks every twenty four hours

1975—First Coca-Cola Collectors Convention is held in Atlanta

1975—Coca-Cola acquires the Thomas Company, the last parent bottler

1975—The "Easy-Goer" bottle is first introduced

1975—November 7th, the Shelly Goldstien collection is sold through Ben Cornings Mail-Bid Auction, creating one of the biggest fiascos in Coke collecting history

1976—March 14th, Allan Petretti publishes his first Mail-Bid Auction devoted to Coca-Cola memorabilia through Nostalgia Publications, Inc.

1976—Bill and Jan Schmidt present their Coca-Cola Museum in Elizabethtown, KY., at the second Annual Coca-Cola Collectors Convention

1976—May 11th, "Coke Adds Life To . . ." advertising campaign begins on national television

1977—Coca-Cola acquires Taylor Wine

1977—Allan Petretti publishes his first *Coca-Cola Collectibles Price Guide*

1979—Mean Joe Green advertising campaign begins

1979—June 13th, "Have A Coke And A Smile" advertising campaign begins

1982—February 4th, "Coke Is It" advertising campaign begins

1982—July 9th, Diet Coke introduced

1985—March 7th, Robert W. Woodruff dies

1985—April 23rd, new formula Coca-Cola is introduced

1985—July 10th, Coca-Cola Classic returns

1985—July 31st, Coca-Cola is the first soft drink consumed in space

1985—October, plastic cans are test marketed

1985—Cherry Coke first introduced

1986—Coca-Cola celebrates its 100th Anniversary

# MANUFACTURERS, PRINTING COMPANIES, LITHOGRAPHERS, AND ADVERTISING AGENCIES

Following is a list of some of the more important manufacturers, printing companies, lithographers, and advertising agencies which produced advertising and production material for The Coca-Cola Company. Some of these names may be helpful to collectors in identifying pieces in their collection. This list is generally pre-1970 and is by no means complete.

A.T. Cross Co.
Acton Mfg. Co.
Advertising Attractions, Inc.
Ambo
American Art Works
American Can Co.
American Chinaware Corp.
American Colortype Co.
American Flyer
American Lithography
American Pullmatch Corp.
Armstrong Packaging
Atlanta Litho Co.
Atlantic City Poster Adv. Co.
Atlantic Playing Card Co.
Auto Car Trucks
Baird Clock Co.
Baltimore Enamel Co.
Bastian Bros. Co.
Barklay
Bill's Novelty
Bond Crown & Cork
Brown Mfg. Co.
Brunhuff Mfg. Co.
Buddy L
Budgie
Calvert Litho Co.
Camco
Carolina Sign Co.
Cavalier
Charles W. Shonk Mfg. &
    Litho Co.
Chas. Lippencott & Co.
Chattanooga Glass Co.
Chilton
Cincinnati Adv. Products Co.
Clauds Neon Co.
Cleveland Worsted Mills
Consolidated Litho
Continnental Can Co.
Cornelius Company
Courier-Journal Printing Co.
Crockery City Ice &
    Products Co.
Crosley Radio
Cross Press & Sign Co.
Crown Cork and Seal Co.
Crystal Mfg. Co.
Dan Mercer Potter
D. Peres Solingen
D'arcy Advertising Agency
Dasco Sign Co.
Diamond Gardner Corp.
Diamond Match Co.
Diner-Thomas Corp.
Dinky

Dole Mfg. Co.
Dole Valve Co.
Doremus Vending Machine
Dualite Displays, Inc.
Dupont Co.
Duro-Products, Inc.
Duro-Products Mfg. Co.
E. L. Ruddy Co.
E. M. Knowles China Co.
Edwards & Deutsch Litho
Electron Sign Co.
Embosograf Corp. of America
Empire Corp.
Empire Ornamental Glass Co.
Federal Glass
F. L. Jacobs
Frigidaire
General Electric Co.
Gilbert Clock Co.
Glascock Mfg. Co.
Globe Superior Co.
Goso
Grady Sign Co.
Hamilton-King Co.
Hammer Brand
H.D. Beach Co.
H.D. Lee Co.
Hanover Neon Co.
Hansen Fittings
Hemp And Co.
Henry Sears & Son
Hickok Co.
H.O.I. Plastics
Holden Book Cover Co.
Honeywell Co.
Hubbs Mfg. Co.
Hubley
Hutchinson
Hyatt Mfg. Co.
Icy-O
Ideal
Ingraham Clock Co.
Ingraham-Richardson Mfg. Co.
International Truck
Jackson Mfg. Co.
J. Ottmann Litho Co. NY
J.B. Carroll
J.L. Clark Mfg. Co.
Kansas City Slide Mfg. Co.
Kaster & Co.
Kaufman & Strauss
Kay Displays
Kent Mfg.
Ketterlinus Co.
L.G. Balfour Co.
Lee Co.

Lima Neon Products Sign Co.
Lincoln Logs
Linemar
Lionel
Marx
Massengale Adv. Co.
Masterack
Matchbox
McCandlish Litho
McCampbell and Co.
McCann-Erickson Inc.
Meek and Beach Co.
Meek Co.
Merchants Publishing Co.
Metalcraft Mfg.
Metropolitan Art Glass Co.
Mills Mfg. Co.
Milton
Milton Bradley
Milton Sturm & Co.
Mirro-Products Co.
Morrison Co.
Multiplex Faucet Co.
Mundet Cork Corp.
Nappe-Smith Co.
National Bottled Drink
    Cooler Co.
Neon Products, Inc.
N.J. Aluminum Co.
N.Y. Metal Ceiling Co.
Niagara Litho
No-Drip Co.
Nylint
Ohio Artcraft Sign Co.
O. J. Gude Co.
Ornamold co.
Owens Illinois Glass Co.
Pam Clock Co.
Passaic Metalware Co.
Permanent Sign & Display Co.
Pike Stained Glass Co.
Pittsburgh Mosaic Glass Co.
Playtown
Poster Advertising Co.
Progress
Progress Gas Fixture Co.
Ralstoy
Remington
Remke Traker Co.
Ridgeway Clock Co.
Riverside Mfg. Co.
Robertson, Inc.
Rome Box Mfg. Co.
Ronemous & Co.
Rosko
Roy G. Booker

Rushton
Royal Mieco, Inc.
Selmix Dispenser Corp.
S. L. Whitten Co.
Sentenne & Green
Sesco
Sherwin Williams Co.
Smith Miller
Snyder & Black
Southern Can Co.
Standard Advertising Co.
Stelad Signs
Street Railways Advertising
Co.
Superior Co.
Superior Decals Co.
Sweet Heart Straws
Swihart Products
Technofix
Temco Inc.
Temprite Mfg. Co.
Tenn Enamel Mfg. Co.
The Federal Quality Corp.
The Gardner Board &
    Carton Co.
The M-C-A Sign Co.
The Woodstock Mfg. Co.
Thos. Cusack Co.
Tindeco
Tippco
Tomica
Troy Sunshine Co.
Tuscarora Adv. Co.
Tyco
United Advertising Corp
U.S. Printing & Litho Co.
Vaughn
Vend-All
Vendo
Venorlator
Victor Mfg. Co.
Vienna Art Plates
Welch Clock Co.
Wellsville China Co.
Westinghouse
Wheeling Pottery Co.
W. H. Hutchinson & Sons
White Motor Co.
Whitehead & Hoag Co.
Wiking
Williams Ice-O-Matic
Winchester
Wolf & Co.
Zell Products Co.
Zippo

# PERSONALIZED COLLECTING

The Cola-Cola Company used many movie stars, celebrities, sports figures, and opera stars to advertise their product. Advertising pieces featuring these celebrities are always prized by collectors. These pieces can be made so much more interesting and valuable when combined with that person's signature. It becomes personalized, and when nicely matted and framed with other information or mementos relating to that person, it actually gives a whole new dimension to the piece. Obtaining autographs and other information provides a new challenge to collecting. Keep in mind that some of these autographs are rare and valuable. Prices are based not only on the piece, but also the autograph and the additional work in putting the group together.

1905 . . . . . . . . . . . . . . . . . . . . . . . . $750
Lillian Nordica coupon ad, original Dupont
cabinet card, autographed
(signed Nordica cabinet cards are rare)

1952 . . . . . . . . . . . . . . . . . . . . . . . . $750
Sugar Ray Robinson cardboard sign, autographed
photo, and June 23, 1952 "Maxim vs Robins"
on fight ticket.

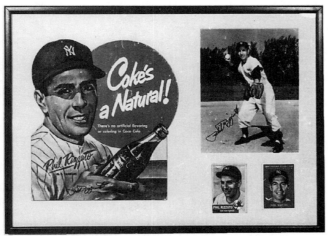

1950s . . . . . . . . . . . . . . . . . . . . . . . . $750
Phil Rizzuto cardboard cutout (autographed and
printed signatures), autographed photo, and two
1950s Rizzuto cards

1932 . . . . . . . . . . . . . . . . . . . . . . . . $850
June Collyer cardboard cutout, autographed photo,
movie still, and caption

1959 . . . . . . . . . . . . . . . . . . . . . . . . $850
Ricky Nelson cardboard sign, autographed photo,
and record with photo jacket. (Cardboard sign is
rare, and Ricky Nelson autograph is rare.)

1947 . . . . . . . . . . . . . . . . . . . . . . . . . $500
Red Grange cardboard sign, autographed photo,
and caption

1954  19" . . . . . . . . . . . . . . . . . . . . $1,400
Eddie Fisher cardboard cutout, autographed photo,
and publicity photo

1947 . . . . . . . . . . . . . . . . . . . . . . . . . $575
Gene Tunney cardboard sign, autographed photo,
and caption

1954 . . . . . . . . . . . . . . . . . . . . . . . . . $175
Eddie Fisher sheet music, publicity photo,
and caption

1947 . . . . . . . . . . . . . . . . . . . . . . . . . $450
Don Budge cardboard sign, autographed photo,
and caption

1954 . . . . . . . . . . . . . . . . . . . . . . . . . $175
Eddie Fisher 45 rpm record, publicity photo
and caption

1950s . . . . . . . . . . . . . . . . . . . . . . . $485
Kit Carson cardboard sign, kerchief, autographed
photo, and caption

1940s . . . . . . . . . . . . . . . . . . . . . . . $200
Andrews Sisters "Rum and Coca-Cola" sheet music
and autographed photo

1933 . . . . . . . . . . . . . . . . . . . . . . . $295
Jean Harlow "Dinner at Eight" magazine ad,
Autographed photo (signed by her mother), original
Harlow autographs are rare, with caption

1950s . . . . . . . . . . . . . . . . . . . . . . . $300
Tony Bennett cardboard sign, record and autographed photo

1932 . . . . . . . . . . . . . . . . . . . . . . . $350
Caludette Colbert and Fredric March ad, autographed photos and "When You Entertain" book,
with caption

1950s . . . . . . . . . . . . . . . . . . . . . . . $75
Tony Bennett record and autographed photo

# BOOKS FOR YOUR LIBRARY

The following books would certainly be a helpful addition to any Coca-Cola collector's library. It is unfortunate that some of these books are out of print, and sometimes difficult to locate. However, they do turn up in out-dated book stores, flea markets, and from other collectors.

*The Illustrated Guide to the Collectibles of Coca-Cola.* Cecil Munsey, 1972, Hawthorn Books, NY

*The Big Drink The Story of Coca-Cola.* E.J. Kahn, 1960, Random House.

*The Real Ones —Four Generations of the First Family of Coca-Cola.* Elizabeth Candler Graham, 1992, Barricade Books, NJ.

*For God, Country and Coca-Cola.* Mark Pendergrast, 1993, C. Scribners & Sons, NY.

*The Real Coke, The Real Story.* Thomas Oliver, 1986, Random House.

*The Wonderful World of Coca-Cola.* M. Shartar & N. Shavin.

*The Schmidt Museum Collection.* $33.95 + $3 postage to: Museum Book, Coca-Cola Bott., Co., P.O. Box 647, Elizabethtown, KY 42701

*Coca-Cola an Illustrated History.* Pat Watters, 1978, Doubleday & Co.

*The Mix Guide to Commemorative Bottles.* Richard Mix, 1997 Edition, P.O. Box 558, Marietta, GA 30061.

*Soda Pop.* Lawrence Dietz, 1973, Simon and Schuster.

*Mr. Anonymous.* Robert Woodruff, The Coca-Cola Co.

*The Coca-Cola Company— An Illustrated Profile.* 1974, The Coca-Cola Company.

*Collectible Coca-Cola Toy Trucks.* Gael de Courtivron, 1994, Collector Books $24.95 + $5 S&H to: Gael de Courtivron, 4811 Remington Dr., Sarasota, FL 34234.

*Vintage Coca-Cola Machines, Vol. II .* Steve Ebner, 1996, Fun-Tronics, Inc., P.O. Box 448, Middletown, MD 21769.

*Classic Soda Machines, 2nd Edition.* Jeff Walters, 1995, Memory Lane Publishing, P.O. Box 2290 Pollock Pines, CA 95726.

*Collectible Picnic Coolers & Ice Chests.* Jeff Walters, 1994, Memory Lane Publishing, P.O. Box 2290, Pollock Pines, CA 95726.

*A Collector's Guide to New and Vintage Coca-Cola Memorabilia.* Randy Schaeffer and Bill Bateman, 1995, 611 North 5h St., Reading, PA 19601.

# SOURCES

## SHOWS

The Indianapolis Antique Advertising
  Show
Indiana State Fairgrounds (South
  Pavilion),
3 shows a year
Kim & Mary Kokles
P. O. Box 495092
Garland, TX 75049

Chicagoland Antique Advertising
Slot Machines and Jukebox Show
St. Charles, IL
Steve Gronowski (708) 381–1234

Game Room Shows
826 West Douglas, Wichita, KS 67203
Atlanta, Ft. Worth, Philadelphia,
  Hackensack
Bob Nelson/Ken McMenamy

Knoxville Bottle and Advertising Show
Larry W. Acuff
220 N. Carter School Rd.
Strawberry Plains, TN 37871

North Alabama Bottle, Insulator and
  Collectible Show
1st Saturday of March
Alan Wright
703 Pratt Ave. N.W. Suite 304
Huntsville, AL 35801

## PUBLICATIONS

*Game Room Magazine*
P. O. Box 41
Keyport, NJ 07735

*The Antique Trader Weekly*
P. O. Box 1050
Dubuque, IA 52001

*The Coca-Cola Collectors News*
Publication of The Coca-Cola
  Collectors
Club International
P. O. Box 49166
Atlanta, GA 30359

## AUCTIONS

Nostalgia Publications
Mail Bid Auctions (Soda Pop)
Published Twice A Year
$10.00 subscription
Nostalgia Publications
21 South Lake Dr.
Hackensack, NJ 07601

Muddy River Trading Co.
(twice a year) Gary Metz
263 Key Lakewood Dr.
Moneta, VA 24121

Frank's Antiques and Auctions
222 South Kings Rd.
Hilliard, FL 32046

James Julia, Inc., Auctions
P. O. Box 830
Fairfield, ME 04937

Noel Barrett Antiques & Auctions, Ltd.
P. O. Box 1001
Carversville, PA 18913

William Morford
Mail Bid Auctions
RD# 2
Cazenovia, NY 13035

Autopia Advertising Auctions
15209 NE 90th Street
Redmond, WA 98052
Mail Bid Auctions

## CLUBS

The following clubs or organizations may be of interest to Coca-Cola collectors, some directly like The Coca-Cola Collectors Club, and others indirectly like Can Collectors, and Advertising Collectors Clubs, etc.

Antique Advertising Assoc. of
  America (AAAA)
P. O. Box 1121
Morton Grove, IL 60053

National Pop Can Collectors
3014 September Dr.
Joliet, IL 60453

The Coca-Cola Collectors Club
  International
P. O. Box 49166
Atlanta, GA 30359

National Association of Soda Jerks
P. O. Box 115
Omaha, NE 68101

Club Soda
P. O. Box 489
Troy, ID 83871

Advertising Collectors Express
  Newsletter
P. O. Box 221
Mayview, MO 64071

Calendar Collector Society
18222 Flower Hill Way #299
Gaithersburg, MD 20879

Figural Bottle Opener Collectors
Nancy Robb
3 Avenue A
Latrobe, PA 15650

American Matchcover Collecting Club
P. O. Box 18481
Asheville, NC 28814

International Lighter Collectors
P. O. Box 536
Quitman, TX 74783

Just For Openers
John Stanley
3712 Sunningdale Way
Durham, NC 27707

National Association of Paper and
  Advertising Collectors
P. O. Box 500
Mount Joy, PA 17552

The Crown Collectors Society Int.
John Vetter
4300 San Juan Dr.
Fairfax, VA 22030

## MUSEUMS

The World of Coca-Cola
adjacent to underground Atlanta
For information call (404) 676–5151

The Schmidt Museum of Coca-Cola
  Memorabilia
Elizabethtown, KY
For information call (502) 737–4000

*Auction Action . . .*

Nostalgia Publications, Inc., sponsors of the world's largest and most respected auctions of Coca-Cola memorabilia, invites you to join the thousands of satisfied subscribers, bidders and consignors.

You can receive the next fully illustrated auction catalogue. Each catalogue pictures and describes hundreds of Coca-Cola, Pepsi-Cola, Hires, Orange Crush, Moxie and other soda-pop related items and other fine quality antique advertising to be sold for the high bid. Auctions are published twice a year, and quality consignments are always welcome. Write for consignment information. We also purchase single pieces or complete collections and offer a complete appraisal service.

Send $10.00 Subscription to:

**NOSTALGIA**
**PUBLICATIONS, INC.**

21 South Lake Dr., Hackensack, New Jersey 07601

# SCHMIDT'S *Coca-Cola* MUSEUM

## ELIZABETHTOWN, KY

The Schmidt Museum contains the world's largest private collection of Coca-Cola memorabilia. Since 1886, through the many years that Coca-Cola has been dispensed, bottled and canned, advertisement of the product has been of great importance. Items such as trays, calendars, glasses, leather goods, jewelry, dishes, playing cards, knives, toys, fans, book covers, sheet music, ashtrays and bottles, large and small, are some of the familiar every-day objects prominently marked with the very familiar script trademark. Unexpectedly, the trademark also appears on cigar bands, candy boxes, chewing gum, hand axes, coffee cups and silverware. Examples of all of these and more are displayed in the collection which covers Coca-Cola advertising dating back over 111 years.

The visitor is taken back in time to reflect on the fashion and way of life during the period of the evolution of Coca-Cola. An 1890s soda fountain, complete with tin ceiling, hanging Tiffany lamp and elaborate stained glass dispensers is a special exhibit in the museum. In another area, a three-foot-tall Tiffany Coke bottle shows its ruby light. The most complete collection of Coca-Cola trays known to exist highlights an entire wall and draws several thousand visitors each year.

The Schmidt Museum is located in the Coca-Cola Bottling Company in Elizabethtown, Kentucky. The Schmidt family has been producing Coca-Cola in Kentucky since 1901 and the third and fourth generations of the family are now responsible for the modern, up-to-date facility which is open to the public. In the lobby, a large pool filled with Japanese Carp reflects the many colors of the very large stained glass mural placed behind it. As the visitor leaves the lobby to enter the museum, he moves along a gallery to watch the modern bottling and canning procedures. After the many thirst provoking sights in the museum, the visitor is offered free ice cold Coke—a very welcomed touch.

**(502) 737-4000**

The Schmidt Coca-Cola Memorabilia Museum is open Monday through Friday from 9:00 a.m. to 4:00 p.m.

Closed every Saturday and Sunday, New Year's Day, Memorial Day, Fourth of July, Labor Day, Thanksgiving and Christmas.

### ADMISSION

| | |
|---|---|
| Adults | $2.00 |
| Senior Citizens and Bus Tour Members | $1.50 |
| Students | $ .50 |
| Pre-Schoolers | *FREE* |

# Schmidt Museum of Coca-Cola Memorabilia

*A nonprofit, independent museum not affiliated with The Coca-Cola Company.*

A new museum destined to attract Coke lovers today and for generations to come!

## "Take part in the creation of this World Class Museum containing the world's largest and finest independent collection of Coca-Cola memorabilia."

*A three story, 90,000 square foot museum dedicated to the display of more than 100 years of marvelous artifacts of Coca-Cola advertising. Thousands of rare and beautiful items in a building worthy of their value on a site easily accessible to one-half of the total population of the United States!*

When making a gift, the donor gains the satisfaction of helping preserve the rich heritage of a unique American product.

### Recognition

Gifts from $1,000 to $100,000 and above, will be listed on a bronze plaque prominently displayed in the museum lobby. In addition, individual plaques representing gifts at the Benefactor level will be placed at specific exhibit areas throughout the museum. Engraved pavers will be placed in the entry walkway area.

Gifts of any amount to the New Museum will be most greatly appreciated. All gifts to the museum are tax deductible and are held in escrow.

### Gift Recognition Levels

| | |
|---|---|
| Benefactor | $100,000 & above |
| Patron | $50,000 |
| Sponsor | $25,000 |
| Supporter | $10,000 |
| Donor | $5,000 |
| Associate | $2,500 |
| Contributor | $1,000 |
| 12" x 12" paver | $500 |
| 8" x 8" paver | $300 |
| 4" x 8" paver | $100 |

**Donors are encouraged to make gifts payable over a five-year period in semi-annual or annual payments.**

To support the New World Class Museum,

I/We pledge: $_____

Paid Herewith: $_____

Remainder: $_____

Name_____

Address_____

_____ Phone _____

Signature_____

Date_____

## Pledge Card

The remainder of this pledge, if any, will be paid:

☐ **Semi-annually**  ☐ **Annually**  Amount $_____

**Date pledge payment to begin:** _____

*Make checks payable to:*

**Schmidt Museum Escrow Account**
**P. O. Box 647**
**Elizabethtown, KY 42702-0647**
**502 737 4000**    **Fax    502 765 5360**

# APPLICATION FOR MEMBERSHIP

**The Coca-Cola Collectors Club International** is a non-profit organization for collectors and their families, who are interested in the history and the memorabilia of The Coca-Cola Company.

## The Coca-Cola Collectors Club International provides:

- International Communication with over 6500 Collectors
- Markets for Buying, Trading and Selling Collectibles
- Informative Monthly Newsletter with Free Classified Ads for all Members
- Special Monthly Merchandise Offerings for Members
- Regional and Local Chapters
- Annual International and Regional Conventions
- Yearly Membership Directory

Annual dues for primary membership are **$25.00** (in U.S. funds.) Additional members of your family may join as associates to your primary membership for **$5.00** per year. An associate member receives all the benefits of membership as listed above, except for the publications of the Club. The dues for overseas primary membership are **$40.00** (in U.S. funds.) and includes FIRST CLASS postage for the monthly newsletter.

The Coca-Cola Collectors Club International is run by unpaid volunteers elected annually from the membership by mail ballot. All primary and associate members may run for elective office.
If you would like to join, complete the form below and return along with one year's dues to:

### The Coca-Cola Collectors Club International
### P. O. Box 49166
### Atlanta, Georgia 30359-1166

| PLEASE PRINT | Please allow 6-8 weeks for delivery. | DUES |
| --- | --- | --- |
| NAME (PRIMARY MEMBER) _____ | | $25.00 |
| ADDRESS _____ | | $40.00 |
| CITY _____ STATE _____ ZIP CODE _____ | | (OVERSEAS) |
| PHONE NUMBER ( ____ ) _____ COUNTRY _____ | | |
| NAME (ASSOCIATE MEMBER) _____ | | $5.00 |
| Give ADDRESS & PHONE only if different from primary's | | |
| NAME (ASSOCIATE MEMBER) _____ | | $5.00 |

**TOTAL AMOUNT ENCLOSED = = = > $** _____

You may use this form for adding associates, but please DO NOT use this form for renewing your own membership.

1990

One legend.

World of Coca-Cola® **ATLANTA**

# Two worlds full of memorabilia.

World of Coca-Cola® **LAS VEGAS**

Now, you have two opportunities to immerse yourself in the history of a legend. See amazing collections of Coke memorabilia. Your all-time favorite commercials. And sample 30 different flavors of international Coca-Cola products. Of course, there are also lots of memories in store for you at 'Everything Coca-Cola', the place to buy Coca-Cola brand merchandise, clothing and collectibles. So c'mon, take a trip around the worlds. You'll be glad you did.

For more information call: World of Coca-Cola Atlanta: 404-676-5151 - World of Coca-Cola Las Vegas: 702-270-5953

# GLOSSARY

The following is a collection of words or terms and their definitions that are commonly used by Coca-Cola collectors.

3-D—Three-dimensional look.

ACL—Applied color labeling.

AIR CAN—Sealed empty can used for test run or display.

ARCIFORM—See fishtail logo.

ARROW SIGN—A sign designed with arrow, often arrow was moveable.

BACK BAR DISPLAY—Display used above the back bar piece in a soda fountain.

BAKELITE—Developed sometime between 1906 and 1909 by Dr. Leo Henrick Baekelan from Yonkers, NY. First synthetic, all chemical thermoset plastic. A mouldable substance set permanently by heat. Manufactured into many products throughout the 1930s and 1940s, became known as "The material of a thousand uses."

BANNER—Long strip of paper, cloth or canvas.

BLOTTER—Piece of thick absorbent paper used to blot excess ink from fountain pens.

BOTTLE DISPLAY—Cardboard or plastic piece displayed on top of bottle.

BOTTLE HANGER—Piece of advertising with die-cut hole to be slipped over neck of bottle.

BOTTLE RINGER—See bottle hanger.

BOTTLERS CATALOG—Yearly catalog sent to bottlers showing available advertising.

BROWN MANUFACTURING COMPANY—Company which produced metal signs and objects such as stationary wall-mounted bottle openers.

BUDDY L—Toy manufacturer producing many toy trucks for Coca-Cola during 1940s through 1980s.

BUTTON SIGN—Disc sign, round, bowl-shaped sign.

CAMEO—Image in an oval or circle.

CARDBOARD CUTOUT—Printed paper applied to cardboard then die-cut in the form of the image.

CARTON INSERT—Giveaway or piece of advertising inserted into carton.

CARTON STUFFER—Piece of advertising, usually an offer, inserted into a six-pack carton

CAVALIER—Manufacturer of vending machines, produced many models for Coca-Cola.

CELEBRITY ADVERTISING—Movie star, sports, or other celebrity appearing on or endorsing Coca-Cola.

CELLULOID—Early form of plastic used to cover and protect.

CHANGE RECEIVER—Glass receptacle for customer's change to be placed in.

CHANGE TRAY—See tip tray.

CHANNEL CARD—Long piece of cardboard, printed and inserted into metal frames or strips.

CHARLES W. SHONK COMPANY—Printing company which specialized in printing on tin.

CHRISTMAS BOTTLE—Coke bottle with December 23, 1923 date embossed on it.

CHROMOLITHOGRAPHY—A picture printed in colors from a series of stones prepared by the lithographic process.

CLOISONNÉ—Color decoration made of enamels poured into divided area of a design outlined with bent wire secured to a metal base.

COMMEMORATIVE—An object produced to commemorate a time, place or event.

COUNTER SIGN—Sign designed to be displayed on top of counter.

D'ARCY—Advertising agency which produced a great deal of advertising for Coca-Cola

DECAL—Water-soaked transfer sign.

DIAMOND CAN—Coke can with diamond design.

DIE-CUT—See cardboard cutout.

DINKY TOY—Toy manufacturer produced Coke toy truck, in 1960s.

DISPLAY BOTTLE—Bottle used in store windows or point of purchase—often large sizes in glass, plastic, styrofoam, etc.

DISTRIBUTOR PIECE—Piece of advertising given away by local stores or distributor usually imprinted with their name.

EASEL BACK—Fold out cardboard stand glued to back of display pieces.

EDWARDS & DEUTSCH LITHO COMPANY—Litho/printing company producing blotters and other pieces for Coca-Cola.

EMBOSSED—Machine process of pressing the back to highlight letters or specific areas on paper and tin.

FANTASY—A piece that has been created with no original like it.

FESTOON—Cardboard cutout display usually hung over back bar.

FISHTAIL LOGO—Logo design similar to fish tails used from 1958 to early 1960s, actual name is "arciform."

FLANGE SIGN—Two-sided sign with a flange at a right angle to be hung and visible from both sides.

FOXING—Discoloration or browning on paper, common on celluloid covered pieces such as the pocket mirror.

FULL COLOR—Multi-color printed piece.

FULL PAD—Calendar pad which is complete with all calendar months.

GLASCOCK—Manufacturer of coolers and vending machines, produced many Coca-Cola coolers and machines.

GROMMET—An eyelet of firm material to strengthen or protect an opening.

HAMILTON KING ART—Art produced by the artist Hamilton King.

HANGING SIGN—Cardboard, tin, or glass sign with a string or chain hanger.

HOBBLE SKIRT BOTTLE—Shape of Coke bottle after 1915, sometimes called "Mae West."

HOME CALENDAR—Small-size calendar given away for home use.

ICE PICK—Metal shaft attached to wood or metal handle used to split ice.

ICE TONGS—Metal handled clasps used to pick up large chunks of ice.

ILLUMINATED SIGN—Plastic or glass lightup sign.

IMAGE—A visual representation, an illusory form, a graphic representation.

IMPRINTING—Printing a name or message on a pre-printed piece of advertising.

INSERT SIGN—Cardboard signs designed to insert into existing wood or aluminum frames.

KAY DISPLAYS—Company producing many specialty signs for Coca-Cola during 1930s through 1950s.

KICK PLATE—Tin strip sign used on bottom of doors.

KIT CARSON—1950s TV cowboy program sponsored by The Coca-Cola Company.

LABEL UNDER GLASS—Ornate label applied to glass bottle and covered with glass.

LEATHERETTE—Embossed paper or cardboard made to look like leather.

LIGHTUP—Sign or clock with lighting unit for more appeal.

LINEMAR—Toy manufacturer producing Coke toy trucks for Coca-Cola during 1950s.

LITHO—Short for lithography or lithograph.

# GLOSSARY

LITHO INSERT—Cardboard sign designed to insert into gold wood frames.

LITHOGRAPHY—The process of printing from a smooth stone or metal plate on which the image area is ink receptive and blank area is ink repellent onto paper, cardboard, tin, etc.

LOGO—Insignia or design created and used to identify a company or product.

MARX—Toy manufacturer producing many toy trucks for Coca-Cola during 1940s-1950s.

MASONITE—Material made from steam treated wood fiber, used on many signs during WWII.

MATCH SAFE—Small metal box used to hold matches.

MEISEL PRINT—Series of 30 color photographs mounted on artboard or canvas and framed, titled "50 Years of Nostalgia 1976." The 30" prints were offered to bottlers. Produced by Meisel Photochrome Corp., Atlanta, GA.

MENU BOARD—Display board used to list food or drink.

METAL STRIP—Thin strip of metal that runs across top or bottom, or both, on calendars and paper signs.

METALCRAFT—Toy truck manufacturer, manufacturing toy Coke trucks in the early 1930s.

MIB—Mint in box.

MINIATURE (Mini)—Small size version of larger object.

MILTON BRADLEY—Game manufacturer which produced many games for Coca-Cola.

NECK RINGER—See bottle hanger.

NEW LOGO—1970s so-called wave logo "Dynamic Ribbon."

NIAGARA LITHO—Printing company which produced paper and cardboard signs for The Coca-Cola Company.

PALM PRESS—See push plate.

PAT. D. BOTTLE—Next bottle change after Coke Christmas bottle. Patent number embossed on bottle.

PEDESTAL SIGN—Sign mounted on a pole with heavy metal base.

PITTING—Corrosion on metal surface, usually caused by moisture.

PORCELAIN—Baked-on enameled finish used for outdoor signs.

PRESS PROOF—Sample copy pulled off press as the job is running to check color, etc.

PRIVILEGE PANEL—Blank spaces left on sign for the store name to be imprinted.

PUB MIRROR—Term given to ornate (recently produced) wood frame mirrors, fantasy items.

PUSH PLATE—Small (usually porcelain) sign placed on door used to push door open.

PULL DOWN SIGN—Paper sign with metal strip top and bottom.

PURE AS SUNLIGHT—Slogan used by Coca-Cola during the 1920s.

PUSH BAR—Long sign or bar attached across door for easy opening or closing.

RACK SIGN—Metal rack used to display 6-packs or cases of Coke.

RARE—A piece considered by collectors to be very hard to find.

RELIEVES FATIGUE—Slogan used by Coca-Cola mainly during 1907 and 1908.

REPRODUCTION—A piece that has been remade as an exact copy or close facsimile of an original piece.

REVERSE GLASS—Painting or screening on the back side of glass in reverse.

ROCKWELL ART—Art produced by the artist Norman Rockwell.

ROYAL PALM—Soda water brand bottled by some Coca-Cola bottlers.

SALES AID—Object used by salesman to help promote his point.

SALESMAN SAMPLE—Miniaturized version of an item carried by salesman to present as a sample.

SELF FRAMED—Tin or cardboard sign with raised or embossed edge to form a frame.

SELTZER BOTTLE—Glass bottle with metal siphon top used in soda fountains and homes for seltzer.

SEPIA—A print or photograph of a brown color.

SIDEWALK SIGN—Metal frame with legs used to insert two signs back to back to be displayed in front of store.

SILK SCREENED—Printing process used in printing some cardboard, tin and masonite signs.

SMITH MILLER—Toy manufacturer producing many toy trucks for Coca-Cola during 1940s through 1950s.

SNYDER AND BLACK—Advertising agency producing much of the Coca-Cola advertising over the years.

SPIDER WEBBING—Hairline cracks in finish of china, and tin trays which looks like spider web.

SPRITE BOY—Image of a young boy with soda jerk cap or bottle cap hat used in Coca-Cola advertising mainly during 1940s and 1950s.

STOCK ARTWORK—A piece of advertising that is produced in quantity with blank areas where advertising can be imprinted.

STRAIGHT SIDE BOTTLES—Shape of Coke bottles pre-1915; sides of bottle are straight.

SYRUP BOTTLE—Glass bottle used in early soda fountain which held various soda syrups.

SYRUP JUG—Glass or pottery container, usually one gallon, which held syrup.

T.V. TRAY—Large tin litho tray for serving snacks or meals.

TABLE TENT CARD—Fold over advertising card which forms a tend and sits on table.

TABLET—Writing pad given away to school children.

TALLY CARD—Score card used in bridge.

TEAR SHEET—Copy of advertising to be used by newspapers and magazines.

TIN OVER CARDBOARD—Tin sign with cardboard backing.

TIP TRAY—Small tin litho tray left on table with customer's change.

TIRE RACK SIGN—Display rack for automobile tires.

TOPPER—Ornament or sign displayed on top of another object, such as a bottle, cash register, etc.

TRADE CARD—Small card given away to potential customers to promote a product.

TRIMMED—A piece that has been cut down from its original size.

TROLLEY SIGN—11" x 21" cardboard sign inserted into racks around top inside edge of trolley car.

VENDO—Manufacturer of vending machines, produced many models for Coca-Cola.

VERY RARE—A piece considered by collectors to be one of only a few known to exist.

VIENNA ART PLATE—Trade name for tin-litho plate, some with advertising on reverse, used as giveaway or premium.

WATCH FOB—Decorative metal attached to a strap used to attach to a pocket watch.

WESTINGHOUSE—Manufacturer of vending machines and coolers, produced many models for Coca-Cola.

WINDOW DISPLAY—Large cardboard displays used in store windows.

WITH BOTTLE—Piece of advertising with bottle visible (bottle sales).

WITH GLASS—Piece of advertising with glass visible (fountain sales).

WOLF & COMPANY—Printing company produced many early pieces for Coca-Cola.

# INDEX

# INDEX

# IMAGE INDENTIFICATION SYSTEM INDEX

# IMAGE INDENTIFICATION SYSTEM INDEX

# IMAGE INDENTIFICATION SYSTEM INDEX

# IMAGE INDENTIFICATION SYSTEM INDEX

# IMAGE INDENTIFICATION SYSTEM INDEX

# IMAGE INDENTIFICATION SYSTEM INDEX